Micros

Azure Architect Technologies and Design Complete
Study Guide

Microsoft
Azure Architect Technologies and Design Complete
Study Guide
Exams AZ-303 and AZ-304

Benjamin Perkins

SYBEX®
A Wiley Brand

Acknowledgments

Transforming an idea into content that can be consumed in a friendly and logical manner requires actions greater than the capacity of a single human being. The skillsets and experiences of a team do increase the reach, inclusiveness, and clarity of the subject being discussed. Here is a list of those who played a significant part in the creation of this book and the organization of its content:

- Mary Ellen Schutz, project editor
- Barton Mathis, technical editor
- Rodney Fournier, technical editor
- Barath Kumar Rajasekaran, production editor
- Kim Wimpsett, copy editor
- Nancy Carrasco, proofreader
- Potomac Indexing, indexer

Writing this book was probably the most mentally challenging experience of my life. If not the most, it is definitely in the top three. I want to call out my parents, Rual and Donna Perkins, who raised me free from limits, free from critique, with maximum freedom of choice. You will come across people who tell you that "you can't," but neither of them ever uttered such a phrase to me. That time in my life gave me the strength I need now to overcome obstacles and finish the stuff I start, no matter what. I also need to call out my family who continued to live life and carry on while I worked on this project. Andrea, Lea, and Noa, I thank you and love you from the bottom of my heart.

About the Author

Benjamin Perkins is currently employed at Microsoft in Munich, Germany, as a senior escalation engineer for IIS, ASP.NET, and Azure App Services. He has been working professionally in the IT industry for more than two decades. He started computer programming with QBasic at the age of 11 on an Atari 1200XL desktop computer. He takes pleasure in the challenges that troubleshooting technical issues have to offer and savors in the rewards of a well-written program. After completing high school, he joined the United States Army. After successfully completing his military service, he attended Texas A&M University in College Station, Texas, where he received a bachelor's of business administration in management information systems. He also received a master's of business administration from the European University.

His roles in the IT industry have spanned the entire spectrum including programmer, system architect, technical support engineer, team leader, and mid- level management. While employed at Hewlett-Packard, he received numerous awards, degrees, and certifications. He has a passion for technology and customer service and looks forward to troubleshooting and writing more world-class technical solutions. "My approach is to write code with support in mind, and to write it once correctly and completely so we do not have to come back to it again, except to enhance it."

Benjamin has written numerous magazine articles and training courses and is an active blogger. His catalog of books covers C# programming, IIS, NHibernate, open source, and Microsoft Azure.

- Connect with Benjamin on LinkedIn:

   www.linkedin.com/in/csharpguitar

- Follow Benjamin on Twitter:

   @csharpguitar - twitter.com/csharpguitar

- Read Benjamin's blog:

   www.thebestcsharpprogrammerintheworld.com

- Visit Benjamin on GitHub:

   github.com/benperk

   Benjamin is married to Andrea and has two wonderful children, Lea and Noa.

The publisher and editors will to acknowledge William Panek's work on earlier unpublished chapters for previous Azure Architect exams that were retired before that book could be published. Although ultimately no part of that work is part of this book, we are grateful for his time and effort during those early Azure Architect certifications.

William Panek is a Five-Time Microsoft MVP Winner. He has taught at Boston University, Clark University, and the University of Maryland, and presently conducts live online classes for StormWind Studios www.stormwind.com.

Contents at a Glance

Contents

Table of Exercises

Introduction

I was speaking to one of my colleagues who didn't have much understanding of what the cloud was, so I explained it from two perspectives, one being from a consumer perspective and the other commercial. From a consumer perspective, the cloud is mostly based on software as a service (SaaS) where individuals store their files on OneDrive, Google Drive, Dropbox, etc., or consume content not residing on a computer in their house like with Netflix or Spotify. So, from a consumer perspective, the cloud is mostly about the consumption of products that historically required individuals to have compute power and local storage space of their own.

From a commercial perspective, the cloud takes on a whole other meaning, whereby a commercial user of the cloud consumes compute resources for the purpose of providing cloud services to the consumer. Providing these services to consumers requires great compute capacity, because customers have become intolerant and impatient when it comes to receiving cloud services. A small outage, an unexpected pause in a movie, or a latent download of a file can lose customers and sometimes make the news. Having extra or idle compute capacity to scale instantly has become a necessity for companies, but buying and managing this capacity is not cost efficient.

I like to think that the birth of the cloud happened because of the Black Friday event that happens in the United States. Black Friday takes place the day after Thanksgiving and is one of the largest, busiest shopping days of the year. Amazon, wanting to make sure it could withstand the surge of traffic it would receive on this day and through the weekend, added a massive amount of compute power specifically for this day. Once the weekend passed, they had to answer the question, now what shall we do with all these extra computers? Having an entrepreneurial mindset, someone likely thought about how to make some money from the servers and the idea of renting them out to companies popped up. And this was the birth of infrastructure as a service (IaaS) from Amazon Web Services (AWS) and what we call the cloud today.

The cloud, from a commercial perspective, is simply a place for companies or individuals to rent computers hosted in a cloud provider's private data center. Cloud providers such as Microsoft, Amazon, and to some extent Google are in the market to provide a cloud platform for companies that want to, in turn, provide a great performant product experience to their customers. From all of this, we have arrived at the next era of IT and computing, which is the cloud.

In 2013, I wrote a book titled *Windows Azure and ASP.NET MVC Migration.* In the introduction of that book, I mentioned the retirement of Windows Server 2003. My primary point in that introduction was to avoid moving an application that originally targeted Windows Server 2003 directly to the cloud. Instead, take the opportunity for a reboot, a refreshing rewrite, and a new start for the application. From a coding perspective, I recommended using some new technologies such as REST, LINQ, and ORM; change from XML to JSON; and use a cross-platform coding language like .NET Core. From an operating system and compute resource perspective, I, as one would expect, drove the reader toward the Microsoft Azure and Azure App Service compute products.

At that time, in 2013, I drove the recognition of the emergence of the cloud and how significant this new platform would become. I predicted this because I knew, firsthand, the complexities, time, and effort involved in adding new compute capacities to an existing on-premise IT solution, needless to mention the cost. I saw that it was now possible, in the cloud, to add 1, 10, 20, or 200 new servers to a web farm with a simple click of a button. And a most impressive part is that when I no longer wanted them, I pressed a different button and removed them. I literally just got goose bumps while I wrote this paragraph, by simply remembering my first experience with this autoscaling capability.

The years have passed, and there has been no slowing of cloud progress with the delivery of more capabilities that make the life of an IT professional simpler and the costs of a software product more manageable. That comment doesn't imply, or even hint, that understanding the cloud product and features is by any means simple—not even close. But there should be no doubt that the arrival of the cloud has provided a platform to deliver products to customers who have a new, much more elevated set of expectations. This book will help improve your understanding of the Microsoft Azure platform and features, with an emphasis on the successful completion of your Azure Solutions Architect Expert (AZ-303 and AZ-304) exams.

Who This Book Is For

This book is for anyone who wants to learn about Microsoft Azure products and features and ultimately attain the Azure Solutions Architect Expert certification. This book is not intended for absolute beginners; however, beginners may gain some greater insights into Azure and how to consume and configure its products and services. Gaining the Azure Solutions Architect Expert certification means that you can comprehend, design, and implement technical solutions using the following:

- Azure Active Directory and security
- Azure networking
- IaaS, PaaS, and serverless compute models
- Azure Storage, Azure SQL, and Cosmos DB
- Hybrid cloud models, compliance, and messaging services
- How to design and program applications for the cloud
- Deploy and migration techniques
- Monitoring and recovery

That is a broad range of topics, and the number of possible scenarios in which to apply them is equally as great. This book will provide insights into each of those topics, but it is expected that you have some experience with each.

What This Book Covers

This book covers everything you need to know to greatly increase the probability of passing the Azure Solutions Architect Expert exam. But most important, the contents in this book, once you learn them, will result in you being an Azure cloud architect. Which is most important to you? Both for sure, which is the goal and purpose of this book. You will learn about Azure security, Azure networking, Azure compute, Azure data stores and storage, Azure messaging services, Azure migration tools, Azure monitoring tools, and Azure recovery tools. That is a lot to learn about, and in addition to learning about what those products are and do, you will work through some real examples to implement and use them.

How This Book Is Structured

Good design really is everything. Unless you plan before doing, it is highly probable that the result won't quite measure up to the expectations. Really, in many instances, even with good planning, the result could still not measure up or even be successful. There are many priorities and areas to be concerned with when planning a big project. The same is true when you are migrating existing on-premise workloads to Azure or creating new applications and infrastructure directly on Azure. In both scenarios, security, networking, compute, and data storage all come into focus. The chapters are provided in the order of priority, which means when you plan your migration or deployments, make sure each of those phases is part of your plan. The order in which those IT components are analyzed, designed, and implemented is important and is the reason the book is constructed in this way.

- Security
- Networking
- Compute
- Data and storage
- Hybrid, compliance, and messaging
- Developing for the cloud
- Migrate and deploy
- Monitor and recover

Security is by far the most important point of concentration. Networking must exist before you place your compute workloads into it, and keep in mind the network needs to be secured before placing your workloads into it. Then your data, compliance and governance, messaging concepts, development concepts, and deploying your application initially and applying updates cannot be ignored or missed. Once deployed, the lifecycle of your application is really just beginning; monitoring it and having a failover and disaster recovery plan designed and tested are musts for production IT solutions.

Following this design pattern laid out by the chapter flow will help you become a great Azure Solutions Architect Expert. Note that when you take the Azure Solutions Architect Expert exam, you sign a nondisclosure agreement (NDA) stating that you will not discuss the questions or any of the content of the exam. That is important, so the credential you gain when passing the exam maintains its integrity and value. This book will help you learn the skills and gain the experience an Azure Solutions Architect Expert should have. By learning and exercising the techniques contained within this book, your probability of passing the exam is greatly increased. The point is, the book is geared toward building your experiences and skills on the Azure platform; with those skills and experiences, you can then master the skillset and gain the certification.

Chapter 1, "Gaining the Azure Solutions Architect Expert Certification"   This chapter provides an overview of the path toward the Azure Solutions Architect Expert certification. It describes each of the new AZ-100, AZ-200, AZ-300, and AZ-400 roles and defines the AZ-300 and AZ-301 knowledge requirements in detail. I give a short overview of how I achieved the certification and closes with a brief overview of 12 of the most common Azure products. Knowing the internals of those 12 products, their features, and their dependences are must-learn curricula for the successful completion of the AZ-303 and AZ-304 exams. The products are introduced in this chapter; the internals are covered in the following related chapters.

Chapter 2, "Security and Identity"   Let's do this! Assuming you already have an Azure subscription, it is time to take the next step and move your company into the cloud. Initially, you need to set up the people who will have access to the subscription and decide what they can and cannot do with it. But there is a whole other world, solar system, and universe when approaching these two topics. Do not under-estimate this chapter; read it fully, because it will touch on the topics necessary to pass the exam, but it doesn't stop there.

Chapter 3, "Networking"   At this point, you have good knowledge of the Azure security and identity capabilities, especially those around the management of your Azure resources. Now it is time to begin planning and building the infrastructure on which your application will operate. The Azure platform runs within the most sophisticated data centers and in more than 50 regions around the world. Each data center is an isolated network, with secure links to the internet and ultrafast connectivity with Azure resources in its other regions. By setting up your own virtual network inside the Azure data centers, you gain an even greater level of security and flexibility. Making hybrid connections over ExpressRoute and VPNs, or simply using HTTPS, is simple and cost effective. This chapter discusses all these topics and a few more.

Chapter 4, "Compute"   Now that security and networking are clarified and configured, it's time to jump into the heart of Azure. Compute is at the center of the cloud and is the reason companies move to Azure. Companies need CPUs and memory to run their software applications or process data. Compute is the heart of Azure because it is surrounded by both security and networking products and features. In this chapter, you learn about the many Azure compute products and features, such as Azure virtual machines (VMs). Azure VMs (i.e., IaaS) are the most popular type of compute offering (Azure VMs was one of the first Azure products), but by no means the only or last. Azure App Service, Azure Kubernetes Service (AKS), Azure Functions, Azure Batch, and Service Fabric also provide compute power for specific business case scenarios. In addition to learning those compute products in depth, you will learn which scenario is best for each compute product. Concepts such as PaaS, event-driven, serverless (FaaS), High Performance Computing (HPC), microservices, and containerization (CaaS) will also become clear.

Chapter 5, "Data and Storage"   If you have made it this far, then you are close to being ready to take the exam. Security, networking, and compute take up a majority of the Azure Solutions Architect Expert exam questions. Those are the concepts that need the most focus and concentration. However, data and storage are quite important. Without them, what does the security procedure you have implemented so far protect? What is the value of the networking capabilities that allow connectivity between nodes, workstations, and clients then provide? Why do you need compute resource to run workloads and application code? The reason is there is some data that needs processing and that data needs to be somewhere for the compute to get the data from. That data needs to be accessible from anywhere in the world and protected from anyone without proper authentication and authorization to do so. Application code is what runs on compute and is something that does work, but if there is nothing to do the work on, then there is no reason for the code. The data, and how and where it gets stored, is the next logical step in your learning and/or migration of your IT solution to the cloud.

Chapter 6, "Hybrid, Compliance, and Messaging"   Moving right along to some additional important concepts, one advantage Microsoft Azure has over all other cloud server providers is its hybrid cloud capabilities. The concept of running hybrid solutions on the Azure platform was introduced in Chapter 1. There was also a discussion about hybrid Azure Identity solutions in Chapter 2, hybrid networking in Chapter 3, and hybrid compute (aka cloud bursting) in Chapter 4. When you read this chapter, the concept of what a hybrid solution is should already be in your back pocket. In this chapter, you get a refresher and maybe some new insights about hybrid clouds. Compliance is a big deal for companies that want to handle financial transactions, work on government contracts, and comply with GDPR laws. There are numerous Azure features and example models that can help you achieve this when running those kinds of workloads on Azure. Finally, you will learn about a portfolio of Azure products that manage the storage and management of messages from IoT or offline transaction processing. Product services such as Service Bus, Event Hub, and Azure Storage Queues shouldn't at all be something new at this point. Prepare to get much deeper into them and other messaging products in more technical and use case details.

Chapter 7, "Developing for the Cloud"   You will not find many questions on the exam about development and coding. The Azure Solutions Architect Expert exam is focused more on which tools to use in which scenario and in the most efficient and cost-effective way. Nonetheless, you can design the most sophisticated security, networking, compute, data store, and messaging solutions, but if the code is unstable, is unreliable, or has many bugs, then nothing really works right. You are protecting an application that doesn't really work, and running on highly tuned and precisely targeted compute resources won't compensate for bad code. This chapter will cover some details about best-case cloud coding patterns so that you can at least have some background if you ever get confronted with such a situation.

Chapter 8, "Migrate and Deploy"   In this chapter, you might begin to recognize that everything is starting to come together. Security, networking, compute, data stores, data storage, messaging services, and your application are all ready to go. Your RBAC controls have been implemented, and those who need access to different Azure products have it. The VNets contain some Azure VMs in numerous subnets protected by NSGs and Azure Firewalls. Your database is idle waiting for some data to process, and your application code is tested, approved, and ready for action. Your heart is pumping with excitement, and all the hard work is ready to pay off. The time has come to move your data and application code to the Azure platform. It is time to reap the benefits of your efforts by watching your customers and employees gain from all the benefits the Azure platform has to offer them. Once you complete this and all previous chapters, you too will experience these events.

Chapter 9, "Monitor and Recover"   Once you're here, for all intents and purposes you have achieved what most do not. You now have a functional application running on the Azure platform. Whether you migrated it or created it from scratch, your application is secure, you have optimized your compute and data consumption, plus you are certain to be compliant with all regulations in the countries where your company operates. That is something worthy of celebration. Take a second to reflect and celebrate your accomplishments. Take a minute actually, but only a minute, and then recognize that you are not quite finished. Although you have done so much, and a very good job as well, you need to make sure the solutions you have running on Azure continue to work properly. If they stop running, you need to quickly determine why. If it turns out that it will take some serious time to get things back up and running, you need to have a BCDR plan. Although this is the last chapter, after completing it, your journey is really just beginning.

What You Need to Use This Book

The following items are necessary to realize all the benefits of this book and to complete the numerous exercises:

- A computer/workstation

- Internet access

- An Azure subscription

- Visual Studio 2019 Community edition (free)

- Azure DevOps free account

Many of the exercises require you to consume Azure resources that have an associated financial cost. Make sure in all cases that you understand the costs you may incur when creating and consuming Azure products. Most of all, once you complete an exercise that required the creation of an Azure product, you'll want to remove it. However, in many cases throughout the book, you rely on the Azure products created in the previous exercises to complete the current one. Those scenarios are called out as much as possible.

Conventions

To get the most out of this book, certain conventions have been utilized throughout. Exercise I.1 shows an exercise.

Exercise I.1

This kind of activity is an exercise that you should work through; following the exercise, some details about what you did are explained. There is an attempt to proactively answer any questions that may come up when working through them.

1. The exercises usually consist of a set of steps.

2. Each step is numbered.

3. The completion of all the steps is required to successfully complete the exercise.

 A note provides tips, tricks, hints, or asides that are related to the current discussion.

Here are the formatting text styles used throughout the book:

- We use *italics* to indicate when a new key term is introduced.
- Keyboard strokes are sometimes represented as Ctrl+Shift+B.
- Filenames and inline code are represented like the following:
  `string csharpGuitar = String.Empty;`.
- Web addresses are provided in this format: `portal.azure.com`.
- Code snippets, PowerShell cmdlets, and Azure CLI commands are presented as follows: `Get-AzVM`.

Source Code

You can find the source code for this book on GitHub here:
    `github.com/benperk/ASA`

 Go to `wiley.com/go/sybextestprep` to register and gain access to this book's interactive online learning environment and test bank with study tools.

AZ-303 Objective Map

Table I.1 shows where in the book the AZ-303 objectives are covered.

TABLE I.1   AZ-303 Objectives to Chapter Mapping

Exam Objective	Chapter
Implement and Monitor an Azure Infrastructure	
Implement cloud infrastructure monitoring	**Chapter 9, "Monitor and Recover"**
monitor security	Chapter 2, "Security and Identity"
monitor performance	Chapter 9, "Monitor and Recover"
monitor health and availability	Chapter 9, "Monitor and Recover"
monitor cost	Chapter 9, "Monitor and Recover"
configure advanced logging	Chapter 9, "Monitor and Recover"
configure logging for workloads	Chapter 9, "Monitor and Recover"

Exam Objective	Chapter
initiate automated responses by using Action Groups	Chapter 9, "Monitor and Recover"
configure and manage advanced alerts	Chapter 9, "Monitor and Recover"
Implement storage accounts	**Chapter 5, "Data and Storage"**
select storage account options based on a use case	Chapter 5, "Data and Storage"
configure Azure Files and blob storage	Chapter 5, "Data and Storage"
configure network access to the storage account	Chapter 3, "Networking"
implement Shared Access Signatures and access policies	Chapter 5, "Data and Storage"
implement Azure AD authentication for storage	Chapter 5, "Data and Storage"
manage access keys	Chapter 5, "Data and Storage"
implement Azure storage replication	Chapter 5, "Data and Storage"
implement Azure storage account failover	Chapter 9, "Monitor and Recover"
Implement VMs for Windows and Linux	**Chapter 4, "Compute"**
configure High Availability	Chapter 4, "Compute"
configure storage for VMs	Chapter 4, "Compute"
select virtual machine size	Chapter 4, "Compute"
implement Azure Dedicated Hosts	Chapter 4, "Compute"
deploy and configure scale sets	Chapter 4, "Compute"
configure Azure Disk Encryption	Chapter 4, "Compute"
Automate deployment and configuration of resources	**Chapter 8, "Migrate and Deploy"**
save a deployment as an Azure Resource Manager template	Chapter 8, "Migrate and Deploy"
modify Azure Resource Manager template	Chapter 8, "Migrate and Deploy"

TABLE I.1 AZ-303 Objectives to Chapter Mapping *(continued)*

Exam Objective	Chapter
evaluate location of new resources	Chapter 6, "Hybrid, Compliance, and Messaging"
configure a virtual disk template	Chapter 8, "Migrate and Deploy"
deploy from a template	Chapter 8, "Migrate and Deploy"
manage a template library	Chapter 8, "Migrate and Deploy"
create and execute an automation runbook	Chapter 8, "Migrate and Deploy"
Implement virtual networking	**Chapter 3, "Networking"**
implement VNet to VNet connections	Chapter 3, "Networking"
implement VNet peering	Chapter 3, "Networking"
Implement Azure Active Directory	**Chapter 2, "Security and Identity"**
add custom domains	Chapter 2, "Security and Identity"
configure Azure AD Identity Protection	Chapter 2, "Security and Identity"
implement self-service password reset	Chapter 2, "Security and Identity"
implement Conditional Access including MFA	Chapter 2, "Security and Identity"
configure user accounts for MFA	Chapter 2, "Security and Identity"
configure fraud alerts	Chapter 2, "Security and Identity"
configure bypass options	Chapter 2, "Security and Identity"
configure Trusted IPs	Chapter 4, "Compute"
configure verification methods	Chapter 2, "Security and Identity"
implement and manage guest accounts	Chapter 2, "Security and Identity"
manage multiple directories	Chapter 2, "Security and Identity"

Exam Objective	Chapter
Implement and manage hybrid identities	**Chapter 2, "Security and Identity"**
install and configure Azure AD Connect	Chapter 2, "Security and Identity"
identity synchronization options	Chapter 2, "Security and Identity"
configure and manage password sync and password writeback	Chapter 2, "Security and Identity"
configure single sign-on	Chapter 2, "Security and Identity"
use Azure AD Connect Health	Chapter 2, "Security and Identity"
Implement Management and Security Solutions	
Manage workloads in Azure	**Chapter 4, "Compute"**
migrate workloads using Azure Migrate	Chapter 8, "Migrate and Deploy"
implement Azure Backup for VMs	Chapter 9, "Monitor and Recover"
implement disaster recovery	Chapter 9, "Monitor and Recover"
implement Azure Update Management	Chapter 4, "Compute"
Implement load balancing and network security	**Chapter 3, "Networking"**
implement Azure Load Balancer	Chapter 3, "Networking"
implement an application gateway	Chapter 3, "Networking"
implement a Web Application Firewall	Chapter 3, "Networking"
implement Azure Firewall	Chapter 3, "Networking"
implement the Azure Front Door Service	Chapter 3, "Networking"
implement Azure Traffic Manager	Chapter 3, "Networking"
implement Network Security Groups and Application Security Groups	Chapter 3, "Networking"
implement Bastion	Chapter 4, "Compute"

TABLE I.1   AZ-303 Objectives to Chapter Mapping *(continued)*

Exam Objective	Chapter
Implement and manage Azure governance solutions	**Chapter 6, "Hybrid, Compliance, and Messaging"**
create and manage hierarchical structure that contains management groups, subscriptions and resource groups	Chapter 2, "Security and Identity"
assign RBAC roles	Chapter 2, "Security and Identity"
create a custom RBAC role	Chapter 2, "Security and Identity"
configure access to Azure resources by assigning roles	Chapter 2, "Security and Identity"
configure management access to Azure	Chapter 2, "Security and Identity"
interpret effective permissions	Chapter 6, "Hybrid, Compliance, and Messaging"
set up and perform an access review	Chapter 6, "Hybrid, Compliance, and Messaging"
implement and configure an Azure Policy	Chapter 6, "Hybrid, Compliance, and Messaging"
implement and configure an Azure Blueprint	Chapter 6, "Hybrid, Compliance, and Messaging"
Manage security for applications	**Chapter 2, "Security and Identity"**
implement and configure KeyVault	Chapter 2, "Security and Identity"
implement and configure Azure AD Managed Identities	Chapter 2, "Security and Identity"
register and manage applications in Azure AD	Chapter 2, "Security and Identity"
Implement Solutions for Apps	
Implement an application infrastructure	**Chapter 4, "Compute"**
create and configure Azure App Service	Chapter 4, "Compute"

Exam Objective	Chapter
create an App Service Web App for Containers	Chapter 4, "Compute"
create and configure an App Service plan	Chapter 4, "Compute"
configure an App Service	Chapter 4, "Compute"
configure networking for an App Service	Chapter 4, "Compute"
create and manage deployment slots	Chapter 4, "Compute"
implement Logic Apps	Chapter 4, "Compute"
implement Azure Functions	Chapter 4, "Compute"
Implement container-based applications	**Chapter 4, "Compute"**
create a container image	Chapter 4, "Compute"
configure Azure Kubernetes Service	Chapter 4, "Compute"
publish and automate image deployment to the Azure Container Registry	Chapter 4, "Compute"
publish a solution on an Azure Container Instance	Chapter 4, "Compute"
Implement and Manage Data Platforms	**Chapter 5, "Data and Storage"**
Implement NoSQL databases	**Chapter 5, "Data and Storage"**
configure storage account tables	Chapter 5, "Data and Storage"
select appropriate CosmosDB APIs	Chapter 5, "Data and Storage"
set up replicas in CosmosDB	Chapter 5, "Data and Storage"
Implement Azure SQL databases	**Chapter 5, "Data and Storage"**
configure Azure SQL database settings	Chapter 5, "Data and Storage"
implement Azure SQL Database managed instances	Chapter 5, "Data and Storage"
configure HA for an Azure SQL database	Chapter 5, "Data and Storage"
publish an Azure SQL database	Chapter 5, "Data and Storage"

AZ-304 Objective Map

Table I.2 shows where in the book the AZ-304 objectives are covered.

TABLE I.2   AZ-304 Objective to Chapter mapping

Exam Objective	Chapter
Design Monitoring	
Design for cost optimization	Chapter 9, "Monitor and Recovery"
recommend a solution for cost management and cost reporting	Chapter 9, "Monitor and Recovery"
recommend solutions to minimize costs	Chapter 9, "Monitor and Recovery"
Design a solution for logging and monitoring	**Chapter 9, "Monitor and Recovery"**
determine levels and storage locations for logs	Chapter 9, "Monitor and Recovery"
plan for integration with monitoring tools including Azure Monitor and Azure Sentinel	Chapter 9, "Monitor and Recovery"
recommend appropriate monitoring tool(s) for a solution	Chapter 9, "Monitor and Recovery"
choose a mechanism for event routing and escalation	Chapter 9, "Monitor and Recovery"
recommend a logging solution for compliance requirements	Chapter 6, "Hybrid, Compliance, and Messaging"
Design Identity and Security	
Design authentication	**Chapter 2, "Security and Identity"**
recommend a solution for single-sign on	Chapter 2, "Security and Identity"
recommend a solution for authentication	Chapter 2, "Security and Identity"

Exam Objective	Chapter
recommend a solution for Conditional Access, including multi-factor authentication	Chapter 2, "Security and Identity"
recommend a solution for network access authentication	Chapter 2, "Security and Identity"
recommend a solution for a hybrid identity including Azure AD Connect and Azure AD Connect Health	Chapter 2, "Security and Identity"
recommend a solution for user self-service	Chapter 2, "Security and Identity"
recommend and implement a solution for B2B integration	Chapter 2, "Security and Identity"
Design authorization	**Chapter 2, "Security and Identity"**
choose an authorization approach	Chapter 2, "Security and Identity"
recommend a hierarchical structure that includes management groups, subscriptions and resource groups	Chapter 2, "Security and Identity"
recommend an access management solution including RBAC policies, access reviews, role assignments, physical access, Privileged Identity Management (PIM), Azure AD Identity Protection, Just In Time (JIT) access	Chapter 2, "Security and Identity"
Design governance	**Chapter 6, "Hybrid, Compliance, and Messaging"**
recommend a strategy for tagging	Chapter 6, "Hybrid, Compliance, and Messaging"
recommend a solution for using Azure Policy	Chapter 6, "Hybrid, Compliance, and Messaging"
recommend a solution for using Azure Blueprint	Chapter 6, "Hybrid, Compliance, and Messaging"
Design security for applications	**Chapter 2, "Security and Identity"**
recommend a solution that includes KeyVault	Chapter 2, "Security and Identity"
recommend a solution that includes Azure AD Managed Identities	Chapter 2, "Security and Identity"

TABLE I.2   AZ-304 Objective to Chapter mapping *(continued)*

Exam Objective	Chapter
recommend a solution for integrating applications into Azure AD	Chapter 2, "Security and Identity"
Design Data Storage	
Design a solution for databases	**Chapter 5, "Data and Storage"**
select an appropriate data platform based on requirements	Chapter 5, "Data and Storage"
recommend database service tier sizing	Chapter 5, "Data and Storage"
recommend a solution for database scalability	Chapter 5, "Data and Storage"
recommend a solution for encrypting data at rest, data in transmission, and data in use	Chapter 2, "Security"
Design data integration	**Chapter 5, "Data and Storage"**
recommend a data flow to meet business requirements	Chapter 5, "Data and Storage"
recommend a solution for data integration, including Azure Data Factory, Azure Data Bricks, Azure Data Lake, Azure Synapse Analytics	Chapter 5, "Data and Storage"
Select an appropriate storage account	**Chapter 5, "Data and Storage"**
choose between storage tiers	Chapter 5, "Data and Storage"
recommend a storage access solution	Chapter 5, "Data and Storage"
recommend storage management tools	Chapter 5, "Data and Storage"
Design Business Continuity	
Design a solution for backup and recovery	**Chapter 9, "Monitor and Recovery"**
recommend a recovery solution for Azure hybrid and on-premises workloads that meets recovery objectives (RTO, RLO, RPO)	Chapter 9, "Monitor and Recovery"

Exam Objective	Chapter
design and Azure Site Recovery solution	Chapter 9, "Monitor and Recovery"
recommend a solution for recovery in different regions	Chapter 9, "Monitor and Recovery"
recommend a solution for Azure Backup management	Chapter 9, "Monitor and Recovery"
design a solution for data archiving and retention	Chapter 9, "Monitor and Recovery"
Design for high availability	**Chapter 9, "Monitor and Recovery"**
recommend a solution for application and workload redundancy, including compute, database, and storage	Chapter 9, "Monitor and Recovery"
recommend a solution for autoscaling	Chapter 4, "Compute"
identify resources that require high availability	Chapter 4, "Compute"
identify storage types for high availability	Chapter 5, "Data and Storage"
recommend a solution for geo-redundancy of workloads	Chapter 4, "Compute"
Design Infrastructure	
Design a compute solution	**Chapter 4, "Compute"**
recommend a solution for compute provisioning	Chapter 4, "Compute"
determine appropriate compute technologies, including virtual machines, App Services, Service Fabric, Azure Functions, Windows Virtual Desktop, and containers	Chapter 4, "Compute"
recommend a solution for containers	Chapter 4, "Compute"
recommend a solution for automating compute management	Chapter 4, "Compute"
Design a network solution	**Chapter 3, "Networking"**
recommend a solution for network addressing and name resolution	Chapter 3, "Networking"

TABLE I.2   AZ-304 Objective to Chapter mapping *(continued)*

Exam Objective	Chapter
recommend a solution for network provisioning	Chapter 3, "Networking"
recommend a solution for network security	Chapter 3, "Networking"
recommend a solution for network connectivity to the Internet, on-premises networks, and other Azure virtual networks	Chapter 3, "Networking"
recommend a solution for automating network management	Chapter 3, "Networking"
recommend a solution for load balancing and traffic routing	Chapter 3, "Networking"
Design an application architecture	**Chapter 4, "Compute"**
recommend a microservices architecture including Event Grid, Event Hubs, Service Bus, Storage Queues, Logic Apps, Azure Functions, and webhooks	Chapter 6, "Hybrid, Compliance, and Messaging"
recommend an orchestration solution for deployment of applications including ARM templates, Logic Apps, or Azure Functions	Chapter 8, "Migrate and Deploy"
recommend a solution for API integration	Chapter 7, "Developing for the Cloud"
Design migrations	**Chapter 8, "Migrate and Deploy"**
assess and interpret on-premises servers, data, and applications for migration	Chapter 8, "Migrate and Deploy"
recommend a solution for migrating applications and VMs	Chapter 8, "Migrate and Deploy"
recommend a solution for migration of databases	Chapter 8, "Migrate and Deploy"

Assessment Test

1. Which of the following protocols are commonly used for making a remote connection to administer an Azure virtual machine? (Choose all that apply.)

   A. SSH

   B. Remote Desktop Protocol (RDP)

   C. FTP

   D. Azure Bastian

2. Which of the following Azure Database products are specifically designed to provide a key/value pair data store? (Choose all that apply.)

   A. Azure SQL

   B. Azure Cosmos DB

   C. Azure Table Storage

   D. SQL managed instances

3. If you wanted to make sure that any person creating an Azure Storage container allowed HTTPS only, which of the following Azure products would you use to achieve that?

   A. Azure Blueprint

   B. Azure Resource Manager

   C. Role-based access control

   D. Azure Policy

4. Which of the following products are available on Azure?

   A. Azure Delta

   B. Azure Attack Vector

   C. Azure Cluster Services (ACS)

   D. All of the above

   E. None of the above

5. Which of the following inbound NSGs will prevent resources from being accessed from the internet?

   A. Priority: 65000, Name: AllowVnetInBound, Port: Any, Protocol: Any, Source: VirtualNetwork, Destination: VirtualNetwork, Action: Allow

   B. Priority: 65001, Name: AllowAzureLoadBalancerInBound, Port: Any, Protocol: Any, Source: AzureLoadBalancer, Destination: Any, Action: Allow

   C. Priority: 65500, Name: DenyAllInBound, Port: Any, Protocol: Any, Source: Any, Destination: Any, Action: Allow

   D. Priority: 65501, Name: DenyAllInternet, Port: Any, Protocol: Any, Source: Any, Destination: Any, Action: Deny

6. Which of the following outbound NSGs will prevent connectivity between the subnets in the same virtual network?

   A. Priority: 65000, Name: AllowVnetOutBound, Port: Any, Protocol: Any, Source: VirtualNetwork, Destination: VirtualNetwork, Action: Allow

   B. Priority: 65001, Name: AllowInternetOutBound, Port: Any, Protocol: Any, Source: Any, Destination: Internet, Action: Allow

   C. Priority: 65500, Name: DenyAllOutBound, Port: Any, Protocol: Any, Source: VirtualNetwork, Destination: VirtualNetwork, Action: Deny

   D. Priority: 65501, Name: DenyVnetOutBound, Port: Any, Protocol: Any, Source: VirtualNetwork, Destination: VirtualNetwork, Action: Allow

7. Which of the following are Azure resources where you can apply an NSG? (Choose all that apply.)

   A. A network interface

   B. An Azure virtual machine (VM)

   C. An Azure subnet

   D. An Azure virtual network (VNet)

8. Which of the following is true when you have a matched value of None for NextHopType in an Azure route table?

   A. The data transmission is dropped.

   B. Traffic is routed to the Internet.

   C. The data packet is routed within the virtual network.

   D. No action is taken.

9. Which of the following is true when you have a value of Internet for NextHopType in an Azure route table?

   A. The data transmission is dropped.

   B. Traffic is routed to the Internet.

   C. The data packet is routed within the virtual network.

   D. No action is taken.

10. Which of the following is true when you have a value of VirtualNetwork for NextHopType in an Azure route table?

   A. The data transmission is dropped.

   B. Traffic is routed to the Internet.

   C. The data packet is routed within the virtual network.

   D. No action is taken.

11. Which of the following is true in regard to an address prefix of 0.0.0.0/0 in your routing table?

   A. The data transmission is dropped if matched.

   B. It depends on the value of the NextHopType bound to 0.0.0.0/0.

    C. The address prefix of 0.0.0.0/0 only supports the NextHopType value of VirtualNetworkGateway.

    D. The default address prefix of 0.0.0.0/0 cannot be customized.

12. How many IP addresses would you get with this CIDR prefix: 172.19.3.0/27?

    A. 62

    B. 1,022

    C. 14

    D. 30

13. Which of the following are true given the CIDR prefix? (Choose all that apply.)

    A. 10.0.0.0/16 provides 65,534 IP addresses.

    B. 10.0.0.0/32 provides 32,766 IP addresses.

    C. 10.0.0.0/32 provides 1 IP address.

    D. 10.0.0.0/64 provides 16 IP addresses.

14. Which of the following are true? (Choose all that apply.)

    A. By default all resources within a virtual network can access each other on any port.

    B. By default all resources within a virtual network can access each other using any protocol.

    C. By default all resources within a virtual network can access the internet.

    D. By default all resources within a virtual network can access each other on ports 22, 80, 443, and 3389.

15. Which tool is helpful for managing your Azure costs?

    A. Azure Spending Control

    B. Azure Cost Management

    C. Azure Monitor

    D. Azure Spending Throttler

16. Which of the following statements are true? (Choose all that apply.)

    A. You can have multiple virtual networks in a single subnet.

    B. You can have multiple subnets in a single virtual network.

    C. You can have multiple virtual networks in a single resource group.

    D. The same virtual network can be placed into multiple resource groups.

17. Which one of the following Azure products is intended for detecting and diagnosing application problems?

    A. Azure Monitor

    B. Application Insights

    C. Log Analytics

    D. Azure Automation

18. Which one of the following Azure products is intended for detecting Azure infrastructure problems?

    A. Azure Monitor

    B. Application Insights

    C. Log Analytics

    D. Azure Sentinel

19. Which ARM template element is used to define a dependency between resources?

    A. contingentUpon

    B. dependentResource

    C. childDependency

    D. dependsOn

20. Which of the following can be used to provision an Azure resource using ARM? (Choose all that apply.)

    A. Azure Portal

    B. PowerShell

    C. Azure CLI

    D. Visual Studio

21. You want to package your application code, dependencies, and operating system into a single deployable unit. This concept is often referred to as which of the following?

    A. Container

    B. Docker

    C. Azure Kubernetes Service (AKS)

    D. Autonomous Deployable Unit (ADU)

22. Which of the following technical concepts apply to a relational database? (Choose all that apply.)

    A. NoSQL

    B. SQL

    C. JSON

    D. Foreign key

23. Which of the following technical concepts apply to unstructured (aka nonrelational) data store products? (Choose all that apply.)

    A. Documents

    B. JSON

    C. Foreign key

    D. NoSQL

24. The term used to describe the process of ensuring you are who you say you are is most commonly called which one of the following?

   A. Authentication

   B. Identity validation

   C. Authorization

   D. Managed identity

25. The term used to describe the process of ensuring you are allowed to access a specific restricted resource is most commonly called which one of the following?

   A. Authentication

   B. Access control verification

   C. Conditional access

   D. Authorization

26. Which of the following correctly describes the hierarchical structure of the management of Azure resources, from top to bottom?

   A. Resource, resource group, subscription, management group

   B. Management group, resource group, subscription, resource

   C. Management group, subscription, resource group, resource

   D. Subscription, resource group, management group, resource

27. What is the purpose of a service tag?

   A. Logical grouping of resources similar to a resource group

   B. Used with NSGs so you don't need to know IP addresses of dependent Azure resources

   C. A marker used with Update Manager that notifies the administrator of missing updates

   D. A notification mechanism for your customers when you are down for maintenance

28. What is an Azure region?

   A. The organizing of Azure data centers per continent (North America, South America, Europe, Asia, etc.)

   B. The organizing of Azure data centers into geographical locations (West Europe, East US, South Central US, etc.)

   C. A highly redundant location within a data center for applications that require very high availability solutions

   D. A geographical location with two or more Azure data centers

29. Which of the following is true in regard to a private endpoint and a service endpoint?

   A. A private endpoint is not discoverable.

   B. By default, a service endpoint is not discoverable.

   C. It is possible to make a service endpoint nondiscoverable.

   D. It is possible to make a private endpoint discoverable.

30. Which of the following Azure products support a microservice-based solution? (Choose all that apply.)

   A. Azure Kubernetes Service (AKS)

   B. Azure Container Instances (ACI)

   C. Azure Microservice for Virtual Machines

   D. Azure Service Fabric

Answers to Assessment Test

1. **A, B, D.** Using the FTP protocol allows connectivity but does not provide any means to configure the VM. The other options are all valid.

2. **B, C.** It would be possible to create a two-column table using SQL, one named Key and the other named Value; however, it would not be as performant as an Azure Cosmos DB or Azure Table Storage product. Both options B and C have features that are specifically designed for key/value pair database implementations.

3. **D.** Azure Policy provides the capability to restrict and enforce resource management and governance-based restrictions. The built-in Azure Policy templates target specific regional and/or industry regulations. It is also possible to create and apply custom policies and apply them subscription-wide.

4. **E.** Remember that you need to know all of the products available on Azure, be able to describe each of them, and understand each product's use case. This will get you very far on the exam.

5. **D.** Any correct answer would need to contain the Action value of Deny to be a possible answer since the question is about preventing the connectivity flow. Only option D contains a Deny value and therefore is the correct answer.

6. **C.** To prevent connectivity using an NSG, the Action value must be Deny. The name of the NSG in option D isn't an optimal name, but the name has no influence on the rule. Option C is the only possible answer.

7. **A, C.** When you apply an NSG, it is realized on a network interface and an Azure subnet. There is no possibility to bind an NSG to an Azure virtual machine or virtual network.

8. **A.** When the value for NextHopType is None, the packet is dropped. This will result in the client receiving a packet dropped error message.

9. **B.** As the name of the value implies, data transmissions that match the NextHopType of Internet are routed to the internet.

10. **C.** As the name of the value implies, data transmissions that match the NextHopType of VirtualNetwork are routed to resources within the virtual network to which the route table entry is bound.

11. **B.** You can create a custom user-defined route (UDR) and link that prefix to any supported NextHopType value. Therefore, the answer is that it depends on what it is linked to. By default it is linked to the internet.

12. **D.** $2^{32-27} = 2^5 - 2 = 30$. Two IP addresses are subtracted for network addressing (for example, 172.19.3.0) and broadcasting (for example, 172.19.3.30).

13. A, C. $2^{32-16} = 2^{16} - 2 = 65,534$ and $2^{32-32} = 2^0 = 1$. The math doesn't work out for option B, and /64 is not a valid prefix at all.

14. A, B, C. The ports presented in option D can be enabled when you initially create an NSG or later, but they are not enabled by default.

15. B. There are no Azure products named Azure Spending Control or Azure Spending Throttler. Azure Monitor is not used for monitoring costs, but rather applications and Azure platform services. This leaves option B as the correct answer.

16. B, C. You cannot have multiple virtual networks in a subnet, nor can you place a virtual network into multiple resource groups. Options B and C are valid.

17. B. Option D has nothing to do with monitoring. Azure Monitor is mostly focused on the Azure platform infrastructure. Log Analytics is a database for storing logs generated by Azure Monitor. Application Insights is mostly focused on application monitoring.

18. A. Azure Monitor is mostly focused on the Azure platform infrastructure. Log Analytics is a database for storing logs generated by Azure Monitor. Application Insights is mostly focused on application monitoring. Option D has nothing to do with monitoring.

19. D. Only option D is a valid ARM template element and is used to define deployment dependencies between Azure resources.

20. A, B, C, D. It is possible to deploy code and provision Azure resources from all of those tools.

21. A. A container is the word typically used to describe the packaging of an application in the described manner. Docker is a tool that can create containers, and AKS is a platform that can run an application in a container. There is no such technology called ADU.

22. B, D. Relational databases are those that organize data broken into numerous tables linked by relations between them using foreign keys. The technical approach for extracting data from those tables uses SQL.

23. A, B, D. Documents, NoSQL, and JSON are terms that you are commonly exposed to when in the context of a nonrelational data store.

24. A. Authentication is the answer. Authorization is the process of confirming someone or something has the correct privilege to access a resource. There is no process called identity validation, and managed identity is similar to a service principle useful for linking a resource to an identity.

25. D. Authorization is the answer. Authentication is the process of confirming someone is who they say they are. There is no process called identity validation, and managed identity is similar to a service principle, which is useful for linking a resource to an identity.

26. C. The only correct Azure resource hierarchy is option C. The others are not supported.

27. B. Service tags are used for grouping IP address ranges by Azure resource. When you create an NSG that needs inbound or outbound access, instead of needing to find and maintain the IP addresses, Microsoft does this for you via service tags.

28. B. A region is usually a group of data centers that exist in close proximity to each other, like in the same city. However, they are far apart enough to be able to not be impacted by natural disasters like weather. Option B is the closest valid answer.

29. A. Discoverable means that there is a URL or host name that is accessible on the internet. Service endpoints will restrict all the traffic to the endpoint, but it will not make it private. Options C and D are not supported, leaving only option A.

30. A, D. AKS and Service Fabric are Azure products created for running microservices. Options B and C are not specifically designed for this purpose.

Chapter

1

Gaining the Azure Solutions Architect Expert Certification

The Azure Solutions Architect Expert certification is one of the more complicated/senior certificates to earn when compared to the other currently available Azure certifications. Table 1.1 describes their level of complexity. Visualize an organization that creates a solution running on Azure. Preferably, a group of *Azure Developer Associates* will code and test the solution based on best-case cloud design patterns as explained and designed by the Azure Solutions Architect Expert.

TABLE 1.1 Azure Certifications

Level	Azure Certificate	Description
100	Azure Administrator Associate	Implement, monitor, and maintain Microsoft Azure solutions, focusing on security, network, compute, and storage
200	Azure Developer Associate	Design, build/code, test, and support cloud applications and services
300	Azure Solutions Architect Expert	An expert in security, network, compute, and storage for designing solutions to run on Azure
400	Azure DevOps Expert	An expert in managing processes, people, and technologies for continually delivering solutions on Azure

An *Azure Solutions Architect Expert* will design and likely configure the security, network, compute, and storage on the Azure platform. Once the application is coded and tested and the platform is ready to run the application, the *Azure DevOps Expert* will collaborate with all concerned parties and deploy the application to the platform. Any further changes will be managed by the Azure DevOps Expert through the proactive engagement of key stakeholders and the adherence and compliance to their processes and will be redeployed using several possible technologies. Finally, the *Azure Administrator Associates* will monitor and maintain the implemented Azure features, designed by the Azure Solutions Architect Expert, developed by the Azure Developer Associates, and deployed by the Azure DevOps Expert.

Every role plays a significant part in the overall success of the solution running on the Azure platform. The solution can be as simple as an Azure Function or as complex as a hybrid Azure VM Scale Set running across multiple virtual networks in multiple regions/data centers. To attain this higher level of Azure certification, senior IT professionals must recognize that although these are four separate certifications, they all play a distinct role toward the design, creation, deployment, and maintenance of the solution.

Let's now discuss getting on the path for Azure Solutions Architect Expert certification.

The Journey to Certification

As Ralph Waldo Emerson wrote, "Life is a journey, not a destination." The same can be said about the approach for achieving the Azure Solutions Architect Expert certification. The experiences you pick up while working with and learning Azure features are the true purpose of your goal and not necessarily the certification itself. An IT professional can be an expert at designing Azure solutions without taking the exams and earning the certification. Simply having the certification is commendable, but without the knowledge and wisdom learned along the way, how much value does it really denote?

Unlike life, where a destination is reachable with potentially an infinite number of experiences and from multiple directions, the path to the Azure Solutions Architect Expert certification is simple. Previously, the exams required to become a certified Azure Solutions Architect Expert were AZ-300 and AZ-301. As you can see in Figure 1-1, those exams were retired in September of 2020. The replacement exams are AZ-303 and AZ-304.

FIGURE 1.1 Azure Solutions Architect Expert Certification path

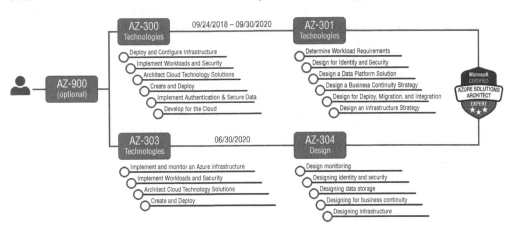

The *AZ-303 Azure Architect Technologies* exam is focused on these components:

Implement and monitor an Azure infrastructure curriculum contains designing monitoring solutions in terms of capturing diagnostics, exceptions, and performance data. Using Azure Monitor, Log Analytics, and Application Insights will provide a place to store and analyze that data. Data can be captured from Azure Active Directory, Networking, VMs, Azure App Services, and Data storage products, to name a few. How to configure, store, and analyze them is something you need to know.

Implementation of management and security solutions curriculum contains designing management solutions using tools like Update Management, Azure Backup, and Azure Migrate. Once your compute, data, and security products are provisioned, you need to know how to configure and support them. Additionally, proper security implementations with Key Vault, RBAC, and network appliances like Azure Firewall, Azure Front Door, and Azure Traffic Manager are also products and use cases you need to know.

Implementation of solutions for apps curriculum contains designing compute workloads using Azure App Service, Azure App Service Web App for Containers, Azure Functions, and Azure Kubernetes Services (AKS). You will need to know when to use these products and the benefits and constraints for choosing them.

Implementation and management of data platforms curriculum contains designing data stores like Azure SQL, Azure Cosmos DB, and Azure SQL managed instances. Each of them store data, and you need to know when to choose which one and how to configure them.

The *AZ-304 Azure Architect Design* exam is focused on these components:

Design monitoring curriculum contains designing monitoring with Azure Monitor and Azure Sentinel. Keep in mind that cost is always a factor and you need to know how to implement such solutions in the most cost effective manner. How to design and configure a monitoring solution include not only capturing and viewing, but also alerting and taking actions when an identifiable event takes place.

Designing identity and security curriculum contains designing security which is the most important aspect of computing today. Tools like Azure Active Directory (AAD), Azure Policy, and Azure Blueprint are helpful for managing and enforcing authentication. Additionally, concepts like multifactor authentication (MFA), Conditional Access, Single Sign-on (SSO), and Privileged Identity Management (PIM) are must know concepts, not only what they are and how they are used, but also how to implement and monitor them.

Designing data storage curriculum contains designing the data stores for storing your application or big data. Learning about relational vs. non-relational data stores, Azure Data Factory, Azure Data Bricks, and Azure Synapse Analytics are necessary to clear this portion of the exam.

Designing for business continuity curriculum contains designing redundancy and failover solutions. Azure Backup and Azure Site Recovery (ASR) are the tools primarily used in this area. Concepts like retention policy, snapshots, and archiving must be known and not only understood, but implemented and monitored.

Designing infrastructure curriculum contains designing your compute, network, storage and messaging requirements. Almost every company has something unique about their IT applications. Knowing the internals of Azure VM's and Azure App Services and choosing which one best fits their requirements is a key knowledge element. Event Hub or Service Bus are messaging products; why use which one? You need to know this and will learn it in this book. How to effectively implement and monitor all Azure products and features and the use case for each is best known by candidates taking this exam.

The amount of technologies, Azure features, and concepts that one must comprehend to pass these exams is relatively high. I recommend that you take the optional AZ-900 Azure Fundamentals exam prior to attempting the AZ-303 and AZ-304 exams. Doing so will provide a taste of what is to come, may help define areas needing more study, and can provide a more gradual descent, or should it be more eloquently stated, assent into the clouds.

A Strategy to Pass the Azure Exams

Now that your head is spinning with all the knowledge required to take the exams, let me provide a few tips to help pass them. Reading through the requirements of AZ-303 and AZ-304 and knowing what is covered in this book, you will be in good shape to pass.

- Use Azure daily.
- Read Azure articles, keeping yourself current.
- Learn to recognize Azure product names, features, and functionality.
- Gain a deep knowledge of a few, along with some knowledge of many, Azure products and features.

Before taking most Microsoft certification exams, candidates are prompted to accept certain terms and conditions, as well as committing to abide by a nondisclosure agreement (NDA). Therefore, the following sections contain activities and efforts that will most likely play a role in helping you achieve the Azure Solutions Architect Expert certification. No specifics about the exam are provided as per the NDA.

Use Azure Daily

It shouldn't be a stretch to imagine that using the product often will play a large role in gaining the required knowledge tested on the exam. In my specific case, I successfully completed the 70-533 Developing Microsoft Azure Solutions exam in October 2015 and had been fully engaged with Azure for a few years prior to that. Then I completed the Azure Solutions Architect Expert certification in February 2019. This means I have been working with Azure on a daily basis for about six years. According to Wikipedia, Microsoft Azure was announced in 2008 and went live in 2010, meaning I have worked on Azure almost since its existence.

My role has been primarily supporting customers who want to migrate existing or create new solutions to run on Azure App Service. Originally, Azure App Service was named Azure Web Sites (AWS), but over time that acronym caused some confusion with a solid competitor with the same acronym, so the name was changed. Even today when an Azure App Service solution is created, the default URL is `*.azurewebsites.net`.

Azure App Service will be discussed in more detail in later chapters, but Azure App Service as an entry point into Azure is a good one for customers and for those wanting to learn Azure. Azure App Service can expose you to the following additional Azure features:

- Azure Monitor and Application Insights
- Deployment techniques

- Azure Active Directory, OAuth, and managed Identity (MI)
- Backup and recovery techniques and Traffic Manager
- SSL/TLS certificates
- Hybrid Connection Manager, Azure VNet, and Azure CDN
- WebJobs
- Autoscaling

The list could go on and on, with many more Azure features and products. The fact is that once the entry point is discovered, the path toward getting visibility into other Azure features becomes well-defined. The pace of learning quickly increases, and the visibility of how tightly these products and features are all integrated with each other also becomes obvious.

 A typical entry point into the Azure platform is based on where the company currently is at regarding its Azure consumption. In addition, the entry point depends on the role of the individual and the type of solution being created or migrated to Azure. This topic was discussed in the introduction, and you'll learn more at the conclusion of this section.

The point is that using Azure and its many features is necessary to prepare for and ultimately pass the exam. Daily interaction and usage builds depth into many products, which usually results in the horizontal consumption of others.

Read Azure Articles, Keeping Yourself Current

Once upon a time there was a saying in IT that "things change faster than the internet." Having been part of that era, I confirm that the rate at which things changed, primarily for the better, was intense. Changes to hardware, changes to operating systems, and changes to products such as Internet Information Services (IIS), as well as the programming capabilities created to run on them, were all happening at once. Keeping up was a challenge, but there was the internet itself to search for ideas, tips, and solutions.

Not much has changed from an intensity perspective since then, but the saying mostly used today is that "we are moving at cloud speed" or "we are moving at the speed of the cloud." Things are changing very fast still, and it is hard to keep up. The ability to stay current on all Azure features exceeds the capacity of a single human mind. Therefore, tools, teamwork, and logical groupings of information are necessary to have a chance of remaining current and relevant. It is possible to have Azure change notifications pushed directly to your email inbox. As shown in Figure 1.2, on GitHub it is possible to be notified based on specific scenarios.

Table 1.2 describes the scenarios.

FIGURE 1.2   Possible GitHub notifications

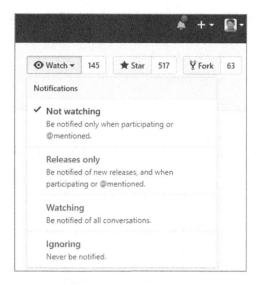

TABLE 1.2   GitHub Change Notification Types

Type	Description
Not Watching	Be notified only when participating or @mentioned.
Releases Only	Be notified of new releases and when participating or @mentioned.
Watching	Be notified of all conversations.
Ignoring	Never be notified.

For example, the Azure Functions host is open source and hosted on GitHub here:

github.com/Azure/azure-functions-host

If you would like to be notified of changes or conversations, then select the type of notification to receive. Additionally, to get notifications when announcements or changes occur to the Azure App Service environment, sign up here:

github.com/Azure/app-service-announcements

Many Azure features are hosted on GitHub and not only support the ability to be notified of changes but also allow people to contribute to the enhancement of the product.

A list of changes to all Azure features is stored here:

azure.microsoft.com/en-us/updates

A graphical representation is accessible here:

aka.ms/azheatmap

Additionally, a list of all Azure products is available here:

docs.microsoft.com/en-us/azure/#pivot=products&panel=all

Click the product of interest to get a great set of documentation for that specific product. Finally, here is a link to the official Azure blog:

azure.microsoft.com/en-us/blog

Here you can access and/or integrate an RSS reader to read new posts in your email client, for example. Each of these information sources will help you get into the flow of information required to remain current on Azure.

A final suggestion on how to remain current (or even be a little ahead) is to engage in private previews and in previews of new features being created for Azure. To engage in a private preview, you generally need to attend a Microsoft conference where new features get release, have someone inform you, or watch videos posted on Channel 9 that contain this information, for example. Not all private previews are open to the public, and sometimes joining is possible only through invitation from Microsoft product managers. If you are interested in working with private previews, attend a Microsoft conference to hear about them and ask for instructions on how to become engaged.

After a new feature leaves private preview, it enters the public preview phase, often known as *beta testing*. The feature becomes available on the portal, presented by its name followed by a "(Preview)" tag, similar to that shown in Figure 1.3.

FIGURE 1.3   Typical Azure feature preview

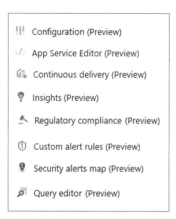

This is a manual way to find newly released features for a given product. It is at this point that it is fully open and Microsoft is eager for customers and users to test and provide feedback if nonintuitive scenarios are found or bugs are experienced. Finally, after testing is considered successful, the feature reaches "Generally Available" status and is fully supported by Microsoft Support. In many cases, products or features in preview are supported, because Microsoft wants you to test them and give feedback. However, a root cause solution for the issue is commonly not provided as part of the request, but a fix will come later.

It is important that IT professionals not only remain current with the new features, products, and technologies, but that they learn about what already exists and go deeper into how the technology actually works, all the way down to the bits. IT professionals need to learn in both forward and backward directions; otherwise you might miss why a feature was created in the first place.

Recognize Azure Product Names, Features, and Functionalities

The more products and features that pass in front of your eyes and get stored into your subconscious, the easier it will become to answer certain types of questions. For example, assume this question is presented to you in one of the exams:

> Which of the following are considered an Azure Storage product or feature? (Choose all that apply.)
>
> A. Blob Storage
> B. Data Storage
> C. Queue Storage
> D. File Storage

Having some experience with Azure Storage accounts, you might remember that Azure Storage accounts support multiple service types. The types of storage services are Blob, Files, Tables, and Queue. Based on that knowledge, it is for certain that options A, C, and D are the correct answers. But are you certain that there is no Azure product or feature called Data Storage? During the exam you must recollect if you have ever seen, heard, or read about an Azure Data Storage product or feature. You need to be confident in choosing the correct answer. In fact, there isn't an Azure product or feature called Data Storage in this context. You can check all the Azure products here to be sure:

docs.microsoft.com/en-us/azure/#pivot=products&panel=all

Continuing on that same thought process of name recognition, once you gain enough experience with the kinds of Azure products that exist, then learning what they do and what they are used for is the next step. Knowing the functional purpose of the product or feature will help to answer questions like the following:

> Which of the following Azure products provide messaging management capabilities? (Choose three.)
>
> A. Service Bus
> B. Event Hub
> C. ExpressRoute
> D. Queue Storage

Service Bus, Event Hub, and Queue Storage are all products that receive messages from endpoints for later processing. ExpressRoute is not a messaging product; rather, ExpressRoute allows an on-premise network to connect over a private link into the Azure cloud using a connectivity provider. Therefore, the answer is A, B, and D.

In conclusion, knowledge of and experience with a large majority of all existing Azure products and features are needed. Without knowing the products that exist, there is no chance of knowing what they do. Knowing both what products exist and what they do is a necessity to achieve the Azure Solutions Architect Expert certification.

Strive for a Deep Knowledge of a Few, Some Knowledge of Many, and a Basic Knowledge of All

Up to now, the words *product* (aka service) and *feature* have been used numerous times. There is a subtle difference between them. When the word *product* is used, it refers to an object like Azure Virtual Network, Azure App Service, Azure Web Apps, or Azure SQL. The product is something that is bought; it is the item that is selected after clicking the + Create A Resource link in the portal, as shown in Figure 1.4.

FIGURE 1.4   The + Create A Resource link

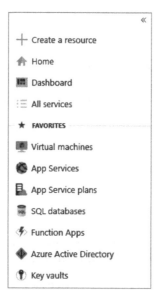

The products are also in the Favorites section, also shown in Figure 1.4.

Features, on the other hand, are additional, usually optional, capabilities that can be added to the product. For example, it is recommended that the Application Insights *feature* is combined with an Azure App Service web app. Also, there is an Azure Search feature that works well with Azure SQL. Backup is not a product and cannot be used on its own; it is a feature that is bound to a specific product. Not all features are available on all products;

some scenarios wouldn't make sense such as having the Backup feature for Event Hub. Other features such as SSL/TLS or custom domain features for an Azure Function make good sense.

From an exam perspective, it is important to have a broad knowledge of all Azure products and features. The following list shows how many products fall into different Azure categories:

- Compute (13)
- Networking (13)
- Storage (14)
- Web (7)
- Mobile (6)
- Databases (12)
- Security and identity (19)
- Containers (8)

That is a large number of products/services to comprehend, and the number is continuing to grow. The recommended approach is to pick a few of the products that are of most interest to you (Azure VM, Azure App Service, Azure Functions, Azure Database, Azure Security, and so on). Then, based on personal preference, create and configure those products and study them deeply to become an expert in them. Experience how those products interact with each other and learn all the available features available to them. The knowledge gained using this approach, via creating and configuring Azure products and integrating them with other products and features, leads to mastering a few and knowing others rather well.

 I gathered the previous list of categories from here:

docs.microsoft.com/en-us/azure/#pivot=products&panel=all

This list contains the Azure products that relate mostly to the Azure Solutions Architect Expert exams. You will learn how to configure and integrate some of the Azure products and features in later chapters.

Do not think that it is required to know all products and features down to the bits to pass the Azure exams. However, deep knowledge in the security, compute, network, and databases categories is expected. This is obvious in the outlines of the exams on the Microsoft Certification website.

docs.microsoft.com/en-us/learn/certifications/exams/az-303

docs.microsoft.com/en-us/learn/certifications/exams/az-304

Therefore, learn a few products deeply and learn *something* about the other many products. You will be expected to at least notice if a product is presented as an Azure product but is not. You can then exclude it from the possible correct answers.

Next, read more about the products and features in the next section. These are the ones that are highly recommended to know in detail.

An Introduction to "Must-Know" Azure Features

Recognizing a feature name and its functions can help you pass the Azure Solutions Architect Expert exams. This section discusses some of the more well-known and utilized Azure products in a little more detail. Later in the book, you will get the opportunity to create and utilize these products as well as numerous other Azure products in a more complete scenario.

Azure Active Directory and Security

Security is one of the most important aspects of an IT solution. If you cannot manage the access and manage who has what rights on the system, then it is unlikely the solution will have much value. Azure provides many products and features to help create, enforce, maintain, and monitor your features, from a security perspective.

Whether you realize it or not, the first significant product created when you begin consuming Azure products and features is an Azure Active Directory (AAD), sometimes referred to as a *tenant*. The first time you set up an Azure subscription, a requested option is the initial domain name. This name must be unique on Azure and is prefixed with `*.onmicrosoft.com`, where * is the unique name provided by the creator. The tenant must always be sent to AAD when requesting authentication.

 Azure Active Directory also can be referred to as an *identity as a service*. AAD is used for authenticating sign-ins and identity protection.

Let's take a step back and touch quickly on how AAD came to be. The first authentication technique was a simple user ID and password data store. However, this broke down because each application typically had their own data store and an account was required for each application. As the number of systems being used increased, so did the maintenance and complexity of gaining access to an application. Therefore, the Active Directory concept was created to store all corporate user credentials, user profiles, and permissions in a central global location. (We are discussing enterprise authentication at this point, not private user accounts.) Active Directory worked just fine; all applications implemented with Integrated Windows Authentication (IWA) could log in to any system on an intranet, without having to sign in multiple times as users moved from one application to the next.

Since the size of a typical corporation is relatively small when compared to all possible users accessing the internet, Active Directory worked well internally. There have been attempts to create a global authentication provider for the internet; however, those attempts have failed.

What Azure Active Directory does is to provide those same authentication and authorization capabilities but on the Azure platform. The Azure Active Directory tenant can be used to link and authenticate software as a service (SaaS) capabilities like Bing, Office 365, or Dynamics CRM. Additionally, AAD can be synchronized with an on-premise Active

Directory so that users inside an internal network can use the same credentials to authenticate on a compute resource running on the Azure platform. The tool to use for this synchronization is called *Azure AD Connect*, which will be discussed in much more detail in the next chapter.

In addition to having detailed knowledge of AAD, to increase the probability of successful exam completion, it is necessary to know these Azure security features and technologies and their use cases:

- Azure AD Connect
- Custom domain names
- RBAC
- Key Vault
- Azure Active Directory for Domain Services
- Managed Service Identity (MSI)
- Storage Access Signature (SAS)
- AAD conditional access policies
- AAD domain services
- Azure confidential computing
- Multifactor authentication
- Single sign-on (SSO)
- Security Center
- Encryption techniques, data-at-rest, data-in-transit
- Certificate authentication, SSL/TLS, certificate authority (CA)
- Forms, token, OAuth, JWT, and claims authentication techniques

This list contains not only products and features available on Azure but also technologies and models for securing application and resources. Knowing which type of authentication is best used in a given scenario is helpful when taking the exam. Additionally, having some practical experience with the tools improves your knowledge of the limits and constraints imposed by each, which leads to making good designs with specific products and features based on a given scenario. More detail, a few scenarios, and exercises are covered in later chapters.

Networking

Using any of the Azure Infrastructure as a Service (IaaS) or Platform as a Service (PaaS) offerings, a network infrastructure is provided as part of the service. Azure VM, App Service, or Azure Functions is allocated an IP address (internal and external), and in most scenarios, the endpoint becomes immediately and globally accessible.

Keep these two topics in mind:

Cost   Although the network is provided as a service, that doesn't mean it is free. Network attributes such as public IP addresses, inbound and outbound global/regional peering, and inbound and outbound data transfers between availability zones all have a cost; it is nominal, but it is not free. Data transfers between resources within the same virtual network are free, however. The task of managing, planning, and calculating costs is a significant part of managing an Azure subscription. It requires so much that Microsoft purchased a company named Cloudyn in 2017. Cloudyn is a tool that helps manage and monitor costs, and it can provide some tips on how to optimize the consumed Azure resource. Read more about Cloudyn here:

    docs.microsoft.com/en-us/azure/cost-management/overview

Configuration   There are some significant configuration activities to consider once you have deployed to Azure. Internet connectivity into an Azure data center, firewalls, DMZs, and other basic networking devices and configurations provide only the fundamental capabilities for the deployed application.

The number of configurations depends a lot on the requirements of the solution being created or migrated to Azure. From a default perspective, typical configuration includes the following: inbound and outbound port/firewall rules, network security groups (NSGs), enabling security via the Azure Security Center, and any load balancing rules. These are some other products and features that may require configurations:

- Azure Virtual Network, VNet peering
- Azure DNS
- Azure Availability Zones
- Azure Load Balancer
- Azure Application Gateway
- Azure Content Delivery Network
- Web Application Firewall
- Azure DDoS Protection
- Azure ExpressRoute
- VPN capabilities

Other tools that are useful to know from the context of Azure networking are as follows:

- Network Performance Monitor (NPM)
- Azure Log Analytics
- NPM for ExpressRoute
- Azure Monitor
- Azure Network Watcher

These costs, configuration requirements, network products features, and monitoring capabilities are "must-know" topics for an aspiring Azure Solutions Architect Expert candidate.

Azure Virtual Machines

Azure Virtual Machines (VM) is Microsoft's IaaS product offering. Azure VM was one of the first cloud products Microsoft offered on the Azure platform and is a highly scalable and enterprise-ready compute platform. IaaS means that all the hardware necessary to run a server, for example, CPUs/compute, memory, and storage, is provided by the cloud service provider, in this case Microsoft. Additionally, the networking capabilities, summarized previously, are provided and supported. The customer is responsible for the operating system, configuration, updates, and applications that run on top of that.

When choosing Azure VM to handle your compute requirements, there are many important considerations to make that help ensure a successful deployment or migration. The top three are operating system, location, and size. Azure VM supports Windows and Linux operating systems and is available in each of the 54 Azure regions around the world. There are many different sizes of virtual machines ranging from a one-vCPU machine and 1GB of RAM up to 128 cores and 432GB of RAM. The offerings in Azure change rapidly; the point is that there is a great range of available virtual machines in Azure VM.

It is most common to migrate from either Hyper-V, VMware, or a physical server to Azure VM. Any virtual machine must be in the form of a virtual hard disk (VHD), and common deployment mechanisms are either using Azure Site Recovery or placing the VHD in a Blob container as a Block blob. You'll learn more about this and Azure Migrate later in the book.

In addition, to have an expert grasp of Azure VM to increase your chances of passing the exam, it is necessary to know these features and their use cases:

- OS disks, data disks, and managed disks
- Availability set
- Configuration
- Identity
- Disaster recovery and backup
- Update management
- Configuring alerts and monitoring

You should also know about the following tools/products for planning, configuring, deploying, securing, and maintaining virtual machines on Azure VM:

- Azure Migrate
- Azure Site Recovery
- Azure Backup
- Azure Automation

IaaS can require more support and maintenance costs when compared to other Azure compute products. However, these costs may be justified because of missing features or constraints in the PaaS offerings.

Azure App Service

Azure App Service is Microsoft's PaaS offering. This means that in addition to the network infrastructure being the responsibility of the cloud provider, the operating system and its patching are no longer a concern to the customer. Azure App Service comes in four flavors.

- Azure Web Apps/WebJobs
- Azure App Service Web App for Containers
- Azure Mobile Apps
- Azure API Apps

There is one additional flavor—an enterprise-grade app known as the App Service Environment (ASE). ASE is an isolated Azure App Service tenant that belongs solely to the customer who creates it. There are some capabilities available only in ASE, for example, configuring cypher suite order. That specific example makes sense in the public App Service tenant because all customers running in that tenant may not want the cypher suite configured in that order.

Azure App Service offers both the Windows and Linux operating systems and supports a large majority of coding languages, both Microsoft and open source such as .NET Core, Java, Ruby, Node.js, and so on. All flavors of Azure App Service support built-in autoscaling, load balancing, integration with AAD and OAuth providers, and great deployment capabilities with integration with Git, DevOps (formerly Visual Studio Team Service [VSTS]), and GitHub.

From an Azure Web Apps perspective, use one of those source code repositories for hosting a custom web application or for running content management systems (CMSs) such as WordPress, Umbraco, Joomla!, or Drupal. The WebJobs service is used for longer-running workloads that don't require an HTTP connection to remain connected from start to finish. Consider a WebJob instance to be something like a batch job or a small program that runs offline in the background that is triggered by a cron scheduler; these are referred to as a *triggered* WebJob. WebJobs can also be continuous/AlwaysOn. In this case, they monitor a queue of some kind, and when a message enters the queue, the WebJob performs some action on it. A WebJob can also be configured as a singleton or set up to run on all the instances of the application.

A container allows you to add all the dependencies of an application into a single package. This includes the application/custom code, its binary dependencies, and the operating system on which it runs. This allows the application to be portable across many platforms as all the dependencies are in a package that is fully functional on its own.

Azure App Service Web App for Containers supports Windows- and Linux-based containerized applications. When using the noncontainerized web app, the application runs within a sandbox, which imposes certain limitations. For example, writing the registry, accessing the event log, working with COM, and changing the order of the default cypher suite as mentioned before are not supported in the Azure Web Apps sandbox. You can, however, do all the previously mentioned activities in a Azure App Service Web App for Containers instance. Azure App Service Web App for Containers is even more flexible than ASE in many cases. As already stated, as a designer and an Azure architect, you must know the requirements of the application and the capabilities of the product for which you are planning your migration. It is possible to build your own container in Visual Studio or use an existing one hosted on Docker Hub, the Azure Container Registry, or GitHub.

Azure Mobile Apps was at one time called Zumo and is similar to Azure Web Apps but is optimized for a mobile scenario. Simple integration with a data source, easy integration with multiple authentication providers, and the ability to send push notifications to mobile devices are some of the specific features of an app on Azure Mobile Apps. As mobile apps typically operate on multiple operating systems such as iOS, Android, and Windows, there is a cross-platform SDK specifically created to work in this context. Autoscaling, monitoring, load balancing, and other basic features are the same between Azure Web Apps and Azure Mobile Apps.

Finally, let's take a look at Azure API Apps. Don't confuse Azure API Apps with API Management discussed later in this book. Azure API Apps is the quickest way to deploy and create RESTful APIs. While the apps require no infrastructure management, Azure API Apps has built-in support for Swagger. Azure App Webs instances would typically have some kind of a GUI or an interface for an individual to interact in some way with the application. API Apps instances do not have a GUI or page to interact with; instead, they are endpoints that usually exchange and process JSON documents.

The following are some related products, features, and concepts to know in the Azure App Service context:

- Cloning
- Application Insights
- Backups
- Custom domains
- Managed identity
- SSL/TLS, App Service certificates
- Scale-up versus scale-out
- KUDU/SCM
- Cross-origin resource sharing (CORS)

Azure App Service is one of the main points of entry onto the Azure platform. This product can be configured to utilize and interface with almost all other Azure products and features. It is a cost-effective product, but keep in mind the sandbox in which the application must operate in; see the full list of products here:

github.com/projectkudu/kudu/wiki/Azure-Web-App-sandbox

Azure Functions

Azure Functions is the serverless product offering from Microsoft. This doesn't mean that the code somehow executes without having any supporting compute resource; rather, it means that when the application is not in use, it is not allocated to a server/compute resource. There are currently two scenarios in which you can configure an Azure Function: a Consumption plan and an App Service plan.

Running in the Consumption plan means that after 20 minutes of nonuse, the resources will be deallocated and placed back into a pool of compute resources, and the application gets shut down. This is the biggest difference when compared to the App Service plan. Running in Consumption mode is dynamic, which is why the Consumption plan is often referred to as *dynamic mode*. In addition to the shutdown difference, when running in Consumption, the following limitations apply:

- The combined consumption is limited to 1.5GB of memory per Functions app.

- Scaling is handled by a scale controller; there is no manual or autoscaling.

The 1.5GB memory limit is based on the Functions app. A Functions app can contain many functions. Functions are always bound to a trigger like on Storage Queue, Cosmos DB, or HTTP. The combined memory consumption of all functions within the Functions app would constitute the limit threshold. Unlike running in the App Service plan's Consumption mode, where scaling is managed by a scale controller, the controller executes custom algorithms per trigger type and scale based on their unique attributes. As a consumer of an Azure Function, scaling is something that you should not be concerned about in dynamic mode.

Since Azure Functions runs on the same architecture as Azure App Service, when running in that mode, the function has access to the same compute resources as App Service would. This means that the Functions app can consume more than 1.5GB of memory, up to the maximum allowed to the selected App Service plan's SKU; scaling based on custom rules is supported, and enabling AlwaysOn is supported. The ability to enable AlwaysOn means that after 20 minutes of nonuse, the application/function will not be shut down; this helps avoid any latent cold-start or warmup issue. Finally, running Azure Functions on an existing Azure App Service plan (ASP) may be more cost effective if you already have an ASP that has spare or unused compute capacity.

From an Azure Functions perspective, these additional topics should be of interest:

- Azure Cosmos DB

- Azure Event Hub

- Azure Event Grid

- Azure Notification Hubs

- Azure Service Bus (queues and topics)

- Azure Storage (blob, queues, and tables)

Azure Functions is more useful for smaller workloads that resemble a single method. Therefore, the approach toward their consumption should be based on what typically runs within a single function/method of a typical nonserverless application. The point is, do not overload a single Azure Function with a massive workload. Although it will scale, it may not work as expected. Instead, break any large workload into smaller work sets and implement them using the Durable Functions model.

API Management

Azure API Management (APIM) is a virtual gateway that is placed between consumers and actual APIs. You can think of APIM as a proxy or gateway in front of other APIs that reroutes the request to the proper API based on the parameters and signature of the URL. Why would this product be implemented? APIM provides the following benefits:

- Can expose separate APIs to external and internal consumers
- Hides the actual landscape from the consumer, which reduces complexity and confusion
- Controls usage and limits consumption
- Includes monitoring capabilities and error detection
- Connects to any and multiple APIs on the internet and exposes them via a single endpoint
- Allows group-based access control to APIs

The following are the scenarios in which APIM will be most beneficial:

- Integration
- Hybrid solutions
- Migration

From an integration perspective, assume that two companies have merged; both companies have internal and external APIs that are fundamental to the success of their company. Assume also that each of those APIs exposes a different endpoint, so managing, documenting, and knowing which to use and where to access it becomes possibly more complex than the API itself. What APIM can do is to expose a single endpoint where all APIs are accessible and manageable. This greatly simplifies the consumption, management, and maintenance of all APIs.

Hybrid solutions are when a company has created a product that depends on components hosted on-premise and in the cloud. Some customers want or need to keep some content or processes in-house for compliance or legal reasons. APIM can be used as a gateway between both of these on-premise and cloud-hosted APIs. APIM can be configured to run within a virtual network; then the virtual network is configured using a VPN or ExpressRoute to access on-premise resources. As mentioned already, APIM has solid authentication capabilities that are relatively simple to implement, directly in the portal.

Finally, imagine a scenario where a company has an API app running on an Azure App Service plan. This API would have a unique endpoint for all consumers to access so that its use case can be accessed. A change to the endpoint would require all consumers to update their code, which is a large ask, and sometimes an impossible one, so avoiding this from the beginning is most optimal. Having APIM manage all the requests to APIs in a company's solution helps with that scenario. If the backend API endpoint needs to change, the APIM endpoint remains the same. A change to the routing via the Azure Portal, PowerShell, or CLI would result in the migration to the new API endpoint.

APIM supports the configuration of many API types, as listed in Table 1.3.

TABLE 1.3 Azure API Management–Supported API Types

Type	Description
OpenAPI	Non-language-specific but standard interface to REST APIs
WADL	An XML description of an HTTP-based web service, RESTful
WSDL	An XML description of an HTTP-based web service, SOAP
Logic app	Scalable and hybrid workflow management, visual
API app	An API hosted using the Azure App Service product
Functions app	Event-driven, serverless compute via the Azure App Service product

The following are other topics that are helpful to know in the context of API Management:

- CA certificates
- Client certificates
- OAuth 2.0
- Delegation
- Custom domains
- Managed Service Identity
- Virtual networks

APIM is a useful product for managing migrations and integrations between companies and IT solutions.

Azure Monitor

Migrating an application or a solution consisting of numerous applications to a cloud provider is a big decision that requires many considerations. Properly estimating the compute requirements, configuring the security configuration, and organizing resources into supportable groups are just a few items to keep in mind. One significant consideration is how to monitor the solution and make sure it remains available and performant after deployment. Azure provides a product called Azure Monitor for just that.

Azure Monitor includes both Log Analytics and Application Insights. Combined, this feature supports end-to-end monitoring of applications that can identify how a customer consumes a product, can locate bottlenecks, and even can recommend some actions to improve experiences using the recommendations analyzer. Azure Monitor combines the capabilities of both these other products; or, Log Analytics and Application Insights can continue to be used on their own.

 Features and terminology change over time. For the most up-to-date Azure Monitor terminology, check this page out:

docs.microsoft.com/en-us/azure/azure-monitor/terminology

Log Analytics stores application and diagnostic logs into a query-able data source based on *Azure Data Explorer*, which is a highly scalable service for logging and storing telemetry data. The Log Analytics portion is the interface to create the workspaces that capture the data and to query the data source to gather performance, usage, and application behavior information. The query language used to extract the data is called KUSTO, and it is relatively simple and well-documented.

Here is an example that scans a table called Event, which stores content typically found in the event logs on a typical Windows server. Additionally, the query retrieves only those with an EventLevelName value of Error from one day ago.

```
Event
| where EventLevelName == "Error"
| where TimeGenerated > ago(1d)
| summarize count() by Source
```

Application Insights, on the other hand, is more metrics driven. It represents a set of data in a graphical calculation over a given time frame. The outcome of that calculation is a chart showing a value. For example, if a chart is created to show the availability of a specific product, per day, then the chart would show the availability from 0% to 100%. Application Insights offers great charting capabilities found in a product called *Metrics Explorer*, which monitors the availability, performance, and usage of web applications. Application Insights can monitor applications hosted on Azure and on-premise.

In addition to charting metrics data, Application Insights can trigger alerts, which can find bottlenecks in code executions using a profiler based on *PerfView*, and can build an application map that identifies dependencies between different Azure products.

In conclusion, Azure Monitor is the go-forward name for the previous products Log Analytics and Application Insights. Knowing the capabilities included in Azure Monitor is a great asset. Pulling data from different products, querying that data using KUSTO, graphing that data to define performance metrics, sending alerts based on captured data, and finding dependencies between the different products that make up the solution are all impactful features.

Azure SQL

Azure SQL is Microsoft's database as a service (DaaS) offering. It provides data storage, allows you to configure and optimize data without needing to be a database administrator (DBA), and removes the requirement for managing the server on which the database runs.

Four fundamental activities are required for placing your data into a relational database on the Azure platform:

- Creating the database
- Configuring security
- Migrating the data
- Monitoring the database

Two scenarios allow the consumption of a SQL Server database on the Azure platform:

- Azure SQL Database
- SQL Server on an Azure virtual machine

Azure SQL Database provides the following options:

Single Database   The single database option is a database that runs inside an Azure SQL Database instance but has its own resources and is manageable using a SQL Database server. A single database is the typical entry point for new applications that desire to start small and then scale up as consumption increases. When choosing elastic pools, a customer would have multiple databases, and each would reside on the same Azure SQL Database server. However, the ability to predict the amount of capacity required per database is unknown or overly complicated. Elastic pools help solve that problem by having the platform provide the performance capacity (elasticity) per database within a defined budget.

Elastic Pool   Elastic pools like single databases are priced using the database transaction unit (DTU) pricing model, or eDTU for elastic. DTU is the term created by the Azure SQL team that measures reads, writes, CPU, and memory consumption. The number of DTUs allocated to a single or elastic pool is determined by the selected service tier, for example, Basic, Standard, or Premium. The more you pay, the more DTUs you get; it's that simple.

Managed Instance   The price of managed instances is not calculated using the DTU model, rather the vCore-based purchasing model. This model is straightforward and is similar to the way prices are calculated for on-premise SQL Server databases. This offering is as close as you can get to a replica of an on-premise installation of SQL Server, while still getting the benefits of DaaS.

A *relational database (RDBMS)*, such as SQL Server, Oracle, and Azure SQL, organizes data into tables consisting of columns and rows. Each row typically has a primary key, which can be the foreign key of one or more other related tables. The data in those tables is accessible using the Structured Query Language (SQL).

In the unfortunate event that an on-premise SQL Server installation has dependencies or requirements that prevent using any of the DaaS offerings, Azure provides an option to run SQL Server on a virtual machine. In this scenario, you simply choose the configuration (SQL Server and Windows version) and determine the license agreement and size of the virtual machine. From that point, it is the same procedure for your own on-premise SQL Server instance running on IaaS.

For security, Azure SQL provides a firewall-setting feature. By default, all Azure resources pass through the firewall, and all other resources external to Azure (determined based on IP) are not allowed through. The Azure SQL database is not inside a virtual network and has a globally accessible endpoint. Azure SQL does currently support connectivity to a virtual network, but it doesn't exist in one. A product called VNet Service Endpoints changes this, but as of this writing, it is in preview. The globally accessible endpoint is a point of interest/concern for some customers, and VNet Service Endpoints is expected to resolve this issue. If having a global endpoint is a showstopper, then the options are strong firewall settings or a SQL Server on Azure Virtual Machine that can be contained in a VNet.

Once the type of database required has been provisioned, the next step is to migrate the data to it. The available tools are based on the type of database chosen. For both a single pool and an elastic pool, use the *Data Migration Assistant (DMA)* to confirm the source database is compatible with the destination database. Once confirmed, export the source database, which creates a BACPAC file. Import that file into the destination database using the Azure Portal or a SqlPackage. This procedure is not intended for migrating production databases as there could be extended downtime. To move a production database and reduce downtime, use the *Data Migration Service (DMS)*.

The process for migrating data to a managed instance or to a SQL Server instance on Azure Virtual Machine is the same for on-premise installations. First use DMA to identify and resolve any conflicts; then use the native SQL Service restore capabilities, via a BAK file, to migrate the data to Azure.

Once the database is provisioned, secure, and populated with data, monitoring/optimizing it is the next and final step (excluding maintaining it, of course). Here are the numerous products and tools capable of monitoring an Azure SQL database. Note that monitoring and tuning a SQL Server instance on Azure Virtual Machine is the same as on-premise SQL Server and IaaS (via Log Analytics).

- Query Performance Insights
- Query Store
- XEvents

Setting up an Azure SQL database is quick and easy. The connection string is found with ease, and as the endpoint is globally accessible, making a connection to it from code is just as quick.

Remember to whitelist the IP address of the client (for example, your development workstation) connecting to the database. Otherwise, access will not be possible.

Azure Cosmos DB

Unlike Azure SQL, which is a relational DBMS, Azure Cosmos DB is classified as a NoSQL database. Cosmos DB includes databases, containers, and items exposed by numerous APIs. When choosing a data store for an application, if the following scenarios match the data storage requirements, then Azure Cosmos DB would be an optimal decision:

- Utilizes key/value pairs
- Needs document storage capability
- Graphs data stores
- Globally replicates data
- Provides results in JSON format
- Exposes data using a RESTful API

 The MongoDB API is to Cosmos DB like ADO.NET is to Azure SQL/SQL Server. Cosmos DB is compatible with the Mongo API, Cassandra API, Gremlin API, and Etcd APIs. Therefore, any solution currently using those databases can be migrated to Cosmos DB without any changes. This allows customers to gain the benefits such as a 99.999 SLA and global availability without rewriting their solutions.

When Cosmos DB is provisioned from Azure, one required attribute to select is the API, which also dictates which database type to implement. The currently supported Cosmos DB types are as follows:

- Core (SQL)
- MongoDB
- Cassandra
- Azure Table
- Gremlin (graph)

The database/API dictates the entity type, referred to as a *container*; see Table 1.4.

TABLE 1.4   Azure Cosmos DB Container Entities

Database/API	Azure Cosmos DB Container
Core (SQL)	Collection
MongoDB	Collection
Casandra	Table
Azure Table	Table
Gremlin (graph)	Graph

Table 1.5 describes how Azure Cosmos DB refers to items.

TABLE 1.5   Azure Cosmos DB Item Entities

Database/API	Azure Cosmos DB Container
Core (SQL)	Document
MongoDB	Document
Casandra	Row
Azure Table	Item
Gremlin (graph)	Node or Edge

There is a slight terminology barrier for implementing a Cosmos DB, but this is common for all types of technologies and their corresponding features. Figure 1.5 shows the relationship between the database account, database, container, and item entities listed in Table 1.5.

The important takeaway from this section is that you should understand under what scenarios one would choose to use Cosmos DB and the differences it has compared to a relational DBMS. Primarily, Cosmos DB exposes its data via a RESTful API, communicates in the format of JSON, and is, by default, platform independent.

Azure Storage

There is not much you can accomplish without storage. This is true regardless of running workloads in the cloud. Although it is possible to store large amounts of content in memory, that content must come from some physical location. Azure Storage provides some useful capabilities for storing content that is globally accessible, secure, scalable, and durable.

FIGURE 1.5   Database account relationships

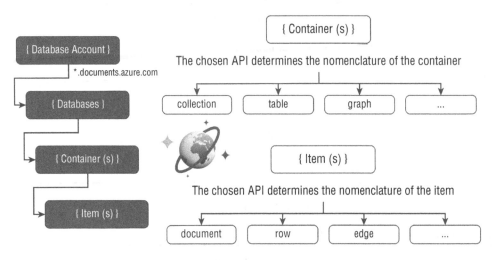

Azure Storage provides four data services, which are described in Table 1.6.

TABLE 1.6   Azure Storage Services

Type	Description
Azure Blob storage	Scalable object store for binary and text data
Azure File storage	Managed file shares
Azure Queue storage	Messaging store and queuing
Azure Table storage	NoSQL data store, now part of Cosmos DB

To utilize Azure Storage, you must first create a storage account from within Azure Portal via a REST API, via the CLI, or by using an ARM template. Once an account is created, from within the portal you would see something like that shown in Figure 1.6.

FIGURE 1.6   Creating a storage account

It is possible to have multiples of each service types within a single storage account.

A *blob* is typically a file, for example, an image, a video, or an audio file. These and any other file type can be stored in Azure Blob storage. The following are some common uses of Azure blobs:

- Support the upload of large files from a website.
- Back up and restore, archival or disaster recovery.
- Writing logs

There are numerous reasons to support the uploading of files from a form on a website. Consider YouTube, which supports the upload of very large files—files so large that an HTTP connection made for the upload would likely time out before the transmission of the data completes. Using the `System.Web.UI.WebControls.FileUpload` class isn't an option in this scenario. Instead, one would use `Microsoft.WindowsAzure.Storage .Blob.CloudBlobClient` and upload the large file to an Azure Storage blob container that is designed specifically for this purpose, instead of storing it directly on the hard drive running the app.

Performing backups of a database or website and storing a VHD image of an IaaS instance as a block blob for quick recovery are also common scenarios for blobs. In case of a disaster situation, pulling data, content, or an image from a blob is a feasible recovery strategy. Writing logs to a blob file makes a lot of sense if there is a need to expose them to some other entity. For example, accessing IIS logs typically requires access to the server and then performing a manual effort to consolidate them. It is possible to configure Azure App Service to write IIS logs to a blob's storage container. Accessing/analyzing them is then much more efficient, because the logs are in a single location and globally accessible.

The following are important topics to know in this context:

- Locally redundant storage (LRS)
- Zone-redundant storage (ZRS)
- Georedundant storage (GRS)
- Read-access geo-redundant storage (RA-GRS)
- Encryption at rest
- Immutable blobs
- Page and block blobs

Azure File storage is somewhat synonymous with what we commonly refer to as a *file share* that uses the Server Message Block (SMB) protocol. Historically in Windows Explorer, when you right-click a folder and select Share, then all those who are given access can read, write, and/or delete the content of that directory. That scenario, however, is restricted to those within an intranet. True, there are some configurations using WebDav via IIS that could provide access to internal shares externally. However, that configuration can be complicated to configure and maintain. Azure files simplify that by providing the same mapping capabilities as one would expect from doing what was just described globally.

Mapping a drive to an Azure files share is supported on Windows, Linux, and macOS and is configured by using a PowerShell cmdlet: net use, sudo mount, or mount_smbfs. An Azure file share is globally accessible via *.file.core.windows.net, where * is the name of your storage account. Finally, Azure files are utilized by Microsoft for its own products; one specifically is Azure Functions.

Azure Queue storage is a big deal and is discussed in more detail later in the book. There is a lot to consider when deciding on a messaging and queueing solution, and it is not made simpler because Microsoft offers numerous messaging capabilities:

- Azure Queue storage

- Azure Event Grid

- Azure Event Hub

- Azure Service Bus

Each one provides similar offerings, specifically, messaging/queuing capabilities, but each has a specific use case that warrants their existence. An Azure queue is specifically designed for storing a message, which is, for example, a short string up to 64KB in size that is accessible via authenticated HTTP or HTTPS calls. The message may be a location (blob URL) to a file that needs to be processed offline by WebJobs or may contain details of the size of an image to be generated. Thus, you would use an Azure blob when you need to store an entire file and an Azure queue to store a message.

 LRS, ZRS, and GRS redundancies apply to both Azure blobs and Azure queues.

Azure Table storage, as previously mentioned, is now part of Cosmos DB. Regardless of the reclassification, an Azure table remains a NoSQL datastore. The datastore accepts global authenticated access and is most useful for storing massive amounts of data (terabytes) where the data is not bound by complicated stored procedures, joins, or foreign keys. Again, it is common that Microsoft has numerous products that provide similar capabilities, in this case, Azure SQL and Cosmos DB. Both of those products provide a solution to a specific use case.

The product you choose to store the object in—which your commissioned compute power processes, whether it be a file (blob or files), a message, or a NoSQL entity—has numerous design considerations. Having a thorough understanding of your business need/use case is fundamental in the decision driving the consumption of the storage solution.

Service Bus

Service Bus is one of the messaging capabilities mentioned in the previous section that focused on Azure Storage. As you certainly recollect, one of the four Azure Storage services is Azure Queue storage, which naturally leads to the question of why both, and even why four, messaging features exist. Service Bus has a specific and defined set of unique faculties.

If the following fall within the defined requirements of your solution, then Service Bus is the correct choice, as they are currently unique to Service Bus:

- Consumes messages in batches
- Requires AMQP 1.0 support
- Guarantees FIFO
- Restricts the message size: greater than 64KB and less than 256KB
- Requires RBAC and greater control over senders and receivers
- Supports high throughput and parallel processing
- Restricts the queue size to less than 80GB

Both Service Bus and Event Hub utilize a protocol beginning with `sb://` that maps to a hostname of `*.servicebus.windows.net`. This means they are built upon each other. Table 1.7 summarizes the messaging services and should provide clarity toward choosing Service Bus over other Azure messaging services.

TABLE 1.7   Azure Messaging Services

Type	When to Use	Purpose
Service Bus	Financial processing and order processing	Highly valued messaging
Event Grid	Status change reactions	Reactive programming
Event Hubs	Data streaming and telemetry	Big data pipeline

Service Bus can be categorized into two distinct entities.

- Queues (explained earlier in this chapter)
- Topics and subscriptions

After the creation of a Service Bus namespace, the option to create either a Service Bus queue or a topic exists, as shown in Figure 1.7.

FIGURE 1.7   Creating a Service Bus queue or topic

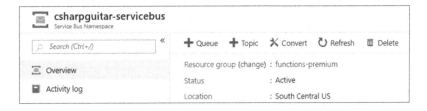

Messages within a Service Bus Queue can be processed by a single consumer. Where a consumer may be an Azure Functions app or perhaps a WebJobs app, that's a one-to-one relationship. I know you already know what topics and subscriptions they provide. You guessed it—it's a one-to-many form of communication. We're talking high volumes here— big data, machine learning scale, where the message is made available to each subscription registered to a specific topic.

The mapping of a message to a subscription is useful for scaling compute resources so that multiple instances/services/consumers can process a message as fast as possible upon its arrival in the queue. Like an older product called Stream Analytics, a Service Bus message can be analyzed using a filter and sent to a specific subscriber that executes an anticipated, delicate, or uniquely subtle code sequence. The creators of the Azure messaging capabilities have given great thought to many use cases and are eager to understand any you encounter that have no provision. Choose the one that meets the needs or your business requirements.

Site Recovery

Even when a solution has been migrated to the cloud, a disaster recovery solution remains a necessity. Often and only after something unexpected occurs does one recognize the need of a recovery plan. This plan is commonly referred to as a *business continuity and disaster recovery (BCDR) strategy*. Some failures can be a simple transient issue that corrects itself, while others can result in some major downtime. In the worst case, data or source code is lost, and sometimes it is not recoverable.

One should not expect that simply because a solution exists in the cloud that there are built-in redundancies and backups. There are some built-in redundancies on the Azure platform—be certain of that—but those are for the stabilization of the platform and infrastructure, not for your app. Ask yourself this question, "How could Microsoft know what parts of a solution should or should not be backed up?" The answer is that Microsoft cannot know this; customers have so many varied requirements, and the storage of the backups and the configuration of redundancies have a cost. Backup is not something provided by default or for free.

It is up to the individual subscribing entity to design the BCDR strategy. Remember, the strategy should specifically match the explicit requirements of the subscribing entity and operate within its given cost constraints. To help with not only the recovery of IaaS-based solutions but also with the migration and movement of them to and within Azure, Microsoft has a product named *Site Recovery*. Note that Site Recovery is focused on IaaS. Other non-IaaS components of a BCDR strategy are discussed later in the book. You will need to know this product in depth for the Azure Solutions Architect Expert exams.

From a recovery perspective, Site Recovery protects IaaS solutions in the following scenarios:

- Azure VM
- Physical servers
- VMware virtual machines
- Hyper-V virtual machines

From a BCDR perspective, the use of Site Recovery has two main configurations:

- To act as a BCDR solution for your on-premise solution and servers
- To act as a BCDR solution for your Azure-hosted IaaS compute workloads

Setting up a BCDR strategy for a company's servers running in their own privately funded and maintained data center is commonplace. This is expensive because although you could get some failover support when servers are in the same data center, what happens if the entire data center suffers an outage? The point is, to implement a real, enterprise BCDR strategy, you would need two data centers, with mirror replication of the hardware, software, and data, and they must be in different regions. Instead of setting up a second data center, a company can utilize Azure. Connecting, creating, replicating, and maintaining an Azure BCDR environment can occur over any secure means for those procedures, such as an ExpressRoute or a VPN similar to that shown in Figure 1.8.

FIGURE 1.8 Secure means for connecting, creating, replicating, and maintaining an Azure BCDR environment

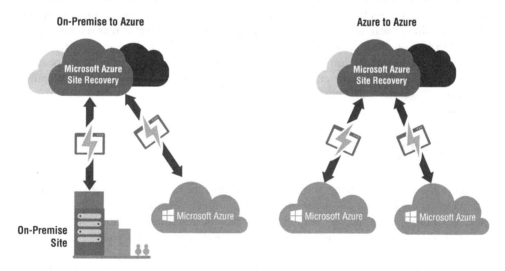

Additionally, running in a single data center on Azure can create a solution that requires massively high availability vulnerable to a natural or data-center-wide outage. Therefore, by using Site Recovery, you can build the same on-premise to Azure BCDR strategy as one that would exist between two Azure regionally dispersed data centers.

A tool called the *Site Recovery Deployment Planner (SRDP)* is helpful in the planning portion of the building of a BCDR instance or for migrating an IaaS virtual machine from one region to another. SRDP provides a compatibility assessment report on the following attributes, for example:

- Number of disks, disk size, IOPS, OS version
- Storage type, number of cores, virtual machine size recommendation
- Estimated cost

No IT solution is a complete solution without a BCDR plan, whether the solution is hosted completely on-premise, is a hybrid on-premise to Azure solution, or is hosted completely on Azure. In the last two scenarios, Site Recovery can help create a BCDR plan and assist with moves from IaaS to Azure, as well.

Azure Bastion

Making a remote connection to one of your Azure IaaS compute resources is typically performed using either RDP over port 3389 or SSH over port 22. By default, when you connect to those machines from your company or from home, the connection traverses the internet. If you do not want the connection to your machines to travel across the internet, you can instead access the console using Azure Bastion from within the Azure portal. When you do this, the connection takes place over port 443 from within the Azure portal to the machine. This Azure product makes connecting to your provisioned Azure compute more secure.

Summary

This chapter provided the starting point for the path toward earning the Azure Solutions Architect Expert certification. Feel confident that if you are already comfortable with the Azure products covered in this chapter, what you need now is some additional hands-on practice and some test questions to get your brain neurons connected to this Azure knowledge.

The next chapters cover the approach to take if you are planning to migrate an organization to the cloud, starting with creating the subscriptions, setting security and access, and then deciding which compute and storage resources to use. Finally, implement some management capabilities to help the transition, such as monitoring, and don't forget the BCDR strategy. You will create, configure, and monitor in each of these scenarios, so get ready to get your hands and brain moving.

Exam Essentials

Make sure you are on the right Azure path.   There are numerous Azure certification paths. Make sure you are on the path that best fits your career's objects. Azure Solutions Architect Expert certification is for system administrators or system architects, whereas someone who is more development-focused might consider the Azure Developer or Azure Dev Ops Engineer certification.

Gain experience with Azure.   To pass this exam, you will need experience with the platform. Do not expect any book or training to get you through this without having worked on the platform for some amount of time. If you do that, then this certification will have greater meaning to you and others.

Keep up-to-date by subscribing to online resources.   The Azure platform is constantly changing and requires daily actions to keep your skills up-to-date. Here are some of the most popular resources to read on a regular basis:

azure.microsoft.com/en-us/blog

blogs.technet.microsoft.com/blog/tag/azure

docs.microsoft.com/en-us/azure

Know what products exist in Azure.   Sometimes answers to questions contain products that may not be Azure products. They read like they are, but they are not. Knowing what really is available will help you remove at least one possible answer to a few questions.

You need to know at least one Azure product deeply, numerous products well, and a little about them all.   No one knows everything, but you can be an expert in one or two Azure products and features. Those products and features usually have a connection or dependency to other Azure features, and you could then learn some internals about them. There are some products and features that are not related to any other directly. For example, there is no direct relationship between Azure Cognitive Services and Azure VNet, but it would be useful to have at least a basic knowledge of the benefits each provides.

Focus on certain products.   The Azure Solutions Architect exam is heavy on Azure Active Directory, networking, compute (specifically IaaS), and migration from on-premise to Azure. Make sure you have a good understanding of the products and features and their limits. Having those will provide you with the best chance of passing the exam.

Key Terms

Azure AD Connect

Azure Administrator Associates

Azure Data Explorer

Azure Developer Associates

Azure DevOps Expert

Azure Solutions Architect Expert

Building and Deploying Applications

Business continuity and disaster recovery (BCDR) strategy

Configuring and Deploying Infrastructure

Data Migration Assistant (DMA)

Data Migration Service (DMS)

Designing a Data Solution

Designing an Infrastructure Strategy

Designing for Continuity and Recovery

Designing for Migration, Deployment and Integration

Designing for Security and Identity

Determining Workload Requirements

Developing for the Cloud

Error

Event

Implementing Security and Authentication

Implementing Security and Workloads

Metrics Explorer

PerfView

Platform as a service (PaaS)

Product

Site Recovery

Site Recovery Deployment Planner (SRDP)

Review Questions

Many questions can have more than a single answer. Please select all cori
answer choices.

1. Which security feature can you implement to protect Azure App Service fr
   internet access? (Choose two.)

   A. Azure Active Directory

   B. Role-based access control (RBAC)

   C. Managed identity

   D. Single sign-on (SSO)

2. When choosing a compute resource to execute your workload, what are the Azure options?
   (Choose two.)

   A. Azure VM

   B. Azure ExpressRoute

   C. Azure Functions

   D. API Management

3. A custom domain can be bound to which of the following Azure products? (Choose all
   that apply.)

   A. Azure App Service

   B. Azure Storage Account

   C. Azure VM

   D. Azure SQL

4. Azure Storage consists of which of the following service types?

   A. Blobs

   B. Queues

   C. Files

   D. Only A and B

5. You need to decide on the most cost-efficient Azure Storage redundancy solution, and you
   must store the data in multiple data centers. Which of the following would you choose?

   A. LRS

   B. ZRS

   C. GRS

   D. RA-GRS

You need to grant access to products running on Azure to another product or feature. Which Azure product or feature would you use?

   A. Key Vault

   B. AAD conditional access policies

   C. Managed identity

   D. Role-based access control (RBAC)

7. Which of the following is a valid business continuity and disaster recovery (BCDR) Azure product for an IaaS workload solution?

   A. Azure Availability Sets

   B. Azure Automation

   C. Azure Availability Zones

   D. Azure DNS

8. What is the most current supported SSL/TLS version for Azure App Service?

   A. SSL 3.0

   B. TLS 1.0

   C. TLS 1.2

   D. TLS 1.3

9. Which of the following is *not* a supported Azure VPN Gateway configuration?

   A. Point-to-point

   B. Site-to-site

   C. VNet-to-VNet

   D. Point-to-site

10. An Azure Active Directory tenant has which of the following?

   A. `*.atmicrosoft.com`

   B. `*.onmicrosoft.net`

   C. `*.onmicrosoft.com`

   D. `*.contoso.com`

11. You need to run an offline process that typically consumes 2GB of memory, takes 80 percent of two CPUs, and runs four times per day. Which Azure product is the most cost efficient?

   A. Azure Functions

   B. Azure VM

   C. Azure App Service WebJobs

   D. Azure Batch

12. What is multifactor authentication?

    A. User ID and password

    B. Something you know and something you have

    C. Client certificate and PIN

    D. Windows Hello for Business

13. Which product is most useful for monitoring the health of an Azure solution?

    A. Azure Monitor

    B. Application Insights

    C. Log Analytics

    D. Security Center

14. What Azure features are available for Azure VM? (Choose all that apply.)

    A. Azure Automation

    B. Disaster Recovery and Backup

    C. Azure Migrate

    D. Azure Site Recovery

15. True or false: Cross-origin resource sharing (CORS) restricts access to the rendering of a web page based on IP address.

    A. True

    B. False

16. In what scenario would you use the Azure API Management product? (Choose two.)

    A. An API that needs to scale based on consumption, regardless of limits

    B. Integration

    C. Managing access permission

    D. A REST API endpoint that will not change

17. Senior management requires you to run your workload on Azure App Service. You need to implement autoscaling. Under load, which of the following would you do?

    A. Scale out

    B. Scale up

    C. Both A and B

    D. Neither A nor B

18. A solution needing migration to Azure requires the registration of an assembly into the Global Assembly Cache (GAC). Which Azure product would you choose to run the workload?

    A. Azure Functions

    B. Azure App Service

    C. Azure VM

    D. None of the above

19. Which of the following options describe a RESTful API? (Choose all that apply.)

    A. Supports cross-platform software

    B. Is the fundamental concept underlying the Windows Communication Foundation (WCF) library

    C. Typically converses using JavaScript Object Notation (JSON)

    D. Is supported by Cosmos DB

20. Which of the following describes an Azure Web App for Containers instance? (Choose two.)

    A. Can have slow startup times when compared to Azure Functions

    B. Is compatible with Azure files

    C. Currently supports Linux only

    D. Can consume GPU resources

Chapter

2

Security and Identity

EXAM AZ-303 OBJECTIVES COVERED IN THIS CHAPTER:

✓ **Implement and Monitor an Azure Infrastructure**

- Implement Azure Active Directory
- Implement and manage hybrid identities

✓ **Implement Management and Security Solutions**

- Manage security for applications

EXAM AZ-304 OBJECTIVES COVERED IN THIS CHAPTER:

✓ **Design Identity and Security**

- Design authentication
- Design authorization
- Design security for applications

What's the first rule of security? It's the same as the first rule of fight club. There is really no reason to openly discuss your patching strategies, what versions of software you are running, or the ports/protocols that are open on your corporate firewalls. The fact is, the less someone knows about how you protect your stuff, the less likely they are to get it. As a side note, IIS by default sends its version as a header variable in an HTTP response. I have personally worked many cases where companies want to remove that, and the same goes for ASP.NET. Never, without any doubt, underestimate the importance of IT security. Security is so important that it is the first subject discussed in detail in this book.

Protecting personally identifiable data, protecting intellectual property, and securing physical resources are all integral parts of an IT organization. Without an implemented security strategy, a firm loses its integrity and the confidence of customers. Neither customers nor employees want their identity or private information leaked, stolen, and then sold. We don't really know yet what is happening to the data that has been stolen from the security breaches reported recently where hundreds of millions of records have been compromised. It is best to take every precaution in advance so you don't need to worry as much about that happening to your company.

In addition to protecting your solutions and data from external threats, you need to consider how to protect or restrict access to internal assets from employees. Configuring security that restricts access to the applications you host on Azure, creating compute workloads, and making sure your data is safe, at all times, are all discussed in this chapter. Once you complete this chapter, your understanding of Azure Active Directory, role-based access control (RBAC), hardware, networking, and some other generic security features available in Azure will be clear. You must understand these topics when preparing for the Azure Solutions Architect Expert exam.

Azure Active Directory

I am assuming you have an Azure subscription, which means you have an *Azure Active Directory (AAD)* to go with it. You can get a free Azure subscription here: azure.microsoft.com/en-us/free. You will notice the name of your AAD flash into and out of the address box in your browser when logging in to the Azure Portal. It resembles *.onmicrosoft.com, where * is the name of your Azure Active Directory.

By default, the AAD name is generated via an algorithm that uses the identity of the person who created the subscription. On the Azure Active Directory blade in the portal, there is a Create A Directory link. I created a preferred new AAD and reallocated my subscription to it. I didn't like the one defaulted to me. The AAD name is used in so many places that it's nice to have a friendly name you like.

AAD in Azure terms is often referred to as *directory name* or *tenant*. It can be used to manage access to numerous Microsoft software as a service (SaaS) products such as Office 365 and Dynamics 365, for example. Additionally, the Azure AD tenant is necessary when coding authentication into an application to use Azure Active Directory or to integrate with other third-party SaaS applications such as Salesforce, Box, or SAP. Figure 2.1 represents this visually.

FIGURE 2.1   Connection between Azure AD and other SaaS offerings

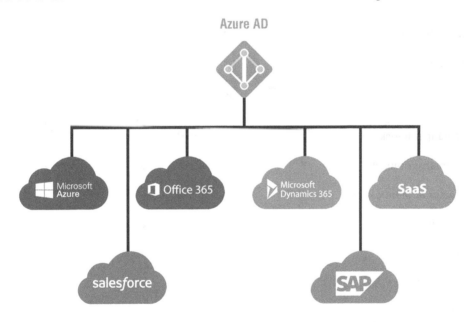

There are four editions of Azure Active Directory. The one created with the subscription is the Free edition. The other editions are Basic, Premium P1, and Premium P2. Single sign-on (SSO), AAD Connect, and self-service password reset are available in all editions. See Table 2.1 for an overview of the central features per AAD edition.

TABLE 2.1   Azure Active Directory Features per Edition

Feature	Free	Basic	Premium P1	Premium P2
Directory objects	500,000	Unlimited	Unlimited	Unlimited
SSO	✓	✓	✓	✓
B2B collaboration	✓	✓	✓	✓
Self-service password change	✓	✓	✓	✓
AAD Connect	✓	✓	✓	✓
Self-service password reset		✓	✓	✓
Company branding		✓	✓	✓
Application proxy		✓	✓	✓
SLA		✓	✓	✓
Self-service password reset/change/unlock			✓	✓
On-premise writeback			✓	✓
Multifactor authentication			✓	✓
Connect Health			✓	✓
Identity manager			✓	✓
Conditional access			✓	✓
SharePoint access			✓	✓
OneDrive for Business Access			✓	✓
Identity protection				✓

It is important to know which features are available in different AAD editions. Exam questions may ask you to choose the required version of AAD given a use-case scenario. Before we discuss some of these features in more detail, let's do a few exercises.

Which Azure tool can be used to synchronize all users in an on-premise Active Directory with Azure Active Directory?

A. Connect Health

B. AAD Connect

C. Identity Synchronizer

D. Active Directory Updater

Read on to learn the answer.

You should already have an Azure subscription, an Azure AD tenant, and an understanding of the different AAD editions (Free, Basic, P1, and P2). The next step is to give other people access to the tenant. Adding users to the Azure AD tenant will be done manually in a later exercise instead of using AAD Connect to synchronize existing users from an on-premise Active Directory. Had you used AAD Connect, then all the identities and groups would be migrated automatically. Keep in mind that we are still discussing AAD; we haven't begun discussing role-based access control, which is coming in the next section.

When creating an Azure Active Directory user in the portal, you have the following three options: User, Global Administrator, or Limited Administrator (see Table 2.2). Having these default roles simplifies permissions management because they contain a prebuilt permissions list that can be used as a guide.

TABLE 2.2 Azure Active Directory Roles

Directory Role	Description
User	Basic user type with limited access to most directory resources
Global Administrator	The credential used to create the Azure subscription originally is created as a Global Administrator. This role has full administrative access to all features in the Azure Active Directory.
Limited Administrator	Is added to a specific nonglobal administrative role upon creation. Examples include Application Admin, Help Desk Admin, Service Admin, and about 30 other built-in roles.

To add a user who utilizes a custom domain, you must first add the custom domain to the Azure AD. If this is not done, then you will see an error similar to Figure 2.2. It is also possible, if you have no custom domain, to add users with the default Azure AD tenant name, for example, user@*.onmicrosoft.com, where * is the name of your tenant.

FIGURE 2.2   Adding a user to Azure AD

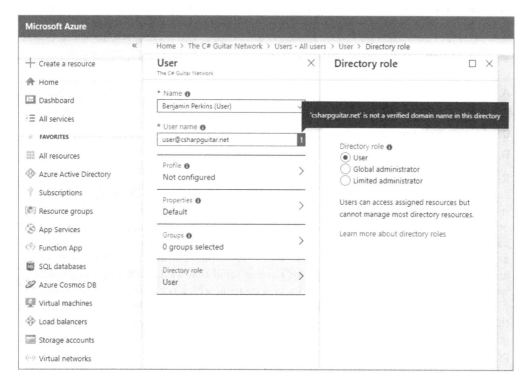

Complete the following to add a custom domain to your Azure Active Directory.

Add a Custom Domain to Azure Active Directory

In Exercise 2.1, you will add a custom domain to your Azure Active Directory. By doing this, you will be able to add users with that custom domain as part of their identity.

EXERCISE 2.1

Adding a Custom Domain to AAD

1. Log in to the Azure Portal at portal.azure.com.

2. Click the Azure Active Directory link, select Custom Domain Names, select + Add Custom Domain, enter your custom domain in the Custom Domain Name text box, and click the Add Domain button. See Figure 2.3.

FIGURE 2.3 Configuring a custom domain name

3. Log in to your domain hosting provider (for example, GoDaddy) and add the preferred DNS record that validates that you own the domain. (There is information about DNS and DNS records in Chapter 3.) See Figure 2.4.

FIGURE 2.4 Validating a custom domain name in Azure

4. Once you've added the record, click the Verify button. It can take up to 72 hours for the Domain Name System (DNS) change to propagate, but it usually takes much less time. In my scenario, it took less than five minutes.

5. Once it's verified, click the Make Primary button and then Yes. Keep in mind that this is a test scenario; take caution if you are working in a live, production scenario. See Figure 2.5.

FIGURE 2.5   A verified custom domain

6. Navigate back to the Azure Active Directory link. Select Custom Domain Names, and you will see the new custom domain marked as Primary as well as the default tenant. See Figure 2.6.

FIGURE 2.6   A validated custom domain

As mentioned, it is possible to use the default domain extension to create users. For example, user@*.onmicrosoft.com will work fine. The previous example is for those who have a custom domain, which most companies have. Also, this does not redirect an application or website that currently is hosting the domain on the internet.

When the Azure subscription is first created, the credentials used during its creation are automatically assigned the Global Administrator role. You can confirm this after logging into the portal, selecting Azure Active Directory ➤ Users ➤ *your account* ➤ Directory Role. See Figure 2.7.

FIGURE 2.7   A list of Azure AD user accounts

Now, let's add a few more users to different roles so later you can learn firsthand the differences between their access rights. Make sure to keep a list of the usernames and passwords in a secure place.

Create New Azure Active Directory Users

In Exercise 2.2, you will create numerous user accounts with different Azure Active Directory roles.

Creating Azure Active Directory Users

1. Log in to the Azure Portal at `portal.azure.com`.

2. Click the Azure Active Directory link, select Users, select + New User, and then create an additional Global Administrator. Add the required information, as shown in Figure 2.8, and click the Create button.

FIGURE 2.8 Adding an Azure AD user template

3. Notice that in the user list there are now two Global Administrators, one where the source is Microsoft Account and the other is Azure Active Directory. The identity used for authentication must come from the Azure Active Directory source in order to use and configure numerous Azure features. See Figure 2.9.

FIGURE 2.9 A list of Azure AD users

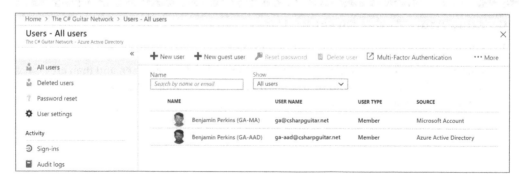

4. Create three more users where the directory roles are as follows:

- User

- Limited Administrator ➤ Application Developer

- Limited Administrator ➤ Cloud Application Administrator

5. Once completed, the list of users should resemble Figure 2.10.

FIGURE 2.10 A list of Azure AD users

When you sign in using one of the created users, the account will not be able to create any Azure resources. The reason is that the accounts are not linked to any subscription. This becomes apparent when navigating to the Subscription blade, which lists the subscriptions that are linked to the account. If the user clicks the + Add button, then they can create their own subscription that allows them to create Azure resources. In Exercise 2.6, you will grant a user access to a subscription.

There is a difference between Azure Active Directory and the security mechanism used within Azure to control access specifically to Azure resources. This is called *role-based access control*, as discussed in the next section. The point to note here is that AAD is a tenant that can be used to authenticate users across different products, while RBAC controls access to the Azure resources within the Azure Portal. When RBAC is covered in the next section, you will grant users access to the subscription and restrict access based on roles and groups.

Let's now get into the details of other Azure Active Directory products and features.

AAD Connect

AAD Connect, as shown in Figure 2.11, is used to create a hybrid identity solution existing between an on-premise Active Directory and an Azure Active Directory. One feature of

AAD Connect is that it configures Azure so that users with an on-premise AD can access
Azure resources.

FIGURE 2.11   Azure AD Connect wizard

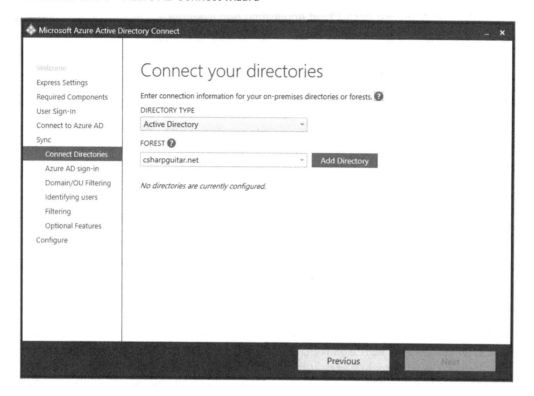

In addition to the support for configuring three sign-in scenarios (password hash synchronization, pass-through authentication, and ADFS, discussed later), AAD Connect helps
with synchronization. The synchronization support creates directory objects such as users,
devices, and groups existing in your on-premise AD to the cloud. In the Azure Portal, navigate to the Azure Active Directory blade and click Azure AAD Connect, and you will see
the sync status of the Azure AAD Connect process. Figure 2.12 represents how this looks
before and after a successful synchronization.

To complete the Azure AAD Connect synchronization, it is necessary that the account
used to synchronize is a Global Administrator that exists in the Azure Active Directory.
This is likely not the case. Initially, as shown in Figure 2.13, the user I used to create the
subscription has a source equal to Microsoft Account while the other has the source equal
to Azure Active Directory.

FIGURE 2.12   Azure AD Connect status

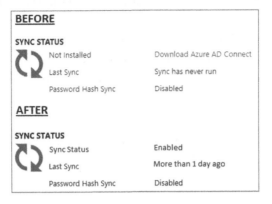

FIGURE 2.13   AAD versus Microsoft accounts in the Azure Portal

You must use an account with the source Azure Active Directory when running AAD Connect, and the account role must be a Global Administrator.

Connect Health

It would not be a stretch of the imagination to think that when you are syncing two or more data repositories that one or more of them may get a little or a lot out of sync, meaning updates, inserts, or deletes in one repository are not reflected immediately, not reflected at some point later, or not ever reflected in another repository at all. Transient issues or longer outages can have some impact on the consistencies of your data. This applies to more than just to an Active Directory but to any data repository.

Azure AAD Connect Health is a monitoring service that replaces older tools such as DirSync and Azure AD Sync and is a service agent that helps monitor the health of features such as the following:

- Sync errors with Azure Active Directory (missing, out-of-date, or duplicates).
- Identify IPs that are bad actors attempting ADFS logins.
- Monitor and alert on health issues of Azure Active Directory Domain Services (discussed later).
- Configure alerts based on error types.

Azure AAD Connect Health is configurable from the portal by clicking the Azure AAD Connect Health link. See Figure 2.14.

FIGURE 2.14   Azure AD Connect Health

Directory Objects

Directory objects consist of items such as users, devices, and groups. Remember that Azure Active Directory is an identity provider or authority and is the location where a user's identity is authenticated. Once authenticated, applications can utilize groups where the identity exists to authorize access. Therefore, the limit of 500,000 objects in the Free edition will be enough for most customers. However, that edition is missing many other necessary corporate features for running secure workloads in the cloud. When comparing Azure Active Directory capabilities with an on-premise Active Directory implementation, specifically for service accounts and machine accounts, some differences may not initially be obvious. For example, you are not able to add Azure VMs, for example, to an Azure Active Directory without implementing and configuring numerous other Azure products and features.

Single Sign-On

As mentioned in the previous chapter, needing a user ID, password, and profile for every application required to perform a job is not optimal. Therefore, the creation of a global intranet capability was created called an Active Directory. This entity contains the identities and group assignment for all users in a company. After a single sign-on (for example, logging into a workstation that is connected to an intranet), any other application in that intranet can reuse those credentials without asking for them again. The same applies to cloud-based resources, meaning any cloud-based application that authenticates using AAD will not request credentials again if the user has already been authenticated in your corporate network.

When implementing SSO in an AAD, there are three notable hybrid identity sign-on methods to consider.

Password Hash Synchronization   Here AAD Connect synchronizes a hash of the hash of a user password from on-premise to an AAD. Then users sign on to services on Azure using the same password as they would when connecting to on-premise applications. This method requires the least amount of effort.

Pass-Through Authentication   Here are some scenarios where a company would want to authenticate a user on their on-premise Active Directory to enforce adherence to specific security procedures and password policies. The approach requires the download and configuration of an authentication agent, which manages the authentication between AAD and an on-premise AD.

Active Directory Federation Service (ADFS)   In this scenario, all user authentication happens on-premise. ADFS is therefore a group of domains that have a trusting relationship with each other. An on-premise domain administrator wanting to create a trust relationship with an AAD can federate the on-premise environment with Azure AD.

To access the single sign-on capability in the Azure Portal, click the Azure Active Directory link and click Azure AAD Connect; you will see the current configured state, similar to Figure 2.15.

FIGURE 2.15   AAD Connect state

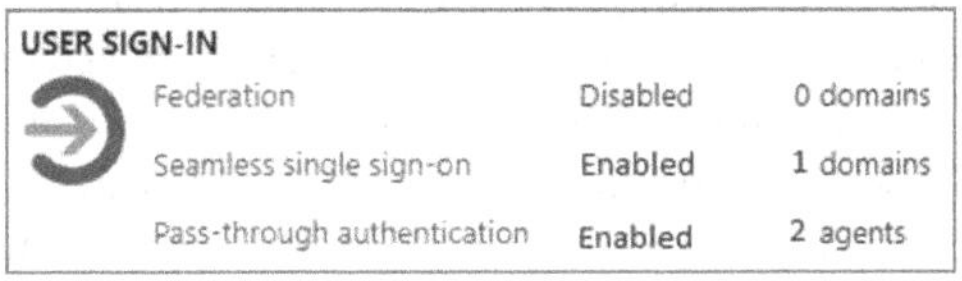

USER SIGN-IN		
Federation	Disabled	0 domains
Seamless single sign-on	Enabled	1 domains
Pass-through authentication	Enabled	2 agents

B2B Collaboration

B2B collaboration is a business-to-business concept that allows a company to share services and applications with guest users from other businesses. The connection is secure and allows the entity doing the sharing to maintain control over their own corporate data. As shown in Figure 2.16, the implementation of B2B collaboration is performed by clicking the + New Guest User button and inviting an individual to the Azure Active Directory.

Once the guest users have been requested to join, you can control their access to corporate content using the conditional access capabilities discussed later. Additionally, you can add guests to Azure Active Directory and role-based access security roles. Therefore, guest accounts and B2B collaboration are a simple way to get an individual into your AAD using their own current identity. There is also an Azure AD B2C capability that exists for a different use case. Whereas B2B is for granting individuals to help collaborate on a project or product, the B2C capability is for authenticating users of the products created via the B2B concept, for example.

FIGURE 2.16 A list of users in Azure Active Directory

Home > The C# Guitar Network > Users - All users
Users - All users
The C# Guitar Network - Azure Active Directory
New user
New guest user
Reset password
Delete user
Multi-Factor Authentication
More
All users
Deleted users
Password reset
User settings
Activity
Sign-ins
Audit logs
Name
Search by name or email
Show
All users
NAME
USER NAME
USER TYPE
SOURCE
Benjamin Perkins (B2B)
guest@csharpguitar.com
Guest
External Azure Active Directory
Benjamin Perkins (GA-AAD)
ga-aad@csharpguitar.net
Member
Azure Active Directory
Benjamin Perkins (GA-MA)
ga@csharpguitar.net
Member
Microsoft Account

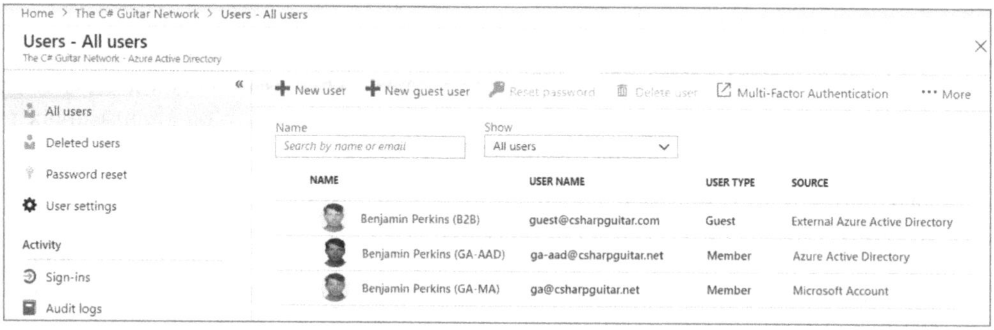

Self-Service Password

Changing, resetting, and unlocking accounts created a lot of work for support teams before the invention of global identity repositories like Active Directory. The in-house development teams quickly got this feedback and built self-service features for changing, resetting, and unlocking passwords into their application.

With the Free edition, the only supported capability is the ability to change a password. If the user is mostly in Azure, this is done here: `myapps.microsoft.com`. In some standard use-case scenarios, a custom security policy can provide a trigger that requires users to change their password every 30 to 90 days.

The functionality to reset and unlock accounts is available with the Free edition; however, it is self-help—back to the old days. In the Basic and Premium editions, there are built-in self-service capabilities for resetting and unlocking passwords. This is an optimal place to perform cost analysis. In other words, take the number of accounts you have and multiply that by the cost per user, and include the probability of how often users would need to unlock or reset their password. Is that amount greater than or equal to the cost of running Azure Active Directory in Basic or Premium?

Application Proxy

This feature reminds me a bit of the Hybrid Connection Manager (HCM), which will be discussed in the next chapter, where we hash out Azure networking. The similarity comes from the fact that there is a connector service, aka connection manager, that is downloaded from the Azure Portal and is typically installed on a server within an on-premise customer network. Navigating to the Azure Active Directory blade and clicking the Azure Proxy link renders a link for downloading the connector, as shown in Figure 2.17.

FIGURE 2.17 Application Proxy link

Application proxy

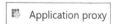

The *application proxy* allows users to access an on-premise application remotely. A proxy, as you know, is a physical or virtual layer that exposes an endpoint, like a URL. That URL then, using the incoming data sent along with the request, can be analyzed so the request can be sent to a different endpoint. This helps from a security perspective because the actual address of the application is not known and also helps from a maintenance perspective because if the hidden endpoint changes, only the proxy needs to be updated, not all the remote clients accessing the endpoint.

Once you have installed the Microsoft Azure Active Directory Application Proxy Connector on a server in an on-premise data center, you need to log in to your Azure account to connect the server hosting the connector and the application proxy. Logging in using a Global Administrator account with the source of an Azure Active Directory endpoint causes an entry to appear on the Application Proxy blade. Then you configure an app, providing the requested information, as shown in Figure 2.18.

FIGURE 2.18   Adding an application proxy

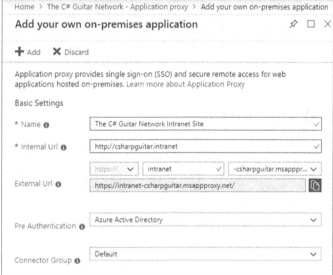

Provide the configuration name, the internal URL to which the request will route, and an external endpoint. Based on the pre-authentication configuration, those attempting access to the external URL will be authenticated against AAD prior to getting access to the internal URL. As shown in Figure 2.19, after a request to the external URL, which is the application proxy service (which is configured similar to that shown previously in Figure 2.18), the credential is validated against your Azure Active Directory; once it's validated, access to the internal URL is granted.

FIGURE 2.19   Application proxy flow diagram

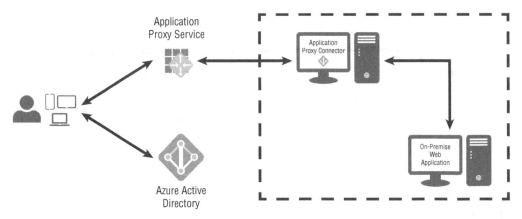

There are also use cases for reducing latency between different data centers. It is good practice to place the content your employees need, and what your customers or partners want, as close to them as possible. This simply makes the whole experience better because connectivity happens faster. Simply install the Application Proxy Connector onto a server anywhere, as close to the people who need the information as possible. Then configure the external endpoint URL for that specific connector and deliver it to those individuals.

Service Level Agreement

A service level agreement (SLA) typically describes how available a specific product is guaranteed to be during a certain time frame. Usually, when the SLA is breached, partial refund for the price of the product is provided upon request. The Free edition of Azure Active Directory does not have an SLA, as shown previously in Table 2.1. The Basic and Premium editions have the same SLA terms, as shown in Table 2.3.

TABLE 2.3   Basic and Premium Azure Active Directory SLAs

Monthly Uptime Percentage	Service Credit
< 99.9%	25%
< 99%	50%
< 95 %	100%

The monthly uptime percentage is calculated using the following algorithm:

(User Minutes – Downtime) / User Minutes × 100

where User Minutes is the sum of the amount of Downtime and the number of impacted users. SLAs are important, but that doesn't mean Microsoft Support will turn their backs on you just because you are running in Free mode. At the same time, if you are running mission-critical or business workloads that have great impact, I recommend running in an edition that has a commitment to uptime. It simply makes good business sense, and any issue can start without needing to have that conversation in the first place.

Identity Protection

From a security perspective, a company is only as strong as its weakest employee. Getting unauthorized access into a corporate network often uses an approach commonly referred to as *phishing*. The sophistication of these attempted accesses through this attack vector has improved to the point that even veteran IT professionals can sometimes become victims of them. Getting access to a corporate network only requires an unsuspecting victim to double-click an executable, open an attachment, or visit a link that installs malicious software. An interesting approach some bad actors take is that they get administrative access and don't take any action right away. They let you forget that you made the mistake. But the consequences do not go away. The vulnerability might be employed right away, stay dormant until the attacker needs it, or simply lie in wait until the exploiter gets around to engaging and probing the network.

That reads kind of scary, but there are some ways to protect against this, for example with identity protection. Even if you forget about a detected threat and even if you don't recognize any odd behaviors on your system, the actions taken on the exploited system expose certain patterns and in many cases act within a definable pattern of activities. These activities can include the following:

- Sign-ins from anonymous IPs (for example, accessing from Tor)
- Sign-ins attempted from multiple locations within a time frame that is suspicious due to impossible travel times
- Sign-ins from unfamiliar locations
- Sign-ins from infected devices

The previous points read like common sense, but the massive amount of authentication-related data being sent back and forth can make attacks difficult to catch. This is what Identity Manager provides; it provides features to monitor the behaviors of users who are authenticated but appear to have been compromised.

When you first created your subscription, you had the option to enable a 30-day free trial of the Premium edition of Azure Active Directory. Most exercises in this chapter require Premium. Please plan your time accordingly so that you can get through this chapter or book before the free trial expires; or, of course, you can simply pay for it.

Add Azure AD Identity Protection

In Exercise 2.3, you will add Azure AD Identity Protection to protect an enterprise from exploited accounts and identity spoofing. Identity Protection also provides visibility into existing threats and vulnerabilities.

EXERCISE 2.3

Adding Identity Protection

1. Log in to the Azure Portal at `portal.azure.com`.

2. Click the Marketplace link, search for *Identity Protection*, and click the Create button, as shown in Figure 2.20.

FIGURE 2.20   Create Azure AD Identity Protection

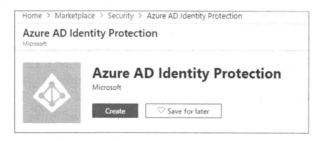

3. Select the directory into which to install Identity Protection, for example The C# Guitar Network, as shown in Figure 2.21.

FIGURE 2.21   Selecting a directory for Azure ID Identity Protection

4. Click the Create button and open the Azure AD Identity Protection blade by clicking the link, as shown in Figure 2.22.

FIGURE 2.22   Azure AD Identity Protection

Installing this Marketplace feature is required to utilize some of the conditional access policies discussed in the next section. Identity Protection provides the reporting capabilities as well as the interface for creating the remediation policy. For example, consider that I want to create a remediation policy after a sign-in attempt has been flagged as High. The controlled remediation can be to enforce multifactor authentication. Continue reading about conditional access; then perform Exercise 2.4 to create a policy.

Conditional Access

Security, security, security—it can't be said enough to a point where it equals the importance of the topic. There have been reports just in the past year that the number of invasive intrusion attempts have increased by almost 300%. So, there are a lot of bad actors attempting to find vulnerabilities in IT solutions and then exploit them. Ransomware, for example, is a lucrative undertaking. It doesn't specifically focus on private data or corporate intellectual property (IP) like many security administrators might be focusing on. Rather, ransomware attempts to prevent the access to the data and the Internet Protocol (IP) itself. The point is that bad actors are very inventive about discovering new ways to exploit IT vulnerabilities. Therefore, security consultants and those who want to prevent and protect must come up with and implement new ways to protect their assets.

 Be careful! You can implement so much security that it inhibits employee productivity and access to your products and services by customers. Remember, bring-your-own-device (BYOD) policies, remote workers, and the different types of devices accessing your resources all make the work more efficient. However, consumption of IT resources is much more complex. Each of those scenarios needs specific attention and a specific approach toward the implementation of a security solution.

Conditional access is a useful method and somewhat of an efficient approach to thwarting many of the newer types of security attack attempts. Conditional access consists of policies that are implemented after the first-factor authentication completes. Thus, it makes sense that *multifactor authentication (MFA)* is implemented as a conditional access policy that happens after the initial authentication. In addition to MFA, some common conditional access policies are as follows:

- Device platforms
- Locations
- Sign-in risk

Managing IT device resources within a company is no small feat. Microsoft Intune is specifically designed to make this easier. Using Microsoft Intune, it is possible to know with high probability what kind of operating systems are running within your company, or at least you know which operating systems you support and will allow to access your internal network. A device platform policy can at least help you prevent malicious devices running any number of operating systems from gaining access to your internal network. For example, if you do not want to support macOS, then you can restrict access based on that operating system. It is also possible to restrict access to cloud apps based on whether the device is domain-joined. There is a capability in Azure known as AAD Connect, which helps you synchronize an on-premise domain-joined device with your Azure AD tenant so that a domain-joined policy can be implemented.

Real World Scenario

How Did They Get There?

Like with supported operating systems or domain-joined devices, you will know most normal scenarios such as where your employees would typically connect from or where they wouldn't ever likely connect from. In this case, you can create a location conditional access whereby if the first-factor authentication is successful but the location of the login is from an unexpected place, then you could block or force them to walk through an additional authentication step, such as MFA.

Take a look at Figure 2.23. A named location called CSHARPGUITAR HQ was created to contain a range of valid IP addresses that are known to come from that location.

FIGURE 2.23   Configuring conditional access

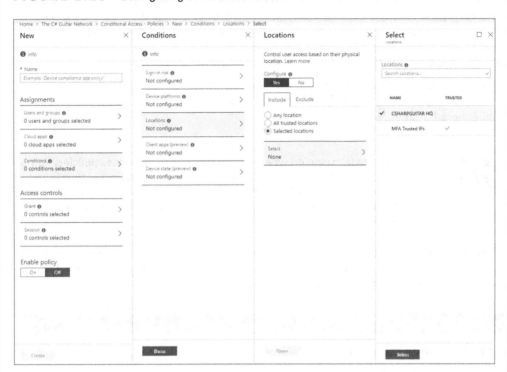

It would then be possible to configure a conditional policy based on what happens when a device connects from that location. Notice that both Include and Exclude options exist. That means if I want a policy to be applied to allow access for the IP address range configured for the named location CSHRAPGUITAR HQ, then I include that range and exclude the rest.

Remember that conditional policies occur after the first-factor authentication. Conditional access policies are an added layer of security and are useful in this new era of constant security exploits.

Sign-in risk is a calculated value that results in the classification of High, Medium, or Low. AAD analyzes each login and determines based on an algorithm whether the sign-in is suspicious. A suspicious sign-in can be from an unusual location, as discussed previously, or when the IP address of the client is hidden or anonymous. Based on the real-time analysis of the sign-in attempt, a conditional access policy can be applied. Complete Exercise 2.4 to practice implementing a conditional policy for blocking suspicious sign-ins.

Create a Conditional Access Policy

In Exercise 2.4, you will create a *conditional access policy* that will block all guest users who have a suspicious sign-in with a calculated value of Low when accessing the Azure Management Portal.

You need to take caution when you create conditional access policies. You can lock yourself out with ease. Make sure you have multiple accounts just in case you lock yourself out. There is the "What If" feature to check who is impacted by the new policy, but this is available only after you have applied it. Be careful.

This is a rather restrictive policy; however, I want to make sure no guest has any chance of abusing their access in any way. To clarify, the algorithm to calculate the risk level is proprietary and part of AAD. You simply need to configure it.

EXERCISE 2.4

Creating a Conditional Access Policy

1. Log in to the Azure Portal at portal.azure.com.

2. Click the Azure Active Directory link, select Conditional Access, select + New Policy, and select Users And Groups. Now, select the Users And Groups check box and select all the Guest accounts; the result is shown in Figure 2.24.

FIGURE 2.24   Creating a conditional access policy

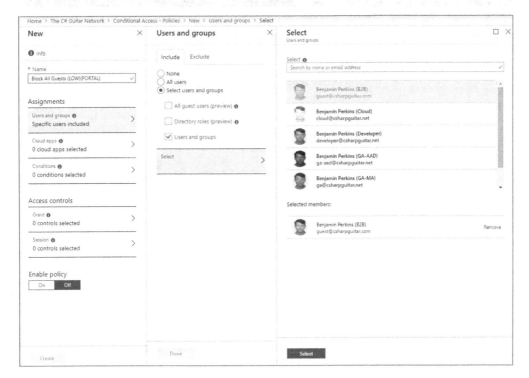

3.   Click Select and Done.

4.   Give the new policy a name. The name should be a good description so you can tell what it does. If you need to look at the configuration to determine what it does, then the name is not good enough. In this example, the conditional policy blocks all sign-ins where the risk is identified as Low.

5.   Next, select Cloud Apps ≻ Select Apps ≻ Select ≻ Microsoft Azure Management, shown in Figure 2.25.

FIGURE 2.25   Configuring a conditional access policy

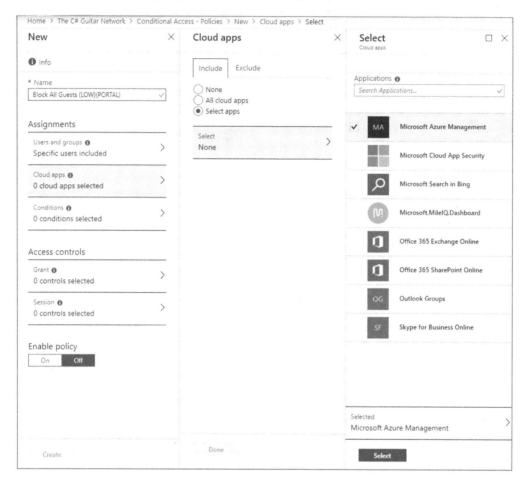

6. Click Select and then Done.

7. Select Conditions ➢ Sign-In Risk ➢ Yes. Select the Low check box.

8. Click Select and then Done.

9. Select Grant ➢ Block Access, as shown in Figure 2.26.

FIGURE 2.26 Creating a conditional access policy

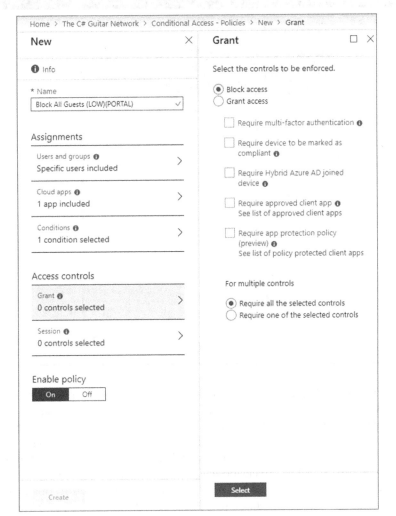

10. Click Select ➢ Enable Policy ➢ On and then click the Create button.

11. You will see the policy show up in the list. Click the What If button to check if the policy applies as you expect.

12. Attempt to log in to the Azure Portal, for example, using the Tor browser. You will get an error that looks like Figure 2.27.

FIGURE 2.27 Access policy access right violation pop-up

You will recall that Figure 2.25 showed the cloud apps that are to be restricted. That exercise was intended to restrict access to the Azure Portal. This is the reason you made the Microsoft Azure Management selection. There is another interesting possible selection, which is Microsoft Cloud App Security. With the creation of any conditional access policy, a cloud app is a required value. Microsoft Cloud App Security (MCAS) is a full-featured product for the enterprise for implementing security for your proprietary cloud apps. It provides tools and reporting focused on protecting sensitive data, protecting files, and discovering shadow IT. The implementation of this capability is mostly focused on compliance details, which are covered in more detail in Chapter 6. Once those details are defined, they are applied using a conditional access policy. The policy is then applied to that particular cloud app.

Multifactor Authentication

No one uses the same user ID and password more than once, says no one. Each application or website you visit, you always use a unique ID and password, right? Well, maybe some people do. Reusing credentials makes security that much more complicated because if one of the sites or products you use is compromised, then an attacker could try those same credentials on other websites, like your email or bank account. The fact is, most passwords are simply hashed and stored in a database table. There are different strengths of hashing, but in the end, it is still just a hash. All hashes are vulnerable because all you need is a supercomputer, a rainbow table, and time. At some point, a match will be found, and your password can be translated into plain text.

This is one reason why many security policies make employees change their password every 30 to 90 days. The strongest hashed password will take 30 to 90 days to be compromised on the fastest supercomputers, so to keep the employees ahead of that, the policy of changing passwords is enforced. Not being allowed to use the previous two to three passwords is also good practice for achieving a higher level of security. Therefore, relying only on a user ID and password should be considered as a first line of defense, or the first level of authentication to confirm before moving to the next phase.

We have discussed already some of the conditional access policies that can be implemented as the second, third, or fourth layers of authentication, for example location or expected operating system of the device. Another, more popular access policy is called *multifactor authentication*. MFA is typically implemented by having two or more of the following:

- Something you know
- Something you are
- Something you have

Something you know can be a user ID and password, but it can also be a set of multiple-choice questions that only you would know. For example, what is your favorite fruit, or what color was your first car? However, these days many of those questions could be compromised by information shared on social media, so just those questions about some individual alone aren't enough to prove someone's identity with high confidence. Therefore, something else must be included in the authentication process.

Biometrics, for example, are something you are. A fingerprint, facial recognition, and retinal scan are identifiers owned only by a single individual. No one has the same fingerprint or retinal pattern as anyone else; they are unique. Some think that having only a retinal scan or fingerprint alone is enough; this might be the case, but two forms of identification are better than one. I have seen a few movies where biometric vulnerabilities are exposed, and it is not pretty.

Lastly, something you own, for example, is a mobile device, digital certificate, or smart card. The validation of any two methods, as shown in Figure 2.28, would be legitimate options for a multifactor authentication process.

FIGURE 2.28   Types of multifactor authentication options

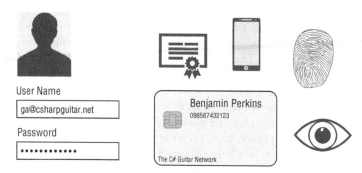

Once a conditional policy is executed based on its assignments, the Access controls which are either to Grant/Deny access or to restrict Session actions of the user are applied. In the previous exercise, the action taken was to block the login attempt. Instead, it is possible to grant access based on several different criteria. One or all need to be met to proceed with authentication.

- Require multifactor authentication.
- Require a device to be marked as compliant.
- Require a hybrid Azure AD–joined device.
- Require an approved client app.

As already mentioned, MFA requires more information than a simple user ID/password combination; it requires also something you have or something you are. Table 2.4 describes the supported scenarios for implementing MFA on your AAD.

TABLE 2.4   Supported MFA Authentication Methods

Authentication Method	Description
Password	This method is always available and enabled.
Microsoft Authenticator app	Once installed, the app receives a notification that a sign-in attempt has been attempted. The person must then approve the notice.
SMS	The user is prompted with a request to enter a six-digit code, which is sent as a text to their mobile device. Once received, enter the code and proceed with authentication.
Voice call	The user receives an automated phone call where the voice provides a six-digit code. Enter the code, and the authentication process proceeds.

Perform Exercise 2.5 to enable multifactor authentication.

Enable Multifactor Authentication

It turns out the conditional access policy created in the previous exercise was too aggressive, and it locked out our partner even though we wanted the account to be authenticated. In Exercise 2.5, you will modify the conditional access policy that blocked all Guest users who have a suspicious sign-in with a calculated value of Low. Instead of blocking the authentication from proceeding, as long as the partner has a valid mobile device that can receive a verification code, we will allow access.

EXERCISE 2.5

Enabling Multifactor Authentication

1. Log in to the Azure Portal at portal.azure.com.

2. Click the Azure Active Directory link, select Conditional Access, click + Select, and select the policy created in the previous exercise, as shown in Figure 2.29. In this case, Block All Guests (LOW)(PORTAL) is selected.

FIGURE 2.29   Enabling multifactor authentication

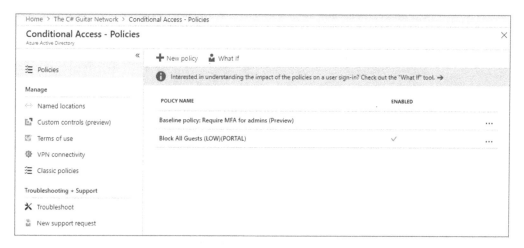

3. In the Access Controls section, select the Grant ➢ Grant Access radio button. Select the Require Multi-factor Authentication check box. Click the Select button and click Save. See Figure 2.30.

FIGURE 2.30 Enabled multifactor authentication, granting access

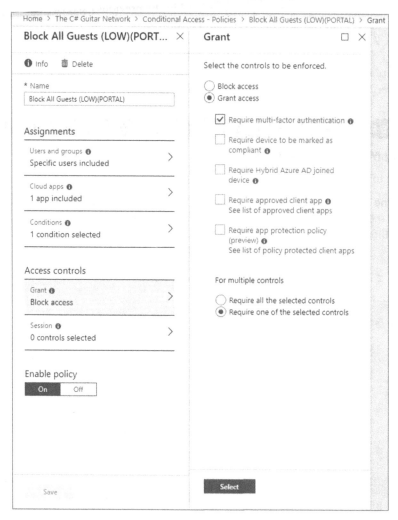

4. Wait a few moments to ensure the policy gets applied (just a few moments) and then attempt to log in to the Azure Portal with the credential you selected to apply the conditional policy to. The user should receive the pop-up shown in Figure 2.31.

FIGURE 2.31 Multifactor authentication pop-up window

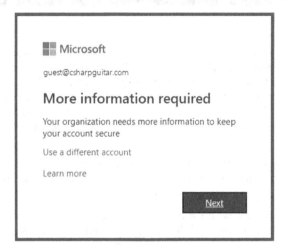

5. As this would be the first time the user is accessing AD with this policy in effect, it is likely they would need to provide some additional details.

   a. For the Step 1 screen, MFA requests more information about how to contact you, as shown in Figure 2.32.

FIGURE 2.32 Multifactor request for more information page

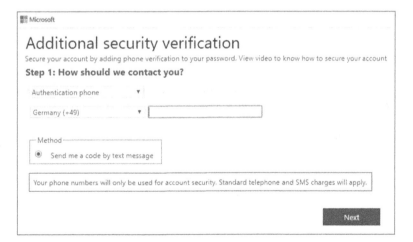

If your security neurons are firing, you are contemplating all the different scenarios in which this approach has flaws. It does, and it doesn't. Because step 5 took place after the user ID/password, first-factor authentication step, we can have some confidence this person is who they say they are. If you wanted to be more secure, you could select more check boxes on the screen in Figure 2.30 so that all those controls are enforced along with MFA.

b. On the Step 2 screen, select the country code, enter the phone number, and then click the Next button. The Step 2 information box opens with the message, "We've sent a text message to your phone at: #####."

c. On the Step 3 screen, wait for the text message to arrive at your cell/mobile phone, enter it into the text box, and then click the Verify button. (See Figure 2.33.)

FIGURE 2.33   MFA additional security information request page

6. If the verification is successful, click the Done button. The user account is now configured to use MFA, as shown in Figure 2.34.

FIGURE 2.34   MFA security verification page

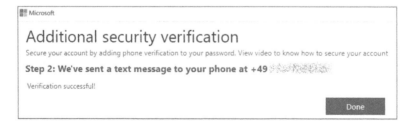

7. In this scenario, for this conditional access policy, the sign-in attempt always triggers the MFA control. The user always is prompted to provide a verification code, as shown in Figure 2.35.

FIGURE 2.35   MFA window for verification message entry

There are many ways to create and apply conditional policies. It really is up to you or the security officer/adviser.

The point of the previous two exercises is that there is a balance between security and productivity. Initially, the conditional access policy was aggressive and blocked any guest no matter what. I have actually seen this approach implemented after a security administrator leaves the company or there is an apparent loss of control of the security solutions. Just lock everyone out and then revalidate them all based on new policies. That is not an approach with low impact, but. . .is it better than doing nothing when you know there is a vulnerability? Blocking everyone isn't realistic in a company with thousands of employees and partners. The human resources' costs would be too prohibitive. That approach is not something I would ever recommend; instead, in a best-case scenario, plan, design, and implement your policy right the first time.

Just keep in mind that security is fundamental, but you need to let the people work and not have a security policy prevent them from doing that. If your policy does have a negative impact on productivity, then you have a bad security solution. In Chapter 9, where we discuss monitoring, you will come to learn how you can see the impact of your security policy on productivity. Additionally, you can use the "What If" feature, discussed in Exercise 2.4, to check how impactful the policy will be.

Privileged Identity Management

Giving a group or individual user access to a resource is standard practice. This measure protects unauthorized individuals from gaining access and potentially causing the company or customer harm. There may be a scenario where just being authenticated or authorized to access the resource isn't restrictive enough; for example, providing a user with read access to a database so that the individual can analyze behaviors to find new features for a product or to find unexpected behaviors due to poor code path execution in the application. Perhaps an individual needs to make a remote desktop connection to a server to troubleshoot an issue or give someone access to a certificate's private key.

In each scenario, the security administrators have the justification to grant access, but the issue is how long they need access, because some of the resources being accessed are more sensitive than others and would therefore need some additional security policies. How can that be implemented? How can additional security levels be applied based on a specific resource? The solution is Privileged Identity Management (PIM). Simply, PIM is a feature for controlling, managing, and monitoring access to highly critical or sensitive resources within your company. This is performed by adding authentication capabilities to resources on the Azure platform based on an individual's AAD identity, AAD group assignment, or Azure resources through RBAC (RBAC is discussed later in this chapter). Table 2.5 shows the additional authentication features available through PIM.

TABLE 2.5 Privileged Identity Management Authentication Features

Authentication Feature	Description
Audit history	A report for analyzing who has accessed which resource, when, and how often
Notifications	Notification when a group or user is granted privileged access to a resource
Multifactor authentication	Additional layer of authentication
Time-bound	Apply start and end dates for the privileged access.
Access reviews	Reports that identify if access is still required for the specific user or group
Justification	Create rules for requested access, like a work item must be provided along with the request.

Approval	Implement an approval process for granting privileged access.
Just-in-time	Request access when you need it and it gets approved JIT. JIT means the user is given acces at the moment it is required and then is removed when the access is no longer required.

To enable PIM, you must navigate to the Azure AD Privileged Identity Management blade, as shown in Figure 2.36, and click the Consent To PIM link.

FIGURE 2.36   Azure AD Privileged Identity Management

The verification is multifactor, just like what was configured in the previous section. Once verification is completed and consented to and your account is signed up, you can then begin using the feature to add that extra layer of security and control around your company's most sensitive products and data. Finally, PIM provides monitoring and review capabilities that help ensure your security solution is functioning as expected.

Managed Identities

Up to now we have only discussed accounts that are associated with physical beings, like a person. These people are logically assigned to groups, and those groups are granted or denied access to certain resources. There is another common scenario when running applications that benefits from a resource having an identity, for example, an instance of Azure App Service, Azure Functions, or Azure VM. Most Azure resources within a given subscription can be granted access to any other resource so long as those resources have a managed identity stored in the Azure Active Directory.

This is commonly referred to as *credential leaking*. This is when credentials are stored in source code, configuration files, or application settings. These passwords are generally for connecting to a database, connecting to a third-party application, or connecting perhaps to a REST API. Regardless, any resource connected from any other resource that requires authentication needs to store those credentials someplace. The original solution for this was Azure Key Vault, which stores a secret or connection string in a secured, encrypted location. The secret string is then accessed using a key.

The key, though, has to also be stored somewhere, which creates the credential leak mentioned earlier, where the credential is stored in a secure place but can still be accessed by using the key stored in a less secure location. What finally came into being was a feature called Managed Identities (MI) for Azure resources, formally called Managed Service

Identity (MSI). Once MI is implemented for a given resource, then that specific resource has permission to get the secret, and the authentication is handled using MI and AAD.

In Chapter 7, there is an exercise where you will create an Azure App Service instance and an Azure Key Vault, configure MI, and access a secret within it. As we have yet to cover the creation of compute resources (covered in Chapter 4), there is not enough explanation yet to perform those activities.

Azure AD Domain Services

Azure Active Directory Domain Services is useful for a scenario called *lift-and-shift*. This means that a company that has on-premise application workloads or other domain-dependent assets wants to package the IT solution and deploy it as is to the Azure platform. Consider, however, the scenario where that workload has Lightweight Directory Access Protocol (LDAP), NT LAN Manager (NTLM), or Kerberos requirements. As you should already know, those features run on an on-premise Active Directory and are not supported on the Azure platform out of the box with AAD.

There are numerous workarounds to get those three features working on Azure, such as creating a site-to-site connection between Azure and an on-premise AD. Other possibilities are creating an AD domain using an actual Azure virtual machine or replicating the domain in the cloud. Those solutions are valid, but they require significant monitoring and administration and can be vulnerable to latency and transient network issues. Therefore, Microsoft created Azure AD Domain Services as the best solution for lift-and-shift workloads.

There are two supported scenarios:

- Azure AD Domain Service for hybrid solutions
- Azure AD Domain Services for cloud-only solutions

In a hybrid solution, a company has infrastructure resources both in its on-premise data centers as well as on Azure. The company additionally has a requirement or a desire to synchronize identities between its on-premise AD and its Azure AD tenant. As shown in Figure 2.37, resources are in a virtual network. (Virtual networks are discussed in Chapter 3.) Those resources connect to AAD using Azure AD Domain Services, and then AAD uses Azure AAD Connect, discussed earlier, to synchronize the identities.

The configuration for a cloud-only solution is like that for the hybrid; the only difference is that there is no synchronization happening between AAD and an on-premise AD using Azure AD Connect.

So, that's Azure Active Directory and many of its additional features and related security and identity products. It would be possible to write an entire book about Azure Active Directory; I know there are a few. If this subject is of particular interest to you, then make it one of the topics that you learn a lot about.

FIGURE 2.37   AAD Domain Services flow diagram

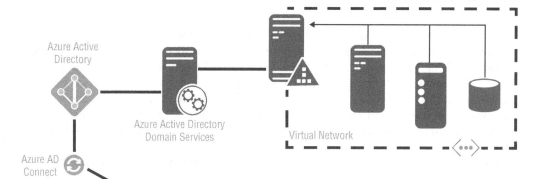

Let's now turn our attention to the next section where we discuss role-based access control. But before that happens, look at the following table, Table 2.6 to see the differences between AAD and RBAC.

TABLE 2.6   Differences Between AAD and RBAC

Azure AD	Azure RBAC
Role-based information is accessible using Microsoft Graph and Azure AD PowerShell.	Role-based information is accessible using the Azure Portal, Azure CLI, Azure PowerShell, and REST.
Custom roles are not supported.	Custom roles are supported.
Manage access to Azure AD resources.	Manage access to Azure resources.
Scope is AD tenant roles and groups.	Much more granular scope capabilities for resources and artifacts

The most important aspect to recognize is that Azure AD has a scope greater than that of Azure, while RBAC is specifically focused on the resources accessible via the Azure Portal.

Role-Based Access Control

Role-based access control (RBAC) is neither a new concept nor unique to the management of access to resources in the Azure Portal. Azure Active Directory is where we authenticate the credentials of individuals desiring access to a restricted resource. After authentication, we are certain that the client attempting to connect to that resource is who they say they are. However, this is not enough; not only must the identity and credentials be validated, permission to access the desired resource must also be allowed. This kind of permission check is referred to as *authorization*—a method for specifying access rights or privileges to resources.

There has already been a discussion about how Active Directory (the on-premise flavor) resolved the issue of requiring an identity authority per application. The management of the profiles and passwords for each application quickly became unmanageable as the number of applications required to perform a task increased. Take that same authentication concept and apply it to authorization. Here, instead of managing and validating credentials in each application identity database, the management of an individual's rights once authenticated would be managed by each application. It is easy to grasp how quickly this model broke down as the effort required to maintain it is too great as the number of users increase.

Part of the migration from *application-bound identity provider databases* to Active Directory required the mapping of tasks to an identity. For example, if many systems provided human resource, financial, accounting, or logistic data and capabilities, the question becomes, who can access what data and who can execute which activities? Should someone in Finance see details about the last time an employee called in sick? Should someone in Human Resources be able to approve the payment of an invoice from a third-party vendor? Probably not, so there needs to be a scalable way to grant or deny individuals access to the data, actions performed upon the data, and activities that have significant consequence.

It would not take long to realize that granting access to data or actions on an individual basis won't scale. Perhaps in a very small company this could be a possibility; however, in a larger corporation, the more maintainable approach is to create *roles*. Active Directory supports creating groups, as does AAD. However, AAD groups are not what are used for managing access to Azure resources. Instead, an Azure implementation of RBAC is the means for granting access to resources within Azure to users.

You will find three common RBAC roles in Azure: Owner, Contributor, and Reader (see Table 2.7). In total there are about 40 built-in Azure RBAC roles, and in addition, it is possible to create custom roles. Creating custom RBAC roles is discussed later in the section.

TABLE 2.7   Most Common Built-In Azure RBAC Roles

Name	Permissions (Brief Overview)
Owner	Access to all resources; can delegate this right to others
Contributor	Same as the Owner, but cannot delegate this right to others
Reader	Can only view existing Azure resources; cannot create or delegate

Each role has a set of permissions, and instead of assigning an individual a permission, you assign permissions to a role and then add an individual to that role. We all know that individuals perform many tasks and perform many roles that require access to many resources. The RBAC feature in Azure supports this scenario, where individual accounts can be assigned multiple roles, which allows them to execute and perform many tasks.

 It's important to note again the difference between AAD and the RBAC model available in the Azure Portal. It is true that AAD supports groups; however, AAD can be considered as a level higher than RBAC. AAD can be used to authenticate individuals within applications, workloads, and other SaaS products; RBAC cannot. RBAC is the feature for controlling access to the resources on the Azure platform from within the Azure Portal, not the access to the application or code running on the Azure resources.

The permissions for the Owner RBAC role in Azure can be viewed in the portal by selecting Subscriptions, choosing an Azure subscription accessible to the signed-in user, and then choosing Access Control (IAM) ➢ Roles ➢ Owner ➢ Permissions. Finally, click the Load More link a few times. You will then see the list of permissions for the given role, something similar to Figure 2.38.

FIGURE 2.38   RBAC permissions overview

Home > Subscriptions > Pay-As-You-Go - Access control (IAM) > Owner > Permissions (preview)	
Permissions (preview) Owner	
Microsoft Web Apps	All
Microsoft.AlertsManagement	All
Microsoft.Archive	All
Microsoft.Attestation	All
Microsoft.Azure.Geneva	All
Microsoft.BizTalkServices	All
Microsoft.Cdn	All
Microsoft.ChangeAnalysis	All
Microsoft.ClassicInfrastructureMigrate	All
Microsoft.ClassicSubscription	All

Left navigation: Create a resource, Home, Dashboard, All services, FAVORITES, All resources, Azure Active Directory, Subscriptions, Azure AD Identity Protection, Azure AD Privileged Identit..., Azure AD Connect Health, Resource groups, Virtual machines

Click one of the permissions categories, for example, Microsoft Web Apps, and you will see the access controls (Read, Write, Delete, and Other) provided for the role. (See Figure 2.39.) Click a check mark for more information about what kind of access is granted when the permission is established.

FIGURE 2.39 RBAC permissions detail

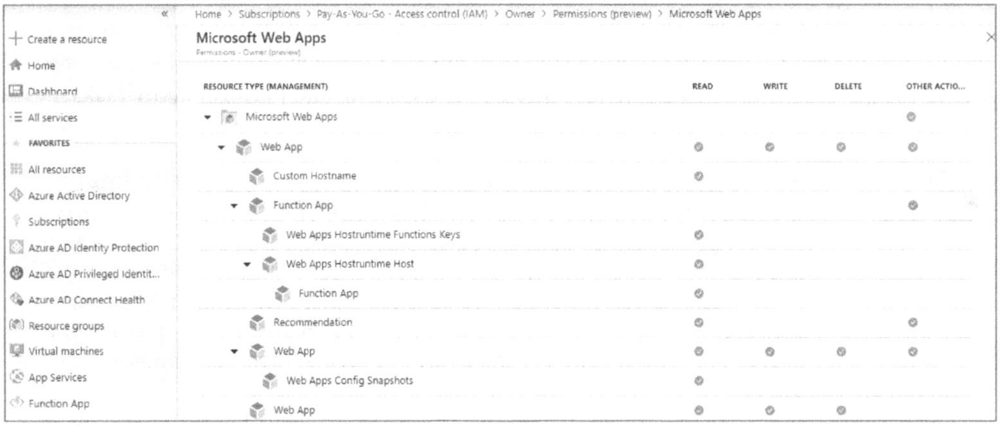

If the account you used to access the portal does not yet have access to a subscription, complete Exercise 2.6 and grant access to it. If you created the users as demonstrated in previous exercises, then none of those accounts will be associated to any subscription. Up to now, only the account that created the subscription has access. Consider logging into the Azure Portal using the account created in a previous exercise. Then click the Subscription link and you will find none; instead, there is a link that allows you to create a new subscription. Additionally, while logged in, it will not be possible to create any kind of resource as the account is not yet associated to any subscription.

EXERCISE 2.6

Granting Access to an Azure Subscription

1. Log in to the Azure Portal at portal.azure.com.

2. From the navigation panel on the left side of the display, select Subscriptions. From the list of subscriptions that opens, select one for granting access. (See Figure 2.40.) In this case, there is only a single subscription. From the two drop-down lists, My Role and Status, select the values to apply to the list of subscriptions. Notice that you can only set the values for subscriptions that you (or other logged-in users) can access. Therefore, it is possible to filter based on the roles a logged-in user has for a given subscription. You can also filter on the active or disabled status of the subscription.

FIGURE 2.40   Azure subscription list

3. Select Subscription ➤ Access Control (IAM) ➤ Role Assignments. Click the + Add button and select Add Role Assignment. You will see something similar to that shown in Figure 2.41. The + Add button also presents the option to select Add Co-administrator. If you choose to add a co-admin, no Role or Assign Access To drop-down list appears. Co-admins are granted the same access as the original administrator automatically.

FIGURE 2.41   Azure subscription details

The Role drop-down list contains the roles or groups the user can be assigned to. For example, you might see Owner, Contributor, or Reader. (You'll learn more about assigning access later in this exercise.)

4. Click the Role drop-down list and notice the numerous roles available for selection. Next to each there is an information circle to click that will provide more details about that role. In this scenario, create an Owner. Refer to Table 2.7 to confirm what permissions this provides.

5. From the Assign Access To drop-down list, leave the default. The plan is to grant this role to an Azure AD user.

6. Search for the Azure AD user to add to the Owner role and click the Save button.

7. Log in using that account; the subscription will now be visible, and the permission to create and consume resources within it exists.

As you worked through Exercise 2.6, many concepts and much technical jargon were introduced. Some were obvious and intuitive, while others were not so and touched on a number of behind-the-scenes concepts. The first one is the *subscription*, which we know by now is the entity into which resources are organized and billed. An Azure subscription is only one component of a greater hierarchy that is commonly referred to as *scope*. Figure 2.42 shows the scope concept as designed in Azure.

FIGURE 2.42   Azure scope relationship hierarchy

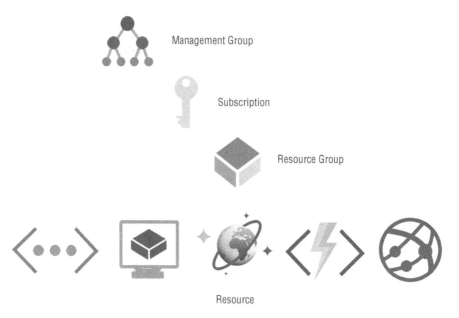

Management Group

Subscription

Resource Group

Resource

At the top of the hierarchy is an entity called a *management group.* This newest member of the hierarchy was introduced in 2019. (Management groups will be discussed in more detail in Chapter 6. They help with the governance and compliance aspects under which some enterprises must operate.) There can be only one root management group; however, the limit for submanagement groups is constrained only by one's imagination, up to 10,000 down to a depth of six levels. Management groups can be designed after the structure of an organization. For example, consider the following management groups:

Root Company Group

> Marketing

> Human Resources

> IT

> Finance

> Accounting

Within each of those management groups, one or more subscriptions and/or one or more groups can exist. A Human Resources management group may contain child regional groups, while the IT management group could contain Production, Testing, and Development groups. Then each one of these groups is assigned a subscription, which would be helpful with managing and estimating costs, as well as providing an option for the application of access controls.

 The higher the level a group or role is granted access to on the hierarchy, the greater the impact their actions can have. The best approach is to grant roles the least amount of privileges required to perform the required work.

To create a management group, perform the steps described in Exercise 2.7.

EXERCISE 2.7

Creating a Management Group

1. Log in to the Azure Portal at portal.azure.com.

2. Search for *management groups* in the search box found at the top of the page. Navigate to the Management Groups blade.

3. If this is the first management group being created, click the Start Using Management Groups button to create one. Otherwise, click + Add Management Group.

4. Add a management group ID, for example: **CSHARPGUITAR-IT**.

5. Add a management group display name, such as: **The C# Guitar Network – IT Department**.

6. Click the Save button.

When a subscription is created, by default an Azure AD tenant is created, as already mentioned. Also, by default a management group named Tenant Root Group is created. The subscription is automatically assigned to that root management group. If you want to move items between management groups, for example, a subscription, click the ellipsis next to the item and select Move, while on the Management group blade.

The next level down in the scope hierarchy is the subscription, which has already been covered. Next is a *resource group*, which is another method for logically grouping Azure resources. The best use of a resource group is to group together all the Azure products and features that make up an application or solution. For example, a web application may contain an Azure App Service instance, a Cosmos DB instance, an Azure Blob Storage container, and a Key Vault instance. Each of these products is required to provide the service that the application provides, which is an optimal use of a resource group. Resource groups are mentioned or used in many more chapters in this book. In Chapter 3, there is an exercise to create one.

The lowest level on the scope hierarchy is the resource itself. As mentioned, Azure App Service, Cosmos DB, and Key Vault instances are the actual entities that an administrator is restricting access to. Here are the four scope hierarchy levels:

- Management group
- Subscription
- Resource group
- Resource

Where a resource group can contain many resources, a subscription can contain many resource groups, and a management group can contain many subscriptions. However, there can be only one root management group per Azure AD tenant. Overall, the scope hierarchy is helpful in the organization of the Azure resources and controlling who and what have access to them. The final questions are as follows:

- How do you control who or what has permission to the Azure resource?
- How do you provide permissions to Azure resources?
- How are the permissions controlled in the portal? What about the CLI, PowerShell, or REST APIs?

How to Control Who or What Has Access

Up to now we have discussed both users and groups and have experienced how they can be granted permission to an Azure resource. In Exercise 2.7, the Assign Access To drop-down was left at the default. The role assignment was being performed on a user. Figure 2.43 shows some other available options, which are referred to as *security principals*.

Each of these security principals has been discussed already except service principal. Nonetheless, Table 2.8 provides an overview of each type.

FIGURE 2.43   Azure users, groups, managed identity, and service principal icons

| User | Group | Managed Identity | Service Principle |

TABLE 2.8   Security Principals

Type	Description
User	A person or individual who exists in the Azure AD tenant
Group	A collection of users in the Azure AD tenant
Managed identity	An identity managed by Azure
Service principal	A security identity used by applications to access Azure services

A *service principal* is synonymous with a service account that one would create on a Windows server. This account is used to manage permissions between machines. A common use of a service account is in IIS when companies want to implement an intranet web farm with Kerberos. The context in which the identity of the IIS process runs must be within the Active Directory. It wouldn't be good practice to assign that process to a real user; instead, the account is a generic one that is not linked to a specific person. Additionally, running scheduled tasks that need access to restricted data stored on a file share need to run with a given identity. Simply run the task in the context of a service principal/service account and grant that identity permission to the file share. Again, it wouldn't be prudent to run the scheduled task as a real user.

The difference between managed identities and service principals is subtle. Service principals are no longer recommended for services that support managed identities. Managed identities are effectively "managed service principals" and remove the need for storing credentials in the application's configuration and instead inject certificates into the resource that the managed identity is created into.

How to Provide Permissions to Resources

At each level in the scope hierarchy, as shown in Figure 2.42, you will find the Access Control (IAM) menu option; IAM stands for "identity and access management." You likely remember this menu option from Exercise 2.7 when granting a user permission to a subscription. In the Azure Portal, open any subscription, resource group, or resource and you'll find the Access Control (IAM) link, which provides the interface for granting access.

As discussed in the previous section, it is possible to grant access to any of the entities in the scope hierarchy to any of the four security principals. Ask yourself this, would it be practical to grant user access at the resource level? Why? Why not? The answer is no; it would not be practical, because the effort required to maintain such an approach would be the greatest compared to all the other possible scenarios. It is unlikely that a single user needs access only to a single Azure resource, so in addition to adding that single user to all the necessary resources, it would be necessary to add all users to all resources. This approach would quickly break down.

The best-practice approach is to grant users access to Azure resources via roles. Figure 2.44 visualizes the most common roles (Owner, Contributor, and Reader) mapped to the scope hierarchy.

FIGURE 2.44 Azure roles and relationship hierarchy

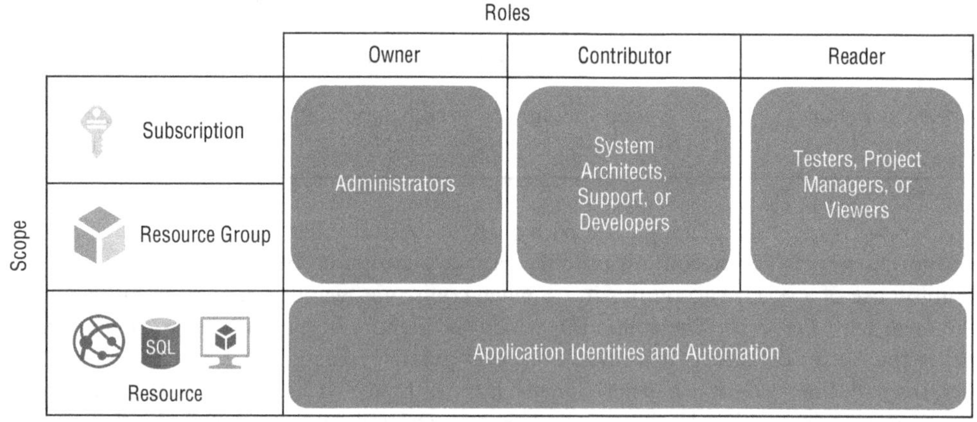

Notice that in addition to the roles and scopes shown, Figure 2.44 provides a more detailed visualization of some additional job titles that may fit well into some of the already existing RBAC roles. Irrespective of that, it is most beneficial to grant from a group or role perspective and give the role the least amount of access to Azure features as required. The Contributor role for example, may only need access to a specific application that is in a resource group and not all Azure resources within a subscription. In that case, the necessity for additional roles, one per project or region, for example, with contributor access may be required.

Lastly, observe that the only recommended time to assign any role or user to a specific resource is when the identity is used by the application. The assignment would not utilize a user account, rather a managed identity or a security principal, for the reasons just discussed.

How Are the Permissions to Resources Controlled?

It should now be clear that permissions are granted to one of the four security principals, and those security principals should be grouped together in a role. Then that role is granted permissions at one of the three levels (subscription, resource group, and resource) in the scope hierarchy. The question is now, how does Azure implement RBAC so that when someone attempts to access an Azure resource from the portal, the CLI, PowerShell, or a REST API, that authentication happens? The answer is *Azure Resource Manager (ARM)*. One cannot fully understand the implementation of RBAC in the Azure Portal without also comprehending the Azure Resource Manager.

Covered in more detail in Chapter 8, ARM is an API discussed most often within the context of deployments, but ARM can also be used for auditing, tagging, and controlling access to Azure resources. The API is accessed from the Azure Portal, Azure PowerShell, REST APIs, and Azure CLI, for example. ARM provides the means for logically structuring a company's workload and compute solutions. This structure makes it possible to implement access control on a resource, a group of resources, resources that make up an entire solution, or even all resources within a given subscription. As shown in Figure 2.45, ARM is the heart of RBAC, and nothing happens to Azure resources without flowing through it in some way.

FIGURE 2.45   Azure and the resource manager relationship

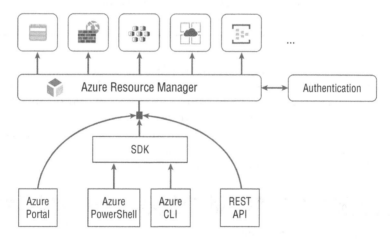

If you are interested in learning more about ARM immediately, jump forward to Chapter 8 for more in-depth coverage.

Custom Roles

What happens if one of the 40 or so built-in roles do not match your specific need? The answer is to create a custom role. Although the developers and designers of the RBAC roles available in Azure have done great diligence to provide as many roles as possible, there are cases where there is not an absolute match for what you need. This is the greatness of technology and the platform that Azure provides. The platform provides the capability to create exactly what you need to meet your requirements.

Custom roles, like the built-in Azure roles, can be granted using the same scope hierarchy and service principals as previously discussed. There is nothing different in that respect. By default, however, not every user can create custom roles as you would expect. Instead, only Owners or User Access Administrators, for example, would have this privilege as they would be the ones who have an overview of what roles already exist.

The specific actions required to create a custom role can be manually assigned to a custom role, as shown in Table 2.9.

TABLE 2.9   Actions Required to Create a Custom Role

Operation	Type
`Microsoft.Authorization/roleDefinition/read`	View a custom role
`Microsoft.Authorization/roleDefinition/write`	Update a custom role
`Microsoft.Authorization/roleDefinition/write`	Create/delete a custom role

Therefore, if a user needs to have the permission to create custom roles and support cases only, then that would be a case for creating a custom role. Let's call that role Security Support Engineer; complete Exercise 2.8 to create an Azure RBAC custom role. Before you begin, take notice that there is no capability to create custom roles in the Azure Portal. This is possible only when using Azure PowerShell, when using the Azure CLI, or when calling the REST API directly. It is expected that you already know one or more of those clients and can use it for this exercise. This exercise utilizes Azure PowerShell.

EXERCISE 2.8

Creating an RBAC Custom Role

1. Log in to the Azure PowerShell console using the `Login-AzureRmAccount` cmdlet. Enter **Login-AzureRmAccount** and enter the same credentials as you would when accessing Azure using the portal. You will be prompted for your credentials automatically.

2. Just for fun, execute **Get-AzureRmRoleDefinition | FT Name, IsCustom**, which lists
    all the existing roles with the associated identifier that distinguishes whether the role
    is custom or built-in (False if built-in and True if the role is custom).

3. If there is a built-in role that has many of the permissions required for the
    new custom role, consider exporting that role in JSON format and then
    updating it to include the additional permissions. To achieve that, execute
    Get-AzureRmRoleDefinition "Support Request Contributor" | ConvertTo-Json
    and save the output to a file.

4. Copy the content, similar to that found here, into Notepad or Visual Studio and save
    the file as **sec-support-eng.json**.

```
{
    "Name":  "Support Request Contributor",
    "Id":  "cfd33db0-3dd1-45e3-aa9d-cdbdf3b6f24e",
    "IsCustom":  false,
    "Description":  "Lets you create and manage Support requests",
    "Actions":  [
                "Microsoft.Authorization/*/read",
                "Microsoft.Resources/subscriptions/resourceGroups/read",
                "Microsoft.Support/*"
            ],
    "NotActions":  [ ],
    "DataActions":  [ ],
    "NotDataActions":  [ ],
    "AssignableScopes":  [ "/" ]
}
```

5. Modify sec-support-eng.json and add the new permissions identified in Table 2.9
    along with the Azure subscription represented by the # sign in sec-support-eng
    .json. The content of the file should resemble the following:

```
{
    "Name":  "Security Support Engineer",
    "Id":  null,
    "IsCustom":  true,
    "Description":  "Create and manage Support requests and Custom RBAC roles",
    "Actions":  [
                "Microsoft.Authorization/*/read",
            "Microsoft.Authorization/roleDefinitions/write",
                "Microsoft.Resources/subscriptions/resourceGroups/read",
                "Microsoft.Support/*"
            ],
```

```
        "NotActions":   [ ],
        "DataActions":   [ ],
        "NotDataActions":   [ ],
        "AssignableScopes":   [ "/subscriptions/######-#####-######-#####" ]
    }
```

6. Execute **New-AzureRmRoleDefinition -InputFile "C:\ASA\Chapter02\ sec-support-eng.json"**. If successful, the output should resemble Figure 2.46.

FIGURE 2.46 Azure custom role PowerShell output

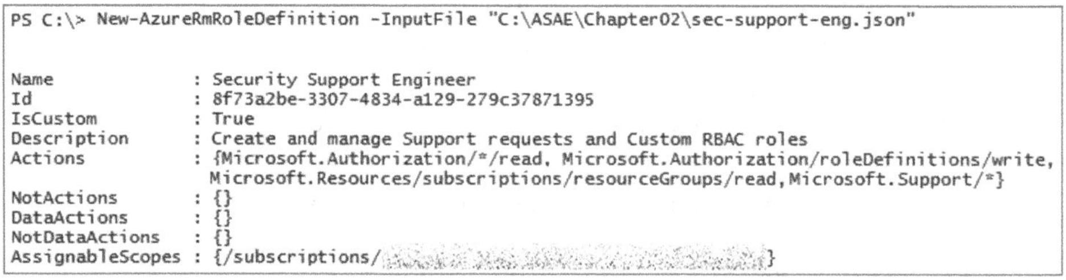

```
PS C:\> New-AzureRmRoleDefinition -InputFile "C:\ASAE\Chapter02\sec-support-eng.json"


Name              : Security Support Engineer
Id                : 8f73a2be-3307-4834-a129-279c37871395
IsCustom          : True
Description       : Create and manage Support requests and Custom RBAC roles
Actions           : {Microsoft.Authorization/*/read, Microsoft.Authorization/roleDefinitions/write,
                    Microsoft.Resources/subscriptions/resourceGroups/read,Microsoft.Support/*}
NotActions        : {}
DataActions       : {}
NotDataActions    : {}
AssignableScopes  : {/subscriptions/                                              }
```

7. Again, execute **Get-AzureRmRoleDefinition | FT Name, IsCustom** and you should see the newly created custom role, and the IsCustom property is True as expected.

8. Log in to the Azure Portal at portal.azure.com. Navigate to the subscription that the custom role was created for and then click the Access Control (IAM) blade. Select Roles and search for the custom role you just created. When in the Azure Portal, you will notice a role with the value of CustomRole in the type column instead of the default BuiltInRole type, similar to Figure 2.47. The CustomRole type identifies the role as custom; you can also provide a custom name for the rolefor example Security Support Engineer.

FIGURE 2.47   List of roles and the custom role just created

Home > Subscriptions > Pay-As-You-Go - Access control (IAM)

Pay-As-You-Go - Access control (IAM)
Subscription

×

🔍 Search (Ctrl+/)   «   **+** Add   ⬛⬛ Edit columns   ↻ Refresh | 🗑 Remove

ⓘ Overview

▲ Access control (IAM)

✘ Diagnose and solve problems

🔘 Security

⚡ Events

Cost Management

💲 Cost analysis

🕐 Budgets

☂ Advisor recommendations

Check access   Role assignments   Deny assignments   Classic administrators   **Roles**

A role definition is a collection of permissions. You can use the built-in roles or you can create your own custom roles. Learn more ⬈

Name ⓘ
| Support |

Type ⓘ
| All   ⌄ |

Showing 2 of 124 roles

	NAME	TYPE	USERS	GROUPS	
	Security Support Engineer ⓘ	CustomRole	0	0	...
	Support Request Contributor ⓘ	BuiltInRole	0	0	...

An electronic copy of the `sec-support-eng.json` script can be found here:

github.com/benperk/ASA/tree/master/Chapter02

Once the custom role is created, you can assign it to any of the levels of the scope hierarchy. There is one element that is consumed in the previous exercise—but it's not obvious. The consumed element is called a *resource provider*. Resource providers are an integral part of ARM, discussed in more detail in Chapter 8. To view the resource providers referenced from the Security Support Engineer customer role, click the custom role shown in Figure 2.47. Choose Permissions, and the blade presented shows the resource providers; click each to see and choose the type you need.

RBAC is an important, critical concept to understand, design appropriately, deploy, and manage. The permissions you grant to users of subscriptions, resource groups, or resources can have significant financial impact. But more than financial impact, access to your company's intellectual property and customer data is at risk here as well. It is crucial to manage this with attention to detail, perform regular reviews, and make modifications when deemed necessary.

Hardware and Network Security

The authentications and authorizations into the local portal and into the Azure Portal covered so far provide portal access and resource access, but not compute access (getting onto the actual resources). Creating an Azure resource doesn't immediately grant access to any actual resource; there are additional identities for that. Most compute resources that get created usually have a global endpoint. Anyone in the world could conceivably ping (or access) the compute resource, depending on how you have protected it.

Understand that you are responsible for the vulnerabilities inside your code and from your Azure endpoints. Like other cloud providers, Azure is responsible only for the security of its software and infrastructure; the options it provides are for increasing security and perhaps for plugging some holes that are not simple to fix. The cloud hosting provider focuses on protecting the platform. No cloud provider can know what vulnerabilities exist within your code or the packages used by your customers. That is left up to the customer. Additionally, if you deploy older, legacy applications known to have attack vectors that are too risky or expensive to change/update, you must accept the risk. Lastly, when you deploy to the cloud, it really isn't a bad idea to add some extra layers of security if your team has the skills, and there is no increase in latency.

Azure provides a few products and features that can help improve the level of security for customers of all kinds. Table 2.10 briefly describes many of them. Each one is discussed in greater detail here and in even greater detail in later chapters.

TABLE 2.10   Additional Azure Security Features

Azure Product	Description
Microsoft Trust Center	A location to gather security and compliance information
Security Center	A feature to analyze Azure workload and find vulnerabilities
Azure Network Security	A collection of controls, appliances, and facilities for defending the integrity of a network
Application Gateway/WAF	A public endpoint that can load balance or restrict access to backend endpoints
Azure DDoS Protection	Real-time traffic monitoring that can catch DDoS attacks and take action
Azure Confidential Computing	The means for protecting data at rest, data in transit, and data being processed

These additional features are presented in the sequence in which they should be approached, designed, and deployed. Begin with the research and design of security, then network, then compute, and finally your application code and dependent resources.

Microsoft Trust Center

The Microsoft Trust Center is a location for learning about security compliance. What is security compliance, why is compliance important, what does it mean to be compliant, and what happens if my Azure product is not compliant? All these answers are found at the Microsoft Trust Center and are discussed in great detail in Chapter 6.

www.microsoft.com/en-us/trustcenter/default.aspx

Security Center

Security Center is a full-fledged Azure product that helps support the implementation and maintenance of security policies. This is accomplished within the context of the following Support Security Center concepts:

- Policy and compliance
- Resource security hygiene
- Advanced cloud defense
- Threat protection

Security Center is a service found within the Azure Portal. Log in and search for *Security Center* and then click the link. It looks like Figure 2.48.

FIGURE 2.48 Security Center icon

There are two tiers of the Security Center: Free and Standard. The Free tier is just that— it has no associated cost, but as you may imagine, it comes with fewer capabilities than Standard. The costs are based on a combination of consumption and/or hours of usage. See Table 2.11 for some details about the differences in tiers.

Clicking the Security Center link opens the Security Center blade that gives an overview of all resources within the linked subscription. Expect something similar to Figure 2.49.

Let's look at each of the major components of the Security Center in more detail.

TABLE 2.11   Azure Security Center Tier Differences

Resource Type	Free Tier	Standard Tier
Virtual machine	✓	✓
App service	✓	✓
IoT devices		✓
Azure Blob storage		✓
MySQL		✓
PostgreSQL		✓
SQL database		✓

FIGURE 2.49   Security Center overview portal blade

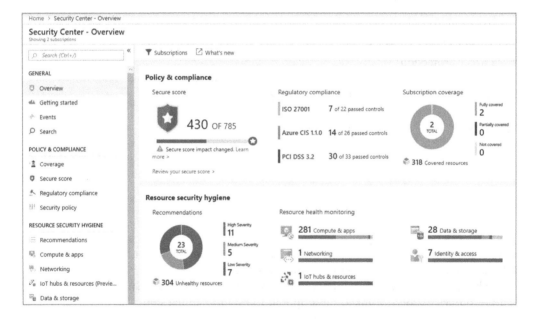

Policy and Compliance

Most of the policy and compliance capabilities found in the Security Center are covered in Chapter 6. The links found under this header provide a more detailed view of what is presented on the Overview blade shown previously in Figure 2.49. The information includes the coverage of subscriptions included with the feature, regulatory compliance, and security policies, which are discussed in detail later in this chapter.

The Secure Score feature is an interesting one in that specific actions, such as enabling MFA, enabling advanced data security, or applying JIT network access, all have an associated value. The more security compliance recommendations that are implemented, the higher the score. The Secure Score blade provides an overall score for all resources in the subscriptions as well as a breakdown per category, such as compute, data, storage, networking, and identity.

The calculation of the total possible points and the current points is one of the main benefits of Security Center. All the supported resources in the subscription are constantly reviewed with an algorithm that compares the current configuration with a recommendation database. If differences or missing applications of policy or procedures are found, then the points are not granted but are identified in a resource recommendation list, along with the attainable points when implemented. The recommendation report is found within the next group of capabilities.

Resource Security Hygiene

This category provides a list of overall security-related recommendations by subscription as well as by resource type. For example, by clicking the Recommendations link, you'll get a list of all recommendations, the score received for implementing them, the number of resources by type that are impacted, and the severity of each one. Figure 2.50 shows the output.

FIGURE 2.50   Security Center recommendations

Clicking a specific recommendation opens a new blade that describes it and provides some general information, what the threats are, and the steps to remediate it. The other resource types such as Compute & Apps, Networking, IoT Hubs, Data & Storage, and Identity & Access list recommendations specific to those types of resources. Finally, the Security Solutions feature allows the integration of third-party tools, non-Azure resources, and next-generation security capabilities.

Advanced Cloud Defense

In the cloud, companies pay for compute resources. Sometimes the required compute power is significant, and it can be very costly. In an IaaS setup where you can make a remote connection to a VM, checking what is running on the machine can lower your costs. In an IaaS scenario, you are charged for all the consumed compute anyway, so there is not much concern there. However, consider PaaS or serverless compute when you do not have access to the VMs that are running your code. How can you be certain that only your application is running on the machine?

From a cost perspective, compute consumption does have some impact, but not as much as it has from a security perspective. Running on a machine without knowledge of the owner is how malware works; malware somehow gets executed on a machine without permission. It wouldn't use up much compute to stay under the radar, but malware can still do some damage and expose sensitive data or intellectual property to bad actors. The way to prevent things like this from happening is to configure some adaptive application controls. These controls are similar to a whitelist on a firewall whereby only IP addresses specifically identified in the list will pass through. An adaptive application control is a list of processes allowed to run on any given compute resource on the Azure platform. This control prevents any unexpected process foe or friend from running on your compute resources without specific allowances. It of course requires that you know specifically which processes are required, from your application perspective. Platform processes would be whitelisted by default.

JIT access has already been mentioned; it is also an advanced cloud defense capability and is the concept of providing access to a resource, in this case a VM, when it is required and only for a specific amount of time. The request should be linked to a work item that defines the need for the access, which is then reviewed and approved. Once the time frame has passed, access to the resource is revoked.

File Integrity Monitoring (FIM) provides the capability to monitor changes to files, application software, or registry settings since the last scan. FIM requires the Standard tier of Security Center and provides a report on the number of changes per the types just stated (file, registry, etc.) along with whether the action taken was an update, addition, or removal. The platform cannot determine whether the changes were intentional or not; however, some patterns that have been linked to certain types of malicious attacks are recognized. These kinds of anomalies are displayed in the output of the FIM report as well.

Threat Protection

Recall from earlier in this chapter where you created a conditional access policy and one of the attributes was to validate the risk level of the attempted sign-in. The calculation of the risk level is simply a service that is provided as part of Azure Active Directory. Think of Microsoft Threat Protection in the same way.

Microsoft is in a unique position to capture telemetry from many products and services, which produces an enormous opportunity. This telemetry contains failed and potential successful exploitation of both Microsoft's own products as well as customer products that are implemented on them.

As the collection of this telemetry grows, using machine learning and AI, patterns, behaviors, and anomalies begin to emerge for many different types of scenarios. The scenario here is that some bad actor is taking some action that matches a pattern mapped to what has historically been considered a threat or an action that appears to have malicious intentions. The ability to capture this telemetry, learn from it, present details about it, and alert about its existence is a benefit from configuring and using this Azure product.

One product that is focused on using AI to monitor and react to security issues on the cloud is Azure Sentinel. Check it out here:

`azure.microsoft.com/en-us/services/azure-sentinel`

The internals of Microsoft Threat Protection are proprietary to Microsoft; however, these three points are worth a deeper dive:

- Types of threats
- Threat intelligence
- Detecting threats

The number and kind of threats you might encounter are limited only by the imagination of the bad actor who attempts to perform them and the kind of tools and resources that are used. However, there are some common actions that have been linked to potential malicious activities that may warrant an alert and some follow-up. Here are a few:

- Brute force
- Botnet
- DDoS
- Malicious software

There are too many types of threats to mention every one that may exist; this is true in day-to-day life, not just regarding technology and Azure. Many threats are specific to the type of resource being exploited. The attack vector for Windows would be different than IIS, Linux, Azure Blob Storage, or a database. Just keep in mind that the Threat Protection feature can help to identify them, but covering all of them would require a security expert and a security-focused book.

With that said, it is the act of gathering threat intelligence that makes this feature so valuable. The massive amount of telemetry being generated, when harnessed, is most useful for linking an actual exploitation with the actions taken to implement it. We expect that normal operational behaviors occur within a given range of activities. When something outside that range occurs, the activity can be logged, and you can get an alert for it. Those boundaries are set by the collection intelligence via telemetry, compared to learned behaviors from previous attempted or successful attacks. Here are a few example actions that are sometimes linked to events that are considered questionable:

- Clearing event logs
- Creating or modifying a firewall rule
- Attempting suspicious connections on known default ports
- Deleting files

You can detect these threats when the Security Center product is enabled for the resources within the Azure subscription. I would expect Microsoft to have capabilities like this enabled for the Azure platform, but as some telemetry coming into and going out of customer's resources on Azure contains sensitive and proprietary information, the data is not captured by default. The customer needs to agree to have this data collected so that threats can be detected and investigated. Microsoft respects customers' privacy—have no doubt about that!

Azure Network Security

The internals of Azure Networking are discussed in the next chapter, Chapter 3; however, as this is the security chapter, it makes sense to touch on some network security concepts here. Concepts such as isolation, connectivity traffic filtering, and routing are require security-related knowledge, as well as knowledge of the actual feature.

From an isolation perspective, Azure Networking offers the concept of *virtual networks*. A virtual network simulates the networking scenario one would have in their own on-premise network, utilizing private IP addresses, implementing access control policies, and defining subnets. These options separate the virtual network containing Azure resources from all other resources running on the Azure platform. While outbound internet connectivity is enabled by default, the capacity for any source to connect to products and features within a virtual network requires explicit allowances and configurations.

To filter inbound and outbound virtual network traffic, configure the *network security groups (NSGs)* feature. The identification of IP address, port number, and protocol in real time at the edge of the virtual network is useful for allowing or denying the traffic to leave or enter. An NSG provides the capability for this deny or allow rule. Finally, routing tables are important to security to ensure all communications into and out of the virtual network happen through a single network appliance. This reduces the maintenance of multiple NSGs and reduces the likelihood of unauthorized devices from entering or exiting the virtual network subnet.

Application Gateway/WAF

Again, Azure Networking is covered in detail in Chapter 3, but the Application Gateway provides a capability to secure an application running on the Azure platform. The

Application Gateway is a network security appliance that, in addition to load balancing, managing session affinity, and URL rerouting capabilities, provides a web application firewall (WAF).

Web applications are one of the most vulnerable endpoints for exploitation. The reason is simple: they are globally available to anyone and anything that also has connectivity to the internet. Keeping up with known vulnerabilities and patches to prevent them can be a significant undertaking depending on the size of your application or number of applications. There are vulnerabilities not only from a platform perspective but also from an application one. For example, SQL injection, XSS, common misconfigurations, or probing from bots and crawlers are all application-level vulnerabilities.

A *web application firewall (WAF)* can be implemented to help detect and prevent such application weaknesses. In Chapter 3 there is an exercise where a WAF is configured on an Application Gateway device. For now, recognize that the detection and prevention of malicious activities on the WAF is constructed by applying a rule set with the configuration. Supported rule sets are CRS 3.0, CRS 2.2.9, and OWASP CRS 3.0; the contents of each are outside the scope of this book but are fully documented elsewhere. Once you've determined which rule set to apply to the WAF, determine whether the requirement is to detect and log the attempt or to prevent the request from proceeding past the WAF if the occurrence is observed.

Azure DDoS Protection

A distributed denial-of-service (DDoS) attack is when some source consumes all the available resources an application has that stops other clients or customers from getting access. There are two tiers for this product on Azure: Basic and Standard. By default, DDoS protection is enabled automatically and is constantly monitoring traffic in real time. If an attack is recognized, then the same defensive capabilities Microsoft uses to protect its online services are applied to customers running on Azure. In the Standard tier, the additional features are diagnostic and attack metric reports, resolution details if an attack happened, and the authorization to consult DDoS experts. This is a great benefit, but for most cases and purposes this protection is free.

Azure Confidential Computing

Moving extremely sensitive data to the cloud has historically been one of the most discussed concerns customers have. It is a valid concern and one that has been taken seriously by the development of two concepts:

- Encryption of data at rest
- Encryption of data in transit

Each of those techniques helps ensure data is secured. Up to now, the security topics have mostly focused on keeping bad actors or malicious code from getting access to a resource hosted on Azure. Let's assume this happens and that a bad actor gets access to your database or to one of the VMs running your application within your virtual network. What then? This is where data at rest and data in transit come into view.

Data at Rest

There are numerous Azure locations and formats in which data can be stored such as data backups, archived data, VHDs, files on hard disks, and content stored in an Azure Storage container. Without taking an action to encrypt those objects, they are vulnerable if the other methods protecting them are compromised.

There are numerous approaches for encrypting your data while it is at rest, in other words, not in use. The simplest is to encrypt the data or content before it is deployed to the Azure platform using a client-side encryption key. When the data is accessed, the private key can be used to decrypt the data and expose it to an authenticated individual or service. Another method is server-side encryption where part of the process for capturing and storing data is encrypted as it arrives, or shortly thereafter, and then stored encrypted in a secure location. When the data is requested via an application, the application can get the server-side encryption key, decrypt the data, and render or provide the data to the authenticated entity. Both of these approaches requires a key that leads to the question of where the key should be stored. The answer is Key Vault, which is discussed in the next section.

 Encrypted hard disks, Azure Storage features like blobs, and data stored in a database can all be encrypted and made secure in case the other measures taken to prevent access have somehow failed.

Data in Transit

Two of the most common protocols for moving data between servers are Server Message Block (SMB) and Hypertext Transfer Protocol (HTTP). All VMs running on Azure are running SMB 3.0. Earlier versions of SMB have been disabled as there have been some vulnerabilities identified within them. SMB 3.0 supports the encryption of the content available from file shares. Administrators can enable the SMB encryption for all shares on a server or limit it to only a specific group. SMB encryption is enabled by default on Azure.

Data sent using HTTP is delivered in plain text; therefore, it is highly recommended to instead communicate using HTTPS. By using HTTPS/TLS, a secure tunnel is created between the client and the server, and then the content is encrypted using an agreed-on cipher. When using, for example, TLS 1.2, you can be confident that the communication is safe. It is common that TLS is offloaded by some edge endpoint like an Application Gateway, for example, where the traffic from that point to other resources within the virtual network or Azure platform is sent unencrypted. If the communication or data being sent is extremely sensitive, make sure HTTPS is not terminated at any point between the client and the server by any network appliance. You can determine this by looking at the port on which the connection was made; if the port is 443, then most probably the connection was made using HTTPS.

Data in Use

The previous two encryption methods (data-at-rest and data-in-transit) have been part of Azure and part of any organization that wants to ensure the security of the data in those scenarios. There was a missing level of vulnerability, however. The missing component was a level lower; consider that the data is unencrypted at some point when it is going through the process of encryption and decryption. Visualize a process running on Windows, where a process is an executable (EXE). This process could be storing the encryption key in memory, and it is storing the data in either the encrypted or unencrypted state while in the processor or in caches. Assuming a bad actor has made it to the VM and is able to execute some malicious code that accesses the memory allocated for the given process, it could then locate and capture the key or access the data while unencrypted and store it in some remote or local location for later retrieval.

This is one of the use cases for Azure Confidential Computing (ACC), which is focused on the encryption of data while in use. There are two implementations of ACC, which help protect data in this scenario; they are a hardware version and a software version, as illustrated in Figure 2.51. Both of those implementations are known as *trusted execution environments (TEEs)*. The hardware TEE creates a protected container, called an *enclave*, around a portion of the available memory and processors existing on the VM. This is supported using Intel SGX–capable hardware. The code that can run in that memory or processor location must be specifically authorized. If this reads familiar, it is similar to the adaptive application control that is part of the Security Center offering. Microsoft does often reuse the products it creates and introduces them into a more consumable additional product or products.

FIGURE 2.51   Trusted execution environment

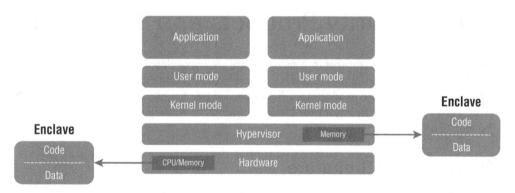

The software enclave that runs the TEE is created at the hypervisor level and is called *virtualization-based security*. The concept in the software enclave is similar as it is for the hardware; however, instead of the configuration at the hardware level, the hypervisor basically creates a virtual memory partition that is restricted from other memory on the host including any administrator who can access the machine.

Another fascinating scenario that fits into ACC is the ability to combine multiple data sources. A noteworthy example comes from within the healthcare industry. Hospitals have significant amounts of patient data; however, that data contains personally identifiable (PI) data that cannot be shared with other entities, other hospitals, or research firms. This is logical as the protection of data, and the privacy of patients, is regulated by the law. The data from a single hospital creates an effective machine learning (ML) model that has proven to supply valuable findings. If the data, however, was shared between many other hospitals, then those models would produce even greater discoveries, because ML is fed by data.

When data from multiple entities is uploaded, the data can/should be encrypted on the client side using a private key. The ML can decrypt using the key and produce a result by running the analysis in an enclave. The results have been positive in that running the datasets from multiple entities through an ML model have increased the predictability of some ailments when compared to running the same ML model on a single dataset.

Azure Confidential Computing is available as a Marketplace product called Confidential Compute VM Deployment, illustrated in Figure 2.52.

FIGURE 2.52   Confidential Compute VM Deployment

This is an exciting area, and I expect many advancements to come from this in the future.

Azure Security Products and Techniques

This section covers some features in Azure that are security-related but are not part of AAD, RBAC, networking, or computing. These products and techniques are either application-specific, Azure product-specific, or procedures happening behind the scenes. In Chapter 7, where developing for the cloud is covered, the configuration of some of the following is discussed in more detail.

Shared Access Signature

Shared Access Signature (SAS) is used for controlling access to blob, file, table, and queue storage containers. When an Azure Storage account is created (we'll discuss this in Chapter 5) and a client attempts to connect to a storage container, instead of using the access keys for the storage account, it is a best practice to generate a SAS key (aka token). You would not want to share an access key since it is like a root password to all the containers existing within the Azure Storage account. An access key resembles something like the following and looks very similar to a token:

```
aWgiDojznGEZoY+9Ivrt+Wmr1MsI9VO+qtEB8+RLL+88jk7cNnurEb3vWPvLdJxf7y
7vpeP6OUqfpNRKOA==
```

For example, in a scenario where there are multiple clients that will upload a blob, it would not be secure to provide the root password to each client, since if one of them is compromised, then all clients will need to be reset or updated with the new key. That is not an optimal or maintainable scenario. Instead, you can expose an API for clients to be authenticated and then receive a SAS key that allows the API to perform CRUD operations on a specific storage container. The API that generates the SAS key does need the access key to generate the SAS key for the clients. A connection string for the Azure Storage account is necessary to achieve that. This connection string resembles the following:

```
DefaultEndpointsProtocol=https;AccountName=<name>;AccountKey=<key>;EndpointSuf
fix=core.windows.net
```

There have been many references made to keys up to now, and it is for certain that those keys be stored in a secure and restricted location. The means to store keys, connection strings, and other secrets are achieved by using an Azure feature called Azure Key Vault, which is discussed next.

Azure Key Vault

Azure Key Vault is a product that stores secrets. Anything, almost, that an application needs to function that needs protection, provides access to sensitive data, or cannot be stored in plain text at any time or anyplace can be stored in Azure Key Vault. Items such as tokens, certificates (.pfx), passwords, and encryption keys can be encrypted and stored in a vault. To access any item stored in a Key Vault, you must first be authenticated.

Azure Key Vault supports the following authentication capabilities, which have been previously discussed:

- Service principals
- Managed identities

Knowing that the secret stored in the Key Vault is accessible only using an authentication method that doesn't utilize any hard-coded metadata, it is a reliable solution to common problems. For example, when two systems want to communicate with each other and use a secret key, then it would be prudent to encrypt the secret before sending it across the internet. If it is not encrypted, then it could be seen and simply added to a request to allow unauthorized access. Sure, in most cases the communications are handled using SSL/TLS; however, there are scenarios in which this extra level of security is justified.

Complete Exercise 2.9 to create a key and a secret in Azure Key Vault. In later chapters, both the key and secret will be made accessible and utilized to encrypt/decrypt a secret message between two entities and make a connection to a storage account using a connection string.

EXERCISE 2.9

Creating an Azure Key Vault

1. Log in to the Azure Portal at portal.azure.com.

2. Click + Create Resource (top left) and select Key Vault ➢ Create.

3. Give the Key Vault a name, select the subscription to place it in, and then select that location.

4. If you have not already created a resource group (this will be done in Chapter 3 when we begin creating Azure resources), then click the Create New link and create a new one. Remember when RBAC was discussed that a resource group is one of the locations in the scope hierarchy to which service principals can be granted access. It is important to provide a name for the resource group that reflects what is contained within it. Select the resource group into which the key value will be created.

5. Leave the pricing tier, access policies, and virtual network access at the defaults, and click the Create button.

6. Select the Key Vault, click the Keys link, and then click + Generate/import.

7. Set Options to Generate, enter the name, leave the other entries at the defaults, and then click Create.

8. Select Secrets ➢ + Generate/Import.

9. Leave Upload Options set to Manual, enter a name, and add a value like the following string:

   DefaultEndpointsProtocol=https;AccountName=<name>;AccountKey=<key>;
   EndpointSuffix=core.windows.net

 This is not a valid connection string; it will be updated in a later chapter.

10. In the Content Type text box, enter This is an Azure Storage Account, leave the other options at the defaults, and then click the Create button.

11. Finally, click the Access Policies link to see who or what has access to the Key Vault.

Both the key and the secret are now in a secure location accessible only to the service principals identified in the portal. This is a secure location and can be trusted.

Easy Auth

Easy Auth is a managed IIS custom module that contains built-in authentication and authorization capabilities. This feature can be utilized from either Azure App Services or Azure Functions and is not enabled by default. The Easy Auth module is subscribed to the authentication event in the IIS execution pipeline; when the event is fired, the request is handed over to this module for continued execution. Once the Easy Auth code is executed successfully, the request is placed back into the pipeline and continues down the pipeline into the execution of your application code. If the authentication fails, then a 401 HTTP status code is returned to the client.

Figure 2.53 shows the authentication providers supported by Easy Auth.

FIGURE 2.53   A list of authentication providers

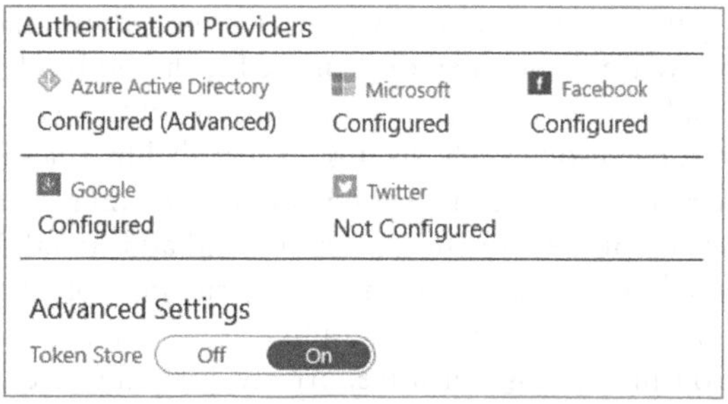

Microsoft, Facebook, Google, and Twitter all use the OAuth tokens for the management of their authentication provider, while Azure Active Directory utilizes the classes and methods contained within the `Microsoft.Identity` namespace. This feature is a quick and simple way of protecting an instance of Azure App Service or Azure Functions from unauthenticated access. Keep in mind, however, the designers and developers must manually create an authorization model, like RBAC, and implement it into the security layer of the application.

Notice also in Figure 2.53 the existence of an advanced setting named Token Store. Tokens are granted by an authentication provider; as a developer, if I choose to trust that authentication provider and the validation of the token is successful, then I can allow access to my protected resource. Tokens stored in the token store can be used in the same manner as managed identities or service accounts. Instead of the request coming from an actual user, the request is sent on behalf of someone or something else. This something else needs to have a valid token and can be stored in the token store and retrieved using code in real time.

NOTE   Tokens typically have a life span of 60 days. Therefore, those stored in a token store must be refreshed from time to time. Each authentication provider has their own design and requirements for refreshing a token. It's similar to sending a GET request to /.auth/refresh when the status result from an authentication request results in an expired token error.

In Chapter 4, you will configure Easy Auth as part of creating an Azure App Service instance, and the contents of an authentication request and response are described and presented in Chapter 7.

Summary

In this chapter, we covered the most important step when migrating to the Azure platform: security. The fact that Azure Active Directory (AAD) is the feature that authenticates the access to the portal, via Azure PowerShell or Azure CLI, should be clear. AAD additionally provides an API that can be consumed from code running on the Azure platform to provide authentication into the application. Authorization is handled by role-based access control that protects the Azure resources within a subscription based on role and scope.

There are threat prevention, networking, compute, and additional Azure products and features that increase the level of security from a platform and application perspective such as WAF, Confidential Computing, Easy Auth, and NSGs. Combined, Azure provides all the necessary capabilities to run the most sensitive, private compute executions, house sensitive data, and comply with the most stringent security policies and restrictions.

Exam Essentials

Understand Azure Active Directory.   Know how to configure the most common features within AAD to pass the Azure Solutions Architect Expert exam. The most common have been discussed in this chapter. Understand that AAD provides security around the Azure Portal and is used to authenticate users. AAD also authenticates when calling a REST API, executing Azure PowerShell cmdlets, or running Azure CLI commands on Azure resources. AAD can be configured to authenticate for other Azure SaaS resources such as Office 365 or Dynamics Online.

Understand role-based access control.   RBAC is an authorization model that exists within the Azure Portal. It comes with more than 40 built-in roles that are useful for granting permissions on create, read, update, and delete (CRUD) operations for Azure resources. Individuals are added to a role, and then that role is granted permission to an Azure resource at either the subscription, resource group, or resource level. RBAC also supports custom roles if one of the built-in roles does not meet your needs.

Know AAD Connect.   Have a good understanding about what this feature is used for. This is a tool that mid to large companies will use to migrate an on-premise Active Directory to Azure Active Directory. Additionally, this tool can keep profiles and permissions synchronized in case a hybrid solution is implemented. It supports password synchronization between instances that helps support SSO.

Understand conditional access.   This feature is a second-level security feature, meaning it is triggered after a client has provided credentials, such as a user ID and password, that are authenticated successfully. The feature can be configured to check the location of the access, which platform or OS the client is on, and a risk assessment performed on the access request. If either of those second-level security checks fails, then the client is not allowed to access the resource.

Understand multifactor authentication.   This feature is becoming more mainstream every day. This also happens after an initial authentication is successful, which is based on something the client knows. The second factor is something the client has or is, such as a retinal scan or a phone that can be sent a number to provide to the authentication provider.

Review Questions

1. What features does Azure Active Directory provide? (Choose all that apply.)
   - **A.** Authentication
   - **B.** Authorization
   - **C.** Retinal scan capabilities
   - **D.** Synchronization with on-site Active Directory

2. What is true about data-at-rest encryption?
   - **A.** Data stored in memory cache is encrypted.
   - **B.** Streamed content is encrypted.
   - **C.** Data stored in a database is encrypted.
   - **D.** Archived data is encrypted.
   - **E.** Both A and D

3. Which of the following role-based access controls are free?
   - **A.** Custom roles
   - **B.** Built-in roles
   - **C.** Both
   - **D.** Neither

4. What does AAD Connect do?
   - **A.** Authenticates Active Directory service principals
   - **B.** Exposes a REST API for querying AAD profile details
   - **C.** Synchronizes passwords between on-premise and AAD
   - **D.** Both B and C

5. Conditional access can be configured for which of the following scenarios?
   - **A.** Location of login attempt
   - **B.** To require a client certificate
   - **C.** Both A and B
   - **D.** Neither A nor B

6. Which permission is required to create a custom RBAC role?
   - **A.** A. `Microsoft.Authorization/roleDefinition/read`
   - **B.** B. `Microsoft.Authorization/roleDefinition/write`
   - **C.** C. `Microsoft.Authorization/*/write`
   - **D.** D. `Microsoft.Authorization/roleDefinition/*`

7. What is the underlying almost invisible feature that protects Azure resources from unauthorized access within the portal?

   A. Azure Resource Manager (ARM)

   B. Role-based access control (RBAC)

   C. Azure Service Manager (ASM)

   D. Just-in-time (JIT) access

8. What is false about data-in-use encryption?

   A. It encrypts all data while stored in memory.

   B. It encrypts data while executing in the CPU.

   C. Both A and B

9. You can use a SAS key for user authentication on which of the following Azure products?

   A. Azure Message Storage Container

   B. Azure Functions

   C. Azure Blob Storage Container

   D. Azure Cosmos DB

   E. Both A and C

10. Which of the following can you store in Azure Key Vault?

   A. A secret

   B. A key

   C. A .pfx file

   D. All of the above

   E. Only A and B

Chapter

3

Networking

EXAM AZ-303 OBJECTIVES COVERED IN THIS CHAPTER:

✓ **Implement and Monitor an Azure Infrastructure**

  ▪ Implement cloud infrastructure monitoring

✓ **Implement Management and Security Solutions**

  ▪ Implement load balancing and network security

EXAM AZ-304 OBJECTIVES COVERED IN THIS CHAPTER:

✓ **Design Monitoring**

  ▪ Design for cost optimization

✓ **Design Infrastructure**

  ▪ Design a network solution

Many steps are required to move IT solutions to the cloud, and the order of occurrence is worthy of attention. Customers do not generally view networking as their first point of entry. Nor do customers or companies first consider security. But security is the first and most important step, followed by networking. Security must encompass every aspect of the Azure products, features, and solutions you run. The networking topology, once created, can only exist within the realm of security you created.

Networking and networks have been around for a long time, some as early as the 1950s. In those early days, the sharing of data and resources among the connected nodes was limited mostly to governments and a few (maybe five) big organizations. It wasn't until the 1990s that the capacity to make connections to other computers became mainstream. In other words, an individual didn't need a doctorate in computing to configure a *local area network (LAN)* anymore.

The 1990s also saw the first recorded occurrence of the term *World Wide Web (WWW)*. The World Wide Web required a network connection and the same technology used as when networks first appeared. Today, the *www* host name prefix, social media apps, and video streaming used by billions of client devices still use that basic networking principle (with TCP/IP being the basis of connectivity). Connectivity to these networks (i.e., intranet and internet) and the resources that support it are often erroneously considered simple. The service offered through networking is without doubt an expected default feature of computing that must function without manual intervention. Networking gets overlooked because this layer of technology is unseen but expected to work just like the devices connecting to the network.

Before we begin digging into the details of the Azure networking products and features, there are three high-level networking concepts that need explanation.

- Microsoft's global network
- Hybrid Azure networks
- The Azure Virtual Network service

To attain the Azure Solutions Architect certification, you must comprehend these concepts, their differences, and their use cases.

Microsoft's Global Network

Microsoft has data centers in more than 50 locations worldwide, and they are accessible to more than 140 countries, as shown in Figure 3.1. These data centers are referred to as *regions* that are interconnected by Microsoft's global *wide area network (WAN)*. These data centers are capable of hosting applications requiring email, IoT, video streaming, search, storage, and cloud capabilities. Not only do these data centers host the Azure cloud platform, they accommodate other Microsoft SaaS offerings such as OneDrive, Xbox, Office 365, and Bing. This means when you run on Azure, you get the same infrastructure as Microsoft uses to run its own products.

FIGURE 3.1   A global map of the Microsoft Azure network

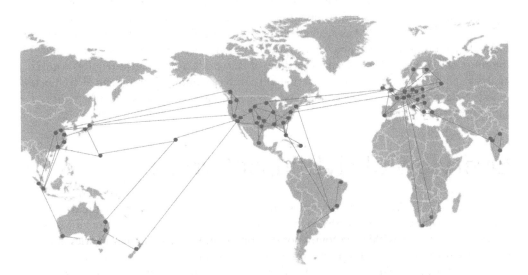

The connectivity between resources hosted in different regions and the traffic sent between them remains inside the WAN. If you have a primary database in the East US data center and synchronize data to another database instance, for example in North Europe, none of the data being transferred across the Atlantic will travel through the public internet. This is an often overlooked security gain that is provided essentially for free and isn't a benefit that smaller cloud companies can offer to customers.

Responsiveness is crucial, and having the Azure cloud as close to companies and their customers as possible is what is expected from cloud platforms and online service providers. The speed at which data transmits across the WAN is nearly at the speed of light; the path of the data transfer determines the latency. The number of *hops*, which can be found using a tool called `tracert`, identifies how many hardware appliances the request travels through from client to server or from server to server. For more details about `tracert`, take a look at this web page:

docs.microsoft.com/en-us/windows-server/administration/windows-commands/tracert

The number of hops and appliances a request flows through affects the latency and perceived responsiveness. How these requests are routed within the WAN is discussed in more detail later in the "Network Traffic Routing" section of this chapter.

As the cloud infrastructure matured, it was determined that the existing hardware-based routing capabilities alone did not keep up with the demands of customers. Microsoft, being a software company (well, maybe not 100% anymore), came up with a cloud-optimized, software-based architecture to manage its WAN. This architecture is referred to as a *software-driven WAN* (SWAN).

A SWAN is a system that optimizes the utilization of inter-data-center network capacity. The concept is based on the redirection of network traffic from one network segment/switch to one that currently has available bandwidth. We all know that an overutilized network will result in latency, but that overutilization is confined to a segment and not the entire network topology. Keeping the flow of network traffic efficient requires regular analysis and maintenance as the utilization of resources running within them also changes. A SWAN keeps an eye on transient network congestion and reroutes traffic where the capacity exists to satisfy the demand.

Overview of Hybrid Networks

The entire "Hybrid Azure Networking" section covers hybrid networks in more detail later in the chapter, but it is worthy to touch on the topic now. Whenever the word *hybrid* is used, it is typically within the context of the combination of two similar entities into a single, usually more efficient, object. For example, there are hybrid cars that utilize components historically linked to an automobile but with a change to the source of power—electricity instead of combustion. Likewise, there are hybrid computing models that combine compute and data resources that are within different network boundaries like on-premise and cloud. A hybrid network, then, combines two separate network topologies into one, which renders benefits from their synergy.

A few realized benefits of creating a hybrid network with Azure are access to modernized capabilities and an increase in bandwidth. Creating a data center, and the architecture that runs it, is without argument inconceivably expensive, and that's just to build it. Maintaining it takes another pile of cash. Once that investment is made and time passes, technological advancements to the infrastructure components that were originally configured come on the market, which may justify their replacement. Additionally, the amount of space in the data center may have been less than required, so you need more room for growth. Replacing or reconfiguring data centers is expensive and potentially disruptive, so why not combine networks, making a hybrid one? Figure 3.2 shows an example of a generic hybrid network.

FIGURE 3.2   An Azure hybrid network example

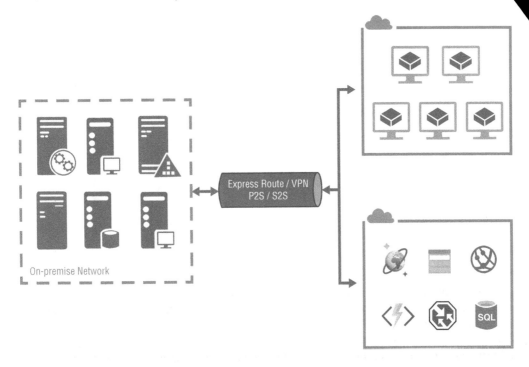

From a bandwidth perspective, a data center will typically have an enterprise-level network connection to the internet backbone through a telecommunications company. Even the networking devices and capacities of telecommunications companies come under duress and need updating. On-premise data center owners can review the contracts with third parties regularly and request better resiliency, when required. Keep in mind that connectivity from an on-premise data center to an Azure data center using express routes, VPNs, or point-to-site offerings is managed by third-party companies. The outbound traffic to the internet and connectivity between Microsoft data centers, however, is managed by Microsoft. This means it is fast, efficient, and best of all supported by Microsoft, and that is a good thing!

Azure Virtual Network

All Azure resources reside within the Microsoft Azure network, as discussed. Every Azure resource, on the other hand, does not exist within *Azure Virtual Network*. Azure products such as SQL Azure, Azure Storage Containers, and Azure App Service run within the Microsoft network but not within Azure Virtual Network. Figure 3.3 represents this scenario where you see Azure virtual machines (IaaS, Azure VM) within Azure Virtual Network, while other products are not.

Azure virtual machines embedded within the Microsoft Azure network

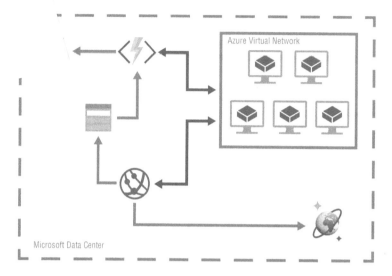

The other products are within the Microsoft network and are accessible via a global endpoint from anyplace on the internet. Azure VMs are accessible via the internet, but not without performing a configuration that specifically allows that, usually at creation time. Additionally, products within the Microsoft network can connect to other Azure products and features within a VNet, but again, not by default—the VNet must allow that specific connection. Lastly, all products within the VNet can connect to each other by default. The next section provides the details for VNets.

The key takeaway is that all Azure products do not function within or need a VNet, nor do they need to communicate with resources hosted within one. The solution that is moved to Azure may also not need to communicate with an on-premise source and instead can run completely on Azure instead of being a hybrid solution. Table 3.1 lists some scenarios.

TABLE 3.1 Scenarios Requiring a VNet

Frontend	Backend/Data Source	VNet Required
Azure App Service	SQL Azure	No
Azure VM	Managed Azure SQL	Yes
On-premise	In Azure	Yes/No
In Azure	On-premise	Yes/No

If you run a website on Azure App Service that connects to a SQL Azure database, then no VNet is required. Both products run within the Microsoft network. If you run a website on an Azure virtual machine that needs connectivity to a managed Azure SQL instance running on a VM, then those products must run within a VNet. If the design calls for an on-premise server, for example, to process data from a data source in Azure, then, again, a VNet is required. Finally, if the frontend, whether it is part of the presentation layer or compute power, runs in Azure and connects to a secured on-premise data source, then a VNet would indeed be required. Simply, a hybrid network requires a VNet and so do Azure virtual machines.

From an Azure Solutions Architect Expert perspective, you should know those scenarios that require a VNet, whether there are any alternatives to a VNet (such as Hybrid Connection Manager, discussed later in the chapter), and which features live only in the Microsoft network.

Azure Virtual Networking

An Azure VNet is an isolated and secure network unit inside the Microsoft network. The Microsoft networking infrastructure is fundamental to the Azure IaaS and PaaS cloud offerings. A central trait making an IaaS offering valuable is that the cloud provider is responsible for the networking infrastructure; the same goes for PaaS and even SaaS. The procedure to place another network inside the cloud provider can be regarded as placing a network within a network, where the cloud provider's network has the actual hardware and network appliances and the customer's is a "virtual" network, operating mostly on an abstracted software layer that simulates the network appliances.

This isolated and secure network unit (aka a VNet) consists of one or more subnets, where a subnet is a technique used to segment or to create the boundary where the resources inside the VNet operate. Specifically, the technique used for segmentation is based on a unique IP address range specified in the *Classless Inter-Domain Routing (CIDR)* format, for example 10.0.0.0/24. Finally, the VNet and the subnets contained within it are configured to run in a region, which is synonymous to a data center, as described earlier. Let's take a closer look at regions and some key VNet capabilities; then we'll get into the networking aspects of running VNets and subnets on Azure.

Regions

In Chapter 1 we touched on the top three considerations to make when deploying or migrating to Azure, one of which was location. There are more than 50 locations that customers can choose from to deploy their applications. So, which one should you create your VNet in, and what are some of the considerations when deciding?

Well, note the following considerations between a region and a VNet:

- The VNet and the resources within it must exist in the same region.

- The resources being added to a VNet must also exist within the same subscription.

- VNets in different regions and different subscriptions can connect with each other by means of peering or VPNs.

- How much resiliency does the application hosted on Azure require? Does it warrant Availability Zones?

- Are the consumers of the application hosted on Azure in the vicinity of an Azure region?

- Are there any legal, compliance, and sovereignty considerations for the application?

The first three bullet points are relatively clear in that an Azure VM that exists in the North Europe region cannot be added to a VNet that is in a West US region/data center, regardless of whether they are in the same subscription. However, with peering or VPNs, discussed later, the resources within different VNets can connect with each other, regardless of region or subscription. The latter makes more sense, in that the resources in a VNet can be configured to connect to an on-premise non-Azure corporate intranet, which is not in an Azure data center and certainly not in an Azure subscription. Therefore, you can conclude that a VNet can be connected to any other network so long as the security rules allow it.

The remaining points need a bit more explanation, starting with *Availability Zones*. The analogy between a region and data center has been made numerous times, but in some instances, there is more than a single data center per region. So, although that analogy is correct, it is a little restrictive. The reason for having multiple data centers in a single region is to provide redundancy in case of a catastrophic data-center-wide failure. These kinds of failures are typically caused by weather, electrical power disruption, network outage, or some other scenario that is profound and totally unpredictable. The numerous data centers in Azure regions may be across the street from each other, across town, or in different towns, but they are close enough to be useful for redundancy and to be considered within the same region.

All that being said, as visualized in Figure 3.4, an Availability Zone is an instance of a customer's resources in one or more Azure data centers in the same region. These Availability Zones provide redundancy and high availability capabilities to protect against any single point of failure that can occur from a region or data center perspective. The question is, does your application running on Azure need to have this level of redundancy? This offering has an associated cost: it is not free to have this replication and extra level of redundancy. This is a question that is answered on a case-by-case basis because it depends on the criticality of the application itself.

FIGURE 3.4 Availability Zones within an Azure region

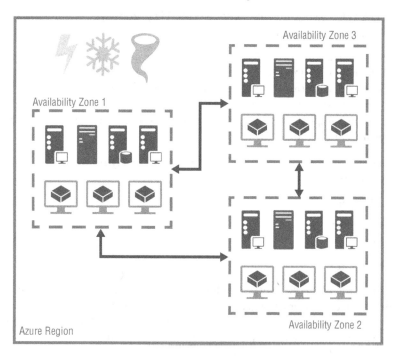

Finally, not all Azure regions offer Availability Zones, and regions that do offer them do not support all Azure product and features. Therefore, you must know whether your workload being moved to the Azure platform needs Availability Zones, and you must know what products and features are required and then choose the location of deployment. It wouldn't be prudent to place this list in written form because it can and does change at a relative quick pace. See Table 3.2 for a short summary of regions with Availability Zone support and the supported products within them.

TABLE 3.2 Regions, Availability Zones, and Products

	Central US	East US	North Europe	Southeast Asia
Virtual machines	✓	✓	✓	✓
Managed disks	✓	✓	✓	✓
Azure VPN Gateway	✓	✗	✓	✓
Azure ExpressRoute	✓	✗	✓	✓
Azure Load Balancer	✓	✓	✓	✓
Azure Cosmos DB	✗	✗	✗	✓

This list is updated online here:

docs.microsoft.com/en-us/azure/availability-zones/az-overview# services-support-by-region

Note that Table 3.2 shows that Azure VPN Gateway and ExpressRoute are not supported in the East US region; in other words, those products are not supported across Availability Zones. That means if there is an unexpected outage in an Availability Zone in East US and you have one of those products configured, then you will be impacted. Take a look at the following question which will test your knowledge concerning how to test latency between Azure Regions.

Which Azure tool can you use to measure network latency between a region and specific location?

A. Network Logger

B. Network Watcher

C. Wireshark

D. Network Monitor

The answer is *Network Watcher*, which you will use in Exercise 3.1. There is no product called Network Logger, at least not an Azure one. Both Wireshark and Network Monitor can be used to monitor network traffic, but neither is optimal for measuring latency between an Azure region and a specific location.

Chapter 1 introduced Azure Storage. We will go deeper into that product in Chapter 5. Remember the terms LRS, ZRS, GRS, and RA-GRS? Not only are those options critical to Azure Storage, but they are the backbone that provides the capability offered by Availability Zones. These redundancy options are must-know concepts.

Once you have considered how redundant your application needs to be and have narrowed down which Azure region provides all the required products and features, you can progress to the next step, which is to find the region closest to your customers or employees. Keep in mind, customers are not tolerant of latent or poorly performing applications. Perhaps they will revisit at a later time or simply navigate to a competitor and never return. From an employee's perspective, where latent applications must be used to perform a job, the slowness results in great frustration and a loss in productivity.

Answering the question may be simple if the workloads are for internal consumption. The location of the Azure region would simply be the one closest to the company's location. The situation gets a little more complicated as the number of locations in which the company exists increases and, at some point, becomes global. Then there is a question of if the application is for customers, where are they mostly located? Is there even a single or small group of locations, or is your customer base global? Those are questions that need to be answered by the company. The following exercise can help to provide input for making such critical decisions.

In Exercise 3.1, you will host your workloads in the Central US region, which is in Iowa. Central US supports Availability Zones, and all Azure products and features that can run within them are supported as well, excluding Azure Cosmos DB. At some point in the near term, you expect to place corporate offices in Germany and Japan and would like to test latency from those locations (see Figure 3.5).

FIGURE 3.5 Testing connectivity from the Central US region to other regional and global locations

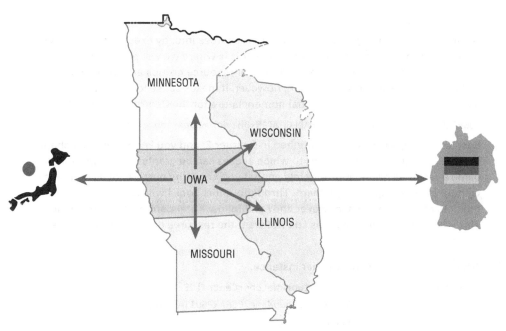

To test latency between these three locations, complete Exercise 3.1. There is currently no Azure Portal interface for performing this activity; instead, you will use PowerShell.

EXERCISE 3.1

Testing Network Latency from a Region to Other States and Countries

1. If you have not already installed the new Az PowerShell cmdlets, run the following command after opening the Windows PowerShell ISE as an administrator. Power-Shell is installed by default on a Windows machine.

```
Install-Module -Name Az -AllowClobber -Force
```

2. Once PowerShell is installed, log in using the `Connect-AzAccount` cmdlet. Type **Connect-AzAccount** and press Enter. You will be prompted for your credentials automatically. Enter the credentials as you would when accessing Azure via the portal.

3. Once authenticated, make sure you are in the desired Azure subscription context. This is relevant only if you have multiple Azure subscriptions. Execute the following cmdlets to set the Azure subscription. Add your subscription as the value of `SubscriptionId.$subscription = Get-AzSubscription -SubscriptionId "########-####-######"`.

    ```
    Set-AzContext $subscription
    ```

4. Create a resource group to place the Azure resources into, by executing the following cmdlet. The location is Central US because this is where we will place the Network Watcher instance. There is no requirement for resource groups and the resources within them to be in the same region; however, it makes sense to do so from a maintenance perspective. (DM1 is internal nomenclature for the Central US region.)

    ```
    New-AzResourceGroup -Name CSHARPGUITAR-DM1-RG -Location centralus
    ```

    Resource groups have been mentioned in Chapter 2, and you know from that chapter that they are groups of resources to which access can be granted. It is important to name a resource group appropriately so that you know the purpose of its contents without having to go through them. Throughout this book I will add resources to multiple resource groups; however, they will follow a standard naming convention. This will help me delete them as I do not want the resource once I have completed an exercise.

5. Next, create the Network Watcher instance.

    ```
    New-AzNetworkWatcher -Name NetworkWatcherCentralUS `
                         -ResourceGroupName CSHARPGUITAR-DM1-RG `
                         -Location centralus
    ```

6. The Network Watcher instance is created and is ready to perform some tests. First, generate a Reachability Report between the Central US region and the State of Minnesota. Execute the following:

    ```
    Get-AzNetworkWatcherReachabilityReport `
      -NetworkWatcherName NetworkWatcherCentralUS `
      -ResourceGroupName CSHARPGUITAR-DM1-RG `
      -Location "Central US" `
      -Country "United States" `
      -State "minnesota" `
      -StartTime "2019-05-25" `
      -EndTime "2019-05-30"
    ```

7. The output may resemble the following. The report has a start time and end time spanning five days. The maximum is 30 days, and data exists for only a rolling 30-day period.

```
AggregationLevel   : State
ProviderLocation   :
{
 "Country": "United States",
 "State": "minnesota"
}
ReachabilityReport :
[
 {
  "Provider": "Comcast Cable Communications, LLC - ASN 7922",
  "AzureLocation": "Central US",
  "Latencies": [
  {
   "TimeStamp": "2019-05-29T00:00:00Z",
   "Score": 96
  },
  {
   "TimeStamp": "2019-05-28T00:00:00Z",
   "Score": 94
  },
  {
   "TimeStamp": "2019-05-27T00:00:00Z",
   "Score": 98
  },
  {
   "TimeStamp": "2019-05-26T00:00:00Z",
   "Score": 98
  },
  {
   "TimeStamp": "2019-05-25T00:00:00Z",
   "Score": 98
  }]
 }
]
```

8. The Score value is a range from 1, which is the worst (and probably means there is an outage), to 100, which is perfect and rarely attainable. From that report it seems the 28th had some less than perfect latency, but it's still OK versus the previous day, which was near perfect. The fact that the Central US region is so close to the tested location, we would expect no latency to minimal relative latency. Next, see what it's like from Germany.

9. Execute the following and review the results:

```
Get-AzNetworkWatcherReachabilityReport `
  -NetworkWatcherName NetworkWatcherCentralUS `
  -ResourceGroupName CSHARPGUITAR-DM1-RG `
  -Location "Central US" `
  -Country "Germany" `
  -State "bavaria" `
  -StartTime "2019-05-25" `
  -EndTime "2019-05-30"
```

10. The output of the Reachability Report between Central US and Germany, as expected, shows scores between 93 and 94, which is still acceptable considering the distances between the location and country. Try the following Reachability Report from within the country itself, and the resulting score will be much better, 98 and 99 when I performed them:

```
Get-AzNetworkWatcherReachabilityReport `
  -NetworkWatcherName NetworkWatcherCentralUS `
  -ResourceGroupName CSHARPGUITAR-DM1-RG `
  -Location "Germany Central" `
  -Country "Germany" `
  -State "bavaria" `
  -StartTime "2019-05-25" `
  -EndTime "2019-05-30"
```

11. The test is happening between the Germany Central region and country itself. If a company started getting large consumption from their customers or employees from Germany, then it might make sense to put that workload closer to them.

12. To generate a list of supported locations, countries, states, and cities, execute this cmdlet:

```
Get-AzNetworkWatcherReachabilityProvidersList `
  -NetworkWatcherName NetworkWatcherCentralUS `
  -ResourceGroupName CSHARPGUITAR-DM1-RG
```

You can find the PowerShell script named NetworkWatcher.ps1 used for this exercise on GitHub.

github.com/benperk/ASA/tree/master/Chapter03/Ch03Ex01

There are some techniques one can implement to improve latency, like a *content delivery network (CDN)* or a *traffic manager*, discussed later. Both of them are potential alternatives to making the investment required to deploy an application into another region and configure any required replication that goes along with that. But for now, we will leave it here knowing that choosing the region for your initial Azure workload pertains to the location from which your customers, employees, or consumers utilize the capabilities within it.

The last most common decision point when deploying your first or next resource to Azure is to determine whether the application must comply to any legal regulation and data residency. Some configurations could trigger some copying of data between regions, and some regions allow only governments or companies doing business in that region to store data there. Also, there are three regions that are completely isolated from the other Azure regions.

If globally redundant storage (GRS) is configured for blob or table storage, then that data will be replicated to another region. Does the data your application stores or captures have any privacy restrictions or legal issues that come with it? If you do not know, then you should figure that out before configuring GRS. You should also learn all the Azure products that, when configured, perform this kind of replication for redundancy reasons. There is one point to make here, however, that makes the replication a little more tolerable. Remember that I likened regions to data centers and that a region can have multiple data centers to support Availability Zones. Those data centers are in the same vicinity as each other. A *geography* is another concept that applies here, as shown in Figure 3.6.

FIGURE 3.6 An Azure geography for a given region and Availability Zone

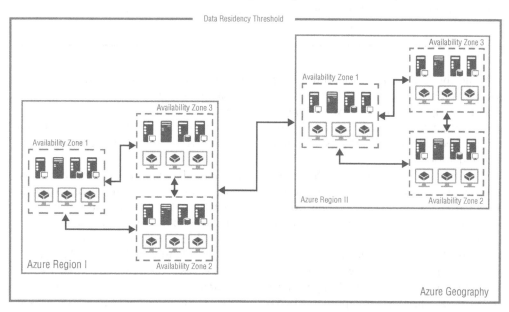

You can see that multiple regions are contained within a geography and that each region contains two or more Availability Zones. Any data that replicates to another region so that any region-wide catastrophic incident can be avoided remains within the data residency threshold and will not leave the geography unless configured to do so.

If you take a closer look at the regions in a given country, you will see that there is rarely only one. Table 3.3 shows that four identified geographies have at least two regions within them. This is not the complete list; there are many more regions per geography. The fundamental point here is that when the data is replicated for redundancy for a specific region, the data remains in the geography, which in most cases resolves any residency and redundancy concerns.

TABLE 3.3   Azure Geographies and Compliance

Geography	Region	Sovereign	Available To
Americas	North Central US South Central US	No	All
Europe	Germany Central Germany Northeast	Yes	Germany only
Asia Pacific	Australia Central Australia East	No	Australia only
Middle East/Africa	UAE Central UAE East	No	All

Remember that some Azure products replicate data from a region to another outside the geography. For example, LUIS, Azure Machine Learning, or quite often products and features running in beta or preview are handled this way. Each of these products makes some sense as the data generated is used to improve the product itself. You, as the Azure solution expert, need to know these things, engage your legal department, and ask the privacy-related questions.

Finally, in Table 3.3, notice the Sovereign and Available To columns. A *sovereign region* means that it is not connected to the global Microsoft Azure network, and there is no data being moved out of the region to any other. This benefit is mostly for government organizations that want to place higher restrictions and control on the data and how they are supported. Currently, the United States, Germany, and China are the only countries with a sovereign cloud Azure implementation. The Available To column simply means that when you are in the portal, it knows your business location because you provided it when the Azure subscription was created. If your business location is not, for example, in Germany or Australia, when you attempt to create Azure resources, those regions will not show as a selectable option. An error will be thrown if you attempt to use the regions via PowerShell, a REST API, or any other supported client.

It is possible to configure a subscription-wide Azure Policy instance that restricts where VNets and other resources can be configured. This prevents accidentally placing any resources into a region that doesn't comply with customer, country, or company requirements. Azure Policy is discussed in more detail in Chapter 6. Also, Chapter 6 discusses the Microsoft Trust Center, which provides a lot of information about compliance and policy making. If you are urgently wanting to learn more about those topics, skip forward and take a look. If not, continue reading to learn more about some key Azure virtual networking features and capabilities.

Key Features and Capabilities

In the previous section, we touched briefly on how the location of resources impact or restrict inclusion in a VNet. We also touched a bit on the connectivity between VNets running on Azure and the connections of those VNets with perhaps an on-premise frontend or backend resource. In this section, I discuss this area a bit more, starting with some key VNet benefits and then concluding with some coverage of filtering and routing traffic in the networks.

The following are the areas covered in this section:

- Connecting with other Azure resources
- Connecting with other Azure VNets
- Connecting with the internet
- Connecting with on-premise resources
- Filtering network traffic
- Routing network traffic

The terms Azure *products* and *features* have been the common expressions for defining what Azure entity is specifically in scope at the time. The Azure products SQL Azure, Azure VM, and Azure App Service, for example, come with a calculable price. Features bound to a product generally have no charge. This is the case, for example, for EasyAuth, network security groups (NSGs), and network interfaces. Going forward, using the term Azure *resource* encompasses all Azure products and features. It is likely you are now able to differentiate between calculated price and no charge anyway.

Some Key Azure VNet Features and Capabilities

It should come as no surprise that the primary reason to use a VNet is to isolate a group of Azure resources into a segmented group, where the isolation comes in the form of the VNet and the segmentation as the subnet within it. When a VNet is created, as you will do in Exercise 3.2, it is required to provide an address range for the VNet. A typical starting value for this is 10.0.0.0/16, which provides a range of IP addresses from 10.0.0.0 to

10.0.255.255 and is a total of 65,535 unique addresses. When the subnet is created, you must then also select its address range, which may be something like 10.0.0.0/24. All of this is covered in the "VNets and Subnets" section later in the chapter. The point is that the subnet's IP address range is within the VNet's IP address range. Azure resources are added to the subnet and are the method where their segmentation is achieved. It is possible to have multiple subnets per VNet.

The Azure resources contained within a VNet probably need to communicate with resources outside the subnet. Azure VNets provide many options for securely connecting to resources outside the subnet. Azure resources within a subnet can connect using the following capabilities, all of which are discussed in detail later in this chapter:

- VNet to VNet
- VNet to on-premise
  - Site-to-site (VPN gateway)
  - ExpressRoute
- VNet to Azure resource not in a VNet
  - Directly using the global endpoint
  - Using subnet delegation and service endpoints
- VNet to internet

If the configuration allows access, no mainstream or semi-mainstream scenario prevents resources within an Azure VNet from connecting with other networks accessible over the internet, assuming the configuration to allow the access has been made.

When it is determined that connectivity with a resource in another location is required, you might want to use a host name instead of the IP address. In this case, Azure provides two options. The first is to use the Azure-provided name resolution services. It should be already understood that DNS is the service that provides the translation of a host name to an IP address. Without DNS there would be no domain names, and accessing a website would require the client to know the IP address, which is not so friendly. If, however, how DNS works is not clear, then you can get up to speed in the "Using Azure DNS" section. The Azure platform also provides the capability to create, configure, and manage your own DNS instance on an Azure VM within a VNet.

From a security perspective, which is of upmost importance, *network security groups (NSGs)* control access into (inbound) and out of (outbound) each subnet using NSGs.

Where Are NSGs Bound by Default for Azure VMs?

By default, an NSG is bound to the network interface card of the Azure VM. It is recommended that this default setting is changed and the NSG bound to the subnet instead. You can see how to do this in Exercise 3.9 later in this chapter.

An NSG can restrict traffic based on a protocol, port, and specific IP address. This is a tight and secure way to manage what can access the resources within the subnet. Outbound traffic can be controlled, as well. The outbound request originates from one of the IP addresses in the subnet, and it will pass any restrictions placed elsewhere; therefore, making sure the traffic is flowing over the expected port using the expected protocol could also be warranted. This is covered in greater detail in the "Network Security" section.

Once the VNet is configured, you can sleep well knowing that it is being monitored and supported by Microsoft. To fully understand this complexity, you need to look at this from an Azure (or any other cloud hosting company) perspective. Neither entity can predict when a customer creates a VNet if it is for fun, for testing, or if it will be a full-blown data-intensive bandwidth-hungry monster. From that perspective. Microsoft has you covered from three perspectives. The first is that the network is monitored for bandwidth and will scale as your workload requires it. Second, if your workload is in a section of the data center with other customers and they start consuming massive amounts of network capacity, it gets handled. Finally, the network is constantly monitored from a health and wellness perspective and gets auto-healed when telemetry-based thresholds are breached.

Connecting with Other Azure Resources

Recall from Figure 3.3 that some Azure resources *must* reside within a VNet, some can exist in a VNet, while other Azure resources cannot exist in a VNet or do not by default. Table 3.4 provides a compact view of which Azure resources can/cannot be deployed into an Azure VNet. As this list changes frequently, conduct a search on the internet for the most current information. Table 3.4 contains those items most likely to be covered when taking the Azure Solutions Architect Expert exam.

TABLE 3.4   Azure Resource VNet Support

Type	Azure Resource	VNet Deployable
Web	Azure App Service	✕
Compute	Azure VM	✓
Networking	Azure Application Gateway (web application firewall)	✓
Web	Azure Logic Apps	✓
Security	Azure Key Vault	✕
Data	SQL Azure	✕
Web	API Management	✓
Networking	Azure Firewall	✓

TABLE 3.4   Azure Resource VNet Support *(continued)*

Type	Azure Resource	VNet Deployable
Containers	Azure Kubernetes Services (AKS)	✓
Data	Azure Cosmos DB	✗
Web	App Service Environment	✓
Storage	Azure Storage	✗
Data	Managed Azure SQL	✓
Messaging	Azure Event Hubs	✗

This doesn't mean these Azure resources cannot connect with each other simply because one exists within a VNet while the other doesn't. It means that if there is a need for it, additional actions are required to make it happen. Take, for example, a common scenario where there is a web application with a SQL server database backend. There are numerous scenarios that one can design to deploy this, as depicted in Figure 3.7.

- App Service web app and managed SQL Azure instance
- Azure VM and managed SQL Azure instance
- Azure VM and an on-premise backend data source
- App Service web app and an on-premise backend data source
- App Service web app and SQL Azure

As listed in Table 3.4, an App Service instance does not exist within a VNet, while a managed SQL Azure instance does. Remember from Chapter 1 that a managed SQL Azure instance is the full version of the SQL Server DBMS running on an Azure VM. Since Azure VMs must run within a VNet, so must a managed SQL Azure instance. Also mentioned in Chapter 1, an Azure App Service instance runs within a sandbox. This means things like spawning child processes or writing to the Windows Registry are not supported. If your web application requires unsupported capabilities on an App Service instance, then an option could be to run it on an Azure VM. An Azure VM can connect to a managed SQL Azure instance or an on-premise backend data source. It is also possible to connect an Azure App Service instance to an on-premise data source and an Azure SQL database that is not in a VNet.

FIGURE 3.7   Different web application/database solutions

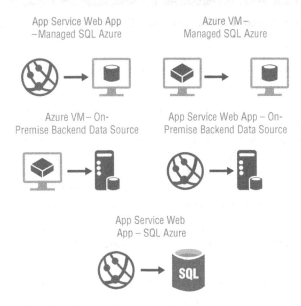

Each of those solutions must be deliberated and a decision made based on which solution bests meets the requirements of the application. An important point about running an Azure resource that is not in a VNet is that the resource exposes a global endpoint, which means it is accessible to the internet and suggests that routing is likely different. In addition, some additional security questions arise. Indeed, routing is different; however, the Microsoft networking infrastructure is intelligent enough to determine whether the resource being requested is an Azure one. If it is, the traffic takes more hops, but it remains on the Microsoft backbone. Additionally, having the endpoint of an internal or highly sensitive website globally identifiable is not something every customer would want. Although there are steps that can be taken to secure the endpoint, like a WAF or IP restrictions, why expose that attack vector for no reason? There have been many cases where that is a red flag, which is an immediate showstopper for many customers.

A solution could be an internal load balancer App Service Environment (ILB ASE) or an Azure VM to run the web application and restrict the access using an NSG. But that is not all; there is another, more recent feature called *virtual network service endpoints*. Before we discuss service endpoints in detail, let's do an exercise. In Exercise 3.2 you will create an empty Azure VNet and enable service endpoints.

EXERCISE 3.2

Creating an Azure Virtual Network and Enabling Service Endpoints

1. Log in to the Azure Portal at portal.azure.com.

2. Click + Create Resource at the top left of your screen, search for *Virtual Network*, and click the Create button.

3. Give the VNet a name (for example, CSHARPGUITAR-VNET-A), select the subscription, and select the resource group. I plan on placing these resources into North Europe (code DB3); therefore, the resource group name will be CSHARPGUITAR-DB3-RG. Remember the restrictions when it comes to what resources can be added to a VNet? Only resources in the same resource group can be added to a VNet. Therefore, if at some point in the future you would like to add an Azure VM to this VNet, it must be created in the same resource group.

4. Select the location, select the region where the VNet will reside, consider placing it into the location where the resource group is based, leave the remaining option at the defaults, and then click the Create button.

5. Navigate to the Virtual Networks blade and select the VNet you just created.

6. Click the Service Endpoints link, click + Add, expand the Service drop-down list, select Microsoft.Web, expand the Subnets drop-down, check Select All, and finally click Add.

7. When saved successfully, something like that shown in Figure 3.8 is rendered. I did provide my subnet with a specific name (csharp) instead of accepting the default.

In Chapter 2 we introduced resource providers; notice how the options in the Service drop-down are resource providers (for example, Microsoft.Web). In Chapter 8 we cover resource providers extensively within the context of ARM.

FIGURE 3.8   A service endpoint configured for an Azure VNet

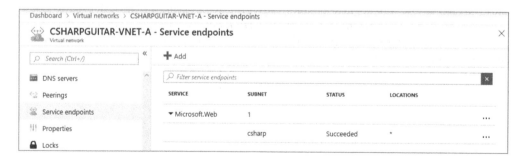

In the next section we discuss subnets, but you couldn't have missed that one of the required fields for the VNet was the CIDR subnet address range. Generally, the default address range for a subnet in Azure is 10.0.0.0/24, which means the available IP address range is from 10.0.0.0 to 10.0.0.255. That range of IP addresses is commonly referred to as a *virtual network private address space*. These IP addresses provide an additional means to identify the resources within a VNet. As an administrator, you know which Azure resources exist in which VNet and what range of IP addresses they have and can therefore create restrictions based on the resources within that range of IP addresses.

In Exercise 3.2, you selected Microsoft.Web, which means the VNet will delegate support to Azure App Service because that is the resource provider to which Azure App Service instances are bound. There were numerous others like Microsoft.EventHub, Microsoft.KeyVault, Microsoft.AzureCosmosDB, and Microsoft.Sql. Why service endpoints are so powerful is that once you configure one on an Azure resource that is not deployed to an Azure VNet, then only IP addresses from the subnet (which are private IP addresses) will be allowed to connect to that resource. This is shown in Figure 3.9.

FIGURE 3.9   Connectivity between a VNet and Azure resources using a service endpoint

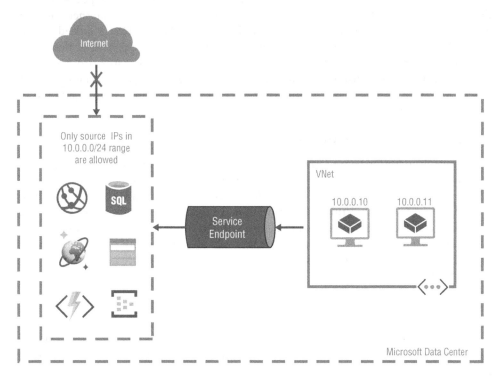

Also, no access from the internet is permitted because the IP addresses won't be in that range either. I want to call out the statement "from the configured VNet." The question is,

"Isn't it possible that more than one VNet on Azure can have the same private IP address range of 10.0.0.0/24?" The answer is yes. However, up to now you have only enabled service endpoints for the default subnet; you haven't yet configured the Azure resource. A step in that configuration requires the selection of the subscription, virtual network, and subnet that exist in that subscription. That is a tight and secure configuration.

Connecting with Other Azure VNets

Making a connection between two VNets in the same region is referred to as *VNet peering*. Even without VNet peering, it would be possible to connect to resources by providing a public IP address to the Azure resources existing within it. This has a downside because the connectivity would then happen over the internet, or at minimum the number of hops between the two resources would be more than if the VNets were peered. Specifically, that means that when two or more VNets are peered, the traffic between them remains inside the Microsoft network and can utilize private IP addresses. The same goes for Azure VNets hosted in different Azure regions.

Connecting Azure VNets that exist in different Azure regions is called *global VNet peering*. The benefit is again that the traffic between the VNets remains on the Microsoft backbone, and private IP addresses are utilized. In addition, you would expect that because the traffic remains on the Microsoft backbone and doesn't traverse the internet, the latency would be low and the amount of required bandwidth would exist. That is indeed the case.

Bandwidth and latency are crucial factors when running large applications that are in multiple regions. Many of these applications require data synchronization from a global source to more regional instances nearer to the customer or employee. The movement of this data is much faster and much more fault-tolerant when performed through the Microsoft backbone versus the internet.

Connecting with the Internet

By default, the outbound connectivity of Azure resources contained within a VNet can connect to any other resource on the internet. If, for example, a company exposes a REST API that an application within a VNet needs to access, then there are no configurations required from an infrastructure perspective to make that happen. This can be visualized by viewing a default NSG, as shown in Figure 3.10. Notice that the outbound security rule named AllowInternetOutBound allows traffic across all ports and all protocols from all sources to access the internet. This is the default and would therefore not restrict any outbound traffic for any reason.

The opposite is the case for inbound. Notice also in Figure 3.10 that there is no AllowInternetInbound rule or anything at all similar to that. This means that by default inbound connectivity to resources within the VNet is not possible. It is also not possible to simply create an inbound rule to allow internet traffic because by default there is no public endpoint for an Azure VNet. There are two Azure products that come into play in this context.

- Public IP addresses
- Azure Load Balancer

FIGURE 3.10   Default inbound and outbound security rules

A public IP address is just that; it's a way to make the resource within a VNet accessible to other resources running on the internet that are connected by any other means. The public IP address, which can be created to make a VNet-hosted resource public, has its own configurable settings. For example, should the IP address be IPv4 or IPv6, should the address be dynamic or static, or should it run across Availability Zones? As well, what kind of resource will the public resource route to—a virtual machine, an application gateway, or load balancer?

Although it is possible to route a public IP address directly to an Azure NIC, you might consider linking it to Azure Load Balancer. There are two primary reasons for using Azure Load Balancer, which are the better management of inbound and outbound internet connectivity. From an inbound perspective, having the public IP address map to a specific resource is risky because it would be a single point of failure. Additionally, if there were any direct links to the IP address from any client and the IP address changes, then those clients would stop functioning. Azure Load Balancer can act like a proxy and can be configured to route requests to a specific IP address to one or more other resources in the VNet.

The outbound scenario is a much more complicated one and is covered in more detail later in the "Connecting with the Internet" section. It boils down to what you want the outbound IP address to be. In the scenario where the IP address is bound directly to the resource, when there is no difference between the inbound and outbound IP addresses, this is called an *instance-level public IP (ILPIP)* address. However, this is not the most efficient configuration because there are costs and limits on the number of IP addresses that one can consume per subscription. Beyond that, the workloads could experience *source network address translation (SNAT)* exhaustion, which means there are no more ephemeral ports available to PAT. When you alternatively use Azure Load Balancer, it employs *port address translation (PAT)*, which conceals the private IP addresses behind a single public one. There is some reuse of outbound IP addresses happening; it's not a one-to-one mapping.

The final scenario is that the outbound IP address has no significance. In this scenario the outbound IP address is not configurable and doesn't count against any subscription limits, but it can change many times for many reasons. A word of caution: if this last scenario is selected, although most cost efficient, there is no means to whitelist or perform any kind of dependable restricting of access by those resources.

Connecting with On-Premise Resources

Figure 3.2 shown previously illustrates connectivity from Azure and on-premise resources completely. An Azure VNet can be configured to connect with an on-premise data center using one of the following:

ExpressRoute   An *ExpressRoute* instance is the only connection between an Azure VNet and an on-premise network that does not cross into the internet. The connection is private and managed directly by an ExpressRoute partner. This connectivity scenario is mostly reserved for large enterprises with large workloads. The solution is relatively expensive when compared to the others, so checking out the price in advance using the Azure calculator would be advised. See `azure.microsoft.com/en-us/pricing/calculator`.

Point-to-Site Connection (VPN)   A *point-to-site (P2S)* connection, on the other hand, is an inexpensive solution for connecting any supported Azure resource to one existing in another network. If you are just getting started or are a developer wanting to give it a test run, start here. P2S is typically implemented using the *Hybrid Connection Manager (HCM)*, which is based on Azure Relay, or you can just simply use Azure Relay itself. P2S sends traffic through an encrypted tunnel between a computer and a virtual or on-premise network. Figure 3.11 illustrates that P2S connections can be made from within a VNet to an on-premise server, from an Azure App service/Azure Function to an on-premise server, and from an Azure App service/Azure Function to a server within a VNet.

Site-to-Site Connection (VPN)   Like P2S, traffic passing through a *site-to-site (S2S)* connection is sent within an encrypted tunnel across the internet. The primary difference is that the connectivity happens between Azure VPN Gateway and an on-premise VPN device.

Which Azure to on-premise connection would you recommend for a company just getting started with Azure but doesn't want their traffic to go across the internet?

A.   Site-to-site

B.   ExpressRoute

C.   Point-to-point

D.   Point-to-site

E.   Both B and C

The answer is site-to-site. When the traffic cannot traverse the internet, ExpressRoute is the only solution that provides that capability.

FIGURE 3.11   The network flow of a point-to-site connection

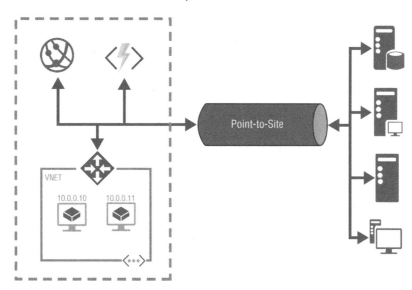

Network Traffic Filtering

The most common or popular means for filtering traffic on Azure, and likely on-premise, uses NSGs (aka *security rules*). As shown in Figure 3.10, an NSG restricts (filters) inbound and outbound traffic based on a set of security rules. Another Azure feature that is helpful for filtering network traffic is an *application security group (ASG)*. An ASG provides the ability to group a set of Azure VMs and define NSGs specifically for that group. Take Figure 3.12, for example. Notice that all three Azure VMs exist in the same subnet; two of them are associated with an ASG named CSHARP-ASG, and one is associated with an ASG named GUITAR-ASG.

Look again at Figure 3.10 and notice the Destination column. Later when you create an NSG and an ASG, you will find that the supported values for Destination are Any, IP Addresses, VirtualNetwork, and of course Application Security Group. And just like any NSG, the rule will be applied when a request to that destination is sent. For example, you want to allow inbound internet traffic on both the ASGs, but for Azure VMs in the CSHARP-ASG, only HTTPS (port 443) is supported. In that case, the NSG would deny HTTP (port 80) when the destination is CSHARP-ASG. That security rule would not apply to the Azure VM in the GUITAR-ASG.

NSGs and ASGs for App Services, Azure Storage, and More

Many Azure resources that are not deployed into an Azure VNet do have some capability for restricting access based on IP address ranges or configured service endpoints. Those capabilities can be found as a feature for a resource in the Azure Portal.

FIGURE 3.12   How application security groups filter network traffic

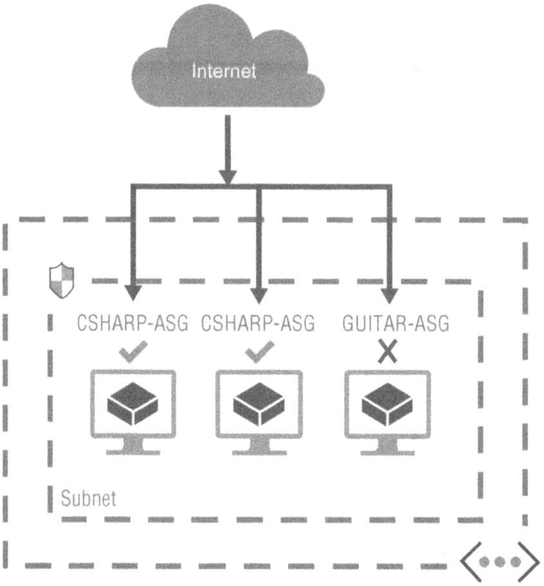

When NSGs and ASGs are discussed by IT professionals working with Azure, those conversations generally occur within the context of Azure resources such as Azure VNets and Azure VMs. This is because you cannot currently configure NSGs or ASGs for Azure resources that exist outside of a VNet. There are no Azure-wide capabilities to configure NSGs or ASGs for Azure App Service, Azure Storage, or Azure Event Hub. For example, there is no interface nor is there an implementation to apply and enforce NSG or ASG configurations for those Azure products. Instead, a customer could implement a network appliance like an Azure Application Gateway web application firewall or a third-party solution found on the Azure Marketplace. For example, Barracuda, FortiGate, Cisco ASA, or Kemp, to name a few, might be useful.

Network Traffic Routing

The key term *hop* has been mentioned a few times already in this chapter. In simplest terms, a hop occurs each time a packet of data being transferred between two network-connected machines touches a node. A *node* is considered a server, which is also connected to the network and helps get the packet of data to its desired location. Based on that definition, it is easy to imagine that the fewer the hops, the faster the packet is delivered.

Consider sending an invitation to your next-door neighbor. Because you know how to get there, you simply walk out the door and place the letter into their mailbox. Imagine that you would also like to send an invitation to a few friends who live at different locations around town. You know where they all live, but the most optimal route to each location is something you do not know, but you do know where the nearest mailbox is. Finally, consider that an invitation needs to be sent to a family member who you haven't seen for a long time and who lives in another state. You have an address but don't really know where they live. In each of these scenarios, the concept of a routing table is applicable. A *routing table* is where the next hop on route to the final destination is stored. See Figure 3.13 for an example of the default Azure system route table.

In the first scenario, it is true that the invitation could have been sent through the post office, but that would not be the most optimal route. The routing table was in your head, and you chose to get the invitation to the neighbor using a route with the fewest hops, which is none in this scenario. In the second scenario, it would make sense to send the invitations via mail. The routing table stored in your head knows where to place the invitations (into the mailbox), but after that, you have no information about the route taken to deliver the invitations. The invitations would then proceed to a node where the post is sorted. Each node would know the next hop to pass the invitation based on the content stored in the routing table on that node.

A similar scenario exists for the third example. You would expect more hops and more nodes to be involved in the invitation's delivery because the final destination is farther away. Take note that a node only knows where to send the data packet next; this keeps the routing tables small. A node does not know the data packet route from end to end. The routing of data inside the Azure network functions along similar lines. When the outbound request remains within the Azure platform, then, as you know, the routing remains on the Microsoft backbone and does not enter the internet. Outbound traffic from an Azure resource that does traverse the internet uses the nodes and routes managed by multiple internet service providers. In summary, the routing of data between source and destination is not unique to Azure. Networking is typically considered a low-level TCP/IP-based process used everywhere to support the connectivity of nodes and the transmission of data. Azure provides many products on top of this, but you will find that the same networking concepts that apply to Azure also apply to all networks in general.

The remainder of this section will cover in a little more detail how Azure routes outbound network traffic originating from an Azure VNet. The routing decision is based on a combination of the destination IP address and an algorithmic match to a route in the route table based on the longest address prefix. To explain that more, assume in the route table that there are two routes: one is 10.0.0.0/16, and the other is 10.0.0.0/8. If the outbound IP address is 10.0.0.4, then the chosen route would be 10.0.0.0/16. Looking at Table 3.5, it is obvious that 10.0.0.4 is in both routes, but 10.0.0.0/16 has a longer prefix and is therefore chosen. It would be most prudent to add a route for 10.0.0.0/24, which would likely reduce the number of hops; however, currently, it is not present. Again, see Figure 3.13.

TABLE 3.5 CIDR to IPv4 Conversion

CIDR Range	Start IP	End IP	Total Host
10.0.0.0/24	10.0.0.0	10.0.0.255	256
10.0.0.0/16	10.0.0.0	10.0.255.255	65536
10.0.0.0/8	10.0.0.0	10.255.255.255	16777216

The prefix is based on a bit mask where each of the four octets in the IP address is converted to bits, and the chosen route map entry is the one that has the most overlap of the CIDR range. /8 means that the first eight bits of the octet are the same, whereas /16 means the first 16 are equal. To get much further into this complex area, it is time to create an Azure VM. Although we get into the details of computing in the next chapter, it will be hard to provide good examples without a VM. In Exercise 3.3, you will create an Azure VM to use for the analysis of the networking infrastructure created around it.

Azure Resources Have an Associated Cost

This is the first time so far that you will create an Azure resource that will have a direct cost. Even if you never use it, when you complete step 12, there will be a charge. Take note of this because as we progress, we will create resources that have a cost. I will not notify you each time. At the end of each exercise, you may consider deleting the resource group; however, examples from this point will likely build upon each other and call upon resources created in previous exercises.

EXERCISE 3.3

Creating an Azure Virtual Machine

1. Log in to the Azure Portal at portal.azure.com.

2. Enter **Virtual Machine** into the Search Resources, Services, And Docs box at the top of the portal. Select Virtual Machines + Add.

3. On the Basics tab, select the subscription and resource group into which you want the Azure VM to be placed (for example, CSHARPGUITAR-DB3-RG).

4. Provide a name for the Azure virtual machine (for example, CSHARPGUITAR-VM). Remember that VM names are limited to 15 characters.

5. Select the region; it can be the same as the one for the resource group, but it doesn't have to be.

6. Leave the availability options at the defaults and choose Windows Server 2019 Datacenter as the image. Leave Size at the default.

7. Enter a username and password and confirm the password.

8. Select the Allow Selected Ports radio button and enable all ports: HTTP, HTTPS, SSH, and RDP.

9. Specify that you do not already have a license; if you do, then select Yes. Click the Next: Disks button.

10. Leave the defaults and click the Next: Networking button.

11. Select the VNet that you created in Exercise 3.2 and the corresponding subnet (for example, CSHARPGUITAR-VNET-A and csharp).

12. Leave everything else at the defaults and click the Review + Create button. Feel free to navigate through the other tabs; however, no other configuration is required at this time. When you have finished exploring, click the Create button.

13. After the deployment has completed successfully, you can view the default system route table by executing the following PowerShell cmdlet. The output will be something similar to that shown in Figure 3.13, but the value for `-NetworkInterfaceName` will be different in every case.

```
Get-AzEffectiveRouteTable -NetworkInterfaceName csharpguitar-vm810 `
 -ResourceGroupName CSHARPGUITAR-DB3-RG | Format-Table
```

FIGURE 3.13   PowerShell cmdlet output of the System route table

Name	DisableBgpRoutePropagation	State	Source	AddressPrefix	NextHopType	NextHopIpAddress
	False	Active	Default	{10.0.0.0/16}	VnetLocal	{}
	False	Active	Default	{0.0.0.0/0}	Internet	{}
	False	Active	Default	{10.0.0.0/8}	None	{}
	False	Active	Default	{100.64.0.0/10}	None	{}
	False	Active	Default	{192.168.0.0/16}	None	{}
	False	Active	Default	{13.64.73.110/32...}	VirtualNetworkServiceEndpoint	{}

Notice in Figure 3.13 that there are columns named NextHopType and NextHopIpAddress. Once the destination IP address finds the best match for the route, NextHopIpAddress defines where to send the data packet next. It is possible to update the routing so that it is optimized for the specific application. How to do that would best fit into a book that covers networking specifically. However, there is one point that needs to be made concerning what happens when there are additions made to the route table that could then match an outbound request equally. For example, what happens if there is an additional route added with the address prefix of 10.0.0.0/8 with NextHopType set to VirtualAppliance? In Figure 3.13, you can see that a route of 10.0.0.0/8 already exists. The answer is that Azure will recognize *user-defined routes (UDRs)* with higher relevance than those in the default system route table. UDRs are touched on numerous more times, so if this term is not yet clear, it will be soon.

The 0.0.0.0/0 Address Prefix

This routing prefix is added to the routing table by default in Azure. It routes all traffic with a destination IP address that does not exist within the 10.0.0.0/16 range to the internet. This can be confirmed by checking NextHopType on the routing table for that address prefix.

Table 3.6 describes each of NextHopType values shown in Figure 3.13 in more detail. The address prefix associated to the VnetLocal NextHopType is 10.0.0.0/16, which is the address range of a default VNet. Any request with a destination IP address within that range remains within the VNet.

TABLE 3.6   NextHopType Details

Next Hop Type	Description
VnetLocal	Routes traffic within the VNet
Internet	Routes traffic to the internet
None	Traffic is dropped
VirtualNetworkServiceEndpoint	Routes to public IP addresses of service endpoint

Any request with a destination IP address outside of the 10.0.0.0/8, 100.64.0.0/16, and 192.168.0.0/18 address ranges will be dropped and respond with an error like "connection dropped." Any request with a destination IP address outside of all four of those address prefixes (10.0.0.0/16, 10.0.0.0/8, 100.64.0.0/16, or 192.168.0.0/18) will be routed to the internet. Finally, VirtualNetworkServiceEndpoint is not created by default; it was added to the route table during the completion of Exercise 3.2 where a service endpoint was partially configured. Once the configuration is completed later, a request with the destination IP address within the associated address prefix will route to that service endpoint.

The routing of data in the Azure network isn't exceedingly unique when compared to network routing in general, excluding the fact that there is a giant backbone at the customers' service. There is a lot more to do and learn about VNets and subnets, so keep on reading.

VNets and Subnets

Albert Einstein once said, "Organized people are just too lazy to go looking for what they want." Like the relational hierarchal structure of a management group, subscription, and resource group, a VNet and subnet provide similar capabilities for the organization of Azure resources, keeping things structured and maintainable. VNets and the subnets within them offer many more benefits and complex technical concepts than simple organization. That notion and thoughtful deployment of a resource shouldn't be overlooked. As with a resource group, and even a subscription, it is prudent to keep its contents limited to the resources making up an IT solution. The same goes for VNets and subnets where you would want to keep the contents within them constrained by a designed context so that their contents are intuitive.

I can assure you that you need to know about VNets in some depth if you want to pass the Azure Solutions Architect Expert exam. The best way to do that is by creating, configuring, and using the product and its features. Now that all the preliminary networking subjects are complete, it's time to really take a deeper look at VNets. The following will be covered in this section:

- Additional networking concepts and tools
- Azure networking patterns
- Azure networking limits
- VNet to VNet
- Site-to-site (S2S) overview
- VNet-to-Azure resources
- VNet to internet

Once you read, understand, and then complete the exercises in this section, your grasp of Azure virtual networking will be in good shape.

Additional Networking Concepts and Tools

Four topics are covered here. At first read they may seem a bit disconnected, but I can assure you they are all related and are networking subjects that must be understood. If the networking area is one that is of specific interest and you have a burning desire to take it to the limit, master the topics IPv6, SNAT and port exhaustion, 65535, and network routing.

Up to now all the IP addresses discussed have been in the IPv4 structure, which is the most common format. An IPv4 address is 32 bits long, broken into four 8-bit octets. Take, for example, the loopback network interface IPv4 address of 127.0.0.1, which is, at initial glance, four integers separated by periods, referred to as *dot-decimal notation*. Convert that into bits and you get the binary result shown in Figure 3.14.

FIGURE 3.14   Dot decimal IPv4 address in binary

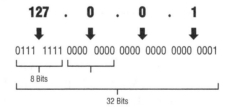

The range of IPv4 addresses is between 0.0.0.0 and 255.255.255.255. Why? When you convert the integers into binary, it becomes clear. The binary values of 0.0.0.0 and 255.255.255.255, respectively, as shown in Figure 3.15, recognize that the range contains all possible 32-bit values. The maximum range of IPv4 addresses is therefore 4,294,967,296, which is 2^{32}.

FIGURE 3.15   IPv4 address in binary from 0 to 255

The initial design of IPv4 had the address divided into two parts. The first three digits of the address make up the *network identifier*, while the remaining digits are called the *host identifier*. The host identifier is used to uniquely distinguish a device within a given network, which is identified by the network identifier. The first digits (i.e., the network identifier) originally had a total of 256 possible unique networks (0000 0000 to 1111 1111, or 2^8), which was promptly found to be insufficient. In hindsight, presuming there would only be a need for 256 global networks is now inconceivable. The solution was to create five IP address classes (Class A to Class E); three are described in Table 3.7.

TABLE 3.7   IPv4 Classful Definitions

Class	Total Networks	Network Addresses	Start	End	CIDR
Class A	128 (2^7)	16,777,261 (2^{24})	0.0.0.0	127.0.0.0	/8
Class B	16,384 (2^{14})	65,536 (2^{16})	128.0.0.0	191.255.0.0	/16
Class C	2,097,152 (2^{21})	256 (2^8)	192.0.0.0	223.255.255.0	/24

The three IPv4 address classes (A, B, and C) are classified as unicast addresses or one-to-one connectivity between a sender and a receiver. This is the most common scenario and most relevant to the Azure Solutions Architect Expert exam. The other classifications are broadcast (one to many) and multicast (many to many). These classful definitions effectively increased the number of total global networks and increased the number of possible internet IP addresses. Note that we are discussing public IP addresses here, and that below them subnets can exist and can't contain private IP addresses. These subnets, since they are not exposed globally, can implement any desired IP value or range.

What's So Special About 127.0.0.1?

The 127.0.0.1 IPv4 address is commonly referred to as a *loopback address*. The IP address is typically mapped to the host name *localhost* and can be referred to as *home*. This is useful when accessing a website hosted on the machine that you are currently logged into. For example, `http://localhost` accesses a website hosted on the currently logged into machine. The IPv6 address for localhost is ::1. As they say, "There's no place like 127.0.0.1."

Even after this improvement, there was still an issue with public IP address exhaustion. Many companies that received a Class C IP address from the *Internet Assigned Number Authority (IANA)* ran out of network addresses. The Class C IP address range is limited to 256. Companies that requested a Class B address, which was exponentially larger, and many of the 65,536 addresses were not utilized. This change increased the possible number of global networks from 256 to just under 16,500, which is still a restrictive number. The newest version (1998) of the Internet Protocol (IP), which hopes to be the solution to avoid IP address exhaustion, is IPv6.

IPv6 is supported on numerous Azure products such as Azure Load Balancer, NSGs, within a VNet (Preview), and for routing to Azure VMs. Supporting IPv6 doesn't happen with some configuration; however, the ability to support IPv6 addresses is there. Azure App Service web apps, Azure Functions, and instance-level public IPs (ILIPs), for example, do not support IPv6.

As already stated, the IPv4 address range is bound to 32 bits, which is 2^{32} of addresses space. IPv6, on the other hand, is bound to 128 bits, which provides an address range of 2^{128}. That's a lot of numbers and looks like this, which is 340 undecillions:

$$340,282,366,920,938,463,463,374,607,431,768,211,456$$

An IPv6 address is structured into eight groups, separated by colons, in hexadecimal format. It looks something like Figure 3.16.

FIGURE 3.16   An example of an IPv6 address and its hexadecimal conversion

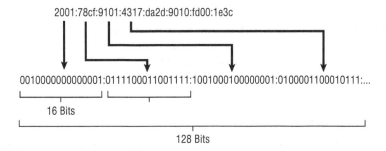

IPv6 addresses are most commonly implemented when creating infrastructure for the internet of things (IoT) and mobility-based solutions. Those kinds of solutions are best designed for handling viral events or the exponential growth of concurrently connected IoT devices. In those scenarios, the number of IP addresses could easily exceed the range of a Class B IPv4 range (65,535). Keep in mind that the number of IP addresses in version 6 is much greater than version 4 and that version 6 is the most reliable solution for the two scenarios stated earlier. Finally, when the original creators of IPv4 designed it on a 32-bit range base, that number was probably mind-boggling, and no one ever thought there would be a need for so many devices that depend on an IP address. I wonder if the same will be true for IPv6. No one knows the future, but a solution with a 2^{128} range of IP addresses seems like the logical next step. I won't begin to find out what that number is!

The next concepts to be discussed are *source network address translation (SNAT)*, *network address translation (NAT)*, *port address translation (PAT)*, and *ephemeral ports* as they are all relevant when discussing Azure networking topologies. Remember when you created a VNet in Exercise 3.2? The address ranges used for the VNet and the subnet were 10.0.0.*, which are not addresses that are accessible on the internet (they are private). A NAT, as illustrated in Figure 3.17, translates the private IP address into a public one. The router/NAT device has both a private IP address as well as a public one; the public one is provided by an internet service provider. The NAT technique is good at concealing the private IP addresses of your internal networks or VNets from the internet. However, NATs are typically a one-to-one mapping between private and public IP addresses.

FIGURE 3.17   An example of NAT IP address translation

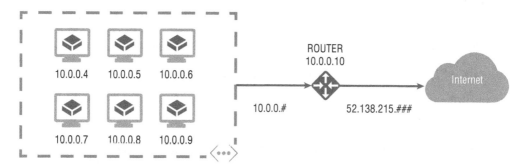

As the number of IPv4 addresses began to reach an exhausted state, the concept of PAT was introduced. PAT implements a one-to-many mapping of private and public IP addresses and is often referred to as *IP masquerading*. Consider that each IP packet sent between a client and a server has both a source address and destination IP address.

What Is a Router?

Most people who have an internet connection in their house also have a router. The router is what is connected to the internet. A common IP address for your router is 192.168.1.1; just open your browser and enter it. That router has the internal IP address as just mentioned, and there is likely software for managing all the devices that can connect to your router. These days, a router is also the device that exposes your WiFi signal. Your router also has a public IP address; without that, the server responding to your request wouldn't be able to get the requested information back to you.

The private IP address (source) would have the source address of, for example, 10.0.0.4 and would route to some public IP address like 51.140.49.239 (the Azure Portal), which is the destination address. The source IP address gets translated into the public IP address of the router, 52.138.215.### , and then forwards the request to the destination. That seems easy when sending packets outbound, but what about getting the answer back to the private 10.0.0.4 address? There must be more to it than that. How does the router know the response from 51.140.49.236 that has the destination address that is now 52.138.215.### needs to be directed to 10.0.0.4? The answer is found by digging into a *socket*.

A socket is the combination of an IP address and a port number. More specifically, it has a source IP address, source port, destination IP address, and destination port, and each side (source and destination) has 65,535 available ports, which is $2^{16} - 1$. These ports are what we refer to as *ephemeral ports*. For each TPC/IP session there will be an ephemeral port allocated and sent with each packet for the duration of the communication. The router, using the details of the socket, can determine where to send the response. A tool called netstat is useful for monitoring the connections on a specific machine. Execute netstat from a CMD console and you will see something like Figure 3.18. That netstat command was performed on the Azure VM created in Exercise 3.3.

FIGURE 3.18 netstat connection output from an Azure VM

Finally, SNAT is the term used for translating an IP address as it traverses the router. You have read that this is done when converting the private IP address to the public IP address and back again. You can consider this as the counterpart of *destination network address translation (DNAT)*, which manages the destination IP address translation. You may be wondering whether this is important from an Azure perspective. The answer is, yes, it is. You might think that when you create an Azure VM that you would get all 65,535 ports, but this is not the case. You might encounter port exhaustion without proper planning and understanding.

The most common scenario to deploy an Azure VM is the one used in Exercise 3.3. In that scenario, the VM, by default, was allocated an instance level IP. In this case, you are provided with all the expected ephemeral ports within the default range (see Figure 3.19).

FIGURE 3.19   netsh default dynamic port range output from an Azure VM

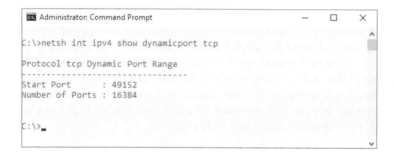

Execute the following command on an Azure VM to get the output shown in Figure 3.19:

```
netsh int ipv4 show dynamicport tcp
```

It is possible to create an Azure VM that does not have an ILIP and instead have the public IP address mapped to the availability set. (I will discuss these in the next chapter.) This approach is often used to secure the VMs from being individually accessible from the internet, instead exposing them via another network device like a load balancer. In that scenario, your SNAT ports are allocated based on the size of the pool of VMs in your availability set. Table 3.8 shows those default SNAT port allocations.

TABLE 3.8   SNAT Allocation per VM Pool Size

SNAT Ports per IP Address	Number of VMs in Pool
1024	1 to 50
512	51 to 100
256	101 to 200
128	201 to 400
64	401 to 800
32	801 to 1000

Table 3.8 is relevant when the Azure VM does not have its own ILIP and instead shares an outbound IP address with the other VMs in the pool. To determine whether your VM has an ILIP, navigate to the Networking blade in the portal for the VM. You will see something like that shown in Figure 3.20. Notice the NIC public IP address.

FIGURE 3.20 Azure portal view of the NIC public IP address

Take note that all Azure features that make outbound connections to the internet will have some dependency on TCP/IP, PAT, SNAT, or ephemeral ports. Make sure you recognize that this is not an Azure restriction; it is TCP/IP and the way networks function. You won't need to know this level of detail for the Azure Solutions Architect Expert exam; however, a quality Azure Solutions Architect Expert would have some knowledge of this. They would know the scenarios where you get all 65,535 addresses or just a subset of them. The Azure Solutions Architect Expert would also need to know how to troubleshoot and provide some optimizations. More about this will be covered in Chapter 7.

If you haven't noticed, $2^{16} - 1$ or 65,535 is mentioned a lot in networking discussions, so I would therefore like to call attention to the areas where that number is relevant for networking. The "minus one" is present because the count begins at zero. 65,535 is as follows:

- The default TCP receive window buffer size
- The upper limit for TCP and UDP ports
- The highest number represented in 16-bit binary
- The maximum number of private IP addresses per VNet
- The maximum number of NICs per subscription
- The number of IP addresses with the /16 CIDR prefix

65,535 is a common number in computer science; just keep in mind that there are some limits around that number. It's also cool to have an answer or comment about that number in case you see it when troubleshooting some issue: "Did you know that 65,535 is 2^{16}?"

TCP and UDP

TCP and UDP are supported on Azure VMs. UDP is a transport protocol that is best suited for media streaming like videos. UDP doesn't mind if there are some missing packets that may cause a slight blip in the video. Using TCP for video streaming wouldn't be prudent because a missing packet would be retransmitted, causing the video to hang while it waits for the packet. For scenarios where more accurate transmission of data is required, TCP is the best choice.

It has been stated that all resources created within the same VNet will automatically have connectivity with each other. This is true so long as the NSGs support the protocol and port over which the request is being received. To prove this, complete Exercise 3.4. Here you will create a subnet within the existing VNet, add an Azure VM to it, and test the connectivity between them.

EXERCISE 3.4

Testing Connectivity Between Subnets

1. Log in to the Azure Portal at portal.azure.com.

2. In the search box at the top of the portal, enter **Virtual Network** and click Virtual Networks.

3. Click the VNet you created in Exercise 3.2 (for example, CSHARPGUITAR-VNET-A) and then choose Subnets + Subnet.

4. Add a subnet (for example, Name = guitar), leave all the defaults, and then click OK. Notice that the CIDR address range is 10.0.1.0/24, and the subnet created in Exercise 3.2 (for example, csharp) is 10.0.0.0/24.

5. Add an Azure VM to this new subnet. Enter Virtual Machines in the search box (located at the top of the portal) and then select Virtual Machines + Add.

6. On the Basics tab, select the subscription and resource group into which you want the Azure VM to be placed (for example, CSHARPGUITAR-DB3-RG). This must be the same resource group as the one that was created in Exercise 3.2.

7. Provide a name for the Azure virtual machine (for example, CSHARPGUITAR-V1; there is a limit of 15 characters, which a VM name can have).

8. Select the region; this should be the same as the one for the resource group, but it doesn't have to be.

9. Leave the availability options at the defaults, choose Windows Server 2019 Datacenter as the image, and leave the size at the default.

10. Enter a username and password and then confirm the password.

11. Select the Allow Selected Ports radio button and enable all ports: HTTP, HTTPS, SSH, and RDP.

12. Indicate whether you have a license and then click the Next: Disks button.

13. Leave the defaults and click the Next: Networking button.

14. Select the virtual network you created in Exercise 3.2 and the subnet created earlier in this exercise (for example, CSHARPGUITAR-VNET-A and guitar).

15. Leave everything else at the defaults and click the Review + Create button. Feel free to navigate through the other tabs; however, no other configuration is required at this time. Click the Create button.

16. Once the VM is created, navigate to it on the Overview blade, select Connect, click Download RDP File, and connect to the VM.

17. Open PowerShell and execute the following command:

```
Install-WindowsFeature -name Web-Server -IncludeManagementTools
remove-item C:\inetpub\wwwroot\iisstart.htm
Add-Content -Path "C:\inetpub\wwwroot\iisstart.htm" `
            -Value $("Hello from " + $env:computername)
```

18. Once the PowerShell cmdlets are complete, on your local workstation (from a computer not in Azure), enter the following command. The result should be similar to that shown in Figure 3.21. The public IP address is provided on the Overview blade of the Azure VM. See where to download `curl` in Table 3.9.

```
curl -G <Public IP address>:80
```

FIGURE 3.21   Azure VM accessible from the internet

19. A successful response means the Azure VM is accessible from the internet using the public IP address, but what about the private IP address, also shown on the Overview tab? Write it down; it will likely be 10.0.1.4.

20. Make a remote desktop connection using RDP to the Azure VM created in Exercise 3.2 (for example, CSHARPGUITAR-VM) and execute the following `curl` commands. You would see something like Figure 3.22.

```
curl -G <Private IP address>:80
curl -G <VM Name>:80
```

FIGURE 3.22   Azure VM accessible an Azure VM in a different subnet

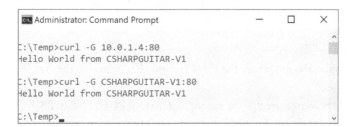

EXERCISE 3.4 *(continued)*

21. There is another tool called `psping` that can quickly check the connectivity between Azure VMs. Try executing these commands to confirm connectivity:

    ```
    psping <Private IP address>:80
    psping <VM Name>:80
    ```

22. Note that `ping` does not work due to the protocol it uses; ICMP is disabled. Now you should feel confident that the Azure VM created here, which is bound to a subnet (for example, guitar), can access VMs in another subnet.

TABLE 3.9   Networking Tools

Tool	Location
curl	curl.haxx.se/download.html
psping	docs.microsoft.com/en-us/sysinternals/downloads/psping
tcpping	github.com/benperk/ASA/tree/master/tools
nameresolver	github.com/benperk/ASA/tree/master/tools

If you run into problems with the connectivity using `curl` or `psping`, try using the Network Watcher instance that you created in Exercise 3.1. Complete Exercise 3.5 to test the IP Flow Verify and the next hop feature available through the Network Watcher.

EXERCISE 3.5

Using Network Watcher to Troubleshoot Connectivity Issues Between Subnets

1. Log in to the Azure Portal at `portal.azure.com`.

2. In the Search box at the top of the portal, enter **Network Watcher** and then click Network Watcher from the drop-down. Now, click IP Flow Verify.

3. Enter the following:

   a. For the subscription, enter the subscription that contains the Azure VM created in Exercise 3.4.

   b. Enter the resource group (for example, CSHARPGUITAR-DB3-RG).

   c. Enter the virtual machine (for example, CSHARPGUITAR-V1).

    d. Enter the network interface. It should default to the one bound to the Azure VM.

    e. For the local IP address, enter the private IP address of CSHARPGUITAR-V1, for example, 10.0.1.4.

    f. For the local port, enter **5555**.

    g. For the remote IP address, enter **10.0.0.4**, which is the private IP address of the address Azure VM created in Exercise 3.3 (for example, CSHARPGUITAR-VM).

    h. The remote port should be a port that is allowed inbound in the NSG; try port 22, which is the SSH port. The packet details section should resemble something similar to Figure 3.23.

FIGURE 3.23   The identified NSG that allows or denies the request between Azure VMs

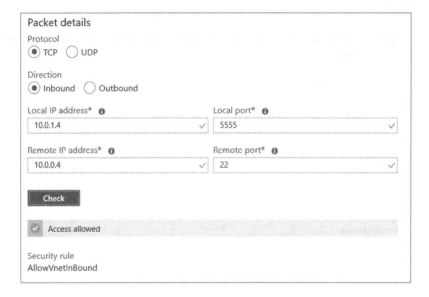

4. The result from the IP Flow Verify will identify the NSG rule that is allowing or blocking the request. You can then take action to add or modify the rule that is causing the failure.

5. Click the Next Hop link and enter the following:

    a. For the subscription, enter the subscription that contains the Azure VM created in Exercise 3.4.

    b. Enter the resource group (for example, CSHARPGUITAR-DB3-RG).

    c. Enter the virtual machine (for example, CSHARPGUITAR-V1).

    d. Enter the network interface. It should default to the one bound to the Azure VM.

    e. For the source IP address, enter the private IP address of CSHARPGUITAR-V1, for example, 10.0.1.4.

    f. For the local port, enter 5555.

    g. For the destination IP address, enter **10.0.0.4,** which is the private IP address of the address Azure VM created in Exercise 3.3 (for example, CSHARPGUITAR-VM).

6. Click the Next Hop button. Notice, as shown in Figure 3.24, that the output shows the next hop type that is used to route the request. You can then confirm that the address prefix for the given next hop type is the one expected. If not, you can add a user-defined route.

FIGURE 3.24 The next hop type is used to route a request from the source IP address to the destination IP address.

Later in this chapter, and in many places throughout this book, you will learn more about routing, networking, and Azure VMs.

Azure Networking Patterns

There are some fairly common Azure networking patterns that customers typically implement. Here is a short list of the most popular ones:

- Isolated
- Hybrid network
- DMZ
- Hub and spoke

An isolated network pattern is like the one created in Exercise 3.2. It was illustrated in Figure 3.17 and is the simplest form of network to implement. It is simply a single VNet with connectivity to the internet. It might encounter limitations as the consumption and deployment of workloads into it increase. Azure networking limits are discussed in the next section, but keep in mind that this networking pattern is usually where customers begin. Knowing the other patterns will help you configure and design with this growth in mind.

Hybrid networks, as discussed earlier in this chapter, can be visualized by reviewing Figure 3.2. This is simply the connectivity between on-premise compute or data resources with the same or similar resources contained within an Azure VNet. (Hybrid connections will be discussed later in this chapter and will cover some additional details about forced tunneling.)

A demilitarized zone (DMZ) is an approach that adds a layer of security around your deployed workloads. As shown in Figure 3.25, notice that, in this pattern, Azure VMs no longer have public IP addresses. They cannot be accessed from the internet or from on-premise directly. To make the Azure VMs reachable from another network like an on-premise network, a VPN gateway, an application gateway (web application firewall [WAF]), or a load balancer will be configured in front of them. Those network hardware components are often referred to as a *network virtual appliance (NVA)*. NVAs can restrict and route traffic for the Azure VMs configured behind it.

The hub and spoke pattern is a variation of the DMZ where the routing can span multiple subscriptions, VNets, DMZs, and/or workloads. As shown in Figure 3.26, the internet traffic has been routed to a specific WAF. Perhaps there needs to be a different set of NSGs applied for connectivity via the internet when compared to connectivity coming from an on-premise endpoint. Then, from the WAF, there are three different VNets represented. Each could have their own subscription. In another scenario, the VNets may play a specific role for the deployed solution.

One reason for splitting VNets into different subscriptions is the separation of costs. Production, testing, and development environments might need to separately monitor usage, data storage, and costs. Assume that the VNets in the previous figure represent just that. This pattern can also provide an isolation perspective. The three environments—production, testing, and development—can be completely isolated from each other. It is important that any kind of performance testing on a test environment does not impact the production system. There are many different patterns, designs, and approaches. It really depends on what your application requires for security and necessary capabilities. The point is to keep in mind that the first default VNet you create will likely not be the end solution. Consider all the options and don't knowingly implement any pattern that can restrict your growth. You can achieve this by having the long-term pattern for your application in mind at design time and building the VNet and surrounding infrastructure with that in mind.

FIGURE 3.25   An Azure DMZ networking pattern

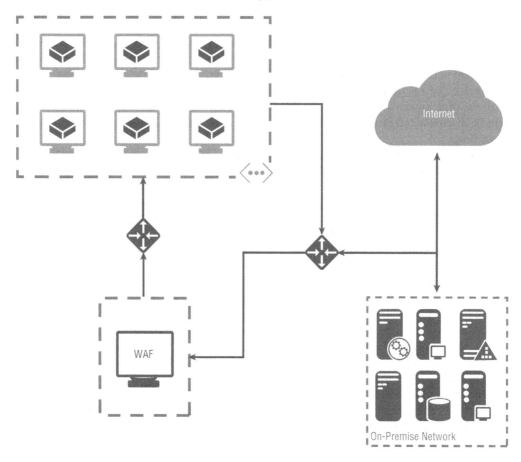

FIGURE 3.26   An Azure hub and spoke networking pattern

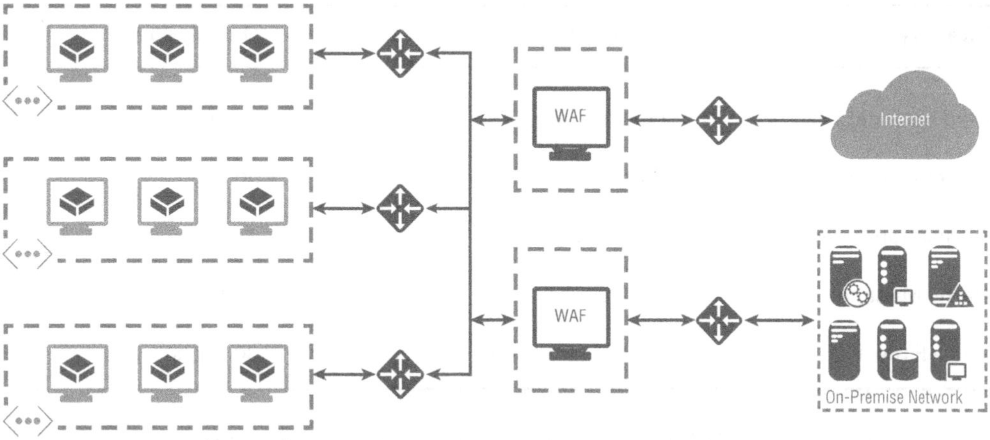

Azure Networking Limits

Sometimes, there is a misconception that the cloud equals limitless capacity and bandwidth. Those with that perception will quickly discover that limitless capacity and bandwidth are not realistic in any computing environment. The cloud offers great capacity and bandwidth with very fast scale-out and up times, but compute capacity (hardware) and bandwidth are not infinite. Table 3.10 describes some of these limits within the Azure Networking context per region and per Azure subscription.

TABLE 3.10   Azure Networking Limits

Category	Resource	Default Limit
Networking	VNets	1,000
	Subnet per VNet	3,000
	Private IP address per VNet	65,536
	Network security groups	5,000
	User-defined route tables	200
Public IP addresses	Dynamic	1,000
	Static	1,000

TABLE 3.10   Azure Networking Limits *(continued)*

Category	Resource	Default Limit
Load balancers	Load balancers	1,000
Express route	Circuits	10
Application gateway	Gateways	1,000
Traffic Manager	Profiles	200
Azure Firewall	Data throughput	30 Gbps

The limits are mostly the defaults and can be increased via a support ticket if more is required. The default settings are there to protect applications from running away with all the resources, which might indirectly impact other customers in the same region; this is commonly referred to as a *noisy neighbor*. The list provided in Table 3.10 is a summary. There are many more default limits. The limits change often, usually to increase the benefits to the customer.

docs.microsoft.com/en-us/azure/azure-subscription-service-limits# networking-limits

In the following sections there will be many exercises that will increase your knowledge of networking topics. The best way to learn is to configure and consume the products and features.

VNet to VNet Integration

In Exercise 3.6 you will create a second VNet in a different region and resource group. This is referred to as *peering*. Actually, when VNets are connected to each other in different regions, it's called *global VNet peering*. When the VNets exist within the same region, it is simply *VNet peering*. Remember, as mentioned in Exercise 3.2, only resources in the same resource group as the VNet can exist within it. The resource group created in Exercise 3.2 was named CSHARPGUITAR-DB3-RG, and it is in the North Europe region. A summary of the resources contained in that resource group follows. These are the resources that the new VNet created here will connect to:

VNet: CSHARPGUITAR-VNET-A

Subnet: CSHARP (10.0.0.0/24)

Azure VM: CSHARPGUITAR-VM

Region: North Europe (DB3)

Although the VNet can also be in another subscription, in this scenario, both VNets will be in the same subscription but will exist in a different region and resource group.

Before starting the exercise, there is a point that needs to be discussed. When you created the first VNet in Exercise 3.2, the portal logic provided the address space for the VNet and address range of the subnet. Are those defaults enough for you? Might you need more than 65,353 addresses for the VNet and about 256 addresses for the subnet? How do you calculate the optimal CIDR even if you know the number you need? Well, remember in Chapter 2 when we discussed conditional access policies? I specifically mentioned that you need to know which operating systems your customer or employees use, as well as the locations they commonly use for access, to effectively create the policy. How many IP addresses your solution requires isn't something Azure or Microsoft can anticipate, so you need to know the answers to these questions, just like you need to know your access control policy requirements. You can find a table that shows how many IP addresses are made available per CIDR prefix here:

```
en.wikipedia.org/wiki/Classless_Inter-Domain_Routing
```

Keep in mind that Azure needs four to five IP addresses to manage the infrastructure per subnet, but this matters only if you are creating very small subnets. A mathematical equation to calculate how many IP addresses exist per CIDR prefix is 2 to the power of (address length minus 2 to the power of the prefix length). For IPv4, the address length is always 32. For example, if the prefix is /29, the equation is $2^{29} - 2^2 = 2^3 = 8$ addresses. In Exercise 3.6, the default range and space are used, but keep in mind to ask or at least think about whether these will be enough. Be aware that you can only change the number of addresses by deleting the VNet or if the VNet is empty.

EXERCISE 3.6

Configuring Global VNet Peering

1. Log in to the Azure Portal at `portal.azure.com`.

2. In the search box at the top of the portal, enter **Resource Groups**, click Resource Groups from the drop-down, and then click + Add.

3. Select the desired subscription and provide a different resource group name. In this example, I create the resource group named CSHARPGUITAR-SN1-RG. SN1 is the designation for South Central US. You can name the resource group as desired; however, make sure it is not in the same region as the VNet created in the earlier exercise.

4. In the search text box at the top of the portal, enter **Virtual Networks**, click Virtual Networks in the drop-down list, and choose + Add.

5. Enter **CSHARPGUITAR-VNET-B** for the VNet name. Take note of the default address space for the VNet (10.1.0.0/16) and the default address range for the subnet (10.1.0.0/24). Select the subscription and resource group as done in step 3, set the subnet name to **csharp**, leave the defaults, and then click the Create button.

Global VNet Peering

Recall that when you created the first VNet, the default address space for the VNet was 10.0.0.0/16, and the default for CSHARPGUITAR-VNET-B is 10.1.0.0/16. Why did the portal decide to default to a different default address space between the VNets? It is possible to have the address range the same for both. However, If the address spaces are the same within two VNets, then they wouldn't be able to peer. There can be no overlap in subnet IP addresses when setting up peering. The portal helps to prevent this from happening by defaulting to another space for VNets in the same subscription and renders a warning. However, it is not prevented, and you can have them overlap, but then peering wouldn't be successful.

6. In the search text box at the top of the portal, enter **Virtual Machines**, click Virtual Machines from the drop-down list, and click + Add.

7. Select the desired subscription and resource group (the same as done in step 3).

8. Provide the Azure VM with a name (for example, CSHARPGUITAR-V2), select the region (for example, South Central US), select Windows Server 2019 Datacenter from the Image drop-down list, and provide a username and password.

9. Select the Allow Select Ports radio button and enable all the available ports, for example, HTTP (80), HTTPS (443), SSH (22), and RDP (3389). Click Next : Disks : Networking, set Virtual Network to CSHARPGUITAR-VNET-B, set the subnet to csharp, leave the remaining components at the defaults, click the Review + Create button, and click the Create button.

10. Once the deployment is complete, do a quick check of the contents of the route table. Execute the following PowerShell cmdlet, and you should get output like that shown in Figure 3.27. The output is also like Figure 3.13 shown previously for CSHARPGUITAR-VM.

    ```
    Get-AzEffectiveRouteTable –NetworkInterfaceName csharpguitar-v2713 `
      –ResourceGroupName CSHARPGUITAR-SN1-RG | Format-Table
    ```

FIGURE 3.27   PowerShell cmdlet output of the system route table

Name	DisableBgpRoutePropagation	State	Source	AddressPrefix	NextHopType	NextHopIpAddress
	False	Active	Default	{10.1.0.0/16}	VnetLocal	{}
	False	Active	Default	{0.0.0.0/0}	Internet	{}
	False	Active	Default	{10.0.0.0/8}	None	{}
	False	Active	Default	{100.64.0.0/10}	None	{}
	False	Active	Default	{192.168.0.0/16}	None	{}

11. Make a remote desktop connection using the Remote Desktop Connect (RDP) application to CSHARPGUITAR-V2 and execute the following curl command, just to make sure the connectivity is not working. Recall from Figure 3.21 and Figure 3.22 in

Exercise 3.4 that this `curl` code was from CSHARPGUITAR-VM to CSHARPGUITAR-V1. In this scenario, you are testing the connectivity between CSHARPGUITAR-V2 and CSHARPGUITAR-V1. See Figure 3.28.

```
curl -G <Public IP address>:80
curl -G <Private IP address>:80
```

FIGURE 3.28   Using curl to test Azure VM accessibility

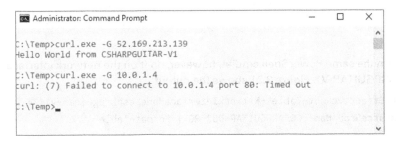

12. As expected, using `curl` for the public IP address works, but not the private IP address. Remember that CSHARPGUITAR-V2 is in San Antonio, Texas, and CSHARPGUITAR-V1 is in Dublin, Ireland. Let's peer the VNets together so the private IP address will work. Navigate to CSHARPGUITAR-VNET-B, click Peerings, and then click + Add.

13. Provide a name for the peering (for example, CSHARPGUITAR-PEER-B2A). In the Virtual Network drop-down list, select CSHARPGUITAR-VNET-A and then name the peering in the other direction (for example, CSHARPGUITAR-PEER-A2B). Leave the remaining defaults and click the OK button.

14. Once the configuration has completed, access CSHARPGUITAR-V2 again and use `curl`. See Figure 3.29.

FIGURE 3.29   Using curl to test Azure VM accessibility

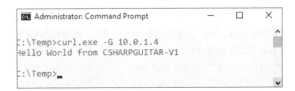

15. Execute the same PowerShell cmdlet as in step 10, and you will notice there is a route added to the table (Figure 3.30).

FIGURE 3.30   PowerShell cmdlet output of the system route table

Name	DisableBgpRoutePropagation	State	Source	AddressPrefix	NextHopType	NextHopIpAddress
	False	Active	Default	{10.1.0.0/16}	VnetLocal	{}
	False	Active	Default	{0.0.0.0/0}	Internet	{}
	False	Active	Default	{10.0.0.0/8}	None	{}
	False	Active	Default	{100.64.0.0/10}	None	{}
	False	Active	Default	{192.168.0.0/16}	None	{}
	False	Active	Default	{10.0.0.0/16}	VNetGlobalPeering	{}

16. Perform the same PowerShell cmdlet; however, do it on the network interface for CSHARPGUITAR-V1. Figure 3.31 shows the output.

    ```
    Get-AzEffectiveRouteTable –NetworkInterfaceName csharpguitar-v1434 `
      –ResourceGroupName CSHARPGUITAR-DB3-RG | Format-Table
    ```

FIGURE 3.31   PowerShell cmdlet output of the system route table

Name	DisableBgpRoutePropagation	State	Source	AddressPrefix	NextHopType	NextHopIpAddress
	False	Active	Default	{10.0.0.0/16}	VnetLocal	{}
	False	Active	Default	{0.0.0.0/0}	Internet	{}
	False	Active	Default	{10.0.0.0/8}	None	{}
	False	Active	Default	{100.64.0.0/10}	None	{}
	False	Active	Default	{192.168.0.0/16}	None	{}
	False	Active	Default	{10.1.0.0/16}	VNetGlobalPeering	{}

Nice work! It is now possible to communicate from servers hosted in South Central US and North Europe within the Microsoft global network. There are three settings that should be covered in more detail that were present when configuring the peering.

- Allow Virtual Network Access
- Allow Forwarded Traffic
- Allow Gateway Transit

Allow Virtual Network Access is enabled by default and, as shown in Figure 3.32, is configurable for both traffic directions between VNET-A and VNET-B. In this configuration, if the need ever arises that you do not want to support the traffic in one direction or both directions, then that channel can be disabled. This is easier than deleting and re-creating it later.

Allow Forwarded Traffic has to do with supporting the traffic from a network appliance in the virtual network but doesn't originate from the virtual network itself. This scenario has a lot to do with the design of the network and how traffic is being routed through your solution. The simple point is if you have VNET-A, VNET-B, and VNET-C and not all are peered, but there is a network appliance in one that is peered, then that traffic can be routed through if configured to do so.

FIGURE 3.32   Additional Azure peering configuration options

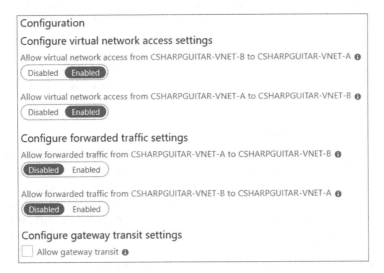

For Allow Gateway Transit, which we have not covered in detail yet, has to do with on-premise connectivity. The implementation of either a VPN gateway or ExpressRoute could necessitate allowing gateway traffic. By enabling them, traffic will be allowed to flow between the gateway and the peered VNets.

Site-to-Site Overview

The section "Azure Relay/Hybrid Connection Manager" gets into a little more detail about the internals of S2S connectivity. In this context, S2S means the connection between a VNet in Azure or the series of VNets (i.e., pattern dependent) and some other network not on Azure. As illustrated in Figure 3.33, the connectivity is managed through a gateway subnet and a VPN tunnel.

FIGURE 3.33   Site-to-site configuration

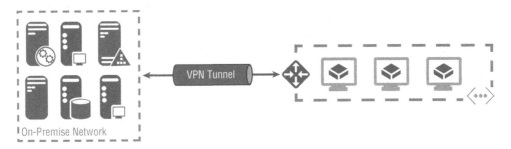

There are numerous steps required to successfully configure S2S connectivity; many of the Azure components required to complete this activity have not yet been discussed such as the creation of a gateway subnet, an optional Azure DNS, and the VPN gateway. One of the more complicated parts, as it is very reliant on the on-premise endpoint, is the configuration and connection from Azure to the on-premise VPN endpoint. You can find more discussion about S2S in the later section "Azure Relay/Hybrid Azure Networking" and in Chapter 6. By then all the components required to make this configuration will have been covered.

VNet to Azure Resources

Not all Azure resources exist within an Azure VNet. As you are already aware, when you create an Azure VM, part of the setup is to select the VNet instance that it will be placed on. This is not the case when creating, for example, an Azure Function instance, an Azure App Service instance, or an Azure SQL database. Each of these three Azure products exposes a globally accessible endpoint, for example, *.azurewebsites.net, where * is the name of the Azure Function or Azure App Service instance and is accessible from any client able to make HTTP calls.

An Azure SQL database has an endpoint of *.database.windows.net, where * is the name of the Azure SQL server on which the database is hosted. To show that you can connect to an Azure SQL database from an Azure VM, complete Exercise 3.7. There are a few prerequisites that will not be detailed in the exercise like the creation of an Azure SQL database. The creation of an Azure SQL database will be detailed in Chapter 5. Also, there are many sources that can provide this activity in detail; for example, this is one of them:

docs.microsoft.com/en-us/azure/sql-database/sql-database-single-database-get-started

When creating the Azure SQL database, be sure to select the Allow Azure Services To Access Server check box. This will make sure there are not IP restrictions that prevent the connection from internal Azure resources. From an Azure VM perspective, you will need to install three utilities. Table 3.11 describes what they are and where to find them.

TABLE 3.11   Database Networking Tools

Utility	Location
2017 C++ redistributable	aka.ms/vs/16/release/vc_redist.x64.exe
ODBC Driver 17 SQL	www.microsoft.com/en-us/download/details.aspx?id=56567
SQLCMD	docs.microsoft.com/en-us/sql/tools/sqlcmd-utility

Once the utilities are successfully installed on an Azure VM, perform Exercise 3.7.

EXERCISE 3.7

Connecting to Azure SQL from an Azure VM

1. Make a remote desktop connection to the Azure VM on which you have installed the utilities identified in Table 3.11.

2. Open a command prompt and enter the following, also visualized in Figure 3.34. `sqlcmd` is installed by default into `C:\Program Files\Microsoft SQL Server\ Client SDK\ODBC\170\Tools\Binn`. Navigate there to run `sqlcmd`, or add the path to your environment variables, as I have done, which allows execution from any location. Be sure to replace `<uid>` and `<password>` with your credentials.

    ```
    sqlcmd -S *.database.windows.net -d <dbname> -U <uid> -P <password>
    select database_id, is_read_only, compatibility_level from sys.databases
    go
    ```

FIGURE 3.34   Connecting to Azure SQL from an Azure VM

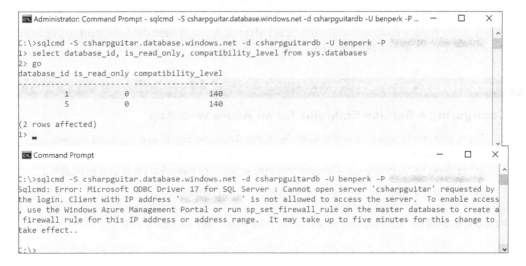

3. A successful execution of the `SELECT` query from the Azure VMs confirms the connection is successful.

4. The second command prompt output in Figure 3.34 was run from my local workstation. Remember, you needed to allow Azure services to access the database when creating the Azure SQL database. Since the IP address of my workstation is not an Azure service, then the connection request was denied. To make it work, the client IP address would need to be whitelisted on the database. You'll learn more about this in Chapter 5.

The endpoints of an Azure SQL database instance are exposed, but they are not simply open for database connections; credentials are required. It is a similar scenario with Azure App Service; however, as App Service instances are locations that customers typically run internet applications on, there are no IP restrictions implemented by default. It is possible; Azure App Service has the capability to add a list of white- or blacklisted IP addresses. Remember also that when making the connection between Azure resources, whether they have global endpoints or not, the traffic is routed inside the Microsoft global network.

Try accessing an Azure web app from the same Azure VM and from a workstation, not on Azure using curl, something like the following:

```
curl -G csharpguitar.azurewebsites.net/api/values
```

The output should be something like the following:

```
["csharp","guitar"]
```

In Exercise 3.8, let's configure a service endpoint on the Azure web app so that its endpoint is accessible only from within a VNet. Recall from Figure 3.13 and Exercise 3.2 that when you created the VNet, you also enabled Microsoft.Web from the Service Endpoints drop-down. This added a route to the table that was bound to the Azure VM at the time. You might consider running the PowerShell cmdlet and checking the route table prior to enabling the service endpoint and then again after, just to get into the habit and to confirm the configuration works as expected.

EXERCISE 3.8

Configuring a Service Endpoint for an Azure Web App

1. From any workstation or client outside of the Azure network, use curl, as shown in Figure 3.35. This is to make sure that access is not restricted so that you have something to compare your access attempt to after the service endpoint is enabled.

   ```
   curl -G csharpguitar-se.azurewebsites.net/api/values
   ```

FIGURE 3.35   Connecting to an Azure Web App from an Azure VM

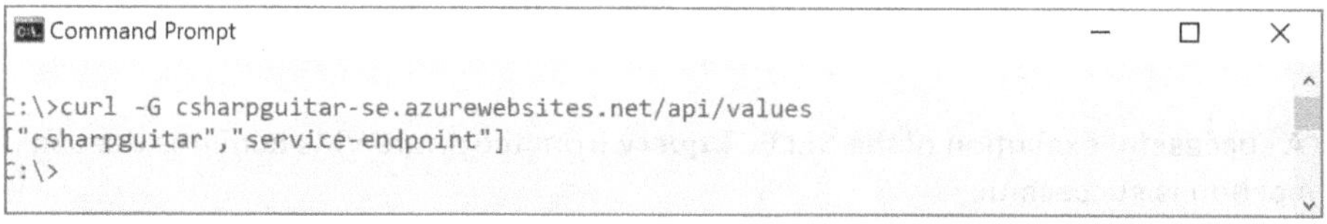

2. Log in to the Azure Portal at portal.azure.com.

3. Create an Azure App Service following these instructions, and place the Azure web app into the same resource group as the Azure VM and VNet for which you want to configure the service endpoint for.

   docs.microsoft.com/en-us/azure/app-service/

4. Navigate to the Azure web app created for this exercise. Select Networking Access Restrictions Configure Access Restrictions and click the + Add rule.

5. Add a name (for example, ALLOW CSHARPGUITAR VNET A GUITAR); then select Allow, set Priority to 300, and provide a description. From the Type drop-down list, select Virtual Network, select the subscription, select the virtual network (for example, CSHARPGUITAR-VNET-A), select guitar from the Subnet drop-down list, and click the Add Rule button. Notice the message stating that the `Microsoft.Web` service endpoint will be enabled on the selected Subnet (guitar).

6. Navigate to the Subnet details, and you will see that it is indeed selected. Additionally, check the effective routes, and you will see the *VirtualNetworkServiceEndpoint* Next Hop Type added.

7. Perform the same `curl` as done in step 1; you should now get a 403 – Forbidden HTTP Status response. Make a remote desktop connection using RDP into an Azure VM within the CSHARPGUITAR-VNET-A and subnet guitar and perform the same steps, and the request will be successful.

The source code that runs on the csharpguitar, csharpguitar-se, and the Azure web apps are default versions of an ASP.NET Core 2.2 Web API; instructions can be found at the following site:

`docs.microsoft.com/en-us/aspnet/core/tutorials/first-web-api`

Make just a small change to the default `ValuesController.cs` to customize it if desired.

Chapter 8 will explain in more detail how to deploy the API to the Azure App Service platform. A service endpoint, as shown in Figure 3.36, is a way to grant inbound network traffic to numerous Azure products on a subnet while denying access to those endpoints from the internet.

This is a useful feature for an additional level of security to protect Azure features that have global endpoints. I specifically used inbound previously to call out the fact that just because the VNet supports the connectivity for inbound traffic, outbound using the private IP address isn't automatically configured. For example, the Azure VM that was tested using `curl` had a private IP address of 10.0.1.4; the outbound traffic was to the now protected global endpoint. However, that Azure Web App would not be able to access the Azure VM using 10.0.1.4. The public IP address of the Azure VM is accessible, if the NSG is set up to allow it. Each of the numerous endpoints that support service endpoints set up their own configuration requirements and subtle differences, but the purpose is the same in each case, which is to prevent inbound internet traffic on the global endpoint.

Another term, subnet delegation, can be found on the same blade where the configuration of the service endpoint is located. Subnet delegation allows the creation of service-specific resources into the subnet. Take, for example, the *Microsoft.Batch/batchAccounts* resource. This resource has privileges such as read, write, and delete. When you delegate that resource to the subnet, the Azure Batch product will have those permissions on resources within the subnet.

FIGURE 3.36 A visualization of a service endpoint

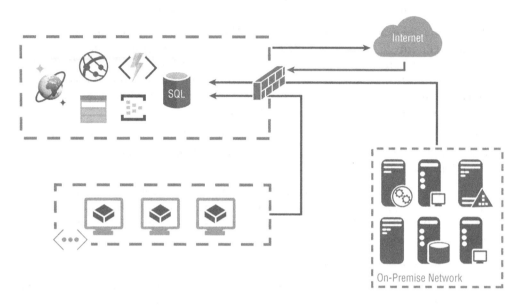

VNet to Internet

Outbound internet connectivity is enabled by default, and there is nothing you need to do to open it. It is possible to restrict certain ports and protocols using an NSG that has already been discussed and will be elaborated on in the next section. The simplest way to test the connectivity is to use curl on a website such as www.bing.com or www.stackoverflow.com. Or perhaps open a browser and navigate to the URL.

Recall the route table with the CIDR prefix of 0.0.0.0/0, which defines the next hop as the internet. This is matched when the destination IP address doesn't fall into any of the other routes. The request is routed out of the Microsoft global network and onto the internet backbone. You should now understand Azure VNets and subnets. The remaining sections cover security, DNS, hybrid networks, and some other general networking products and features. Read on.

Network Security

There have already been a few points made about the network security capabilities available on Azure. For example, we've talked about network security groups (NSGs), application security groups (ASGs), network filtering, network virtual appliances (NVAs), and service endpoints. In this section, we will get a little deeper into network security as it pertains to Azure; the specifics are as follows:

- Traffic filtering with NSG, ASG, and NVA
- Azure Application Gateway/WAF

- Azure Firewall
- IP restrictions
- Network map and topology

Before starting, answer the following question:

Which of the following are considered an Azure network pattern?

A. Hybrid

B. Hub and spoke

C. DMZ

D. All the above

E. B and C

The answer is that all of these are patterns that can be implemented into the Azure networking architecture.

Traffic Filtering with NSG, ASG, and NVA

When I read the word *filter*, my first visualization is coffee. That's kind of old-school because these days the beans are ground and the coffee is made without a filter in these ultramodern mechanized appliances. But many may relate to the brown paper that formed a barrier when placed into a coffee machine, followed by some previously ground coffee beans that hot water flowed over, brewing an element of satisfaction. The same could be said about the filtering of network traffic, in that instead of the barrier being brown paper, it's an NSG, an ASG, or an NVA.

An NSG was introduced earlier in Figure 3.10. Table 3.12 describes the properties of an NSG. Note that there is a limit of 5,000 NSGs per Azure subscription.

TABLE 3.12   NSG Property Descriptions

Property	Description
Priority	The order in which the rule is applied. Rule #1 processes before rule #2, and processing stops after the first match.
Name	The name of the NSG; it must be unique.
Port	Can be a single port or a range of ports
Protocol	TCP, UDP, or Any
Source	Private IP CIDR range, specific IP(s), service tag, or ASG
Destination	Private IP CIDR range, specific IP(s), service tag, or ASG
Action	Allow or Deny

Table 3.12 is relatively clear excluding the source and destination properties, which require a bit more explanation. Recall from the discussion about SNAT and PAT that IP addresses are finite resources and need to be translated so the resource is preserved as much as possible. This is why the NSG source and destination properties are based on the private IP addresses and not public when specifying an Azure resource. SNAT happens before the inbound source IP address engages with the resource protected by the NSG. Outbound traffic, as well, engages with the NSG before the SNAT engagement happens. The "engagement" happens at the `tcp.sys` level prior to leaving the physical hardware. Public IP addresses and ranges of public IP addresses are supported. Just when you configure an NSG for an Azure resource, it's recommended to use its private IP address.

Another option available from the source drop-down list is Service Tag. A *service tag* is a grouping of IP addresses that are bound to a specific Azure product. For example, the *Azure Traffic Manager (ATM)*, discussed later in the chapter, can probe a set of servers to gather a health status. These requests are inbound requests to a specific Azure VM. Those IP addresses would need to be allowed to make the connection. Instead of expecting the customer to create an NSG that supports the ATM, Microsoft will manage those IP addresses via a service tag. Azure architects need not worry about the maintenance of those NSGs. See Figure 3.37 for a visualization of the inbound and outbound rules.

FIGURE 3.37   A visualization of a service endpoint

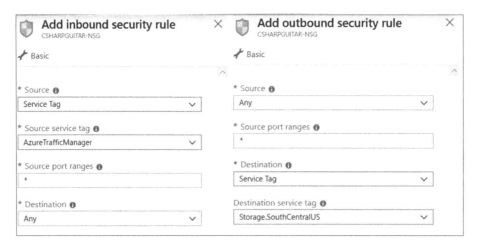

The similar scenario for outbound NSGs applies as well, where, for example, an Azure VM needs to make a connection to an Azure Storage container. Instead of creating an NSG specifically for that container and having to possibly manage any changes to the IP addresses, instead select Storage from the Destination Service Tag drop-down list. It is possible to further constrain this to a specific region of storage container. For example, one could select Storage.SouthCentralUS from the Destination Service Tag drop-down list so that all Azure Storage–related IP addresses are allowed via the NSG. Table 3.13

summarizes the different Azure products that service tags support. The table also provides the expected implementation of the service tag, indicating whether it should be an outbound or inbound NSG.

TABLE 3.13 Service Tags and Azure Products

Azure Product	Regional Support	Inbound or Outbound
Azure Load Balancer	✕	Inbound
Azure Active Directory	✕	Outbound
Storage	✓	Outbound
Internet	✕	Both
SQL	✓	Outbound
Azure Key Vault	✓	Outbound
Azure Cosmos DB	✓	Outbound
API Management	✕	Both
App Service	✓	Outbound
Gateway Manager	✕	Inbound

Being able to select an Azure product instead of trying to figure out which inbound or outbound restriction is needed based on an IP address adds great value. Service tags are helpful in reducing maintenance and support efforts in that respect. Let's do an exercise and implement a best-practice, recommended NSG configuration. In Exercise 3.9, you will bind an NSG to a subnet instead of the network interface that is bound to a specific Azure VM.

EXERCISE 3.9

Binding an NSG to a Subnet

1. Log in to the Azure Portal at portal.azure.com.

2. In the search box at the top of the portal, enter **Application security groups**, click Application Security Groups in the drop-down, and click + Add.

3. Select the desired subscription, select the resource group (for example, CSHARPGUITAR-DB3-RG), provide a name (for example, CSHARPGUITAR-ASG), select the desired region (for example, North Europe), click the Review + Create button, and click the Create button.

4. Once that's complete, in the search box at the top of the portal enter **Network security groups**, click Network Security Groups in the drop-down, and click + Add.

5. Provide a name (for example, CSHARPGUITAR-NSG), select the desired subscription, select the resource group (for example, CSHARPGUITA-DB3-RG), select the location (for example, North Europe), and then click the Create button.

6. Navigate to the CSHARPGUITAR-VNET-A blade in the Connected Devices list. There you should find a list of the network interfaces belonging to CSHARPGUITAR-VM and CSHARPGUITAR-V1 Azure VMs (Figure 3.38). If you have followed the exercise up to now, the two network interfaces will be in different subnets: 10.0.0.0/24 (csharp) and 10.0.1.0/24 (guitar).

FIGURE 3.38   Connected devices VNet list

Connected devices			
🔎 *Search connected devices*			
DEVICE	**TYPE**	**IP ADDRESS**	**SUBNET**
csharpguitar-vm810	Network interface	10.0.0.4	csharp
csharpguitar-v1434	Network interface	10.0.1.4	guitar

7. Remove the NSG from the network interface attached to the csharp subnet, click the network interface bound to 10.0.0.4 (csharp guitar subnet), select the Network Security Group link then Edit, and then select the currently bound NSG. Select None and Save.

8. Navigate back to the CSHARPGUITAR-VNET-A VNet, select Subnets, click csharp, select CSHARPGUITAR-NSG from the network security group in the drop-down list, and then click Save. Now the NSG is bound to the subnet and not to a specific Azure VM.

9. Navigate to CSHARPGUITA-NSG, select Inbound Security Rules, and click + Add. Now, select Application Security Group from the Source drop-down list, select CSHARPGUITAR-ASG from the Source Application Security Group drop-down list box, set Protocol to TCP, set the destination port range to 443, give the NSG a name (for example, allowOnlyHTTPS), and then click the Add button.

Now, when you add Azure VMs to this subnet (csharp) by default, the Azure VM is bound to this NSG and the inferred ASG. Application security groups, which were introduced with Figure 3.12, is also an option you can choose from the Source and Destination drop-down lists for an NSG. How to apply an ASG and what ASGs are should now be clear.

A network virtual appliance (NVA) and its implementation are highly sophisti-cated enterprise-level architecture devices. NVA is a general term that can be used when describing a DMZ, for example. A DMZ is often described as having an internet-facing NVA in front of a group of edge servers and another NVA behind those servers that per-form an extra layer of filtering. Perhaps the internet-facing NVA will support the HTTP protocol only, while the backend NVA does not. The fact that there are two locations where the NVA exists in a DMZ makes the location between the two an unknown, which is confusing to bad actors. The design of a DMZ and its dependent and supporting compo-nents is specific to the dependencies and requirements of the application and can, therefore, be illustrated in Figure 3.39 only as a basic default scenario.

FIGURE 3.39   Enterprise NVA VNet architecture diagram

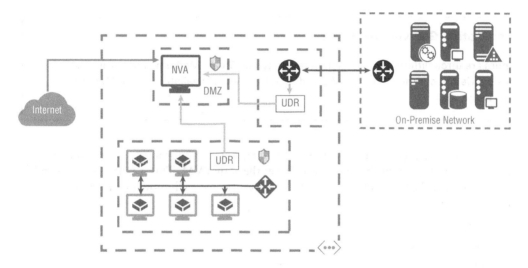

The point to take away from Figure 3.39 is that the traffic to and from on-premise and the internet flow through a DMZ where the traffic can be greatly scrutinized and con-trolled. Doing that increases the level of protection of the resource behind the DMZ. This concept is also commonly referred to a *forced tunneling*. The name matches the action in that all traffic is forced through an NVA tunnel prior to reaching any resource behind the two firewalls (aka NSGs). An item that has not been discussed much in Figure 3.39 is *user-defined route (UDR)*. UDRs are custom routes placed into the routing tables of the VNet. These UDRs would contain routes to the gateways, express routes, or VPNs connecting the different networks. More on UDRs is still to come.

Application Gateway/WAF

Application gateways provide more capabilities than a *web application firewall (WAF)*; however, in this section only the WAF part of the product is discussed. The other available features are covered in detail later in this chapter. When you begin approaching security for a web-based application at the application level, i.e., coding or configurations, it wouldn't take long until you ask yourself, "Is there a better way?" That's because from an application perspective your focus is on the code and keeping security patches up-to-date on all the instances. For smaller implementations, it may be not be so hard, and for PaaS you need not worry about those patches. However, from an Azure VM perspective, those are valid concerns. In both scenarios, finding vulnerabilities in your application code is a significant but worthy undertaking.

Application Gateway Types

There are three different application gateway types: Small, Medium, and Large. Each has a different cost and associated set of features. WAF is available only in Medium and Large.

One answer to the "Is there a better way?" question is to put some protection in place to prevent known exploits before they arrive at the actual VM. This is where Azure Application Gateway (WAF) can help. A WAF can prevent some well-known vulnerabilities, like the following:

- Cross-site scripting (XSS) attacks
- Bots, scanners, and crawlers
- SQL-injection attacks
- HTTP response splitting
- HTTP request smuggling

These protections are enabled by applying a rule set based on CRS or OWASP, which was discussed in Chapter 2. Review that for more information on CRS. When new vulnerabilities surface, the protections against them are automatically added to the rule set and applied to the WAF, without action on the system administrators' side. Application Gateway WAF performs this protection at layer 7 of the OSI model, which is the application layer. Table 3.14 summarizes the OSI model.

TABLE 3.14 The OSI Model

Level	Layer	Description
7	Application	High-level APIs and resource sharing
6	Presentation	Character encoding, compression, encrypt/decryption
5	Session	Manages back and forth communication between two nodes
4	Transport	Manages transport of data between two points
3	Network	Controls addressing, routing and traffic control
2	Data link	Physical layer data transmission
1	Physical	Physical transmission on a physical medium

The reason the OSI level of the WAF is important is because there are certain capabilities that are allowed only when the transmission is touched at that certain level. For example, it is not possible to perform URL-based routing or SSL termination in OSI levels 1–4, because the data isn't in a state to be touched at that time. Only at OSI level 7 can those two activities take place. Azure does have other options for firewalls discussed later; until then, take a look at Figure 3.40 to better understand the architecture of a VNet with Application Gateway WAF protecting an Azure VM configured into what is called a *backend pool*.

FIGURE 3.40 Application Gateway web application firewall diagram

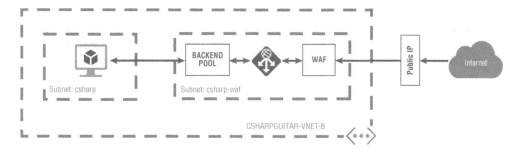

In Exercise 3.10 you will create and configure an Application Gateway WAF. Application Gateway can be configured only on an empty subnet; therefore, the first action is to create one.

EXERCISE 3.10

Creating and Configuring an Application Gateway WAF

1.   Log in to the Azure Portal at portal.azure.com.

2.   Navigate to CHSARPGUITAR-VNET-B, click the Subnets link, and then click + Subnet. Provide a name for the subnet (for example, csharp-waf), accept the defaults, and click the OK button.

3.   In the search box located at the top of the portal, enter **Application gateways**, click Application Gateways from the drop-down, and then click + Add.

4.   On the Basics tab, select the desired subscription, select the resource group (for example, CSHARPGUITAR-SN1-RG), provide a name for the AGWAF (for example, CSHARPGUITAR-SN1-AGWAF), and select the region (for example, South Central US, which is the same location as the resource group).

5.   In the Tier drop-down list, select WAF, set the instance count to 1m, make the SKU size Medium(m), leave the other defaults, and then select the virtual network to configure the WAF for (for example, CSHARPGUITAR-VNET-B). This VNet was already created in the SN1 region. Now, select csharp-waf from the Subnet drop-down list, confirm that the final configuration resembles that shown in Figure 3.41, and then click the Next: Frontends button.

6.   Select the Public radio button, click the Create New link under the Public IP Address drop-down list, enter a name for the frontend (for example, CSHARPGUITAR-WAF-ip), click OK, and finally click the Next: Backends button.

7.   Click + Add Backend Pool, provide a name (for example, CSHARPGUITAR-WAF-BACKEND-POOL), select Virtual Machine from the Target Type drop-down list, select the network interface of CSHARPGUITAR-V2 from the Type drop-down list, click the Add button, and then click the Next: Configuration button. You should see something like that shown in Figure 3.42.

FIGURE 3.41 Basics tab, application gateway creation

| ① Basics | ② Frontends | ③ Backends | ④ Configuration | ⑤ Tags | ⑥ Review + create |

* Subscription ❶

Microsoft (25)

└── * Resource group ❶

CSHARPGUITAR-SN1-RG

Create new

Instance details

* Application gateway name

CSHARPGUITAR-AGWAF

* Region

(US) South Central US

Tier ❶

WAF

* Instance count ❶

1

SKU size ❶

Medium

Firewall status ❶

○ Disabled ◉ Enabled

Firewall mode ❶

◉ Detection ○ Prevention

HTTP/2 ❶

◉ Disabled ○ Enabled

Configure virtual network

* Virtual network ❶

CSHARPGUITAR-VNET-B

Create new

* Subnet ❶

csharp-waf (10.1.1.0/24)

Manage subnet configuration

FIGURE 3.42 Configuration tab, application gateway creation

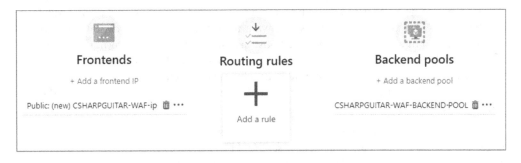

Frontends	Routing rules	Backend pools
+ Add a frontend IP		+ Add a backend pool
Public: (new) CSHARPGUITAR-WAF-ip 🗑 •••	➕ Add a rule	CSHARPGUITAR-WAF-BACKEND-POOL 🗑 •••

8. Click the + Add A Rule button, enter a rule name (for example, CSHARPGUITAR-WAF-HTTP80), enter a listener name (for example, CSHARPGUITAR-LISTENER), select Public from the Frontend IP drop-down list, select the Backend Targets tab, select CSHARPGUITAR-WAF-BACKEND-POOL from the Backend Target drop-down list, click the Create New link under the HTTP Setting drop-down list, provide the setting a name (for example, CSHARPGUITAR-HTTP-SETTING), and click the Add button.

9. Click the Next: Tags button, click the Next: Review + Create button, and click the Create button.

10. Once that's created, open the Application Gateway blade for CSHARPGUITAR-AGWAF, copy its IP address and place it into a browser, and attempt to connect. If IIS is not installed on the VM in the backend pool, make a remote desktop connection using RDP and execute the following PowerShell cmdlets:

```
Install-WindowsFeature -name Web-Server -IncludeManagementTools
remove-item C:\inetpub\wwwroot\iisstart.htm
Add-Content -Path "C:\inetpub\wwwroot\iisstart.htm" `
        -Value $("Hello from " + $env:computername)
```

11. The request to the public IP address of the WAF routes to the Azure VM configured into the backend pool and responds with the "Hello from CSHARPGUITAR-V2" string.

There is one more configuration that needs more discussion—Firewall mode. You might have noticed it on the Basics tab in step 5 of Exercise 3.10. Firewall mode has two options: Detection and Prevention. As the names would lead one to believe, when detection is selected and an access matches a pattern similar to what is considered a malicious intrusion (for example, some JavaScript in a web form), it is logged. The request can flow through and be processed. I assume someone would want to do this if their application is for some reason designed in a way that an expected post matches a malicious pattern. Other times, you want to let the bad actors think they are going undetected but come back and get them later. Lastly, perhaps the application under attack has strong enough resistance to known vulnerabilities. As you can see, there are certainly numerous additional reasons for allowing the traffic through.

Prevention, on the other hand, will not let a request/post pass through the WAF if it is flagged as malicious. Instead, the client is sent an HTTPS status code of 403 – Forbidden. The attempt is still logged for later review and analysis, but the bad actor is immediately informed of their denial or failed attempt at potentially causing harm. Chapter 9 contains more details of monitoring. Azure does provide another firewall product called Azure Firewall; read on to learn about it.

Azure Firewall

Azure Firewall (AF) acts like the Application Gateway WAF but with a few differences, or a few capabilities exist with Azure Firewall that do not with a WAF. They are summarized in the following list:

- Azure Firewall is stateful.
- It has unrestricted scalability.
- It allows the creation of allow or deny network filtering rules.
- The cost of Azure Firewall is considerably more than an Azure Gateway WAF.

Remember, since the WAF runs on OSI level 7 and AF can monitor traffic from layer 3 to layer 7, traffic at level 5 is supported. OSI level 5, as documented, is the layer in which the session can be monitored. (A session has some kind of unique identifier that exists between two nodes and remains for the duration of a series of back-and-forth communications.) AF is able to identify each request and can perform actions based on multiple transmissions between two nodes. It might set a timeout or route the request to a specific location or server, keeping the request sticky to the server.

It is true that WAFv2 supports scaling, however. WAF alone does not. Recall from the previous exercise that we set the instance count to 1. This was chosen only for the example; a minimum of 2 is recommended for redundancy. This cannot scale out more after it is provisioned. This is not the case with Azure Firewall. The scaling capabilities are built in and will scale as much as needed based on the traffic flowing through them, without anyone needing to take action.

It is possible to set up NSG-like rules for Azure Firewall. Once they're created, there is a link called Rules that opens a blade showing the three supported types of rule collections. See Figure 3.43.

- NAT rule collection
- Network rule collection
- Application rule collection

A NAT rule collection is set to *destination network address translation (DNAT)*, which translates and filters inbound traffic to the subnet. As already discussed, DNAT, SNAT, NAT, and the like have to do with the translation of IP addresses from internal to external or for the reuse of dynamic IP addresses in an effort to avoid SNAT exhaustion. This rule feature provides the ability to place a rule on the translated address and translated port in addition to the expected source and destination properties. A network collection rule is like what is seen with an NSG that gets bound to a subnet; instead, here the rule is enforced on Azure Firewall. The rule contains, as expected, the source IP address, source port, destination IP address, and destination port (socket). If there is a match, the allow or deny action is executed. Finally, the Application role collection can be configured to check *fully qualified domain names (FQDNs)* as well as protocols such as HTTP or HTTPS. Both of those are generally specific to applications and are therefore allowed or denied at this point.

FIGURE 3.43   Azure Firewall rule collections

The application of the rules occurs in the following order:

1. NAT rule

2. Network rule

3. Application rule

Once there is a match for any of the rules in any collection, the request is either allowed or denied, and no other rule is processed.

Lastly, the cost of Azure Firewall is considerably more than an Azure Gateway WAF. Costs change, and perhaps the amount warrants the additional capabilities only available in the AF. Either way, watch out for the prices, but if the feature exists only in AF, like maintaining session, and your application requires it, then you have to take that approach.

IP Restrictions

There are lots of ways to protect your application from a networking perspective, no? Up to now these protective solutions have been placed on a device, whether virtual or physical, which doesn't run the actual application. Neither do the solutions run directly on a database or other Azure product. IP restrictions are most commonly implemented on the compute hardware on which the resource being protected is also running. Take *Internet Information Services (IIS)*, for example, which is a web service that runs on a Windows server and hosts a web application of some kind. IIS provides two kinds of IP restrictions: IP Security and *Dynamic IP Restrictions (DIPRs)*.

The IP Security capability is the typical whitelisting and blacklisting of IP addresses. If clients have an IP address existing on the whitelist, the request will be responded to; otherwise, the request is denied. If the source IP address is on the blacklist, then the request is blocked, while all others are then allowed. This implementation could become maintenance heavy if the IP addresses in the whitelist/blacklist change frequently. The IP Security feature is also not very optimal for preventing malicious kinds of activities as changing the source IP address is a nonissue once it gets placed into a blacklist. The IP Security feature is best used when you know the IP addresses, which will be included or excluded, and the list remains static. DIPRs, on the other hand, are very well suited for handling malicious attacks. DIPR can be configured to block based on the number of concurrent requests from the same source IP address or by the total number of requests over time. Once the source IP address exceeds any of those set thresholds, future connections are denied for the configured timeframe.

From an Azure perspective, an Azure VM running IIS would have those capabilities discussed previously and would be implemented directly on the VMs themselves. Other Azure products provide similar capabilities, such as Azure App Services, Azure SQL, and Azure Storage. On Azure App Services, the attributes displayed in Figure 3.44 seem similar to an NSG; however, these rules are managed by the Azure App Service product directly.

FIGURE 3.44 IP restrictions for an Azure App Service

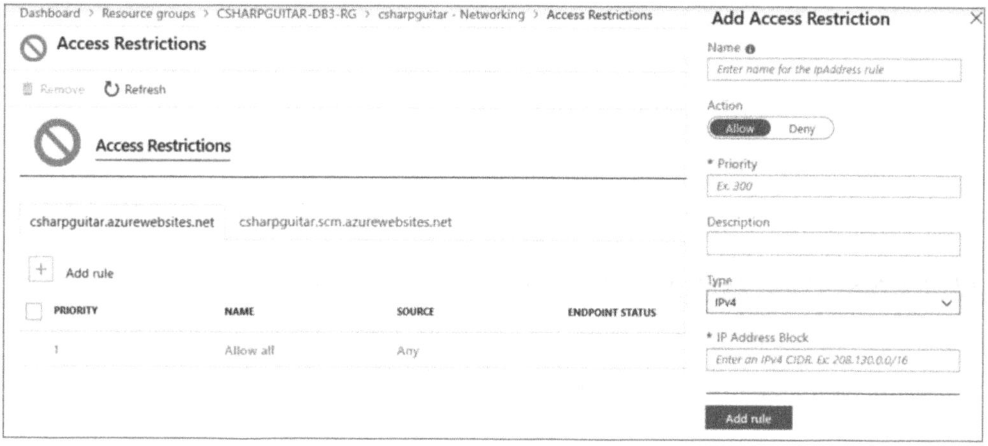

As shown in Figure 3.45, setting a firewall/IP restriction on a SQL Azure database configured directly on the SQL Azure database blade in the portal. Notice that the portal identifies the IP address of the client you are connecting from and lets you click a button to add it, which makes things easy during development mode.

On the Azure SQL blade in the portal, it is also possible to allow access from resources running in an Azure virtual network (VNet). Another Azure product that supports restricting access directly on the product itself is an Azure Storage account, as shown in Figure 3.46.

After navigating to the firewalls and virtual networks blade from the Azure Storage account page, you again see the capability to configure both VNet access and specific ranges of IP addresses. As time progresses, more and more Azure products will support this kind of configuration. It is important to recognize that an Azure architect needs to design with supportability in mind, and having NSGs, Azure Firewall, WAFs, and IP restrictions configured can cause some seriously complicated troubleshooting scenarios. Imagine that an IP address of an endpoint changes. Which rule needs to change, and what does it need to change to? You get the picture—now that I've mentioned it, to get a picture, there is a cool feature discussed in the next section called a network map.

FIGURE 3.45   IP restrictions for a SQL Azure

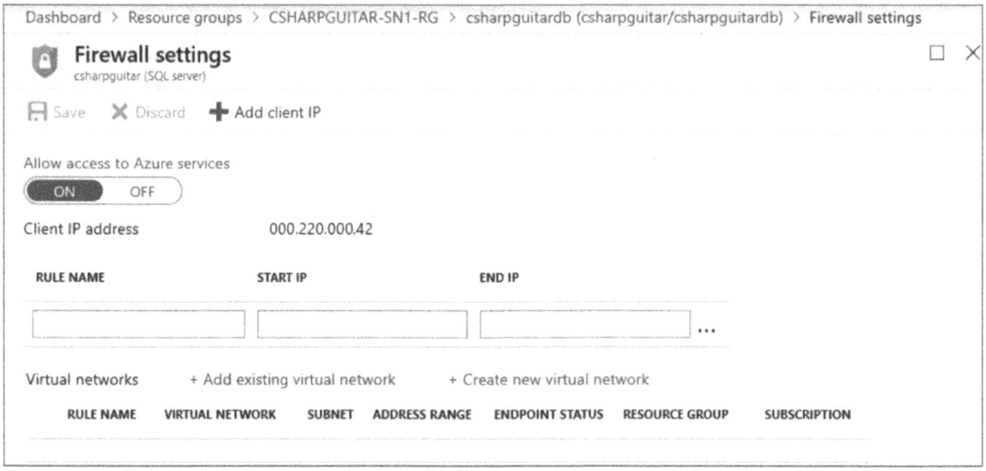

Dashboard > Resource groups > CSHARPGUITAR-SN1-RG > csharpguitardb (csharpguitar/csharpguitardb) > Firewall settings

Firewall settings
csharpguitar (SQL server)

☐ Save   ✕ Discard   ➕ Add client IP

Allow access to Azure services
(ON   OFF)

Client IP address   000.220.000.42

RULE NAME	START IP	END IP

···

Virtual networks   + Add existing virtual network   + Create new virtual network

RULE NAME	VIRTUAL NETWORK	SUBNET	ADDRESS RANGE	ENDPOINT STATUS	RESOURCE GROUP	SUBSCRIPTION

FIGURE 3.46   IP restrictions for an Azure storage account

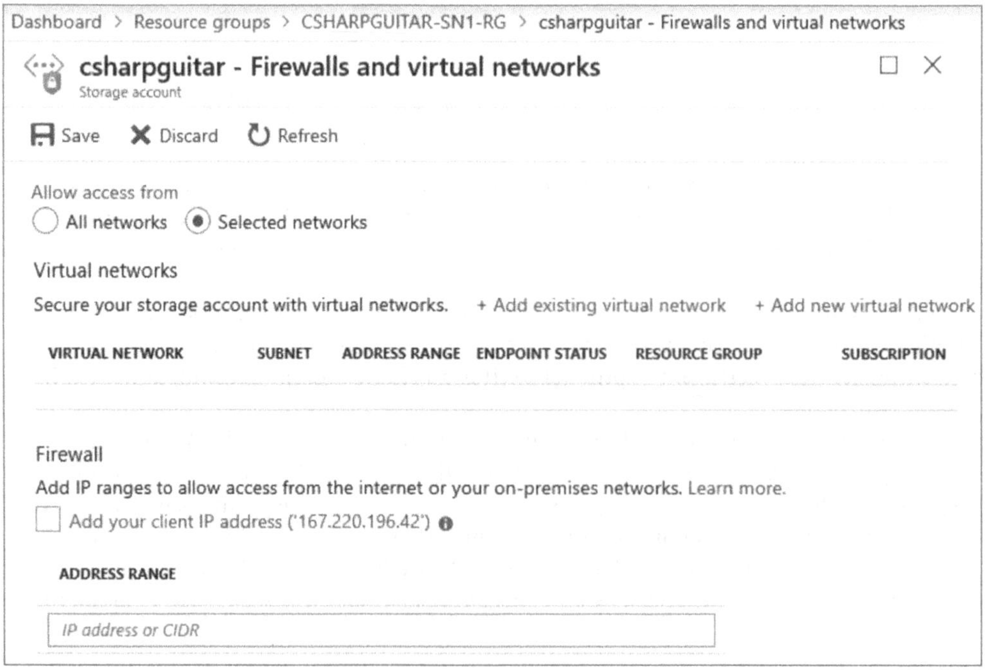

Dashboard > Resource groups > CSHARPGUITAR-SN1-RG > csharpguitar - Firewalls and virtual networks

csharpguitar - Firewalls and virtual networks
Storage account

☐ Save   ✕ Discard   ↻ Refresh

Allow access from
◯ All networks   ⦿ Selected networks

Virtual networks
Secure your storage account with virtual networks.   + Add existing virtual network   + Add new virtual network

VIRTUAL NETWORK	SUBNET	ADDRESS RANGE	ENDPOINT STATUS	RESOURCE GROUP	SUBSCRIPTION

Firewall
Add IP ranges to allow access from the internet or your on-premises networks. Learn more.

☐ Add your client IP address ('167.220.196.42') ⓘ

ADDRESS RANGE

IP address or CIDR

Network Map and Topology

There are two cool features that can help customers get a nice overview of their network topology. The first one is called a *network map* and is accessible via the Security Center, which was discussed in Chapter 2. Simply navigate to the Security Center, click Networking on the navigation menu, and click Network Map on the Networking blade. As shown in Figure 3.47, the connectivity between VNets, subnets, and the Azure VMs within them are displayed.

FIGURE 3.47   Security Center networking map topology

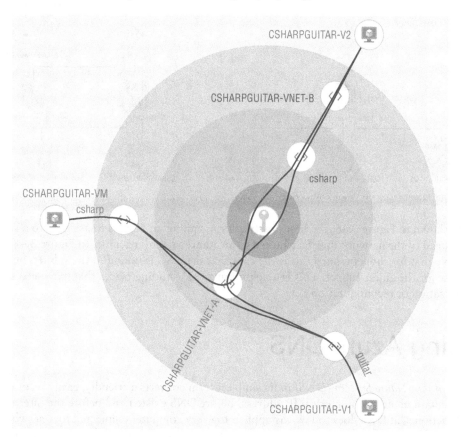

The lines flowing between them show the allowed traffic flow between all the resource in the selected Azure subscription. The Azure subscription is depicted by the key in the center of the image. Had there been an Azure VM that wasn't able to make connection with another, this map would help visualize why this could be.

Another helpful visualization of network topology within a given resource group is available using the Network Watcher. Navigate to this feature, select Topology from the navigation menu, and select the subscription and resource group. Figure 3.48 shows a graphical representation of the network topology for the resources in resource group CSHARPGUITAR-DB3-RG.

FIGURE 3.48   Network Watcher topology view

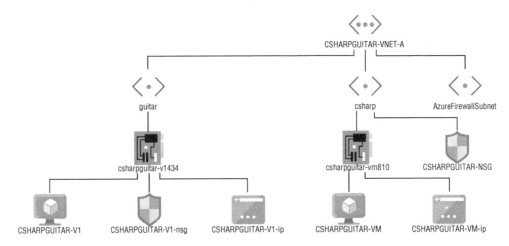

As shown in Figure 3.48, the best practice for assigning an NSG is to assign it to a subnet instead of the network interface linked to an Azure virtual machine. In Figure 3.48, it is visible that for subnet csharp this is the case that the NSG is bound to the subnet, but not the case for the guitar subnet. This is a helpful image for finding places that may need some optimization or reconfiguration.

Using Azure DNS

The *Domain Name System (DNS)* in its simplest term converts a friendly, easily recognizable domain name to a numerical IP address. Before DNS existed and before the internet, the function that DNS does today was applied to every computer connected to a network. If you look into your C:\Windows\Systems32\drivers\etc directory, there will be a file named hosts. This file contains a mapping between a friendly name and the IP address to which it routes. As you can imagine, this is neither a scalable nor a secure way of managing where domain names map to. The configurations in that file would apply today and can be used to route, for example www.bing.com, to any desired IP address, but keep in mind that works only for the computer with that configuration in the hosts file.

DNS is today maintained by numerous trusted internet authorities. Name servers are the nodes that house the DNS database of domain name to IP address mappings. When you decide to expose a custom domain to the internet, you typically contact a domain hosting provider, like GoDaddy, for example. Once the domain is purchased, their portal allows you to choose the name servers that will host the DNS entry and to insert, update, and delete DNS records. There are a large number of possible DNS records; however, in the context of Azure, the most popular and utilized records are shown in Table 3.15.

TABLE 3.15   DNS Record Types

Type	Description
A	Binds the domain name to an IP address
CNAME	Configures an alias for a domain name
MX	Used for configuring email exchanges and capabilities
NS	Delegates a DNS zone to use specific authoritative name servers
SOA	Specifies information about an authoritative name server
TXT	This is commonly used for verification of ownership.

A TXT record, as stated, is often used to validate ownership of the domain. It is common that the domain is purchased from a domain provider, and then the website is hosted someplace else, like on Azure. To bind that domain to a website on Azure, there needs to be a way to prove that the person attempting the bind really owns it. It is rightly assumed that if someone has the required access to add a DNS record, they indeed own it. During the binding process, you are asked to add a unique code as a TXT record. The verification process reads the DNS record for the domain, and if the unique code is found and matched, then the system allows the binding to occur.

An MX record is used a lot with configuring Office 365, as this is where email is often configured. It simply contains the name of the mail server to route the sending and receiving of SMTP traffic. (NS and SOA are discussed later in regard to private DNS and DNS zones.) CNAME records are bound to an alias; for example, an alias of www is bound to csharpguitarnet.azurewebsites.net for domain www.csharpguitar.net, while an A record binds a naked domain for example, csharpguitar.com (a domain name without a prefix) to a specific IP address. Use nslookup on www.csharpguitar.net and csharpguitar.com to see how the DNS records look. The output should be similar to Figure 3.49.

FIGURE 3.49   Using nslookup to view CNAME and an A record DNS configurations

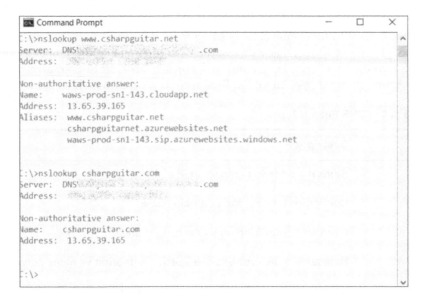

The output also identified the DNS server and the IP address of the DNS server that resolved the DNS query. The IP address of the DNS server is helpful to know because of the many different servers that can provide this service. Sometimes the data on the servers can get out of sync. Consider needing to change the IP address of a website hosting csharpguitar.com. You can imagine that a lot of DNS servers need to be updated; every name server on the entire internet needs to be updated, and the time lag can be up to 48 hours.

In the context of performing updates, two specific topics need some more attention. The first is the A record versus CNAME and *time-to-live (TTL)*. As just mentioned, it can take up to 48 hours for a change to replicate throughout the internet, so when you have an A record bound to a static IP address and that IP address needs to urgently change, you may have some downtime. Cloud-based IP addresses have a reputation of sometimes changing, and if the IP address of the website the domain is bound to changes unexpectedly, you're down. That's why using a CNAME is much more redundant. It is bound to an alias; if the IP address of the alias changes, there is no problem because the domain name still points to the alias. Watch out for that.

The reason it can take up to 48 hours to replicate a change is that there are different layers of DNS servers. To keep that database stable, other DNS servers that help manage the load draw from the official source and cache the values on other servers. When you configure a DNS record, part of that configuration is the TTL value. The TTL value is an amount of time that the record is stored in cache before attempting an update. Keep in mind that the shorter the time frame, the more load it places on the authoritative servers and the name servers, so keep a balance, and the internet will run faster.

Azure-Provided DNS

DNS servers are hosted inside the Microsoft global network and are optimized in a way so that requests needing name resolution access the nearest DNS name server, which speeds up the transmission. This feature is provided by default. Configuring the public DNS is simple; complete Exercise 3.11 to see how.

EXERCISE 3.11

Configuring Azure DNS for an Azure VM

1. Log in to the Azure Portal at `portal.azure.com`.

2. Navigate to one of the Azure VMs that has been created in a previous exercise (for example, CSHARPGUITAR-V1) on the Overview blade. There will be an item named DNS Name with a value of Configure, which is a link; click it.

3. When the Configuration blade for the associated public IP address of the VM is rendered, add a DNS name label to the text box (for example, csharpguitar-v1) and click Save.

4. The FQDN will then be accessible from the internet. Open a browser and enter the FQDN (for example, `csharpguitar-v1.northeurope.cloudapp.azure.com`).

5. Make a remote desktop connection using RDP to the Azure VM and perform an `nslookup` for both the FQDN and the NETBIOS name, which is the server name without the extension. Notice that in Figure 3.50, the FQDN query returns the public IP address and the NETBIOS returns the private IP address. The Azure-provided DNS service manages this data and service.

FIGURE 3.50   Azure-provided DNS `nslookup` queries

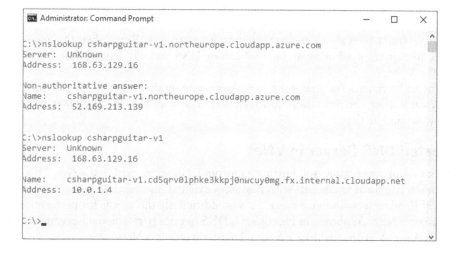

It is not possible to use Azure DNS to purchase a domain name; a service named App Service Domains is the place to make that purchase. Azure DNS is used to host information about domains as records. If you do choose to purchase a domain from Microsoft, using App Service domains, the process creates what is called a *DNS zone*.

Azure Public DNS

A DNS zone is synonymous with having a public DNS. Typically, the management of DNS records has been performed using the portal provided by the domain provider, like GoDaddy. A DNS zone supports the movement of that capability into the Azure Portal. The benefit is that you have one less portal to access and one less profile and credentials required to perform tasks.

This is where the two DNS records mentioned earlier come into play with Azure: NS and SOA. An NS entry into the DNS records is necessary to migrate the DNS management into the Azure Portal. The hosting provider does usually provide a group of four name servers; however, if you would like to move this to Azure, then Azure provides you with the name servers, and the name server records at the domain hosting company would need to be updated with Azure's. Additionally, an NS record must be added to the DNS zone. When the NS record is created, the SOA record type is also automatically inserted. A *start of authority (SOA)* record notifies that the maintenance of the domain will no longer be happening at the parent domain hosting company; instead, it is being delegated to the authority identified in the SOA record.

Azure Private DNS

Private DNS hosting is a feature that allows the configuration of DNS entries for Azure VMs hosted in VNets to be accessible using a domain name. This is different than what was performed in Exercise 3.11 in two ways. First, the domain name of the Azure VM is publicly accessible; anyone in the world with internet access can reach the endpoint.

The other difference is that the provided domain name ends with azure.com, which is not your own. The custom domain bound to an Azure VM can be something like private.csharpguitar.net. Then any Azure VM bound to this would be accessible using csharpguitar-v1.private.csharpguitar.net. Remember, though, that this domain resolved using an internal private DNS and will work only for servers within the VNet.

In a hybrid scenario, you may need to make custom modification to a DNS server, which is not possible using the procedures just reviewed. The next section covers how to implement a scenario like that.

Dedicated DNS Server in VNet

Azure does support creating and hosting a custom DNS server within a VNet. This is helpful for when you want to connect with resources existing on-premise using a friendly name instead of IP addresses, and vice versa. This is additionally the means for performing the same across VNets. As shown in Figure 3.51, DNS queries performed on-premise can be routed to Azure VMs hosted in a VNet and across multiple VNets.

FIGURE 3.51   Dedicated Azure DNS server

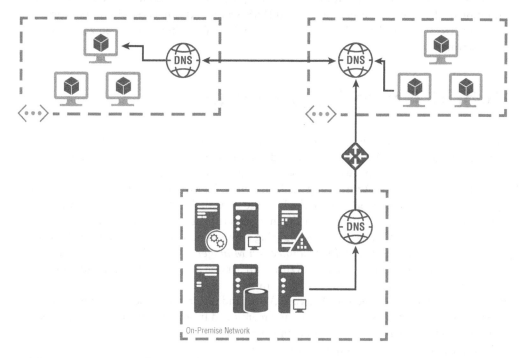

This scenario is a sophisticated one requiring lots of configurations, design, and maintenance. Only larger corporations would need to implement such a scenario. Nonetheless, it is useful to know that this capability exists. The feature is accessible on the VNet blade into which you would like the DNS server to be active. It looks something like Figure 3.52.

FIGURE 3.52   Dedicated Azure DNS server configuration

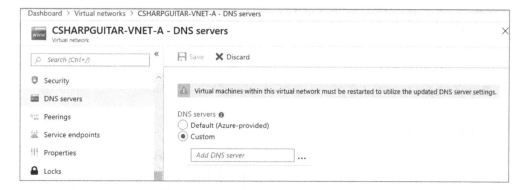

If this is a chosen implementation requirement, then the DNS server software and configuration of the server identified in the Add DNS Server text box is required. As shown also in Figure 3.52, the Azure VMs in the VNet will need a reboot to recognize the DNS server settings.

Hybrid Azure Networking

Hybrid networking has been described in numerous contexts, and this chapter's introduction includes a solid description of hybrid networking. In summary, a hybrid Azure network is a combination of two networks, most commonly an on-premise network and a network that is hosted on Azure using an Azure virtual network. Two fundamental advantages of hybrid Azure networking are the increase of available data center capacity and the ability to upgrade the sophistication of the infrastructure at a reasonable price.

There are numerous methods for configuring a hybrid network connection, such as site-to-site, point-to-site, and the *Hybrid Connection Manager (HCM)*. HCM uses Azure Relay to create a secure connection between Azure App Service and any accessible endpoint. You will configure HCM in a later exercise, but, for now, know that it is a useful tool for making simple and secure connections between Azure and on-premise resources. Numerous other connectivity options have been already mentioned in the "VNets and Subnets" section. Additionally, there is more to come in Chapter 6.

Before we continue, here's a question for you:

> True or false: A custom DNS is required to create a connection between a VNet and an on-premise network.
>
> The answer is false. A custom DNS is necessary if the connections will use friendly names instead of IP addresses to connect with servers between a VNet and on-premise network.

In this section, the additional hybrid Azure networking topics are discussed in more detail.

- ExpressRoute
- Site-to-site (S2S) VPN gateway
- Forced tunneling

ExpressRoute

ExpressRoute is the only way to connect to an on-premise network from and to Azure without traversing over the internet. All other connection methods do. A benefit of ExpressRoute is its built-in redundancy. The redundancy is realized with *ExpressRoute circuits,* where a circuit consists of two connections to two *Microsoft Enterprise edge (MSEE) routers.* These routers support layer 3 connectivity and implement *Border Gateway*

Protocol (BGP) sessions. BGP sessions are a means for efficiently routing data transmissions between on-premise and Azure-hosted resources. See Figure 3.53. ExpressRoute also guarantees the speed and bandwidth available to customers, which depend on the selected pricing tier.

FIGURE 3.53   ExpressRoute diagram with circuits

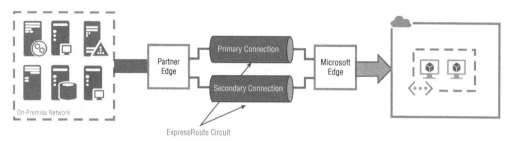

Other benefits are the connectivity options between regions and global and government clouds. Regional connectivity is actually a connection within a geopolitical region. Recall from Table 3.3 that geopolitical regions are groups of regions within a geography. For example, a customer can connect through ExpressRoute configured for North Central US and have connectivity to all Azure cloud services in South Central US as well. There is also an option to have global access to Azure cloud services, whereby ExpressRoute crosses geopolitical boundaries. Government clouds, which require a different configuration, are excluded but still supported.

The interconnectivity between cloud resources in different geopolitical regions is important in merger and acquisition scenarios. Take, for example, two fictional companies, CSHARP INC and GUITAR GmbH, that decided to merge so that synergies could be realized and IT costs could possibly be reduced. CSHARP INC was primarily running operations from the South Central US (SN1) Azure region, and GUITAR GmbH was doing operations in Europe and hosted its Azure resources in North Europe (DB3). Both companies had existing ExpressRoute configurations. The companies desired connectivity between the Azure resources in both Azure subscriptions and on-premise networks. This would require full support of cross-geopolitical network connectivity similar to that shown in Figure 3.54.

Notice from the figure that the connectivity between the two VNets in the different subscription is configured by simply using VNet peering. Global VNet peering is what was configured in Exercise 3.6 previously and provides verification that this kind of connectivity does support any network with a reachable endpoint, regardless if the endpoint is between subnets in a VNet, between VNets in the same subscription but in different regions, or between endpoints in VNets in different subscriptions. That is a flexible product. One final note to be covered now has to do with the connectivity between the ExpressRoute configurations of both companies, CSHARP INC and GUITAR Gmbh. Connectivity is configured on the ExpressRoute circuits using routing tables and the associated virtual network gateways, which are discussed in more detail next.

FIGURE 3.54 Cross-geopolitical ExpressRoute networking

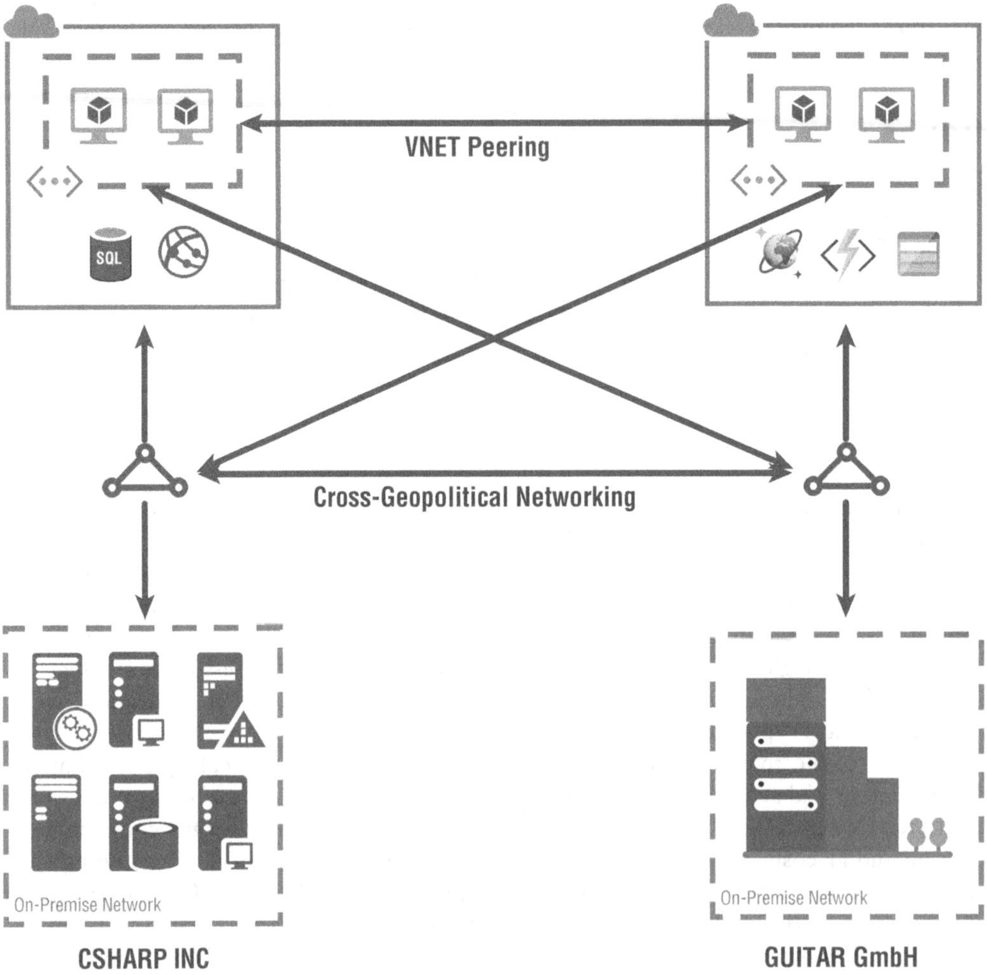

CSHARP INC   GUITAR GmbH

Site-to-Site VPN Gateway

If you need a refresher about what an S2S diagram looks like, refer to Figure 3.33. That diagram shows an on-premise network connecting through a secure tunnel to a VPN gateway and into the Azure VNet. You may also recall Exercise 3.6, where a VNet-to-VNet configuration was performed. A difference between S2S and VNet-to-VNet configuration (VNet peering) is that no VPN gateway is required to make the connection between the two VNets. This leads people to question what specifically a VPN gateway is and what role does it play regarding S2S. The answer to those questions will play out in the following text.

There are two pieces of the equation to successfully configure an S2S connection that is not available on Azure. The first piece is a VPN device that exposes an internet-accessible IP address that allows traffic into and out of the on-premise network. The second is of course the on-premise network. Those two parts are relatively unique, proven by the fact there are lists of supported VPNs devices; see the list here:

`docs.microsoft.com/en-us/azure/vpn-gateway/vpn-gateway-about-vpn-devices`

Some VPNs are not supported. Some VPN devices have compatibility issues that can be resolved with some low-level configurations and configuration scripts requiring execution on those on-premise side VPNs. Having a good scenario for that would be hard to realize, and therefore the steps required to create the S2S are discussed here instead of a full-blown exercise.

There are seven steps required to configure S2S connectivity between an Azure VNet and an on-premise one.

1. Create a virtual network.

2. Specify a DNS server.

3. Create a gateway subnet.

4. Create a VPN gateway.

5. Create a local network gateway.

6. Configure your VPN device.

7. Create the VPN connection.

Create a Virtual Network

For certain it isn't possible to make a connection from a VNet to an on-premise network without having a VNet. In Exercise 3.2, a VNet named CSHARPGUITAR-VNET-A was created. Then later in Exercise 3.6 where global VNet peering was performed, CSHARPGUITAR-VNET-B was created. It is safe to say that if those two exercises have been completed, then you know how to create a virtual network.

Specify a DNS Server

In the previous section "Dedicated DNS Server in VNet," the purpose of a dedicated DNS server was discussed. Additionally, Figure 3.52 provided a graphic depiction of how to configure the DNS server into a VNet. The existence of a dedicated DNS server in a VNet is optional and is added when the use of friendly host names for accessing on-premise servers is desired over IP addresses. The default for utilizing DNS services is the Default (Azure-provided) DNS server.

If the dedicated DNS server names do not resolve as expected, be sure to reboot the Azure VMs in that VNet after the DNS servers. A tool named `nameresolver` can expose the DNS server the Azure VM is using to perform the host name to IP address conversion. Copy the `nameresolver` program to the Azure VM and execute the following command:

`nameresolver CSHARPGUITAR-V1.`

Figure 3.55 illustrates the output of the previous code line, where CSHARPGUITAR-V1 is the name of the Azure VM in the VNet.

FIGURE 3.55 Determining which DNS is resolving host names

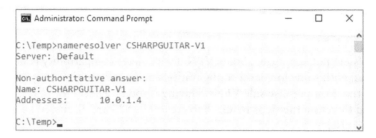

Notice that the value for Server is Default, which identifies that the Default (Azure-provided) DNS server is the one that resolved the DNS name to an IP address. If there was a dedicated DNS server configured, you would expect to see the name of that DNS server.

Create a Gateway Subnet

Each time a VNet is created, a default subnet is created, as well. Take, for example, when an Azure Firewall instance is created; it must exist in a subnet named AzureFirewallSubnet. The same goes for the creation of a VPN gateway. The VPN gateway must be created as a gateway subnet (not a regular one) named GatewaySubnet. You may recall from a previous exercise when creating a subnet that you navigated to the Virtual Networks blade, selected Subnets, and selected + Subnet. In this case, as shown in Figure 3.56, you need to select + Gateway Subnet instead.

FIGURE 3.56 Adding a gateway subnet

Notice the subnet name is grayed out and cannot be modified. Subnets are containers defined by address ranges (for example, 10.0.3.0/24), which are allocated to servers existing within them. But why is this subnet required, and what goes into it that helps make the connection between a VNet and an on-premise network? Read the next section for that answer. Just as a teaser, a VPN gateway requires physical or virtual hardware to work.

Create the VPN Gateway

A gateway subnet is created to accommodate Azure VMs that are responsible for routing data transmissions between Azure and the on-premise network. Basically, they house the routing tables that are necessary for managing the movement of data, as you now certainly know. The Azure VMs placed into this subnet are not accessible or configurable; they are managed and maintained by the Azure platform.

A complete S2S configuration is not going to be implemented in this book, but let's go ahead and create a VPN gateway just to see how it is done and perhaps learn some more interesting facts. (You need a physical on-premises VPN device to complete Exercise 3.12.)

EXERCISE 3.12

Creating an Azure VPN Gateway

1. Log in to the Azure Portal at portal.azure.com.

2. Navigate to an existing VNet (for example, CSHARPGUITAR-VNET-A), select Subnets from the navigation menu, click + Gateway Subnet, leave all the defaults, and then click the OK button.

3. In the search box (you can find it at the top of the portal) enter **Virtual Network Gateways**, click Virtual Network Gateways in the drop-down, and click + Add.

4. Select the desired subscription, provide a name (CSHARPGUITAR-DB3-VPNGW-A), and select a region. (The region should be the same as the location of the VNet where the gateway subnet was created in step 2.)

5. Select Basic from the SKU drop-down and then select Virtual Network from the drop-down, which should be populated with the VNet selected in step 2.

6. Create a new public IP address and provide a name for the address (for example, CSHARPGUITAR-DB3-VPNGW-A-IP). On the Basics tab (similar to that shown in Figure 3.57) click the Review + Create button, and then click the Create button.

FIGURE 3.57   VPN gateway basic configuration

There are a few options that remained at their default settings. Let's discuss them a bit more now, starting with Gateway Type. It is correct to assume that the configuration of ExpressRoute also requires a VPN gateway where the type is ExpressRoute. When you select the ExpressRoute radio button, the list of SKU types changes to those available for that type. The scenario for Exercise 3.12 is for a VPN, and therefore the default remained as VPN. The options available in the SKU drop-down list concern price, the number of tunnels, connections, and redundancy. Table 3.16 summarizes the limits.

TABLE 3.16   VPN Gateway SKU Types

SKU	Tunnels/Connections	Throughput	Zone Redundant
Basic	10/128	100 Mbps	✗
VpnGw1	30/128 to 250	650 Mbps	✗
VpnGw3	30/128 to 1000	1.25 Gbps	✗
VpnGw1AZ	30/128 to 250	650 Mbps	✓
VpnGw3AZ	30/128 to 1000	1.25 Gbps	✓

The SKU limits and pricing change frequently, so only a summary is provided. One would expect that the more capacity and redundancies in the SKU, the higher the price. This is the reason for selecting a basic SKU in Exercise 3.12—just to avoid any price shock during the exercise. Your needs for a required SKU will be company-specific. Keep in mind, however, that it is not possible to scale from Basic up to a higher-level SKU. It is, however, possible to scale from VpnGw1 to VpnGw2/3 or from VpnGw1AZ to VpnGw2/3AZ, so in a real-world application, avoid Basic unless you are certain scaling up will not be required in the future or if you simply want to test a product.

The next set of radio buttons are Route-based and Policy-based. This configuration determines how the VPN will decide to allow IP traffic through the VPN tunnel or not. If a route-based VPN is selected, then the routing table (the ones hosted on VMs in the GatewaySubnet) makes the decision to allow the traffic. If the route exists, then the traffic is allowed in; otherwise not. A policy-based VPN doesn't use routing tables; policy-based VPN are constrained to the Basic VPN SKU. It is a legacy configuration that requires special hardware and additional configuration.

The Assignment set of radio buttons, Dynamic and Static, apply to the public IP address, and the names imply the meaning. To be allocated a static public IP address requires the selection of a SKU of VpnGw1/2/3AZ. Additionally, when either of those three SKUs is selected, a drop-down box containing the type of zone redundancy required for the VPN gateway is presented. Zone redundancy was discussed earlier in this chapter, as well as in Chapter 1; it will also be discussed in Chapter 5 and Chapter 9. The same redundancy concepts apply here. The selection is dependent on how reliable the connectivity must be. This is solution-specific and has significant cost considerations. Finally, by enabling active-active mode, the VPN gateway is allocated with a second public IP address. This provides a level of redundancy in addition to the zone redundancy capabilities. It does make sense to have redundancies that avoid a single point of failure for mission-critical IT solutions, which is what configuring active-active mode for the VPN gateway does.

Congrats on the successful configuration of a VPN gateway; that wasn't so hard! The remaining steps happen outside of Azure and the testing of the connectivity after completing the S2S connection.

Create a Local Network Gateway

The Azure feature named *local network gateway* requires configuration to make an S2S connection from Azure to an on-premise network. The most significant requirements for this configuration are the IP address of the on-premise VPN gateway and the CIDR address ranges, which exist within the on-premise network. The IP address is the one that is linked to the device configured in the next step. The IP address is a public IP address, which is accessible by any device with a connection to the internet. The CIDR address ranges cannot overlap each other. Up to now, the exercises have used the address ranges 10.0.0.0/24, 10.0.1.0/24, 10.0.2.0/24, 10.0.3.0/24, 10.1.0.0/24, and 10.1.1.0/24. The on-premise address range should not overlap any of those existing ranges; for example, an on-premise address range of 10.0.0.0/24 would overlap, as would any of the other examples. Remember, however, that in this example the defaults were always used. Those CIDR ranges can be configured for any private IP address ranges.

Configure Your VPN Device

This is the place where configuration happens 100% outside of the Azure platform, and its configuration is unique to the company making the S2S configuration. These are some helpful documents:

- List of VPN devices:

  docs.microsoft.com/en-us/azure/vpn-gateway/vpn-gateway-about-vpn-devices

- Cryptographic VPN requirements:

  docs.microsoft.com/en-us/azure/vpn-gateway/vpn-gateway-about-compliance-crypto

- Known compatibility issues:

  docs.microsoft.com/en-us/azure/vpn-gateway/vpn-gateway-about-vpn-devices#known

There is a lot more helpful documentation, examples, and scripts available online. In addition, if you get stuck and need some advice, it is possible to open a support case with Microsoft, which will help you be successful. Don't forget about that option.

Create the VPN Connection

The VPN connection is created on the VPN gateway, which you created earlier in Exercise 3.12 (i.e., CSHARPGUITAR-VPNGW-A). Navigate to that VPN gateway, click the Connections option in the navigation menu, and click + Add. The blade illustrated in Figure 3.58 provides the template for entering the required information for creation.

FIGURE 3.58 S2S VPN connection

The Connection Type drop-down list contains VNet-to-VNet, ExpressRoute, and Site-to-Site. We are configuring a site-to-site connection here. The local network gateway is the one that contains the on-premise public IP address and the address ranges within the on-premise network. There is a shared key that acts like a password or token that must match the value set when configuring the on-premise VPN. This gets validated after the OK button is clicked (see Figure 3.58) and the connectivity between the two VPNs is tested. On the Connections blade for the given virtual network gateways, the list of connections along with their status is displayed. If the status shows Connected, then the configuration is successful.

The connectivity can be tested in the similar manner as tested when setting up VNet peering in Exercise 3.6. Log in to an Azure VM on the VNet. If the server is running a web service that can respond to HTTP requests, you can attempt to curl to a server in the on-premise network using a private IP address.

```
curl -G <Private IP address>:80
```

If the response is a successful one, then mission complete! That really wasn't so complex; the most difficult part is getting the connectivity between the two public VPN devices to work out. It is complicated only if the details of the VPNs are unknown. When performing this, make sure all the people with the knowledge are present to discuss this implementation and, by all means, contact Microsoft early on if there are problems.

Forced Tunneling

Forced tunneling can have more than a single meaning. When it was mentioned earlier, it was in the context of a DMZ (see Figure 3.59). In this context, forced tunneling is the process of routing traffic from an Azure VNet that is intended to access an internet-hosted resource through the S2S connection into the on-premise network. Once the traffic enters the on-premise network, it can then flow out into the internet. A reason for this kind of routing is for auditing and inspection reasons. Figure 3.59 illustrates this forced tunneling application.

FIGURE 3.59   Forced tunneling diagram

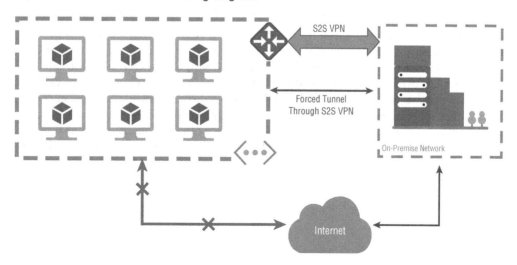

The way forced tunneling works is through the configuration of the user-defined routing table entries. Take a look back at Figure 3.13. By default any destination IP address that does not match an existing route defaults to the address prefix of 0.0.0.0/0 and is assigned a NextHopType of Internet. This means that even after the configuration of an S2S connection and the VPN gateway, traffic to the internet from an Azure VM hosted in the VNets will go directly to the internet. To force that traffic through the VPN gateway, the S2S connection must be set to the -NextHopType for 0.0.0.0/0 to VirtualNetworkGateway.

There currently is no Azure Portal interface to perform this action. The recommended way to set the NextHopType value is to use PowerShell. The following PowerShell script adds forced tunneling to the S2S VPN gateway:

```
New-AzRouteTable -Name "CSHARPGUITAR-DB3-ROUTE-TABLE" `
                -ResourceGroupName "CSHARPGUITAR-DB3-RG" `
                -Location "North Europe"
$rt = Get-AzRouteTable -Name "CSHARPGUITAR-DB3-ROUTE-TABLE" `
                -ResourceGroupName "CSHARPGUITAR-DB3-RG"
Add-AzRouteConfig -Name "ForcedTunnelRoute" `
                -AddressPrefix "0.0.0.0/0" `
                -NextHopType VirtualNetworkGateway `
                -RouteTable $rt
Set AzRouteTable -RouteTable $rt
$vnet = Get-AzVirtualNetwork -Name "CSHARPGUITAR-VNet-A" `
                -ResourceGroupName "CSHARPGUITAR-DB3-RG"
Set-AzVirtualNetworkSubnetConfig -Name "csharp" -VirtualNetwork $vnet `
                -AddressPrefix "10.0.0.0/24" `
                -RouteTable $rt
Set-AzVirtualNetwork -VirtualNetwork $vnet
```

You can find this PowerShell script here:

github.com/benperk/ASA/blob/master/Chapter03/ForcedTunnelRoute.ps1

It is not possible to change the default routing rules provided by Azure. To implement any kind of change, it is necessary to create a new routing table and add, update, or delete routes from there. This is what the previous PowerShell script does. Once the routing table named CSHARPGUITAR-DB3-ROUTE-TABLE is created, it is bound to the csharp subnet, which exists in the CSHARPGUITAR-VNET-A virtual network. Remember that routes with a Source value equal to User take a higher precedence over a route with the same prefix created by default. This is the case here since after adding the previous route for the VirtualNetworkGateway there would be two routes with an AddressPrefix value of 0.0.0.0/0.

Execute the next PowerShell cmdlet to see the effective routes after the addition of the route that implemented forced tunneling:

```
Get-AzEffectiveRouteTable -NetworkInterfaceName csharpguitar-vm810 `
 -ResourceGroupName CSHARPGUITAR-DB3-RG | Format-Table
```

Figure 3.60 provides the output of the cmdlet.

FIGURE 3.60   Forced tunneling route table example

Name	DisableBgpRoutePropagation	State	Source	AddressPrefix	NextHopType	NextHopIpAddress
	False	Active	Default	{10.0.0.0/16}	vnetLocal	{}
	False	Active	VirtualNetworkGateway	{10.5.0.0/24}	VirtualNetworkGateway	{40.115.104.24}
ForcedTunnelRoute	False	Active	User	{0.0.0.0/0}	VirtualNetworkGateway	{}
	False	Invalid	Default	{0.0.0.0/0}	Internet	{}
	False	Active	Default	{10.1.0.0/16}	VNetGlobalPeering	{}

Lastly, recognize in the PowerShell script that the subnet to which the forced tunnel is applied was provided. Recall that CSHARPGUITAR-VNET-A has two subnets, csharp and guitar. The script applied the forced tunnel route only to the csharp subnet and therefore to all the Azure VMs within that subnet. It wasn't applied to the guitar subnet. That means that although the VPN gateway is bound to CSHARPGUITAR-VNET-A, routes are applied to the subnet, and the Azure VMs in the guitar subnet will have internet traffic routed straight to the internet. They are not forced tunneled through the S2S connection through the on-premise network.

Additional Azure Networking Products

The remainder of this chapter covers some networking products that haven't fit into any other previous discussion points. These are networking-like products but are not always mentioned when discussing networking. The additional networking components covered here are as follows:

- Azure Application Gateway (not WAF)
- Azure Load Balancer
- Azure Front Door
- Azure Content Delivery Network
- Traffic Manager
- Azure Relay/Hybrid Connection Manager

The first product is Application Gateway, which has been discussed previously; however, only the WAF portion of it was discussed. Application Gateway provides many more capabilities other than a WAF.

Application Gateway

Since the late 1990s running a web application on multiple servers behind some kind of network balancing device has been the norm. This architectural configuration is referred to as a *web farm*. It makes a lot of sense to have multiple servers running the same application from a redundancy perspective. There is no single point of failure. Since the 1990s those network balancing devices have become much more sophisticated and have enhanced their capabilities to more than just a simple device that directs traffic to a group of servers configured behind it.

The web application firewall capability found in the Application Gateway product is world-class. It provides network capabilities primarily focused on OSI level 7, which means it can make routing decisions based on attributes contained within HTTP requests such as request header values and requested resource path. This provides additional capabilities over other network appliances that are restricted to the content available in a socket (source IP, source port, destination IP, destination port).

In addition to a WAF, the Application Gateway virtual appliance can act as a load balancer, an SSL termination point, and a redirector, plus many other features. Many of those additional features are discussed in more detail. If you have not already completed Exercise 3.10, consider doing it now. The following content expects that you have some knowledge of what Application Gateway is and how it is configured.

SSL Termination

Secure Sockets Layer (SSL) is the old, legacy name for a procedure that encrypts the transmission of data between a client and a server using the HTTPS protocol. These days *Transport Layer Security (TLS)* is the proper term. It encrypts the same as SSL but is more secure. SSL is the most common term used; it is probably OK to continue using it because people will know what you're talking about, but the days of SSL are over. The encryption/decryption of data between a client and server does have some overhead in terms of resource utilization. At some point between the two, there may be a device that is configured to terminate the secure connection, which will eliminate encryption/decryption, resulting in faster transactions and less resource consumption.

The termination of this secure connection is called *SSL termination* or *SSL offloading*, and it usually happens on an edge device like a gateway, intelligent firewall, or frontend server. By edge device, I mean a network device that sits at the entry point of a network, and after the transmission enters the network, encryption is no longer necessary. It is assumed that the network is secure, and therefore the infrastructure doesn't need to take the additional performance hit and overhead of SSL decryption communicating in a secure tunnel once inside. In addition to the improved performance, the termination of the secure connection and the decryption of the request content provide opportunities to route the request more intelligently. Attributes such as headers, the URL, cookies, and the like can be used for routing rules and logic.

Application Gateway provides the capability for both SSL termination and end-to-end SSL encryption. Some customers or applications may require encryption from end to end. Applications with highly sensitive scope or those that transmit highly sensitive data may justify this encryption type when it's required for compliance reasons. What is really neat about Application Gateway is that, even with end-to-end encryption, it is still possible to access the request attributes. Application Gateway still terminates the SSL session upon arrival; however, it encrypts the outbound traffic again before sending it onto the backend pools. Recall from Exercise 3.10 where you created a backend pool (for example, CSHARPGUITAR-WAF-BACKEND-POOL) and added an Azure VM (for example, CSHARPGUITAR-V2) to it. Configure SSL termination in Exercise 3.13 using the application gateway created previously in Exercise 3.10 (for example, CSHARPGUITAR-SN1-AGWAF).

EXERCISE 3.13

Configuring SSL Termination on an Application Gateway

1. Log in to the Azure Portal at portal.azure.com.

2. Navigate to an existing application gateway (for example, CSHARPGUITAR-SN1-AGWAF), select Listeners from the navigation menu, and click + Basic, which renders the Add Basic Listener blade.

3. Enter a name (for example, CSHARPGUITAR-LISTNER-HTTPS), enter **port_443** for the Frontend Port name, enter **443** as the port, and select the HTTPS protocol.

4. Upload the csharpguitarnet.pfx certificate, downloaded from github.com/ benperk/ASA/tree/master/Chapter03/Ch03Ex12. Or create your own using the New-SelfSignedCertificate PowerShell cmdlet.

5. Provide the name (for example, CSHARPGUITARNET), enter the password Csh@rpGu!tarN3t, and click the OK button. The form should resemble something similar to Figure 3.61.

6. Next add an HTTP setting. Click the HTTP settings from the navigation menu. Click + Add. Provide a name (for example, CSHARPGUITAR-HTTPS-SETTING). Select HTTPS as the protocol. Provide a certificate name (for example, CSHARPGUITAR-HTTPS-CER). Select the CER certificate and download a test CER from github.com/benperk/ASA/tree/master/Chapter03/Ch03Ex12. Leave the rest at the defaults and then click the OK button.

FIGURE 3.61 Application Gateway SSL termination template

7. Add a rule by selecting the Rules menu option. Select + Basic to provide a name (for example, CSHARPGUITAR-RULE-HTTP443). Select the listener created in step 3. Select the backend pool from Exercise 3.10, then select the HTTP setting created in step 6, and finally click the OK button.

8. Open a browser and access the Application Gateway virtual appliance's public IP address prefixed with HTTPS://. You should get an error because the certificate wasn't created by a trusted certificate authority; it is only a test certificate. Proceed to the site. The output for the request should resemble Figure 3.62.

FIGURE 3.62   Application Gateway SSL termination test

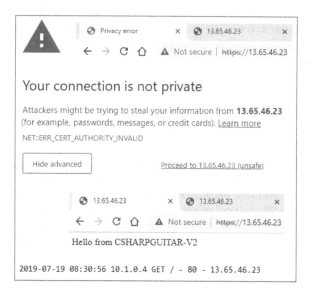

At the bottom of Figure 3.62, notice that the IP address of the client is the IP address of the Application Gateway virtual appliance that forwarded the request to CSHARPGUITAR-V2 with IP 10.1.0.4. The port used for access was 80, meaning the request did not utilize SSL. A request that used SSL would have been on port 443. That confirms the configuration of SSL termination on the Application Gateway virtual appliance is working as expected.

Auto Scaling

Auto scaling is one of the most amazing, useful, and cost-saving capabilities provided in the cloud. Auto scaling delivers enough capacity to handle the load being placed on an application. The load can come as a burst or during regular business hours. When the load is gone or those who were consuming the system go home, the resources made available to handle the load are no longer needed. When this happens, costs are reduced by scaling down and deallocating the resources.

Auto scaling is available only with the version 2 tiers of Application Gateway, Standard_v2 and WAF_v2. Figure 3.41 shows WAF as the selected tier followed by a text box showing the static number of instances. The number can be modified after creation, but the change is manual. An added complexity of manual scale is that you must guess how many instances are required and when those instances are needed. When a version 2 tier is chosen, scaling out and scaling in are based on utilization algorithms without any manual intervention. You are prompted to provide the minimum and maximum number of instances during setup.

Application Gateway Version 1 or Version 2

As a side note, version 2 also supports Availability Zones; version 1 does not.

Why would anyone use version 1 of Application Gateway and knowingly avoid auto scaling and redundancy? It all comes down to cost. The version 2 tiers cost more because they offer more features. If those features warrant the additional cost or are required to run your implementation performantly, then by all means use version 2. However, for smaller companies that don't need those features, there is an affordable tier of Application Gateway for consumption.

Hosting Multiple Websites

Application Gateway can be used to route internet traffic to different backend pools based on the host name provided in the request. This redirection is not based on load or any other algorithm other than a straight analysis of the host name and the execution of a rule based on the value of that parameter. As shown in Figure 3.63, a client sends a request to the Application Gateway endpoint based on the host name. The request is then routed to a different set of backend pools.

The backend pools can be Azure VMs of different sizes and would likely have a different set of application software running on each one. A solid use case for this is the efficient maintenance and organizational opportunities. Up to 100 hosts can be configured on a single Application Gateway virtual appliance, all of which would be routed to the same IP address. The administrator would then have a single location to configure and support all websites for a given company. The backend pool concept provides a layer of isolation between the Azure VM or group of Azure VMs, which respond to requests to a given host name.

URL Path-Based Redirection

Redirecting requests to a different set of servers through a network device based on an OSI level 7 attribute is helpful in numerous scenarios. Take, for example, two different types of requests: one is to run a report, and another is to process a customer order in real time. Running a report can be intense, taking time and resources from your compute services. Someone running a report, depending on the constraints it is running under (for example, annual versus daily sales summary), will have different expectations toward latency than someone placing an order. An annual report would run long because there exists more data to process than a daily report. Reporting systems are known to be slow sometimes.

FIGURE 3.63 Hosting multiple sites flow diagram

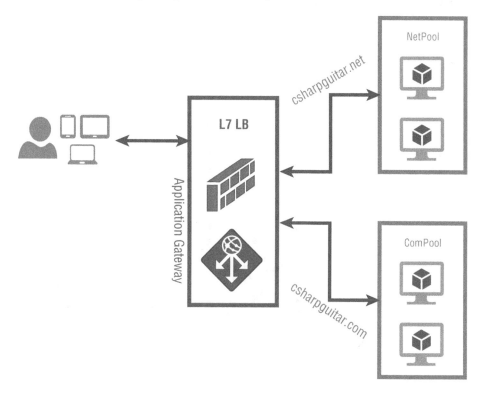

A customer placing an order expects the transaction to be very fast with little to no visible latency. If an architect for some reason hosts both types of requests on the same server or groups of servers, the resource consumption that happens with a reporting request may negatively impact the response time of an order. This is not optimal. URL path-based redirection is something that can help in that scenario. Figure 3.64 illustrates a request that contains `report` in the URL. The request is sent to a pool of Azure VMs that respond to reporting requests. Those VMs can have a higher stock-keeping unit (SKU) ratio, have a more optimal SKU with more memory, or require more CPU of the hosted reporting service.

Alternatively, when the request contains `transaction` in the URL, it in turn is routed to a separate pool. Those Azure VMs are dedicated to processing the transaction fast and furious so the customer has a great experience and returns later to make more purchases. The requests are sent to separate pools based on the URL. This improves the overall performance of the IT solution by separating requests that could impact each other and instead running them on separate machines. Perform Exercise 3.14 to configure URL-based routing.

FIGURE 3.64   URL path redirection request flow diagram

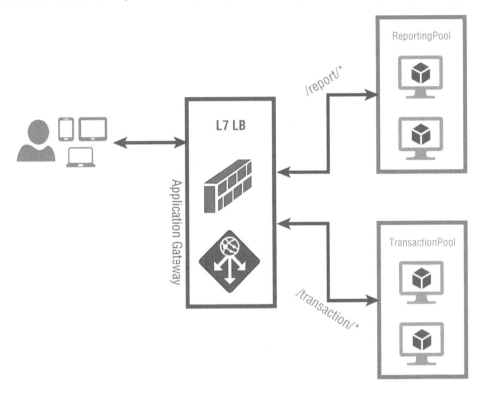

EXERCISE 3.14

Configuring URL Routing on Application Gateway

1. Log in to the Azure Portal at portal.azure.com.

2. Create a new Windows Server 2019 Azure VM (for example, CSHARPGUITAR-V3) in the same resource group as the Application Gateway virtual machine used up to this point. Be sure to enable inbound ports 80 and 3389. Once created, make a remote desktop connection using RDP and run the following PowerShell script:

```
Install-WindowsFeature -name Web-Server -IncludeManagementTools
New-Item -ItemType Directory -Force -Path "C:\inetpub\wwwroot\report"
Add-Content -Path "C:\inetpub\wwwroot\report\iisstart.htm" `
          -Value $("Hello from the report directory on " `
          + $env:computername)
```

3. Open a browser, enter the public IP address of the new Azure VM, and include the `report` path in the request. The request should resemble something similar to that found at `<public IP>/report/`.

4. Navigate to an existing Application Gateway virtual machine (for example, CSHARPGUITAR-SN1-AGWAF), select Backend Pools, select + Add, provide a name for the pool (for example, CSHARPGUITAR-REPORT-BACKEND-POOL), select Virtual Machine from the drop-down, select the Azure VM created in step 2 and its associated network interface, and then click the Add button.

5. Once the save completes, select Listeners from the navigation menu, click + Basic, provide a name (for example, CSHARPGUITAR-LISTENER-REPORT), provide a front-end port name (for example, port_8080), set the port to 8080, leave all other settings at the defaults, and then click the OK button.

6. Select Rules from the navigation menu, click + Path-based, and provide a name (for example, CSHARPGUITAR-REPORT-RULE).

7. The listener created in step 5 should be preselected; if it's not, select it. Select the backend pool created in Exercise 3.10 (for example, CSHARPGUITAR-WAF-BACKEND-POOL) as the default backend pool and then select a default HTTP settings value (for example, CSHARPGUITAR-HTTP-SETTING).

8. Next, provide a name (for example, REPORT) and path (for example, /report/*), select the backend pool (for example, CSHARPGUITAR-REPORT-BACKEND-POOL), select the HTTP setting (for example, CSHARPGUITAR-HTTP-SETTING), and then click the OK button. The final rule should resemble that shown in Figure 3.65.

FIGURE 3.65   URL path redirection Application Gateway rule

Dashboard > CSHARPGUITAR-AGWAF - Rules > CSHARPGUITAR-REPORT-RULE

CSHARPGUITAR-REPORT-RULE
CSHARPGUITAR-AGWAF

✎ Edit   🗑 Delete

Name	CSHARPGUITAR-REPORT-RULE
Type	Path-based
Listener	CSHARPGUITAR-LISTENER-REPORT
Default backend pool	CSHARPGUITAR-WAF-BACKEND-POOL
Default HTTP settings	CSHARPGUITAR-HTTP-SETTING

NAME	PATHS	BACKEND POOL	HTTP SETTING
REPORT	/report/*	CSHARPGUITAR-REPORT-BACKEND-POOL	CSHARPGUITAR-HTTP-SETTING

9. Enter the following URLs into a browser:

    ```
    <application gateway Public IP>
    <application gateway Public IP>:8080/report/
    ```

    You can find the Application Gateway virtual machine's public IP on the Overview blade associated to the frontend public IP address attribute. Figure 3.66 shows the output of those URL requests.

FIGURE 3.66   URL path redirection output

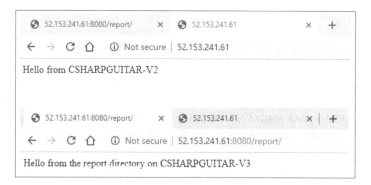

Note that the more rules, listeners, and settings you have, the more likely it is to get them to conflict. If you are working on the previous exercise and it is not working, consider removing the existing Application Gateway completely (we are in testing mode) and perform Exercise 3.13 from scratch. Notice also that in Figure 3.65 there are default settings for the rule (specifically the default backend pool, but also default HTTP settings). This means if the value entered for the path doesn't exist in the request, then the request is routed to the group/pool/setting of Azure VMs. This means that if the request included a /transaction/* in the requested URL that the request would be sent to the CSHARPGUITAR-WAF-BACKEND-POOL because there is no rule that matches. If you would like to check that out, then you need to add the transaction directory to the Azure VMs that exist in the pool (for example, CSHARPGUITAR-V2); otherwise, a 404.0 Not Found error is rendered. To achieve this, make a remote desktop connection using RDP to the server and execute the following PowerShell script:

```
New-Item -ItemType Directory -Force -Path "C:\inetpub\wwwroot\transaction"
Add-Content -Path "C:\inetpub\wwwroot\transaction\iisstart.htm" `
            -Value $("Hello from the transaction directory on " `
            + $env:computername)
```

Once executed on the Azure VM in the default backend pool, a request to either of the following URLs would be routed to the Azure VM on that backend pool (for example, CSHARPGUITAR-V2).

```
<application gateway Public IP>/transaction/
<application gateway Public IP>:8080/transaction/
```

As you begin to use this feature more, it becomes clear there are some constraints, in that it is possible to have only one listener per port, which is why port 8080 was used. Each rule must be linked to a unique listener. Figure 3.67 illustrates the hierarchy of dependencies (listener, port, HTTP settings) and the overall request pipeline.

FIGURE 3.67   Application Gateway configuration hierarchy

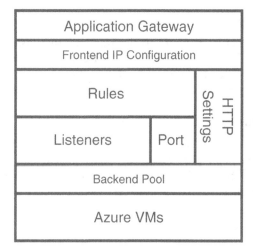

Azure Load Balancer

Having a web application running on multiple dedicated servers or VMs is a common scenario. This design provides redundancy in case one of the servers experiences a transient or fatal system issue. There also could be an application error or resource exhaustion on one server, so having others fill the void in those situations is a good design decision. A *load balancer* is a network device that is placed in front of all those servers before routing the request to a particular server in the backend pool of VMs. The load balancer exposes a single public IP address and then manages the routing of the request to one of the backend servers.

OSI Layers and Their Association to Network Appliances

Azure Firewall runs on OSI layer 3, Application Gateway and Azure Front Door both run on OSI layer 7, and Azure Load Balancer runs on layer 4. The choice of network appliance depends on the application requirements.

In the previous section, you read about a similar capability with Application Gateway. Application Gateway does provide many capabilities and features and is a valid choice for this similar scenario. The reason for having multiple products for similar scenarios is just that the scenarios are only similar; some designs or some applications running on Azure need additional or different features, and instead of putting all features into one product, many products get created. One must know the requirements of the application moving to Azure and which Azure product provides the best set of tools to meet those requirements. Azure Load Balancer provides some unique features that are discussed in the remainder of this section.

- Public load balancer
- Internal load balancer
- Health probes
- Outbound connections

Azure Load Balancer has two SKUs available, Standard and Basic. For any new implementation, it is recommended that you use the Standard SKU. It is the most secure, robust, and scalable of the two. Availability Zones, an internal load balancer, the configuration of outbound security rules, and an SLA are only available with the Standard SKU.

Public Load Balancer

During the creation of an Azure Load Balancer instance, one must choose whether it will be internal or public. Choosing a public load balancer will generate a public IP address for clients to use for connecting to the servers configured in the backend pool. Figure 3.68 illustrates the flow of a request from a client to servers in a pool of Azure VMs.

FIGURE 3.68   Public load balancer flow

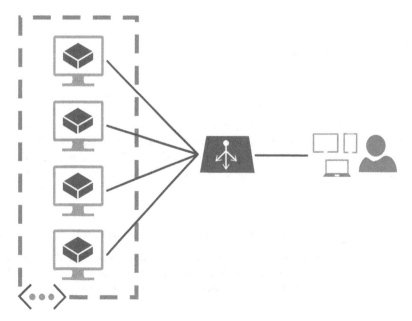

Both internal and public load balancers by default will route traffic equally to the Azure VMs configured into the backend pool. This is often referred to as *round-robin*. Using a five-tuple hash that consists of source IP, source port, destination IP, destination port, and the protocol, the load balancer routes the request to the same Azure VM for the entire transmission session. Any change in the hash values will result in the request being sent to a different server. This may be an issue if there is a need to maintain a session between the client and server. If this is the case, then Azure Load Balancer does support this using the feature called *source IP affinity mode*. This mode uses a hashed version of the source IP, destination IP, and/or the protocol to route requests to the same Azure VM for the life of the session.

Internal Load Balancer

An *internal load balancer (ILB)* will not have a public IP address and is instead configured into an existing virtual network. As shown in Figure 3.69, traffic is load balanced across a group of Azure VMs, and the connectivity from those VMs to other servers in the VNet is managed using an ILB.

FIGURE 3.69   Internal load balancer flow

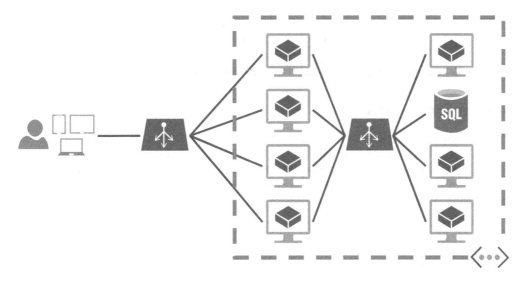

The ILB could be managing access to a group of database servers, REST APIs, or some other kind of resource needing this added level of security and resiliency.

Health Probes

Health probing is a feature that monitors the status of Azure VMs configured in the back-end pool. There are three probe types, TCP, HTTP, and HTTPS. (HTTPS is available only in Standard SKU.) The TCP probe will start a three-way TCP handshake on the configured port (for example, 80) for a given interval and will trigger an alarm if it fails more than the value placed into the unhealthy threshold box. For example, if the interval to run this probe is set to 5 seconds with an unhealthy threshold of 2, it means that if the probe fails twice in 10 seconds, then it will be removed from the pool of VMs that receive traffic. The same scenario applies to HTTP and HTTPS. The additional piece is the path, which will be probed, for example, a simple HTML.

After the creation of the load balancer, you would create the backend pool and the health probe. Then when creating the load balancing rule, you select which backend pool to route the requests to and which health probe to use for that backend pool.

Outbound Connections

Outbound connectivity has been discussed previously; however, this is a fairly complicated topic for many and deserves an additional comment. When a request arrives to the load balancer, the load balancer routes the request to one of the Azure VMs in the backend pool. Those VMs exist in a VNet and would have private IP addresses. That's no problem, but what IP address is used when the response is returned to the client? It uses the public IP address of the load balancer. Remember that this port masquerading is referred to as SNAT. The load balancer will rewrite the private IP address of the VM and replace it with the public frontend IP address of the load balancer.

Having only a single exposed IP address for an application also helps in cases of catastrophe. For example, if for some reason servers in a VNet go offline, the IP address can be mapped to another load balancer with backup instances of your application. Additionally, having only a single outbound IP reduces any whitelisting maintenance activities.

Azure Front Door

Azure Front Door is one of the newer networking products. Again, it is a product that has similarities to other networking products but targets a specific use case and type of customer. In this case, the company or organization needs to be international and have multiple instances of their Azure solutions hosted in different regions around the world. Azure Front Door offers the following features and services:

- URL-based routing
- SSL termination
- Session affinity
- Multisite hosting
- URL redirection
- Custom domains and certificate management
- Application layer security
- IPv6 and HTTP/2
- URL rewrite

Most of those features are understood simply by the name, and many have already been discussed. A few of them may not be so clear and need a little more explanation.

Multisite Hosting

Similar to the URL-based routing, URL redirection, and the URL-based redirection configured with Application Gateway in Exercise 3.13, multisite hosting is a feature that routes requests to different backend pools based on the requested URL. The primary difference with this feature is that the configuration of the domain names linked to Front Door is performed on the blade for the product being configured. Multiple domain names and subdomains can be hosted and configured directly on the Front Door portal blade. Requests to those domains will route directly to Front Door.

Custom Domains and Certificate Management

To support the multisite hosting feature, Front Door needs to support custom domains. In addition to custom domains, SSL certificates are also supported for communicating over HTTPS. The configuration of those two capabilities is built into the portal and also available using PowerShell.

Application Layer Security

Application layer security is synonymous with a web application firewall. The WAF contained within Front Door is primarily focused on attacks that happen at layer 7 such as SQL injection, cross-site scripting (XSS), and session hijacking. These kinds of vulnerabilities generally happen using the HTTP and HTTPS protocols. The concepts are the same with regard to Azure Firewall, Application Gateway (WAF), and Azure Front Door (WAF). A policy that decides whether to prevent or detect an attempted exploit is created. Review Exercise 3.10 if this is not ringing any bells. Once the policy has been created, a group of rules (commonly rules that would prevent the known vulnerabilities listed in the OWASP top 10 list) is applied. When you apply those configurations to a network device, you can sleep a little bit better knowing your application is as safe as possible.

One last capability that is available has to do with backend pools. Up to now the only resource types that could be configured into a backend pool have been Azure VMs contained within a VNet. Azure Front Door also supports products such as App Service, Azure Functions, Azure Storage, and some others. This feature allows much more control and provides more configuration opportunities. Placing a WAF in front of an Azure Functions instance or directing a specific host name to an Azure Storage container are options that come to mind.

Azure Content Delivery Network

A *content delivery network* (CDN) is used to get content as close as possible to the clients who need access to it. Azure has data centers all over the world. These result in better performance for those closest to the regional locations. However, there can be some significant improvement for customers or employees by getting the content hosted physically closer to them. In Exercise 3.1, you used Network Watcher to measure latency between two locations. Now may be a good time to go review it to see the possible latencies your customer could expect and perhaps how much faster the responsiveness of the site can be with a CDN.

To learn more about Azure Content Delivery Network, perform the following exercise. Chapter 4, "Compute," covers creating the App Service web app required to complete this exercise. If you are not familiar with that process, consider skipping Exercise 3.15. When you have completed Chapter 4, come back to this exercise.

EXERCISE 3.15

Configuring a CDN for Azure App Service

1. Log in to the Azure Portal at portal.azure.com.

2. Create an Azure App Service web app (for example, csharpguitar). See Chapter 4 for more details or follow the online instructions at docs.microsoft.com/en-us/ azure/app-service.

3. Click the Networking link in the Navigation blade and then click Configure Azure CDN for your app.

4. In the New Endpoint section, create a new endpoint (for example, CSHARPGUITAR-CDN-ENDPOINT). Select the pricing tier (for example, Standard Microsoft) and CDN endpoint name (for example, CSHARPGUITAR) and then click the Create button.

That was easy because all the magic happened behind the scenes. Configuring a custom domain (for example, www.csharpguitar.com) is most optimal in this scenario. During that process you would bind the custom domain to the azureedge.net domain so that requests made to the custom domain are responded to from the CDN. This works in the background based on the 120+ *point-of-presence (POP)* locations around the world. These POPs have edge servers that are cached with the content you want to deliver to those requesting it. A request to the domain of the site is routed to the nearest edge server for response generation. It is expected to be faster because the content is closer. It really can be significant if the content is large such as videos, audio files, or any content that consists of multiple megabytes.

A few additional features provided by an Azure CDN follow:

- CDN caching rules
- Geofiltering
- File compression
- Dynamic site acceleration

CDN Caching Rules

Managing the way content is cached, and when it gets updated, is an important aspect of a CDN. If there is ever a change to the origin server (the server that is the home to the actual production content and application), then the content on the edge servers must be updated as well. The default CDN setting expires what is cached every two to seven days depending on the selected pricing tier selected during creation. (In Exercise 3.15, the selected pricing tier was Standard Microsoft, which expires the cache every two days.)

Geofiltering

There may be some countries or locations where you do not want to have your content stored. When you set up a CDN and point it to an origin source, the content gets cached as the requests begin to flow in. Geofiltering can be used to prevent Azure CDN from caching content based on country code.

File Compression

Compressing a file simply means it will be smaller at the time of transmission, which results in faster transfer times. If a file is 30MB uncompressed but 15MB compressed, it will for certain result in faster download times when compressed. There are two methods to implement file compression in the Azure CDN context. The first is to simply implement file compression on the origin server prior to caching the content on the edge servers. This passes the compressed file from the origin to the edge server. The other method is known as *compression on the fly*, where file compression is configurable on Azure CDN. There is a navigation item in the portal named Compression on the CDN blade. The compression is based on MIME types, which classifies the kind of file being served (for example, `text/xml`, `text/css`, `application/json`, or `application/javascript`). Compression is enabled by default; however, some configuration may be required if the MIME type of your content is not in the list.

Dynamic Site Acceleration

Caching content is effective for speeding up delivery for static content. Static content means that it doesn't change. This isn't always acceptable because many applications generate content that is unique based on information posted in the request body or based on information sent in the request header. That kind of scenario isn't made for a CDN. There are some enhancements that can be made to improve the delivery of dynamic content. This is a product that comes with an additional cost called *dynamic site accelerator*. This uses new capabilities such as route and TCP optimization and prefetching. The most important takeaway here is that CDNs are most optimal for static content, and if your site is mostly dynamic, then you may not get great improvements using one.

Traffic Manager

Like Azure CDN, Azure Traffic Manager routes a request to the closest location relative to the client requesting it. This is referred to as a *geographic routing method*. In addition to the geographic routing method, ATM provides numerous other features such as a performance routing method, which monitors the endpoints and redirects requests to only healthy servers. ATM can also route requests to resources not hosted in Azure. In that scenario, consider that you are already successfully running an application on-premise. A rule of thumb is, if it's not broke, don't fix it, which means let it keep working instead of taking some action that could cause downtime. But, if that on-premise application is configured in Azure Traffic Manager, you would be able to manage bursts of traffic by having the extra elastic capacity hosted in Azure. The cost of having extra capacity waiting for a burst is not economical, but having the capacity to scale out and in when it happens is one of the most beneficial aspects of the cloud.

If the intention is to migrate the on-premise to Azure, then you can implement a weighted routing method. This means routing some traffic to one version of your application hosted on-premise while routing others on an Azure version. Once you have confidence that the application on Azure is running perfectly, disable the on-premise endpoint. If there is ever a scenario where the on-premise version is again needed, like a disaster recovery scenario, then it is a quick and easy configuration to get back up and running again.

If those scenarios make a lot of sense in the context of your application requirements, then consider the options. Don't neglect the fact that both Application Gateway and Azure Load Balancer have similar capabilities. Consider all the options of each product and make the most educated decision based on the design requirements and cost.

Azure Relay/Hybrid Connection Manager

Azure Relay is a product that provides a one-to-one or peer-to-peer connection from Azure into an on-premise network. The connection into the on-premise network doesn't require any firewall configurations, VPN gateways, or modification. The reason that it works out of the box, so to say, is because it works using ports and protocols that are typically configured and supported for other applications already. Those are ports 80 and 443 and protocols HTTP/HTTPS and WS/WSS, the latter being Web Sockets.

The way it works is that Azure Relay is built upon a service bus global endpoint (service bus is explained in greater detail in Chapter 6). This global endpoint, which is a URL similar to `csharpguitar.servicebus.windows.net`, is protected by an SAS key, which was discussed in Chapter 2. Within the portal on the Azure Relay blade there is a place to create a hybrid connection; call it, for example, `csharpguitar`. The result is a connection string that resembles something similar to the following:

```
Endpoint=sb://*.servicebus.windows.net/;SharedAccessKeyName=accsKey;
    SharedAccessKey=..
```

This connection string is then used in code to make the connecting bridge between a client and a server. Figure 3.70 illustrates the flow between the client and server.

FIGURE 3.70   Azure Relay and hybrid connection flow diagram

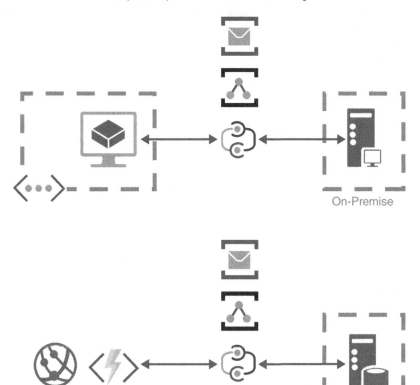

Notice that connectivity between an Azure VM and on-premise network is not the only compute resource that can make a connection like this. Additionally, Azure Functions and Azure App Service can be configured to use Azure Relay via a hybrid connection.

There is one piece missing, which is the code. Both the client and the server require custom code to manage the authentication and connectivity with the endpoint. Using the `Microsoft.Azure.Relay` NuGet package, the connectivity can be configured. Explaining how to perform the coding is outside the scope of the book, and it's not required to know this for the Azure Solutions Architect Expert exam. However, knowing this capability exists and what the purpose is would be beneficial to understand.

A use case that works well in this scenario was illustrated in Figure 3.70, where you see a frontend that exists in Azure and the backend in an on-premise network. The frontend is an App Service web app that exposes an interface for placing orders, and the data source for orders is stored is an on-premise database. Being able to scale out the frontends during a marketing campaign and then scale back in once the merchandise is sold works well with this architecture. Storing all data in the cloud has been a pressure point for some companies, and this may be a solution.

There is also a feature called the Hybrid Connection Manager, which is directly related to App Service. You'll find an exercise for this configuration in the next chapter; until then, if you have an App Service web app, click the Networking navigation menu item, and you will see Hybrid Connections in the list of networking features. If you click it, you get a link to download a connection manager. The connection manager is the server-side application that would need to be coded if you were to use connectivity from an Azure VM. Microsoft has created its own feature that uses Azure Relay for making peer-to-peer connectivity simple. The most significant aspect of the configuration of a hybrid connection between App Service and a server in an on-premise network is how simple and quick it is to do.

Key Terms

Application security groups (ASGs)

Availability Zones

Azure Firewall (AF)

Azure Traffic Manager (ATM)

Azure Virtual Network (VNet)

Border Gateway Protocol (BGP)

Classless Inter-Domain Routing (CIDR)

Content Delivery Network (CDN)

Curl

Destination network address translation (DNAT)

DNS zone

Domain Name System (DNS)

dot-decimal notation

Dynamic IP restrictions (DIPRs)

Ephemeral ports

ExpressRoute

ExpressRoute circuits

forced tunneling

Fully qualified domain names (FQDNs)

Geographies

Global VNet peering

Hop

Hops

host identifier

Hybrid Connection Manager (HCM)

Instance-level public IP (ILPIP)

Internal load balancer (ILB)

Internet Assigned Number Authority (IANA)

Internet Information Services (IIS)

IP masquerading

Local area network (LAN)

localhost

Summary

In this chapter, we covered a lot, including VNets, the Microsoft global network, SNAT, hybrid networking, TCP/IP, CIDR, VNet peering, forced tunneling, firewalls, NSGs, WAF, IP restrictions, DNS, ExpressRoute, CDN, and a lot more. Those topics introduce some sophisticated products, options, and functions. Being able to comprehend and apply these will have great impact on your path toward Azure Solutions Architect Expert certification.

Networking is a fascinating topic as it touches all aspects of computing, the internet, and certainly Azure. It shouldn't take too much convincing that one could spend their entire IT career just focusing on networking and all its techniques and concepts. Therefore, consider this chapter as simply an overview of networking; there is much more, enough to fill a few volumes of books specifically dedicated to TCP/IP, firewalls, and network security.

The fundamental intent of this chapter was to give you enough of an overview of the capabilities of Azure networking so that you can have a good chance of passing the Azure Solutions Architect Expert exam. The content in this chapter exceeds the amount of information required to pass the exam. If this area of IT interests you, then get deeper into it.

Exam Essentials

Understand Azure virtual networking.   Azure Virtual Network is the focal point for networking on the Azure platform. Understanding CIDR, subnets, and VPN connectivity is a fundamental point of focus and required expertise when migrating to Azure. Knowing how to optimally design your network requirements prior to deployment is key to success, in addition to knowing the limits and constraints in which a VNet must run.

Understand network security.   As discussed in the previous chapter, security is the most important element of an, IT solution. This applies to network security as well. Having learned about NSGs, WAFs, firewalls, and IP restrictions, you are well on your way to having a grasp of this topic. Firewalls and WAFs work on different layers of the OSI model and by doing so provide different types of security like capabilities. Applications will have different types of security requirements; however, no application should be vulnerable to known exploits. Therefore, in all efforts, apply what you know about network security by default and seek professional advice when necessary.

Understand Azure DNS.   Azure DNS is provided by default to Azure VMs so that domain names can be resolved when used. It is possible to configure a private DNS server, which is useful with the configuration of a site-to-site connection. This will allow the resources hosted in a VNet to use friendly names when connecting to servers existing in the on-premise network. Additionally, knowing DNS record types like CNAME, A, and TXT is useful, especially because they can have different impacts on applications when their IP addresses are changed.

Understand hybrid Azure networking.   Connecting two networks to gain some synergy that didn't exist when on their own is a result of hybrids. Using a VPN gateway or ExpressRoute to connect a VNet and on-premise network is the path to implementing a hybrid network. ExpressRoute doesn't send any of the traffic over the internet, while traffic through a VPN gateway does. The VPN is a secured tunnel; however, it still routes through the public internet. Channeling all outbound internet traffic from an Azure VNet through an on-premise network is referred to as forced tunneling. This is helpful for monitoring and controlling the traffic from resources hosted in an Azure VNet.

Understand Azure networking products   There are many Azure networking products, and they all have specific use cases and sets of features. Knowing the features of each, and knowing the requirements of your application are crucial in making the decision about which to use. This is important because many of the products have overlapping capabilities but also include unique features not available in other products. Azure Load Balancer, Application Gateway, and Azure Traffic Manager all have the capability to route traffic to a group of backend pool resources, for example; however, they are all a little different.

Review Questions

1. Which of the following CIDR configurations will result in the greatest number of available IP addresses?

   A. 10.0.0.0/8

   B. 10.0.0.0/24

   C. 10.0.0.0/16

   D. 10.0.0.0/32

2. Which of the following network devices offer SSL termination?

   A. Azure Front Door Service

   B. Application Gateway

   C. Load Balancer

   D. A and B

3. Which of the following offer the most optimal web application firewall for a small company needing layer 7 capabilities?

   A. Application Gateway

   B. Azure Firewall

   C. Azure Front Door

   D. Traffic Manager

4. What is true about gateway subnets?

   A. A gateway subnet must be named gwSubnet.

   B. There can be only one gateway subnet per VNet.

   C. A gateway subnet must be named Gateway-Subnet.

   D. Both B and C

5. True or false: Connectivity between resources in a VNet is enabled by default.

   A. True

   B. False

6. Which of the following is true?

   A. VNet peering connects two or more VNets that exist in the same region.

   B. VNet peering connects two or more VNets in different regions.

   C. Global VNet peering is when all VNets in a subscription are interconnected.

   D. Global VNet peering is the connection between three or more Azure regions.

7. If you want to maintain a TCP session at the firewall level, which Azure product must you implement?

    A. Application Gateway

    B. Load Balancer

    C. Azure Firewall

    D. Azure Traffic Manager

8. Which of the following is not a supported networking design pattern in Azure?

    A. Point-to-point

    B. Site-to-site

    C. Frontend-to-backend

    D. Point-to-site

9. Which of the following is not a requirement for the configuration of a hybrid site-to-site connection?

    A. VNet

    B. Gateway subnet

    C. DNS

    D. VPN

10. Which of the following cannot route web requests to a specific server in a backend pool based on information sent in the request?

    A. Azure Content Delivery Network (CDN)

    B. Azure Load Balancer

    C. Azure Front Door

    D. Azure Application Gateway

Chapter

4

Compute

EXAM AZ-303 OBJECTIVES COVERED IN THIS CHAPTER:

✓ **Implement and Monitor an Azure Infrastructure**

 ▪ Implement VMs for Windows and Linux

✓ **Implement Management and Security Solutions**

 ▪ Manage workloads in Azure

✓ **Implement Solutions for Apps**

 ▪ Implement an application infrastructure

 ▪ Implement container-based applications

EXAM AZ-304 OBJECTIVES COVERED IN THIS CHAPTER:

✓ **Design Infrastructure**

 ▪ Design a compute solution

 ▪ Design an application architecture

Companies or developers expose their applications to consumers or employees via a computer. A computer is often visualized as a workstation or laptop that is on the desk or table in front of you. However, the computer I am referring to here is a server in a data center whose sole purpose is to provide a service instead of consuming it. That's clear, right? But, because servers play such a significant role in the existence of an application, often compute products are wrongly chosen as the first point of entry and design into Azure. *Compute*, aka the hosting model, is not the most optimal entry point for production workloads. As you already know, security and networking components need to be considered prior to compute.

Beginning with the creation of an Azure compute resource before the other two steps (security and networking) can lead to growing pains or leaving your application vulnerable to bad actors. For example, did you make your subnet too small for the planned number of resources being placed into it, or do you have control over who can create Azure resources in your subscription? Do you need to synchronize your on-premise Active Directory with Azure to run restricted applications on compute resources hosted in the cloud? What region do you need to place your compute resources into? Those are just a few of the questions needing answers that could be overlooked by jumping straight to compute.

By no means am I attempting to convince you to underestimate the importance of compute. Compute is where the magic happens and should be considered the heart of your IT solution. Without it, there is no place to run the service your program was written to provide. With no compute, there is no need for a network nor any kind of security implementation. You can even argue the importance of compute from a database perspective. It is great to have data, and companies have a lot of it, but without a computer to capture, interpret, manipulate, and present it, what value does data have? The point is that compute is a place where you can realize impact and show progress the quickest, which makes it a favorable entry point. However, doing so would showcase short-term thinking and lack of structured planning. Therefore, it is recommended you follow the process discussed so far (first security, then networking, then compute). By doing so, the odds of successful migration or creation of your solution onto Azure will greatly increase.

> "Excellence is never an accident. It is always the result of high intention, sincere effort, and intelligent execution; it represents the wise choice of many alternatives—choice, not chance, determines your destiny."
>
> —*Aristotle*

Although Aristotle was referring to life in that quote, the same principle can be applied to choosing Azure compute products; there are a lot of choices, and making the wrong choice, as in life, can have undesirable consequences. Moving to or creating a new solution on Azure unfortunately doesn't get much easier at this point. Compute is simply the next level of technical competency required to progress toward your ultimate goal of Azure proficiency. Choosing which Azure compute resources you need, how much of them, how much they cost, and how you get your application configured to run on them, can be a great challenge. But with good intentions and sincere effort, it is possible.

An Overview of Compute (Hosting Model)

This chapter explains the details of Azure compute, which is synonymous with the hosting model. To make sure you know what *hosting model* means, take a look at the exam objectives covered in this chapter. To call out a few, Azure VMs, Service Fabric, App Services, and Azure Functions are hosting models. Each of these compute products has specific benefits, use cases, and limitations that require clarity so that the best one is chosen for the workload being created or moved to Azure. The specifics of each hosting model will be discussed in more detail in their dedicated sections. Until then, let's focus on two key elements: cloud service models and how to choose the right hosting model.

Cloud Service Models

I expect you to already know these cloud models if you are now preparing for the Azure Solutions Architect Expert exam; however, a review will cause no harm. You will know them as IaaS, CaaS, PaaS, and FaaS. There are numerous other "-aaS" acronyms for cloud service models; however, those listed previously are the most common in the Azure context. Refer to Figure 4.1 for a visual representation of them and read on for their description.

Infrastructure as a service (IaaS) was one of the earliest cloud service models, if not the first. This model most resembles the long-established on-premise architecture where a software application executes on a stand-alone or virtual server. The server is running an operating system and is connected to a network. As shown in Figure 4.1, the cloud provider (i.e., Microsoft) is responsible for the hardware and its virtualization, while the operating system (Windows or Linux) is the responsibility of the customer. The customer's responsibilities include, for example, updating the OS version and installing security patches. The customer has great control and freedom with this model, but with that comes greater responsibility. Microsoft only commits to providing the chosen compute power (CPU and memory) and ensuring that it has connectivity to a network. All other activities rest in the hands of the customer. Azure Virtual Machines, discussed in more detail later, is Microsoft's IaaS offering.

FIGURE 4.1 Cloud service models and their responsibilities

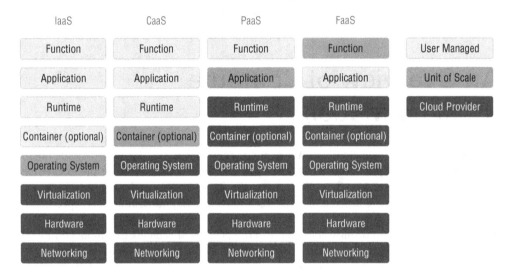

A *container as a service (CaaS)* is one of the newer cloud service models on Azure. CaaS delivers all the benefits available in IaaS, but you drop the responsibility for maintaining the operating system. This is visualized in Figure 4.1 as the operating system box is now the same shade as the hardware and virtualization boxes. A popular containerization product is *Docker*, which allows the bundling of software, dependent libraries, and configurations into a single package. Then that package can be deployed into and run on a container hosting model. Azure Kubernetes Service (AKS), Azure Container Instances, Azure Service Fabric, and Web App for Containers all provide the service for running containerized packages on Azure, all of which are discussed later.

Platform as a service (PaaS) is an offering for customers who want to focus only on the application and not worry about the hardware, network, operating system, or runtimes. This offering comes with some restrictions, specifically in regard to the *runtime*. A runtime is the library of code that the application is dependent on, for example .NET Framework, .NET Core, Java, PHP, or Python. The dependency on the runtime is defined during development. For example, if your application targets Python 3.7.4 but that runtime is not available on the PaaS hosting model, then your application will not run. The same goes for .NET Core 2.2. If you target 2.2 during development but that runtime is not yet on the platform, then it also will not run. Making changes to the runtime is not allowed when running on a PaaS platform. There are other constraints such as changing or deleting operating system–level configurations. This isn't allowed because they may cause damage, and as you are not responsible for the operating system, you cannot make changes to it.

Notice the shaded Unit of Scale box on the far right of Figure 4.1. The boxes with the similar shades under the titles IaaS, CaaS, PaaS, and FaaS symbolize where scaling rules (or manual scaling) are applied when executed. Scaling is a standard PaaS feature but can also be realized using virtual machine scale sets in IaaS. When a scale command is executed, a duplicated instance of your application is brought online for user consumption. The duplication is from the virtualization level upward, whereby the VM on which the PaaS runs will have the same specification. For example, if four CPUs and 7GB of memory (a common size of a single-instance PaaS production workload) are chosen, then the operating system with all patches, the runtime, the containers, and the application code will be scaled, making all the instances identical.

Autoscaling or scaling has not been discussed in much detail so far, but the concept has been touched on. Again, scaling is the most valuable and cost-effective offering that exists in the cloud, from a compute perspective, because it optimizes utilization, which reduces the overall cost of compute power. Products such as Azure App Service and Cloud Services (deprecating) are Microsoft's PaaS offerings.

The final cloud service model to describe is *functions as a service (FaaS)*. FaaS is most commonly referred to as *serverless computing* and is offered via a product called Azure Functions. Unlike the previously discussed cloud service models, FaaS does not require the creation of a compute instance. When creating an instance of Azure VM or an Azure App Service, each of those services requires the selection of an SKU, which describes the number of CPUs, amount of memory, and storage capacity. In the FaaS context, this is not required; instead, you simply create the Azure Function and deploy your code to it. The platform is then responsible for making sure there is enough compute capacity to execute the code. This simply means that the scaling is done for you. There are some restrictions such as the length of time an Azure Function can run, and there is a limit on the amount of capacity you can get allocated. Both of those limits and other limitations to watch out for will be covered in more detail later in the chapter.

How to Choose the Right Hosting Model

Buying the right Azure compute product and getting it to work properly depends greatly on understanding your own application's requirements. Can your code run successfully using Azure Functions (FaaS), or does your solution require options only available through Azure VM (IaaS)? You might be thinking, "I know my application well. I know its dependences, but I don't know what is and what is not supported on each of the Azure compute products. How do I get started?" I can relate to that due to the sheer number of Azure compute options; it can be an overwhelming situation and a cause of great uncertainty.

One reason you may be unsure as to which compute option to use is because you have not finished reading this chapter yet. All the details you need to know to make an educated decision are included in this chapter. But to get started, take a look at the decision diagram presented in Figure 4.2. The diagram is intended only to get you started and to narrow down the number of possible options to a more manageable amount. Notice there are seven possible compute options presented in the diagram; if it helps you reduce the number of options to two or three, then consider that a good thing.

FIGURE 4.2   Compute selection decision tree

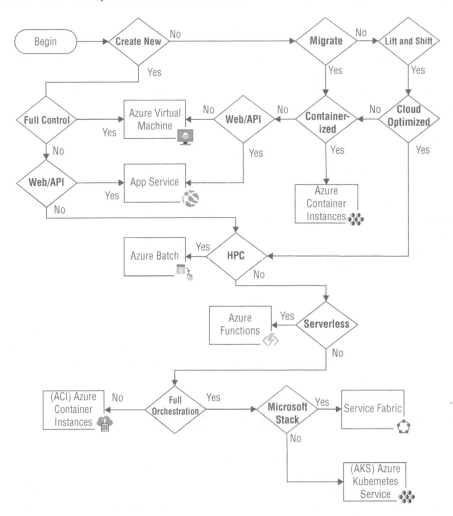

Let's walk through the decision tree together starting with the choices for creating a new application or migrating an existing one (bold words in the discussion relate to a step in Figure 4.2). For the Azure Solutions Architect Expert exam, understanding the migration of existing solutions to Azure is most important, so let's focus specifically on that path. The answer to **Create New,** therefore, is no. The next decision point is **Migrate**. This may be a bit confusing, because of course you are migrating, but the question to answer here is whether you plan on making any cloud optimizations to the solution. Cloud optimizations are discussed later in the "Azure Compute Best Practices" section. But for now, the decision is, will you simply *lift and shift (aka rehost)*, or will you do some optimizations to make the program behave better on cloud architecture?

Assuming you will simply lift and shift with no cloud optimizations (not *Cloud Optimized*) immediately reduces the number of recommended options to three Azure compute products.

- Azure Container Instances
- Azure Virtual Machines
- Azure App Service

Can your solution run within a container; can it be **Containerized**? If yes, then use the Azure compute product for your application code and proceed toward Azure Container Instances. If no, is the product a *Web Application* or a *Web API*? If yes, then the best option for Azure compute would be an Azure App Service. If the code being migrated to Azure is not web/internet-based, then your best choice is an Azure VM.

Web Application, Web API, and Other Application Types

Web applications are typically code that is executed from a client browser using the HTTP protocol. Some common programming languages used here are ASP.NET, PHP, and Node.js. Web APIs are also triggered via the HTTP protocol, but they typically return a JSON document and have no user interface (no GUI). Other application types are background tasks that may manipulate data on a scheduled frequency or a constantly running service that checks for the existence of an item in a queue and, if found, processes it.

Now go back and take a look at the decision tree where we chose no for making cloud optimizations; this time choose yes for *Cloud Optimized*. Notice that electing to make cloud optimizations to your existing application increases the number of available compute options. This is a good decision because many of the Azure compute products that support the most technically advanced cloud capabilities require tweaking to get the code functional; just a simple lift and shift is not enough to get the most advanced technical benefits. In many cases, these other cloud-optimized compute options are more cost effective. Lastly, as you will learn in Chapter 7, "Developing for the Cloud," there are some specific technical concepts that exist in the cloud that you must be aware of. These concepts may not be intuitively obvious to those having only experience with creating and maintaining IT solutions on-premise.

Next answer the question about HPC. *High Performance Computing (HPC)*, aka Big Compute, is a IT solution that uses a large amount of CPU, GPU, and memory to perform its function. These kinds of workloads are typically used in finance, genomics, and weather modeling. The amount of compute power for these processes is huge. If your application falls into the HPC category, then Azure Batch is the place to begin your research and analysis. If not, can your application run in a serverless context? Azure Functions is the Microsoft serverless compute offering. The primary difference between Azure Batch (HPC) and Azure Functions is the size and scale required for processing. The program triggered from an Azure Batch job can be small and compact, but the amount of compute power required to run would likely consume more CPU and memory than is available from an Azure Function. Azure Functions too, should be small and compact. The amount of CPU and memory would be more mainstream and can be large, just not jumbo. In both cases, HPC and serverless are scaled dynamically for you so that the program will successfully complete; the scale is what is different. This will become clearer as you read through the chapter. Don't worry.

In reality, all Azure compute products are running on Azure VMs behind the scenes. Azure App Services, Azure Batch/HPC, Azure Functions, Azure Containers, Service Fabric, and Azure Kubernetes Service (AKS) all run on Azure Virtual Machines. The remaining three compute options are focused primarily on, but not limited to, deployment, maintenance, and failover tasks. These capabilities are commonly referred to as the *orchestration* of containerized workloads. I would go so far and confidently state that most legacy enterprise applications cannot simply be containerized and orchestrated without significant investment in both application redesign and IT employee training. The concepts of containerization, orchestration, and maintenance didn't exist a little more than a decade ago. That being said, if the application would not benefit from **Full Orchestration**, then Azure Container Instances is a recommended point of entry for the solution. Service Fabric is focused on the **Microsoft Stack** (.NET and Windows), and AKS is focused on open source stacks (PHP, Python, Node.js, and Linux).

Operating Systems

Microsoft Azure supports both the Windows and Linux operating systems for all compute offerings. If there are a few compute products that are still Windows only, be assured that Linux support is on the way.

The decision tree is intended as a starting point. I hope after reading the previous text and viewing the flow chart, things are not as overwhelming as you might have initially thought. Before we get deeper into the specific Azure compute products, take a look at the following two sections, which contain some general information to consider as you begin the procurement of Azure compute.

Architectural Styles, Principles, and Patterns

The decision-making process surrounding Azure compute products requires a solid understanding of the technical requirements of your application. Proficient knowledge of the application's style and architectural pattern is an added necessity. The style of application has great impact on the combined architectural pattern and its defined use cases. Here, *use cases* refers to the services that provide the application's purpose. The following bullet points give a quick overview of the three topics that are discussed briefly in this section:

- **Styles:** Big Compute, Big Data, event-driven, microservices, n-tier, web-queue-worker
- **Principles:** Self-healing, redundancy, scaling, data storage
- **Patterns:** Circuit breaker, gatekeeper, retry, sharding

A previous discussion around the decision tree flow had to do with HPC versus Azure Functions. There, I linked HPC with its Big Compute style. The Big Compute style is a rather standard architectural pattern. In general, there is a scheduler, like Azure Batch, which also coordinates the tasks on the provisioned Azure VM worker pool (see Figure 4.3).

FIGURE 4.3   An HPC diagram with Azure Batch

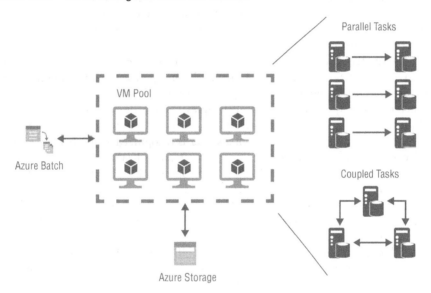

The tasks are commonly either run in parallel when there is no dependency between them or coupled when more than a single task needs to run on the same resource in sequence. Perhaps the use case here is number computation for Monte Carlo simulations. The point is that a Big Compute architecture pattern would mimic Figure 4.3 to some extent most of the time in this application style. If you implement a different pattern for that style, then you may have availability or performance issues because the wrong approach was implemented. Take next, for example, Azure Functions, which is event-driven. This style would have an event producer, event ingestion, and one or more event consumers, as visualized in Figure 4.4.

FIGURE 4.4   An event-driven architecture diagram

An event producer could be numerous IoT devices that are measuring humidity and updating a Service Bus message queue. The Service Bus is providing the event ingestion service. The humidity reading is then consumed or processed and stored into a database, for example by the Azure Function, i.e., the event consumer. Each style has a recommended or common architecture pattern, and each pattern is covered in detail in Chapter 7. Keep in mind that the architecture on which the application executes also has best-practice design principles and patterns. This means that in every case one must understand which compute product to use, know how it works, and then build the application following the best-case patterns for that hosting model; read Chapter 7 for those details.

To touch only briefly on Azure design principles, there is one that jumps out and is worthy of mention here and again later. The principle is referred to as *design for self-healing*. Self-healing means that when a server is recognized as not being healthy, then the platform, in this case Azure, takes an action to make it healthy again. In many cases, this a reboot of the virtual machine. In the cloud context, there is a term called *hyperscale*, which means there is so much capacity being added and removed so quickly that its complexity exceeds that of human capacities. There is no chance that Microsoft could hire enough people with the right skills to manage all the servers that exist in the Azure cloud today; it must be automated.

The health of an application is not the responsibility of the cloud provider; however, an unhealthy application can cause the host (i.e., the virtual machine) to become unhealthy. For example, when there is a memory leak, the storage capacity is 100% consumed or there is a fatal *Blue Screen of Death (BSOD)*, so the server and the application will not be usable anymore. Some action would need to happen to bring the application back online, and that action cannot be a manual one. That action is called *auto-heal* or *self-heal*. That brings you to the conclusion that when writing code, your application must be able to withstand a self-healing when a fail occurs.

One cloud design pattern for handling self-healing is called *retry*, as illustrated in Figure 4.5. Assume that for some reason the VM that the Azure App Service is making a connection to was determined to be unhealthy and is performing a recycle of the website.

FIGURE 4.5   A retry cloud design pattern diagram

If the site has high traffic, then during that recycle, it is probable that a request to the VM will fail. In the application code, you must handle the exception and perform a retry of the request that just failed. It does depend on the scenario and requirements of your application. It might be okay to simply return an exception message to a client requesting a document, for example, while not so acceptable if an exception is returned while placing an order. The preceding few sentences should now clarify my previous comment that you must be aware of specific technical concepts that exist in the cloud that may not be intuitively obvious to those having only experience with creating and maintaining IT solutions on-premise. It is for sure that exceptions happen when running applications on-premise, but most on-premise applications have support teams that can connect via RDP to the machine and manually correct the problem. This is not always the case in the cloud; the scale is simply too large for manual activities to be the norm. Therefore, instead of manual actions, recovery is performed by the platform automatically. All styles, principles, and patterns are discussed in detail in Chapter 7; if you are interested in learning more about them now, skip ahead and learn more.

Azure Compute Best Practices

Chapter 7 has in-depth coverage of cloud best practices, styles, principles, and patterns. The awareness of these concepts at this point, however, is necessary because each will influence the decision of which Azure compute product to deploy or create your application on. From a best-practice perspective, some decision points are again based on the requirements of the application. There are best-practice recommendations for applications that utilize and expose APIs and for applications that are background jobs. In addition, best-practice guidelines exist for implementing autoscaling, monitoring and diagnostics, caching, and how to best recover from a transient failure.

From an API best-practice perspective, applications would be best suited for supporting clients and consumers if they were to implement a *Representational State Transfer (REST)* API. REST APIs are endpoints that expect and deliver responses in the form of JSON documents. There are numerous other technologies that support this kind of internet API capability, such as *Electronic Data Interchange (EDI)*, XML documents, Tuxedo, *Simple Object Application Protocol (SOAP)*, and the *Windows Communication Foundation*

(WCF) framework. Each of those techniques would work, but best-practice recommendations, when your requirement is to expose an API using the HTTP protocol, are to use the REST API architectural style.

From a background job perspective, there are as many options as there are scenarios in which background jobs operate. A background job is a program that runs on a computer that does not have a user interface and typically processes data and delivers the results of the processing. There are two primary scenarios to discuss regarding background processing: how to trigger it and where to run it from. Triggering refers to how the program gets started. As mentioned, there is no interface with a button to click that tells the program to run. Instead, the background process can be scheduled to run at certain intervals or triggered when an event takes place. Running at a scheduled interface is relatively straightforward; CRON is the most common scheduler for this scenario. The other scenario is much more dependent on the type of event and what the requirements are. An event is somewhat synonymous with a message, and all the messaging Azure products are discussed in Chapter 6. There are a number of them, and all have their best-case scenarios, use cases, and *software development kits (SDKs)*. In short, the background process would be hooked into a queue of some kind where a message would be sent (remember the event-driven diagram from Figure 4.4). When a message is received, the hook is triggered that invokes the background job, which then performs the code contained within it. Which hosting environment to use also plays an important role as many Azure compute products can be used to run APIs and background jobs. Azure App Service WebJobs and Azure VMs are well suited for running background jobs and supporting APIs. Azure Batch and Azure Kubernetes Service (AKS) can also be used for running background jobs, but Azure Batch is not intended to host APIs as you would imagine. By the time you complete this chapter, it will be clear which model to use for which application style; however, you will need to know what patterns your application implements and then search the best-practice patterns for that one specifically.

If you intended on implementing autoscaling, any custom monitoring, or diagnostics capabilities or caching, there are some good examples of how to do this. Again, these are discussed in Chapter 7. A description of a transient failure and the expectation of its occurrence in the cloud are worthy of some initial discussion. From an on-premise perspective, transient errors or any error caused by a network virtual appliance hang, memory failure, or hard drive crash are not expected. This is because those hardware components are of trademark quality and are expected to have a high level of stability (which you pay a premium for). In the context of hyperscale cloud architecture, the hardware is more of a commodity. That means when it fails, it simply gets replaced, and the old one is trashed. That's fine, but those failures can have what is called a *transient event,* or an event that happens and is self-healed after some short amount of time. This is something that isn't expected often when running on-premise but needs to be coded for when running in the cloud because it can and will happen more often. The application must gracefully recover from short, random, nonreproducible moments of downtime as a matter of design.

In conclusion, each best-practice example is bound to a cloud service model, hosting model, style, principle, and patterns that are implemented into or required by your application. Figure 4.6 illustrates a Venn diagram to visually represent the relationship between these concepts.

FIGURE 4.6 A Venn diagram that visually links the cloud service model, hosting model, style, pattern, design principles, and patterns together

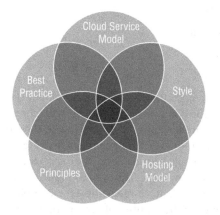

The sweet spot directly in the middle of those five concepts is where you want your application to land. Finding that spot is no easy task; however, knowing the requirements to make an educated decision is the first step. The remaining comes from experience. You will gain some of that experience as you complete the exercises in this chapter. You should be able to answer questions like the following:

Which two of the following compute hosting models provide the highest level of customization?

- Azure Virtual Machines
- Azure App Service
- Azure Functions
- Azure Container Instances

The answers are Azure Virtual Machines and Azure Container Instances. As you will learn, both Azure App Services and Azure Functions run within a sandbox that limits some kinds of supported configuration activities. You have more freedom with a virtual machine and a container. This will become crystal clear as you read more.

Azure Container Instances

The Azure Container Instances (ACI) is Microsoft's container as a service offering and is an entry point for customers with applications that run within isolated containers, where a container is an application or program that is packaged with all dependencies and deployed onto a server for its execution. The package is often referred to as an *image*, while the container is often referred to as the *runtime*. The following are a few benefits for running application code in containers:

- Containers are portable.

- Containers are lightweight.

- Containers are flexible.

- Containers are scalable.

From a portable perspective, containers allow a developer or release manager to have confidence that the code in the container will run anywhere, on a local development environment, on a corporate on-premise physical server, or in the cloud. It will run anywhere without making any configuration or coding changes because it has no system dependencies. A container is lightweight because it reuses the operating system of the host; there is no need for an operating system to be deployed along with the container. It is flexible because all kinds of programs—small, large, simple, or complex—can run in a container. They are scalable, which means the number of servers that can simultaneously run the container can be added to provide more compute power when usage increases.

When a container package is deployed to ACI, it receives a public-facing IP address and domain name with the extension `*.<region>.azurecontainer.io`, where * is the name of the ACI container that must be unique for the given region. A region, as covered in detail in Chapter 3, is the geographical location that the ACI will be installed into. This is selected during the container's creation. Regions are, for example, northeurope or southcentralus. Keep in mind that ACI is not yet available in all Azure regions; however, the deployment globally is ongoing and will reach worldwide scale in the short term.

ACI offers support for containers running on either Windows or Linux. The container concept has been mostly focused on the open source community and therefore Linux, so you will find the number of supported features for Linux images is greater than that currently for Windows. Table 4.1 lists the currently supported Windows base images on ACI.

TABLE 4.1 ACI-Supported Windows Images

Server Version	Edition	Version
Windows Server 2016	Nano Server	10.0.14393.*
Windows Server 2016	Server Core	10.0.14393.*
Windows Server 2019	Nano Server	10.0.17763.*
Windows Server 2019	Server Core	10.0.17763.*
Windows Server 2019	Windows	10.0.17763.*

The thing about Linux is that there are a lot of versions and editions. And when I write "a lot," I mean *a lot*. In reality, there can be an infinite number of versions and editions because the Linux operating system is open source, and if I were so inclined, I could create my own version and edition of Linux, and it would run on the ACI platform. Therefore, there is no table that defines which Linux images will run on ACI. Be assured, however, that mainstream versions of Linux will deploy and run as expected on the Azure Container Instances platform.

OS Virtualization, Containers, and Images

If you are like me, meaning most of your career has been in the Microsoft world of Windows and the .NET Framework, then the concept of images and containers may be a bit of a mystery. This is common because like I wrote earlier, this concept was mostly confined to the open source community, which until recently Microsoft was not actively engaged in. Although there are numerous products that provide *OS-level virtualization*, the most common one is Docker. The Docker software is less than a decade old, which may seem like a long time when considering "cloud speed" but in reality is not. Docker became a publicly available open source product in 2013 and only became supported in Windows Server 2016, which was shipped that same year. Based on that, I am confident that you will agree containers are a relatively new concept, especially from a Windows perspective. Be assured, however, that this area is picking up steam and will become a must-know skill set, especially for an Azure Solutions Architect Expert.

Let's look at what OS-level virtualization is in a bit more detail. Take a look at Figure 4.7, which compares a virtual machine with a container. We have not discussed Azure Virtual Machines in detail yet; that is coming in the next section. However, I would expect anyone reading this book to have a decent understanding of what a virtual machine is. You should have also created a number of Azure VMs in the previous chapter.

FIGURE 4.7 Comparison of virtual machines and containers

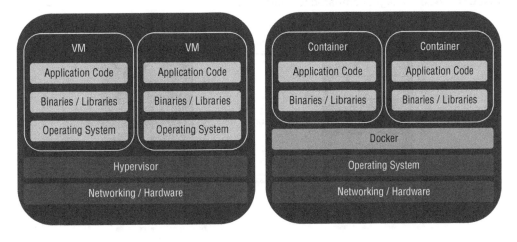

Notice that the primary difference between running application code on a virtual machine and a container is that the operating system is abstracted away. When you create a virtual machine, part of the process is to choose the operating system that is installed along with the acquisition of the CPU, memory, and storage resources. In many cases, a program you want to run doesn't warrant the existence of an operating system, because the operating system itself consumes more of the compute power than the application. In that scenario, having an alternative to run a program on a host in an isolated container, without having a dependency on an operating system, is a desirable option.

Accessing the Kernel

Both Linux and Windows have modified their kernel to support the Docker engine. This is the way a container can run on a host without an operating system. In other words, it gets access to the kernel of the host. In Windows Server 2016, container support was still a hardware virtualized offering and wasn't coded into the kernel. Kernel support was released with Windows Server 2019 through a capability called *Windows Subsystem for Linux (WSL)*.

So, what is an image exactly? I will explain it here, but note that in one of the exercises later in this chapter, you will get to create an image. It will become clearer as you read on. An image is the package of files, configurations, libraries, and a runtime required by a program to run. If your program is written in ASP.NET Core, then the code itself, its dependent libraries, and the runtime in which the code can execute together constitute the image. The image is defined in text form and then built, most commonly, using the Docker program. Once the image is created, you can deploy it to Docker Hub for private or public consumption. Figure 4.8 illustrates the relationship between an image and a container visually, which may help with your understanding of those terms.

FIGURE 4.8   Images compared to containers

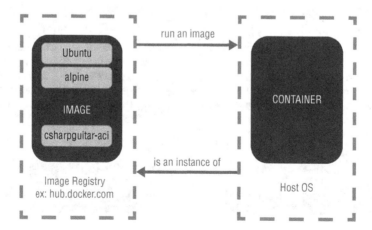

A container, on the other hand, is an instance of the image runtime. When an image is deployed to, for example, Azure Container Instances (the host), initially it will only consume space on some form of storage provider, like a hard drive. In that state, it is still an image. Once the image is instantiated, accessed or run, and loaded into memory, it becomes a container. The container becomes a process that comprises the runtime and application code for responding to requests, messages, or web hooks. In summary, a container is a living instance of an image on a host, while an image is a package of code, libraries, and a runtime waiting to be used.

Container Groups and Multicontainers

A container group, as one would imagine, is a group of containers. So what is a container? Can you answer that without reading forward or backward? A container is an instantiated image or an image that is loaded into memory ready to execute and perform its intended purpose. Therefore, a container group is a group of images running on a host ready to do some work.

It is possible to have multiple container groups, but it is currently only possible to have multiple containers in a single container group when running in a Linux container. This means when you consider a container group as the unit that runs on a virtual machine and the container as a process running on the virtual machine, you can run many containers within the same process. If you know something about IIS, a synonymous scenario is when you run multiple websites within the same application pool, assuming the application pool maps to a single process. See Figure 4.9.

FIGURE 4.9   A representation of multiple containers in a single container group

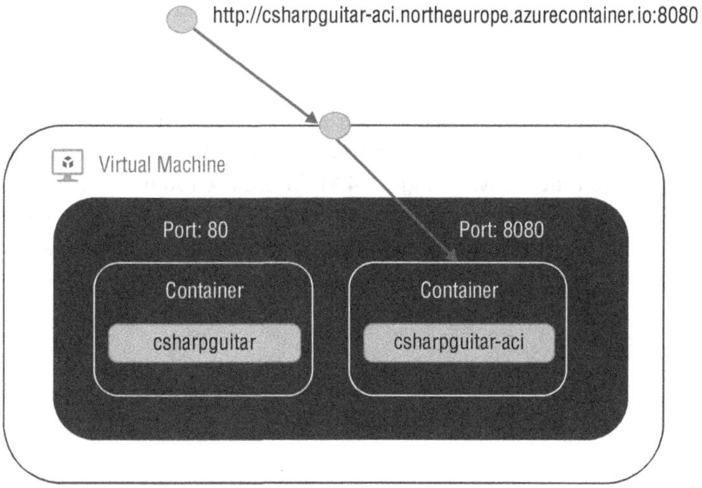

Visualize the virtual machine where the container group consists of two websites (i.e., containers), both of which are running within the same process, where a process means all the EXEs running on the machine that are presented when you open Task Manager or Process Explorer. The container is one of those EXEs. The caveat here is that each container in the container group must be bound to a unique port. As shown in Figure 4.9, one of the containers is bound to port 80, while the other is bound to port 8080. Now that you have some understanding about images and containers, complete Exercise 4.1, which will help you get a workstation configured to enable the creation of an image and the local execution of a container. If you do not want to install the third-party software required to create an image and run a container, that is not a problem. You can skip Exercises 4.1, 4.2, and 4.3. Exercise 4.4 and the following exercises are not dependent on those three exercises; complete them if you want to get hands-on experience with Docker.

EXERCISE 4.1

Configuring a Workstation to Create a Docker Image

1. Download and install Git from `https://git-scm.com/download/win`.

2. Once it's downloaded, begin the setup wizard. Accept all the defaults. Once the installation is complete, enter the following command into PowerShell and then click Run As Administrator. The output will be something similar to Figure 4.10.

    ```
    git --version
    ```

FIGURE 4.10 Output of the `git version` command

```
PS C:\> git --version
git version 2.23.0.windows.1
```

3. Docker requires BIOS-level virtualization support. To confirm this is enabled on a Windows workstation, check the Performance tab in Task Manager. You should see something similar to that shown in Figure 4.11. There are too many scenarios for enabling BIOS-level virtualization to provide instructions on how to enable them all. However, a simple search using Google or Bing for this phrase *How to enable BIOS level virtualization for <enter OS version>* will render the necessary results.

FIGURE 4.11   How to confirm the enablement of BIOS-level virtualization

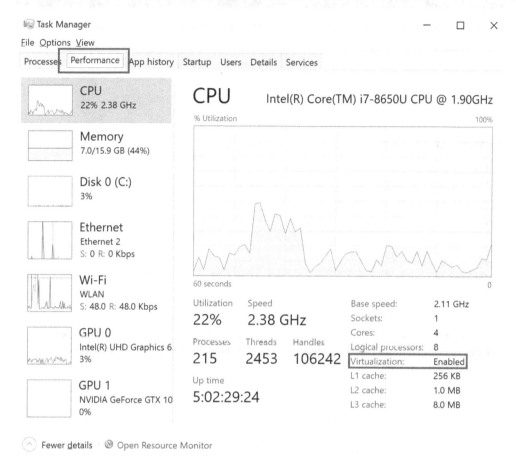

4. Install Docker from this site:

   `https://www.docker.com/products/container-runtime`

   Scroll down, click the Download Docker Engine button, and select the version based on the operating system running on your workstation. In this example, because I am running Windows, download Docker Desktop for Windows. You will need a Docker account to download the free software.

5. Once downloaded, double-click the Docker Desktop Installer. Accept the default options on Windows. Hyper-V and container features must be enabled. If requested, install them and reboot.

6. Enter the following commands into PowerShell and then run as the administrator:

```
docker --version
docker run hello-world
docker images
```

The result of those commands should resemble Figure 4.12.

FIGURE 4.12   Running Docker from PowerShell

```
PS C:\> docker --version
Docker version 19.03.2, build 6a30dfc

PS C:\> docker run hello-world

Hello from Docker!
This message shows that your installation appears to be working correctly.

PS C:\> docker images
REPOSITORY          TAG              IMAGE ID          CREATED        SIZE
hello-world         latest           fce289e99eb9      8 months ago   1.84kB
```

The first time you run docker run hello-world, you may get an exception because the hello-world image isn't yet downloaded. Docker will download it for you the first time and then run it for you.

That's it—your workstation is ready to create images and run Docker containers.

As alluded to in Exercise 4.1, the variety of operating systems that exist such as Linux, Windows, and iOS would make the exercise too repetitive to perform the steps for each one of them. In general, you simply need to get Git and Docker installed and working on your workstation; I am certain this is achievable with the details provided in the Windows-focused exercise.

With newer workstations, BIOS-level virtualization is enabled by default; for older ones it is not. The means for accessing the BIOS of a computer is dependent on the manufacturer of the machine. Although it is common to press F12 or F2 during bootup, it is not a standard activity, nor is the navigation within the BIOS system, as it too is created by the manufacturer.

Before continuing to the creation of a Docker image and running it in a local Docker container, please review these important limitations. These should be understood when choosing to run your application in ACI.

The following are not supported in an ACI:

- *Microsoft Message Queuing (MSMQ), Microsoft Distributed Transaction Coordinator (MSDTC)*, Microsoft Office, UI Apps, and Windows infrastructure roles such as DNS, DHCP, file servers, and NTP are not supported on Azure Container Instances.

- There are limits based on the number of containers that can be created and deleted in a 60-minute time frame (300 creates/deletes per hour and 100 creates/deletes in a five-minute period).

- There is a limit of 100 container groups per subscription and 60 containers per container group.

Docker Components

Before you build a Docker image and run it in a local Docker container, let's learn a bit more about what Docker is and how it works. The five specific Docker components that you need to know are listed next:

- Docker engine
- Docker daemon
- Docker client
- Docker registry
- Docker objects

Docker Engine   The Docker engine is a group of the following Docker components: the daemon, the APIs, and the client.

Docker Daemon   The Docker daemon, `dockerd`, is a listener that responds to requests via APIs that originate from the Docker client or another Docker daemon. These requests concern the management of container, images, volumes, and networks.

Docker Client   The Docker client, which is a *command-line interface (CLI)*, was installed in Exercise 4.1 and is the program `docker` that you used to check the version and run the `hello-world` sample image, also in Exercise 4.1. The client sends the commands to `dockerd`, which is then responsible for routing the request to the correct API that executes the request.

Docker Registry   The Docker registry is a location where you can store Docker images for public or private consumption. The registry is known as Docker Hub and is accessible here: `https://hub.docker.com`. Executing the `docker push` or `docker pull` command with the required parameters will publish an image to Docker Hub or download an image from Docker Hub, respectively. As we are focused on Azure, the image created in the next exercise, Exercise 4.2, will not use Docker Hub. Instead, there is an Azure feature called the *Azure Container Registry (ACR)* that provides the same benefits as Docker Hub.

Docker Objects   Docker objects are considered images and containers, which have already been discussed. In short, an image is a template that includes the instructions for how to create a container. While a container is a runnable instance of the image, the container is executed using the Docker client, docker run, which sends a request to the daemon to spin up an instance of the container.

Finally, there are two more topics that require discussion: the Dockerfile and the runtime of the containers. In the next exercise, you will create a Dockerfile and run it in a Linux container. Here is an example of the Dockerfile that you will create later in Exercise 4.2:

```
FROM http://mcr.microsoft.com/dotnet/core/aspnet:2.2
WORKDIR /app
COPY ./publish .
EXPOSE 80
EXPOSE 443
ENTRYPOINT ["dotnet", "csharpguitar-aci.dll"]
```

The FROM instruction identifies the base image, in this case aspnet:2.2. By doing this, you do not need to start from scratch and manually install all the packages required to run this kind of application. If additional or basic packages are required for the application, you would use the RUN instruction and then the package name. WORKDIR is short for working directory. Once this is defined, it is the reference point from which other instructions operate. For example, the point of entry for the COPY instruction is the /app directory. EXPOSE is an important instruction as it informs the users on which port the application will listen. Ports 80 and 443 are common ports for running web applications. ENTRYPOINT is like the Main() method of a console application. This instruction notifies the Docker build where and how to interface with the image once it's instantiated into a container.

Docker Desktop for Windows supports two container types, Windows and Linux. After installing Docker on your workstation, there will be a white badge that looks like a whale with some ship containers on its back, similar to that shown in Figure 4.13.

FIGURE 4.13   Docker container operating systems

If you click that badge, a menu that displays the type of container you will get when you run the docker build command is rendered. If you see Switch To Windows Containers, it indicates that you are in Linux mode. If you see "Switch To Windows Containers," you are in Windows mode. The sample program you will use in the next exercise is an ASP. NET Core Web API that can run on both Windows and Linux. We will use Linux for the next exercise, so make sure you have it set correctly. In Exercise 4.2, you will create a local Git repository, download an ASP.NET Core Web API hosted on GitHub, create a Docker image, and run it in a Linux Docker container.

EXERCISE 4.2

Building a Docker Image and Running the Container

1. Create a local Git repository by executing the following command in PowerShell (Run As Administrator). The result should resemble something similar to Figure 4.14.

    ```
    git init csharpguitar-aci
    cd csharpguitar-aci
    ```

FIGURE 4.14 Creating a local git repository

```
PS C:\> git init csharpguitar-aci
Initialized empty Git repository in C:/csharpguitar-aci/.git/

PS C:\> cd csharpguitar-aci

PS C:\csharpguitar-aci>
```

2. Download a small ASP.NET Core 2.2 Web API located on GitHub using the following command. Type the command all on one line.

    ```
    git svn clone https://github.com/benperk/ASA.git/trunk/Chapter04/Ch04Ex02/
    csharpguitar-aci -r HEAD
    ```

3. Download the Runtime & Hosting Bundle and install the .NET Core 2.2 runtime from https://dotnet.microsoft.com/download/dotnet-core/2.2. Accept the defaults and execute the following command. The output should be similar to that shown in Figure 4.15.

    ```
    dotnet --version
    ```

FIGURE 4.15 How to check the version of .NET Core

```
PS C:\csharpguitar-aci> dotnet --version
2.2.402
```

4. Restore, build, and publish the ASP.NET Core Web API that you downloaded in step 2 by navigating to the location of the .csproj file. Note the path included in Figure 4.16. When you are finished, execute the following command:

```
dotnet restore
dotnet publish -o ./publish
```

FIGURE 4.16 Restoring and publishing an ASP.NET Core application

```
PS C:\csharpguitar-aci\csharpguitar-aci\csharpguitar-aci> dotnet restore
PS C:\csharpguitar-aci\csharpguitar-aci\csharpguitar-aci> dotnet publish -o ./publish
```

5. To run the .NET Core ASP.NET Web API locally, navigate to the publish directory and execute the following command:

```
dotnet .\csharpguitar-aci.dll
```

6. Open a browser and navigate to the location rendered in the output of the previous command (something similar to http://localhost:5000). If a security warning is presented, ignore it. Click the Click Here link. Notice that the rendered images contain WINDOWS. In PowerShell, press Ctrl+C to stop the application.

7. In Windows Explorer, navigate to the location of the .csproj file, which is the same one as listed in step 4. Create a file named Dockerfile with no file extension. Enter the following contents into the Dockerfile and then save and close the file:

```
FROM http://mcr.microsoft.com/dotnet/core/aspnet:2.2
WORKDIR /app
COPY ./publish .
EXPOSE 80
EXPOSE 443
ENTRYPOINT ["dotnet", "csharpguitar-aci.dll"]
```

8. In PowerShell, navigate to the location of the .csproj and the Dockerfile files. Create a Docker image of that ASP.NET Core Web API by executing the following command. Note that there is an intentional period at the end of the command.

```
docker build -t csharpguitar-aci .
```

9. To run the Docker image in a local Docker container, execute the following command:

```
docker run -p 8000:80 csharpguitar-aci
```

Now, enter http://localhost:8000 into your browser.

10. Click the Click Here link and notice that the image now displays LINUX instead of WINDOWS. This is because Docker is configured to run Linux containers by default.

Azure Container Registry

An Azure Container Registry (ACR) is a location where you can store container images. As mentioned earlier, Docker Hub provides the same capability as ACR; both are places to store containers. The primary difference is that ACR is private only, while with Docker Hub you can make your images publicly consumable. Docker Hub is accessible at https://hub.docker.com and in Exercise 4.4. If you did not perform Exercise 4.1 and Exercise 4.2, use the public Docker image that I created called benperk/csharpguitar-aci. Complete Exercise 4.3 to create an ACR and upload the image you created in Exercise 4.2.

EXERCISE 4.3

Creating an Azure Container Registry and Uploading the Image Created in Exercise 4.2

1. Log in to the Azure Portal at https://portal.azure.com. Click + Create A Resource located in the top-left area of the browser. Click Containers. Click Container Registry.

2. Enter a registry name, for example csharpguitar. Select the Azure Subscription the ACR will be associated with. Select the resource group and the location. Enable the Admin user and leave the SKU as the default. Now, click the Create button.

3. Open PowerShell and run as the administrator. Enter the following command, but replace all instances of csharpguitar.io with the name of the image you used in step 2.

   ```
   docker tag csharpguitar-aci csharpguitar.azurecr.io/csharpguitar-aci:V1
   docker images
   ```

4. Run the docker login command. Look in the Access Keys blade. Find and use the registry name, username, and password. These values were the ones created and used when creating the ACR in step 2 in this exercise. Finally, push the image to the registry by using the docker push command shown next. The output should be similar to that shown in Figure 4.17.

   ```
   docker login csharpguitar.azurecr.io --username "" --password ""
   docker push csharpguitar.azurecr.io/csharpguitar-aci:V1
   ```

FIGURE 4.17   Tag and publish a Docker image to an Azure Container Registry

```
PS C:\> docker tag csharpguitar-aci csharpguitar.azurecr.io/csharpguitar-aci:V1

PS C:\> docker images
REPOSITORY                               TAG       IMAGE ID        CREATED         SIZE
csharpguitar.azurecr.io/csharpguitar-aci V1        934fa1a483b3    23 hours ago    265MB
csharpguitar-aci                         latest    934fa1a483b3    23 hours ago    265MB
mcr.microsoft.com/dotnet/core/aspnet     2.2       45c933779d5c    11 days ago     261MB
hello-world                              latest    fce289e99eb9    8 months ago    1.84kB

PS C:\> docker login csharpguitar.azurecr.io --username "csharpguitar" --password "2FCGu2=cy9CYx5W=MVVtnaTkZU+4/x5E"

Login Succeeded

PS C:\> docker push csharpguitar.azurecr.io/csharpguitar-aci:V1
The push refers to repository [csharpguitar.azurecr.io/csharpguitar-aci]
```

5. Return to the Azure Portal and navigate to the Azure Container Repository you created and click the Repositories blade. Your image should exist in the list.

During the creation of the ACR, you selected an Admin user option and the SKU. I mentioned that images hosted in an Azure Container Registry are private. A username and password are required for access whether you are using the Docker CLI in a client like PowerShell or creating an Azure Container Instances. (You will do that later.) The Admin user option can be enabled or disabled from the Access Keys blade for the given ACR. That blade contains the registry name, login server, the username, and two passwords, just in case you need to change one but have one available at all times.

There are three SKUs for ACR, Basic, Standard, and Premium. As is common, the more resources you need, the higher level of SKU you need. Be aware that those higher levels come with a higher price. However, the great thing about the cloud is that you pay based on consumption instead of a flat fee of the cost for the entire solution, which could be a significant one. I'd like to call out three specific features that are different between the pricing tiers. There are more; check them online if you desire. These three (Storage, Events, and Geo-replication) are the ones worthy of further comment.

Storage is pretty straightforward. Images and containers take space on a hard drive. The more space you need, the higher the tier.

- Basic provides 10GB.
- Standard provides 100GB.
- Premium provides 500GB.

Read and write operations are limited per SKU, as well.

The Events feature of ACR is an interesting one. Though I have not seen this capability on Docker Hub, it may be available with the Enterprise version, but even that won't get too deep into the capabilities of Docker Hub. The interesting thing about the Events feature is that when an image is uploaded or updated, it can trigger an action of some kind. For example, an update to an image or the insertion of a new one could trigger a Logic App or an Azure Function that could then be programmed to execute code. For example, you could enable the copying of site content from a file store to the new image file store or cause the event to write and send a message to Event Hub, Service Bus, or Storage Queue. (Those three products are covered in Chapter 6.) The ability to send a notification to one of those messaging products when a change happens to the ACR image is a cool capability.

Lastly, Geo-replication, which we covered in Chapter 3, replicates your images to other regions. The capability is available in Premium mode only. It is configurable by clicking the Replications link for the given ACR and then choosing which regions you want the ACR replicated into. A benefit is that you deploy once, and that same image is replicated and can be consumed in all regions; this limits the possibility of unintentionally having different versions of an application running at the same time.

Now that the ACR is clear, let's get your hands dirty and create an Azure Container Instance using the image you created or the one that I publicly hosted on Docker Hub (see Exercise 4.4).

Creating an Azure Container Instance

1. Log in to the Azure Portal at portal.azure.com. Click + Create A Resource in the top-left area of the browser. Click Containers and then click Container Instances.

2. Select the subscription and resource group, enter a container name (such as csharpguitar-aci), and then select the region. If you skipped Exercise 4.1 through Exercise 4.3, skip to step 3 now. Otherwise, select the Private radio button and enter the name of the Image you created in Exercise 4.3 (for example, csharpguitar .azurecr.io/csharpguitar-aci:V1). Log into that image with the username and password set using the docker login command in Exercise 4.3. The login server is the registry name with azurecr.io appended to the end, something like csharpguitar.azurecr.io. Remember that the login server, username, and the password can all be found on the ACR Access Keys blade.

3. If you completed Exercise 4.1, Exercise 4.2, and Exercise 4.3, skip this step. Leave the image type as public and enter **benperk/csharpguitar-aci** as the image name. That image is a public Docker image hosted on Docker Hub.

4. Leave the OS type as Linux, the size as default, and then click the Next: Networking button. Add a DNS label (for example, csharpguitar). Note that the DNS label will be appended with the region you selected previously and azurecontainer.io. Click the Review + Create button and then click the Create button. Feel free to review the remaining tabs, but leave the defaults.

5. Enter the public URL into a browser, for example: csharpguitar.westeurope .azurecontainer.io.

Something I found interesting when reviewing the options in the Azure Portal available for ACI was there were not many options. Other than Managed Identity support, which was discussed in Chapter 3, there are not any others worth discussion. Perhaps this is a product in expansion mode or a product that doesn't need any additional features. This means that the image is generally completely packaged and needs no other features because you must consider all the options necessary before deploying the image. Currently, if the application running inside your container is experiencing some unexpected behavior, such as exceptions or performance, due to the product being relatively new, you would have some problems troubleshooting and finding the root cause. (Or perhaps it's just me!) Nonetheless, this entire concept was a black box. Now for me and I hope for you, it is no longer a mystery and all has been clarified. Actually, I found it relatively simple to create, test, deploy, and consume a simple Docker image in a Linux container. That is saying a lot from a Microsoft guy. Someone from the open source community would find it even easier; that's my point.

Orchestration

I often find that when words or concepts are used in technology, they match the meaning when used in a different context. For example, the concept of inheritance in C# can be applied to real life, where properties and attributes are inherited from your parent. Hair color, eye color, and height are all things one would inherit from a parent; the same goes when you inherit from a class in C#.

When I think about the word *orchestration*, the first thing that pops into my mind is music. In that context, an orchestra is a group of performers who play various instruments in unison, such as strings, woodwinds, brass, or percussion. The orchestra has a conductor who orchestrates or organizes the different components of the orchestra. You could say that the conductor is responsible for the conduct of the orchestra. When you then apply that same model to the concept of containers, the model seems to fit nicely. The concept of orchestration in technology is the management (conductor) of different containers (players) that play different instruments (Windows or Linux containers and images). The conventional aspects of container-based orchestration are the following:

- Health monitoring
- Networking
- Scaling
- Scheduling
- Synchronizing application upgrades

Before we proceed into the discussion of those activities, it should be stated again that ACI is the place to run smaller workloads and is best for getting something deployed and running quickly. ACI doesn't provide any orchestration features. When you created the ACI instance, remember that you selected the size of the Azure VM on which it will run. By doing that, you bound your application to that, and there is no automated way to orchestrate that container or multiple instances of that container. The products Azure provides for such orchestration are Azure Kubernetes Service (AKS) and Service Fabric. Refer to Figure 4.2 and you will see that those two products (located toward the bottom of the decision tree) are triggered based on the necessity of orchestration. The point is that ACI is an entry point for using containers on Azure, but if you need greater control and manageability options, then you might outgrow ACI pretty quickly. I will touch on orchestration a little bit more when we cover AKS and Service Fabric later in the chapter, but the activities in the bullet list apply to those products and not to ACI. This just seemed like a good place to introduce this topic.

Health monitoring doesn't need a lot of explanation. When an orchestrator is configured to do so, a service runs that pings the containers to make sure they are still up and responding. If they do not respond or respond in a way that is unexpected, the orchestrator will remove and replace or restart the container. From a networking perspective, you may realize a scenario in which different containers need to communicate with each other. What happens if one of the containers or the host on which a container is running becomes unhealthy and the IP address or location of the container changes? This is what the networking capability of an orchestrator is responsible for—specifically the maintaining and updating the list of containers with location and metadata details. Unlike when you deploy to an ACI and are bound to a single instance of the chosen size, using an orchestrator will allow you to increase the number of container instances and the hardware on which they run based on demand. Of course, you can decrease the consumption when demand slows down, which is very cost effective. Scheduling is the most complicated activity to explain and comprehend, so if you get it, then you are so awesome! But then again, scheduling is just scheduling, and we all have schedules, right? Take a look at Figure 4.18.

FIGURE 4.18 A diagram of how the scheduler activity in a containerized orchestration works

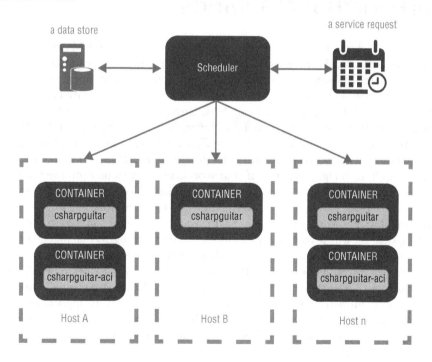

Consider that you have a large number of hosts, which is synonymous with a virtual machine in this context, and you want to deploy some more instances of a container. Do you know if you have existing capacity on some currently deployed hosts, or do you need a new host? That seems like a pretty complicated piece of information to capture without some help. That help comes from the scheduler. Assume there is only a single instance of an image named `csharpguitar` running in a container, and you request that two more instances need to be deployed along with two instances of the `csharpguitar-aci` container images. The scheduler would have knowledge of the current configuration stored in a data source and would make the deployment as required, whether the deployment needs new hosts or if there is enough capacity to run them on existing ones; this is what the scheduler can do. Lastly, the synchronization of application upgrades manages the deployment of the release of new container versions. Some additional capabilities are to avoid downtime and to be in a position to roll back the deployment if something goes wrong.

Azure Container Instances and Docker are young concepts but growing fast on Azure. The consumption rate is one of the fastest at the moment. At this point, you should have a good understanding of what ACI is, what Docker is, and what orchestration is. We will get back to orchestration again later, but let's now move on to Azure Virtual Machines.

Azure Virtual Machines

Azure Virtual Machines is Microsoft's IaaS product offering. Azure VM is by far the most popular and utilized Azure service. This can be attributed to the fact that Azure VM existed before the PaaS, FaaS, or CaaS offerings were available. Some years ago, any company or individual who wanted to utilize compute resources in Azure had only one option to do so, and that option was Azure VM. Even at that early stage of cloud consumption, the savings you could realize by no longer needing to manage the hardware and network infrastructure was great. Recall from Figure 4.1 that networking, hardware, and the virtualization of an instance are owned by the cloud provider when you choose to use IaaS. Also, recall from Figure 4.2 that if your workload is not cloud optimized, if you do not require or desire containerization, and if the workload is of relative complexity, then Azure VM is the place to begin your investigation and consumption. But what is meant by "relative complexity"? Mostly this means that if you need to have some control over the operating system on which your program runs, i.e., you need registry changes, your application instantiates child processes, or the application requires some third-party assembly installation, then it would not work on PaaS, for example. It won't work on PaaS because you have no control over the OS using that cloud model. Also, if you wanted to move an entire application infrastructure that included multiple tiers like web, application, database, and authentication tiers, each of which was running on its own machine, then that would be "of relative complexity" and would best fit in a group of Azure VMs. Figure 4.19 illustrates that kind of architecture.

If someone asked you what a virtual machine was, could you answer that? In your own words, what is a virtual machine? In my words, a virtual machine is a simulated server running on physical hardware that is granted access to CPU, memory, and storage that actually exist on a physical server. There can be many virtual machines on a single physical server. For example, a physical server with 32 CPUs, 128GB of RAM, and 200GB of storage space could realistically host three virtual machines with eight CPUs, 32GB of RAM, and 50GB of storage. The missing one-fourth capacity is necessary to run the OS and programs that manage the physical hardware and the virtual machines. You wouldn't want to allocate all physical resources to run virtual machines, leaving nothing left for the host to use. Related to this, a virtual network is also a simulated network within a physical network, so by understanding the VM concept, you can also visualize the concept of a virtual network.

FIGURE 4.19 An example of a multitier application that fits good on Azure VMs (IaaS)

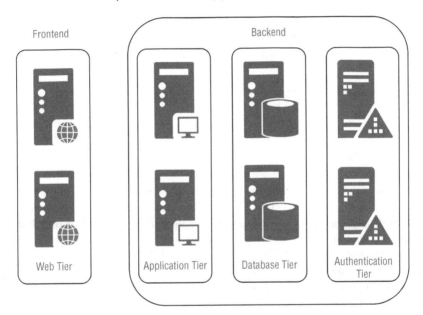

If you read the previous chapter and completed Exercise 3.3, then you already have some experience with Azure VM. Take a look at Figure 4.20 and reflect on that exercise; think about if this is what you had in mind when you created your first Azure virtual machine.

As you may have noticed earlier in Chapter 3, there are a number of additional products and features created when an Azure VM is provisioned. Looking again at Figure 4.20, you will notice a few products such as a virtual network and subnet (if one doesn't already exist), a public IP address, a network interface card (NIC), and managed disks. Each of these you should already have a good understanding of except for managed disks. Although managed disks are discussed in more detail later, since the disk roles OS, Data, and Temp are called out in the figure, a description of them is warranted. On Windows, there is a command named diskmgmt.msc that when entered into a command window identifies the partitions and disks that are configured on the server. Execute this on your workstation or on a Windows Azure VM to see which disks currently exist. Compare the different elements and take away some personal learnings from that.

FIGURE 4.20   How an Azure VM looks with an NIC and hard drives

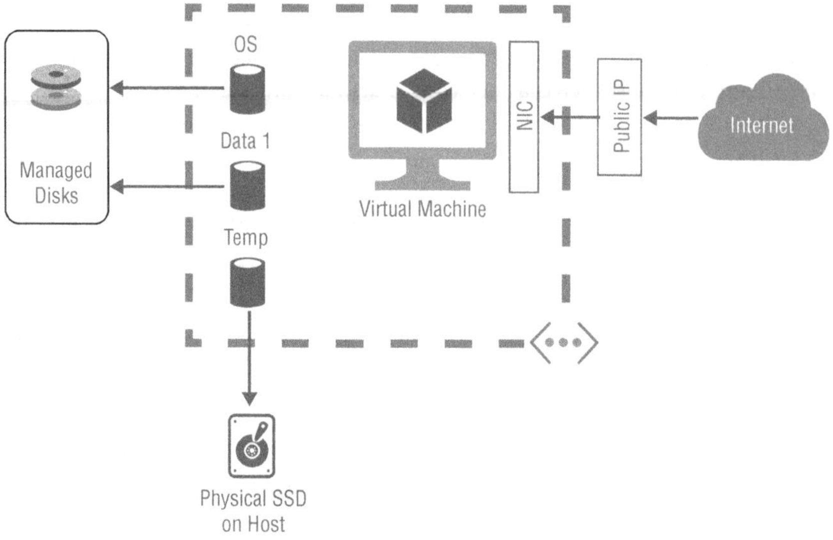

The OS disk is the one that contains the pre-installed operating system that was selected during the creation of the VM such as Ubuntu, Red Hat, Debian, Window Server, or Windows 10. OS disks have a maximum capacity of 2,048GB. A data disk is one that stores application data such as cache, auditing logs, configuration settings, or data in a file or a *database management system (DBMS)*. The number of data disks that can be attached to an Azure VM is based on the size and expected number of *input/output operations per second (IOPS)*. You'll learn more about this later in the chapter, but in short we are talking about a number potentially in the thousands with a maximum capacity of 16,384GB, which is pretty large—actually gigantic. These numbers increase often, so check the Azure documentation for the current maximums.

The temporary disk is a location that is used for storing swap and page files. Those kinds of files exist in the context of managing memory and are used to offload memory from RAM. Recognize that this disk exists and what its intended purpose is, but leave it pretty much alone unless there is a specific reason to change it. I checked using `diskmgmt .msc`, and the temporary storage drive is mapped to `D:/` and has a size of 7GB; on Linux the disk is at `/dev/sdb`. Take note that this disk is temporary, and you should expect that anything stored on that drive can be removed during updates, redeployments, or maintenance, so again, don't use it or change it unless you have a specific need.

Managed disks are available in the following types: Standard HDD, Standard SSD, and Premium SSD. Choosing between a hard disk drive (HDD) and solid-state drive (SSD) comes down to speed, lifespan, reliability, and cost. SSD is the newest and will outperform HDD in all aspects, but it comes with a higher cost. Choosing which disk type and the number of attached data disks depends on what the requirements of the application are.

Now that we've discussed the basics of what a VM is and the related products and features, let's create a few VMs and get into a little more detail.

Creating Azure Virtual Machines

Before creating and provisioning an Azure VM, there are a few items you must consider, such as its location, its size, the quota limits, and the operating system. As discussed in the previous chapter, the location in which you place your workload should be analyzed from a privacy perspective if the application will store customer or personal data. There are laws that dictate the legal requirements of its management. Knowing the regional laws, the concept of geographies, and which data may be sent to other regions outside of the geography are needed pieces of information and were covered in the previous chapter. In addition, you must confirm that all the products required to run your application also exist in the same region. For example, does your application require zone redundancy or a Cosmos DB? If yes, then you would want to make sure those products are in the region you place your Azure VM.

As you would expect, there is a great variety of available sizes of Azure VMs, aka a VM series. To list the available VM sizes in a given region, you can execute this PowerShell command, for example: `Get-AzVMSize -Location "SouthCentralUS"`. The VM size (i.e., the number of CPUs and amount of memory) is greatly influenced by the requirements of the application. In addition, there are different sizes available based on the chosen operating system, for example Windows or Linux. As it is not realistic to determine all the possible customer use case scenarios, both size and quota limits will be discussed later when we focus on Windows and Linux Azure VMs in more detail. There are, however, different categories of Azure VMs that can be applied to both Windows and Linux VMs; take a look at Table 4.2 for more details on the classification. There is more to come in regard to what *instance prefix* means, so please read on.

TABLE 4.2 Azure Virtual Machine Categories

Type	Instance Prefix	Description
Compute Optimized	F	Optimal for batch processing of medium-sized applications
General Purpose	B, D, A, DC	Best for development, testing, and small applications
GPU	NV, NC, ND	Most useful for video editing and graphics
High Performance	H	Powerful CPUs with high network throughput
Memory Optimized	E, M, D, DS	Ideal for in-memory analytics and relations databases
Standard	A	Small VMs not for production, testing only
Storage Optimized	L	Useful for applications requiring high disk I/O and Big Data or SQL databases

Also recognize that there are numerous ways to deploy and create an Azure VM. You may remember when you created your first VM that there was a step where you decided which OS image to use from a drop-down. In that drop-down list there were approximately ten of the most common images, like Windows and Linux, some of which have already been mentioned. But as you will experience in Exercise 4.5, there is also a link below that drop-down that leads to hundreds of public and private images to select from. These other images exist in a place called the *Azure Marketplace*, which is a location for businesses to host their software products for consumption by Azure customers. Microsoft places its software products in the Azure Marketplace just like any other company would do. To learn more about the Azure Marketplace, visit `https://azuremarketplace` `.microsoft.com`.

EXERCISE 4.5

Creating an Azure Windows Server Core VM

1. Log in to the Azure Portal at `https://portal.azure.com` and click + Create A Resource in the top-left area of the browser. Click Compute. Click Virtual Machine.

2. Select the subscription, and select the resource group (for example, CSHARPGUITAR-SN1-RG). Then enter a Virtual machine name (for example, CSHARPGUITAR-SC), select the region (for example, South Central US), and under the Image drop-down, select the Browse All Public And Private Images link.

3. Select Developer Tools from the list (look through some other options and get a feel of what is available), select [Smalldisk] Windows Server 2019 Datacenter Server Core, enter a username and password, select the Allow Selected Ports radio button, and allow HTTP (80), HTTPS (443), and RDP (3389). Click the Next: Disks button.

4. Leave the defaults, click the Next: Networking button, and select the VNET created in the previous chapter (for example, CSHARPGUITAR-VNET-B) or create a new one. Select the subnet (for example, csharp) and leave the remaining as default. Click the Review + Create button, and then click the Create button.

5. Once the provision is complete, connect via RDP to the VM by clicking the Connect button on the Overview blade. Enter **powershell** at the command console, and enter the following PowerShell commands:

```
Install-WindowsFeature -name Web-Server -IncludeManagementTools
remove-item C:\inetpub\wwwroot\iisstart.htm
Add-Content -Path "C:\inetpub\wwwroot\iisstart.htm" `
            -Value $("Hello from " + $env:computername)
```

6. From your workstation enter the public IP into a browser, and you should receive a request saying hello from the server name.

In the previous exercise, you created an Azure virtual machine using a public Azure image and looked through other available images.

Azure Bastion

This Azure feature is new and available for making a remote connection to an Azure virtual machine from within the portal. There may be some organizations that cannot enable ports 3389 or 22, which provide the ability to connect via Remote Desktop (RDP) or SSH to a machine due to security compliance regulations. Additionally, those connections, when made from an on-premise client to a cloud-hosted server, would happen across the internet, which may not be secure enough for some enterprises. By using Azure Bastion to connect to the cloud-hosted servers, you only need port 443 opened, and the connection remains within the secure Azure network infrastructure. Read more about Azure Bastion here:

docs.microsoft.com/en-us/azure/bastion/bastion-create-host-portal

Using Images

An image in the Azure VM context is similar to the definition of an image in the container context discussed in the previous section. An image is a template that defines the environment requirements in which it will run. From an Azure VM perspective, the big difference is that the operating system is part of the image definition. Review Figure 4.7 if you need a refresher on the differences. There are numerous tools that help you to create an image for deployment to an Azure VM, for example, Azure VM Image Builder, System Preparation Tool (SYSPREP), Disk2VHD, snapshots, and export from VMware, VirtualBox, from an already created Azure VM or Hyper-V (VHDs) from the portal. We won't cover all those tools and options in detail now, but an interesting one is snapshots. We have discussed a bit about managed disks, specifically the OS disk. It is possible to create a snapshot of that disk and then navigate to the disk in the portal where you will find a button on the Overview tab that allows you to export it and then create a VM from that snapshot; there are similar capabilities in on-premise virtualization software as well. The simplest way to create an image of an existing Azure VM is described in Exercise 4.6. You would want to do this after the VM that you provisioned is complete and ready to be shared and used in production. In the following exercise, you will create an image from the VM created in the previous exercise and use it to deploy a new VM.

EXERCISE 4.6

Creating an Azure VM Custom Image

1. Connect via RDP or Bastion to the VM you created in the previous exercise and run C:\Windows\System32\Sysprep\sysprep.exe. Enter the settings shown in Figure 4.21. Do not restart the VM; it will shut down automatically.

FIGURE 4.21   How to prepare an Azure VM for imaging using Sysprep

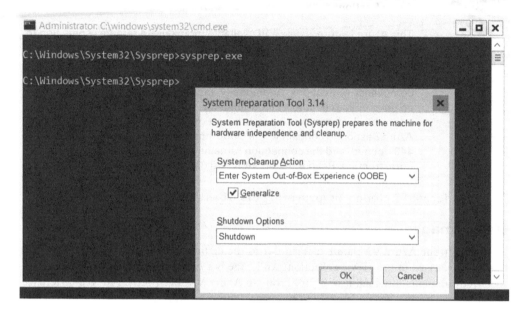

2.   Log in to the Azure Portal at portal.azure.com and then click the Virtual Machine that you created in the previous exercise (for example, CSHARPGUITAR-SC). On the Overview blade, select the Capture link, which opens a Create image blade.

3.   Provide a name for the image (for example, CSHARPGUITAR-SC-IMAGE) and select the check box. This removes the existing VM. Provide a VM from which the image will be taken from (for example, CSHARPGUITAR-SC). That last step is a protection step to make sure you understand that creating this image causes the VM to be deal-located and optionally deleted, which is what you decided to do when you clicked the check box. Now, click the Create button.

4.   Once that's complete, click + Create A Resource in the top-left area of the browser. Click Compute and then click Virtual Machine.

5.   Select the subscription, select the resource group (for example, CSHARPGUITAR-SN1-RG) into which you created the image, enter a new virtual machine name (for example, CSHARPGUITAR-SI), and choose the region, which should be the same as the resource group region (for example, South Central US). Click the Browse All Public And Private Images link below the Image drop-down list.

6. Select the My Items tab at the top of the browser window, and you will see the image you just created. Select it and enter a username and password. Select the Allow Selected Ports radio button and then enable HTTP (80), HTTPS (443), and RDP (3389). Click the Review + Create button, and review the details, specifically the Networking section. Click the Create button. If you used the same resource group and subscription as you did in the previous exercise, the networking values default, for example, to VNET = CSHARPGUITAR-VNET-B and Subnet = csharp.

7. Once deployed, get the public IP address of the VM and navigate to it via a browser.

Now that you have an image that, as in my example created for Exercise 4.6, responds with, "Hello from CSHARPGUITAR-SC." You can use this image you created any number of times as you create redundancy and failover solutions. The image is also available for usage with a *virtual machine scale set (VMSS)*, which will be discussed in more detail later in the chapter. Let's switch gears now and look a little more at the two most popular supported operations systems available for Azure VMs: Windows and Linux. An Azure Solutions Architect Expert must grasp which version of each operating system is supported on Azure. Know, too, that the OS has limits imposed by the subscriptions, CPU, IOPS, RAM, and storage available. You can expect some questions about this on the exam. For example, which of the following types of VMs cannot be deployed to Azure?

Windows

The Windows Server operating system is one of the most used software products for running enterprise-level workloads. In this section and in the following one focused on Linux Azure VMs, we'll focus on the supported OS versions, a subset of recommended VM sizes for those OS versions, and some quota limits specific for the OS and version. Recall from Exercise 4.5 that you selected a prebuilt image of Windows Server 2019 Datacenter Server Core from the Azure Marketplace. Take a look at the following 10 supported Windows images available via the Azure Marketplace in the portal:

- Windows Server 2008 R2 SP1
- Windows Server 2012 Datacenter
- Windows Server 2012 R2 Datacenter
- Windows Server 2016 Datacenter
- Windows Server 2016 Datacenter - Server Core
- Windows Server 2016 Datacenter - with Containers
- Windows Server 2019 Datacenter
- Windows Server 2019 Datacenter Server Core

- Windows Server 2019 Datacenter Server Core /w Containers
- Windows Server 2019 Datacenter with Containers

There are some recommended sizes of an Azure VM based on each of these operating system versions. The recommendations are arranged based on the categories that were presented previously in Table 4.2. Therefore, it is important to know into which category your application falls. Table 4.3 provides a list of recommended Azure VM sizes based on the selected workload category. The values in the Instance/Series column, in my example, DS1V2, represent the grouping of many compute components such as CPU speeds, CPU-to-memory ratio, temp storage ranges, maximum data disks, IOPS, and network bandwidth throughput. The ratio between each of those components is different for each series and therefore has an intended target application category. You can find the specifics of each Windows OS Azure VM here:

docs.microsoft.com/en-us/azure/virtual-machines/windows/sizes-memory.

As an Azure Solutions Architect Expert, you would be expected to recommend the category and VM series when given the specifications of the workload being deployed onto an Azure VM.

TABLE 4.3   Windows Versions to Azure VM Size Recommendation

Windows Version	Category	Instance/Series
2008 R2 SP1	General Purpose	DS1V2, DS2V2, D2SV3, D1V2, D1, DS1, DS2
2012 Datacenter		
2012 R2 Datacenter	Memory Optimized	DS11V2, E2SV3, DS11
2016 Datacenter *	General Purpose	DS1V2, DS2V2, D4SV3, D1V2, D1, DS1, DS2
2019 Datacenter *		
	Memory Optimized	DS11V2, E2SV3, DS11

If you see an asterisk (*), it symbolizes all variants of the Windows versions. As covered later in the "Migrating Azure Virtual Machines" section, it is possible to bring your own on-premise VM to the Azure platform. This means that almost any OS and its configuration that you can export and convert to the *virtual hard disk (VHD)* format can be deployed to an Azure VM. That sounds a bit easier than actually doing it. Sure, you can deploy a VM running Windows Server 2003; however, some capabilities such as cluster failovers, Azure VM agents, or VM extensions will not work or be supported. Some other common Windows Server features that are not supported on Azure are included in the following list:

- Wireless LAN Service
- SNMP Services

- Dynamic Host Configuration Protocol (DHCP)
- Storage manager for SAN
- Hyper-V
- DirectAccess
- Network Load Balancing
- BitLocker Drive Encryption
- RRAS
- Rights Management Services
- Peer Name Resolution Protocol
- Windows Deployment Services

A primary reason for limits and quotas is to prevent the accidental consumption of resources that results in a high, unexpected charge. Most of the limits are considered soft, which means if you need more, then you can get more by contacting Microsoft and requesting more. These limits are typically bound to a subscription or a region. I have seen many customers creating multiple subscriptions or deploying to multiple regions to get around the soft limits instead of realizing that the limit, which is there for protection, can be increased. Contacting Microsoft to get the soft limits increased would make managing your workloads on Azure more intuitive. Moving resources to other subscriptions or regions when those resources are all part of the same solution makes things harder to manage. There are, however, some hard limits, imposed on almost all customers that you must adhere to. Those numbers are big, and most companies wouldn't need (or couldn't afford) so much. They also are not always documented. This is because if the hard limit isn't hard-coded into the product, then it could be increased even more than a documented limit, if the business case is justified. Table 4.4 describes some subscription limits that are related to Azure VMs.

TABLE 4.4   Azure VM Limits

Azure Resource	Soft/Default Limit	Hard/Max Limit
Virtual machines	25,000 per region	Contact Microsoft
Virtual networks	100 per region	1000 per region
Managed disks	50,000 per region	Contact Microsoft
Storage accounts	250 per region	Contact Microsoft
Virtual machine cores	30 per region	Contact Microsoft

Also note that these limits change often. The ones listed in Table 4.4 and most of the numerical and relationship limits existed when the Azure Solution Architect Expert exam was created. Learning these will help you answer any question on the exam regarding this topic. By relationship matching I am referring to Table 4.3 where the links between OS version, category, and VM size are displayed.

The limit of 30 cores per region in Table 4.4 refers to a specific scenario where the limit applies to specific instance/series types. For example, you cannot have more than 30 cores of series A and D VMs in the same region. Additionally, there is a limit of 30 with the Dv2 and F series VMs in the same region. You can, however, have 10 cores of A1 and 20 cores of D1 in the same region equaling 30. You could also have 30 cores of D1 and 30 cores of F1 in the same regions because the instance/series are not grouped together in the limits logic. This is an important point to know when using IaaS; however, I wouldn't expect such a question on the Azure Solutions Architect Expert exam, so just keep it in mind as you progress to being not only a certified Azure Solutions Architect Expert but also a tenured and highly competent one.

Linux

Linux is rapidly becoming the most utilized operating system for running small to medium workloads. Microsoft is helping to support that growth by providing the means for its simple implementation onto the Azure platform. As you have already built an Azure VM, you know how easy that was. The only difference from the previous exercise where you built the Windows VM is that you would choose a Linux image from the drop-down box instead of a Windows one. The other steps are the same; there is no apparent attempt to make deploying Windows VMs easier than Linux. The image defaults to a Ubuntu image. Currently there are six flavors of Linux OS offerings in the Azure Marketplace.

- Ubuntu Server
- Red Hat Enterprise 7
- Container Linux by CoreOS
- Clear Linux OS
- SUSE Linux Enterprise
- Debian

Table 4.5 lists the Azure Marketplace images available for each of those flavors.

TABLE 4.5   Azure Marketplace Linux Versions

Linux OS	Linux Version
Ubuntu Server	14.04 LTS, 16.04 LTS, 18.04 LTS
Red Hat Enterprise	7.2, 7.3, 7.6
CoreOS	Alpha, Beta, Stable 7.5

Linux OS	Linux Version
Clear Linux OS	Basic, containers, machine learning
SUSE Linux Enterprise	15, 12 SP4
Debian	8, 9

There is a concept referred to as *blessed images* or *endorsed distributions* in the context of Linux. As stated earlier, it is possible to build any machine using any OS and configuration and attempt to deploy it to Azure. The key word there is *attempt*. There are so many possible configurations that it would be inconceivable at this time to have 100% coverage. I once tried unsuccessfully to deploy a Linux OS that was not blessed. When you deploy and experience some kind of issue, the place where you tend to turn to is the Serial Console. The Serial Console lets you make a hardware connection to the VM instead of using SSH, which requires a network connection. The Serial Console is listening on a virtual console named tty0 by default. The Linux image I was deploying was configured to listen on tty1, and I couldn't connect to it. Only by chance was I able to figure that out, but this is an example of what happens when you do not use an endorsed or recommended image. There are many "one-offs" that can occur and delay your deployment or, worse, completely prevent it. It is therefore most prudent that your application targets one of the Azure Marketplace images; however, there are more Linux flavors that are considered blessed and endorsed that do not exist in the Azure Marketplace. They are listed in Table 4.6.

TABLE 4.6 Additional Endorsed Linux Flavors

Linux OS	Linux Version
CentOS	6.3, 7.0
CoreOS	494.4
Debian	7.9, 8.2
Oracle Linux	6.4, 7.0
Red Hat enterprise	6.7, 7.1, 8.0
SUSE Linux Enterprise	SLES for SAP, 11 SP4, 12 SP1
openSUSE	Leap, 42.2
Ubuntu	12.04

As with the Windows machines, the recommendations for the VM sizes are based on category and the operating system version. Please find the VM size recommendations per Linux OS flavor in Table 4.7. For greater visibility into the details of the Linux VMs instances, take a look at `https://docs.microsoft.com/en-us/azure/virtual machines/linux/sizes-memory`. As the amount allocated for compute resources increases, so does the cost; therefore, choosing the right size is important.

TABLE 4.7   Linux Versions to Azure VM Size Recommendation

Linux version	Category	Instance/Series
Ubuntu CoreOS	General Purpose	DS1V2, DS2V2, D2SV3, D4SV3, D1V2, D1, DS1, DS2
	Memory Optimized	DS11V2, E2SV3, DS11
Red Hat Enterprise	General Purpose	DS2V2, D2SV3, D4SV3, D2V2, D2V3, D2, DS2
Clear Linux OS	General Purpose	D1, D3, DS3, DS4
SUSE Linux Enterprise	General Purpose	DS1V2, DS2V2, D1V2, D1, Ds1, DS2
	Memory Optimized	DS11V2, DS11

There are no limits or quotas that focus specifically on Azure VMs running Linux; they are the same that were covered previously in Table 4.4. Microsoft fully supports Linux, and there are no policies or practices that knowingly inhibit this operating system.

Azure VM Extensions

Extensions are small programs or automation activities that are helpful for performing post-deployment tasks, security, monitoring, and automated deployments. If you were curious in the previous exercises where we created the Azure VM, there was a tab name Advanced, and on that tab there was a section that allowed you to select an extension. In the exercises I usually skip over those tabs, but you may have looked at them and wondered what all those features are. Consider accessing the portal and simulating the creation of a new Azure VM. First, notice that the list of installable extensions is different when selecting a Linux or Windows-based VM, as well. The region plays a role in the extension list, so again, here is another example of knowing what capabilities are available in each region prior to committing to one.

For Windows there are some nice extensions such as the PowerShell Desired State Configuration extension that will help in post-deployment activities to make sure the VM is configured in the same way in every case. This is important once your workloads get rather complicated and require automated deployments, which are discussed in more detail in the next section. There are anti-malware, cloud security, and other security-related agents that can be deployed, configured, and run on your Azure VM as an extension. When you create your initial Azure VM, you configure all these environment-specific capabilities and then capture your image for use with later automated or manual deployments.

Microsoft provides a lot of monitoring capabilities; however, it fully supports other companies with more specific monitoring capabilities through this extension feature. Some third-party monitoring products available for installation are Datadog, APM Insight, and Dynatrace. Monitoring is covered in more detail in Chapter 9 but will focus on the Azure platform–based capabilities and not third-party extensions in IaaS. If you have an interest in learning more about these extensions, check out this online document:

docs.microsoft.com/en-us/azure/virtual-machines/extensions/overview.

Automated Deployment

Deployment and migrations are covered in Chapter 8, which will target ARM and code deployments (aka content deployments). As you already know, there are many ways to deploy an application and many components that need to be deployed to make it work. If any portions of those deployment tasks can be automated, it decreases the amount of required effort. Consider in many of the previous exercises, after the provisioning of the Azure VM was complete, you were requested to connect via RDP or Bastion to the server and manually install IIS using some PowerShell cmdlets. That is an acceptable approach if you have only one or two servers to deploy that need IIS; however, if you were to deploy 50 or 100, then that option really isn't worth considering. It is not realistic to manually log in to 50+ servers and make manual configurations to each of them. Exercise 4.6 is a similar approach to realize the same outcome, where you create an image and use it as the baseline for all future deployments. Using automated scripting is another option to consider and is useful when you deploy your Azure VMs with PowerShell as well. There are even scenarios when a combination of both these capabilities add great value.

An example of a scenario where both a custom image and an automated deployment script are useful is when there is no public image that has the required utilities installed to run your script. For example, if you wanted to run an Az PowerShell cmdlet, then the image must have those cmdlets installed prior to executing. This currently requires that the following PowerShell installation command be run first; you may remember this from the previous chapter.

```
Install-Module -Name Az -AllowClobber -Scope AllUsers
```

As mentioned in the previous section, there is an option on the Advanced tab of the Azure VM creation blade called Extensions. Clicking Select An Extension To Install opens a window to select an extension to install. The one used for executing custom scripts is named Custom Script Extension for Windows and Custom Script for Linux. When building a Windows OS VM, you can save the following PowerShell cmdlet to a file named, for example, iis.ps1 and upload it when configuring the build properties of the Azure VM in the portal.

```
Set-AzVMExtension `
    -ExtensionName IIS `
    -Publisher Microsoft.Compute `
    -ExtensionType CustomScriptExtension `
    -TypeHandlerVersion 1.4 `
    -SettingString '{"commandToExecute":"Add-WindowsFeature `
                 -name Web-Server -IncludeManagementTools"}'
```

Then, once the Azure VM is created, IIS will be installed using an extension. You can also install, for example, SQL Server and the .NET Framework using extensions. From a Linux VM perspective, in addition to the extensions, there is also the feature on the Advanced tab to implement cloud-init scripts, which can configure users and security and install software packages. The creativity customers and developers have within this tool is greatly varied, and the wonderful point about Azure is it provides a platform to realize that creativity. I recognize this section is a bit abstract. I simply point out this feature as an option to pursue and consider when you are deploying your application to an Azure VM.

You should now have a good understanding of how to create an Azure VM whether it be Windows or Linux. You should also, if asked, know which versions of those operating systems are endorsed and what trying to deploy an image that is not endorsed could entail. You should also know what the different categories/series of VMs mean, such as memory optimized and general purpose. Given a table that shows a list of different VMs with OS, CPU requirements, and memory requirements, you need to know which ones are endorsed by Azure and if the requested resources breach any quota or resource limits.

Azure Dedicated Hosts

When you provision an Azure virtual machine, you receive the compute from a pool of existing virtual machines running on a host. The available pool of compute capacity is commonly used by all Azure customers. Be confident, however, that there is no content or configuration that remains behind after the deallocation occurs. The virtual machine is completely cleaned before being placed back into the pool of available resources. If you wanted or needed all of your virtual machines to run on its own host aka physical machine, which was not deallocated or provisioned from a pool of shared compute resources, then you can choose an Azure dedicated host. Visit this site for more information about this product offering:

docs.microsoft.com/en-us/azure/virtual-machines/windows/
dedicated-hosts.

The cost of the Azure dedicated host is more than running in the shared hosting environment. This is because you would be charged for all the compute power available on the host instead of only the consumed compute power of the host. An advantage of using an Azure dedicated host is the ability to control any infrastructure change that may impact your provisioned resource such as infrastructure or networking kinds of changes. Azure dedicated hosts are not available with VM scale sets.

Managing Azure Virtual Machines

After your Azure VMs are provisioned, it's support time. You should already have solid knowledge about creating Azure VMs. Now it is time to learn some activities that can be done after their creation. This doesn't necessarily mean that the Azure VMs are in production and being actively consumed; rather, it means that you may encounter a scenario in which one of more of them requires a rebuild, a reconfiguration, or a redesign. This section will focus on networking, maintenance, cost and sizing, storage, managed disks, disaster recovery, and backup activities.

Networking

If you followed along with the previous chapter, you are competent from an Azure networking perspective. Even if you didn't complete the previous chapter, the following networking tips may come in handy at some point. The focus of these PowerShell cmdlets is to provide insights into how your network is configured. These are helpful in case you need to find out the cause of unexpected behaviors or transient outages. It would be possible to capture the same information from the portal, but in some cases getting a holistic view of what is going on can be achieved better through running some PowerShell cmdlets. Prior to running PowerShell cmdlets, remember that you must authenticate and then set the focus to a specific Azure subscription, as shown in the following code snippet. From now, I will expect you know this step and will not mention it anymore.

```
Connect-AzAccount
$subscription = Get-AzSubscription -SubscriptionId "#####-####-##########"
Set-AzContext $subscription
```

The following is an example of a PowerShell cmdlet. It lists all the network security groups (NSGs) in a given resource group. It then cycles through all the NSGs and dumps out the NSG name, the direction of the rule, the rule name, and the inbound port. This would be helpful just to get a quick understanding of all the different NSG rules you have in your resource group. The output might resemble something like Figure 4.22.

```
$NSG = Get-AzNetworkSecurityGroup -ResourceGroupName <Resource Group Name>
foreach($nsg in $NSG)
{
    $securityRules = $nsg.SecurityRules
    foreach($rule in $securityRules)
    {
        $nsg.Name + ": " + $rule.Direction + " - " + $rule.Name + " - " `
                + $rule.DestinationPortRange
    }
}
```

FIGURE 4.22   PowerShell output of NSG details per resource group

```
PS C:\> $NSG = Get-AzNetworkSecurityGroup -ResourceGroupName CSHARPGUITAR-SN1-RG
foreach($nsg in $NSG)
{

    $securityRules = $nsg.SecurityRules
    foreach($rule in $securityRules)
    {
        $nsg.Name + ": " + $rule.Direction + " - " + $rule.Name + " - "
                  + $rule.DestinationPortRange
    }
}

CSHARPGUITAR-V1-NSG: Inbound - HTTP - 80
CSHARPGUITAR-V1-NSG: Inbound - HTTPS - 443
CSHARPGUITAR-V1-NSG: Inbound - RDP - 3389
CSHARPGUITAR-V2-NSG: Inbound - HTTPS - 443
CSHARPGUITAR-VM-NSG: Inbound - RDP - 3389

PS C:\>
```

The following are some other helpful PowerShell cmdlets:

- `Get-AzVirtualNetworks`
- `Get-AzVirtualNetworkSubnetConfig`
- `Get-AzNetworkInterface`

There are many, but those are the ones that are most useful. They will require some customization similar to the code snippet previously shown prior to Figure 4.22. The output of those PowerShell cmdlets is often large JSON-formatted documents that contain all the details of the network, subnet, and network interface. Much of the information is unnecessary and can be filtered out with a little creative PowerShell scripting. It is a powerful tool with a large open source set of cmdlets at your disposal.

Maintenance

There is no way around it; once you deploy your workloads to an Azure VM, you can't just walk away from it and forget it. Like a car or your garden/yard, it needs some ongoing attention. Some details you would want to be aware of fall into, but are not limited to, these areas:

- Starting, stopping, and deleting
- Resource locks
- Resizing
- Managing Windows Updates
- Viewing boot diagnostics

In the next section, we'll go into more detail about stopping and starting VMs, but it's most optimal in this cloud service model that you turn off VMs that you don't need. There

are numerous ways to achieve this; one simple way is to execute the PowerShell cmdlet
`Stop-AzVM -ResourceGroupName <name> -Name <VM Name> -Force` to stop a VM
or use `Start-AzVM -ResourceGroupName <name> -Name <VM Name>` to start one.
Stopping and starting VMs can also be achieved via the Azure Portal or via an RDP,
Bastion or SSH session directly on a VM. It is also possible to use
`Remove-AzVM -ResourceGroupName <name> -Name <VM Name>` to delete a VM.
The Remove-AzVM cmdlet can have some significant impact if the VM performs a critical
function in your solution. RBAC controls can be used to restrict this kind of activity based
on individuals or groups. If you wanted to make sure that no one, no matter what, was
allowed to delete a resource or any resource group regardless of RBAC restrictions, then
there is a feature called *resource locks* that will handle that requirement. To test a resource
lock, complete Exercise 4.7.

EXERCISE 4.7

Creating and Testing a Resource Lock

1. Log in to the Azure Portal at `portal.azure.com` and navigate to an Azure VM you
   have created previously (like in Exercise 4.5). If you prefer, create a new VM for use in
   this exercise. Click the Lock link in the navigation bar to open the Locks blade. Press
   the + Add button, which opens a window similar to that shown in Figure 4.23.

FIGURE 4.23   Adding a resource lock to an Azure VM

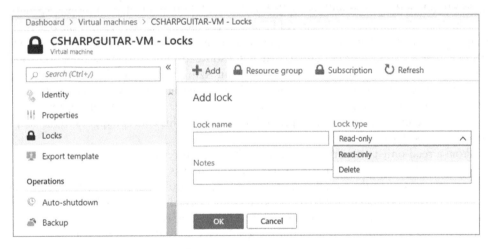

2. Enter a name (such as CSHARPGUITAR-VM-NO-DELETE), and set the Lock type to
   Delete. Enter a note under the lock to prevent the deletion of this mission-critical VM.
   Now, click the OK button.

3. Open a PowerShell session and login attempt to remove the VM you just locked by executing the following cmdlet. You should receive an error similar to the one following the cmdlet.

```
Remove-AzVM –ResourceGroupName <Name> –Name <VM Name>


Remove-AzVM : The scope 'CSHARPGUITAR-VM' cannot perform delete
              operation because following scope(s) are locked:
              Please remove the lock and try again.
              ErrorCode: ScopeLocked
              StatusCode: 409
              ReasonPhrase: Conflict
```

You may have noticed in Figure 4.23 that there were links to the resource group and subscription next to the + Add button. In this context, on the VM blade, you can only add a lock on the given resource, i.e., the Azure VM. However, clicking those other links will show you a list of locks that exist in that resource group and subscription. If you wanted to apply a lock on a resource group or subscription, you would need to navigate to that resource's blade and click the Lock link on that resource. As you would expect, locks placed on the parent will be applied to the child, in that a lock on a resource group will apply to all resources within it. Additionally, the most restrictive lock is the one that is applied if there are locks in both the parent and the child. For example, the drop-down list in Figure 4.23 included not only Delete but also Read-Only. If there is a read-only lock placed on a resource group and a delete lock on an Azure VM within the resource group, then the delete lock is the one that is respected, as it is more restrictive. Refer to Chapter 2 where we discussed scopes if you need a hierarchy refresher in regard to management groups, subscriptions, resource groups, and resources, as this concept applies to the scope model discussed here too.

From a read-only perspective, the meaning here is that resource modifications are read-only, not the operation on the resource. Two examples, if there is a read-only lock placed on a VM, then the size, disks, configuration, or auto-shutdown schedule cannot be changed. However, if someone RDPs or SSHs to the VM, that person will be able to change and/or remove content from the VM itself. Assuming there is a managed SQL Server instance on the VM, the data in the database would be changeable, and the read-only setting applies only to the changes that occur on the VM itself via the portal or other supported client.

The next maintenance-related activity has to do with resizing. Any financially minded person wants to spend the exact amount required to get the job done—nothing more, nothing less. This holds true when choosing an Azure VM because the cost is directly related to the size, i.e., how much compute you get. Starting off small and then growing is an option because resizing is not so complicated. When you create an Azure VM, a default size is selected (for example, D2SV3), but there is a link under it that allows you to change the size. If you decide to keep that size and later determine you need more compute power, there is a link in the navigation bar for the Azure VM named size. Clicking that link opens the Size blade and will show you the existing size and a list of other options, as shown in Figure 4.24.

FIGURE 4.24 Listing different Azure VM sizes

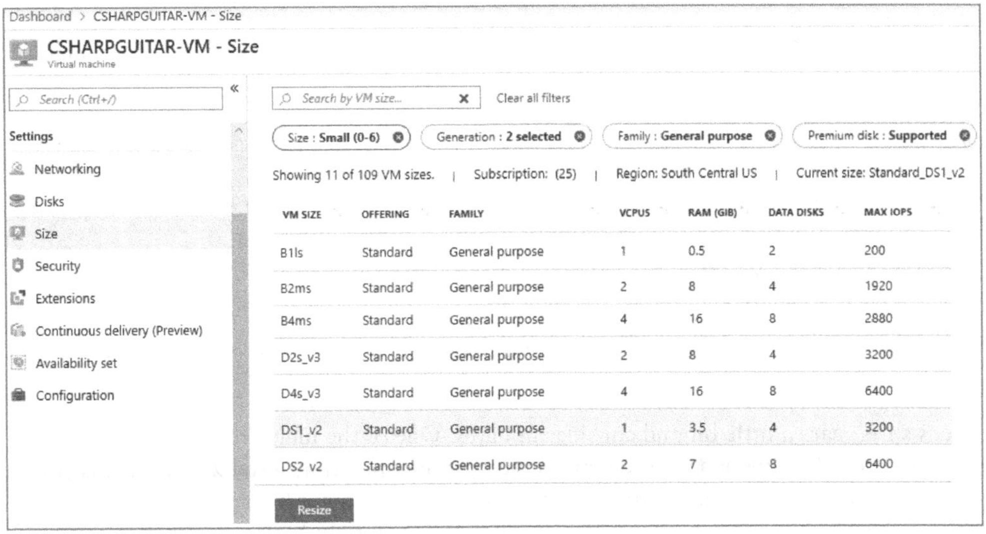

Simply select the desired size, and click the Resize button, and the Azure VM will be scaled up to that size. Note that changing the size will result in a restart of the application, which should be expected since the configuration of the compute power associated to the VM is a significant altercation. It is also possible to make the same change using Power-Shell. Execute the following cmdlets and view the output in Figure 4.25:

```
Get-AzVMSize -ResourceGroupName "<RG-NAME>" -VMName "<VM-NAME>"
$vm = Get-AzVM -ResourceGroupName "RG-NAME" -VMName "<VM-NAME>"
$vm.HardwareProfile.VmSize = "Standard_DS3_v2"
Update-AzVM -VM $vm -ResourceGroupName "<RG-NAME>"
```

The first PowerShell cmdlet lists all the possible VM sizes available for the Azure VM in that region. This is helpful for finding out not only the options you have but also the nomenclature (its name) you need later once you decide on the size. The options in the Azure Portal are a bit more restrictive; you will get an unfiltered list using PowerShell. The next lines of the PowerShell script get the VM into a PowerShell object, set the VmSize, and update it. Wait some time, and then the workload you had running on that VM will be scaled up to the newly allocated compute series. Just as an extra test, update the resource lock you created in Exercise 4.7 to read-only and try the same update process discussed just now. It will fail, because the configuration options for the VM would then be read-only and cannot be changed.

FIGURE 4.25 Resizing an Azure VM using PowerShell

```
PS C:\> Get-AzVMSize -ResourceGroupName "CSHARPGUITAR-SN1-RG" -VMName "CSHARPGUITAR-VM"

Name            NumberOfCores MemoryInMB MaxDataDiskCount OSDiskSizeInMB ResourceDiskSizeInMB
----            ------------- ---------- ---------------- -------------- --------------------
Standard_B2s                2       4096                4        1047552                 8192
Standard_B4ms               4      16384                8        1047552                32768
Standard_B8ms               8      32768               16        1047552                65536
Standard_D1_v2              1       3584                4        1047552                51200
Standard_D2_v2              2       7168                8        1047552               102400
Standard_D3_v2              4      14336               16        1047552               204800
Standard_D4_v2              8      28672               32        1047552               409600
Standard_D5_v2             16      57344               64        1047552               819200
Standard_D11_v2             2      14336                8        1047552               102400

PS C:\> $vm = Get-AzVM -ResourceGroupName "CSHARPGUITAR-SN1-RG" -VMName "CSHARPGUITAR-VM"

PS C:\> $vm.HardwareProfile.VmSize = "Standard_DS3_v2"

PS C:\> Update-AzVM -VM $vm -ResourceGroupName "CSHARPGUITAR-SN1-RG"

RequestId IsSuccessStatusCode StatusCode ReasonPhrase
--------- ------------------- ---------- ------------
                         True     OK OK
```

Let's shift gears a little bit and consider updates. One of the major responsibilities that you have when choosing IaaS is the management of the operating system. This means you need to schedule and manage security patches, bug fixes, and hot fixes (i.e., from a Windows perspective KB patches). There is a product called Update Management that will help you with this. Update Management is used in collaboration with Log Analytics, which is discussed in Chapter 9. Once you configure Update Management, it will perform an analysis of the targeted VM and provide details about any missing updates. This works on both Windows and CentOS, Red Hat, SUSE, and Ubuntu Linux VMs. If any updates are found to be missing, there is an additional feature found within the capabilities of Update Management that allows you to schedule an update deployment. The update can be scheduled to run once or be recurring, and you can configure whether to reboot after the update is applied or not. That is an important option, i.e., whether to allow a reboot. Early in my IT career there was some high risks involved in installing operating system patches. On numerous occasions the patch simply wouldn't install and killed the server, or the patch installed and went down for a reboot and never came back up. In both scenarios, the only option we had was to rebuild the entire server, which was the easy part. Installing, configuring, and testing the freshly built application was the hard part. I am so thankful for images, backups, and deployment slots that can now save me many hours, late nights, and weekends. The experience is to simply point out that selecting the reboot options and automating OS patch installation needs to have some thought about rollback or troubleshooting scenarios. There is another feature for Azure VMs called *boot diagnostics* that can help if after an update is installed the VM doesn't come back up or simply for any reason after a reboot the VM is hanging.

Setting a Resource Lock to Read-Only on a VM

In the previous two paragraphs I discussed resource locks, and in Exercise 4.7 you created a resource lock of type Delete. I also discussed the read-only lock type and moved onto update management. It turned out that you cannot configure update management when there is a read-only lock on the VM. I was getting some errors, and it took me some minutes to figure out what was going on. It is so easy to get spun around on Azure. Keep going and keep learning.

To keep your head from spinning too much, an overview of what is going on in your subscription and resource group can help to give some clarity. Those monitoring topics are covered more in Chapter 6 where we cover compliance topics and in Chapter 9 when we cover monitoring. However, the Inventory link on the Azure VM navigation menu lets you enable change tracking on the VM. Once it's configured, you can get an overview of what software, files, Windows registry, and Windows services have been added, changed, or deleted. For Linux VMs, the software, files, and Linux daemons are monitored for changes. I am confident you will agree that knowing what is happening on your machines is helpful toward their maintenance and support. If something stopped working, you could look on the Inventory blade and check whether something has changed without needing to RDP or SSH to the VM and looking manually.

Finally, if you recall from the numerous times you have created an Azure VM, on the Management tab there is a feature named Boot Diagnostics. It is enabled by default and stores some helpful pieces of information. A helpful one is that it captures a screen shot that may be a BSOD, or for Linux there may be some text shown on what you'd normally see on a monitor when running on-premise and directly connected to the machine. There is also a Serial log, which provides some potentially helpful logs with errors and exceptions that may lead to a root cause and a fix. Another useful tool is the Serial console, which provides a COM1 serial connection to the VM. I mentioned earlier about tty0; this was the place where I was working when failing at the deployment of an unblessed Azure VM image. I was using the boot diagnostics and the Serial console (which I couldn't connect to) trying to get the Azure VM to work. Both of those features are useful for maintenance and trouble-shooting efforts.

Costs and Sizes

Choosing the right compute size is important because the cost is static for an Azure VM, unlike when running a consumption mode Azure Function, for example. You do not want too much, nor do you want too little, but hitting the precise size from the beginning can be challenging. If you decide to start small and then increase or decrease as you go along, that is a good plan. The Azure VM resizing capabilities as shown in Figure 4.25 can help you proceed with that approach. Also, starting and stopping the VM when it is not being used is also a means to reduce costs. There are numerous ways to stop and start a VM; you know already that you can use PowerShell cmdlets Start-AzVM and Stop-AzVM to achieve that. However, in that context, you need to watch out for a few things. As shown in Table 4.8, there are numerous Azure VM power states that you need to understand.

TABLE 4.8   Virtual Machine Power States

Power state	Detail
Deallocating	The VM is in the process of releasing allocated compute resource.
Deallocated	Allocated compute resources are no longer consumed.
Stopping	The VM is in the process of being shut down.
Stopped	The VM is shut down; compute resources remain allocated.
Starting	The VM is in the process of being activated.
Running	The VM has been started and is ready for consumption.

The important point in those VM power states is that if you simply stop the VM, you will continue to incur a charge because the compute resources remain allocated to the VM. You need to make sure that you deallocate the VM if it is no longer needed. Deallocation is achieved when you use the Stop-AzVM PowerShell cmdlet or click the Stop button on the Overview blade in the portal. If you want to use the Stop-AzVM PowerShell cmdlet but not deallocate the virtual machine, pass the -StayProvisioned parameter along with the command. By contrast, if you have an RDP connection to a Windows VM and click the shutdown button, the VM is not deallocated; it is simply stopped. An important note is that when a VM is deallocated, the Public IP address is placed back into the pool, and when you start it back up again, it is likely that it has a different public IP address. That has an impact if your solution has any dependencies on that IP address. You will notice that when you click the stop button in the portal, you get warned of the loss of the IP address and are asked if you want to keep it. If you choose to keep it, the IP address is changed to a static IP address, and there is a cost associated with that. The default public IP address setting is dynamic, which is why it can change when the VM is deallocated.

You may have also noticed during the creation of an Azure VM in the portal that on the Management tab there is an option called Auto-Shutdown. This is configurable during and after the creation of the VM. This feature allows you to deallocate the VM at a given time each day so you do not have to worry about forgetting to stop it all the time. Additionally, you can provide an email address to be notified when the auto-shutdown feature is executed; it includes the name of the VM it ran on as well. Up to now we have focused on Windows VMs; in Exercise 4.8, you will create a Linux VM and execute some Azure CLI commands using https://shell.azure.com.

EXERCISE 4.8

Creating and Managing a Linux VM Using Azure CLI

1. Log in to the Azure Portal at `https://portal.azure.com` and click + Create A Resource in the top-left area of the browser. Next, click Compute and then click Virtual Machine.

2. Select the subscription and the resource group (for example CSHARPGUITAR-SN1-RG). Enter a virtual machine name (like CSHARPGUITAR-LX) and then select the region (for example, South Central US). Select Ubuntu Server 18.04 LTS from the Image drop-down list. Click the Password radio button and enter a username and password. Select the Allow Selected Ports radio button and allow HTTP (80), HTTPS (443). and SSH (22). Click the Next: Disks button.

3. Leave the defaults and click the Next: Networking button. Select the virtual network created in the previous chapter (I used CSHARPGUITAR-VNET-B) or create a new one. Select the subnet (mine is csharp) and click the + Next: Management button. Select the On radio button in the Auto-shutdown section, set a shutdown time, set the time zone, and if desired, enable the notification before shutdown option.

4. Leave the remaining as the default, click the Review + Create button, and click the Create button.

5. Once that's complete, open a browser, and enter this internet address: `shell.azure .com`. Enter your credentials and then execute the following Azure CLI commands:

```
az vm get-instance-view --name <VMName> --resource-group <Name>
                        --query instanceView.statuses[1] --output table


az vm stop --resource-group <Name> --name <VMName>


az vm get-instance-view --name <VMName> --resource-group <Name>
                        --query instanceView.statuses[1] --output table


az vm deallocate --resource-group <Name> --name <VMName>


az vm get-instance-view --name <VMName> --resource-group <Name>
                        --query instanceView.statuses[1] --output table
```

The result should be similar to that shown in Figure 4.26.

FIGURE 4.26   Changing the power state of Linux VM using Azure CLI

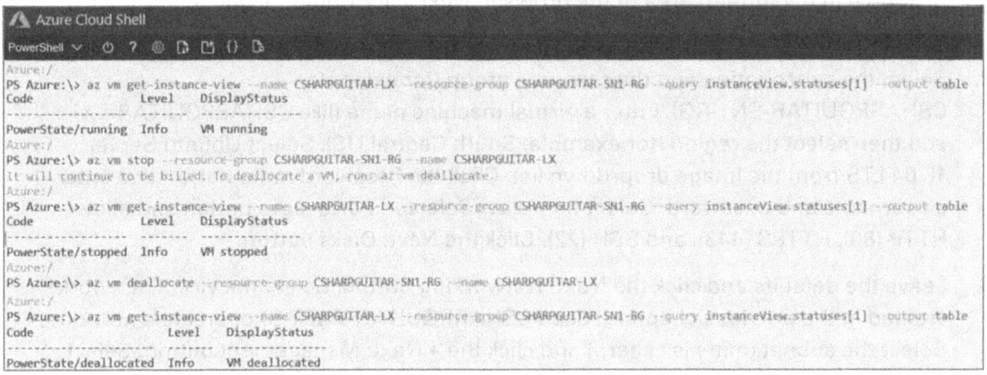

It is possible to install Azure CLI onto your workstation and use it remotely, that same as with PowerShell, but I wanted to show you this Azure Cloud Shell feature. One advantage and something I like about it is that I do not have to constantly execute `Connect-AzAccount` to get logged in. I am prompted for my credentials when I first access the site. Another experience you may have noticed is that `az vm stop` doesn't deallocate the VM like `Stop-AzVM` does; you must instead use `az vm deallocate`. That is an important point to be aware of, and it is mentioned when executing `az vm stop`. However, had you run this as an automated script, perhaps it could have been missed.

When all is said and done and you no longer need the allocated Azure compute power, you can simply remove the resource group, and all of its contents are removed. This is a good reason to keep all your resources grouped together in a resource group when you are testing or developing. Have all the resources being used for a given project or application so you know what the provisioned resources belong to. There is a concept called *tags* that we will discuss in Chapter 6 that provides a similar capability, but for now, put every related Azure resource into a resource group, and when you're done, run `Remove-AzResourceGroup -Name <Name> - Force` in PowerShell or `az group delete --name <Name> --no-wait --yes` using Azure CLI.

Finally, when you have completed the project and the resources can be deleted, you can check the bill. The bill includes the ability to download a CSV file that contains a daily breakdown of resource usage and the associated charge. This is useful not only in hindsight but also to check and see whether there are any resources consuming Azure compute without any real purpose. You could then remove them. To get that report, navigate to the Subscription blade and select the desired subscription. In the Billing section, select Invoices, which renders the option to download the Usage + Charges report, similar to that shown in Figure 4.27.

FIGURE 4.27   Download Azure consumption charges from Azure Portal

It is important to keep an eye on costs, not only from an Azure VM perspective but from a subscription-wide perspective. I sit next to some Microsoft employees who work on the Subscription and Billing team and hear how customers get a shock with the bill and try to reason their way out of it because they didn't expect it to cost that much. I don't get to hear or see the result, but I don't think the charge gets forgiven 100% of the time. So, be careful and keep a close eye on this.

Managed Disk Storage

A managed disk is a virtual hard disk (VHD), and whether you know it or not, you have already created many of them. Each time you created an Azure VM you used the Disks tab where you could select the OS disk type from a drop-down list, the option to add one or more data disks, and an Advanced section. Azure managed disks are not physical disks that use, for example, *Small Computer System Interface (SCSI)* or *Integrated Drive Electronics (IDE)* standards to connect a hard drive to a physical server. Instead, the managed disk is a construct of a *page blob* in an *Azure Container Storage* account. If you by chance do not know what a blob is, consider it to be a file (for example, DOCX, PHP, VHD, or PNG) that has content like text, source code or an image contained within it. Instead of saving the content of the file into a database, for example, you would store the entire file as a blob type. Data and storage concepts are covered in Chapter 5, so we won't go too deep into the topic now. Instead, just know that the hard disk really is a VHD, and the internals of how that works can be left to the Azure platform and accepted as part of the service in which the platform provides.

The alternative to a managed disk is called an *ephemeral disk*, which is found on the Disks tab during the creation of the VM. Expand the Advanced contents to see the option to create one. As you can see in Figure 4.28, an ephemeral drive is connected to the local virtual machine (VM) instead of the abstracted page blob. There are specific use cases for choosing this kind of drive; for one, ephemeral disks are free, unlike managed disks. They also perform better if your workload needs to be reset or reimaged, which makes sense because the disk is physically connected to the VM. Also, if your workload is stateless, you might consider an ephemeral disk. Considering both managed and ephemeral disks, it would mean that your VM can come up, go down, and be reimaged often with no impact on the application or your customers. If that is the case, then the ephemeral drive type might be an option. Most use cases would fit best on managed disks.

FIGURE 4.28   An advanced option to choose ephemeral drives instead of managed

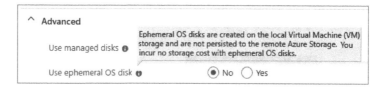

Managed disks have a 99.999% availability threshold, and you can currently create up to 50,000 disks per subscription per region. Five nines is achieved by duplicating your data on the disk to three different instances. All three disks would need to fail before there would be an outage, which is unlikely. Managed disks are deeply integrated with VMSS, which is discussed later and provides protection against impact because of a segment failure from within a data center (you'll learn more about that later in the chapter). Managed disks support Availability Zones, which were covered in the previous chapter and can be encrypted. Remember encryption at rest from Chapter 2? Table 4.9 provides more details about managed disk types.

TABLE 4.9   Managed Disk Types

Offering	Premium SSD	Standard SSD	Standard HDD
Disk Type	SSD	SSD	HDD
Maximum Size	32,767GB	32,767GB	32,767GB
Maximum IOPS	20,000	6,000	2,000
Max Throughput	900 MB/s	750 MB/s	500 MB/s
Usage	High-performance productions	Web servers, dev and test	Backup, noncritical

The managed disk types in the table should be familiar to you; they were the options in the drop-drop list for the OS disk type on the Disk tab when creating an Azure VM in the portal. As a side note, notice that the maximum size of the disks is 32,767GB, which is 2^{15}. There is also an Ultra Disk type that is currently limited to a few regions, and the max size of that is 65,536, which is the number again that I called out specifically in the previous chapter, 2^{16}. When I see things like that, it makes me feel like there was some real thought behind them. Let's get back to the topic at hand; up to now we have only added an OS disk to the VM, which resulted in a disk configuration like that shown in Figure 4.29. This is displayed after connecting via RDP to the VM and running diskmgmt.msc.

FIGURE 4.29   The default disk configuration on an Azure VM

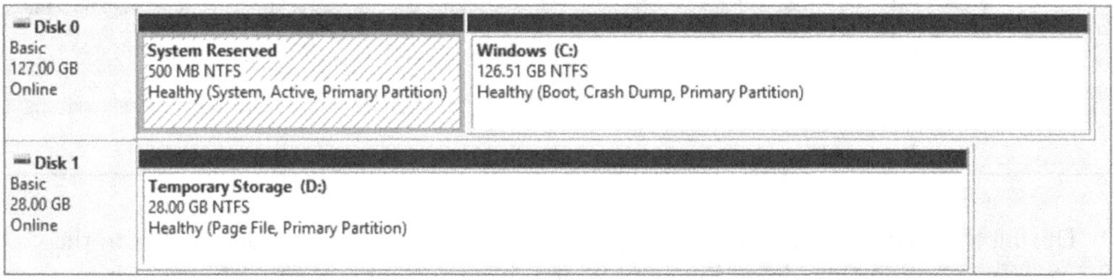

In Exercise 4.9 you will add a data disk to an Azure VM. If you are not clear on the different types of disks available to a VM, refer again to Figure 4.20.

EXERCISE 4.9

Creating and Managing a Linux VM Using Azure CLI

1. Log in to the Azure Portal at portal.azure.com and navigate to a virtual machine that you completed previously. Click Disks from the navigation menu and then click the + Add Data Disk button. You will see the OS disk that is bound to the VM.

2. Below that you will see Data disks. Click the drop-down, click the Create Disk link, and enter a name (I used CSHARPGUITAR-VM-DD1 in my example). Leave the defaults and click the Create button.

3. Once the allocation is complete, the focus returns to the Disks blade for the VM. Click the Save button at the top of the Disks blade.

Run diskmgmt.msc on the VM again, and you will see the disk has been added. See Figure 4.30 as an example. A PowerShell cmdlet like Get-AzDisk or the az vm disk Azure CLI command can also provide insights into the details of the disks bound to the VM. Try either of those on your own if desired.

FIGURE 4.30   A data disk added to the default disk configuration on an Azure VM

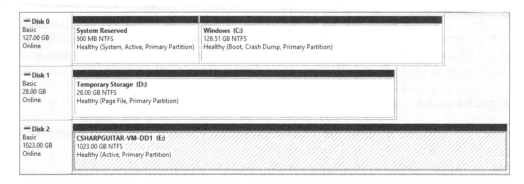

During the creation of the data disk, you may have noticed a drop-down next to the Storage Type option. The drop-down contained three options; we chose None as it was the default, meaning we simply want a blank disk. There was also an option to build the disk from a Storage blob, which was mentioned earlier. This means you can make a VHD of any VM, store it in a blob container, and then reference it as the source for a managed disk. That is cool, and you'll learn more about it in the next chapter. The final option was Snapshot.

Think about what a snapshot is in the real world. When you take a picture of something, the state of the subject of the picture is frozen in time and won't change. Similar to a custom VM image, which you created in Exercise 4.6, a managed disk snapshot is a copy of the contents of the disk at a point of time that can be used as a backup or as a means to build another identical VM for troubleshooting. If you navigate to one of the managed disks you created, you will notice the + Create Snapshot link at the top of the Overview blade for the selected disk. After you create a snapshot, if you do Exercise 4.9 again and select Snapshot instead of None as the storage type, then the one you created is listed in the drop-down.

Backup, Redeploy, and Reset Password

There is an entire chapter, Chapter 9, that covers monitoring and recovery, so only some basic concepts will be discussed here. If you recall from Chapter 1 and Chapter 2, we have already discussed Azure Site Recovery. We will again touch on it with a comparison with the Azure VM backup feature, but the real, in-depth coverage is in Chapter 9. The specific topics covered in this section are provided in the following list:

- Backup and redeploy
- Azure Backup versus Azure Site Recovery
- Resetting the password

The whole point to backing up data and software is to protect your intellectual property and your business. I cannot quote any specific incident, but imagine you have a program with 100,000 lines of code that cost the value of 2 million hours of labor. Imagine too that the data it accesses and analyzes is on the same server and is a set of values captured over the course of the last 10 years. Imagine there is neither a backup of the source code nor the data. That's a scary thought. What happens if the server crashes and you cannot get any of that data or code. If this happens, then the business disappears. This is an avoidable situation if you simply back up. A less impactful scenario discussed in the previous section is what can happen after an update to the operating system that requires a reboot. When you configure Update Management to install updates, you might consider scheduling a backup some hours or a day before the scheduled patching process. There is a Backup link in the navigation menu on the Azure VM blade that allows you to schedule a backup based on a configured policy. The policy can be based on daily or weekly frequencies. Once configured, there is a link at the top of the Backup blade, which allows you to back up manually. In the background, the backup creates and stores a snapshot that can be used later to provision a new Azure VM.

The Redeploy navigation menu item is a bit different than you might initially think. This can be easily misunderstood to mean that it is the feature used to rebuild a VM with a snapshot or a backup. However, when you click the menu item, it becomes quickly apparent that instead of recovery, the feature moves the application to a new host. That concept is interesting because it is only possible because the managed disks are not physically attached to the VM. It is therefore possible to attach those disks to another VM and boot it up, almost in real time, which is amazing. That is what happens when you redeploy and this model is used with VMSS, PaaS, and FaaS. Take note that with ephemeral disks, this kind of redeploy action is not possible because the disks are attached, but as mentioned, the reimaging is faster. You just need to determine which is best for your given use case.

The scenario of losing your business because you don't back up or haven't backed up should give an Azure Solution Architect Expert goosebumps. If I were to reflect on the model being proposed in this book (security, network, compute), I think the next consideration would be a *business continuity and disaster recovery (BCDR)* plan, mentioned in Chapter 1. That leads to the comparison between Azure Backup and Azure Site Recovery. From a backup (Azure Backup) perspective, your context is singular and granular. Where you are backing up a VM and then recover from that backup, you are thinking about files, machine state, or specific folders. You can see that in practice when you click the Backup navigation item for a VM versus when you click the Disaster Recovery Navigation menu item. The Disaster Recovery menu item is the entry point into Azure Site Recovery. Azure Site Recovery is, in old terms, *disaster recovery (DR)*. DR means something big happened, everything on the machine is permanently gone, and likely everything in the data center will be down for many hours. Having a BCDR plan or contingency plan is built upon Azure Site Recovery; jump to Chapter 9 if you urgently need to learn more about that.

Migrating Azure Virtual Machines

Migration is covered in detail in Chapter 8, but it is worth a mention here in the VM context. VMs are the most common cloud service model that is "migrated" to Azure. That's either because, like I mentioned, it was the first offering from Azure or it is an entry point for enterprises to deploy their existing applications that require virtual networks and have multiple tiers of compute requirements. Refer to Figure 4.19 if you don't know what I mean by multiple tiers. In this section we will touch briefly on the following migration topics:

- Migrate from on-premise
- Change regions, zones, subscriptions, or resource groups

Migrate from On-Premise

First, it would be prudent to know what is meant by migration. Say you have a website running on a virtual machine constructed using Hyper-V. Hyper-V is Microsoft's virtualization offering that offers the same capabilities as VMware. The website could also be running on a physical server where no virtualization software is in place. Migration means that you want to move the workload from one place, usually in an on-premise data center, to an Azure VM. You would want there to be an automated process to achieve that. It should be an automated process that avoids the manual rebuild and reconfiguration of the server and application, a simple cut-and-paste scenario if you may. There are some advanced capabilities that help streamline a migration, but unfortunately they are not as simple as cut and paste. It is, however, as simple as preparing the on-premise machine by generating the proper configuration and data files and then packing them and deploying them onto a disk, which can then be used for the Azure VM provisioning. That process is presented in Chapter 8. For now, just know that some tools are called Azure Site Recovery and Azure Migrate; more manual tools include AzCopy, Disk2VHD, SYSPREP, *Microsoft Virtual Machine Converter (MVMC)*, Hyper-V, and VMware.

Azure Site Recovery and Azure Migrate are the tools you will use if you have a large enterprise solution with multiple tiers and many machines. That scenario would be one where the number of servers being migrated is too great to even consider a manual provision. The other mentioned tools are for smaller migration projects, where much of the work can be accomplished by performing manual tasks and is performed by a single person or a small team.

Change Resource Groups, Subscriptions, Regions, or Zones

What happens if you realize you have placed your VM workloads into the wrong resource group, subscription, or region? Perhaps, if you realize it early in the deployment cycle, a simple delete and re-create won't have any impact, and that is the simplest and cleanest way to move the workloads. However, if you realize this after some significant configuration has been performed on a VM or there are now other resources with a dependency on a given VM, re-creating that VM isn't really an option. It's not an option because the impact would be too large. Moving the VM into another resource group is actually easy. As you recall, a resource group is only a logical grouping; there is nothing physical about it. On the Azure Portal on the Overview blade, the resource group to which the VM is associated is displayed. Directly after the words *resource group* there is a link named Change. Simply click that and change it. The same goes for the subscription, as shown in Figure 4.31.

FIGURE 4.31   Azure Portal view of changing resource group or subscription

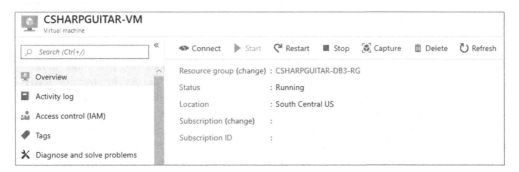

There are three points to call out here, as shown in Figure 4.31. First, although the resource group did change, its physical location did not. The VM was in CSHARPGUITAR-SN1-RG (South Central US), and I changed it to CSHARPGUITAR-DB3-RG (North Europe), but the physical location of the VM did not change. It does kind of make sense in that there may be IT solutions that are global, and I'd want workloads in different regions in the same resource group because they play a part in the overall solution. However, the name of the resource group no longer makes sense. The second point is that only the VM was moved, and there are more components to a VM than just the host. For example, if you enabled boot diagnostics, there would be a storage account for the VM, and there is a network interface, possibly an NSG, and a static public IP address and the disks. You would want to move all the pieces and not leave them separated. You would lose oversight of them quickly. I hope you are realizing more and more how important it is to organize your resources and that there are some good features in Azure to achieve that. Lastly, the name of the VM cannot already exist in the resource group to which it is being moved. The unique key in a resource group is name + resource type, which means you can name everything the same as long as the type of resource is different. An Azure SQL instance, a VM, a Cosmos DB, a Storage account, and an Azure VM can all be named CSHARPGUITAR since they are different types of resources.

Now we come to the more difficult scenario where you actually want to physically move the workload from a region or zone. There are two points to mention about moving like this in this chapter; you cannot move from any region to any region, and Azure Site Recovery is the recommended tool for achieving that kind of move. In the previous chapter, we discussed the Azure network, and the concept of a geography was provided. Well, that is the limit in which you can physically move an Azure VM. One of the reasons for that limit has to do with the sovereignty of the data or intellectual property running on your VMs. It is in a way a protective barrier so you cannot by mistake move restricted data into a location where there is a risk of its presence being prohibited. You know from the previous chapter that geographies are usually in the same area of the world. For example, West Europe and North Europe are in the same geography, and there may be less chance of breaching a Global Data Protection Regulation (GDPR) when moving between those two regions than any other region not in Europe. Moving between South Central US, West Central US, and North Central US is also supported, for example. You'll learn more about that and more on Azure Site Recovery in Chapter 8.

We also discussed what an Availability Zone was in the previous chapter. Simply, it means Microsoft has your back, and all of your compute is not running in a single data center. For a given region, there are multiple data centers, either across the street or across town, but your data and workload are replicated into both, making sure that your solution remains available even if an entire data center experiences a catastrophic event. If you recall from Exercise 4.5, on the Basic tab of the Azure VM creation process there was a drop-down list named Availability Options. In the exercise so far, the value was left at the default because infrastructure redundancy has an associated cost, and it wasn't ready to be discussed then. However, if you return and view the contents of the drop-down, you will find the availability zone and availability set. Both of them are touched on in the next section; however, if after creating a VM with no infrastructure redundancy, you decide you need it, then you can move it into a zone using Azure Site Recovery.

Availability Sets and VM Scale Sets

Availability is a big deal. If you were to deploy a workload to the Azure platform and then the application experiences more unavailability than it had on-premise, some serious questions would be asked. In Chapter 2, we discussed what an SLA is, and it will be touched on again in Chapter 9, but from an Azure VM perspective we'll touch on it a bit because it has something to do with the topic in hand. Basically, if you deploy only a single VM, the SLA commitment for its availability is 99.9%, which translates to approximately 45 minutes of allowed downtime per month. Is that good enough? It would depend on the criticality of the code running on the VM. If you need more, than you have to take some actions to add redundancies across availability sets and Availability Zones.

As you know, when you choose IaaS, the cloud provider is responsible for managing the hardware and infrastructure. Those components do sometimes experience transient outages or require some maintenance. If you have only a single instance of your VM, then there will be downtime if the hardware or infrastructure updates a component that requires a reboot or inhibits traffic transmission from arriving to or departing from your VM. For example, hardware driver updates or a memory module fails. If you create multiple instances of your VM, Microsoft has implemented two concepts to help manage outages during transient or maintenance activities called *fault domains* and *update domains*. When you place your VMs into those domains, the SLA increases to 99.95%, which allows about 20 minutes per month, which is less than half the downtime when compared to running on a single VM. There is a cost for the additional instance, but no cost for the domain feature. If you then go so far as to place multiple domain instances into multiple zones, then the SLA increases to 99.99%, which is a very low amount of downtime at 4.5 minutes per month. Again, it costs more, but the cost may be justified based on the workloads running on the VMs. You may be asking yourself, have we spoken about these domains? The answer is not really, but by the end of this chapter, you will create some and add some VMs to them. You should certainly know what an Availability Zone is because it was discussed in the previous chapter. You will also add VMs to an Availability Zone later.

Availability Sets vs. Scale Sets

In Chapter 3, I stated that more would be covered regarding availability sets. That will happen in the coming paragraphs. In addition to that, it will be good to include scale sets in this discussion now. They kind of read the same and sound the same if spoken; some might even think they are the same, but they are not. An availability set is like a DR environment or primary secondary architectural configuration. While a virtual machine scale set is a group of identically configured VMs. Both do have something in common, in that they benefit from fault domains and update domains. See Figure 4.32 for an illustration.

FIGURE 4.32 Fault domains and update domains

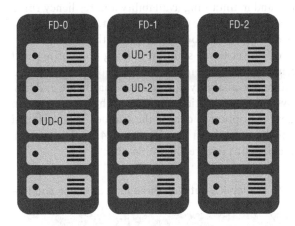

A fault domain is a grouping of VMs that share the same network switch and power source. An update domain is a group of VMs that can be rebooted at the same time after a maintenance activity has been performed. That would mean it would be prudent to place VMs that shouldn't be rebooted at the same time into different update domains. The platform is intelligent enough to place primary and secondary VMs into different update domains on a best-effort basis. For both availability sets and VMSS, you have the fault domains feature and get up to three for availability sets and a default of five for VMSS. There are five update domains created into each fault domain. Finally, note that neither fault nor update domains will prevent downtime caused by application or operating system exceptions. Let's now get into a little more hands-on detail for both Azure products.

Availability Set

As mentioned just previously, an *availability set* is most useful for disaster recovery environments or primary/secondary environments. From a DR or failover perspective, consider you have a web farm that is an internet/intranet application running on many different servers behind some kind of load balancing device. The reason for having many servers running the application is for redundancy. If you have only one server and it goes down, then your business is down. Therefore, have numerous servers each of which is acting as a DR or failover instance of the other. The issue comes when there is a power outage or transient network issue. Fault domains will prevent your servers from being dependent on the same power supply and network switches. When you create your VMs, you select the availability set to place them into, and the platform decides which fault domain to place them into.

Each VM in an availability set is uniquely named, and each can be configured and added to an application gateway or load balancer. Additionally, if you are running a managed SQL Server instance, you would want to have a secondary copy of the database in case of outage, again both being in separate availability sets. Finally, if you were performing updates to your VMs, installing patches, or doing an OS upgrade, you wouldn't do it on all the machines and then reboot them all at the same time. It is actually a tedious process for installing updates and maintaining availability and resiliency throughout that process. It is no small undertaking. But in the simplest context, you would install a patch on one and test to make sure all is well, before moving onto the others. From a database perspective, you may want to failover to the standby, making it the primary after the upgrade and then upgrade the primary, which then becomes secondary. The update domain concept is intended to help maintain availability during Azure hardware and infrastructure updates and not operating system or application upgrades. When you create an availability set in Exercise 4.10 you have the option to choose the number of fault domains, from 1 to 3, and the number of update domains, from 1 to 20. Figure 4.33 simulates the organization of five VMs into five update domains in three fault domains.

FIGURE 4.33   An availability set with three fault domains and five update domains

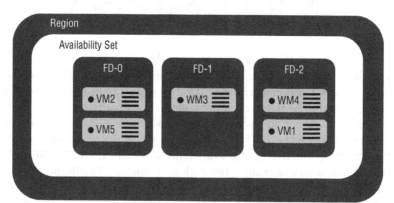

Complete Exercise 4.10 to create an availability set and then add some VMs to it. Note that you can only add a VM to an availability set during VM creation. You cannot move a VM into an availability set after creation; it must be deleted and re-created. However, with what you know about images, disks, and backups, that shouldn't be a significant issue. Just keep that in mind.

EXERCISE 4.10

Creating and Configuring an Availability Set

1. Log in to the Azure Portal at `portal.azure.com` and then click + Create A Resource. Enter Availability Sets into the Search box and then press the Enter key. Now click the Create button.

2. Select the subscription into which you want to add the availability set. Select a resource group (CSHARPGUITAR-SN1-RG), provide a name (for example, CSHARPGUITAR-SN1-AS), and select a region. The region should be in the same as the resource group location. Set the number of fault domains to 3 and the number of update domains to 5. Click the Review + Create button then click the Create button.

3. Create a new Azure virtual machine as you did in Exercise 4.5, but in this case, pay special attention to the Availability Options drop-down list. After selecting both the resource group and region, the contents of the list box would contain both the availability set and Availability Zone. When you select the availability set, a drop-down list box is rendered. Select the availability set you just created in step 2.

4. Complete the remaining steps to create the VM. Refer to Exercise 4.5 if you need more detailed instructions. Repeat step 3 to create a second VM into the availability set.

5. Navigate to the just created VMs. Select Availability Sets from the navigation menu and check which fault and update domains they were placed into. Navigate to the Availability set created in step 2 and select Virtual Machines. View the information, which should be similar to that shown in Figure 4.34.

FIGURE 4.34   A portal view of an availability set containing two Azure VMs

CSHARPGUITAR-SN1-AS - Virtual machines				
Availability set				
Search (Ctrl+/) «	Search virtual machines			
	NAME	STATUS	FAULT DOMAIN	UPDATE DOMAIN
Overview				
Activity log	CSHARPGUITAR-A1	⊘ Running	1	1
Access control (IAM)	CSHARPGUITAR-AS	⊘ Running	0	0
Tags				
Settings				
Virtual machines				

In Figure 4.34, notice that of the two created VMs placed into the availability set, one is in fault domain 0, update domain 0, while the other is in fault domain 1, update domain 1. This means that I can have, for example, either a primary and secondary database or two web servers running the same application behind a load balancer on those machines while they are highly isolated from each other. Additionally, recall from step 3 in Exercise 4.10 that the drop-down allowed the choice between either availability sets or Availability Zones. When you choose Availability Zone, you will get the availability set replicated into each of the zones, which is like a redundancy within a redundancy. You get the realized redundancies from the domains within a single data center replicated to other data centers (zones) within the region. That is great! Lastly, 2,000 availability sets are allowed per region, per subscription, with a maximum of 200 VMs per availability set. That is a large number, but maybe your business will take off due to its high performance and availability, and you need that many. Let's hope so.

Virtual Machine Scale Sets

As mentioned already, scale sets are identical instances of a VM that can scale out based on traffic and load. VMSS provides redundancy capabilities but for a different use case than availability sets. Instead of the primary/secondary or DR scenario, one VMSS benefit is to automatically scale out more instances of the VM based on load. As illustrated in Figure 4.35, the scaling minimum and maximum number of VM instances can be set from 0 to 1000; the default setting is a minimum of 1 and a maximum of 10. You will see that image in practice when you complete Exercise 4.11. From an autoscaling perspective, the default setting is to scale out when the average CPU percentage for all instances is greater than 75%. When that happens, the platform will create another instance of your VM up to a maximum of ten. If later the CPU consumption on the running VMs goes below an average of 25%, then the number of instances will be reduced by one until there is only one left. This scaling rule can be changed after creating the VMSS.

FIGURE 4.35 Autoscaling rules for a virtual machine scale set

To get more knowledge about a VMSS, create one in Exercise 4.11. Before proceeding, however, you will need either an application gateway (Exercise 3.10) or a load balancer. Both of these were discussed in the previous chapter. For Exercise 4.11, an application gateway is utilized because we walked through the creation of one in the previous chapter.

EXERCISE 4.11

Creating and Configuring a Virtual Machine Scale Set

1. Log in to the Azure Portal at `https://portal.azure.com`. Then click + Create A Resource. Enter a virtual machine scale set into the Search box and press the Enter key. Click the Create button.

2. Give the VMSS a name (for example, CSHARPGUITARVSS), and select an operating system disk image by clicking the Browse All Public And Private Images link. Click the My Items tab and the custom image you created in Exercise 4.6 (for example, CSHARPGUITAR-SC-IMAGE). Select the subscription into which you want the VMSS placed, select the resource group and region, select Zone 1, Zone 2, and Zone 3 from the Availability Zone drop-down list, and add a username and password.

3. Set Instance Count to 3 (one for each zone), choose the size (for example, leave it as the defaulted recommendation), enable Autoscale, and leave the defaults.

4. In the networking section, select the Application Gateway radio button and choose the resource group in which the application gateway exists. (It should be the same as the VMSS that you are creating now.) Select the Allow Selected Ports radio button, check HTTP (80), HTTPS (443), and RDP (3389), and then click the Create button.

5. Once the deployment has completed, navigate to the Application Gateway blade. Click the Backend Pools link in the navigation menu. Notice that a default backend pool has been added. Click that backend pool. Notice that the backend target has been populated with the Target type of VMSS and Target, which is the name of the VMSS you created in step 4

   Remember that successfully configuring an application gateway requires the frontend IP configuration, listeners, rules, and the Backend pool setting to all align. If you need a reminder on how to do that, refer to Chapter 3.

6. Enter the IP address of the application gateway in a browser, and the output of the image (for example, CSHARPGUITAR-SC-IMAGE) will render into the browser.

In Exercise 4.11, we did not create public IP addresses for the instances that will live in the VMSS pool. The radio button for the public IP address per instance was left at the default of Off, since all the VMs will reside behind an application gateway and will not be directly accessible from the internet. Next, if you click the Instances navigation menu item, it will list the three VM instances created. Click one of the instances, and on the Overview blade you will see its location, which also includes the zone in which is resides. Since, per the instructions, you selected all three zones, each VM is placed into a different zone, which gives maximum redundancy. Note that also, behind the scenes, the concept of fault domains and update domains is at play and implemented for an ever-greater level of resiliency when the number of VMs increases.

On the Scaling menu item, you can modify the autoscale configuration created originally or manually scale to a static number of instances. Those decisions, like many others, are dependent on the requirements of the application. The Storage menu item is an interesting one and one of the nice benefits of a VMSS. Remember that you chose a custom image when you created the VMSS. This means that each of the three VMs that got created used the same image. The content and configuration of all three VMs are therefore identical, making the deployment of new instances of the image into the VMSS quick and easy with no chance of having an error occur due to a wrongly configured VM. Before this kind of service existed, servers had to be built manually, and there were often scenarios where one of the servers in the pool didn't act like the others. It was hard to find which one it was and sometimes not possible to find out why it was misbehaving, so we just rebuilt from scratch and hoped we got it right the next time. That manual scenario would not be possible in an environment with numbers close to the maximum number of VMs per VMSS of 1,000 instances, 600 of which can be based on the same image. This is per region, per subscription. At that scale, all instances must be identical, which is what is achieved with VMSS using a single base image for all VM instances within it. Finally, if you decide you need a larger VM size, click the Size menu option and scale to a larger size, no problem.

Managed Disks

You might be wondering about the dependencies an Azure VM host has on the disks that are attached to it like the OS disk, data disk, and temp, as you might recall from Figure 4.20. As inferred earlier, the contents of a managed disk that is attached to an Azure VM is stored as a page blob in an Azure Storage container. Storage is covered in Chapter 5; however, the concepts relating to storage such as LRS, ZRS, and GRS have been touched upon already and are relevant here. To see why they are relevant, execute this Azure CLI command from https://shell.azure.com/

```
az disk show --ids <disk-id> --resource-group <name>
```

Notice the output for "sku": { "name": "Premium_LRS" } and make a quick assessment of what that means from a redundancy perspective. LRS means the disk, although copied three times, is locally redundant and has domain redundancies within the data center, but not outside of it. The same goes for a VMSS. To confirm that, navigate to the Instances menu item on the VMSS blade where you can find the name and the numeric InstanceId of the disk. To view the details of the disk attached to a VMSS instance, run this PowerShell cmdlet. Be sure to replace the contents within *< name >* variables with your specific/unique values.

```
(Get-AzVmssVm -ResourceGroupName <name> -VMScaleSetName <name> `
    -InstanceId <#>).StorageProfile.OsDisk.ManagedDisk.StorageAccountType
```

That cmdlet dumps out the account type into which the disk is stored, in this case `Standard_LRS`, which means locally redundant storage (LRS). The important point here is simply that you know that, and you know the dependencies your solution has also impact the availability of your solution. Considering that an availability set is local but redundant across the fault and update domains, you can instead choose to deploy the VM into availability zones and get ZRS reliance in addition to the domain features. Lastly, the `Get-AzVmssVm` PowerShell cmdlet that ran previously was for a single managed disk on a single VM. Remember that in Exercise 4.11 you created a VM in three zones; therefore, if you ran that command on all three managed disks, it would still show `Standard_LRS`, but each one would be in a different zone.

Securing Azure Virtual Machines

Chapter 2 covered security, but not specifically focused on the context of an Azure virtual machine. Let's discuss this a bit more now. There are three aspects of security that need some extra discussion.

- Who can access the VM via the portal or client?
- Who can access the VM using SSH or RDP?
- Who can access the application running on the VM?

The Azure Portal, Azure PowerShell, Azure CLI, and REST APIs all allow great administrative capabilities. You know already the method in which to restrict who can do what is via RBAC and the Access control (IAM) menu item on the VM portal blade. Determining who can do what to which resource at which level in the resource hierarchy requires thought, design, and maintenance. I mean, at the click of a button, a VM can be deleted. That may not be so bad, knowing what you do now about images and how managed disks work. The VM can relatively quickly be recovered, but what if the disks or images get deleted. . .on accident? You need to prevent that. And you should already know how to do that.

When you create the VM, part of the process is to create an administrator username and password. You need to protect them and make a conscious decision as to who gets the credentials. Instead of sharing the admin credentials, create specific accounts with a minimal set of permissions using a just-in-time access policy and monitor the connection activity using the Connection Monitor menu link on the VM blade in the portal. Microsoft doesn't back up the content of your disks on your behalf, but you can, and it's recommended. Microsoft simply lets you do with the provisioned resource as you wish while keeping it highly available. Once someone gets onto the server with mischievous intentions, if they have the credentials, then there isn't a lot you can do to prevent accidents or unwanted behavior. Removing files, replacing files, running some malware, or planting an exploit are things that you must be cognizant of when running your workloads. If you ever feel the credentials of a VM have been compromised, then there is a Reset password menu item on the VM blade. This is also helpful if you happen to forget it, which happens sometimes since you never write them down because that's a no-no. There is also a Security menu option that is an entry point into Azure Security Center (ASC). ASC helps monitor for activities that have been discussed in this paragraph.

From an application perspective, it depends greatly on your chosen identity provider and how it is implemented. You can, however, add safeguards like network security groups, an Azure Policy that enforces TLS 1.2 and HTTPS, and perhaps Managed Identity. All of these application-level security techniques are helpful in securing your application running on a VM. There is one last technique that we also covered in Chapter 2, and that was the concept of encryption of data at rest. This is important if the contents of the managed disks need to be encrypted due the storage of very sensitive data, intellectual property, or the code that runs the application. To encrypt a managed disk, complete Exercise 4.12.

EXERCISE 4.12

Encrypting a Managed Disk

1. Remember in Exercise 2.9 when you created the Azure Key Vault key? You will need that again to complete this exercise. Open an Azure PowerShell session and execute the following cmdlet. The output should resemble Figure 4.36.

```
Get-AzVmDiskEncryptionStatus -ResourceGroupName <name> -VMName <name>
```

FIGURE 4.36 Checking the encryption status of a managed disk using PowerShell

```
PS Azure:\> Get-AzVmDiskEncryptionStatus -ResourceGroupName CSHARPGUITAR-SN1-RG -VMName CSHARPGUITAR-A2

OsVolumeEncrypted          : NotEncrypted
DataVolumesEncrypted       : NotEncrypted
OsVolumeEncryptionSettings :
ProgressMessage            : No Encryption extension or metadata found on the VM
```

2. Notice that the OsVolumeEncrypted status is set to NotEncrypted. Execute the following Azure PowerShell cmdlets to encrypt the OS drive:

```
$KeyVault = Get-AzKeyVault -VaultName <name> -ResourceGroupName <name>
$DAR = Get-AzKeyVaultKey -VaultName <name> -Name <name>

Set-AzVMDiskEncryptionExtension -ResourceGroupName <name> `
    -VMName <name> -DiskEncryptionKeyVaultUrl $KeyVault.VaultUri `
    -DiskEncryptionKeyVaultId $KeyVault.ResourceId `
    -KeyEncryptionKeyVaultId $KeyVault.ResourceId `
    -KeyEncryptionKeyUrl $DAR.Id -SkipVmBackup -VolumeType All
```

3. When prompted, read the warning message about a potential reboot and the possible duration of the encryption. Enter Y and then press Enter to encrypt the drive. When the encryption is complete, execute the following cmdlet to check the OsVolumeEncrypted status. Notice the value is now Encrypted, as shown in Figure 4.37.

```
Get-AzVmDiskEncryptionStatus -ResourceGroupName <name> -VMName <name>
```

FIGURE 4.37   Checking the encryption status of a managed disk using PowerShell

```
PS Azure:\> Get-AzVmDiskEncryptionStatus -ResourceGroupName CSHARPGUITAR-SN1-RG -VMName CSHARPGUITAR-A2

OsVolumeEncrypted          : Encrypted
DataVolumesEncrypted       : NotEncrypted
OsVolumeEncryptionSettings :
ProgressMessage            : No Encryption extension or metadata found on the VM
```

4. Encrypting a managed disk is also possible via the Azure Portal. Log in to the Azure Portal at portal.azure.com. Navigate to the VM where a disk needing encryption is attached and click the Disks menu item. Click the Encryption item on the Disks blade and select your OS and data disks from the Disks To Encrypt drop-down list. Enter the Key Vault. (It should be prepopulated if it exists in the same resource group.) Enter the key and version, and then click the Save link at the top of the Encryption blade. Execute the following cmdlet. The output should be similar to that shown in Figure 4.38.

    ```
    Get-AzVmDiskEncryptionStatus –ResourceGroupName <name> –VMName <name>
    ```

FIGURE 4.38   Checking the encryption status of a managed disk using PowerShell

```
PS Azure:\> Get-AzVmDiskEncryptionStatus -ResourceGroupName CSHARPGUITAR-SN1-RG -VMName CSHARPGUITAR-A2

OsVolumeEncrypted          : Encrypted
DataVolumesEncrypted       : Encrypted
OsVolumeEncryptionSettings :
ProgressMessage            : No Encryption extension or metadata found on the VM
```

There you have it. After reading this section, you now know Azure VMs in some depth. You should feel confident that going into a meeting or to the Azure Solutions Architect Expert exam that your knowledge is ready for use. To make sure, answer the following question, and then move on to learn about other Azure Compute products.

What is the best tool for moving an on-premise server or VM to an Azure Virtual Machine?

Azure Migrate

SYSPREP

AzCopy

Azure Site Recovery

The answer is Azure Site Recovery, which is helpful not only for planning and recovering from a disaster but also for moving on-premise workloads to Azure VMs. SYSPREP and AzCopy are not useful for moving VMs, and Azure Migrate is more for planning the move versus doing the actual move.

Azure App Services

Azure App Services are Microsoft's PaaS offerings. This product grouping offers Web Apps, API Apps, Mobile Apps, Web Apps for Containers (Linux), App Service Environments, and Azure WebJobs. PaaS removes the responsibility of operating systems maintenance from the customer. In Chapter 3, I mentioned the concept of a sandbox and that Microsoft PaaS offerings operates within one. The sandbox is what restricts the actions that you and your code can do. For example, no writing to the registry, no access to the Event logs, no out-of-process COM, and no access to User32/GDI32 are a few of the most common impactful limitations. There is a complete list of the restrictions on GitHub specifically at this location:

github.com/projectkudu/kudu/wiki/Azure-Web-App-sandbox

Additionally, supported framework runtime versions (for example, .NET, PHP, Python, Node, etc.), third-party drivers, cypher suites, registry editing, or root certificates are driven by the cloud service provider. This means, for example, if you want to target .NET Core 3.0 or Python 3.8 and the runtime is not on the platform, then you cannot use it. When you decide to run your workloads on a PaaS offering, you gain some value by delegating responsibility of the OS, such as patching, security, and OS upgrades. However, you lose some flexibility when it comes to making custom environmental configurations and targeting new versions of runtimes that include the newest technologies.

Azure App Services come in a variety of pricing tiers and sizes, the combination of those two attributes create what is called an *App Service Plan (ASP)*. From a pricing tier perspective, there are six different options, each having a different set of accompanying features. Free and Shared are the most economical offering and are intended for testing and learning; you shouldn't run any production workload on them as neither of those tiers comes with an SLA, and they have some strict metered capacity constraints. For example, running on the Free plan, your process can consume 60 minutes of CPU minutes per day and 240 minutes in the Shared plan. This may be enough for some small test sites, but as already mentioned, it's not for production workloads. The other four tiers are Basic, Standard, Premium, and Isolated. Isolated is also called an *App Service Environment (ASE)*, which is discussed later. Some features available in Basic, Standard, and Premium are presented in Table 4.10.

TABLE 4.10   Basic, Standard, and Premium Tiers

Feature	Basic	Standard	Premium
Disk space	10 GB	50 GB	250GB
Max instances	Up to 3	Up to 10	Up to 20
Deployment slots	X	✓	✓
Cloning	X	X	✓
VNET Integration	X	✓	✓

Feature	Basic	Standard	Premium
Autoscale	X	✓	✓
Backup/restore	X	✓	✓
Traffic manager	X	✓	✓
Number of Apps	Unlimited	Unlimited	Unlimited

Any of the tiers discussed in Table 4.10 execute in what is called *dedicated mode*. This means the application is running on its own VM and is isolated from other customers. This is not the case in Free and Shared modes. In addition to the different feature limits available per tier, they also come in three sizes: Small, Medium, and Large. Basic and Standard VMs currently run on A-series sizes where:

- **Small:** 1 CPU with 1.75GB RAM
- **Medium:** 2 CPU with 3.5GB RAM
- **Large:** 4 CPU with 7GB RAM

Premium tier, on the other hand, runs on Dv2-series VMs and come with the following allocated compute resources.

- **Small:** 1 CPU with 3.5GB RAM
- **Medium:** 2 CPU with 7GB RAM
- **Large:** 4 CPU with 14GB RAM

A reason I call out the sizes is that there are restrictions based on the size of the chosen VM, which is an important one. It is important because there are some bad coding patterns that occur often that cause troubles with an application running on an App Service. Those patterns will be discussed in Chapter 7. The specific restriction is the number of concurrent outbound connections. There is no limit on the overall number of outbound connections; the limit and the key word here is *concurrent*. In other words, how many open, in-scope connections is the application currently holding? The limit is 1,920, 3,968, and 8,064, per instance, for Small, Medium, and Large, respectively. Per instance means that if you have two instances of a Medium, you can have a total of 7,936 outbound connections, which is 2 × 3968.

Recall some of the options covered in Table 4.10. Let's discuss them a bit more, specifically these options:

- Max instances
- Autoscale
- Number of apps

- Deployment slots
- Cloning

The documented maximum number of instances can be increased if your workload is running in the Premium plan and you need more than 20. Instances were also just mentioned regarding the number of concurrent outbound connections. An instance is a dedicated VM, aka ASP, that is running your application workload. You can increase and decrease the number of instances using an Autoscale rule, as discussed previously for IaaS Azure VM, or you can perform the scale out or scale in manually. The technique to achieve such scalability with App Services is also similar to a VMSS, where the image is stored in a central location and new instances are built from that as needed. The difference with an Azure App Service is that instead of an image, the application source code and its configuration are stored in an Azure Storage container and used when adding a new instance into the pool. An image is not necessary because you are running on PaaS and the operating system configurations are all the same on every VM.

Recall from Table 4.10 that the number of apps per ASP was unlimited. Nothing is really unlimited; it just means that there is no coded limitations on it, like there is for Free (10) and Shared (100). Each time you create a web app, for example, you are effectively creating a website that will run in its own process within the ASP. Each website gets its own hostname, such as the *.azurewebsites.net, which you already know since you created a few in previous chapters already. The limitation isn't on the number of apps but on the amount of compute resource your applications require plus the number of instances per pricing tier. If you can get 1,000 websites onto a one-CPU machine with 1.75GB of RAM to be responsive, great, but I'd find that unlikely. You would need to use better judgment on which apps need how much compute and then balance them across different App Service Plans and instances. This leads nicely into deployment slots, which are test instances of an app on the same ASP. When you create a slot on an ASP for a given app, you are effectively creating a new process to run a newer version of that same app. In Chapter 9, we will cover deployments, but it is safe to write here that deploying straight into production is risky. Deploying to a deployment slot avoids doing that.

Take, for example, that your web app name is csharpguitar.azurewebsites.net and you create a deployment slot named *test*. A new web app will be created named csharpguitar-test.azurewebsites.net. You can then deploy a new version of the csharpguitar web app to the test site and test it. Once you are sure all things are working fine, you can do what is called a *slot swap*. This means the test site becomes production, and the production becomes the test. This happens by switching which process responds to requests made to the hostnames. Both processes and hostnames remain alive, but new requests start flowing to the new version once the slot swap is performed. Finally, cloning, which is like a backup, is a cool feature. It is also helpful in debugging and trying to find the root cause of an issue. From a debugging perspective, some logging or debugging techniques can have negative impacts on application performance and stability. Making an exact replica of the environment and placing it someplace else can give you more options when troubleshooting issues. Cloning is helpful if you want to move your application to another region, for example. From the portal you can move an App Service Plan between resource groups and subscriptions; however, moving to another physical region is not possible via a click activity in the Azure Portal. Cloning will help you achieve that if that is your objective.

Web Apps

An Azure App Service web app is a popular entry point onto the Azure platform from a PaaS perspective. They are limited to no barriers to entry, and you can be up and running with an internet presence in minutes. That is absolutely an amazing feat when reflecting back 15 years or so and the amount of effort to achieve this. Then also, if required, you could scale out to 400 CPUs in a few additional minutes, which is absolutely inconceivable. Let's do a few things with web apps now. If you do not remember how to create an Azure App Service, please refer to Exercise 3.8 in the previous chapter. In Exercise 4.13, you will enable Azure Active Directory authentication for an Azure App Service Web App. This is a feature named Easy Auth and was introduced in Chapter 2.

EXERCISE 4.13

Enabling AAD for an App Service

1. Log in to the Azure Portal at portal.azure.com and navigate to an existing App Service web app. Click the Authentication/Authorization menu item on the navigation bar and turn on App Service authentication. Select Log In With Azure Active Directory. From the Action To Take drop-down, click the Azure Active Directory Authentication provider.

2. Select Express as the Management mode, leave all defaults, press the OK button, see Figure 4.39, press the Save button.

FIGURE 4.39   Enabling AAD authentication for an Azure App Service web app

3. Navigate to the App Service, and you will be prompted to enter your AAD credentials.

You certainly noticed the other authentication providers such as Microsoft, Facebook, Google, and Twitter. As easily as you enabled AAD for authentication for your site, you can do the same using those other providers. Note that this is for authentication only, which means we can only be sure your visitor is who they say they are; it doesn't provide any information about what they can do on the site. That is more application-specific and is the authorization part. We won't cover that in more detail here. One last note is that in step 1 of Exercise 4.13 the action to take was to log in with Azure Active Directory. This means that no one can access your site if they do not have an identity to be validated. It is common to select the other option Allow Anonymous and then let the visitor create a profile on your site. Once the account is validated, the user can have access to other protected features in your site. However, that kind of accessibility requires code in your application to check for the validation tokens. What you did in Exercise 4.13 is simply wrap the entire application with a security protocol; if more granular or more precise authorized access is required, then it will require some code.

In Exercise 4.14, you will configure Hybrid Connection Manager (HCM) to connect to an IaaS Azure VM in a VNET. Instead of using an Azure VM, you can also use an on-premise machine. This is a simple method for connecting a Web App to an on-premise machine or an Azure VM in a virtual network. HCM uses ports that are typically open for allowing internet traffic, so in most cases this configuration works quickly.

EXERCISE 4.14

Configuring HCM on an Azure App Service

1. Log in to the Azure Portal at portal.azure.com then navigate to an existing App Service web app. Scale up to Standard tier by selecting the Scale Up navigation menu item. Select the Production tab and then select S1. Once the scale=up is complete, click the Networking menu item on the navigation bar and select Hybrid Connections. Click + Add Hybrid Connection and click Create New Hybrid Connection.

2. Enter a hybrid connection name (for example, CSHARPGUITAR-HCM), an endpoint host (for example, CSHARPGUITAR-VM), and an endpoint port (for example, 80). Create or select a service bus namespace. The final settings should resemble something similar to that shown in Figure 4.40. Click the OK button. Once the connection is created, click it. The connection will be rendered in the Hybrid Connections blade. Take note of the Gateway Connection String and then download the connection manager by clicking the Download Connection Manager link.

FIGURE 4.40   Configuration settings for a hybrid connection

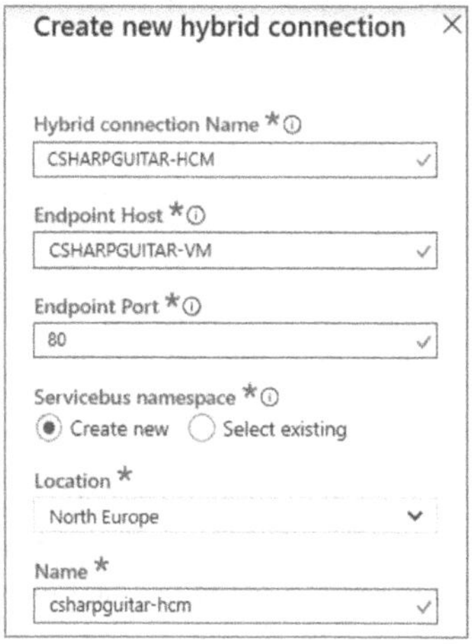

3.   Access KUDU (an administration console for App Services) and select the Advanced Tools navigation menu option. Select the Go link and then select the Debug console at the top middle of the KUDU console. Now select CMD.

4.   In the console window, attempt to CURL to CSHARPGUITAR-VM using the following code snippet:

```
curl http://<Endpoint Host>
```

Notice that CSHARPGUITAR-VM is the endpoint host, as shown in Figure 4.40. It should fail. This step confirms that it doesn't connect by default. A few more steps are required to complete the configuration of HCM.

5.   Copy and install the connection manager you downloaded in step 2 to the server or VM you want to connect to via HCM (for example, CSHARPGUITAR-VM). After instal- lation completes, open the Hybrid Connection Manager UI and click the Enter Man- ually button. Enter the Gateway Connection String, reviewed in step 2, similar to the following, and click Add. After some moments, the Hybrid Connection Manager UI should resemble something similar to Figure 4.41.

```
Endpoint=
sb://csharpguitar-hcm.servicebus.windows.net/;
SharedAccessKeyName=defaultListener;
SharedAccessKey=aHYWXFD&hellip;kW2ULr+T6w=;
EntityPath=csharpguitar-hcm
```

FIGURE 4.41   Server-side HCM configurations for a hybrid connection

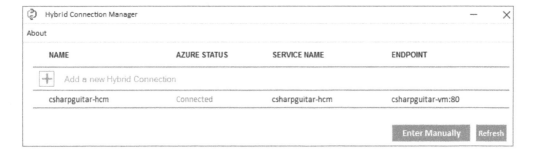

6.   Navigate back to the Azure App Service Networking blade, and you will see the same as this on the Hybrid Connection blade for the given App Service app; see Figure 4.42.

FIGURE 4.42 Successful connectivity between an app service and an IaaS Azure VM using HCM

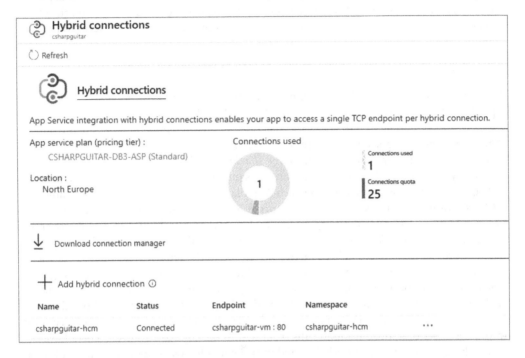

7. Attempt the same CURL commands from step 4, and the request will return successfully. The output resembles something similar to Figure 4.43.

```
curl http://<Endpoint Host>
```

FIGURE 4.43 Successful `curl` connection between an App Service and an IaaS Azure VM using HCM

```
Kudu Remote Execution Console
Type 'exit' then hit 'enter' to get a new CMD process.
Type 'cls' to clear the console

D:\home>curl http://CSHARPGUITAR-VM
   Hello from csharpguitar-vm

D:\home>
```

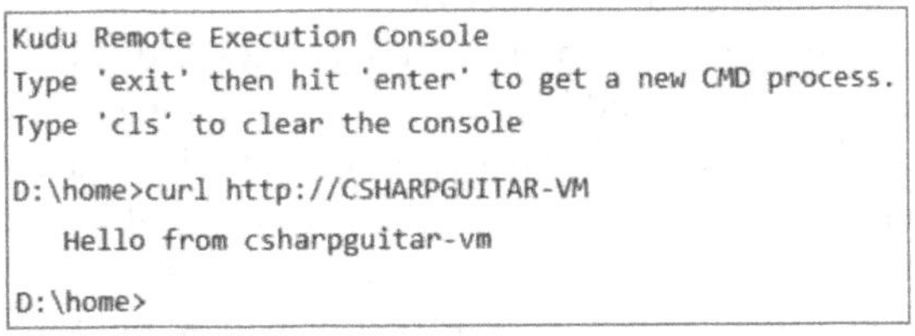

In summary, an Azure App Service web app is a place to run internet applications using Microsoft's PaaS cloud service. It has limited barriers of entry, and you can deploy, scale, and consume at a very fast pace. There are two other products that run on the same PaaS platform as a web app; they are API apps and mobile apps. A brief description of them follows.

API Apps

API apps, not to be confused with API management discussed in the previous chapter, is a product offering that correlates more closely to a Web API versus a web application. In short, an API is an interface that exposes one or more methods that can be called from other applications or consumers; there is no *graphical user interface (GUI)* with an API. API Apps fully support *cross-origin resource sharing (CORS)* and Swagger.

When you create an API app, you follow the same process as when creating a regular web app. The difference is that on the Web App blade there are navigation items named *API definitions* that are used for the configuration and implementation of Swagger. Swagger has numerous capabilities, but its notable feature is making it easy to discover and consume the API app. As you may know, one of the difficulties in consuming an API is trying to figure out the name of all the methods it exposes, the required parameters for them, and the kind of authentication protocol required to communicate with the API. Swagger, when configured, provides this information and greatly simplifies its consumption. There is also a navigation menu item named CORS, which is used for identifying allowed origins. CORS is a security feature that makes sure when code (for example, JavaScript) is running in your browser that any outbound calls from within the code are allowed. There have been cases where scripts are maliciously injected into client-side JavaScript that downloads some snippet of malware. CORS is implemented with the preventions of such injections in mind.

Mobile Apps

Some years ago, Mobile Apps was its own product; today it is running on the same platform as web apps and API apps. It will soon be retired, but it's worth mentioning because of its historical significance. When Microsoft was making its push into the mobile world, this Mobile App was a central point of that. It was planned to be the backend for all the apps that would be published to the Microsoft Store. Well, we all know how that went and it is why we see "no light at the end of the tunnel." Regardless, you create a mobile app like you would an app service and look in the navigation menu for easy tables and easy APIs. Both of those made it quick and easy to set up the backend database or dependent APIs for the mobile app. I expect the feature to be removed, but I am confident it will come back in another shape or form in the next few years. That behavior is a fairly common one (i.e., retire something and then bring it back with a new look and marketing campaign).

Web App for Containers (Linux)

Yes, you can run Linux on PaaS. The version of Linux that Web Apps runs on is Ubuntu Server 18.04 LTS. However, this isn't a showstopper because you can also run Web Apps in a container, which allows you to choose the targeted OS. To create a web app that targets Linux, you begin the same as you have previously, paying special attention to the Publish, Runtime Stack, and Operating System attributes on the Web App creation blade. Figure 4.44 shows how that looks.

FIGURE 4.44   Creating a Linux Azure App Service web app

The first attribute is Publish, which provides the option for code or a Docker container. If you choose Code, it means you will receive a VM that you can then deploy your application code to. The other option is Docker Container, which you should already be an expert in as it was covered already in this chapter. If you choose Docker Container, the Runtime drop-down goes away, and your only option then is to choose Linux or Windows. Choosing a Docker container would result in a VM being allocated to run the container that you create locally or download from Docker Hub, for example.

The contents of the Runtime Stack drop-down is a list of supported, for lack of a better analogy, *common language runtimes (CLRs)*. The runtimes are the frameworks and libraries in different programming languages and their different versions that are available on the platform for your application to target. There are many of them; Table 4.11 displays some of the supported runtimes. For a most up-to-date list, check `https://docs.microsoft.com/en-us/azure/app-service/containers/ app-service-linux-intro#languages`.

TABLE 4.11   Supported Open Source Languages

Language	Versions
.NET Core	1.0, 1.1, 2.0, 2.1, 2.2
ASP.NET	3.5, 4.7
Java	8, 11, SE, Tomcat 9, 8.5
Node	4.x, 6.x, 8.x, 10.x
PHP	5.6, 7.x
Python	2.7, 3.6, 3.7
Ruby	2.x

If a version of the runtime or the total programming language is not supported, then you can simply create a Docker Container to run the workload on PaaS. An interesting scenario you may notice is that when you select, for example, Node or PHP from the Runtime Stack drop-down, the Operating System selection automatically changes to Linux. Even though you can run Node and PHP on a Windows OS, the portal is steering you toward Linux. It's similar behavior for .NET Core. Even though it can run on Linux, when selected, Windows is the selected operating system.

I have a last point to make about Web Apps for Container, and it is an important one. At the beginning of this section I mentioned the sandbox that constrained the configuration that you can perform when running your application with Azure App Services. With Web Apps for Containers, this is no longer the case. Whether you run your application on Windows or Linux, you can create a Docker container and deploy it to the Azure App Service environment. Within the Docker container you can make any modification you desire—registry changes, cypher suite reordering, whatever. The biggest hurdle for most, as I mentioned in the container section, is that this capability is kind of new, and many are reluctant to consume it because it is kind of young. However, for smaller workloads having a less mission-critical role in the IT solution, you should give this a try. It is time to start learning this, and you learn best by consuming, maintaining, and troubleshooting it.

App Service Environments

An App Service environment, aka the Isolated tier, is an instance of the entire Azure App Service capability inside a virtual network accessible to only one entity. When running in other tiers such as Basic, Standard, and Premium, i.e., in a multitenant stamp, although your VMs are dedicated, there are other customers who use some of the shared resources that provide the App Services product. For example, the front ends that load balance and direct requests to the correct web app or to one of the multiple instances of the web app are shared resources in Basic, Standard, or Premium. If you do not want or cannot share resources with other tenants, then you can choose the Isolated tier and get all the shared resources for yourself. You never share VMs running your application in Basic, Standard, or Premium; they are dedicated to you.

There are two benefits that come to mind when running in an ASE that do not exist in other tiers. The first is that you can implement an *internal load balancer (ILB)*, which will prevent direct access to the ASE from the internet. In the context of an ILB, the IP address and the internet end point (i.e., `*.azurewebsites.net`) are not globally accessible and need a gateway VPN connection to allow access. In addition, the ordering of cypher suites is allowed with an ASE. A cypher suite is an encryption algorithm used for encrypting TLS connectivity between a client and server. They are added to an OS in a specific order, and the first match is the one that a client and server agree to use. Sometimes a customer wants to use a stronger or different cipher for many reasons. An ASE allows the reordering; other tiers do not. Table 4.12 shows the feature limitations for an ASE's Isolated tier.

TABLE 4.12   ASE/Isolated Tier Limitations

Feature	Isolated Limit
Disk space	1 TB
Max instances	Up to 100
Deployment slots	✓
Cloning	✓
VNET integration	✓
Autoscale	✓
Backup/restore	✓
Traffic manager	✓
Number of Apps	Unlimited

The VMs are a dedicated Dv2-series with the following specifications:

- **Small:** One CPU with 3.5GB RAM
- **Medium:** Two CPU with 7GB RAM
- **Large:** Four CPU with 14GB RAM

Keep in mind that with ASEs you are getting a few more servers that run the other Azure App Service components that are typically shared in the multitenant environment. Those additional series and the additional benefits come with an additional cost.

This product is most common for large enterprises or customers who have some stringent security requirements and need or desire to run PaaS within their own isolated VNET.

Azure WebJobs

Azure WebJobs is a feature strongly linked to Azure App Services that supports the execution of background tasks. This is similar to the older concept of *batch jobs*. Batch jobs are typically programs that are run at scheduled intervals to process data or to read from a queue and perform some action based on its contents. They typically have filename extensions like .cmd, .bat, .exe, .ps1, and .js, which the operating system recognizes as an executable program. There are two types of WebJobs.

- Triggered (Remote debugging is not supported.)
- Continuous (Remote debugging is supported.)

A triggered WebJob is a program that is scheduled to run using a scheduler scheme named CRON, or it can also be run manually. A common format of CRON is illustrated in Figure 4.45. For example, a CRON schedule of 0 15 8 * * * would run every day at 8:15 a.m.

FIGURE 4.45   CRON schedule format for use with a triggered WebJob

```
r — — — — — — second (0 - 59)
| r — — — — — — minute (0 - 59)
| | r — — — — — — hour (0 - 23)
| | | r — — — — — — day of month (1 - 31)
| | | | r — — — — — — month (1 - 12)
| | | | | r — — — — — — day of week (0 - 6)
| | | | | |
| | | | | |
| | | | | |
* * * * * *
```

There are two common ways to manually trigger an Azure WebJob; the first is from within the Azure Portal. As stated, a WebJob is tied into an Azure App Service, meaning an Azure App Service is required to run a WebJob. To manually run a WebJob, access the Azure App Service where the WebJob is located, select the WebJobs link from the navigation menu item, select the WebJob, and click the Run button. The WebJob blade looks something like that shown in Figure 4.46.

FIGURE 4.46   WebJob portal display

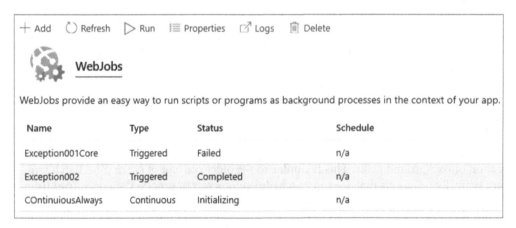

Name	Type	Status	Schedule
Exception001Core	Triggered	Failed	n/a
Exception002	Triggered	Completed	n/a
COntinuiousAlways	Continuous	Initializing	n/a

The other means for manually triggering a WebJob is using the WebJob API. The WebJob is hosted on the Azure App Service platform, which exposes a global endpoint. This means also that the WebJob is globally accessible. When KUDU was mentioned and you accessed it via the Advanced Tools menu item, you may have noticed the URL that you were routed to. It was the name of the web app followed by .scm.azurewebsites.net. If you add /api/triggeredwebjobs/<WebJobName>/run and you access the URL, then the WebJob would be manually triggered from the WebJob API. A final example might resemble the following, where * is the name of your web app:

```
https://*.scm.azurewebsites.net/api/triggeredwebjobs/Exception002/run
```

Just on a side note, this API is one of the foundational technologies on which Azure Functions is built. Azure Functions is discussed later, and you will read briefly about a Timer Triggered Azure Function; just note that the WebJob SDK is a fundamental component of Azure Functions, and it may or may not be recognized without some deep technical review.

The other type of WebJob is one that runs continuously. This is useful for scenarios where you process orders or execute reports in the background but in near real time. Capturing a customer order is something that you always want to make easy, which is why you want to do as little as possible when the place order button is clicked. Perhaps simply place the order details into a queue. In other words, do a simple valuation and then a simple insert into a data source. Then you can have the WebJob continuously monitoring that queue that then processes the order offline. If there are any errors, notify an administrator to correct it and get it reprocessed. Once the order is reprocessed, then the WebJob can send the customer an email notification. Another scenario is running large reports. Many reports take a long time to process, and running them in real time can result in timeouts and not getting any results. Again, you could save the query parameters in a queue that a WebJob is monitoring, and then it can process it. Batch or offline processes typically run longer than real-time web requests, which have built-in timeouts. Once the report is complete, a link to the output is emailed to the user. Easy.

There is a configuration that needs to happen on the Azure App Service to run continuous WebJobs. You must have enabled a capability called Always On. There is a mechanism that conserves resources by shutting down websites that haven't been used in 20 minutes. This shutdown feature can be disabled by enabling Always On, which is found on the Configuration menu item for the Azure App Service. Another point worth considering is what happens if you run multiple instances of your Azure App Service. Does the WebJob run continuously on every instance? The answer is yes, by default it does. However, you can configure the WebJob as a singleton by creating a file named settings.job and placing it into the root directory of where the WebJob is located. The contents of the settings.job file are as follows:

```
{ 'is_singleton': true }
```

Instead of creating the settings.job file manually, if you configure the WebJob from the portal using the + Add button, as shown in Figure 4.46, when you select Continuous as the type, you have the ability to select Multi Instance or Single Instance from the dropdown, as shown in Figure 4.47.

FIGURE 4.47   Adding a continuous or triggered WebJob

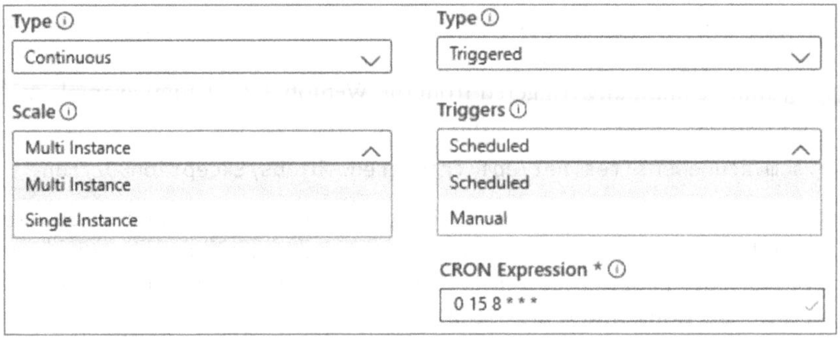

Type ⓘ	Type ⓘ
Continuous ⌄	Triggered ⌄
Scale ⓘ	Triggers ⓘ
Multi Instance ⌃	Scheduled ⌃
Multi Instance	Scheduled
Single Instance	Manual
	CRON Expression * ⓘ
	0 15 8 * * * ✓

Figure 4.47 also illustrates a view of how + Add Capability looks when Triggered is selected.

Azure Batch and HPC

In the previous section, we touched on batch jobs. So, you should have some idea at this point of what they are. However, in that context I would think we are talking about a maximum of 20 to 30 cores and perhaps from 7GB to 14GB of memory to perform a serial execution of a specific task. Let me now introduce you to Azure Batch, which provides you with the tools to run processes in parallel on a large scale. Azure Batch lets you connect thousands of compute instances across multiple *graphical processing units (GPU)* that provide low latency and extremely powerful processing when compared to CPU-only architectures. Tasks such as dynamic image rendering and visual simulations with GPUs, Big Data scientific and engineering scenarios are a few examples of workloads that run using Azure Batch and High-Performance Computing concepts. Those workloads can run on either Windows or Linux, using coding languages like R, Node, PHP, Ruby, Python, Java, and .NET.

There are numerous HPC models, two of which work optimally with Azure Batch; they are InfiniBand and *Remote Direct Memory Access (RDMA)*. As shown in Figure 4.48, InfiniBand architecture provides a metrics-like structure to group together massive, and I mean massive, compute power. The compute power can come from a mixture of CPU, GPU, and XMC processors.

Using Azure Batch, the RDMA architecture, as shown in Figure 4.49, illustrates the sharing of memory between a pool of nodes.

Notice how the access to memory across nodes happens over an Ethernet connection. Both InfiniBand and RDMA support what is called *cloud bursting*. If you recall from the previous chapter, we discussed the concept of a hybrid network, and one use of that hybrid model was to handle extra traffic or unexpected growth when necessary. There is a similar model that allows you to cloud burst from an on-premise HPC architecture to Azure if you happen to run out of or want more compute power. The connectivity works via both ExpressRoute and a VPN Gateway connection. Finally, let's not fail to mention that if you want a super computer, Azure offers you the ability to get a dedicated cray computer placed into one of your private virtual networks so you can crunch and crack those weak encryption algorithms in less than two months. You might be tempted to do that just for fun, but there isn't even a price I could find for that, so if costs matter, then you might want to just consider this as something cool and for NASA or other government organizations to consume.

FIGURE 4.48 InfiniBand architecture

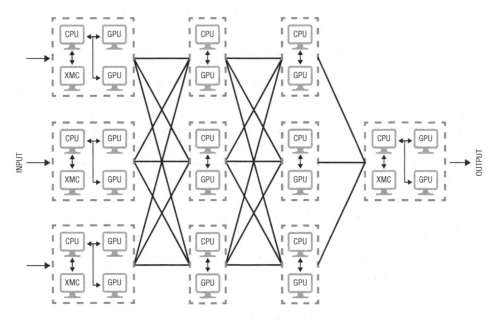

FIGURE 4.49 RDMA architecture

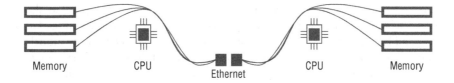

Let's start off with creating an Azure Batch account in Exercise 4.15.

Creating an Azure Batch Account and Running a Parallel Monte Carlo Simulation with R

1. Log in to the Azure Portal at portal.azure.com and click the + Create A Resource link at the top left of the browser window. Click Compute and then Batch Service. Select the subscription into which you want to add the Azure Batch account. Then select a resource group, enter an account name, and select the location.

2. Click the Advanced tab and leave the pool allocation mode as the default. Click the Review + Create button and click the Create button.

3. The Monte Carlo simulation instructions are found at docs.microsoft.com/en-us/azure/batch/tutorial-r-doazureparallel.

Before you attempt the online simulation, let's cover a few things. First, what is the difference between the Batch service and Subscription service that you saw on the Advanced tab? For most cases, you would use the default Batch service, which makes the most of what is going on with compute provisioning behind the scenes. In general, it simplifies the consumption and execution of workloads by handling the server pools for you. If you want to have more control over the server pools or utilize *Azure Reserved VM Instance*, choose the Subscription service. Next, take a look at Figure 4.50 to see more about how Azure Batch and HPC works.

1. Upload the code and data input files into storage.

2. The tasks, jobs, and the pool of compute nodes are created.

3. Azure Batch downloads the application code and data to use for computation.

4. The application is monitoring pool and tasks.

5. The computation completes, and the output is loaded in storage.

6. The application retrieves the output files for conclusion.

An application is the code and data that you are tasking Azure Batch to process. In Exercise 4.15, the source and data are accessible on GitHub and used in the Azure Portal when creating the application within the Azure Batch blade. The pool, as shown in Figure 4.50, is the group of compute nodes. Recall from earlier where you read about InfiniBand and RDMA. You would have noticed that the difference in those models is based on one having massive compute processing power and the other offering massive amounts of memory. Prior to creating your pool, you need to consider which kind of model your HPC workload requires. Consider Figure 4.51.

FIGURE 4.50   How Azure Batch and HPC work

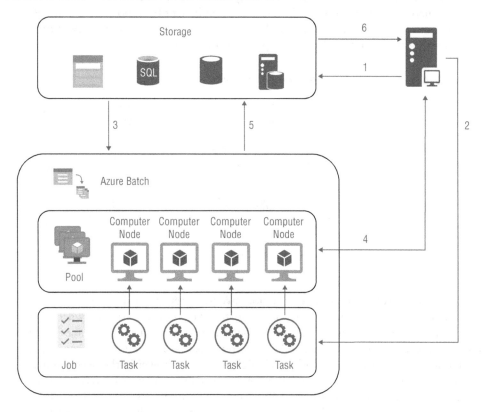

FIGURE 4.51   Ratios between CPU, RAM, and GPU

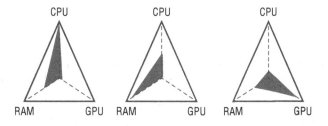

Figure 4.51 symbolizes the different kinds of HPC, where some workloads perform computational activities that require large CPU power for simulations and analytics, while other data analysis programs parse large databases that have been loaded into memory, requiring lots of RAM. If the workload processes images for gaming or real-time images

generation, then the workload would need large amounts of GPUs. There could also be a scenario where you would need a solution that could benefit from both CPU and GPU with a smaller amount of RAM. As shown in Figure 4.52, there are a large variety of options when choosing the kind of VM nodes to place into your pool.

FIGURE 4.52   Choosing a VM node for the HPC pool

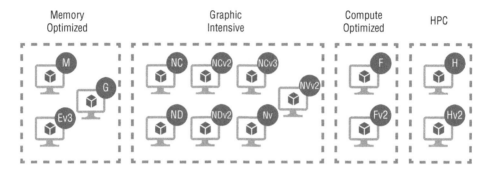

When you run your workload, you do not have to worry about the amount of resources in the pool. When you create the pool in the portal, there is a scale section where you can create a customized scale algorithm to scale out and in with. When I think about VMSS and try to compare it with Azure Batch, a difference is that I do not need a base image, and it looks like there are VMs with much higher resource power in the selection list. I would think that it boils down to the reason you need the compute power. If you are doing intensive graphics simulations or Big Data analysis, then use Azure Batch. If you are running an enterprise web application or other workload type, then use VMSS or even App Services. Also, in Figure 4.50 there were tasks and a job, which is where you specifically specify what method or activity in the application is run in which pool.

Storage

Storage is covered in detail in the next chapter. As you can imagine, images, movies, Big Data, and other kinds of files that get processed by Azure Batch will likely be huge. The space required to store them and the latency you get when retrieving them is an important aspect when implementing a workload using the Azure product. Azure-supported storage products include VMs that are storage optimized (for example, the Ls series), if your workload will store large amounts of data on the physical VM. Also, blob, table, and queue Azure storage containers and Azure files all can be utilized for storing the input and output for your Azure Batch HPC workloads. Let's not forget about a DBMS like SQL Server or Oracle, which can be used to store and retrieve data in such scenarios.

Marketplace

Access the Azure Portal, and in the search textbox at the top of the browser enter **Marketplace**. Then do a search for *HPC*, which will result in numerous preconfigured HPC solutions that can be created, configured, and utilized fast. You might consider taking a look through these to see whether they can meet your requirements prior to investing the time required to build a custom HPC solution.

Azure Functions

Many details of an Azure Function have been touched on in Chapter 1, so review that if you need a refresher. Azure Functions is Microsoft's FaaS product offering and is also commonly referred to as a *serverless* computing model. One of my colleagues once said, "If you have two servers and you take one away, what do you have? You have a server less." Although that is indeed true and kind of funny, it isn't what serverless means in regard to Azure Functions. What it means is that when your Azure Function workload is not running, it is not bound to any compute resource and therefore not costing you anything. The real beauty of serverless is its cost effectiveness. In reality, the product is free, yes, free, as long as you run in Consumption mode and stay under 1,000,000 executions and 400,000 gigaseconds of compute. A gigasecond is an algorithm based on memory consumption and the number of seconds the Azure Function ran. It's a lot of free compute—more than enough to get your hands dirty with and even to run some smaller production workloads. When your Azure Function is invoked/triggered, a feature called a Scale Controller will notify the Azure Function that it has work to do, which results in a real-time provisioning of compute capacity, the configuration of that compute resource, and the execution of the Azure Function code that you have deployed. As you see illustrated in Figure 4.53, the Scale Controller is monitoring supported message sources, and when one arrives, it spins up a VM, configures it, and puts the code on the VM. Then the Azure Function will retrieve the message and then process it, as the code dictates.

FIGURE 4.53   The Scale Controller role and an Azure Function

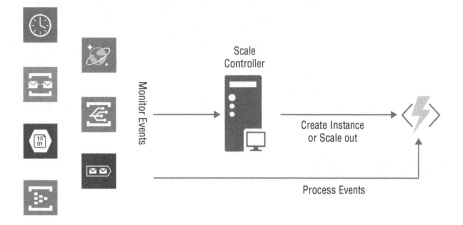

When I spoke to one of my technical friends about serverless, the first question was about the latency of going from 0 to 100, meaning, how long does it take for the Scale Controller to get hardware provisioned, the Azure Function configured, and the function executed? I won't try to pretend that there is no latency, but that would only happen on the first invocation, and it will remain warm for 20 minutes before it times out (using a dedicated or premium hosting plan, you can avoid this timeout and keep the instances warm). The internals of how it all works is proprietary and won't be shared, but there are some steps you can take if you want to improve the cold start of an Azure Function.

There are two ways to make the initial Azure Function invocation faster. The first one is to deploy your code in something called a *run from package*. This requires basically that you publish your code in a ZIP file. When you "zip" a file or a group of files, it compresses them and makes them smaller. As you would then imagine, when the code is being deployed to the VM, it happens faster than if you have many files in an uncompressed form. The run from package is enabled using an App Setting that you will set in a later exercise, and it has much more impact when running in the consumption hosting plan than when in dedicated. The reason for running faster in dedicated is because the VM that is provisioned to run the Azure Function code doesn't get rebuilt after 20 minutes, which means the code is copied once. Take note that since the zip capability discussed here is the Windows variety (in contrast to .7z, .tar, .war, etc.), it means that this feature is only supported on Windows. The second way to reduce latency with the first Azure Function Invocation after a shutdown is to not let it shut down in the first place. Implementing the second approach requires you to run on a dedicated or premium hosting plan instead of consumption. When running in dedicated or premium mode, there is a general configuration setting named Always On, which, as the name implies, keeps the Azure Function warm by disabling the 20-minute timeout threshold.

Efficient Use of Compute and Networking Capacity

Recall from the previous chapter when you read about the software-driven wide area network (SWAN) and that it uses spare capacity in one network to help resolve transmission pressure in other networking areas. Azure Functions operates in a similar manner whereby the compute comes from locations where there is extra capacity. It is not cost effective for a cloud service company like Microsoft to have compute power sitting around idle, waiting to be used, especially when you remember that Azure Functions is mostly free. That is how they end up being free because the compute comes from capacity that is effectively already paid for but isn't being used by other Azure compute products.

The remainder of this section will discuss hosting plans, triggers and bindings, runtime versions, and supported languages.

Hosting Plans

In Chapter 1, I shared two hosting plans, Consumption and Dedicated. There is another, which won't be on the Azure Solutions Architect Expert exam because it is in preview; it is called Premium. I will include Premium in the following text, but keep it in mind that it won't be necessary to know for the exam. The Consumption hosting plan is the one that is considered the serverless model, when you operate in any of the other plans you are running an Azure Function but you have a VM or a group of VMs that are actively provisioned and bound to the workload. Both Dedicated and Premium will have a fixed cost, but the primary difference between Dedicated and Premium is the existence of the Scale Controller. In Dedicated, you are using the scaling capabilities that exist for an Azure App Service that were just discussed. That scaling can be automated using that products feature, but you have to manage it, you can also manually scale out and in. However, in both Consumption and Premium, the Scale Controller manages the scaling out and in of compute resources based on numerous intellectual property algorithms and concepts. Table 4.13 lists additional limits and differences based on hosting plan. Please note that the Dedicated hosting plan is often referred to as the App Service plan.

TABLE 4.13   Hosting Plan Limits

Feature	Consumption	Dedicated	Premium
Storage	1 GB	50 to 100GB	250GB
Maximum Apps per plan	100	Unlimited	100
Maximum memory	1.5 GB	1.75 to 14GB	3.5 to 14GB
Default timeout	5 minutes	30	30
Maximum timeout	10 minutes	Unlimited	Unlimited
Maximum number of instances	200	10 to 20	20

From a storage perspective, note that when running in Consumption mode you are allocated 1GB of storage, which is where you can store the files (source, configuration, log, etc.) required to run and manage your application. Additionally, the content of an Azure Function running in Consumption mode is placed into Azure Files, which is unique to this mode. When running in Dedicated or Premium mode, your content is stored in an Azure Blob container. Both of those storage products are discussed in the next chapter, but they are different, and over time it was found that Azure Files with Azure Functions perform better when there are fewer files needing retrieval from the storage source, which is where the run from package feature came from. The differences in storage limits for the dedicated mode (i.e., 50 to 1000GB, shown in Table 4.13) exist because you have to choose different tiers of VM to run in that mode, like small, medium, and large, each having their own set of limits. The same applies to the amount of memory where each tier has a specific allocated amount; for memory this applies to Premium mode as well. An Azure Function in consumption mode has a limit of 1.5GB for the Function app; if more are required, you can move to one of the other plans to get more allocated memory.

The Maximum Apps per plan means, as a plan is synonymous with a process (EXE), that you can have 100 to an unlimited number of Function apps running on the VM. Remember that you can have multiple Functions per Function app. Also, remember that nothing is really unlimited, but there are large amounts of compute at your call. Realize that in Consumption mode you will run on a single processor, so would you really put workloads that have massive compute needs there? You would consider another hosting plan or compute product if that were the case. The maximum number of concurrent instances, where instances mean the number of VMs that will run your Azure Function, is also limited based on the hosting plan. There is some major compute power there; consider Premium with a max of 20 EP3 tier VMs massive. Finally, there is a timeout duration for the execution of an Azure Function. With Azure Functions there are two JSON configuration files, function.json and host.json. The function.json file is the place where your bindings and triggers are configured for a given Function within a Function app; you'll learn more about triggers and bindings in the next section. The host.json configuration file contains options that are applied to all the Functions in the Function app, one of which is the functionTimeout. It resembles something like the following:

```
{
"functionTimeout": "00:05:00"
}
```

The default is set to five minutes per Function invocation, and an invocation is the same as an execution in principle. For Consumption mode, the values can be from 1 second to 10 minutes. For both Dedicated and Premium modes, the default is 30 minutes. Setting the attribute to –1 means the function will run to completion. You might agree that 30 minutes is a long time for a single method to run, but it's not unheard of; however, I think setting the limit to infinity is a dangerous setting because you are charged based on usage, and what if something gets hung or runs in a loop for a week or so until you get the bill? Ouch. Keep in mind that if you consume the compute power, even if by accident, you will have to pay for it.

Triggers and Bindings

When you think about a regular program, there is a main() method that is the entry point into the program. From there all the if/then/else statements are assessed, and the code within the selected code block gets executed. In the Azure Function context, without getting too much into the coding aspect of this, instead of the main() entry point, there is a method named run(), which is where there are some details about what will cause the Azure Function to be invoked, i.e., the trigger. The simplest kind of Azure Function to create and consume is the HTTP trigger, which is triggered from a browser, curl, or any client that can make a request to an internet address. Take a look at the following code snippet; notice the run() method that has an attribute named HttpTrigger. It defines the kind of trigger that will invoke the Azure Function. The attribute has additional parameters that define the details about the binding (i.e., its metadata).

```
[FunctionName("csharpguitar-http")]
public static async Task<IActionResult>
        Run([HttpTrigger(AuthorizationLevel.Function, "get", "post",
            Route = null)] HttpRequest req, ILogger log)
```

It is also possible to declare the binding in the function.json file instead of in the method definition, as shown here:

```
{
  "bindings": [
    {
      "authLevel": "function", "name": "req",
      "type": "httpTrigger", "direction": "in",
      "methods": [ "get", "post" ]
    },
    {
      "name": "$return",
      "type": "http",
      "direction": "out"
    }
  ]
}
```

To summarize, a trigger is what will cause the function to run, and the binding defines the properties of the type. Take, for example, the previous function.json file that specifies the authentication level of type function, the name of type req (i.e., an HTTP request), and the HTTP methods that are supported, get and post. If the binding was to a database or other storage product, the connection string, the container name, an access key, and a name of a collection of data that the function will receive when triggered are all examples of what can be included in the binding. By doing so, you can implicitly access them in the Azure Function code without declaration. There are numerous kinds of triggers that are supported by an Azure Function, a summary of the most popular ones is shown in Table 4.14.

TABLE 4.14 Azure Functions Supported Bindings

Type	Trigger	Input	Output
Timer	✓	X	X
Service Bus	✓	X	✓
Queue Storage	✓	X	✓
Blob Storage	✓	✓	✓
Cosmos DB	✓	✓	✓
Event Grid	✓	X	X
Event Hub	✓	X	✓
HTTP	✓	X	✓

If an image or file is uploaded into a blob container and there is an Azure Function bound to that container, then the Azure Function gets triggered. The same goes for an HTTP trigger; when it is called, the code within it is executed. Let's look at both the blob and HTTP trigger in a bit more detail, specifically at the binding metadata. If a file is added to a blob container, what kind of information do you think is important to know if your code needs to perform some action on that file? Its name, the location of the file, and perhaps the size of the file are important. All those details and many more will be accessible within the run() method as it was defined in the following blob storage binding example:

```
{
  "bindings": [
    {
      "name": "myBlob",
      "type": "blobTrigger",
      "direction": "in",
      "path": "samples-workitems/{name}",
      "connection": "AzureWebJobsStorage"
    }
  ],
  "disabled": false
}
```

The name attribute is mapped to an element called myBlob that passed from the blob storage to the Azure Function of type System.IO.Stream. The System.IO.Stream class contains properties called name, LocalPath, and Length that are populated with information about the blob and can be accessed via code to provide the details of the blob as previously stated. Additionally, an important object when managing HTTP requests is the HttpRequest object, and as you see in the previous binding example found within a function.json file, it is identified as req and passed into the run() method as an HttpRequest object. That would mean you could access the properties and methods that exist in an HttpReqest object like the query sting and the request body.

To mention the input and output a bit more, consider that the direction of a trigger is always in. You can see that in the previous HTTP bindings example based on this setting: "direction": "in". In Table 4.14 note the triggers that support input bindings; this means you can have multiple input bindings. For example, if you wanted to have a Timer Trigger read some data on a Cosmos DB, because Cosmos DB supports input bindings, the Timer Trigger can be imperatively preconfigured to know the metadata about the Cosmos DB, for example connection string, database instance, etc. Then if you wanted that same Timer Trigger to save the content from the Cosmos DB into a file and place it into a blob container, since blob storage supports an output binding, the details of it can be preconfigured as a binding with a setting of "direction": "out". You can see "direction": "out" as a binding for the HTTP trigger shown previously. It is, of course, supported to define the binding information at runtime (declaratively) using the extensions and SDKs for those given messaging and storage Azure products. There are more actions required to make this happen and more concepts to consider, which won't be discussed here, but it is possible.

Every trigger has a corresponding extension module that must be loaded into the runtime when the Azure Function is started for the first time. All trigger extensions have some configuration settings that can be set in the host.json file. Take the HTTP trigger settings, for example.

```
{
    "extensions": {
        "http": {
            "routePrefix": "api",
            "maxOutstandingRequests": 200,
            "maxConcurrentRequests": 100,
            "dynamicThrottlesEnabled": true
        }
    }
}
```

If you have some experience writing ASP.NET Web APIs, then you know by default the route to the API is prefixed by /api/ after the URL. Then after /api/ is the name of the Azure Function, which in the previous example is csharpguitar-http. Recall from the run() method declaration that included this annotation [FunctionName("csharpguitar-http")]. What the routePrefix allows you to do is change api to something else, like v1 or v2. For more information about the other HTTP trigger settings, take a look at the following online documentation: https://docs.microsoft.com/en-us/azure/azure-functions/functions-host-json#http.

Create an Azure Function that is triggered by an HTTP request by completing Exercise 4.16.

EXERCISE 4.16

Creating and Consuming an Azure Function

1. Log in to the Azure Portal at portal.azure.com and then click the + Create A Resource link on the top left of the browser window. Click Compute and then Function App and select the Subscription into which you want to add the Azure Function. Select a resource group and enter a Function App name (for example, csharpguitar-azf). Select .NET Core as the runtime stack from the drop-down and then choose a region.

2. Click the Next: Hosting button and select a Storage account or create a new one by clicking the Create New link below the drop-down. Choose Windows as the operating system, select Consumption as the plan type, and then click the Next: Monitoring button.

3. Select No to disable Application Insights and then click the Review + Create button. Review the summary and press the Create button.

4. Once created, navigate to it to click the + New function button. Select In-portal as the development environment and then click the Continue button. Click the Webhook + API Function type and then click the create button. Click the </> Get function URL link and copy the link by clicking the Copy link next to the URL. You should see something similar to Figure 4.54.

FIGURE 4.54   An overview of an Azure Function

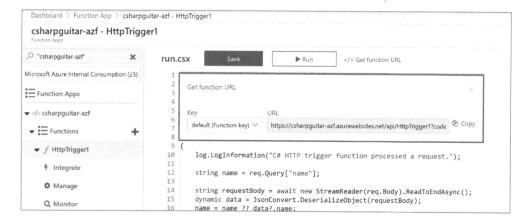

5. Open a CMD window on your local workstation and enter the following `curl` command as a single line. (The command line is broken here to better enable readability.)

    ```
    curl https://<functionName>.azurewebsites.net/api/HttpTrigger1?code=xcEFmx...
    -d "{\"name\":\"Benjamin\"}"
    ```

    The output will be similar to that shown in Figure 4.55.

FIGURE 4.55   Consuming an HTTP-triggered Azure Function using curl

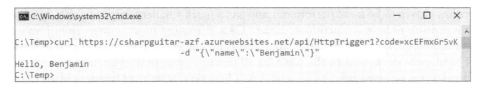

6. To confirm the run from package feature, add an app setting by clicking the function name. Click the Configuration link and click the + New Application Setting link. Enter **WEBSITE_RUN_FROM_PACKAGE** for the name, enter **1** as the value, click the OK button, and finally click the Save button.

    You can test the Azure Function from within the portal by selecting the Test item on the right side of the IDE in the browser and then pressing the Run button.

I'll point out a few things about some decisions made during the creation of the Azure Function. First, all runtime stacks do not support the feature of developing in the portal. For example, both Python and Java require that you develop locally and then deploy; therefore, the exercise chose .NET Core because the example was a bit simpler. You also chose not to enable Application Insights. This is a valuable tool, and again, since this was just an example, it was not enabled. If you are developing an Azure Function to run some live workload, then Application Insights is by all means recommended. Application Insights will be discussed in more detail in Chapter 9, but keep in mind that Microsoft (i.e., the FaaS offering) doesn't record your application errors. Cloud hosting providers are concerned primarily about the platform. You as the owner of the application need to code in exception handlers, and the location where you write those exceptions to is Application Insights. Finally, although the exercise created the Azure Function via the portal, that scenario is more for getting your hands wet and learning a bit about the capabilities. It is recommended for more complicated scenarios to develop and test locally using Visual Studio, Visual Studio Code, IntelliJ, Eclipse, or other open source IDEs.

Runtime Versions

A runtime is an in-memory set of supporting code that helps the management and execution of the custom application running within it. What a runtime is has been mentioned before, so more depth isn't required here. From an Azure Functions perspective, there are three versions of the runtime: version 1, version 2, and version 3. The difference between version 1 and version 2 is quite significant, and by all means, if you are creating a new function, choose the latest version. Version 1 of Azure Functions targets the .NET Framework, which doesn't support cross-platform execution. This means you are bound to Windows and bound to the full .NET Framework library. That isn't necessarily a bad thing; it just isn't the newest thing. Version 2 targets .NET Core 2.x and is cross-platform. .NET Core has proven to be more performant and has a much smaller footprint. Also, in version 1, it is possible to have a function written in C# and another function written in JavaScript contained within the same Function app. This is no longer a supported scenario in version 2. The runtime stack must be the same for all functions within the Function app.

To view the targeted runtime of your Azure Function, from the Overview blade in the portal, click Function App Setting. When the blade is rendered, you will see something similar to Figure 4.56.

FIGURE 4.56   A view of the Azure Function runtime version

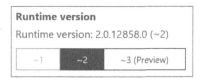

At this moment, version 3 of the Azure Function runtime is in preview; however, it is moving quickly toward *Global Availability (GA)*. Version 3 targets .NET Core 3.x. Notice also the tilde in front of versions ~1, ~2, and ~3. This notifies the platform that when there is a newer version of the runtime released, the code running will automatically target that new version. As you see in Figure 4.56, there is a specific version of the runtime 2.0.12858.0. If there is ever a newer version that your code cannot support, then you can pin your function to a specific version of the runtime using the FUNCTIONS_WORKER_RUNTIME app setting parameter accessible via the Configuration blade in the portal.

Supported Programming Languages

The chosen runtime version is important because it will dictate the operating system the Azure Function runs on and the languages in which you can write code with. As mentioned, version 1 targets the full version of the .NET Framework, which is not cross-platform and therefore can only run on the Windows operating system. However, version 2 and any future version target .NET Core, which is cross-platform and can therefore run on either Windows or Linux.

From a language perspective, C#, JavaScript (Node), and F# are supported in all supported versions of the Azure Function runtime. Java, PowerShell, Python, and TypeScript are supported in version 2 and greater. There is likely work happening in the background to support more languages as time progresses. See Table 4.15 for an overview of supported languages by the Azure Function runtime version.

TABLE 4.15   Azure Function Supported Languages

Language	1.x	2.x	3.x
C#	.NET Framework 4.7	.NET Core 2.2	.NET Core 3.x
JavaScript	Node 6	Node 8 and 10	Node 8 and 10
F#	.NET Framework 4.7	.NET Core 2.2	.NET Core 3.x
Java	X	Java 8	Java 8
PowerShell	X	PowerShell Core 6	PowerShell Core 6
Python	X	Python 3.6	Python 3.6
TypeScript	X	✓	✓

As of writing this chapter, version 3 is in preview, and all those languages in the 3.x column are considered preview as well. There were also numerous other languages considered "experimental" in the context of version 1. I used the past tense because those will remain "experimental" and will never be a fully supported development language for Azure Functions v1. Those languages are Bash, Batch, and PHP.

Which of the following runtime stacks are available for running an Azure Function on Linux?

A. JavaScript

B. .NET Core

C. Python

D. .NET Framework

The answer is A, B, and C because the .NET Framework is not cross-platform and therefore cannot run on the Linux operating system.

Service Fabric

The concept of microservices has been around for quite a number of years. The structural style of *service-oriented architecture (SOA)* may ring some bells. Service Fabric is a platform and an orchestrator to run microservices, which are a variant of the SOA development technique. What are microservices then? You can begin to understand by visualizing a nonmicroservice application, which would run on an Azure VM or an Azure Function, for example. When you create an application to run on virtual machines, the capabilities within it would typically span multiple tiers, i.e., a monolithic approach, as shown in Figure 4.57. The monolithic application solution would have a GUI and possibly these hypothetical built-in capabilities or services: security, order validation, logistics management, order fulfillment, and billing. This kind of monolithic architecture provides the compute using multiple tiers of IT architecture. Recall Figure 4.19 where the IT solution is comprised of the web/GUI, application, database, and authentication tiers.

FIGURE 4.57   Monolithic architecture

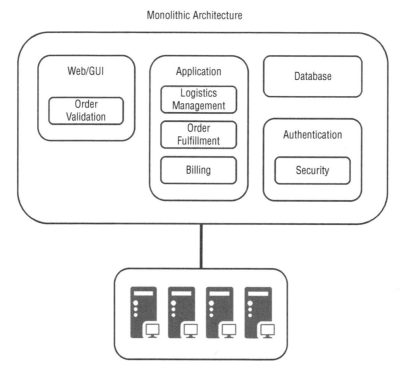

Each of those services (security, ordering, logistics, etc.) has a set of executable code that possibly overlapped, reused, or combined logic and shared libraries. A change to any part of the monolithic application would have some impact on all the services hosted throughout the multiple tiers.

From an Azure Function perspective, you may recognize some similarities with the term *microservices*, in that the unit of work performed by an Azure Function would be a much smaller service than the IT solution running on those multiple tiers. You could consider implementing a Function for each of those services within a given Function app. That scenario is a valid one so long as the number of Functions are manageable and that it can run in a sandbox. However, there is no orchestrator for running a large number of Azure Functions that may or may not be dependent upon each other, and you can only scale a Function App and not specific Functions. This is where Service Fabric and microservices fill a gap. Service Fabric is an orchestrator that helps efficiently execute and manage a massive number of small isolated programs. Take Figure 4.58, for example, where instead of running those capabilities with a dedicated tier bound to a VM or within a Function App, each service can scale and be managed independently.

FIGURE 4.58   Microservices architecture

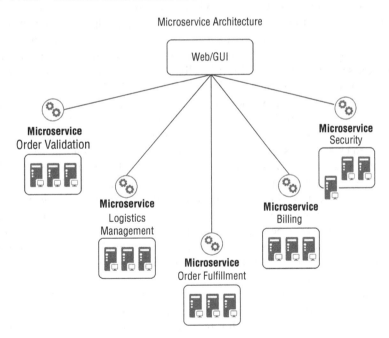

Scaling/managing a microservice independently is an interesting concept. In a monolithic code base, where you have many methods doing many different things, it doesn't take long to find where the bottlenecks are. A common place is performing database *create, insert, update, delete (CRUD)* or Select operations. The fact that all your code runs within the same process, a single slow-running, CPU- or memory-intensive procedure can have significant impact on the other methods running in the same process. There is no simple way to give that specific method more compute power; instead, you need to give compute to the entire tier. The group of services running in the process increases the compute by scaling up to a larger VM. This is not the most cost-effective or stable approach, because the need for extra compute power likely happens in bursts for a single service, and when the burst goes away, you have extra compute sitting idle generating costs. What if by scaling up, the application tier results in greater load on the database tier, again with more scaling until you finally get it right for that burst? The effort to get it right is not a simple one, and contemplating scaling back down and doing it all over again, when the next burst occurs, is often a hard pill to take. With microservices, you can scale more precisely as it is the service that scales and not a tier. Service Fabric handles the scaling; it monitors for health and helps with the deployment of changes.

Clusters and Nodes

There was mention of a node in Chapter 3 within the context of network traffic routing. It was described as a server that is connected to a network that helps route a packet of data to its intended location. A node is a virtual or physical server, and a cluster is a tightly connected group of nodes. Nodes in clusters typically operate with the same operating system, have the same hardware specifications like CPU and memory, and are connected through a high-speed LAN. A cluster in the context of Service Fabric as you would expect isn't concerned about routing networking data packets. Instead, the cluster is concerned with running one or more specific microservices. If you look back at Figure 4.58, connected to each microservice there is a cluster containing three nodes. In reality, the number of nodes for a given cluster can scale into the thousands, and the scaling can be programmatically or manually performed. Recognize that the Service Fabric platform runs on VMSS. That's right, this is another example of an Azure product (i.e., Service Fabric) built on top of another Azure product (VMSS). This means everything you have learned about VMSS in this chapter can be applied here. For example, you know that VMSS scales out using a base image consisting of the operating system and application. Additionally, with that scale out, the concepts of fault domains and update domains are applied. Understanding that, the confidence in the stability and redundancy of the architecture and infrastructure behind Service Fabric should be high.

Recognize that there are durability tiers in regard to the durability of Service Fabric components. They are Gold, Silver, and Bronze. Each of those tiers, as with many of the Azure products, has benefits, different limits, and a different set of capabilities and costs. You might assume that you can choose any series of VMs as your nodes, but this is not true; it is dependent on the tier. The same goes for storing the state. (State management, which is discussed later, is only supported in Silver and Gold.) It is recommended for production workloads that you use either Silver or Gold, because with Bronze, the scheduling of updates and reboots is not respected. The speed in which scaling happens is also dependent on the tier and will scale interestingly slower with Silver or Gold. This is because in those tiers, data safety is prioritized over speed and conversely so in regard to Bronze.

It is the responsibility of the orchestrator to properly deallocate and allocate microservices from or to nodes in the given cluster. This is a complicated activity considering that there can be a different set of microservices on each node. For example, a security and a logistic management service can coexist on the same node. To then properly deallocate a node, Service Fabric must know the state of all other nodes in the cluster so that when moving a service from one node to another, there is no risk of then overloading the new one. All of that scaling logic is happening behind the scenes using the orchestration logic within Service Fabric. When to scale is most commonly based on the consumption of the services or based on the resource usage on the node. There is a concept called *logical load metrics* that allows you to create custom service consumption-based metrics used for scaling. This kind of metric is concerned with elements such as connection count over a given time frame, the responsiveness of the application, or the number of times the application has been running. Based on counters maintained in those custom metrics, it is possible to scale out or in based on your defined thresholds. Another technique that is the most common scaling method is where you scale in or out using usage metrics such as CPU and memory. How all this works together can be better understood by reading more about the Service Fabric architecture, which is coming up next.

Architecture

The Service Fabric orchestration architecture is built upon a layered subsystem of components. Each subsystem component plays a role in making the microservice applications available, fault tolerant, manageable, scalable, and testable. Each component that makes up Service Fabric is shown in Figure 4.59 and discussed in more detail in the following text.

FIGURE 4.59   Service Fabric subsystem components

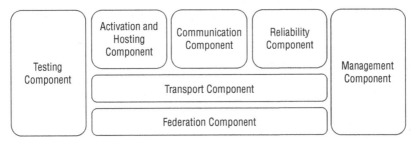

Activation and Hosting   The activation and hosting component is responsible for managing the lifecycle of the application running on each node. It knows which service or services are running on each node, and by interacting with the reliability component it can also determine whether the application is healthy and take appropriate action if not. An appropriate action would be to move the service to another node, move all the services to another node, and/or deallocate the node from the cluster.

Reliability   The reliability component consists of three mechanisms, starting with a replicator that ensures changes are applied to all services on all nodes. A failover manager that monitors when nodes are added and removed from the cluster then can adjust the load to distribute it evenly on the additional or remaining nodes, and finally a resource manager ensures nodes are replicated across fault domains and that the contents within them remain operational.

Communication   The communication component helps resolve service names to a location on any given node in the cluster. As services, aka microservices, can be hosted on multiple nodes, knowing where they are and how to locate them is quite an important feature; consider this as a DNS or naming service within the cluster.

Federation   The federation component is the heart of the Service Fabric product that provides the overview or the entry point for making decisions that need to know the current state of the microservice and nodes running in the cluster. Examples include how many nodes are there, how many of each microservice is running on each node, and what is the health status of each node.

Management   The lifecycle management of the Service Fabric cluster is managed by the, you guessed it, management component. This component interacts with many of the other components for gathering statistics on health, placements, and versioning. In addition, this is where the application binaries are placed and referenced when new services need provisioning.

Transport   The transport component manages the communication between the Service Fabric components and the nodes in the cluster as well as between the nodes and the consumers of the microservices running upon them.

Testing   Finally, the testing component provides a set of tools for simulating failovers, scaling, and deployments without having negative impact on the live application.

Best-Practice Scenarios

There are three areas that I will offer some guidance on regarding Service Fabric.

- Stateless and stateful
- Scaling vertically and horizontally
- Application logging

The HTTP protocol is stateless by design. This means that when an HTTP request is made to a web server, all the required information to respond exists within, for example, the header and/or body. Once the request is responded to, the web server does not remember much if anything about it. The next time you make a request, everything needed to make the request successful again must be sent from the client. A stateful application, on the other hand, could conceivably store some details about the client and the request on the server so that each request didn't have to carry along so much detail. Take a simple example of applications that would not require state like an API that returns the datetime or performs some kind of mathematical calculation, like a calculator. In most cases, neither of those examples would need to store information about a client's previous datetime request or previous calculation. On the other hand, applications that provide capabilities that require multiple steps to complete or need to know the identity of the client sending the request would need to support the maintaining of state. Completing an order online usually takes multiple steps that require clicking a button that sends a request to a web server. Each of those requests would need to know where you are in the order process, as well as who you are. Most websites store that information on the web server (for example, order details and identity token) because it is faster since the order detail doesn't have to be sent each time and because it's safer since just a small time-sensitive encrypted identity token can be sent back and forth instead of reauthenticating with each request.

Service Fabric supports both stateless and stateful scenarios. There is no extra step to take when creating a stateless microservice. However, when the application requires state, then here is a place where the reliability component plays another important role. (Recall Figure 4.59.) Implementing the stateless capabilities into Service Fabric requires coding. The reliability component exposes a set of service APIs that can be consumed to create a `StateManager` for managing and storing the information your application needs to store for subsequent reference. Since the implementation of this technique is code-based and not something you need to know for the Azure Solutions Architect Expert exam, it won't be covered in more detail. However, one important detail that you must understand is that the data that is stored in the `StateManager` exists only on the node where the request is sent. It is important to recognize this in the context of scaling and failover scenarios. The request from a client must always be routed to the same node, and if the node goes away for any reason, so does the data stored on that node for the given session. You need to code for those scenarios.

You should understand what scaling up and scaling out mean. Scaling up means you have chosen to scale from a 1 CPU VM with 32GB of RAM to a VM with 4 CPUs having 64GB of RAM. Scaling out means that when you have one 4 CPU VM with 64 RAM, you add an additional VM with those same specifications that will run the identical application. In the context of Service Fabric, those terms are referred to as vertical and horizontal scaling. Scaling up equals vertical, and scaling out is horizontal. Scaling is recommended using Azure Resource Manager (ARM) templates, which are discussed in Chapter 8, or using the `AzureClient`, which is discussed in more detail here:

docs.microsoft.com/en-us/dotnet/api/overview/azure/service-fabric

Manually scaling the VMSS via the portal or any other interface, vertically or horizontally circumvents the Service Fabric components and can get the management component out of sync with the overall state of the cluster. That is not recommended.

I learned a scaling lesson some years ago while working on support at Microsoft. Previously in this chapter I discussed App Service Environments (ASEs), which are a private PaaS Azure offering. I learned the hard way that ASEs exhibit a different behavior when scaling than what I had experienced many times before. Commonly, when you scale vertically (up/down), it happens within a relatively short amount of time; it is impactful. You will lose state, but the timeframe in which it takes to get running again is usually the same amount of time it would take for a normal reboot of a physical server to happen. What I learned was that for a version 1 ASE environment, it is not the same; the time required to scale an ASE (V1) is much, much longer. I became so comfortable with using this virtual reboot (vertical scaling) as a quick solution for solving downtime, hanging, or badly behaving applications that I used it way too often without much thought. My point is to take caution when scaling. The impact can and sometimes is more impactful based on the product with which you are performing that action. However, recognize that, as stated many times, maybe too many so far, is that the ability to scale compute up, down, in, and out is the most valuable and game-changing offering existing in the cloud from a compute perspective.

Finally, it is important that you implement some kind of logging strategy. The cloud hosting provider does not have the manpower to monitor and resolve all exceptions that are running on the platform; instead, they focus on the platform only. There are limited platform-provided application-focused logging capabilities that are built in by default. It is often the case that, when an exception happens, it gets rendered to the client or shows up in the event viewer on the VM. However, if the application itself, in the form of code, does not implement any kind of logging, the scenario in which the error happened is usually unknown, and it will likely never be figured out. Microsoft provides and recommends tools like the Application Insights SDK, `EventSource`, and ASP.NET Core Logging for Service Fabric microservice deployments. You can learn more in Chapter 9.

Application Insights and Log Analytics, two previous stand-alone features, have been bundled into a single product named Azure Monitor. You will read often about Application Insights, but keep in mind it is bundled into Azure Monitor. The `EventSource` class is found within the `System.Diagnostics.Tracing` namespace available in the .NET Framework. You would need to implement this class in the code of the microservice running on Service Fabric. Part of the implementation requires a configuration in a `web.config` file that identifies where the log file is to be written and whether the logging is enabled. It is advised that you leave logging off unless there is a reason for it being on. Logs can grow fast and large and then have some negative impact on the performance. Watch out for that. Lastly, `EventSource` is dependent on the .NET Framework, which does not run on Linux. If you are targeting an ASP/NET Core application to run on Linux, then you would consider the ASP.NET Core Logging instrumentation. Logging capabilities are exposed via the `Microsoft.Extensions.Logging` namespace, which exposes an `ILogger` interface for implementing the log capturing, but again, this needs design, coding, and configuration. Application logging is a fundamental aspect for resolving bugs in production. If you want to increase the probability of having a successful IT solution running on Azure, then application logging is essential, which is why half of Chapter 9 is focused directly on that.

Azure Integration

It is common when running microservices or web applications on Service Fabric that you also consume and configure other Azure products. For example, when you create the cluster and the nodes within the cluster, there is a need to load balance requests across clusters and to also expose those endpoints to the clients and customers who will consume them. Figure 4.60 shows a common architecture scenario that a customer would implement.

FIGURE 4.60   A common Service Fabric architecture scenario

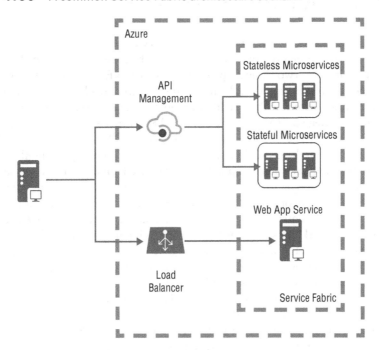

Notice that a load balancer can be used to balance requests across the nodes and microservices hosted in the Service Fabric cluster. The load balancer, as you learned in the previous chapter, can be configured to only support connections from a specific on-premise network, or it can be exposed globally. The same goes for the exposure of the microservice APIs, for example, the logics, ordering, and billing services. API Management can interpret the path in a request and redirect the request to a specific backend pool of compute. This is helpful when changes happen on the Service Fabrics location detail, like a relocation into a new zone, virtual network, or subnet, where its endpoint may receive a new IP address. Those backend changes can be hidden from the client connecting to the exposed endpoint because the API Management configuration can be updated to route to the new location of the Service Fabric cluster as required. The point here is that simply provisioning an instance of Service Fabric doesn't get you up and running. There is coding and some significant configuration requirements to make before this product becomes functional. The barrier to its implementation is a bit high and requires some skilled IT professionals to deploy and support it. However, for large microservice workloads that target the .NET Framework, this has proven to be a good option.

Azure Kubernetes Service

In principle, Service Fabric and Azure Kubernetes Service (AKS) provide similar capabilities. The difference between the two, or, better said, the reason you would choose one over the other, comes down to two things: open source versus .NET Framework (Figure 4.2) and midlevel complexity versus high complexity. While you were reading the previous section about Service Fabric, there wasn't a mention of Docker, Azure Container Instance (ACI), or Azure Container Registry (ACR), for example. AKS is specifically designed toward the consumption of containers created using either the Docker file format or ACR. AKS was not only developed from the ground up using open source technologies but also designed specifically for running open source applications. Service Fabric can run open source code and provide Linux as an operating system to run them on; however its original target was the .NET Framework development stack. Also, AKS is a bit less complicated to get up and running. The barriers to entry are less demanding. When it comes to Service Fabric, the orchestration of the workloads requires coding. When it comes to AKS, the default deployment and management of the workload requires no coding. Both of these orchestrators focus on the containerization of microservices; however, each one is targeted to a specific kind of application (open source versus .NET Framework). Each has a different complexity level of prerequisites and maintenance activities. Figure 4.61 illustrates the AKS concept and that is what will be discussed in this section.

The illustration describes not only the AKS components (like the cluster master) but also its tight integration with Azure DevSpaces, Azure DevOps, Azure Monitor, and container repositories like Docker Hub and ACR. Let's begin with a brief discussion of Kubernetes versus AKS and what existed prior to that on Azure.

Kubernetes vs. AKS

Kubernetes is itself a complete system for automating deployments, as well as scaling and managing applications. If you wanted, you could deploy Kubernetes itself onto the Azure platform and use the Kubernetes product without even touching AKS. What AKS provides is the infrastructure to run the cluster master (the Kubernetes control plane) for no cost. You will see the cluster master in Figure 4.61. Only the nodes within the cluster that run your application incur costs, so simply using AKS, you get some free compute that would otherwise result in a bill. How specifically the cluster master is architected is platform specific and not something you would need to worry so much about; however, it is worth some time to cover the various components that make up the cluster master. The cluster master components are as follows:

- The APIs
- etdc
- The scheduler
- The controller

FIGURE 4.61   An end-to-end illustration of Azure Kubernetes Services

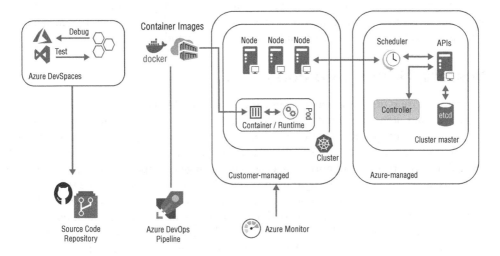

The API server uses JSON over HTTP REST for connecting with the internal Kubernetes API that reads/writes to the etdc data store for configuring the workloads and containers on the nodes in the cluster. The etdc data store is the location where the current state of the cluster is stored. Consider you have numerous pods running on numerous nodes within the cluster and you want to update them with a new version of the container image. How many instances of the pods and on which node they are running are all stored in the etdc, which helps find where the update needs to be rolled out. Additionally, knowing how many instances of a node you have is helpful when it comes to scaling. The scheduler also plays an important role where, if you have multiple instances, then you would not want to deploy a change to all of them at the same time. The scheduler will make sure they are updated one after the other so that the highest availability is achieved. The controller is the engine that maintains the status between the desired state of the cluster and the current state. Consider that you have requested to manually scale out to five instances of a specific node running a specific pod; the request would be sent to the API server. The controller would find out how many instances currently exist via etdc, determine how many more need to be added, and then take on the responsibility of getting them all provisioned, configured, and accepting traffic. Then it would update etdc once the actual cluster state matches the desired state. Imagine if the implementation is very large, there could be a lot going on here. AKS provides you with the cluster master compute and interface for free.

There was a product before AKS named Azure Container Service (ACS) that is being depreciated and replaced by AKS. ACS fully supports the Windows OS for running workloads, which AKS is still in the process of providing full support for. As mentioned, AKS is designed from the ground up on Linux and open source languages. ACS doesn't support the concept of node pools where nodes with the same configuration can target the same underlying VMs. Remember from Figure 4.52, where you read about VMs that are designed specifically for different workloads such as memory, CPU, or storage-intensive work. Pooling the nodes together, which is not possible with ACS, keeps applications that have specific workload requirements together and thereby ensures the best possible performance. ACS is only mentioned here in case at some point you hear or read something about it. You should not target this product for any new projects. Finally, AKS supports 100 clusters per subscription, 100 nodes per cluster, and a maximum 110 pods per node.

Clusters, Nodes, and Pods

A cluster is a group of nodes, where a node is typically a VM. The nodes typically do span update and fault domains so that availability is preserved during transient or other more serious regional outages. Review the "Clusters and Nodes" section in the previous section as the cluster and node concept here is similar to the scenario with Service Fabric. Take a look again at Figure 4.61 and notice the customer-managed component to get a good visual of the cluster, node, and pod configuration in the AKS context. Also note the term *pod*, which wasn't referred to in the Service Fabric context. I like to make the connection between the term *microservice*, which is used in the Service Fabric context, and a *pod*. Each of those references has to do with the location where the application code gets executed. From an AKS perspective and also from a Service Fabric one, you can have multiple microservices or pods running on a single node at any given time. However, from an AKS perspective, the pod is a one-to-one mapping with a container, while in Service Fabric the mapping is with an image (no Docker). From now, in this context, the usage of pod and microservices will carry the same meaning.

Development and Deployment

Creating and deploying an application to AKS is a bit easier than you might expect and is something you will do in a few moments. Before you do the exercise, there are a few concepts I would like to introduce to you or perhaps provide you with a refresher. The first one is a new configuration file called YAML (rhymes with camel) and has a recursive acronym of "YAML Ain't Markup Language." In the context of Kubernetes, AKS, Docker, and even some in Azure DevOps, you will see this file format occurring often. For many this is the "next" iteration of file formatting that started from XML to JSON and now YAML. YAML has yet to show up much in the non-open source world; however, it is likely on its way. There is also some helpful integration of AKS into Visual Studio and Visual Studio Code for deploying to AKS. The Visual Studio IDE allows a developer to develop and test an application on their local workstation and then deploy directly to an AKS cluster. You can see in Figure 4.61 that, once deployed, remote debugging is also possible. What is going on behind the scenes to make that happen is completely abstracted away from the developer by a service called Azure Dev Spaces, which you will see and use later. The final concept I would like to introduce you to briefly here is GitHub and Azure DevOps. Both of those products are designed for the management and storage of application source code. Remember in Exercise 4.2 that with Azure Container Instance (ACI) you got some source code from GitHub to create the application running in that container. The same set of capabilities exist for Azure DevOps as referenced in Figure 4.61 where Source Code Repository and Azure DevOps Pipeline are presented. Much more about Azure DevOps is discussed in Chapter 8 where deployments are covered in detail. Read more about it there if desired.

To learn more about AKS and use Azure Dev Spaces, complete Exercise 4.17 where you will create an Azure Kubernetes Service cluster using Azure CLI and then deploy an ASP .NET Core web application to it using Visual Studio. For this example, I used Visual Studio Community 2019 (16.2.4), which is free to download from here:

visualstudio.microsoft.com/downloads/

EXERCISE 4.17

Creating an AKS Cluster and Deploying an ASP.NET Core Web Application

1. Log in to Azure Shell at https://shell.azure.com and enter the following command, replacing <name> with your resource group and ASK cluster name. Note that the line is broken for clarity; please enter each command on a single line, one after the other. See Figure 4.62, which illustrates a summarized example.

```
az aks create --resource-group <name> --name <name>
    --node-count 1 --enable-addons monitoring --generate-ssh-keys

az aks get-credentials --resource-group <name> --name <name>

kubectl get nodes
```

FIGURE 4.62 AKS Azure CLI commands

```
PS Azure:\> az aks create --resource-group CSHARPGUITAR-DB3-RG --name CSHARPGUITAR-AKS-DB3
                    --node-count 1 --enable-addons monitoring --generate-ssh-keys

PS Azure:\> az aks get-credentials --resource-group CSHARPGUITAR-DB3-RG --name CSHARPGUITAR-AKS-DB3
Merged "CSHARPGUITAR-AKS-DB3" as current context in /home/benjamin/.kube/config

PS Azure:\> kubectl get nodes
NAME                                STATUS   ROLES   AGE    VERSION
aks-nodepool1-20745193-vmss000000   Ready    agent   162m   v1.13.12
```

2. After the commands complete, log in to the Azure Portal at https://portal.azure .com. Navigate to the Azure Kubernetes Services blade, select the AKS cluster that you just created, click Node Pools, and view the nodepool1. Click the Dev Spaces link on the navigation menu, toggle the switch to Yes to enable it, and then click Save.

3. Open Visual Studio 2019 and create an ASP.NET Core Web Application, walking through the creation wizard. Select the project shown in Figure 4.63.

FIGURE 4.63 Selecting the ASP.NET Core Web Application Visual Studio project

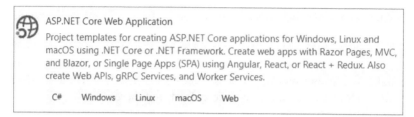

ASP.NET Core Web Application

Project templates for creating ASP.NET Core applications for Windows, Linux and macOS using .NET Core or .NET Framework. Create web apps with Razor Pages, MVC, and Blazor, or Single Page Apps (SPA) using Angular, React, or React + Redux. Also create Web APIs, gRPC Services, and Worker Services.

C#   Windows   Linux   macOS   Web

4. Create a .NET Core/ASP.NET Core Web Application, similar to that shown in Figure 4.64.

FIGURE 4.64 Creating the .NET Core/ASP.NET Core Web Application Visual Studio project

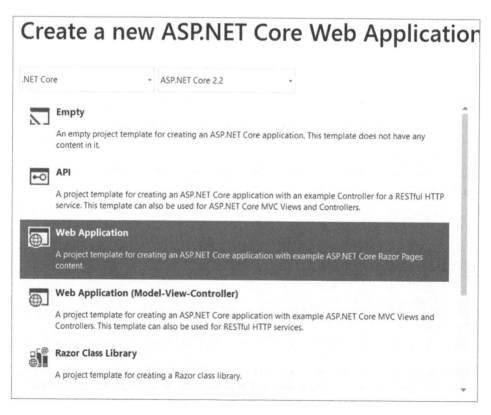

5. Click Azure Dev Spaces, as shown in Figure 4.65.

FIGURE 4.65   How to execute Azure Dev Spaces from within Visual Studio

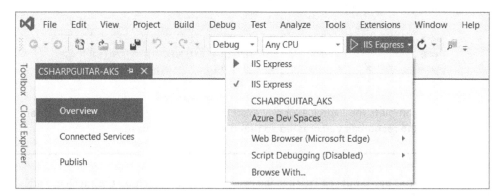

6. When the Azure Dev Spaces window pops up, select the identity, the subscription, and the AKS cluster created in step 1. Keep the other defaults. Check the Public Accessible check box and then click the OK button. Open the Output window in Visual Studio to watch the progress.

7. Once built and deployed, the public IP address will be found in the Visual Studio Output window and will look similar to that shown in Figure 4.66. Access the URL in a browser.

FIGURE 4.66   The AKS public endpoint is displayed in the Output window in Visual Studio.

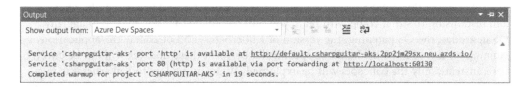

8. Navigate back to Azure Cloud Shell and enter the following command to view additional information about the application running on the AKS cluster:

```
kubectl get service azure-vote-front --watch
```

Figure 4.67 illustrates the command and the potential output.

FIGURE 4.67   Checking the application on an AKS cluster using the Kubernetes command-line tool kubectl

```
PS Azure:\> kubectl get service csharpguitar-aks --watch
NAME              TYPE        CLUSTER-IP   EXTERNAL-IP   PORT(S)   AGE
csharpguitar-aks  ClusterIP   10.0.248.6                 80/TCP    15m
```

9. Once you complete the exercise, or any exercise for that matter, you might consider removing the resources you created so that the cost is minimized.

That wasn't too hard, but realize that the exercise is just scratching the surface, and there is so much more to it. There will be some books written about this at some point if there haven't been already. To explain a bit more about what you just did, I start with the Azure CLI commands. The first one, az aks create, is the one that created the AKS cluster. The second, az aks get-credentials, retrieved and stored the credentials of the AKS cluster so that I would then be able to capture information using kubectl and perform other administrative work on the cluster. The Kubernetes command-line tool kubectl is installed by default when using Azure Shell. A reason I decided to use Azure Shell was to avoid the complexities of installing Azure CLI and kubectl on my workstation. Now that you have created an AKS cluster, developed an application, and deployed it to the cluster, read on to learn a bit about maintaining and scaling the AKS cluster.

Maintaining and Scaling

Since you know that VMSS is used behind the scenes of AKS and you know the roles and responsibilities that come with IaaS, you will recognize that you must manage any OS upgrades, the OS patching, the version of Kubernetes, and of course the application running on the nodes. The details to specifically perform these updates will not be covered here; instead, only the concepts will be explained. When an update to Kubernetes is initiated, it is rolled out using the concept of cordoning and draining. This is done to minimize the impact the update may have on the IT solution. The first action that is triggered from the controller of the cluster master is to cordon one of the nodes and target it for upgrade. There is a waiting period after the node is identified so that any request running on the node can complete; this is considered draining. Once the node is no longer being used, the upgrade proceeds. Once complete, the controller places the node back into the pool and takes out another; the process is repeated until all nodes are upgraded. It is possible to upgrade just a node within the cluster or the entire cluster of nodes. In the Azure Portal on the AKS blade, you will find a navigation link named Upgrade, which will upgrade the entire cluster. Click the Node pools link on the AKS blade, and you will find an option to upgrade each node. Upgrading an application running on the AKS cluster has many available options; you can perform it manually, or you can choose any of the deployment options found by clicking the Deployment Center navigation menu item on the AKS blade. Azure DevOps Repos, GitHub, Bitbucket Cloud, and External Git are all options (as shown in Figure 4.61). Each of those implement CI/CD, which is very helpful when it comes to managing, developing, testing, and deploying application code (more on that in Chapter 8). For upgrading the OS version you have provisioned for AKS, you can find the VMSS instance that was created when you created the AKS cluster. Open the virtual machine scale set in the Azure Portal and navigate to the blade; the name should be prefixed with aks-. On the VMSS blade, click Instances, and then click the instance. The process for upgrading the instances running your AKS cluster is the same as you would do for any other VMSS implementation.

There are two methods for scaling: manual or automated. Manual scaling isn't something you should consider when running a live production application. This kind of scaling capability is most useful during testing where you can learn how your application responds to scaling. You can scale from a pod or node perspective. To manually scale a pod, you can use the Kubernetes command-line kubectl. First use it to get a list of pods so you can see what you have; then once you identify the pod, scale that pod to, for example, five replicas or instances.

```
kubectl get pods
kubectl scale --replicas=5 <podName>
```

To manually scale a node to, for example, three instances, you can execute the following Azure CLI command from either Azure Cloud Shell or from a workstation with Azure CLI configured:

```
az aks scale --resource-group <name> --name <name> --node-count 3
```

From an autoscaling perspective, Kubernetes provides a service called *Horizontal Pod Autoscale (HPA)*, which monitors the resource demand and scales the number of replicas/instances when required. This service does work with AKS but requires an optional component named Metrics Service for Kubernetes 1.8+. The HPA checks the Metric API exposed from the API server, which is part of the cluster master, every 30 seconds. If the metric threshold has been breached, then the scale out is managed by the controller. To check the scale metrics, you can use the Kubernetes command-line kubectl to check, using this command:

```
kubectl get hpa
```

To set the metric threshold, if the previous command doesn't return any configurations, use the following:

```
kubectl autoscale deployment <podName> --cpu-percent=70 --min=2 --max=15
```

This command will add a pod when the average CPU across all existing pods exceeds 70%. The rule will increase up to a maximum of 15 pods, and when the CPU usage across the pods falls below 70%, the autoscaler will decrease one- by one to a minimum of two instances.

Also, you can autoscale a node (the VM on which the pods are running). Although there are some capabilities in the Azure Portal to scale out the number of VMs in the AKS cluster (it is a VMSS product after all), this is not recommended as it will get the AKS cluster controller and etcd out of sync. You can scale a VMSS using PowerShell, Azure CLI, or a supported client. This also is not recommended. It is recommended to always configure scaling or to manually scale using the Azure CLI Kubernetes component, which is accessed via Azure CLI and always followed by aks, for example az aks. The script that follows is an example of how to scale a node:

```
az aks update  --resource-group <name>  --name <name> \
   --update-cluster-autoscaler --min-count 2  --max-count 15
```

Having used the Azure CLI Kubernetes component, as recommended, the AKS cluster is set to have a minimum of two nodes and a maximum of 15. You might be asking yourself, what are the thresholds? Well, in practice, HPA and a node scaler service called *Cluster autoscaler* are used alongside each other. The cluster autoscaler will check the same metrics that were set for the pod every 10 seconds versus 30 seconds like HPA does for the pod. In a similar technique, HPA takes by increasing the number of pods based on the metrics. The cluster autoscaler will focus on the nodes (aka the VM) and adjust them appropriately to match the needs of the pod. You must be running Kubernetes version 1.10.x to get this cluster autoscale feature.

The final topic covered here is one that will handle a burst. I have mentioned the bursting concept a few times in regard to hybrid networks and HPC. That capability is also available when running AKS. In some scenarios, when a rapid burst occurs, there may be some delay with the provisioning of new pods as they wait for the scheduler and controller to get them rolled out; the requested increase in capacity simply hangs in a waiting state until they are added into the cluster. When the burst is unexpected and the number of nodes and pods exceeds the upper limit of your configuration, additional nodes simply are not allowed to be scaled out further. The way to handle this burst a bit better is to use *virtual nodes* and our friend ACI. Virtual nodes and their configuration into AKS is an advanced feature and is mentioned here only for your information. You can find more details here:

docs.microsoft.com/en-us/azure/aks/concepts-scale

Cloud Services

Cloud Services were Microsoft's first PaaS offering. At the time, Cloud Services offered some good capabilities like the all-powerful autoscaling feature. The problem with Cloud Services was the barrier of entry was high. To deploy an application to Cloud Services, the application needed to be reconfigured to run on that environment. This meant existing ASN.NET and ASP.NET MVC applications couldn't simply be deployed to and run from Cloud Services. The application code needed to be migrated to a Cloud Services project in

Visual Studio, which was acceptable for smaller applications, but there was never a good migration process from an existing on-premise web application to Cloud Services. Many customers still use this service, but let it be known that this product is deprecating, and you should not move any workloads to it unless there is a justified business case to do so. There is no need to discuss this Azure product in more detail, but it's worthy of mention because at one time it was the only PaaS Microsoft had, and it was good. It has simply been replaced by better Azure products and features.

Windows Virtual Desktop

The word *virtual* has been popping up a lot in this book, no? Examples are virtual network, virtual machine, and now Virtual Desktop. You should already have an understanding of what *virtual* means in the context of computing now. You should have no doubt that behind the virtual there is a physical layer because nothing exists without some kind of actual connectivity between true existent elements. So, you shouldn't have much difficulty making an educated guess when it comes to Windows Virtual Desktop, right? Take a second now to formalize your definition, and then read on. Try this additional mental exercise and guess why a company would implement or want such a thing.

To answer the first question, *virtual* means that the compute resources allocated to process a workload are allocated from a greater physical pool of compute power. But why would a company want to run a bunch of Windows desktops as virtual machines? The answer to the second question has two aspects. The first is client/server, and the other is cost. From a client/server perspective, before the internet/intranet, the big thing was the creation of GUI (desktop) applications using, for example, Windows Forms, which had very complicated client-side business logic. This design principle certainly existed before *Model-View-Controller (MVC)* and even before the concept of separating presentation and business logic entered into any kind of design-oriented conversation. The referred to computing era was the 1990s. If you recall from the introduction, I mentioned that 2013 was the time companies started migrating to the cloud. Now I also call for the rewriting or rearchitecting of all non-cloud-based applications. It is with limited effort that you should recognize how fast technology moves and why there are possibly many programs from the 1990s that remain too mission critical and complex to attempt such an upgrade or fundamental modification. This is mostly because the people who coded them are long gone, because no one wants to look at the old code, or because the effort required to make the change is too great for most units or people.

The solution was then to create a cost-effective means for a lift-and-shift solution to keep the code and process model intact. That means Windows Virtual Desktop. If you think about the costs involved in running a client/server solution, one is the server side for sure, and this entire chapter has been about the provisioning and configuration of server-side compute power. There have also been some tips on its redundancies and how to control its associated costs. The other side of the equation is the client. Those who need to consume a client/server application need a workstation. It isn't like an internet application where customers have their own workstation to access the code on your server. In this context, it is most commonly an employee, or maybe even a customer, who accesses your application via an in-store kiosk to use some kind of backend server application. The cost comes down to having those machines where they are needed, with ample compute power to run the desktop application.

If the workstation is required to only make a remote connection to a virtual desktop running the actual client-side program, then the employee workstation can be much less powerful than the virtual desktop. In addition, does the employee need to access and use the virtual machine 100% of the time? If not, then the compute power utilized and charged to run the desktop can be reduced. If you purchase a workstation for each employee to run the desktop application, then that compute is 100% allocated to that employee and can be idle sometimes. However, you might be able to save some resources if a shared employee workstation is purchased with lower specifications and the remote shared virtual machine with higher specification is used only on demand and changed only based on its consumption.

To run a Windows Virtual Desktop solution, the following components are required:

- An Azure virtual network

- An Azure Active Directory connected to a Windows Server Active directory via Azure AD Connect or Azure AD Domain Services

- The workstations that connect to the Windows Virtual Desktop solution are not VMs.

There is much more to this area; the topic is worthy of a book on its own. This section should be enough to know the requirements and use case for the Windows Virtual Desktop product. For more information, see docs.microsoft.com/en-us/azure/virtual-desktop/overview. It provides many more details.

Summary

Just like in the previous chapter, we covered a lot, but I hope that you have gotten your hands dirty, created some Azure products, and configured many of the features. You should feel confident that since you now have a solid understanding about Azure security, Azure networking, and now Azure compute, the probability of passing the Azure Solutions Architect Expert exam is rising rapidly.

Specifically, in this chapter, the key takeaways are that although the compute power is advertised as unlimited, there are some limits. For a majority of consumers, however, the limits of that compute will not be reached due to either cost or simply the need for such workload computations are unnecessary. Also, you know that if you do ever hit a compute threshold, if you have a justified business case, those limits can be lifted, and more resources can be provided. The limits are to protect you from receiving an outrageous bill.

Containers and images are gaining a lot of traction and can help simplify the deployments onto IaaS and PaaS architectures, as well as transforming applications to run as microservices or AKS orchestrated solutions. Docker is a leading technology for creating containers. Azure VMs have a vast catalog of VM types, with series that target CPU, GPU, memory, or high storage workloads. You can run the Windows operating system and almost any version of Linux, and remember, when you want to move an on-premise workload to an Azure VM, the tool of choice is Azure Migrate. Also recall the similarity in name between availability sets and VM Scale Sets, which doesn't mean they provide similar capabilities. Availability sets have to do with zones and fault and update domains, and they are usually implemented along with a tiered monolithic architecture model. VMSS is a pool of VMs that get provisioned using the same image.

Azure App Services and Azure Functions provide great platforms for running web applications, Web APIs, and serverless workloads. Being PaaS, they both eliminate the maintenance of operating system and third-party runtimes. That loss can also mean your application cannot run on the platform, but in that case you can either choose to run in a container or move over to IaaS. Don't forget about WebJobs, which run batch jobs, and Azure Batch, which also runs batch processing but at a galactic scale.

Lastly, you learned about Service Fabric and the Azure Kubernetes Service (AKS), which focus on microservices and containerization. Service Fabric can support containers and some open source; however, its primary strength is running and managing .NET-based microservices. AKS is a robust open source orchestrator targeted at containerized open source applications on Linux.

Key Terms

App Service Environment (ASE)

App Service Plan (ASP)

Azure Container Registry (ACR)

Azure Container Storage

Azure Marketplace

Azure Reserved VM Instance

batch jobs

Blue Screen of Death (BSOD)

Business Continuity and Disaster Recovery (BCDR)

Horizontal Pod Autoscale (HPA)

hyper-scale

Infrastructure as a service (IaaS)

Input/Output operations per second (IOPS)

Integrated Drive Electronics (IDE)

Internal Load Balancer (ILB)

lift and shift (aka rehost)

Microsoft Distributed Transaction Coordinator (MSDTC)

Microsoft Message Queuing (MSMQ)

Cloud Bursting	Microsoft Virtual Machine Converter (MVMC)
Cloud Optimized	Model-View-Controller (MVC)
Cluster autoscaler	Orchestration
Command Line Interface (CLI)	OS level virtualization
Common Language Runtimes (CLR)	Page Blob
Compute	Platform as a service (PaaS)
Container as a service (CaaS)	Remote Direct Memory Access (RDMA)
Containerized	Representational state transfer (REST)
Create, Insert, Update, Delete (CRUD)	Resource lock
Cross-Origin Resource Sharing (CORS)	runtime
Database Management System (DBMS)	Service Oriented Architecture (SOA)
Disaster Recovery (DR)	Simple Object Application Protocol (SOAP)
Docker	Small Computer System Interface (SCSI)
Electronic Data Interchange (EDI)	Software Development Kits (SDK)
ephemeral disk	update domains
fault domains	Virtual Hard Disk (VHD)
Functions as a service (FaaS)	Virtual Machine Scale Sets (VMSS)
Global Availability (GA)	virtual nodes
Graphical Processing Units (GPU)	Web API
Graphical User Interface (GUI)	Web Application
High Performance Computing (HPC)	Windows Communication Foundation (WCF)
	Windows Subsystem for Linux (WSL)

Exam Essentials

Understand Azure Virtual Machines and scale sets.   Azure Virtual Machines is the most utilized compute product consumed in Azure. This is also the most important area in compute to completely understand when it comes to the Azure Solutions Architecture Expert exam. Knowing how to migrate, move, and create them, their limits, and the blessed (aka supported by Microsoft) images are must-know concepts.

Understand Azure Container Instances.   Containers are the new thing, and you need to get up to speed with them. This means not only regarding open source technologies, but from a Windows and Azure perspective. Docker is the driver of this concept, but Azure Container Instances, the Azure Container Registry, and AKS are products that prove Microsoft is serious about this.

Understand App Services and Azure Functions.   The PaaS and FaaS cloud services are great for getting your foot into cloud computing. App Services are for running web applications and web APIs, while Azure Functions are for small but rapid processing of messages that arrive in a work queue.

Understand Azure Batch and high-performance computing.   You know about WebJobs and what a batch job is, but Azure Batch and HPC are at another level. Machine learning, AI, Big Data, gaming, and visual rendering are all the aspects of compute that require great CPU, GPU, memory, and storage resources. Compute power is what governments need and use; for example, supercomputers are also products available to Microsoft Azure customers.

Understand the orchestrators Service Fabric and AKS.   Running large-scale .NET-based microservices and open source containerized application images are some of the newer kind of architectural patterns. Using these orchestrators allow an administrator to properly scale, patch, and monitor large-scale workloads using this new architectural design pattern.

Review Questions

1. Which of the following cloud service models allow the customer to control the runtime? (Select all that apply.)

   A. IaaS

   B. FaaS

   C. CaaS

   D. PaaS

2. Which Azure compute product would you choose to host a Web API considering compute cost and maintenance requirements?

   A. Azure VM

   B. Azure Function

   C. Azure App Service

   D. Azure Batch

3. Which of the following Azure compute products support containerization? (Select all that apply.)

   A. Azure Container Instances

   B. Azure App Services

   C. Azure Container Registry

   D. Azure Functions

4. What is the difference between a VM and a container?

   A. Only VMs are allocated a dedicated amount of compute resources; containers are scaled automatically based on load.

   B. A container can scale both out and up while a VM can only scale out.

   C. After provisioning a container image, the originally allocated compute resource cannot be changed without a rebuild and redeployment.

   D. When an Azure container is created, it must target either Windows or Linux OS.

5. Which of the following actions do not deallocate an Azure VM? (Select all that apply.)

   A. `az vm stop`

   B. `Stop-AzVM`

   C. Logging off from an RDP connection

   D. `Remove-AzResourceGroup` on the resource group that the VM exists in

6. What is true about Azure virtual machine scale sets (VMSS)?

   A. VMSS can be deployed into only two Availability Zones at any given time frame.

   B. The VMSS architecture is intended to run tiered applications that contain a front-end tier, a middle tier, and a database or backend tier.

    C. VM instances in a VMSS cluster are identical.

    D. Scaling out additional VMSS instances will not have any negative impact so long as your application is stateful.

7. Which type of WebJob can be remotely debugged?

    A. Continuous

    B. Triggered

    C. Manual

    D. Singleton

8. In which scenarios would you choose an ephemeral disk over managed? (Select all that apply.)

    A. You must use the lowest cost option.

    B. Your application is stateful and cannot be reimaged without impact.

    C. Your disk capacity requirement exceeds 65,535GB (i.e., 2^{16}GB).

    D. Your application is stateless and can be reimaged without impact.

9. Which of the following are true about both Service Fabric and Azure Kubernetes Service (AKS)? (Select all that apply.)

    A. The concept of a node is the same for Service Fabric and AKS.

    B. Both AKS and Service Fabric run on VMSS.

    C. Service Fabric is best suited for .NET Framework development stacks on Windows, and AKS is best suited for open source stacks on Linux.

    D. AKS and Service Fabric are orchestrators that manage clusters and nodes that run microservices.

10. True or False? All of the following components are required to implement a Windows Virtual Desktop solution.

Azure Active Directory

A physical workstation

Azure Virtual Network

Azure AD Connect

    A. True

    B. False

11. Which of the following are true about managed disks? (Select all that apply.)

    A. Managed disks are physically connected to the Azure VM.

    B. Managed disks can be used with both Windows and Linux VMs.

    C. The contents of managed disks are stored on Azure Storage as a page blob.

    D. Managed disks provide better performance when compared to an ephemeral drive.

12. Which of the following represent a use case for running your workloads on Azure Virtual Machines? (Select all that apply.)

    A. Creating a BCDR footprint on Azure

    B. Non-cloud-optimized, lift-and-shift migration

    C. Content-based web application hosting

    D. High-performance compute batch processing

13. Which of the following represent a use case for running your workloads on Azure App Services? (Select all that apply.)

    A. Your website requires a third-party toolkit.

    B. A website that exposes a REST API of relative complexity

    C. A website that requires no operating system–level configurations

    D. A website that is not containerized

14. Which of the following represent a use case for running your workloads on App Service Web App for Containers? (Select all that apply.)

    A. You want to utilize an existing Docker container.

    B. The website currently runs Linux.

    C. You want to run PHP or Node on Windows.

    D. Your website requires a third-party toolkit.

15. Which of the following represents a use case for running your workloads on Azure Functions?

    A. The code requires significant CPU and memory.

    B. Managing your cost is of utmost importance.

    C. Your code has a long startup/warmup time.

    D. Content-based web application hosting

16. True or false? Azure Container Instances (ACI) requires the provisioning of Azure VMs, while Azure Kubernetes Service (AKS) does not.

    A. True

    B. False

17. Which of the following are true regarding Azure Container Instances (ACI)? (Select all that apply.)

    A. Tightly aligned with Docker concepts and features

    B. Supports only the Windows operating systems

    C. Best used for small to medium workloads

    D. Has comparable orchestrator capabilities when compared to Azure Kubernetes Service (AKS)

18. Which of the following are true regarding Azure Kubernetes Service (AKS)? (Select all that apply.)

  A. AKS offers similar capabilities as Service Fabric.

  B. AKS only supports applications that can run on Linux.

  C. JSON syntax is primarily used for configuring AKS.

  D. You can integrate Visual Studio and Azure DevOps into your AKS development and deployment processes.

19. Which one of the following is true concerning the Azure Container Registry (ACR)?

  A. ACR and the Docker Hub serve the same purpose.

  B. ACR containers are private and require a user ID and password to access and deploy.

  C. You can only deploy images contained in ACR into the Azure region where the ACR itself is deployed.

  D. Both A and B

20. Which of the following is true regarding Windows Virtual Desktop? (Select all that apply.)

  A. You must connect to a Windows Virtual Desktop from a physical machine.

  B. An Azure Virtual Network (VNet) is required to implement a Windows Virtual Desktop solution.

  C. You can connect to a Windows Virtual Desktop either from a physical machine or from a VM.

  D. Windows Virtual Desktop reduces costs by optimizing the use of compute resources.

Chapter

5

Data and Storage

EXAM AZ-303 OBJECTIVES COVERED IN THIS CHAPTER:

✓ **Implement and Monitor an Azure Infrastructure**

  ▪ Implement storage accounts

✓ **Implement and Manage Data Platforms**

  ▪ Implement NoSQL databases

  ▪ Implement Azure SQL databases

EXAM AZ-304 OBJECTIVES COVERED IN THIS CHAPTER:

✓ **Design Data Storage**

  ▪ Design a solution for databases

  ▪ Design data integration

In the previous three chapters, you learned about core concepts that require significant experience and knowledge if you plan on taking the Azure Solutions Architect Expert exam. They are security, networking, and compute, in that order. These areas require the most time when you begin a project with start to deploy workloads to the Azure platform. Without compute, there is no place to run your application. Without networking, there is no means to get access to the compute running the application. Without security, both your network and compute are vulnerable to bad actors who may implement some kind of malicious act on you, your customer, or your employees. In Chapter 7, I will discuss more about the application that runs on your compute; however, first I want to speak about data. I chose the path of discussing data before the application because data has more weight on the Azure Solutions Architect Expert exam than coding or designing an application does. Both of these aspects (data and application) are fundamental and highly dependent on each other as you cannot have one without the other.

Take for granted that you have an application at this point. An application is a snippet of code, a full-blown enterprise solution written in C#, a batch job, or a web API. In each scenario, the code will in a high majority of cases interact in some way with data. The snippet of code could be running in an Azure Function that processes a message that was entered into a blob storage account or an enterprise order fulfilment capability for partners that sell, repair, and service guitars. Batch jobs can be used to do many things, as you learned in the previous chapter, such as analyzing petabytes of data as part of a big data machine learning algorithm or doing something as small as updating a value of 1 to 0 every 15 minutes. Lastly, web APIs, which communicate using REST, typically receive a JSON document containing some client-generated data, like an update to an order that would need to be stored. In every case, processing data—whether it is stored, retrieved, or received by the application, no matter how it gets stored, where it gets stored, and how you protect it—is the purpose of the application, the security, the networking, and the compute. Without data, there is no means to reach conclusions through the execution of application code. The criticality of data is further and finally justified by Sherlock Holmes, who stated this:

> "It is a capital mistake to theorize before one has data. Insensibly one begins to twist facts to suit theories, instead of theories to suit facts."

In this chapter, you will learn about Azure Data Stores (databases), other Azure Storage capabilities, how to protect your data from loss, and how to keep it from being improperly accessed. With all of those options, again you are confronted with some decisions. Do you need Azure SQL, Azure Cosmo DB, Table Storage, Azure Files, or Queue Storage? What kind of redundancies do you need: LRS, ZRS, GRS? What kind migration options are available?

What kind of Azure security options exist in the context of data? After reading this chapter, those and many additional questions will be answered. Let's first begin with a summary of the two basic data architectures that the Azure platform is structured for: traditional RDBMS and Big Data.

RDBMS, OLTP, OLAP, and ETL

The first database I ever used was written by yours truly. It wasn't something you would call a database by any means these days, but what I did was instantiate a group of strings with hard-coded sets of data. I suppose in a sense that would be like an in-memory data structure that my code later analyzed and manipulated. That's kind of cool when you think it was almost 40 years ago. It would have never scaled or be a realistic solution now because no single person could ever manually add so much data to a program, nor to a flat file. Flat files existed in the early ages of data manipulation and are text files, for example, that a program would open, read, and then process the contents. The problems started happening as it became hard to know how the content data was organized or categorized and whether there were any logical links between the data in a flat file. That led the industry toward the creation of the *relational database management system (RDBMS)* concept. Simply processing files (which is what a database realistically is), where the files had neither columns that identify what the data element meant nor any ability to recognize any relations between the data, caused misinterpretations and resulted in false conclusions. RDBMS provides the management of data using tables, columns, and relationship mapping between those columns and tables. It was intended to resolve the issues occurring in the previous data management approaches. Figure 5.1 illustrates a typical implementation of an RDBMS data solution.

FIGURE 5.1 A traditional RDBMS scenario

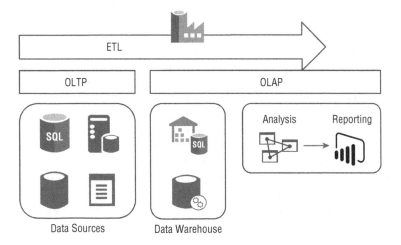

Starting with *online transaction processing (OLTP)*, you see the place where the data is stored most commonly from an interaction with some kind of external system. For example, placing an online order or withdrawing cash from an ATM would both result in insertion, retrieval, and/or an update occurring on a transactional relational database. In contrast, you also see *online analytical processing (OLAP)* components that are focused on storing a rather large amount of data from multiple sources into a single location, such as a data warehouse. The data warehouse is accessed and processed using, for example, *Azure Analysis Services* that creates data models that are useful for rendering human-readable reports using, for example, Power BI. Finally, the process by which the data flows between OLTP and OLAP is referred to as *extract, transform, load (ETL)*, which can be implemented in Azure by using an *Azure Data Factory (ADF)*. Figure 5.1 illustrates a rather sophisticated RDBMS data architecture solution, which is what you would aim for if targeting Azure and your workload requires this solution type. In principle, those are the components, and they can be designed and deployed following numerous other patterns.

Big Data/NoSQL

RDBMS has worked and continues to work for the scenario for which it was designed, such as managing transactions. However, new concepts such as Big Data and machine learning have placed a strain on traditional RDBMS solutions. Two such examples are an RDBMS solution that assumes there is a relationship between the data and making schema changes typically require ontological discussions, which slows the speed of change.

It is possible to make the analogy between RDBMS and Big Data using structured versus unstructured. That in itself explains the first strain Big Data has on RDBMS solutions. The variety of data stored in Big Data is large, including everything from the content of a novel to the current temperature in Dallas. While I was writing Big Data, I attempted to apply my RDBMS design skills to think about a way to do that. Only ugly solutions entered my mind. If the data has no structure, how can you use it? How can you learn anything from it? Azure Analysis Services (mentioned earlier and visualized in Figure 5.1) helps make sense of such data.

Imagine you work in a large enterprise where everything the company does is mapped to your RDBMS schema. Assume you would like to create a new feature or service for the company, but it would require a change to the database schema. The meetings and conversations required to make that happen would increase the time to deploy by many days, weeks, or months. On the other hand, Big Data stores have no structure, so you can simply create the structure how you need it, code the application, and go live.

NoSQL is terminology you will hear often in the context of Big Data. The data stored in the NoSQL database is not structured, and as you can see in Figure 5.2, the nonrelational example lacks a relationship between data existing in the table. The data stored using the NoSQL model is achieved by storing the given entity on a single row, in its entirety. You see that all the models for Fender guitars are stored on a single row where key = 1. This may not seem as the most efficient data structure, considering NoSQL (nonrelational) database models. Many NoSQL database models lack triggers, stored procedures, and join features. To get a list of all the Fender models using a relational database, you would need to perform a join between the Guitars and Models tables using the primary and foreign keys.

FIGURE 5.2   An RDBMS versus NoSQL scenario

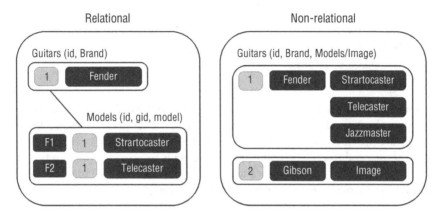

Regardless of a perceived inefficiency, NoSQL structures scale very well when the amount of data is large to gigantic in size—it scales so well that companies such as Facebook, LinkedIn, and Google all use NoSQL database structures to store and access their data. As you likely know, those companies earn money by analyzing and learning from the data collected from their services. Because the storage, analysis, and easy access to the data are fundamental to their business operations, they inherently favor the most effective and efficient data storage technologies.

Choosing the Right Data Storage Solution

The correct data store for the application may have already been decided if you are moving a workload to Azure. However, if you have the opportunity to deploy a greenfield project to Azure, then you must know the requirements of the application in order to choose the proper storage solution. Recall from Chapter 2 that you need to know from where clients will access your application in order to implement a conditional access policy. In Chapter 3 you learned you need to know the number of resources that will exist in a subnet so that you can identify the correct CIDR prefix. Finally, in Chapter 4, you learned you need to know if the application is CPU-, memory-, or storage-intensive, which would then dictate the chosen

Azure VM series. The same applies here. Which of the following data stores fit best with the application you are about to build?

- Document databases
- Graph databases
- Key/value pairs
- Object storage
- RDBMS
- Search engine databases
- Data analytics/data warehouse
- Shared files

The following sections cover the intents and purposes of those database models. In addition to that, the Azure Data Store or Azure Storage product that is designed for each specific model are provided as well. Later in the chapter there will be more depth provided into many of those products. The intent of the following is to provide you with the knowledge to get an understanding of available Azure Data Store and Azure Storage products and which data model they are intended to be used for.

Document Databases

A document database is one that stores data typically in one or more of the following formats: XML, JSON, or YAML. The row in a document database consists of two columns: a key and a document. As you can see in Figure 5.3, the key, being unique, gives a means to retrieve the document directly, allowing the application to parse and process it. A powerful feature of the document database is that you can query the contents of the document itself. You could query all the documents where OriginalOwner is csharpguitar.

The content stored in the document column are relatively small and typically in the form of collections, lists, or scalar items. The document typically includes all the data for the entire entity, which can have a unique schema. What constitutes an entity is based on the requirements of the application. What you see in Figure 5.3 are two entities, one that defines a guitar and the other a programming language. Do those entities provide all the details about a guitar and C#? No, but for my purpose they contain what I need. Although the structure (schema) of the documents looks similar, they have different attributes and are therefore unique. The Azure product that is designed to meet the needs of an application requiring a document database is Azure Cosmos DB, which is described in much more detail later in the chapter.

FIGURE 5.3   A document database table

Key	Document
1618	```{ "GuitarID": 1, "Description": [{ "Brand": "Fender", "Model": "Stratocaster", "Year": 1956, "Color": "Sunburst", "Condition": "Mint", "Accessories": "Case,Strings,Picks" }], "OriginalOwner": "csharpguitar" }```
6174	```{ "LanguageID": 1, "Description": [{ "Name": "C#", "Pronunciation": "see sharp", "Year": 2000, "TargetOS": "Windows", "Crossplatform": true, "CurrentVersion": 8.0 }], "DevelopedBy": "Microsoft" }```

Key/Value Pairs

If you take a quick look at Figure 5.4, you will notice that the structure of the table looks similar to a document database. Both document databases and key/value stores consist of two columns per row; however, there are some significant differences. The first one is the expected size of the data that will be stored, where a key/value store expects that size to be gigantic, which is not so in the document database context. Next, a key/value store does not support aggregation, which means the data cannot be found by querying. You can only retrieve data from the store using the keys' value, as opposed to adding a WHERE clause on the Value column to the selection query.

Finally, you will notice that, in Figure 5.4, the value can be stored as an array of strings separated by a comma, for example. When I first saw this, I had a flashback to my first database experience where I loaded all the data manually into the program and then loaded it into memory, and from there I manipulated, or should I say, played with it. Subconsciously, I additionally noticed the key/value store structure maps very well into a C# dictionary. For example, the first row in Figure 5.4 should be loaded into memory using this code:

```
var guitar = new Dictionary<string, Tuple<string, string, string, string>>()
```

FIGURE 5.4   A key value store

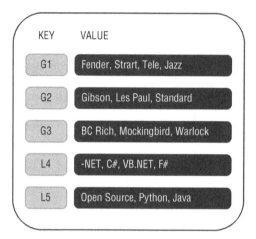

The point is that the structure of the data as it is stored into the key/value table has a seemingly very tight binding with programmatic structural patterns. Therefore, the performance and scalability seem also rooted with each other, that is, tightly bound at the design level. This isn't so much the case as with the document database as the value is an entity, which would need casting and parsing after its retrieval. A common use case scenario for key/value pairs is for data caching. That is why you see data caching mentioned a great deal with the Azure product Azure Cache for Redis, which is discussed later. Azure Cosmos DB also provides the key/value store feature as does Azure Table Storage. As you read through the sections covering Azure Cache for Redis, Azure Cosmos DB, and Azure Table Storage, the reason to choose one over the other may become clearer to you. In summary, the reason for choosing a key/value store versus a document database is based on expected size, the ability to query on the value, and speed.

Graph Databases

Node and edges are two terms to know in regard to a graph database store. A node can be viewed as an entity, in the same way an entity is the value that is stored in a document database in the form of JSON document. The information contained within that node is comprised of all the data that defines it. An edge is what defines the relationships between the nodes. Here again, node and edge are common words that you have read in numerous contexts. It is probably becoming apparent that technical scenarios can get complicated when there is so much overlap in terms. In concept, though, the term node does fit well into the other scenarios in that a node acts like an endpoint, or like I have already written, it's a well-defined entity that has some defined purpose. Taking the same approach as with a node, an edge is the networking infrastructure that connects the nodes. Edges are routes and *Virtual Network Appliances (VNA)* that define and make connections between the nodes.

If you have a group of nodes, for example, VMs, each would have some attributes that together define it as a unique entity. The VMs in the group would have some kind of relationship with each other that is defined by the edge. The following query would return all the databases that a VM named `csharpguitar` is connected to:

```
MATCH (az:vm)-[CONNECTED-WITH]-(database)
WHERE az:name = 'csharpguitar'
RETURN az, database
```

For scenarios where relationships between nodes are complicated, dynamic, and change rapidly, this kind of data store may provide your best solution. Imagine in the previous scenario that the VMs scale in, up, out, and down and the databases are elastic also scaling in real time. That could be considered a dynamic scenario, and if you wanted to get some real-time reporting on that, you may need a graph database store. Azure Cosmos DB is the product that provides graph database capabilities via Gremlin APIs for the creation of entities and the execution of query operations against them. The VM example was used only as an example to help you visualize. VMs can be seen as nodes, but nodes in the graph database context are logical, not physical.

Object Storage

Binary Large Object (BLOB) storage, aka object storage, is an entity comprised of a collection of binary data that is stored into a database system. Blobs were discussed in the previous chapter in the context of managed disks, Azure Batch, Azure Apps, and Azure Functions, all of which use an Azure Blob Storage container for providing their services. This type of storage is optimized for storing and retrieving binary objects such as images, videos, and VHDs, for example. Each entity stored with this type usually consists of the actual data, a unique key, and some metadata such as blob type, size, last modified, timestamp, and such. Later in the "Azure Storage" section, blob storage is discussed in much more detail. What is an object store is pretty clear now, perhaps not so much the details, but those are provided later, so read on. Azure Blob Storage is the product that will fulfill your Object Storage needs.

Relational Database Management System

Azure provides numerous RDBMS products such as Azure SQL Database, Azure Database for MariaDB, Azure Database for PostgreSQL, and Azure Database for MySQL. Each provides capabilities commonly found in RDBMs, such as SQL query capabilities, joins, stored procedures, and triggers. As shown previously in Figure 5.2, a relational database consists of one or more (usually more) tables with rows and columns. A column or a group of columns on a row are used to uniquely identify the data row and is known as a *primary key*. This key can be used when creating relationships between two or more tables. The primary key on a table is used as the foreign key on another table and for making the join between them. Figure 5.2 illustrates a primary key = 1 on the Guitars table is the foreign key on the Models table. The primary key on the Models table is the combination of F1 and 1 or the combination of the primary key and the foreign key.

There are many books written about relations' database structures because they have been around for many decades. However, there are a few concepts I would like to discuss: *atomic, consistent, isolated, durable (ACID)*; transaction; normalization; and schemas. When data is stored on an RDBMS, it occurs in the form of a transaction. To visualize a transaction in the real world, think of a financial transaction. A financial transaction typically contains properties such as an agreement, a buyer, a seller, a payment, and a transfer of goods or services. In the database context, a transaction is guaranteed if it consists of the ACID properties. ACID is an acronym that begins with *atomic*, which means that the transaction executes as a single unit and either completely succeeds or completely fails. Consistency guarantees that the data does not become corrupted, for example having a row with a foreign key without a match on the parent table. Isolation is the concept that manages when the data is readable and modifiable once inserted into a table. In a high-volume application, this is a serious consideration where concepts like dirty and phantom reads are prevalent. Finally, durability ensures a transaction gets committed even if there is an exception or perhaps a power outage. If the transaction is durable, once the data is committed, it remains committed. This is a specialized area, and if you ever get into this, consider consulting a *database administrator (DBA)* for guidance. There are books written about this area, so if it interests you, pursue this further via other books and resources. It is a career in itself.

If you have done database work, you would likely know some concepts like first, second, and third normal form. Those are all models of database normalization. The guiding principle of normalization is to reduce the duplication of data in tables that have a relation with each other. For example, take a look at Figure 5.2 again and assume that instead of having a Models table, you could save all that data into the Guitars table. That would result in having Fender written on in two rows; it is duplicated data that can be removed and be more efficient by creating the Models table, adding the foreign key, and creating the relationship. A schema is the structure or blueprint of the tables and their relationships in an RDBMS. As shown in Figure 5.5, a database schema is usually represented by tables and columns written in text with relationships defined with a line connecting between two or more tables.

FIGURE 5.5   A database schema

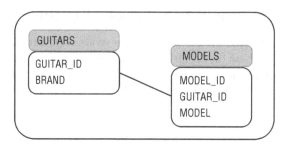

Up to now, the table structure for a data store has been two columns per row, where one column is named Key and the other Value. In that scenario, the client retrieving the data needs to already know what it's retrieving so that it can parse and interpret the data. This is not so with a well-designed RDBMS, in that tables and the columns within them have intuitive names that can be used in code at runtime or design time to determine their purpose and meaning.

RDBMS database scenarios are most useful for reporting, accounting, inventory, and order management. Any scenario where you would want to have clearly defined data and their relationship with data on other tables fit into this data storage scenario.

Search Engine Databases

When you initially read the title of this storage type, you likely thought immediately about Bing—OK, probably Google. It is true that this data store is optimized for scenarios as one would expect to be found for powering search engines, as the name implies. However, there are other usages for this kind of store. One of those scenarios is when you need to store and index large amounts of data as well as provide a quick response from the query match with this storage type. But you kind of want that from all your storage systems, no? In addition to being responsive, when all your database will do is respond with data based on a string of text, this is the correct place to focus. Think about that approach on a traditional RDBMS with columns and rows. How would you formulate a SQL query for such a transaction? There would need to be a column to search for the string of text, and that column would be wide. RDBMS simply doesn't align well with such a requirement.

I remember some years ago I searched for *How search engines work* and stumbled upon a 100-page book on Amazon that cost hundreds of US dollars and discussed the scientific algorithms behind searching. This is another fascinating area worthy of great investigation and career commitment. Instead of the book, I found a technology called Lucene. Since I really liked C#, I was driven to `Lucene.NET`. There I learned what I know about searching. It is an interesting area. In my workings with `Lucene.NET`, I learned that when you search using some string of text, you get many results that need to be ranked in an order using some algorithm or group of algorithms. Those algorithms are highly private and, in many cases, somewhat controversial. These days with the help of *Language Understanding Intelligent Service (LUIS)*, an Azure cognitive service can take some words and interpret their intent. Not only can you get a result based on some text, but you can also attempt to understand what the words mean and then tweak the query even more.

Lastly, there are scenarios in which you place a search database and search engine logic in front of a more traditional structure. You would need to create and populate the search database with searchable fields that link to the means of capturing the true, intended result set from a backend, traditionally structured, or non–*search engine optimized (SEO)* database. Azure Search is the product that will help you down that path if the road is leading you there. Notice that when you look for it, you find the words *cognitive* and *artificial intelligence (AI)* used in the same space. This is an active area in the IT industry these days.

Data Analytics/Data Warehouse

A data warehouse, aka *enterprise data warehouse (EDW)*, is a central data store that receives data from many different sources that is then used for reporting and data analysis. The analysis of the data is typically done to identify business trends, such as customer satisfaction, number of units sold, or marketing spend. The information learned from this analysis is used for predicting future events, which is helpful for the planning resource allocation in preparation for similar events in the future. For example, Black Friday is known for high sales volume, so how much of a product you sold last year would be good to know so that you are certain to have that much in stock. Additionally, you might wonder how much you spent on marketing that product one year compared to the next and then compare the impact it had on sales. One would assume the more spent on marketing, the more sales, but that may not be the case; you could find that out with data.

Data warehousing is a term for where the data is stored, and *data analysis* is the process you use to assist decision making. That might lead you to ask yourself, "What is data analytics?" Data warehousing and data analysis are both components of data analytics, which also includes the techniques and tools used to attain a level of visibility into a company's operations that can help with making decisions, most often decisions about the allocation of human and capital resources.

The data that exists in a data warehouse can be historical or near real-time, but in most cases the data comes from multiple sources and will be in multiple formats. That means part of the process for the movements of data into an EDW requires some modifications to the data so that it can be later analyzed in combination with data from other sources. To achieve this on Azure from a design perspective, there are two data warehouse schemas (star and snowflake) that are designed to work well. Figure 5.6 illustrates the star schema where in the center is the FACT table that contains the keys to all the dimension tables. The analysis algorithms would begin at the fact table and use the data there to access other tables to gather more details and execute further analysis. Figure 5.6 also resembles a star if you use a little imagination.

FIGURE 5.6   A database warehouse star schema

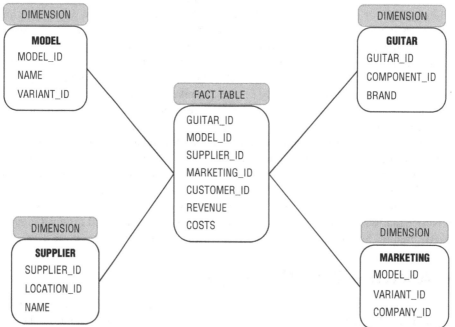

The snowflake schema is built upon or expands outward from the star schema, as illustrated in Figure 5.7. It is simply a more elaborate schema with more dimensions for providing more insights and details helpful for forecasting and planning.

FIGURE 5.7   A database warehouse snowflake schema

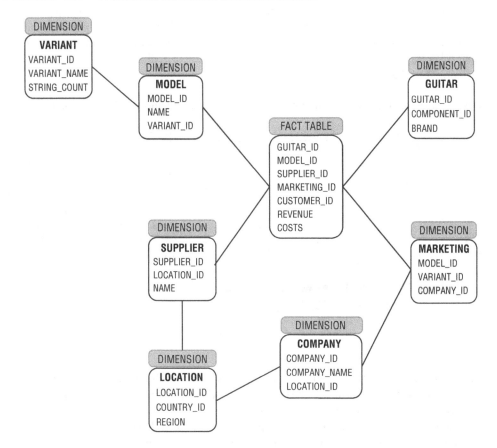

Azure provides all of the components necessary to create, deploy, and execute your data analytics with products such as Azure Synapse Analytics (formerly Azure SQL Data Warehouse), *Azure Data Factory (ADF)*, *Azure Data Lake Store (ADLS)*, Azure Data Lake, and Azure Analysis Services. The next sections provide a summary of each. Keep in mind that for the exam you may need to know the purpose each of the products plays within a data analytics context. The internals of how they work, how to build data warehouse structures, and how to query them are not part of the exam.

Azure Synapse Analytics

Figure 5.2 illustrated two important aspects of the structure of data; relational and nonrelational. The divergence of data storage from relational to nonrelational can be attributed to the creation and collection of data stemming from internet and social media consumption. Relational models simply did not work in that scenario, and a new model, with its supporting tools, needed to be created. Take another look at Figure 5.1, which shows the flow of a traditional relational data solution. Notice specifically the data warehouse portion, and recognize that for nonrelational data, Azure Data Lake is the product to achieve the same or comparable outcome for nonrelational data capture. Figure 5.8 illustrates the data flow of a nonrelational or Big Data model.

FIGURE 5.8   A traditional nonrelational data flow diagram and Big Data pipeline

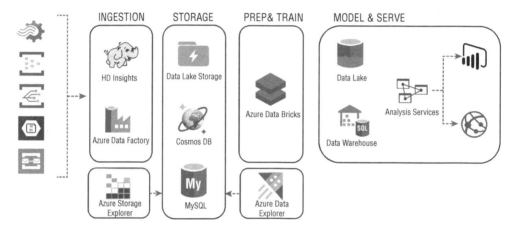

The nonrelational dataflow begins with endpoints from which data in many different varieties, structures, and meaning find their way into the ingestion process. The ingestion of data, in contrast to an OLTP process, must respond extremely quickly, be extremely flexible, and be highly available. These ingestion endpoints do not typically store any data, because that could be too latent; instead, these endpoints get the data queued up and perhaps cleansed in preparation for storage and analysis. Once the data is ingested into the Big Data pipeline, it then gets stored into any number of systems such as Data Lake Storage, an Azure Cosmos DB, or an Azure Database for MySQL. An Azure product called Azure Data Bricks helps with the exploration of the data so that learnings can be found and once found stored in a Data Lake for additional analysis and presentation. Each of the aforementioned Azure products are covered in some more detail next; for starters, take a look at Table 5.1 for a comparison between a data warehouse and a data lake.

TABLE 5.1   Differences Between Data Lake and Data Warehouse

	Data Warehouse	Data Lake
Convenience	Complicated, costly, and hard to make changes	Accessible, cost efficient, and easy to make change
Data Access	Schema on write	Schema on read
Consumers	Business professionals	Data scientists
Data Structure	Managed, relational	Raw, nonrelational
Security	Mature	Maturing
Access Methods	SQL	NoSQL
Scale	Horizontal	Vertical

Azure Synapse Analytics (formally Azure SQL Data Warehouse) is a product that provides the capability to manage both data warehouse and data lake datasets. It is important for you to understand the difference between a data warehouse and data lake, plus to also get an illustration of the big data pipeline (see Figure 5.8) and compare it to the traditional relationship data model (see Figure 5.1). For more detailed information about this product, review the content at this link:

docs.microsoft.com/en-us/azure/sql-data-warehouse

Before proceeding, let's discuss the meaning of the content in Table 5.1 starting with convenience. After data relationships are created, other programs or data sources build dependencies on those relationships over time. Making a change then to a data relation requires analysis on the impact on downstream, dependent systems. This is a common scenario with an EDW, but not so much in a data lake scenario where there is limited to no structure of the data. A benefit of storing unstructured data is that the provisioning of the data source happens much faster. If you were to build or reuse a relational database and store the data into it, the amount of time required to design its structure greatly exceeds that of an unstructured approach. Consider that instead of creating the database structure and code to insert the data, you instead take the data on Azure, place it into a JSON document, and store it straight into an Azure Cosmos DB. That concept brings us to the next row in Table 5.1 where schema on write and schema on read are shown. Remember that a schema is simply the shape, the form, and the relationships of data. From an RDBMS or EDW perspective, schema on write dictates that the schema of the data source is created before data can be written to it. Schema on read expects the structure of the data is applied when it's read. When you think about that fact, you should quickly realize that the concept of schema on read is the basis for the ability to store data in an unstructured manner in a data source.

Another difference between EDWs and data lakes considers who will use the stored data. Enterprise companies, which desire to use corporate data based on sales, location of customers, and marketing costs, would typically use an EDW. The individuals are business professionals who use the data to forecast future trends. It is not that an EDW cannot be used in a big data pipeline; it is just assumed to not be the most efficient when compared to the non-structured, NoSQL approach. Individuals who use Big Data and data stored in data lakes are data scientists who are confronted with a great amount of unstructured data and are tasked with making sense of it. Finally, from a scaling perspective, the typical model for scaling unstructured data is horizontally. Horizontally means that you create additional, identical instances of the same data source usually in different geographical regions to be closer to the clients consuming the data. In contrast, a vertical scale increases compute and storage capacity (CPU and RAM) on a given single server.

Let's take a closer look at each of the Azure products shown in Figure 5.8.

Azure Data Factory (ADF)

The nonrelational data model and the big data pipeline are focused on the ingestion of huge amounts of data from many sources in many different endpoints. Some of those endpoints that an ingestion service may receive data from can come via social media companies such as Twitter or Facebook; from Azure messaging products such as Event Hub, Event Grid, Storage Queues, and Blobs; or from an IoT device. The Azure Data Factory (ADF) is the connector between the data generators and the data storage. Say you are creating a new ADF pipeline, and there are two fundamental elements, the connections and the triggers. When you configure the connection portion, you identify the data source the information will be coming from by providing the endpoint and credentials. The trigger part is then configured to instruct what to do with the data once it is received. You will also notice that Figure 5.8 contains some mention of HD Insights. Note that ADF is intended to manage relational data structures, while HD Insight, which is based on Hadoop, Spark, Kafka, and the like, is more targeted toward nonrelational, NoSQL, and open source solutions.

Azure Data Lake Store (ADLS)

The newest version of Azure Data Lake Storage (ADLS) is built on top of Azure Blob Storage. ADLS is optimized for storing a large amount of data in any format for analytical and reporting purposes. The fact that data can be stored in any format correctly implies that ADLS supports the nonrelational data model concept of semi- and unstructured storage. The data is retrieved from ADLS using the schema-on-read approach as ADLS doesn't require a predefined schema definition. In many ways, storing data in this way is simply collecting without really knowing what you plan on doing with it. It is stored to be sure that nothing is missed; then later, when you have a question for which analysis of the collected data results in an answer, you will be happy you collected the data to begin with. It is a common comment that Big Data and machine learning is being built to answer questions that haven't been asked yet.

There are numerous storage products that ADF and HD Insights can place the collected data into. Azure Cosmos DB and Azure Database for MySQL are two that are discussed later. There are numerous other storage products that can be used to store data on Azure using open source and closed source products. For example, you could transform the data into a file and store it directly into an Azure Blob container or an Apache HBase NoSQL database that is built on Hadoop. Don't forget that it is possible to perform data analytics on relational data. If the data is relational, then for sure you could store in a SQL Server DB or other RDBMS and, once it is refined, progress it into an Azure Data Warehouse product for reporting.

Azure Data Bricks

This product is getting into a different subject matter and touches concepts such as AI, ML, and the data sciences. Azure Data Bricks provides an interface to the data that helps you get an answer to questions that you think can be found in the data. You might use AI to gather some insights into the intention of a data element instead of attempting to convert its meaning. You can use the ML capabilities to ultimately define the algorithms and process flows through which programs can follow once the intelligence has been identified in the data. There is a lot to this new industry, and I won't pretend to be an expert on it. It can easily require a PhD in data science to effectively understand and explain the concept. It is an interesting area that is gaining ground in the IT industry.

Azure Data Lake

Once the data has been prepared and the search and learning outcomes documented, the data is stored in either Azure Data Lake or Azure Data Warehouse for final analysis, conclusion making, and presentation. The primary differences between placing the data into Azure Data Lake versus a data warehouse is based on the size or amount of data being stored and analyzed. Azure Data Lake is intended for scenarios where petabytes of data are being engaged. An EDW is quite a bit smaller and much more structured, making it simpler to analyze and serve. As the amount of data stored in Azure Data Lake is expected to change at a relatively quick pace, scaling is a large part of the Azure offering. In addition, the data stored in Azure Data Lake can be in any form—videos, blobs, documents, or semistructured data sources.

Azure Analysis Services

This product is an Azure PaaS offering that restructures or interprets data, whether it be relational or not, into a *semantic data model (SDM)*. An SDM is data that is modeled and transformed into a more modern model aspiring to capture the meaning of data that may not be realized using more traditional approaches. The fact that this is a PaaS offering means that there is some compute power behind it as that data needs to be analyzed, manipulated, reformatted, and stored before behaving as an SDM. Like many other Azure products, there are numerous tiers: Developer, Basic, and Standard. Each has different features and associated CPU and memory allocations.

When data structures are created initially, there is certainly some logical meaning of the data that is built into the columns, tables, and relationships. The sematic data model attempts to provide a conceptual data structure that is then easily served, for example, to a Power BI report, as shown in Figure 5.9.

FIGURE 5.9   The formation of a semantic data model

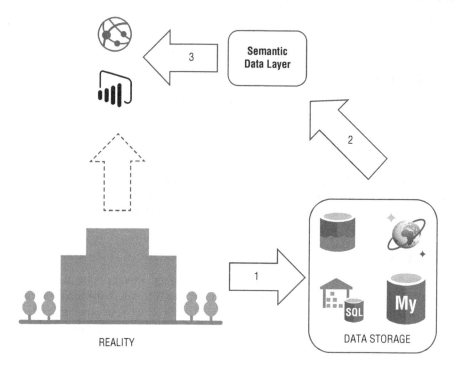

Consider that you have some data that describes a company or a group of companies. You likely have data that includes employees, locations, mission, and inventory. That data is in some storage that is attempting to show or produce an illustration of that company. In the Big Data context, there may be other tables, not structured or with no defined relationship, in the data source that indirectly have some conceptual connection. Assume that one of the companies has a mission to "empower every person and every organization on the planet to achieve more." Analysis Services may be able to get the meaning of that mission statement and use the meaning in the search for more companies with similar missions. That finding would be formalized into an SDM, and by doing so it provides a more feasible source to query against and visualize those results.

Azure Data Explorer (ADX) and Azure Storage Explorer

Once data has been placed into a data store, whether it's structured or not, a tool called *Azure Data Explorer (ADX)* can help you browse and analyze it. This powerful tool provides an interface to query data stored on, for example Data Lake and Azure Monitor. Azure Monitor is discussed in Chapter 9. ADX is used internally by Microsoft. I personally analyze customer issues with Azure Functions. ADX gives me an interface into our logging system, KUSTO, where I can query logs in almost real time to get an understanding of what is going on with the product. We are "eating our own dogfood" as it goes. Azure Storage Explorer, on the other hand, provides an interface for traversing numerous Azure Storage products such as containers, shares, queues, and tables, all discussed later. Azure Storage Explorer resembles that shown in Figure 5.10.

FIGURE 5.10   Azure Storage Explorer

For each Azure Storage product, you first create the storage account for the option you want, such as containers, shares, queues, or tables. Then, within the account you create the container. The account is the location where you can configure firewall rules, logging, and zone redundancy, while the container exposes a more limited set of configurations, for example size and access policies. You can use PowerShell, Azure CLI, .NET, Java, Python, and Node.js to manage and configure Azure storage.

Shared Files

Sharing files has always been a big part of using a computer. Whether it be a `.zip`, a `.gif`, or a `.docx`, it is common that after creating or receiving such files you would want to share them with others. Additionally, you might have numerous computers that need to have access to those files. There is a concept of a file share, which is simply a server that is available on a network. It has lots of storage capacity and shares content in the form of files. The files are stored in folders that make up a logically constructed directory structure.

In Windows Explorer, for example, there is a menu item named Map Network Drive, which then prompts you to enter the server name and share name. The format might be familiar and resembles \\server\share. This works well when all the machines that need access to the file are on the same or a trusted network and the identity used to connect to the share has access.

There are better solutions these days such as Microsoft Teams or SharePoint to store shared files that can be modified in parallel by numerous people at the same time. A file share isn't the primary option for an active collaboration that requires real-time updates to a shared file. The file share solution is more for storing files that may need to be referred to at a later time with updates happening at nonscheduled intervals. It wouldn't be too much of a stretch to think that you have a large number of files that are rarely used or referenced but for some reason you cannot bring yourself to delete. Perhaps an old résumé, old letters, awards, or certificates? Pictures, on the other hand, although not often viewed are precious. You wouldn't want them on a single computer because if it crashes, getting the data off the hard drive is expensive, if possible at all. Placing them on a file share is a nice alternative, perhaps something like OneDrive or the Microsoft Azure file storage product called Azure Files.

Azure Files, like all other Windows file server sharing technologies, is based on the *Server Message Block (SMB)* protocol. It offers LRS, ZRS, GRS, RA GRS, and GZRS redundancies; great amounts of storage capacity; synchronization capabilities; data-at-rest encryption; and an exposed HTTPS API that allows file management customizations. The redundancies are described later in this chapter, in the "Zone Replication" section. Skip forward if you want to get the details now. To learn more about Azure Files, complete Exercise 5.1 where you will create a storage account and then create and configure an Azure Files file share.

EXERCISE 5.1

Creating and Configuring Azure Files

1. Log in to the Azure Portal at https://portal.azure.com and click the menu button on the top-left area of the browser. Click + Create A Resource, click Storage, and then click Storage Account.

2. Select the subscription and resource group into which you want to create the storage account, enter a storage account name (I used csharpguitar), enter a location (should be the same as a resource group location, but it's not required), and select Locally-Redundant Storage (LRS) from the Replication drop-down. Leave all remaining options at the defaults. Click the Review + create button and then click the Create button.

3. Once the provision is complete, navigate to the Overview blade of the storage account. In the center of the blade you will see something similar to Figure 5.11. Click the File Shares link, click the + File Share button, enter a name (for example, guitar), enter a quota (for example, 1), and click the Create button.

FIGURE 5.11   A portion of the storage account overview blade

4.   Open Azure PowerShell and enter the following PowerShell cmdlet:

```
Test-NetConnection -ComputerName <name>.file.core.windows.net -Port 445
```

If port 445 is blocked by your company or private firewall, then the previous Power-Shell cmdlet will not work. Replace <name> with the name of the storage account you created in step 2. The output of the PowerShell cmdlet may resemble something similar to Figure 5.12.

FIGURE 5.12   The output of a PowerShell cmdlet testing file share connectivity

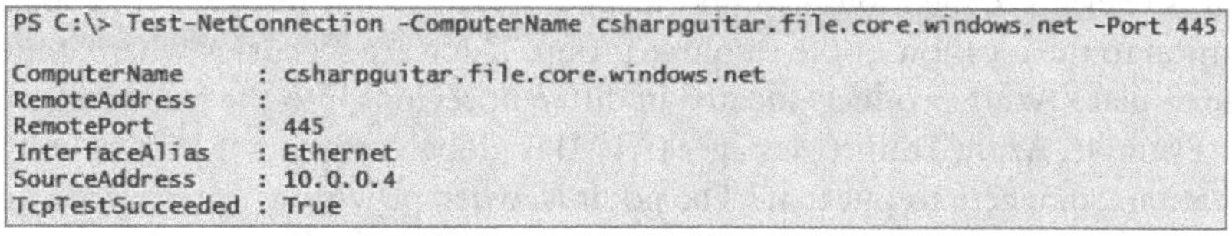

```
PS C:\> Test-NetConnection -ComputerName csharpguitar.file.core.windows.net -Port 445

ComputerName      : csharpguitar.file.core.windows.net
RemoteAddress     :
RemotePort        : 445
InterfaceAlias    : Ethernet
SourceAddress     : 10.0.0.4
TcpTestSucceeded  : True
```

5.   Click the file share you just created, click the Connect button, review the sample scripts provided per operating system, and select your desired OS script.

6.   If the PowerShell cmdlet you ran in step 4 was successful, enter the following to mount/map the drive:

```
cmd.exe /C "cmdkey /add:`"<name>.file.core.windows.net`" ´
        /user:`"Azure\<name>`" /pass:`"<password>""
New-PSDrive -Name Z -PSProvider FileSystem &acute;
            -Root "\\<name>.file.core.windows.net\<shareName>"-Persist
```

Replace <name> with the name of the storage account you created previously in step 2 and replace <password> with the value found in the script presented to you after clicking the Connect button in step 5. Replace <shareName> with the file share name you created in step 3. Figure 5.13 illustrates a successful outcome and how the mounted/mapped drive looks in Windows Explorer.

FIGURE 5.13 The output of a PowerShell cmdlet mounting an Azure File Share and how it looks in Windows Explorer

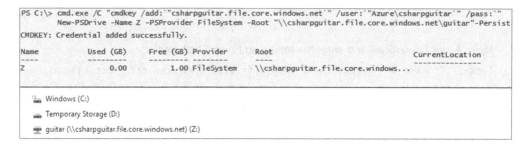

Again, it is relevant to mention the importance of placing your resources in a logical location in relation to the location of the resource group. There are scenarios where it might make sense to place Azure products located in different regions into the same resource group. For example, Azure Traffic Manager (ATM) is global, meaning it isn't bound to a specific location. So, where to put that? The point is, when provisioning resources, group them in a logical way. The grouping doesn't always have to be by location; it could be product or IT solution base. Stay organized as it makes support easier and reduces costs.

Before moving to the next section, take a look at Table 5.2 to get some better insights into which data store technology you should choose for many different scenarios. You need to know the requirements of your application, then using what you have learned in the previous text, you may be better able to decide which data store is best matched to meet those requirements. The table provides a different view of the same information previously provided.

TABLE 5.2 Comparing Data Storage

	Document DB	Key/Value	Object Storage	RDBMS	EDW	Shared Files
Non- or semi-relational	✓	✓	✓	✗	✗	✓
Relational	✗	✗	✗	✓	✓	✗
Aggregation	✗	✗	✗	✓	✓	✗

	Document DB	Key/Value	Object Storage	RDBMS	EDW	Shared Files
Open source	✓	✗	✗	✗	✗	✗
Big Data	✓	✗	✗	✗	✓	✗
OLAP	✗	✗	✗	✓	✓	✗
OTLP	✗	✗	✓	✓	✗	✗
File storage	✗	✗	✓	✗	✗	✓
Vertical scale	✗	✓	✓	✓	✓	✓
Horizontal scale	✓	✗	✗	✗	✗	✗
Encrypt-at-rest	✓	✓	✓	✗	✓	✓

Aggregation   Remember that aggregation means you can run SQL query-like statements against the data source. An RDBMS like Azure SQL is relational and therefore corresponds to that criteria nicely due to the relationships between tables. Although you do run query-like commands against a document DB using an Azure Cosmos DB, those queries are typically run on the document that is retrieved from the data store instead of the data store itself. You will do this later in the chapter after creating an Azure Cosmos DB.

Open Source   The table item "open source" represents that the related data store is most popular, specifically designed for applications written with open source software or typically implementing concepts most paired with that approach.

Vertical Scale and Horizontal Scale   Vertical versus horizontal scaling signifies that the data store is designed for scaling to multiple instances versus scaling to a more powerful single instance. Although vertical scaling is supported by all the data storage products, you might experience greater improvements by scaling horizontal into a closer proximity to your users versus simply scaling to a more powerful VM.

Now that you know a large majority of the possible types of data stores, their use cases, and their strengths and weaknesses, read on to get a bit deeper into the specifics of a few Azure data store and Azure storage products.

Azure Data Store

In this section, you will learn about numerous Azure data store products. Azure SQL Database and Azure Cosmos DB will be covered in depth, while other less popular but worthy of mention data stores such as table storage, MySQL and PostgreSQL are discussed. In addition to those Azure data stores, the following will also be covered:

- Azure Data Store versus Azure Storage
- Database as a service (DaaS)
- Data partitioning
- Datasets
- Azure Database Migration Service

It is a good approach to have a definition of certain terms handy in the event you get put on the spot in a meeting or when you are on the phone with a client or customer. One such question is, what is the difference between a data store and data storage? Aren't they the same thing? Well yes, kind of. They are the same because they both store data. The difference comes in the structure or form of the data. It is simplest to understand by comparing an Azure data store product and an Azure storage product with each other. For example, compare Azure SQL and Azure Blob Storage. The first, Azure SQL, is what you would simply refer to as a database. This implies that it has some tables with columns and rows and can be queried using SQL-like commands. Azure Blob Storage is for storing files like `.gif`, `.docx`, `.vhd`, or `.pfx`, and you would query the storage using the filename and not the contents within the file. Another way of putting it is that you would store raw data in a data store, and you would store files in data storage.

In Chapter 4 you read about the different cloud service models like IaaS, CaaS, PaaS, and FaaS. *Database as a service (DaaS)* is a common acronym for this kind of cloud offering. Other variants include the acronym DBaaS. Be aware that DaaS when expanded can represent data as a service. Another variant represents *desktop as a service (DaaS)*, the Windows Virtual Desktop offering discussed in Chapter 4. That DaaS offering is tasked with storing and delivering data on demand. If you compare it to one of the compute cloud service models where CPU and memory are provided on-demand, the similar analogy can be used with database as a service. It is not that the data is generated for your consumption, but rather the compute resource, data store, and storage are provided to store, process, manage, analyze, consume, and report on the data that you, your customers, your business transactions, devices or your applications produce. How all the storage, processing, and consumption happens may be clear to you now with the content provided at the beginning of this chapter; if not, read it again. Those kinds of products and features that provide the storage, processing, and consumption are what Azure provides as its DaaS.

If you are an architect or a developer, you probably have numerous ideas about tuning an application for performance, scalability, and availability. From an architecture perspective, you should be certain that clients connecting to a database are as close to the data source as possible. If you are tuning a web app, then you would want to make sure that the web tier and the data tier are in the same geographical region. You wouldn't get the most optimal performance if the web tier is in South Central US and the database is in North Europe. From a developer perspective, you might look at projecting the queries better. Here you would remove any SELECT * FROM TABLE and replace the * with exactly the data you need instead of bringing back all data. As an alternative, you could move the query to the data tier and call a stored procedure instead. If you wanted to tune a database itself, for sure it is best to engage a specialist like a DBA, which like security experts and network administrators, are career worthy because each speciality requires lots of experience to be proficient in those fields. However, a world-class Azure Solutions Architect Expert would at least have a few ideas of actions to take directly on a database. One such concept, called *data partitioning*, comes in three forms: horizontal (aka sharding), vertical, and functions. Figure 5.14 illustrates horizontal data partitioning.

FIGURE 5.14   A horizontal data partition

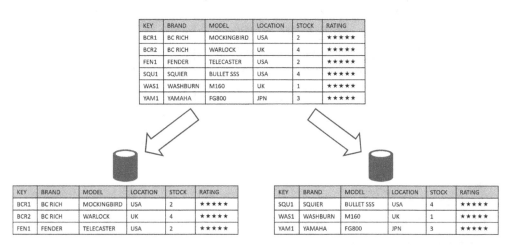

The implementation of horizontal data partitioning, as you may gather from Figure 5.14, breaks or shards a table based on the primary key. There can be numerous shards. It all comes down to how much data is being stored in the table. The point is to reduce the amount of data in a single table in an attempt to improve performance and reduce contention. For example, guitars with a key where the first letter is A–G could be stored in one shard, and H–Z are stored in another shard. You may notice that the A–G is eight letters, while H–Z is nineteen letters, which might not seem balanced. The reason for that is since I know about guitars, I know that there are many more guitar models that start with A–G than with H–Z, and in the end, that distribution of data is more likely to balance. The point is that you should consult an expert because shards are not designed to be changed and need to be designed appropriately from the beginning because the important aspect here is to balance the number of queries across the shards. The separation is not always simply down the middle of the alphabet or a midpoint between numbers. Splitting the data is also often based on performance, latent contentions, or datasets that get accessed most frequently. A program requesting data that is accessed often is more likely to be latent than a program that accesses dormant data. This is because all processes work on threads, and they have to manage access to shared resources such as data. Although this happens fast, with high load there may be contention where requests are queued that decreases performance and increases latency. Both of those can be optimized by implementing horizontal data partitioning. Figure 5.15 shows another model, vertical data partitioning.

FIGURE 5.15 A vertical data partition

KEY	BRAND	MODEL	LOCATION	STOCK	RATING
BCR1	BC RICH	MOCKINGBIRD	USA	2	★★★★★
BCR2	BC RICH	WARLOCK	UK	4	★★★★★
FEN1	FENDER	TELECASTER	USA	2	★★★★★
SQU1	SQUIER	BULLET SSS	USA	4	★★★★★
WAS1	WASHBURN	M160	UK	1	★★★★★
YAM1	YAMAHA	FG800	JPN	3	★★★★★

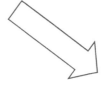

KEY	BRAND	STOCK
BCR1	BC RICH	2
BCR2	BC RICH	4
FEN1	FENDER	2
SQU1	SQUIER	4
WAS1	WASHBURN	1
YAM1	YAMAHA	3

KEY	MODEL	LOCATION	RATING
BCR1	MOCKINGBIRD	USA	★★★★★
BCR2	WARLOCK	UK	★★★★★
FEN1	TELECASTER	USA	★★★★★
SQU1	BULLET SSS	USA	★★★★★
WAS1	M160	UK	★★★★★
YAM1	FG800	JPN	★★★★★

While horizontal data partitioning is focused on balancing queries across the shards, vertical data partitioning is focused on splitting data on a table between the data that is queried more often and the data that is queried not so often. Remember I recently used the technical term *projection*, which means optimizing data queries by retrieving only the data you need. I stated that I was approaching it from the context of the consumer. Here with a vertical data partition, you can provide that same projection as the provider. There are numerous database analysis tools that can provide insights into which tables are queried the most. Additionally, those tools can provide the columns and even rows that are accessed the most. That kind of information would be extremely useful for the creation of a vertical data partition. In the case shown in Figure 5.15, which brands of guitars and how many there were in stock were queried more than the guitar model, location, and rating. Therefore, the data structure was created as shown. As mentioned, this is dependent on what your application does. It is possible not to know at the beginning of a project which part of the data structure will get the most access, so this may be a tuning exercise once your application gets a bit more mature.

Finally, a functional data partition, as the name implies, breaks a group of tables into different data sources based on what is contained within them. Take, for example, a database that contains GUITAR and PROGRAMMING_LANGUAGE tables. Those tables would conceivably have different functions simply based on the name and may benefit from a split based on their functions into a different data source. That is a simple example, but you are sure to get the point. Another example splits a reporting function from an order entry function. In conclusion, many Azure data store and storage products can benefit from one or more of these data partitioning models. As you read, you'll see that any optimal data partitioning recommendations will be referenced back to this section.

I mentioned a dataset in the previous paragraphs but did not follow up with a description. A dataset is a relational database concept. You will not hear the words *dataset* much in the nonrelational or semistructured data context. This is because a dataset is directly related to a table, or a collection of data that has been retrieved from multiple related tables to form a logical unit useful for a computer to run code against. When you think about data, visualize it as being stored in a raw text file. That raw text file has a DBMS to manage that data and respond to queries. By manage, I mean it knows what relationships exist in the data contained in the file. When you execute a query against a database that contains joins between multiple tables, it returns a result that is not similar to any table existing on the database. This result must be stored as an entity, and that entity is a dataset. Additionally, a dataset typically contains properties such as row count. This dataset exposes interfaces for parsing by query engines like LINQ, DataTable, and DataView classes.

The last topic to discuss before you dive into some details about Azure data store products is the *Azure Database Migration Service (DMS)*. DMS aka ADMS is covered in more detail later and again in Chapter 8, but as this may come up on the Azure Solutions Architect Expert exam, it needs to be called out more than once. Since DMS is a tool focused on moving data, this seemed like a fitting place to introduce this product. DMS is the recommended Azure tool for data migration from one or more on-premise data stores to an Azure data platform product. Some important parts of a data migration to consider are to determine the source and target and whether the database will be online or offline during the migration. It would make sense that if you have an on-premise SQL Server database, your target would be Azure SQL. However, what if you have an Oracle database or a MongoDB as the source? Which database would you choose to target on Azure? Also, some databases are huge and might take more than 24 hours to move all the data from a source to the target. Can your database be offline for that long, or does it need to remain online for use? Once the migration is complete, how do you get the data synchronized if the database remained online and accepting CRUD operations during the move? All of those questions are answered later, but the recommended tool for use for production data stores is the Azure Database Migration Service.

Azure SQL Database

A decade or so ago, there really were only two mainstream data stores you could choose from. One was Microsoft Access and the other Oracle. Microsoft Access wasn't scalable and was therefore useful only for small kinds of applications. If you needed a large data store, your only option was Oracle. There were others, but for the sake of argument only those two are mentioned here as both are still relevant today. The first release of SQL Server was in 1989. It took some years to get to a point where it was an acceptable alternative to Oracle. These days it can be said they are about on par with each other. SQL Server is a world-class DBMS system capable of running any kind of workload in today's IT world. The largest decision factor between the two is based on the ecosystem in which you want to run the workload. If you are determined (or required) to run a large percentage of your IT solutions using Microsoft technologies, then a valid choice for a relational database is SQL Server. An alternative ecosystem to Microsoft is perhaps open source with Java as the development language, Oracle as the database, and either Linux or Windows as the underlying operating system. All of those options are available on Azure; however, the remainder of this section is focused on SQL Server and the following topics:

- Selecting an Azure SQL database
- Pricing models and limits
- Configuring and securing
- Migrating data
- Monitoring
- Partitioning data
- SQL managed instance and SQL VM

Before you get into the details, you might consider reading the portion about Azure SQL from Chapter 1. There is good, high-level information there. Perhaps read it just to get into the context a bit. You should recognize that this is an area where a detailed level of understanding is necessary for the Azure Solutions Architect Expert exam. The exam focuses on scenarios in which you need to identify which Azure SQL options to select: the most cost-effective solution, the best method for migrating data, redundancy, and monitoring strategies. Migration, monitoring, and recovery are covered in more detail in Chapter 8 and Chapter 9; however, that information is more general in nature. This chapter and section focuses on Azure SQL databases.

Selecting an Azure SQL Database

When it comes to selecting the right Azure SQL database to run on, you would start with choosing the platform that consists of Azure SQL, SQL managed instances, and SQL virtual machines; see Figure 5.16. Each has a specific use case based on cost, migration options, maintenance, and service level agreements (SLAs). Once you decide the platform, the next step is to determine the tier, for example general purpose, business critical, hyperscale, basic, standard, or premium. Each tier, like the platform, comes with a set of features with an increase in cost as you traverse up to scale or an indirect cost from the maintenance activities you take over based on the chosen platform, aka IaaS. However, before you decide the tier, you need to decide if you will use the vCore, DTU, or serverless purchasing model; the most optimal choice is dependent on your requirements.

FIGURE 5.16   The SQL database platform options

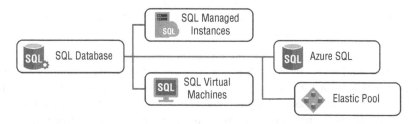

Before getting into the details of each of those different decision scenarios, complete Exercise 5.2 to create an Azure SQL database. The exercise will be followed with some explanation of terms and content, then it will flow into covering all the content just mentioned in the first paragraph.

EXERCISE 5.2

Creating an Azure SQL DB

1.   Log in to the Azure Portal at https://portal.azure.com and enter **Azure SQL** in the top middle search box. Click Azure SQL and click the + Add button to display the Select SQL deployment option blade, as illustrated by Figure 5.17. Locate and click the Create button within the SQL databases box and leave Single Database as the Resource type.

FIGURE 5.17   The Select SQL deployment option blade

Select SQL deployment option
Microsoft

♡ Feedback

How do you plan to use the service?

SQL databases	SQL managed instances	SQL virtual machines
Best for modern cloud applications. Hyperscale and serverless options are available.	Best for most migrations to the cloud. Lift-and-shift ready.	Best for migrations and applications requiring OS-level access. Lift-and-shift ready.
Resource type	Resource type	Image
Single database ⌄	Single instance ⌄	Please select an offer ⌄
Create Show details	**Create** Show details	Create Show details

2. Select the subscriptions and resource group into which you want the database to reside and enter a database name (for this exercise, I used `csharp`). In the Server drop-down box click the Create New link to create a database server. Enter a unique server name (for example, `csharpguitar`) and enter a server admin login and password. After you confirm the password, select the location of the server. It is recommended, but not required, that you place the server in the same location as your resource group. Now, click the OK button.

3. Click the Configure Database link in the Compute + Storage section. Take a look at all the options. The General Purpose, Business Critical, and Hyperscale options are tiers targeted at enterprise applications. For this exercise, click the Basic, Standard, Premium link to view those tiers. Select the Basic tier, and take a look at the cost, the Data max size, and the DTUs. Compare them to the options on the other tiers. When you are finished, verify that the Basic tier is selected and then click the Apply button.

4. Click the Review + create button and then click the Create button.

5. Once the server is created, navigate to the Azure SQL database. On the Overview blade, find the link named Show Database Connection string and click it. Notice that it shows numerous examples of making a connection to your database.

6. Navigate back to the Overview blade and click the Set Server Firewall link. Notice that the Allow Azure services and resources to access this server is defaulted to ON and that the link named + Add Client IP includes an option that allows you to configure a VNet.

    Nice work! You have created an Azure SQL database as well as the server on which the database is hosted.

You know that the three Azure SQL platforms are Azure SQL, which you just created; SQL managed instances; and SQL virtual machines. You might have noticed while creating the Azure SQL database that the provisioning of the SQL database to run it on was simple and had no configuration steps other than a name, user ID, and password. This is because Azure SQL runs on the PaaS compute offering, and you do not have access to the database server; you only have access to the database. The same goes for SQL managed instances. The primary difference between the two is determined by whether you migrate an existing database versus creating a new one. A SQL managed instance is much more like a SQL Server implementation on-premise than an Azure SQL database. This means that migrating an existing database to Azure will be easier because most SQL server features available with on-premise are also available with SQL managed instances. So, what is the difference between a SQL managed instance and a SQL virtual machine? The quick answer is that one is PaaS-like, while the other is IaaS-like. Since you know already the different responsibilities you have between those two cloud service models, the pros and cons don't require much detail. Table 5.3 shows more details, which will help you to choose which Azure SQL platform is required for your database.

TABLE 5.3 Choosing an Azure SQL Product

	Azure SQL	SQL managed instance	SQL VM
SLA	99.995%	99.99%	99.99%
Lift and shift	×	✓	✓
SaaS-like	✓	×	×
PaaS	✓	✓	×
IaaS	×	×	✓
Cost friendly	✓	=	×
Built-in backups	✓	✓	×
Private IP	×	✓	✓
Dynamic Scaling	✓	✓	×

The SLA is higher for the Azure SQL platform offering because of its relation to the PaaS cloud service model. With PaaS you have no means of touching the infrastructure, which limits the chance of making configurations that could cause a disruption of service. Additionally, there are many built-in recovery, security, and intelligence features that help improve its availability. Customers who provision an Azure SQL database cannot access the compute on which it runs, thereby reducing the possibility of making a change that causes a platform disruption. The other two platform options do allow some platform configurations. Lift and shift was mentioned in detail in Chapter 4. Use this option when your plan is to take a database that you have in a private data center (on-premise) and place it, as is, on the Azure platform without making any changes. As you progress through the cloud service models from PaaS to IaaS, the opportunity to make custom changes to the infrastructure increases. The ability to make these customizations increases the probability of successfully completing a lift-and-shift migration. Likewise goes the associated costs. The PaaS-based Azure SQL database offering is more cost effective than the more customizable SQL virtual machine. IaaS with SQL managed instances falls between the two. The cost here is focused on the direct cost of the software and compute resource, not the additional support and maintenance costs that are taken over when you decide to run IaaS (a SQL VM). When you choose a SQL VM, you are responsible for the configuration of backups and patches. If you need to scale the VM to a larger size, there will likely be some downtime, but you get a private IP address that can be accessed from on-premise. The private IP address is useful for running hybrid cloud solutions. Although most SQL Server capabilities and features are supported by Azure SQL or SQL managed instances, not all are. If you realize that you require a feature not available on those other platform models, then a SQL VM is your only option.

An example is perhaps your on-premise database utilizes a third-party tool that needs write access to the registry or you need to run a `.exe` or `.msi` to add binaries on the server that is not supported neither in PaaS nor in PaaS.

Both Azure SQL and SQL managed instances have built-in capability for backups. Azure SQL does not have a private IP, but SQL managed instances does, which allows the connectivity through a VPN Gateway or Express Route, like a SQL VM. It is possible to set firewall rules and configure service endpoints, which were introduced in Chapter 3 to restrict access to the database via the public IP of the Azure SQL database. When you discuss scaling in the context of a database, the method is concerned with scaling up and down and not scaling in or out like you experienced in the context of compute scaling. This make sense as the data store is a single location, it is the source of record, and there can be only one true data value at any given time. So, making a copy of the database onto many instances wouldn't work well unless there is massive synchronization happening or if the data is read-only and updated infrequently. Avoid scaling your database if at all possible because it will cause downtime while the scaling operation is processing. Scaling up and down is relatively quick and easy in the context of Azure SQL and SQL managed instances, not so with SQL VM as it can take a bit longer than the other platform options.

Before proceeding to the tier discussion, you may have noticed in Figure 5.16 there was a mention of a resource type named Elastic Pool, as well; it existed in the Resource Type drop-down box for the SQL databases platform type shown in Figure 5.17. Just in case you missed it, the Elastic Pool option is illustrated in Figure 5.18. Single Database and Database Server exist as well and also deserve some words to describe why you would select one versus the other.

FIGURE 5.18   The Resource Type drop-down box content for a SQL database platform

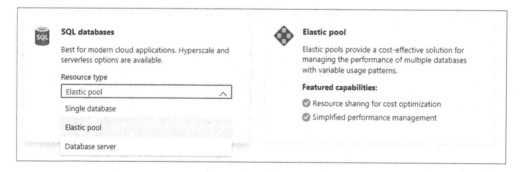

Let's begin with Single Database. That is the one you created in Exercise 5.2. You also created a database server, which is a required necessity for hosting the database. I quickly touched on that previously as well. The maintenance of the PaaS VM on which the database server resides is further alleviated when compared to the PaaS cloud service model. The SQL database server is the location where you perform administrative actions such as setting firewall rules, enabling security monitoring rules, and managing backups. It is also the location where your data is stored and accessed. Setting the firewall rules was mentioned a bit earlier;

however, that was from the context of the database and not the database server. When you configure the firewall rule on the database server, then all databases on that server will allow access from the IP or IP range added to the rule. By default, all Azure services will have access to the databases on the SQL database server. Any other IP address must be added manually. For a tighter level of security, it is recommended to place the firewall rule on the database itself instead of at the higher database server level. There will be more on these options in the coming sections.

It is possible to have multiple Azure SQL databases on a single SQL database server. Log in to the portal and navigate to the SQL database server you created in the previous exercise. On the Overview blade, you will see the + New Database button. When you click it, you are directed to the navigation wizard that walks you through the addition of another database. I did state the addition of another database because there isn't a use case for having only a SQL database server without a database on it, so the expectation is that you create the Azure SQL single database, which requires a SQL database server together. That implies if you access the SQL database server and click the + New Database button, you are adding an additional one. There are two other buttons on that menu bar that are notable. The first one is the + New Data Warehouse button. After reading the previous text, you should know what a data warehouse is. It was often referred to as EDW, for example. There wasn't an exercise that explained how to create one, but now you know where to get started with it if you ever need one. The other button is + New Pool, which is how to move your single database into an elastic pool, which is the third option shown previously in Figure 5.18. An elastic pool has everything to do with scaling and the optimal utilization of resources. Take a look at Figure 5.19.

FIGURE 5.19 Over-provisioning database resources

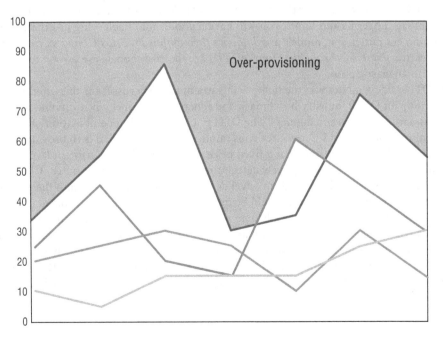

Now, assume you have four Azure SQL single databases, each one with a different use case. The databases are accessed at different times and have different peak times. The four lines on the Figure 5.19 chart illustrate the utilization of compute resources necessary to respond to data request traffic. Historically, you would need to scale your server to a size that is capable of managing the peak amount of traffic, even if that peak happened only once a week or even once per month. Figure 5.19 shows the amount of over-provisioning you would have in that old model; recognize that over-provision carries a cost. An elastic pool allows you to move single databases in and out of the pool. The platform scales out the capacity that is required to handle peaks when they occur instead of having and paying for the extra capacity—even when it is not used. *Elastic* is a good word because you can visualize a rubber band stretching out and back in, which is exactly what the elastic pool does with the size of your database. It expands when required and contracts when the force causing the expansion is removed.

Pricing Models and Limits

It wouldn't come as a surprise that the pricing for an Azure SQL database is rather complicated. It is not only a challenge from an Azure SQL perspective but from many other Azure products. This is why there is a large team at Microsoft whose only job is to answer questions about Azure bills. However, one reason for the new cloud era explosion is because the cost is much less when compared to running the same on-premise. Understanding the costs is one thing, but seeing that the bill is 50% less running on Azure is worth the initial confusion. The intention of the following text is to provide some insights into the costing terms, how they link into different Azure SQL platforms, and some of the limits that constrain the product from going rogue and potentially consuming infinite resources at a great cost. Don't get me wrong, calculating cost is an understandable algorithm and wanting to be able to give an educated guess on the cost of the deployment to an Azure SQL database is feasible. After understanding the terms and limits, you will have a good shot at achieving just that. The two most prominent purchasing models are *database throughput unit (DTU)* and vCore. *Serverless* and *elastic database throughput unit (eDTU)* are the cost models used when running a database in an elastic pool.

The DTU pricing model was the first pricing attempt by Microsoft for this offering. It was based on an OLTP industry benchmark and remains the model when running in the basic, standard, premium pricing tiers. The DTU pricing model is a combination of compute, memory/storage, and I/O resource consumption. Its primary goal is to provide a fixed amount of compute resource at a fixed price while providing a consistent level of performance and stability, preemptively calculating how much of each resource (CPU, memory, and IOPs) a database needs in advance and then translating that into the number of DTUs your database requires. It would be quite remarkable if you were able to achieve it. There are certainly some database tools that will give you a ballpark idea of the maximum amount of CPU consumed, the maximum amount of memory, and the maximum amount of read/write operations for an on-premise database over a given time frame. Using those findings, you could then consider them as the base for calculating the number of DTUs that are required when running the same on an Azure SQL database. With the basic pricing model, the maximum number of DTUs is five, the standard is 3000, and the premium is 4000 DTUs. In Exercise 5.2 you created a basic database with five DTUs. There is no conversion from those DTUs directly into the number of CPUs, the amount of memory, or the maximum IOPS required. Instead, consider that the performance you get when running at ten DTUs is double that when running at five DTUs. Running at the maximum of 4000 DTUs, via premium, would be an 800x increase in compute power (CPU, memory, and IOPS) when compared to running with five. When running in the DTU pricing model, the takeaway is that the price is based on the fixed consumption of CPU, memory, and IOPS. You will not get crystal-clear transparency that translates DTUs into compute. You will need to test and tune the DTUs once you migrate, but the behavior will be consistent enough to get to a stable state after some testing.

The DTU pricing model is fixed, which means when your database consumption hits the threshold, the compute gets throttled. This causes latency, and if the application consuming or creating the data cannot handle such a scenario, then there will be exceptions and potentially lost or corrupted data. After some learnings from customer feedback about DTUs, the concept of elastic pools was realized that included a new pricing model named eDTU. eDTUs provide some flexibility when it comes to the reality of the negative impact, which the fixed DTU concept had on the legacy type of applications that didn't work well when a threshold was hit. Therefore, the option to move a single database into an elastic pool allowed for the dynamic allocation and deallocation of DTUs based on demand.

One of the other problems experienced with DTUs was the bundling of CPU, memory, and IOPS together. What happens if your database needs more of one item than the other? For example, your database can be heavy on IOPS, but not so heavy in regard to memory. You might be required to scale to a very high DTU to get the required throughput, costing a significant amount because the CPU and memory increase are bound to it. The vCore pricing model, which is the recommended model, provides two benefits. The first is that you can scale based on compute, memory/storage, and IOPS, which resolves one of the issues with DTU, making vCore a bit more cost effective. And while we are in the context of costs, the second benefit is that the charging is a bit more transparent. When compared to DTU, you simply had to scale if your database was being throttled. You wouldn't really know if the reason was CPU, memory, or IO bound. Your only option was to increase the number of DTUs. However, with vCore, you can increase the number of cores that get allocated to your database without increasing other items. The final pricing model is called *serverless*, which you may recall mentioned in the previous chapter in the context of compute in the context of FaaS. That concept is the same for an Azure SQL database. In Exercise 5.2 you created the cheapest possible tier and cost model possible. It comes with a fixed monthly price, regardless of its use. As per the serverless model, there is no compute allocated when the product is not being used, and therefore you are not charged. You are charged a specific amount of compute and storage costs based only on its usage and consumption.

So far, you have read about the different Azure SQL products: Azure SQL, SQL managed instances, and SQL VMs. You also learned the differences between DTU/eDTU and vCore-based costing. Let's now take a look into the different available service pricing tiers. The pricing tiers are separated into two pricing categories based on the pricing models of DTU and vCores. General Purpose (w/ serverless), Business Critical, and Hyperscale are priced using the vCore model. Basic, standard, and premium are priced using DTUs. The basic tier is the most cost-friendly option, and it is the one that you created in Exercise 5.2. For development, non-mission-critical applications or just to learn and have fun, this is a valid option. It's similar to standard and premium where you have the same PaaS offering and basic but can get more storage capacity and DTUs. For more details about DTU service pricing tiers, please review Table 5.4.

TABLE 5.4   Basic, Standard, and Premium DTU tiers

	Basic	Standard	Premium
DTUs	5	10 to 3000	125 to 4000
Database size	100MB to 2GB	100MB to 250GB	100MB to 1TB
Read-only replicas	×	×	✓
Run demanding workloads	×	✓	✓
High I/O workload	×	×	✓
Secondary DB	×	1	Active 0 to 4

Having a read-only replica of your data is useful from a failover perspective as well as for performance. From a failover perspective, consider a scenario in which the primary database instance goes down; you could make the read-only instance writable, redirect all the clients to it, and make it the primary database. This may be a faster recovery than troubleshooting and trying to bring the original primary database back online. From a performance perspective, you can tunnel clients that run reports to a read-only database instance. Routing the execution of reports, which typically have large datasets, complicated SQL queries, and extended date ranges, away from OLTP instances, would likely reduce load on the primary database. This would save compute on the primary database for managing OLTP capabilities. It would be hard to define in absolute precision what a demanding workload is, as referred to in Table 5.4. However, it wouldn't be hard to conclude that five DTUs don't provide a production-worthy amount of compute power, when compared to the other two tiers. While standard and premium allow for a high number of DTUs, only premium is designed for high I/O workloads. Premium also includes an active secondary data replication mechanism. This mimics the behavior of what is often referred to as a hot standby. This host standby is not a read-only instance and wouldn't have clients making a connection to it for any reason. It would act as a failover instance in case the primary instances fails. Table 5.5 shows some details about vCore-based service pricing tiers.

TABLE 5.5 General Purpose, Business Critical, and Hyperscale vCore Tiers

	General Purpose	Business Critical	Hyperscale
Availability	99.99%	99.99% to 99.995%	99.95% to 99.99%
Single database	✓	✓	✓
Elastic pool	✓	✓	✗
Managed instance	✓	✓	✗
Database size	5GB to 4TB 32GB to 8TB	5GB to 4TB 32GB to 4TB	Up to 100TB
Compute size	1 to 80 vCores	1 to 80 vCores	1 to 80 vCores
In memory OLTP	✗	✓	✗
Read-only replicas	0	1	0 to 4
Serverless	✓	✗	✗
Backups	7 to 35 days	7 to 35 days	7 days
Autoscaling	✗**	✗	✓*

*   Hyperscale supports the autoscaling of the data storage up to 100TB. The ability to load and access data in memory increases performance as it eliminates the requirement to read the data from disk. This feature, in-memory OLTP, is available only with the Business Critical tier.

**   Serverless is supported only via the General Purpose tier and will autoscale the allocated compute resource. When configuring serverless, you choose the maximum number of vCores, which can be between 1 and 16, and the minimum, which can be between 0.5 and 1.

General Purpose is the tier that offers the most cost friendly option. Although the price is much greater than basic/DTU, you get the added benefits of vCore costing, backups, and greater database sizes to name a few of the compared benefits. It is up to you to decide whether that is enough to justify the associated costs. The Business Critical tier is targeted for the lift and shift of OLTP enterprise databases, which require high resilience to failures and require great responsiveness and availability. Hyperscale is, again, exactly what the name implies. Focused also on OLTP databases models with a need for fluid, high-frequency autoscaling. From an availability perspective, you may notice that Business Critical and Hyperscale have a range of possible values, 99.99% to 99.995% and 99.95% to 99.99%, respectively. To achieve the top end SLA availability, you must add additional replicas or zone redundancies.

The values in Table 5.5 may change over time, so it is always worth checking online for them. Here is a link that will have the current information:

```
docs.microsoft.com/en-us/azure/sql-database/
sql-database-service-tiers-general-purpose-business-critical
```

Notice that Table 5.5 calls out the fact that not all database types are available in each service pricing tier. Hyperscale tier is available only as a single database and will not run on a managed instance, and the database cannot be added to an elastic pool. You may have also noticed that the database size for both General Purpose and Business Critical have multiple values. The first row (5GB – 4TB) is for single database and elastic pool databases, while the second row is for the managed instances platform type.

It is also possible to configure the maximum data storage size, similar to the Hyperscale feature. For General Purpose, it scales between 1GB and 512GB. Finally, the backup capability supports the capturing of a copy of the database and storing it for a given time frame. The specifics of database backups will be provided in more detail later in the "Data Backup, Migration, and Retention" section.

Configuration and Security

A DBA specializes in the analysis and optimization of a database, performs the analysis, and executes actions typically required when running on-premise. If you are a DBA, then the configurations you can make to an Azure SQL database will seem restricted. This is because many of the optimizations and tuning exercises a DBA would do on a database are done automatically or via an approved automated recommendation from the platform. Keep in mind that if you run a SQL Server database on an Azure VM, you would need a DBA. This is a recommended approach when the database is highly specialized, customized, and fits into the confines of a legacy database. Legacy is synonymous with old and can mean that making changes to it would have a great impact; making changes to old things and breaking them is another one of those technical concepts that creep into real-world applications, one which perhaps must simply be dealt with until it retires, which will eventually happen in all scenarios.

Once you decide to break from the legacy constraint, take note that the Azure SQL analysis and optimizations are automated and the algorithms that create those optimization suggestions are written by those who wrote the logic for the DBMS itself. You cannot get a source of tips from a source much better than that. The intelligent performance suggestions you can get when running SQL server databases on Azure aren't the only kind of configuration you get or can make. In addition to configurations that optimize performance and availability, there are also some security-related features. The following are configuration and security concepts that will be discussed further.

- Scaling
- Achieving optimal availability
- Introducing backups
- Security and data encryption

The concept of scaling shouldn't be something new at this point, assuming you have read the previous chapters and previous sections in this book. Scaling simply means adding additional compute resource (CPU and memory) to your IT solution. Perhaps a new scaling area in the context of data stores is the storage itself, or adding hard disk capacity as the data stored on a physical drive requires more space. This may be a requirement in the compute context, true, but it is perhaps more relevant in the storage of data. Regardless, the ability to scale in all those areas is supported for all Azure SQL products, Azure SQL, SQL managed instances, and SQL virtual machines. Keep in mind that scaling from a database perspective is up or down and not out and in. There is one caveat, however. You can scale out the number of read-only replicas, but not ones that allow write operations. (Refer to Table 5.4 and Table 5.5 for tiers that support the scaling out or read-only instances.) You can probably relate that scaling out with read doesn't do much if the issue is with the inbound transmission of data to your database (usually a write process). In that case, the case where the inbound consumption, or perhaps better stated the absorption of data is the cause of compute consumption, the only option you have is scaling up. (Sure, performance tuning is an option, but it's assumed all that has been done already by a DBA or the intelligent performance optimization algorithms provided by the platform.)

In its simplest form, scaling a database up or down is performed by navigating to the Overview blade of the database and clicking the value to the right of the Pricing tier attribute. If you view the database details created in Exercise 5.2, you will see Basic, similar to Figure 5.20.

FIGURE 5.20 The pricing tier on the overview tab of an Azure SQL database

After clicking the Basic link, you will be able to scale to, for example, standard, which has 10 DTUs with 2GB of data storage as the default, and can be configured for up to 3000 DTUs and 250GB of storage. It is also possible to manually scale to the other tiers that use vCores. Moving to general purpose and hyperscale tier allows autoscaling. From a general-purpose autoscaling perspective, you would need to select the serverless, as illustrated in Figure 5.21. The scaling is handled by the setting provided via the max vCores, min vCores, and data max size scroll bar; the platform (aka Azure) handles the rest.

FIGURE 5.21 Setting the maximum and minimum for autoscaling

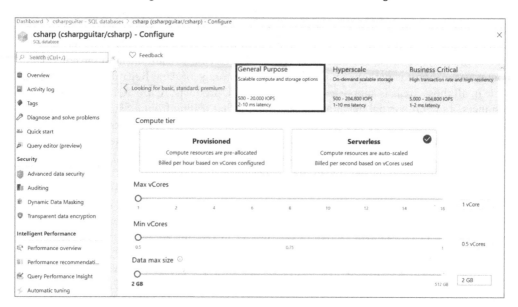

If you wanted to scale from a tier that targeted the DTU pricing model, it would be possible, but only manually. You could scale from basic to standard or premium and then, when demand required it, increase the number of allocated DTUs. In the same context, you could consider using an elastic pool that can target either DTUs or vCores and adding the database to the pool.

SQL Azure Database Server

A SQL database server can contain different tiers and pricing models. It is a virtual grouping of Azure SQL databases that is similar to the construct and purpose of a resource group.

It is an interesting area to pursue, and you should if it interests you. For the exam, the internals of all scaling options are not relevant. Just note that when creating an elastic pool the selection of tier is the primary consideration.

When you decide the pool is a PaaS that is constrained by the offerings within tiers—basic, standard, premium, general purpose, and business critical—hyperscale is noticeably absent. It was interesting to find that in the context of the basic DTU elastic pool pricing model that the minimum eDTUs was 50. This makes sense because it is expected that you would have multiple databases in the pool and would require more than the minimal required via the single database default value of five.

Although disaster recovery is covered in a bit more detail in Chapter 9, there are some interesting components about the built-in continuity features for Azure SQL databases. The type or model of built-in redundancies is bound to the selected pricing tier. The model, which is illustrated with Figure 5.22, is the one that exists for basic, standard, and general-purpose tiers.

FIGURE 5.22   Database availability architecture for basic, standard, and general-purpose pricing tiers

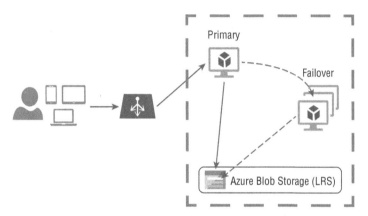

Notice that there is a primary database instance that is being accessed from an application. The data stored in the database is actually hosted, not on the compute resource. Rather, the data is stored as a blob in an Azure Blob Storage container. The data in the blob container is stored using the *locally redundant storage (LRS)* option. The details of that and other redundancy options are covered in detail later in this chapter, but in short, it means that the data is stored only within the given zone. If there is a failure on the primary compute VM, the traffic from the application can be routed to a failover instance, which will point to the data on the blob container. This is also the way an upgrade to the VM or to the database engine would happen. Prior to upgrading the VM, which is managing the processing of queries from your application, the traffic is routed to a new, already upgraded instance. This minimizes downtime and is what helps achieve the 99.99% SLA commitment. An impact you may encounter is one of latency if your solution loads data into memory or has large caching dependencies; that data resides on the VM and must get refreshed on the new VM if/when it gets replaced or patched. Additionally, if there is a data-center-wide issue, which rarely happens (but it has), your application will be down until the issue is resolved. Both of those possible impacts can be minimized or avoided altogether when running in premium or business-critical pricing tiers. Figure 5.23 illustrates that architecture in more detail.

FIGURE 5.23   Database availability architecture for premium and business critical

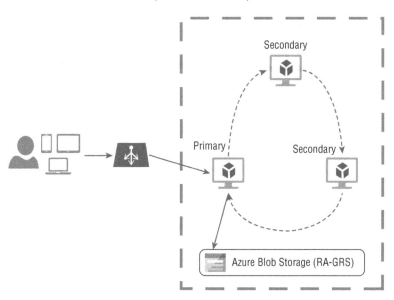

The main difference between the architecture shown in Figure 5.22 and that presented in Figure 5.23 is that the primary database has one or more standby replicas that exactly match the primary database. The cache and memory are loaded and updated with data required by the application. Additionally, the blob container that is hosting the database data runs with the *read-access geo-redundant-storage (RA-GRS)* option. With that option, your data will be readable in the event of a region-wide data center outage. The amazing part of this availability architecture is that it is all managed by the platform as part of the PaaS offering. It is simply there for you even if you never need it. Think about needing that data accessibility or benefiting from it without knowing it exists. There is a similar but much more sophisticated architecture available when you select the Hyperscale pricing tier. It utilizes many of the same concepts, like using an Azure Blob Storage container and secondary replicas as the premium and business-critical tiers do. Hyperscale adds RA-GRS storage options as well.

Azure SQL backups are created automatically and are stored in an Azure Blob storage container running in RA-GRS mode. Full backups are taken weekly, differential backups every 12 hours, and transaction logs backups occur every 5 – 10 minutes. Table 5.5 showed the retention period of a database backup can be between 7 and 35 days, whatever you configured. Once the existing database backup exceeds the age, it will be deleted. This reduces costs because you are charged for the storage of the backups. That cost can be large if your database is large or you forget to enter a threshold and everything is backed up and stored forever—until you get the bill. If you need to keep database backups for more than the maximum of 35 days, use the *long-term retention (LTR)* offering. LTR allows the storage of database backups for up to 10 years. There will be more about data backups later in this chapter.

The security chapter introduced topics such as vulnerability assessments and threat detection. When you click the *Advanced Data Security (ADS)* link on the SQL Database Overview blade in the Azure Portal, Azure provides information about those two security concepts. You can also access data discovery and classification information. The data discovery and classification option provides insights into the confidentiality level of the data stored on tables, rows, and columns, which is important for GDPR compliance. Additionally, it will show who is accessing that data and how often, which of course is important so that you are certain you have control over who or what has access to the data.

A vulnerability assessment scans your database and generates a report that highlights any known security or compliance issues. A vulnerability assessment might find that you have not classified the sensitivity/confidentiality of the data columns stored in your database. It is correct to assume that the Azure SQL database cannot know the meaning of your data, and therefore you must manually classify it. If that classification is not present, then you will get notified and receive a message stating its recommendation. The scan also checks for roles and identities that have access to the database. If for example, some roles and identities are not being used, the assessment can recommend changes to or removal of access. Lastly, threat detection works in a similar way in which it worked with Azure Active Directory authentication discussed in Chapter 2. Where the platform monitors the database activities and through machine learning it is able to identify behaviors which appear to be malicious. For example, SQL injection attempts access from unusual locations or an access using an unexpected credential. If you have threat detection enabled, when you run the report, these kinds of events will be called out to give you visibility and some tips for you to take action on.

Also, previously in Chapter 2 we touched on the two concepts of data at rest and data in transit, which means, from a database perspective, that some or all of the data in the database is encrypted when not being used and remains encrypted until it is rendered on an authorized client machine. This would mean that even if your database gets copied, stolen, or accessed by a bad actor, the data will be encrypted, not being able to be deciphered, making it unusable. In the next section, you will perform an exercise that encrypts data on the database and then later, in Chapter 7, you will see some pseudo-code that will retrieve the data and decrypt it for an authenticated and authorized client consumer.

Migrating Data

Moving your database from an on-premise database to the Azure platform can be complicated depending on the following:

- The size of the database
- The data availability required during the move
- The targeted Azure SQL products

There are three Azure SQL products: Azure SQL, SQL managed instances, and SQL on virtual machines. One of the easiest methods for moving an on-premise database to Azure employs an SQL Server backup. These backups generally have a file extension of .BACPAC. Once you have created a backup of the database, you can upload that file to an Azure Blob Storage container. From there, you can import it into any of the three different product offerings. This method depends greatly on the size of the database and whether it is realistic to transfer terabytes or more of data across a network connection. It might work, but it may not due to transient or network latency problems. Tools like Azure Storage Explorer or AzCopy are your best bet if you want to take that route.

If you do have a large database that you want migrated to an Azure database, consider a service called Import/Export. You can read about it here:

`azure.microsoft.com/en-us/services/storage/import-export/`

This service allows you to send actual physical, tape backups, or hard drives that contain your database to Microsoft. Microsoft then makes them available for importing into the DBMS. You also can use Azure Database Migration Services (DMS) to move data from an on-premise to a SQL managed instance. That method is more tolerant of databases that must remain available during the migration. Using the Import/Export option takes significantly longer and requires much more manual effort. The manual effort involves disk preparation and the application of transaction logs. Transaction logs capture data changes between the time you took the backup and when the database on Azure becomes the primary source of record. You would need to apply those changes to get the DB on Azure current.

Another option to move between two SQL Server databases is *SQL Server Integration Services (SSIS)*. The target in this scenario benefits the SQL virtual machine platform. See Table 5.6, which summarizes the contents of these methods in a more visual form. It is possible to use numerous approaches for migrations from on-premise to Azure; however, the following are the preferred approaches.

TABLE 5.6 Migration Options per Azure SQL Platform Type

	Azure SQL	SQL Managed Instance	SQL VM
BACPAC	✓	✓	✓
Import/Export	×	×	✓
ADMS	×	✓	×
SSIS	×	×	✓

Complete the following Exercise 5.3 where you will import a database using a `.BACPAC` file and then encrypt it using the key stored in the Azure Key Vault you created earlier in Exercise 2.9.

Creating an Azure SQL DB

1. Download a database backup by clicking the Download button located at this location:

   `github.com/benperk/ASA/blob/master/Chapter05/Ch05Ex03/guitar`
   `.bacpac`

2. Log in to the Azure Portal at `portal.azure.com`, enter **Storage Accounts** in the search box at the top middle of the page, click Enter, select the Storage Account that you created in Exercise 5.1 (for example, `csharpguitar`), and click Containers (recall from Figure 5.11). Click the + Container button on the Containers blade, enter a Name (for example, `guitar`), select Blob from the Public access level from the drop-down, and then click the OK button.

3. Click the container that you just created then click the Upload menu item at the top of the Overview blade. Upload the `.BACPAC` which you downloaded in step 1.

4. Navigate to the SQL database server you created in Exercise 5.2 (for example, `csharpguitar`). Click the Import database menu item on the SQL database server Overview blade. Select the subscription into which the database will be imported into then select the Storage that contains the `.BACPAC` you created in the previous step. You should see something similar to Figure 5.24. Click the select button.

FIGURE 5.24 Selecting a SQL database backup from an Azure Blob container

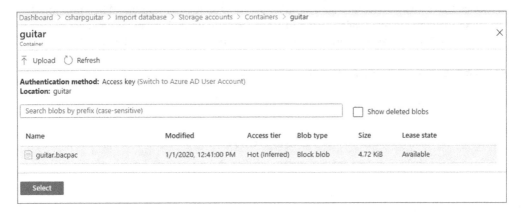

5. Change the pricing tier to Basic, and provide a Server admin login ID and the password which you used in Exercise 5.2. Click the OK button.

EXERCISE 5.3 *(continued)*

6. The import will take some minutes. Once that's complete, click the Azure SQL database you just imported. You will see the list of databases bound to the SQL database server on the SQL database server Overview blade, something similar to Figure 5.25.

FIGURE 5.25   A list of SQL databases bound to a given SQL database server

7. Click the Set Server Firewall menu item located at the top Azure SQL database Overview blade. Click the + Add Client IP menu item and then click Save.

8. Download and install SQL Server Management Studio (SSMS Version 18.4) from this location: aka.ms/ssmsfullsetup.

9. Once that's installed, open Microsoft SQL Server Management Studio. When prompted, enter the connection details, similar to Figure 5.26, and the SQL server database name. The user ID and password are the ones that you created in Exercise 5.2 step 2.

FIGURE 5.26   Connecting to a SQL Server database using SSMS

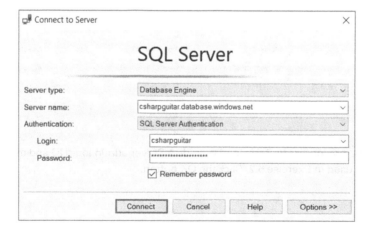

10. In the Object Explorer panel, expand Databases then expand `guitar`. Expand Tables and right-click the dbo.`MODELS` table. Now click Select Top 1000 Rows. Verify that the output resembles that shown in Figure 5.27.

FIGURE 5.27   The data content of the MODELS table

	GUITAR_ID	MODEL_ID	MODEL
1	1	1	Stratocaster
2	1	2	Telecaster
3	1	3	Jazzmaster
4	2	1	Les Paul Custom
5	2	2	Les Paul Standard
6	2	3	Explorer
7	2	4	Flying V

⊞ Results   ▦ Messages

11. In the Object Explorer pane, expand Security and then Always Encrypted Keys. Right-click Column Master Keys and select New Column Master Key. Enter a name for the key (for example, `csharpguitar-DAR`) and then select Azure Key Vault from the Key Store drop-down list. Click the Sign In button and select the subscription and Azure key vault that you created in Exercise 2.9. The configuration should be similar to Figure 5.28. Now click the OK button.

FIGURE 5.28   SSMS-created Column Master Key Configuration visualization

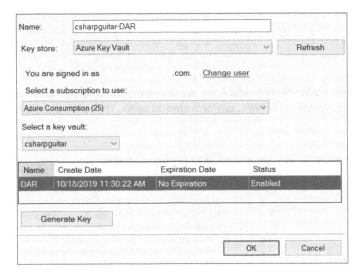

12. In the Object Explorer pane, directly below the Column Master Keys folder, right-click Column Encryption Keys and select New Column Encryption Key. Enter a name for the key (for example, DAR) and then select the master key created in the previous step; click OK. You must enable the following cryptographic operations key permissions on the Azure Key Vault for the operation to be successful: `wrapKey`, `unwrapKey`, `decrypt`, `verify`, and `sign`. Review Exercise 2.9, step 11, which explains how to view the existing key permissions.

13. Right-click the dbo.MODELS table, select Encrypt Columns, and then click the Next button. Select the check box to the left of the MODEL column and then select Deterministic from the Encryption Type drop-down list. If the Encryption Key is not defaulted to the one you created in the previous step, select it (for example, DAR); see Figure 5.29.

FIGURE 5.29   SSMS column selection configuration

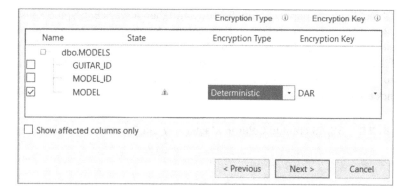

14. Click the Next button three times. After reviewing the Summary click the Finish button. Once the encryption completes, perform step 10 again. The result should be similar to Figure 5.30.

FIGURE 5.30   The encrypted content of the MODELS table

	GUITAR_ID	MODEL_ID	MODEL
1	1	1	0x01C140E221B3C785697FC521C1358DF67E01A1A75F3...
2	1	2	0x01B2EAC12C7ACA922B2F081EB79C5058E946EB5A7A...
3	1	3	0x011737E58AE39D2CDDFC098B749A1D90D907CCBFA...
4	2	1	0x017C85A1A3EF707D9931DE04AB2F2304F4D5056DD3...
5	2	2	0x0152141EEAC5BA1944755ED63D2E4FB70E757EFF80...
6	2	3	0x01A7125442AD9F75A090149BC4E450C2BD345F60ED...
7	2	4	0x01CC1C7944079DD831D89F54717182CE83C0974C82...

The process took quite some time to encrypt the data considering that there were only seven rows on the table. Keep this in mind; I would recommend not doing this procedure directly into production without some testing on nonproduction environments first. I recommend performing this action using PowerShell for large datasets versus the example using the `Set-SqlColumnEncryption` cmdlet. Additionally, the clients need to be modified to support the encryption. Doing this in production without modifying the clients, the consumers of the data, would cause some serious downtime. There will be impacts on the production database during this process such as not being able to perform write operations. Recall that step 7 is where you added your client IP address to the firewall settings white list by clicking the Set Server Firewall menu item; you did the same in Exercise 5.2 when you created your first Azure SQL database. Had this not been done, you would have not been able to connect. When using SSMS, as you did in step 9, a prompt reminds you to add your client IP address to the firewall rules. However, be aware that making a connection using a connection string results in an access denied exception. Your client IP address does not have access to the server; see Figure 3.34 for a previous example using `SQLCMD`.

Another interesting topic is one that was touched on in Figure 5.29 that showed the Deterministic encryption type. The other option is Randomized. The names themselves describe how the different types work. Deterministic encryption generates the same value for a given text each time. For example, the deterministic encrypted value of the word Telecaster will have the same encrypted value of `0x01B2EAC12C7ACA922B....` Randomized encryption would cause the encrypted value to be different each time. Randomized encryption is more secure, as you would imagine. Randomized results do not allow to search, group, join, and index those columns, while deterministic encryption does. It all comes down to how sensitive the data is. In this example, you would likely agree it is not so sensitive; however, identification numbers, birth dates, or any other personally identifiable dataset are. There is more about information concerning migration later in this chapter and in Chapter 8.

Monitoring

The state of a database changes frequently. Data is being inserted, updated, and deleted with great frequency. This can change the way that queries written to perform those actions behave. For example, a SQL query such as `SELECT * FROM MODELS` can work fine if there are just a few records; however, if it grows to thousands or hundreds of thousands of rows, then the code that receives the result set and processes it would perform slower because it has more work to do. Therefore, monitoring, tuning, and optimizing need to be applied to the database. (Such activities are usually performed by a DBA.) Azure SQL databases include built-in intelligence that provides automatic performance tuning and monitoring as well as something called *adaptive query processing*. Adaptive query processing would be helpful in the previous example where the query `SELECT * FROM MODELS` would be monitored and flagged if a query began to perform less than optimally. You can find a section in the portal on the navigation bar for the SQL database server named Intelligent Performance. The same group of capabilities can be found on the page for the specific Azure SQL database along with a few additional features named Performance Overview, Performance Recommendations, Query Performance Insight, and Automatic tuning. Having these features available at

Chapter 5 · Data and Storage

the database level makes the most sense because each database would have its own purpose and clients that access it, resulting in the database having different behaviors and needs.

A beneficial aspect of running your database on Azure SQL is that the built-in intelligence tuning, monitoring, alerting, and optimizing capabilities are written by the team who wrote SQL Server. These people know the internals of the SQL Server database engine better than anyone in the world. You get this capability as part of the PaaS offering and cannot be matched by any other product. The fact that the people who wrote the product also wrote the tools and features to automatically improve your database is mind-boggling and something that has great value. This is all for monitoring for now because there is not much on the Azure Solution Architect Expert exam that requires this knowledge; however, knowing this exists and some details about it is helpful in becoming a great Azure Solutions Architect Expert. There are more details on general monitoring concepts in Chapter 9.

Data Partitioning

Data partitioning from an Azure SQL perspective is best aligned with horizontal (aka sharding). Databases are typically constrained by the amount of data they can contain and the number of concurrent connections they can have. To break through those constraints, you can implement sharding. A basic example of sharding was illustrated previously in Figure 5.14. Using elastic pools, you can horizontally scale your SQL databases and partition them into shards that are distributed across multiple databases. The concept is rather straightforward; however, the implementation is not and is not discussed here as it is well outside the scope of this book. However, consider a database that contains all existing and future information about CSHARP and GUITARS. As that dataset grows, you realize that the size is going to breach the maximum allowed size (16TB), which requires you to take some action. You could split the database into two shards that are managed by something called a *global shard-map manager database*. The e-manager database would understand which shard the request is bound for. (It is referenced in the connection string and makes sure to direct the request to the correct database instance.) When running in an elastic pool, each shard is implemented as an individual Azure SQL database. The visual and physical recognition of the databases is abstracted away via the use of a value in the connection string. Just in case you are not clear on what a connection string is, it is the information required by a client to connect to the database. For example, the server name, the protocol, the port number, the user ID, and the password are all parameters that exist within the connection string, and in this data partitioning example, an additional parameter would be the shard key.

Service Endpoints

Both SQL managed instances and SQL VMs have private IP addresses. There is no global endpoint like the one you accessed in Exercise 5.3 (`csharpguitar.database.windows.net`). Although the global endpoint for an Azure SQL database is protected by a firewall, it is still pingable and discoverable. That is just the way it is designed and how it works. In addition to the firewall settings, there are two additional steps you can take to better secure an Azure SQL database. The first one is to turn off the Allow Azure services and resources to access this server setting. As shown in Figure 5.31, it is enabled by default on the Firewall Settings blade.

FIGURE 5.31   Allow Azure services and resources to access this server setting with a value of ON.

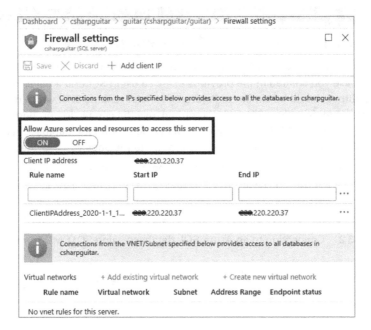

If you set the value to OFF and save, then only the IP addresses in the firewall IP address list will have access to the SQL Server database. Note that these rules apply to all databases on the SQL database server and not just a specific database.

The other security action you can take is to enable service endpoints. Service endpoints were introduced in Chapter 3; see Figure 3.36 for a refresher. You also created a service endpoint in Azure App Service in Exercise 3.2. Remember when you created the service endpoint in the VNet that you configured only the `Microsoft.Web` service, which allowed access from an Azure App Service. Then in Exercise 3.8 you configured an access restriction on the Azure App Service to use that service endpoint. Before the Azure App Service had the service endpoint configured, a `curl` to the global endpoint (for example, `csharpguitar` `.azurewebsites.net`) worked from any client with an internet connection. Once the service endpoint was configured for the Azure App Service, the endpoint was accessible only from a resource within the VNet. An HTTP status of 403 was rendered for all other clients attempting to connect. Note, that in both cases for an Azure Web App and an Azure SQL that the endpoint will always remain discoverable, but the endpoint will deny all access from any client other than resources within the VNet. To support an Azure SQL database service endpoint, you need to enable the `Microsoft.Sql` service and then configure the restriction on the Azure SQL database; this is the same process as with the Azure App Service. Complete Exercise 5.4, which walks you through the setup and testing of a service endpoint for an Azure SQL database.

EXERCISE 5.4

Creating a Service Endpoint for an Azure SQL Database

1. Open a cmd window on your local workstation and make a connection to the Azure SQL database you created in the previous exercise using SQLCMD similar to the following. The output should be similar to Figure 5.32. Refer to Table 3.11, which describes the requirements for installing SQLCMD. If required, use the connection properties you used when connecting via SSMS; see Figure 5.26. Replace * with the database server name and update <dbname>, <uid>, and <password> to the ones you provided.

```
sqlcmd -S *.database.windows.net -d <dbname> -U <uid> -P <password>
select database_id, is_read_only, compatibility_level from sys.databases
go
```

FIGURE 5.32   Connecting to an Azure SQL database using SQLCMD from an Azure VM

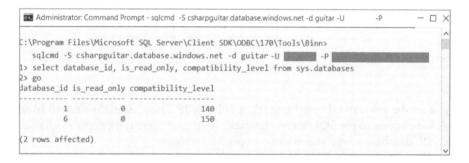

2. Make a remote connection (RDP) to an Azure VM you created earlier. Refer to Exercise 3.3 if you need to create a new one. Attempt the same SQLCMD connection to the Azure SQL database you created in the previous exercise using SQLCMD. The output will be similar to Figure 5.32.

Firewall Settings

For step 1 to work, your client IP must be added to the white-list for the Azure SQL database. For the connection in step 2 to work, the setting Allow Azure Services And Resources To Access This Server must be enabled, set to ON.

3. Navigate to the Azure VNet that you created in Exercise 3.2 (for example, CSHARPGUITAR-VNet-B) or create a new one. The VM in step 2 must be located in

this VNet. Select the Service Endpoints Navigation item and click the + Add menu item button. Then select `Microsoft.Sql` from the Service drop-down. Select the subnet in which the Azure VM you tested from in step 2 (for example, `csharp`) and then click the Add button. The result should resemble Figure 5.33.

FIGURE 5.33   Adding a service endpoint to a VNet and subnet

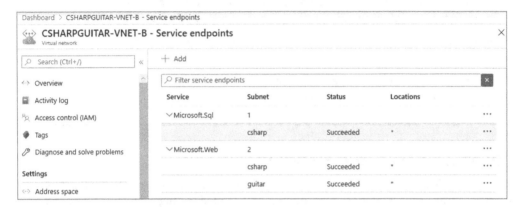

4. Navigate to the Azure SQL database created in the Exercise 5.3 and the one you connected to in steps 1 and 2 on the Overview blade. Select Set Server Firewall at the bottom of the Firewall Settings blade and click + Add Existing Virtual Network. Enter a name and the subscription the rule will reside in. Enter the virtual network (for example, `CSHARPGUITAR-VNet-B`) and subnet name/address prefix (for example, `csharp / 10.1.0.0/24`). The configuration should resemble Figure 5.34; click the OK button.

FIGURE 5.34   Enabling a service endpoint (VNet integration) to an Azure SQL database

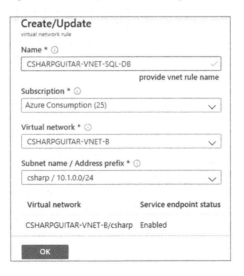

5. Wait some time, perhaps 5 or 10 minutes, and then perform both step 1 and step 2 again. The connection from your workstation should fail while the connection from the Azure VM will succeed. Keep in mind that most likely you have your workstation IP added to the firewall white-list. This will override the service endpoint. Additionally, you likely also have enabled Allow Azure Services And Resources To Access This Server. You need to turn that off; then you will have a secure and locked-down database.

There is more to service endpoints. Read this online documentation if you want to learn more:

```
docs.microsoft.com/en-us/azure/virtual-network/
virtual-network-service-endpoints-overview
```

SQL Managed Instance and SQL VM

Recall from Figure 5.17 in Exercise 5.2 that when you create an Azure SQL database, the selection of the product (aka deployment option) defaulted to Single database. In Exercise 5.2 you selected the SQL databases option, which offered the resource types of Single Database, Elastic Pool, and Database Server, which you could use to group numerous other databases together. It acts kind of like a resource group. The other two options are SQL managed instances and SQL virtual machines. These two SQL platform options are best for projects or solutions that you simply want to lift-and-shift (move to the Azure platform without making many if any changes). With SQL managed instances, you get full integration with VNet, which comes with a private IP. See Table 5.3 to review the differences between the types of Azure SQL database platforms.

Running SQL Server on an Azure VM is the closest you can come to running it on-premise. This is an IaaS offering that requires you to take all the responsibilities for the OS, but with that comes great flexibility. You can pretty much make any change or customization needed to run your database on the Azure platform. The benefit is that your database is now on the Azure network infrastructure, which is fully supported by Microsoft. SQL Server has been around for a long time. It was designed for relational IT solutions, although it can be used for more modern kinds of data store solutions, like the storing of unstructured data.

Let's now take a look at a database that is rapidly coming onto the Big Data and modern database store scene, Azure Cosmos DB.

Azure Cosmos DB

Chapter 1 contained a summary for both Azure SQL and Azure Cosmos DB. Review that chapter before continuing here as some of those details won't be discussed again. Certainly take a quick refresher look at Figure 1.5. I remember the world when Cosmos DB didn't exist, and I distinctly remember when I started hearing about this data store software. In hindsight, initially I assumed that this was simply an open source database IT professional that was new and exciting and simply coincided with the mindset of those in the open source world. At that time, the gap between black-box software and open source was wide, and the distance and approach toward the implementation and support of those technologies felt very foreign. After a while, it became apparent that new industries like machine learning, big data, and artificial intelligence are growing within that open source mindset. Programming languages like Python, Go, R, and Node.js are what most people in those new industries use. They also use Azure Cosmos DB to store their data, because at the time of incarnation of those industries, there really wasn't a database that was designed for storing documents, graphs, or key/value pairs; it was all relational. Although SQL Server can do a good job running those models, the support for those was built in later instead of being created and designed for those nonstructured data model scenarios from the start. It's not so much that one database is so much better than the other; it is simply that Cosmos DB was there, ready to go at the spark/beginning of the industry and is what took traction and got utilized. This isn't to say that there are some advantages for using Azure Cosmos DB when compared to some other DBMSs. Ease of implementation, extreme low latency, and global distribution are a few of the benefits you would realize when choosing this data store product, in addition to the alignment with the other companies and developers working in that industry.

Before proceeding further, create an Azure Cosmos DB by completing Exercise 5.5. This will give lots of opportunities for discussion points afterward. There will be more clarification on what is meant by ease of implementation, extreme low latency, and global distribution; they will become inherently obvious as you progress through this chapter.

EXERCISE 5.5

Creating an Azure Cosmos DB

1. Log in to the Azure Portal at `portal.azure.com` and click the menu button located in the top-left corner of the main page. Click + Create A Resource in the top-left area of the browser. Click Databases and then click Azure Cosmos DB.

2. Select the subscription and resource group into which you want to place the Azure Cosmos DB. Enter a unique account name (for example, csharpguitar), leave Core (SQL) as the API, select a location, click the Review + Create button, and click the Create button.

3. Once the deployment is complete, click the Go To Resource button and then click the Overview link in the navigation menu. Take note of the URI of your Azure Cosmos DB. Click the Keys link in the navigation menu and take note of the value for PRIMARY KEY. The primary key resembles a token.

4. Navigate to `github.com/benperk/ASA/tree/master/Chapter05/Ch05Ex05` and view the contents of `cosmos.py`. (This will be discussed later.)

5. Back on the Overview tab for the Azure Cosmos DB, click + Add Container and add a database ID (`csharpguitar-db`). Add a container ID (`csharpguitar-container`) and then add a partition key (`/Year`) and click the OK button.

6. On the Data Explorer blade, expand the database ID, expand the container ID, click Items, click the New Item link, and add the commented-out content that exists at the bottom of `csharp.py` file (i.e., the code behind #s; do not include the #s) located at the URL in step 4. Click the Save link add another Item using the contents of the `guitar.py` file. Figure 5.35 illustrates how the configuration should look.

FIGURE 5.35   Adding items to an Azure Cosmos DB container

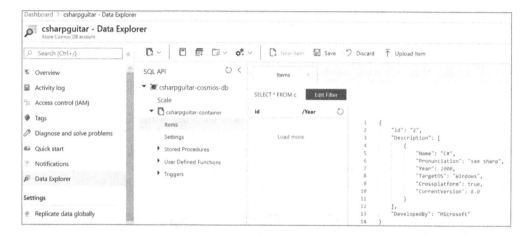

Setting up Visual Studio Code with Python and Cosmos

The code that was linked to in step 4 can also be used from Visual Studio Code to create the same database, container, partition key, and content that you just created manually in the Azure Portal. Getting Visual Studio Code and all supporting libraries is a rather complicated scenario. If you get stuck, start an issue on GitHub at that link.

7. Install Visual Studio Code from here, `code.visualstudio.com/Download` version 1.41.1 was used for this example, install Python from here: `www.python.org/downloads/` version 3.8.1 was used for this example. After download and installation, open a command prompt and enter the following command:

```
py -3 --version
```

Figure 5.36 illustrates the output.

FIGURE 5.36 Adding items to an Azure Cosmos DB container

8. Open Visual Studio Code and install the Python extension. Click View Extensions from the menu. Enter **Python** and install the extension. Select View Terminal and enter the following command:

```
mkdir csharpguitar
cd csharpguitar
code .
python -m venv .venv
pip install azure-cosmos
```

The Python extension and commands will be similar to Figure 5.37.

FIGURE 5.37 What the Visual Studio Code Python extension and environment setup looks like

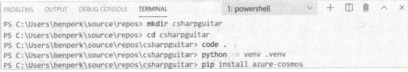

9. Create the files `cosmos.py`, `csharp.py`, and `guitar.py` using the code provided on GitHub (see step 4). In the `cosmos.py` file, change the endpoint and key to match your Azure Cosmos DB, which were called out in step 3. Then save the files using Ctrl+K+S (Save All). Execute the following command to create the database, container, partition key, and items:

```
python .\cosmos.py
```

Let's go over what just happened in Exercise 5.5. Let's also view some of the other Azure Cosmos DB concepts, such as the following:

- Azure Cosmos DB API models
- Databases, containers, items, and partition keys
- The cosmos.py code
- Azure Cosmos DB migration options
- Querying an Azure Cosmos DB
- Global replication concepts

Azure Cosmos DB API Models

In step 2 of Exercise 5.5, you may have noticed a list of Azure Cosmos DB APIs in the drop-down list. Table 5.7 lists those APIs and data model.

TABLE 5.7 Azure Cosmos DB APIs

API Type	Data Model	Container Item
Core (SQL)	Document database	Document
Azure Cosmos DB for MongoDB API	Document database	Document
Cassandra	Relations (Apache/CQL)	Row
Azure Table	Key/value pair	Item
Azure Cache for Redis	Key/value pair	Item
Gremlin	Graph database	Node or edge

When you tell someone that you have created an Azure Cosmos DB, there should be a follow-up statement or a question from that person. This is because, as you see in Table 5.7, behind the scenes an Azure Cosmos DB can be a document database or numerous other database types. For example, it accommodates relational databases that focus on apps designed for Apache Cassandra, which is queryable using SQL-like CQL. It could also contain a key/value pair data structure or a graph database. All of those capabilities sit behind the generic term of Azure Cosmos DB.

Azure Cache for Redis is also a key/value data store and will be covered in more detail later. However, now is perhaps a good place and time to introduce this product and compare it briefly to the Azure Cosmos DB Azure Table API data model. There are two primary differences between those two Azure products, the first being where the data is stored and the second being what happens when scaling happens. Azure Cache for Redis stores the data being referenced by the application into memory. When the application needs to access that data there is no I/O latency because the data is already present within the process. If the data is referenced from the Azure Table key/value store, then a connection to the server hosting the data and a connection to the data store itself is required to retrieve the data, which may be more latent. The benefit for the Azure Cosmos Table API is that when you scale out to multiple instances, your application continues to be bound to a single instance of your data. However, from an Azure Cache for Redis, if a new instance of your application is scaled into the server farm, then the data is retrieved from the data source and loaded into memory. If you have five instances of your application on five VMs, then five copies of the data are loaded into memory. Multiple copies of your data can consume lots of memory, which carries additional costs, but if performance is the driving factor, then you have at least two products that provide you with the feature to meet that given requirement.

Databases, Containers, Items, and Partition Keys

Recall from Chapter 1's Figure 1.5 where the relationships between a database, container, and items were visualized. An Azure Cosmos DB Core (SQL) database is similar in purpose to an Azure SQL database in that it acts as a grouping of the actual data stores that contain data. One caveat is that all databases within the Azure Cosmos DB account must be for the same API. (The APIs were provided in Table 5.7.) You cannot have a Core (SQL) database and an Azure Table in the same Azure Cosmos DB account. This makes sense and has the same behavior as exists when compared to Azure SQL. In the Azure SQL case, there is only one kind of database, SQL Server. Therefore, you can have only that one kind of database within the Azure SQL database grouping. As shown in Figure 5.38, you can, however, have multiple databases with multiple containers within them.

You can also use Azure CLI to list the Azure Cosmos DBs for a given resource group and account using these commands:

```
az cosmosdb sql database list -a $accountName -g $resourceGroupName
az cosmosdb sql container list -a $accountName -g $resourceGroupName \
   -d $databaseName
```

FIGURE 5.38   Using the Data Explorer in the Azure portal to view Azure Cosmos DB and containers

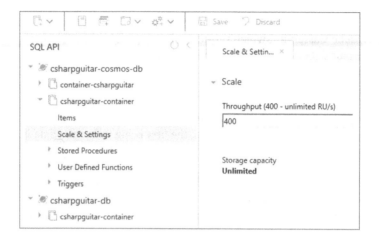

From an architectural context, the container is the most important element in this group. It's most important because it is the location where scaling occurs and the SLA is applied. You can see in Figure 5.38 that the scale settings are managed at a level under the container name. You will also see on the Overview blade of the Azure Cosmos DB account, as shown in Figure 5.39, that the number of RU/s are applied to the container and not to the database or account. You might be asking yourself about the term RU. A *request unit (RU)* is the unit of throughput that identifies the amount of available compute resources available to the container (i.e., CPU, memory, and IOPS). You might remember DTUs from the previous section; it is a similar unit of measure. Like the DTU, an RU is what the cost of the product is; the more you need the more it costs.

FIGURE 5.39   Different scale settings per Azure Cosmos DB container

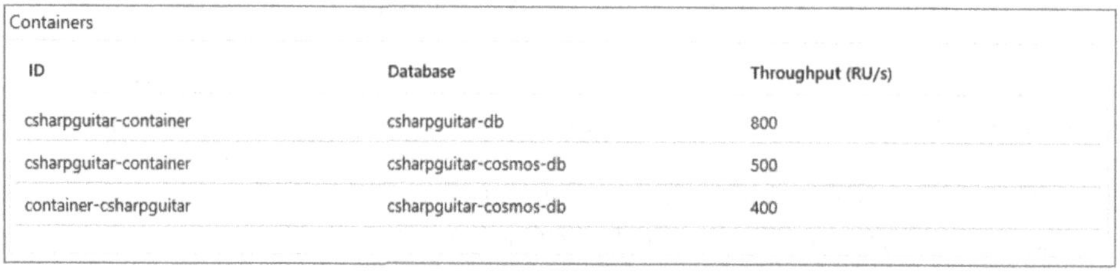

Containers		
ID	Database	Throughput (RU/s)
csharpguitar-container	csharpguitar-db	800
csharpguitar-container	csharpguitar-cosmos-db	500
container-csharpguitar	csharpguitar-cosmos-db	400

To calculate the cost, know that the cost is based on the RUs utilized per hour, plus the amount of storage you consume. It is important to understand that when horizontal scaling happens, the number of RUs are not increased; rather, you receive a new instance of that container in another geographical location. However, if you know that you need 900

RUs between the hours of 8 a.m. and 5 p.m., then one idea is to create an Azure Function that can increase and decrease the number of RUs as required. Basically, because you can update the throughput using Azure CLI and Azure Functions supports that language you can use this command from an Azure Function to run and update the value, which is a simulated scale up and scale down. Have an Azure Function named `scaleUpCosmos` that runs at 8 a.m. that updates the number of RUs to 900. Have another Function named `scaleDownCosmos` that runs at 5 p.m. that sets the value to the minimum your application requires; the minimum is 10 RUs.

```
az cosmosdb sql container throughput update -a $accountName -g \
    $resourceGroupName -d $databaseName -n $containerName --throughput 900
```

The container is also the place where you add things such as stored procedures, *user-defined functions (UDF)*, and triggers. You can see those listed in Figure 5.38. At the beginning of the discussion about containers, I called out the container as the most important element from an architectural perspective. From an Azure Cosmos DB perspective, you would likely consider the data that is stored in the container and database as the most important. The data is stored as Items, and by clicking Items after accessing the database and container on the Data Explorer blade, it executes a `SELECT * FROM c` and lists the ID and the partition key. The item can be represented in numerous forms depending on the selected API. In this case, where Core (SQL) is used, the item is considered a document, which is appropriate as we stored a JSON document in it and refer to this as a *document database*. However, had you used another API, then an item could be any of those shown previously in table 5.7, for example a row, node, or edge. These are important as you begin performing CRUD operations against the data store as they define the types you need to create in the code performing those actions. They will become intuitively obvious as you get more aligned with a specific Azure Cosmos DB API.

Finally, let's talk about the partition key. With each data storage offering, there has been some words about partitioning, and a common key word has been *sharding*, where better performance is achieved based on some kind of logical splitting of data across compute instances. The same goes for an Azure Cosmos DB and is where the partition key comes into the spotlight. In the example used in Exercise 5.5 where `/Year` is set as the partition key, the result would be that partitioning would happen for matching years and be split across multiple servers based on that value. The partitioning is performed automatically by the product, so you need not worry too much about the internals. If you, however, consider reading further about this topic, visit docs.microsoft.com/en-us/azure/cosmos-db/partition-data, which discusses details about logical partitions, which was just discussed, and another type of partitioning called *physical partitions*.

A Walk Through the Cosmos.py Code

Like I mentioned already, the industry in which you are working has an apparent influence on the IDE and language the applications get written in. Although C# is fully compliant and functional with an Azure Cosmos DB and you could use Visual Studio Community edition to create the same program, when I work with individuals who have real-world, in-production applications that use an Azure Cosmos DB, there is a heavy presence of open source languages like Python, Java, Node.js, and Xamarin. A coder with a background using Microsoft technologies would likely use Visual Studio Code. Curious ones would begin moving toward learning and using those languages, which will increase the chances of getting a job as a developer since those are the languages often used with programs supporting machine learning, Big Data, and artificial intelligence industries. Although the initial configuration of Visual Studio Code was somewhat of a challenge, it is one that is achievable after some effort. After that, the coding and testing of a Python application is simple. The first line of code in `cosmos.py` imports the `azure.cosmos` library, which you installed in Exercise 5.5. Next it imports the JSON documents that will be stored in the database once it has been created. The code then creates a client using the endpoint and key; creates the database, the container, and the partition key; and adds two items. Finally, the database is queried using the document IDs. That is straightforward and worked with minimal effort.

When comparing this to a C# project that uses Entity Framework or ADO.NET, it is simple to get the database and application up and running using Python and an Azure Cosmos DB. The approach comes down to how fast the implementation of your project needs to be. The data you store in a document database such as `csharp.py` and `guitar.py` are unrelated; however, they are stored in the same database. Had you done the same using C# and an RDBMS, the timeframe would have been likely some hours if not days longer. In many scenarios, where you need a quick solution, there is a common principle: capture the data and store it. We will figure out what to do with it later, but we don't want to lose any data. That principle fits and aligns in the ML, Big Data, and AI industries, which require a highly skilled data specialist to then make sense of the data.

Azure Cosmos DB Migration Options

If you are moving your data from another cloud hosting provider or from an on-premise, in-house data source, there are numerous tools that help you achieve this. As you can imagine, the tools you choose depend on the type of API site behind the Azure Cosmos DB. The following is a complete document that describes this process:

> `docs.microsoft.com/en-us/azure/cosmos-db/import-data`

It breaks down the required steps based on the API type. Additionally, if you simply have a directory full of JSON documents and you want to load them into a document database so that you can query them, then the *Document DB Data Migration Tool* will do this for you. The tool is an open source project hosted on GitHub.

Querying an Azure Cosmos DB

Recall from the `cosmos.py` file created in the Exercise 5.5 file that there exists a query like this: `SELECT * FROM c WHERE c.id IN ('1', '2')`. This is very much like a typical SQL command you would run when querying a relational database. In the Azure Portal, you will find a feature called Data Explorer in the navigation menu on the Azure Cosmos DB Overview blade. Expand the database you created in Exercise 5.5, expand the container, and a menu item named New SQL Query opens. Clicking that item opens a window that allows you to test SQL queries on the data items that exist in the container. You should see something similar to Figure 5.40.

FIGURE 5.40   Using the Data Explorer in the Azure Portal for querying an Azure Cosmos DB Core (SQL) database

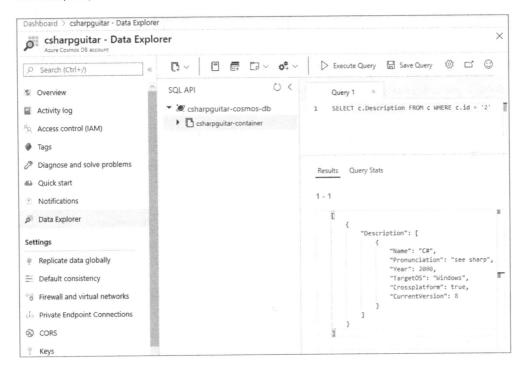

Once you enter a query, click the Execute Query link to execute it. This is a great place to test the queries that you will place into your application later.

Global Replication Concepts

The reasons for getting the data or compute as close to the clients or customers that consume them have been mentioned a few times already. Also, Azure products such as a content delivery network (CDN) or the cloning of application environments in different Azure regions and using Azure Traffic Manager (ATM) to route requests to the closest region to the location where the request came from should be known to you. One of the great features of the Azure Cosmos DB product is its ability to support the global replication of the data stored within it. With this feature comes some relatively complicated concepts like regional and global data distribution, data concurrency, and data consistency. When you create an Azure Cosmos DB, by default you have a single instance of the data source in the region in which you chose to create it in. If you navigate to the Azure Cosmos DB Overview blade, you will see a menu item named Enable georedundancy. If you recall from Chapter 3 where you learned about a geography, there was some discussion about each region having a sister region on the same continent. Having these pairs of regions, for example, West Europe (AM2) and North Europe (DB3) and South Central US (SN1) and North Central US (CH1), helps provide some extra redundancies without having to cross international boundaries. This is helpful if your data had regulatory or compliance issues requiring such data confinement. When you enable geo-redundancy for the Azure Cosmos DB, the databases existing in the Azure Cosmos DB account are automatically replicated to their prospective geo-paired regions. As you might expect, when you enable global replication, the databases in the Azure Cosmos DB account can be replicated anyplace in the world where Azure exists. To enable global replication, navigate to the Azure Cosmos DB account and select the Replicate Data Globally Navigation item, as shown in Figure 5.41.

FIGURE 5.41 How to enable Azure Cosmos DB global replication from the Azure Portal

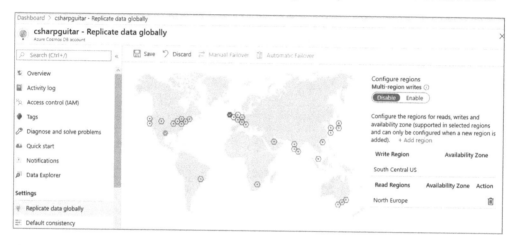

You will notice that the only regions selected are South Central US and North Europe; however, any or all of the shown regions can be selected. By doing that, your databases would be replicated to that location and be much closer to customers in that part of the world. Recognize that for each instance you replicate the cost, you also increase by a factor of 1; if you have three instances, then the cost would be three times the amount as when running on a single instance. This is an important fact not only from a database or backend perspective but also from the frontend. Will you run your frontends from a single location and have all your backends nearer to customer or clients? That doesn't make a lot of sense. The most logical design is to have not only the backend database close to those who need it, but you also need the frontends as well. This increases the cost even more, but you need to make decisions. Speed costs money, and you need to determine if the reduction in latency is worth that cost and if it is something those accessing your application demand. That is the architecture design you must decide on, but there is another concept that needs understanding, design, and implementation. That is, you need to decide how and when the data will be replicated between the different instances. This comes down to the concepts of data concurrency and consistency.

See in Figure 5.41 that there is a button for enabling/disabling multi-region writes. Say you leave the default value of Disable and have only the original instance of your Azure Cosmos DB to be writable. This means that since the Azure Cosmos DB was created in North Central US, all writes would be performed there and then replicated to the instance in North Europe, which is read-only. As you might imagine, the replication of that data may take a second or less or more. This can be a big issue if you have a high transaction database where the consistency of data is crucial. On the other hand, perhaps the speed at which your data is inserted is more important than having all data replicated globally. If that is the case, then enabling the multi-region writes makes sense, because having a real-time application that has to write data to a database across the Atlantic Ocean wouldn't be the most optimal solution. It is totally dependent on what your application does and requires; i.e., what level of concurrency do you require? But what happens if the same data column on the same row in the same database is updated before it can be replicated? Well, this is where consistency comes in.

In Figure 5.41, you see the navigation item Default Consistency. Clicking it opens a blade that shows the five different levels of consistency that Azure Cosmos DB provides; the default is Session. The others are Strong, Bound Staleness, Consistent Prefix, and Eventual. You can read more about those specifics here:

`docs.microsoft.com/en-us/azure/cosmos-db/consistency-levels`

Those different consistency levels provide you with many options for finding the right data integrity and performance that matches those using your application whether it be locally, regionally, or globally. Finally, here is a colorful and active group that discusses Cosmos DB concepts in a very friendly and active manner: `https://azurecosmosdb .github.io/CosmicNotes`. Finish up this section by answering the following question:

If you have an on-premise relational database designed for OLTP scenarios, which database would you choose for a lift and shift to Azure?

Azure SQL single database

Core (SQL) Azure Cosmos DB

Azure SQL managed instance

Azure Table Azure Cosmos DB

Answer: Azure SQL managed instance

Although the Azure SQL single database option has a high probability of meeting your requirements, there are some features that are not present with that offering (discussed earlier) that may negatively impact the deployment. Both answers that include Azure Cosmos DB should have immediately been weeded out as possible answers. The Azure SQL managed instance is the target for OLTP and relational database migrations.

Other Azure Data Stores

Azure SQL and Azure Cosmos DB are by far the most commonly provisioned data stores on Azure and if there are any questions on the Azure Solution Architect Expert exam, they would be about those two. But to become the best Azure Solution Architect Expert possible, you should know some about other data store offerings on Azure.

Table Storage

If you return to Figure 5.11, you will see that Azure Table Storage is contained within an Azure Storage account, just like Azure Files, Queues, and Blob containers. In short, an Azure Table is a place where you can store data in a nonstructured way based on key/value pairs. The ability to store petabytes of data and manage the scaling are the major benefits available for this offering. Both the compute and storage requirements are managed by the Azure platform. When creating the storage account, you decide which redundancy option is required, for example, LRS, ZRS, GRS, and so forth, which is helpful for availability and DR scenarios.

Table Storage is based on two fundamental concepts, the partition key and the row key. Once the table itself is created, either using the portal or, for example, Azure PowerShell, you can configure both of them. After importing the `AzTable` module using `Import-Module AzTable`, when you add data to the table, both the partition key and row key are required. An Azure PowerShell command similar to the following would insert a row into the Azure Table:

```
Add-AzTableRow -table $tableName -partitionKey $pk -rowKey ("FEN1") /
          -property @{"MODEL"="TELECASTER";"LOCATION"="USA"}
```

Figure 5.42 provides a visualization of the Azure table partitioning concept. You will notice the Azure Storage account with two tables. The table can have multiple partition keys that then define the physical partitions created on the disk. This is similar to the sharding technique discussed in the context of numerous other data store products up to now. However, in the case of Azure Tables, the partitioning is done for you, by the platform, so long as you add the data to the table in the appropriate form, i.e., table, partition key, row key, data.

FIGURE 5.42   Azure Table storage partitioning

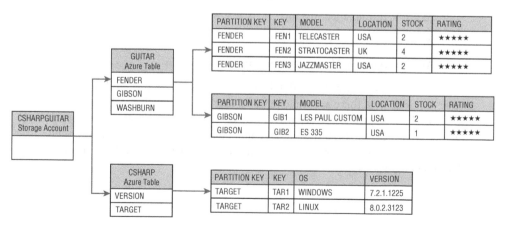

One additional fact to call out here is the relationship between Azure Table storage and the Azure Cosmos DB Azure Table API. The Azure Cosmos DB Azure Table API backend is an Azure Table; however, each has a different use case and purpose. You must map your application's requirements. A big one that was called out specifically in the previous section is the ease and scale that comes with an Azure Cosmos DB. Scaling out globally with an Azure Cosmos DB is quick, simple, and very effective, especially when it comes to getting the data close to those who will access it. Azure Tables does not come with such a feature. You are bound to a single region with an optional secondary read-only instance in that same region. Another is that an Azure Table is optimized for storage versus an Azure Cosmos DB. The Azure Table API is optimized for throughput. So, it is a balance or a decision that is based on your application where you decided if you need greater storage optimization or greater throughput. An Azure Table, for example, has a limit or 20,000 operations per second. The Azure Cosmos Table API can support 10,000,000 per second; there is no documented upper limit. Indexing, latency, and querying capabilities also differ, but the Azure Cosmos DB Table API generally performs better in each of those scenarios. Keep in mind, though, that the cost is more for an Azure Cosmos DB than for Azure Table storage, which is in many cases the most important constraint.

Azure Cache for Redis

Azure Cache for Redis is a very development- or coding-oriented product. It falls into the data store category, however. Even though the data is stored in a solid state, it is loaded from that state into a process (an `.exe`) so the data is accessible in memory at the time the process is invoked. The point being, this isn't really an architecture-like product. Still, you should know that, so if it shows up in some exam question, you have a context for it. You know some details about it if you ever get asked about it by your manager or a customer.

There is an open-source product named Redis at `https://redis.io/` and it is what Azure cache for Redis is based upon. There are five Azure Cache for patterns and three SKU offerings. Let's start with the patterns.

- Cache aside
- Content caching
- User session caching
- Message queuing
- Distributing transaction

The cache aside pattern has to do with the size of the data that you plan on storing in memory. Recognize the many options you have when considering memory-optimized IaaS offerings, the smaller number of offerings with PaaS, and the minimal memory offerings when it comes to FaaS. It all comes down to the fact that a data store can be large, and it isn't prudent to load the entire database into memory. Instead, this model loads data into memory when requested by a consumer of that data. The first time will result in a query to the source; however, the next and all future requests for that same data will come from memory and be much less latent.

Content caching has more to do with the dynamic nature of files. Unlike `.html` files that are static, do not change, and can be loaded and delivered from memory, dynamic files are created per request based on attributes typically sent with an HTTP POST or existing in headers to a web server. However, some of a page that is dynamically generated may not change, perhaps menus, page headers, page footers, or toolbars. Those can be cached and the dynamically generated web responses can be cached using this pattern. The user session caching can be used in a shopping cart scenario. Here you need to store what a customer wants to buy into memory and allow it to remain until the purchase button is selected. Instead of storing this on a data store, store it in memory. There are numerous options for this such as the `System.Web.HttpContext.Session` object in C#.

The message queuing feature in Azure Redis Cache, like user session caching, has numerous options. The purpose of this option is to store, for example, an order that would respond very fast and then actually process the order offline. Performing an `INSERT` into a data store on disk will experience more latency than a write into memory or a technology designed for handling such requirements. (More about messaging in the next chapter.) Just take this pattern as one that makes sure orders that are placed do not fail based on overutilization of a real-time backend OLTP data store.

The final pattern has to do with the concept of an ACID operation, as discussed earlier. Distributing transactions means that you can perform CRUD operations that are dependent on the successful completion of numerous commands. All will be rolled back if one of them fails.

The three Azure Cache for Redis SKU offerings are basic, standard, and premium. Basic does not come with an SLA and is therefore out of the question for any production or enterprise IT solution. Basic is intended for use during development and testing project phases. Standard tier runs on multiple instances (i.e., nodes), which provides redundancy and failover capabilities; the SLA for standard tier is 99.9%. The most obvious benefit when selecting premium is that latency and throughput are much better when compared to standard. This is because premium is run on a compute SKU with higher specifications. Expect a more responsive product when running in premium mode for Azure Cache for Redis.

The data partitioning strategy for Azure Cache for Redis is the same as that for an Azure Table, which is also the basis for the Azure Cosmos DB Table API. Sharding is the approach for all three of those products and can be visualized using Figure 5.42 provided earlier. You might be asking yourself in what scenario you would use Azure cache for Redis versus an Azure Table or an Azure Cosmos DB Table API. The latter has already been explained. However, Azure Cache for Redis comes with a framework that can be consumed within your application code, meaning Azure cache for Redis can be implemented into your application faster than if you chose an Azure Table for achieving the same caching behavior.

Azure Database for MySQL

When I reflect back to the time I had the opportunity to begin a new project from scratch or even when I was coding just for fun and needed a data storage solution, my go-to options were SQL Server and Oracle. Both of those took some serious amount of effort, configuration, and skill to get installed and accessible. Azure Database for MySQL is a relational database, which is helpful for the age of rapid development. This also falls into the area of those who prefer the open source community platforms, communities, and products. It is a fully functional enterprise-ready RDBMS that includes scalability, monitoring, alerts, high-level SLA at 99.99%, and the support for sophisticated security services.

Azure's Azure Database for MySQL solution is considered a database as a service (DaaS/DBaaS) offering that runs on PaaS. This means that scaling out and up based on consumption is supported, making it a cost-effective data store product. There is also MySQL on Azure VMs that run in the IaaS cloud service model. When running in IaaS, there are greater fixed costs but also greater flexibility when compared to running MySQL on PaaS. Choosing a database to store one of the most important resources in your IT solution shouldn't be taken lightly. Azure Database for MySQL is a dependable option and is conceptually bound to the open source and community-driven company and development resources. If the open source mentality or approach is the culture in which your company operates within, consider this data store as the solution for a relational database.

On a side note, remember in Exercise 5.4 where you created a service endpoint for an Azure SQL database. When you did that, the service you selected was `Microsoft.Sql`; review Figure 5.33 if you need a refresher. There is neither a service for MySQL nor PostgreSQL; however, when you select `Microsoft.Sql`, it also gives both of those data stores the ability to configure service endpoints and VNets.

Azure Database for PostgreSQL

This database offering is similar to the MySQL product you just read about. It is an open source relational database built upon the PostgreSQL database engine, which you can read about at `www.postgresql.org`. This Azure product offering comes in two different alternatives: Single Server and Hyperscale (Citus). Running in single-server mode you have three options: basic, memory optimized, and general purpose. Those last two should ring a bell from Chapter 4, where Azure VMs that are available based on the specific expected workload of the application, memory, or CPU bound, and in this case the database were covered. While basic is meant for testing and development phases, it is possible to scale or migrate from basic to larger tiers as your project progresses. You get the whole portfolio of expected features, such as high availability, dynamic scaling, monitoring, high-level security capabilities, and backup. All of those features make this a valid option for running your mission-critical application.

Hyperscale (Citus) is what has made PostgreSQL a popular data store. By the name alone, you should get some idea about what this product is capable of. You should have a good idea about what sharding is now and some general knowledge about how it works by placing data into smaller subsets sometimes on different nodes, which makes querying faster. The PostgreSQL database takes it to another level by placing those shards into different table-like structures by having the ability to have a shard running on a completely independent machine. The database engine can run queries in parallel across these machines, which results in fast responsiveness on large datasets.

Oracle and Marketplace Options

There are many data store products available on Azure, many more than Azure SQL, Azure Cosmos DB, MySQL, and PostgreSQL. Azure provides the opportunity for third-party partners to place prebuilt VMs or installable products from within the portal using a feature called Marketplace. Performing a search there, you would find Oracle, CouchDB, SQLite, MongoDB, and many other data store options. If you do not find a prebuilt or preconfigured VM for the database that you desire, you can build an Azure VM, and if you have a license or follow the required open source guidelines, you can make it work and run that workload on Azure.

Azure Storage

When you think of a data store solution, you typically think of data in a text form that is placed into a table consisting of rows and columns. Realize that the data in that table actually exists in a physical file written to a hard drive or a storage account of some kind. Not only do the files that store your data need a place to exist, but videos, pictures, and documents can be of significant size and of critical importance. As you would imagine, there are numerous considerations to review when determining the product you will use for storing your data on Azure. Concepts such as security, performance, scalability, and redundancy all need some thought.

Consider your data storage requirement from a security perspective asking questions like, does the data need to be encrypted, does the data need to be encrypted while transferred, should it be encrypted at rest, and how secure is accessing the data once migrated to the Azure platform? After reviewing each of the Azure Storage product capabilities and having your own requirements identified, deciding which product provides the requirements of your data security strategy can then be chosen. Security is a big deal as you know already from reading Chapter 2, but there may be some specific compliance requirements from customers, for example, using AES 256-bit encryption or the support of RSA key with a size of 2048. Understanding your requirements and which product supports them is your responsibility, but tips have been given in this book previously, with more to come.

From a performance and scalability perspective, if your data files are stored on HDD drives instead of SSD, would that matter? From a performance perspective, it would. SSD are known to have a much better throughput and IOPS than HHD. Does your storage solution need to handle more than 20,000 requests per second? How many requests per second does your application require? How about the growth of the data that your application or customers generate and that needs to be stored? Does it only grow, or does it expand and contract over a given timeframe? In reality, the amount of storage at your disposal is great, perhaps up to two petabytes; however, there are different limits per region, which makes this an important preliminary question to ask and answer.

Finally, let's talk about data redundancy and concurrency. In the later section "Zone Replication," you will finally get the details about LRS, ZRS, GRS, and the like. Simply put, these are the options you have for making sure you neither lose data nor lose access to it if there is an outage in a given region or zone. Concurrency needs thought. How stringent do you want to be on reading and writing data? Writing, updating, and reading data on hyperscale data storage products might encounter experiences where a row or file is in the process of being written to by different clients at the same time. How do you handle such a scenario? Azure Storage accounts support optimistic or pessimistic concurrency. Optimistic concurrency would not write the second update. With pessimistic concurrency, a lock is placed on the object being written to and remains until the write completes. Any other client must wait until the lock is released before performing the work. In an optimistic scenario, the result is fast; the update would fail. Your application logic would need to handle that and retry. Pessimistic concurrency is slower but should complete after some seconds, if not faster. The Azure Storage products, features, and concepts discussed in the next section consist of the following:

- Storage accounts
- Zone replication
- Azure managed disk storage

Storage Accounts

The storage account product portfolio contains many of the original Azure cloud offerings. When you apply what you have learned up to now (having been exposed to Azure VM and Azure SQL databases), you know that they and many others are completely dependent on Azure Blob Storage and Disks. Both of those products existed prior to other products being used to support them. Azure Blob Storage and Disks continues to be used for running App Services, Azure Functions, and Azure Container Instances. These applications depend on one or more of these Azure Storage products. Don't forget about the Azure Cosmos DB Table API, which is wrapped around the Azure Table. In general, each of these storage account services provides a place to store rows of data or files at great scale but has limited querying capabilities. If these match your requirements, the Azure Storage products in the following list will be a great fit:

- Azure Blobs
- Azure Files
- Azure Queues
- Azure Tables

Take a quick refresher look at Figure 5.11. A common pattern between Azure Storage services is that they have a global endpoint, similar to those shown in Table 5.8. Simply replace the asterisk (*) with your storage account name.

TABLE 5.8 Azure Storage Service Endpoints

Azure Storage Service	Endpoint
Azure Blobs	`https://*.blob.core.windows.net`
Azure Files	`https://*.file.core.windows.net`
Azure Queues	`https://*.queue.core.windows.net`
Azure Tables	`https://*.table.core.windows.net`

These global endpoints like many other Azure products include the ability to create firewall rules to prevent access. In addition to those storage services, there are a few other storage products that will be discussed in this section as well, for example Storage Explorer, Shared access signature, Azure Data Lake Storage, and Azure NetApp Files. To get started, complete Exercise 5.6. Here you will add an Azure Blob container to the Azure Storage account you created in Exercise 5.1. Remember that all of these storage services exist within a single storage account. The storage account is where you configure monitoring, alerts, advanced security, and many other features that would apply to the services within the account.

EXERCISE 5.6

Creating an Azure Blob Storage Container

1. Log in to the Azure Portal at `portal.azure.com` and navigate to the Azure storage account you created in Exercise 5.1. (Mine was `csharpguitar`.) On the Overview blade, click Containers. There is also a Containers link in the navigation menu within the Blob service section. Click the + Container menu option, enter a name (`csharpguitar`), select Blob (anonymous read access for blobs only) from the Public access level, and then click the OK button.

2. Once the Blob container is created, click it. Click the Upload menu button. Select any random file that you would like to upload from your workstation by adding the path in the Files box. Expand the Advanced section and review its contents. Click the Upload button. The Upload blob window should resemble that shown in Figure 5.43.

FIGURE 5.43   Azure Blob Storage Container Upload blob window

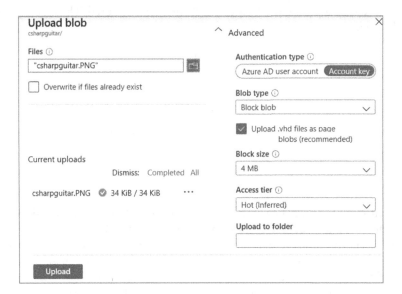

In the previous exercise, you uploaded a file to Azure Blob using the portal. Doing this called the *Azure Storage REST APIs* from the Azure Portal. Those are defined in detail here:

    docs.microsoft.com/en-us/rest/api/storageservices

These APIs can be used for all of the Azure Storage services, not only Azure Blobs. These APIs are useful for migrations that contain a large number of files or data, where manual upload isn't feasible. A command-line tool named *AzCopy* is useful for moving Azure Blobs or files stored in Azure Files from one storage account to another. Finally, an opensource library named the *Microsoft Azure Storage Data Movement Library* is located here:

    github.com/Azure/azure-storage-net-data-movement

It is useful for uploading, copying, and downloading a large number of Azure Blobs or files existing on Azure Files. For more explanation of the settings and actions you took in Exercise 5.6, continue to the next section where Azure Blob Storage is discussed in detail.

Azure Blobs

If you recall from the beginning of this chapter, you will find the term object otorage. The Azure product for storing objects is the Azure Blob storage service. If you view Figure 5.11 again, you will notice the description of "Scalable, cost-effective storage for unstructured data." Having completed the previous exercise, you know that Azure Blobs exist within a container. The container is the location to which an object is stored. The types of objects can be the following:

Images	JSON
CSS	Scripts
Static HTML	Videos
Logs	Office documents
Database backups	PDFs
CSV	VHDs

Notice that small file types like perhaps an HTML or CSS file can be saved to an Azure Blob container just like larger file types such as videos and VHDs. There is no limit to the number of objects you can save to a container, and there is no limit on the number of containers you can have in your storage account. The maximum size of a single object that can be stored in a container is *about* 5TB. There are three types of blobs, something you would have noticed in Exercise 5.6 had you expanded the Blob type drop-down list in the Advanced Settings section when you uploaded the blob. They are block, append, and page.

A *block blob* as its name describes is an object that is large, can be broken into numerous parts (i.e., blocks), and each block uploaded in parallel. It's optimal for streaming files. You could imagine that this can improve the management and speed of upload. Consider the time required to upload a 1TB file and consider during that timeframe you must assume the risk of interruption is greater than if you are uploading a 100MB file, which would happen faster. If you could upload that 1TB file in blocks using multiple machines or connections, it will happen faster. Recall from Exercise 5.6 that in the Advanced window for the blob was a Block Size drop-down list . The value was left at the default of 4MB, and had the file been large enough, the portal logic would have optimized the upload using that block size. The reason for the comment about the 5TB limit is that for a block blob there is a limit on the number of blocks per blob, as well as on the size of block. Those values are 50,000 blocks of 100MB each, which equals 4.75TB.

There is a similar limit on *append blobs*: 50,000 blocks with a maximum size of 4MB, which equals 195GB. Appending means that you add data at the end of a file or in this case a blob. This kind of blob is optimized for updating and should be chosen when you append rather than update the contents contained in your blob.

The last blob type is a *page blob*. You might recall, as illustrated in Figure 5.43, there is a check box with a caption that recommends uploading VHD files as page blobs. If you upload a custom VHD to create an Azure VM, for example, you would select a page blob, which is optimized for that kind of usage. The maximum size of a page blob is 8TB and is written in pages based on the page size defined also during its creation. The maximum size of the page blob is set at creation time. In addition to being the backbone of the Azure IaaS (i.e., VHD) product, this kind of storage is used for storing data for an Azure SQL and PaaS products. In those scenarios, there are benefits for having large data files stored in collections of pages of defined sizes. Remember that sharding breaks data into logical groupings for better query performance. A page blob is one of the design philosophies that provide that. It is the reason that writes to page blobs are committed immediately and written in place.

The last two concepts within the Azure Blob storage context to call out are the public access level of the container and the access tier of a block blob. Recall when you created the Azure Blob container in Exercise 5.6, the only attribute required to create the blob, other than its name, is the public access level. This can be Private, Blob, or Container, as shown in Figure 5.44.

FIGURE 5.44   Public access levels available for an Azure Blob Storage container

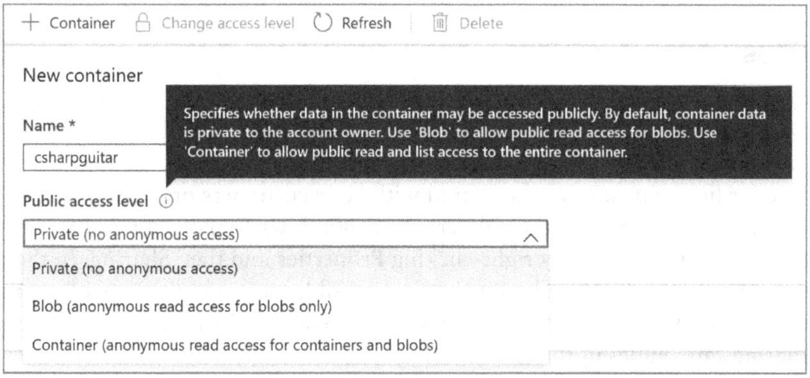

The default is Private (no anonymous access). If you wanted to retrieve a blob stored in that container, the client from which you requested the blob would need to send a valid token along with the request. Using a tool like Postman or the Azure Storage SDK would provide the capabilities to add this token to the request, which is in the form of an HTTP request shown here:

```
csharpguitar.blob.core.windows.net/csharpguitar/csharpguitar.PNG
```

Because in Exercise 5.6 you selected the Blob (anonymous read access for blob only), simply pasting that into a browser will retrieve the blob. The blob is accessible globally from any client that can make HTTP requests and can render a PNG image (blob names are case sensitive; PNG must be uppercase). The third public access level is Container (anonymous read access for containers and blobs). Here you allow all blobs in all containers to be read and listed. You can understand why this setting is at the container level. It has a level that is container wide and not restricted to a single blob or blob container. Also, reading a blob isn't the only capability provided when selecting this level of access. Listing is enabled. Using the Azure Storage SDK or Azure Storage REST APIs, you would have the access to a list of existing blobs within a container and can read the ones that you wanted or needed.

The final Azure Blob feature to discuss is the access tier, which is available only for block and append blobs. There are three different tiers, Hot, Cold and Archive. Hot means the data is accessed more than once in a 30-day period. Cold means the data is accessed greater than 30 but less than 180 days. Archive is anything over 180 days. The reason for these tiers, as you might expect, is based on cost. The more frequently the data is accessed, the more it costs. However, if you know some data will be accessed less often, you can save even more cost by storing the blobs on partitions that wouldn't need to be scaled, for example. Blob partitions are based on a key formed by the `account name + container name + blob name` and are used to load balance the blobs across machines. Therefore, when implementing a solution here, you must consider the names of your blobs, naming the ones accessed often similarly. Making the name of blobs accessed less often differently is good design. The partitions are made by the platform based on the derived name of the partition key.

Azure Files

You might recall from Exercise 5.1 that you created an Azure Storage account and a file share that utilized Azure Files. Take a quick look at the section named Shared Files in this chapter for more details about this Azure storage product. Azure Files is a product that provides storage for files that can then be shared with your customers or employees. It works in the same way as a file share you would create in Windows Explorer by right-clicking a folder. You can then give access by right-clicking Properties and then Sharing. In the case of Azure Files, there is a global endpoint that is accessible from any device with an internet connection running Windows, Linux, or macOS. The SaaS product OneDrive is one that uses such file sharing capabilities in the cloud.

There are two tiers you can choose when setting up an Azure File share, standard and premium. The primary difference is based on the amount of ingress and egress per second. Where ingress refers to incoming throughput, egress is outbound. This is important if you are moving large files that need to be transferred quickly. From a storage capacity limit, the two tiers are the same, with 100TB being the maximum total amount per Azure File share, and the largest size of a single file can be up to 1TB.

Azure Queues

When a person from England is waiting in line for something, instead of using the word line, they say *queue*. Be happy you won't hear my attempt at pronouncing "Look at those people in the long queue" with an English accent. Being able to visualize a line of people queuing for something may help you better understand what a message queue is. A message queue is simply a serially aligned and bottom to top ordered list of messages. Like any line or queue, the person at the front is processed first, and anyone needing that processing gets to the back of the line and is processed when it is their turn. This is most commonly referred to as *first in, first out (FIFO)*, something that Azure Queues does not support. Take a look at Figure 5.45 where you see a storage account named `csharpguitar` that has three storage queues. In the csharpguitar storage queue, there are two messages that need processing.

FIGURE 5.45   The relationship between storage account, storage queue, and messages

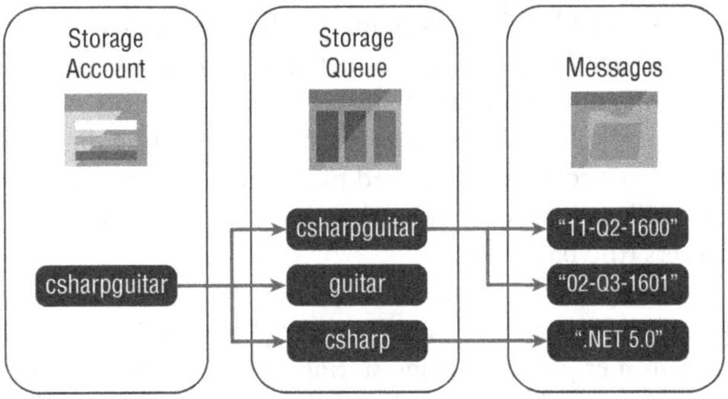

The message at the top of the csharpguitar storage queue, in this case 11-Q2-1600, will be processed before message 02-Q3-1601. If you viewed the messages in the queue via the Azure Portal, they would resemble something similar to Figure 5.46.

FIGURE 5.46   What storage queue messages look like in the Azure Portal

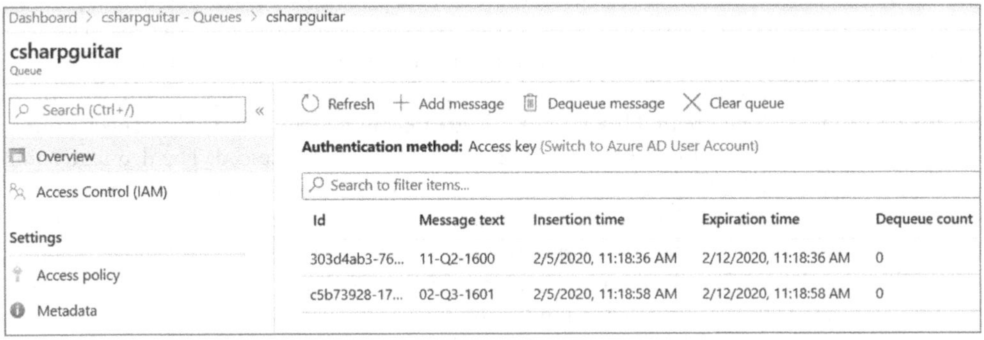

Notice that the Insertion time of 11-Q2-1600 happened before the other message, which is what is used to enforce the FIFO processing of Azure Queue messages. Another interesting attribute of messages is the expiration time that has a default and maximum of seven days; the minimum is one second. After the expiration date threshold is breached, the platform logic removes the message from the queue. Before explaining what the dequeue count means, first read about a use case for Azure Storage Queue messages.

In Chapter 6, there is more in-depth discussion about other Azure Messaging products. The reason Azure Storage Queue is being discussed here is more of a historical or legacy reason than any other. This product was the first messaging product offered on Azure. It also gets created within an Azure Storage account, like blobs, files, and tables; it belongs here based on the group of other Azure products in which it operates. Do note that the Azure Storage Queue is mostly considered a messaging product versus a storage one. That being said, a reason you would use a messaging product is to decouple your applications components from each other. An example of one that has been used before is the execution of long-running reports. Instead of submitting a large query to a reporting database and running the report in real time, your code could instead place the query into a queue, like an Azure Queue, and process it offline. This decouples the web server (the frontend) from the reporting and database servers (the backend).

Another reason for implementing a message queue into an IT solution is to make the system more resilient. For example, when a customer places an order online, you want to be 100% sure that the customer gets a message stating all is okay and thanking them for placing the order. You can increase the probability of this by placing the order information into a queue, which would have a high success rate when compared to making the same insertion into a database before, during, or after a real-time logistics validation. The validation of the order can be done offline, by validation. The order can be checked to see whether the item is in stock and can be delivered. If so, the order can be processed using, for example, a WebJob or Azure Function that updates all the logistical information about the ordered products. Now, let's get back to the dequeue attribute. That attribute counts the number of times the message has been taken from the queue, but not deleted after 30 seconds. The delivery model for an Azure Queue is "at least once" versus "exactly once." An important concept to grasp, it is the developer's responsibility to not process the same messages multiple times. This is as easy as checking the dequeue count and, if it is zero, process it straight up because you know it is the first time it's being read. However, if it is greater than zero, you need to check your system of record to make sure the message hasn't already been processed. The dequeue count is increased by one each time the `GetMessage()` method is called, which is used in code to retrieve the next message in the queue. If it takes longer than 30 seconds to process, there is an exception in the code, or the `DeleteMessage()` method is not called to remove the message in that timeframe, then the count is increased by one. An example of this pattern using the Azure Storage SDK will be provided in Chapter 7.

From a partitioning perspective, the model used is based on the queue name. All messages, which can be a maximum size of 64KB, that are sent to the specific queue name are stored in the partition. If you expect heavy utilization of a given queue, you might consider breaking it into a larger number of queues so that the load is spread across partitions. The maximum size of a single queue is 500TB (huge by all means) and has a maximum request rate of 20,000 messages per second.

Azure Tables

Like Azure Files, Azure Tables has been covered already in great detail. It was introduced first as an option available via the Azure Cosmos DB offering. (See Table 5.7.) Reading a bit further, you would learn of the relationship between Azure Tables and the Azure Cosmos DB Table API and that Azure Tables is a place to store nonstructured data using key/value pairs. The Azure Cosmos DB Table API is most useful for globalizing (georeplication and co-locating the data near those who consume it). Without the Azure Cosmos DB layer, an Azure Table is bound to a single region that may be continents away from the current or potential user base. There isn't much more to say about Azure Table that hasn't already been said. Review Figure 5.42 to see how partitioning works with this product and skim the "Table Storage" section earlier in this chapter if you wound up here out of interest. The reason that Azure Tables exists here at all is because of its grouping into the Azure Storage account structure. (See also Figure 5.10, which illustrates that Blobs, Files, Queues, and Tables all must be contained within an Azure Storage account.)

Other Azure Storage Services

The previous four products constitute the most utilized Azure Storage products. Keep in mind the difference in naming and the role of an Azure Data Store, which are databases versus Azure Storage that store data but have specific use cases, which should be clear now. There are a few other features and products that fall into the context of storage that haven't gotten direct attention but are worthy of that. Examples are the Storage Explorer, a Shared Access Signature (SAS), Azure Data Lake Storage, and Azure NetApp Files.

Storage Explorer

This is a tool you can download that makes the interaction with Azure Storage products simple. Once you download and install the tool, you can create any of the four Azure Storage products to insert, update, and delete blobs, files, messages, or key/value pairs as you need. Prior to this tool, the only means of that was by using Visual Studio, the Azure Storage SDK, or REST APIs. The latter two required some serious coding. Figure 5.47 illustrates how the contents view of an Azure Table using Storage Explorer appears.

FIGURE 5.47   View the contents of an Azure Table using Storage Explorer.

PartitionKey	RowKey	LOCATION	MODEL	Timestamp
FENDER	FEN1	USA	TELECASTER	2020-02-05T12:47:01.563Z
FENDER	FEN2	UK	STRATOCASTER	2020-02-05T12:47:20.717Z
FENDER	FEN3	USA	JAZZMASTER	2020-02-05T12:47:38.260Z

Additionally, some monitoring and administrative capabilities such as clearing queues, creating shares, and viewing usage statistics are also available. This tool is also useful for migrating small to midsize data sources from on-premise to the Azure Platform.

Shared Access Signature (SAS)

Originally introduced in Chapter 2, a Shared Access Signature (SAS) key provides the means to restrict access and rights to a specific resource within an Azure Storage account. In the Azure Portal, navigate to an Azure Storage container, and then click the Shared Access Signature link on the navigation pane. That will open a blade that allows you to create an access key with limited access. For example, you can create a SAS that can only add messages to an Azure Queue. This means any client using that connection string, which includes the SAS token, can only insert messages. That client cannot read, delete, or list any messages. As an alternative, navigate to the Access Keys blade, which contains a master or administrator-level connection string and generates a different token. When clients use that connection string for making the connection to the Azure Queue, they also have access to all storage options in the account, as well as all CRUD operations on them all. The SAS is to be used when your clients connecting to the account cannot or do not utilize Azure Active Directory (AAD), which is the preferred or recommended approach for implementing security on your Azure Storage. There is a bit more about this in the "Securing Azure Data" section later in this chapter.

Azure Data Lake Storage

The first generation of the Azure Data Lake Storage (ADLS) product (Gen1) is based on Azure Blobs and is used for storing data that supports Big Data analytic workloads. With ADLS Gen1 you would rightly expect to receive the same redundancy, capacity, throughput, and scalability as you get with an Azure Blob container. The data that is stored into ADLS is in a staging-like state (a data warehouse). The data can exist in any format from a database dataset to videos. The data remains in ADLS until it is ready to be analyzed. Once analyzed by the Azure Data Lake product, the results are published and viewable using frontend tools like Power BI. The data existing in ADLS is viewable using the Storage Explorer discussed just earlier.

Azure NetApp Files

Azure NetApp delivers the same kind of service as Azure Files with one big difference. You do not need to manage or provision any kind of storage product. Azure NetApp does this for you. It is based on the proprietary but fully supported by Microsoft NetApp software solution found at www.netapp.com. This product helps migrate and run hybrid solutions that require enterprise-level file share solutions. NetApp requires much less manual maintenance when compared to Azure Files, for example.

Zone Replication

Zone replication has been referred to in many places throughout this book. It is a pleasure to provide you now with the details about the numerous Azure Storage redundancy options.

- Locally redundant storage (LRS)
- Zone-redundant storage (ZRS)

- Geo-redundant storage (GRS)
- Read-access geo-redundant storage (RA-GRS)
- Geo-zone-redundant storage (GZRS)
- Read-access geo-zone-redundant storage (RA-GZRS)

Table 5.9 that provides the redundancy, durability, and availability thresholds for each replication option. Before taking a look, notice that two of the options have read-access capability. When you create an Azure Storage account, using an option that includes read-access the copy of the data is only readable. If read-access to the copy is not required, it is more cost effective to use the replication option without read-access. If Microsoft initiates a failover, a step in the process makes the redundant copy readable. In regular usage, that copy is not readable.

TABLE 5.9   Zone Replication and Storage Redundancy

	LRS	ZRS	GRS	RA-GRS	GZRS	RA-GZRS
Node	✓	✓	✓	✓	✓	✓
Data center/zone	✗	✓	✓	✓	✓	✓
Region	✗	✗	✓	✓	✓	✓
Read-access	✗	✗	✗	✓	✗	✓
SLA	99.9%	99.9%	99.9%	99.9%	99.9%	99.9%
Durability	11 9's	12 9's	16 9's	16 9's	16 9's	16 9's

As you read through the specific descriptions of each of the storage options, what node, data center/zone, and region in this context mean will become clear. The details describing each option are coming up next. Read-access was explained in the paragraph preceding Table 5.9, which leaves the SLA and durability options. SLA typically has to do with the availability of the system. Uptime is something most technical people are aware of. It is usually a metric, just like the ones shown in Table 5.9. Durability, on the other hand, has to do with the long-term protection of the data. In contrast to an SLA, which is focused on availability and often focused on redundant hardware, durability is focused on the redundancy of the data and keeping it from becoming corrupted or compromised in any way. Durability of the data is exactly why these storage redundant options exist.

Locally Redundant Storage (LRS)

Take a quick look back at Figure 3.4, which illustrates the concept of a region and a zone. Each zone is considered a data center; all three exist in the same region, but far enough from each other to be able to withstand unexpected outages caused by unforeseen events, like tornadoes or lightning. When you choose LRS, which is the cheapest and most cost effective, data written to the storage account is copied to three nodes in the same zone. Fault and update domains, which add to data redundancy, apply here, as they do for all storage redundancy options. As you may recall from the previous chapter, a node is mostly synonymous with a VM. It is also the only redundancy scenario available for LRS, as listed in Table 5.9. Use this solution if your data can be reconstructed if lost or if you have a compliance constraint that requires the data remain within a specific region. Always use this for the testing and development phases of your project. This setting can be changed after the creation of the storage account.

Zone-Redundant Storage (ZRS)

In Figure 3.4, you will notice that there are typically three availability zones in a given region. As you would easily conclude when choosing ZRS, the data is written into each of the three availability zones in the region. Unlike with LRS, if one of the zones or data center has some outage, then the reading, writing, and updating of data to the storage account would utilize one of the copies in another zone. Microsoft takes the responsibility for performing the failover in accordance with the SLA. You need not be concerned which zone your storage is reading from in this context.

Georedundant Storage (GRS)

Take a look at Figure 3.6. There you will see that each region, from a geographical redundancy perspective, has what is known as a twin region. The twin region exists on the same continent (geography). In addition to redundancy, the twin region provides compliance to the data restrictions would allow data to exist in different countries or states on the same continent but not across continents. West Europe and North Europe are twin regions, similar to North Central US and South Central US or UK West and UK South. A primary purpose of geographies is to provide great recovery options while complying with any data residency requirement. When you select the GRS redundancy option, the data written to the storage account is replicated from, for example, North Europe to a replica in West Europe. The GRS option is simply the replication mechanism. The data in the region once written works in the context of LRS. Although you have a full and automatic copy of your data in another region, the attributes and features that apply to the storage account when in use in the primary regions are identical to those of LRS. In this scenario, the data on the secondary data store is not accessible.

Read-Access Georedundant Storage (RA-GRS)

This is simply GRS, but the secondary copy of the data is readable. In some scenarios, you may be able to increase performance and decrease the load on the primary data storage instance by pointing read operations to the RA-GRS secondary instance.

Geo-Zone-Redundant Storage (GZRS)

When GRS is in operation, LRS rules apply as you just read. That means that the data is in a single zone, but it's in two regions. GZRS still replicates to its twin region, but only when in operation it acts like ZRS and not LRS. Remember that ZRS replicates data to each zone in a region versus three nodes in the same zone as LRS. This gives you greater redundancy and reduces the likelihood of needing to failover. No IT support person wants to experience a failover because it takes a lot of attention and testing before, during, and after the event. Also, steps must be taken to revert to primary once the outage event is over. This has a cost; the cost is the time of the IT support professional. If that is greater than the cost of GZRS versus the other redundancy options, then this option is the one for you. Keep in mind that as you proceeded through these options, the cost for each increased as the number of replicas and the platform requirements increased.

Read-access Geo-zone-redundant Storage (RA-GZRS)

The last option is one you can certainly define without fail. Take a moment before reading forward to describe to yourself what RA-GZRS is. Like RA-GRS, the secondary replicas of the GZRS clusters allow read operations. This may or may not be a requirement for the workload you are moving to or creating on Azure. However, you never want to lose your data or have a scenario in which you cannot access it, right? It simply comes down to how much is access to your data worth. This isn't a useful option for development and test scenarios; rather, use it for highly critical, production data scenarios.

Azure Managed Disk Storage

Managed disk storage was introduced in Chapter 4, but a chapter about storage couldn't be written without including some information about disks. A managed disk is a construct of a page blob that is stored in an Azure Blob container in the form of a VHD. The benefit of having a managed disk is that you can use a snapshot of it as the root or primary disk for use with up to 10,000 Azure VMs. You can have 10,000 identical Azure VMs, which are provisioned using a managed disk built from the same VHD stored as a page blob in an Azure Blob container. Isn't it amazing that after reading the book so far and doing all the examples, you know you can visualize all the technical terms and concepts in that previous sentence. It is amazing. Take note again that Azure Managed Disks is deeply integrated with VMSS. Take a look at Table 4.8 for their limits and constraints.

Data Backup, Migration, and Retention

Data is important to an organization. It's already been written numerous times, but a reminder is often helpful. What does your security protect? What does your network give you access to? What does the provisioned compute resource run the code against? The answer to all these questions is data. Honestly, it would be hard to think of an application or program that provides any value that warrants security, networking, and compute that doesn't consume, create, or analyze some kind of data. This is why protecting it, not only from unauthorized access but also from corruption or loss, is of great importance. Performing data backups, the successful migration of data from an on-premise data source to Azure and the retention of the data backups are all topics that you need to consider when choosing to move your data solutions to Azure. Much of the details for these areas are covered more in Chapter 8 and Chapter 9. However, as this is the chapter about data, it is a good place to introduce you to some of the capabilities. Data backups and migration are covered in the following sections:

- "Tools and Services"
- "Azure SQL"
- "Azure Cosmos DB"

When you create your backup strategy, you need to also consider your data retention policy. This is an area that identifies how long a backup should be stored before deletion. The storage of backups has a cost based on the size of the backup or, put another way, how many megabytes, gigabytes, or terabytes of storage space is required to store the backup? The cost of storage is relatively cheap, but if you make full daily backups of a database that is 100GB, then the amount of space and cost can grow really fast. Take, for example, that Azure SQL supports the retention of database backups for up to ten years. These backups can also be stored in a RA-GRS redundant Azure Blob storage, which will allow the backup to be restored as a new database. That is the maximum any application could configure. You need to know your retention requirements and take appropriate actions to control costs. There is a feature named *long-term retention (LTR)*, which is a framework leveraging standard backup procedures that is helpful for customers requiring longer storage of their historical data. LTR supports *point-time restore (PITR)* so that any of the automatically created backups can be used to recover a database from a historical point in time. Consider that a massive amount of your data was corrupted by some bad code, or a batch job updated millions of records incorrectly. If there is no way to roll back those operations, the only option is to recover your database from a point in time before the time the data was corrupted.

Finally, before moving onto the next sections, I want to introduce a new term called *data resiliency*. In the previous section, you learned about data availability, which typically has to do with SLAs and hardware. You learned also about data durability, which was linked to redundancies and replication using the numerous Azure Storage options such as LRS, ZRS, and GRS. Another term to introduce here is data resiliency. How quickly can you (your application) recover from the loss of a primary data source? The primary difference here is that durability means your data is backed up and won't be lost or corrupted, while resiliency focuses on how quickly you can begin to use the secondary data source.

Tools and Services

Other than the tools that help performing backups, migrations, and data retentions directly bound to the product itself, there are also some stand-alone tools that can help. These tools usually exist for scenarios that do not match perfectly with the built-in product capabilities. For example, the *Data Migration Assistant (DMA)* tool can help you identify any compatibility issues between your current version of SQL Server compared to the targeted Azure SQL version. DMA is a stand-alone tool that you would not find in the Azure Portal. Another helpful tool for planning migration is the *SQL Server Migration Assistant (SSMA)*, which performs similar analysis as DMA when the source database is on-premise databases, which are not SQL Server. Instead, if you are migrating from Oracle, DB2, or MySQL, for example, this tool can analyze the targeted Azure SQL or SQL VM versions and highlight any compatibility issue you may have during a migration. Once you have performed your preliminary analysis and corrected any issue, you can use DMS to perform the migration. Take a look at this online Azure Database Migration guide for additional details:

```
datamigration.microsoft.com
```

Azure Database Migration Service (DMS)

DMA is useful for smaller migrations that wouldn't have an impact on a production or enterprise. The process is similar to what you performed when working Exercise 5.3. In that exercise, you worked with a `.BACPAC` file and applied it to an Azure SQL database, which effectively is a migration. DMA is useful for more simple, non-mission-critical migrations. When downtime is an issue, you should utilize DMS (ADMS), which supports both offline and online database migrations from on-premise to Azure. DMS cannot be used to migrate to an Azure SQL database; instead, the target SQL product must be either an SQL Server Managed Instance or a SQL VM. Use DMS for your larger, enterprise and mission-critical database migrations. You'll learn more about this in Chapter 8.

Archive Storage

When you take a backup of your data source, you need a place to store it. In the previous section, you learned about Azure Blobs and the different blob types, one of which was archive. The archive blob type is intended to store data, which isn't expected to be accessed in a period of less than 180 days. Of course, you can access the data in that tier whenever you want; however, the cost and partitioning of the data in that tier is optimized for the less than 180 days scenario. You might see or hear this archive blob type referred to as a stand-alone product called Archive Storage. Keep in mind when you hear it, that you recognize behind the scenes it is an Azure Blob configured to use the archive blob type (the other blob types are page and block, just to jog your memory).

Azure Backup

Although Azure Backup can be used to back up many Azure products, it is useful in regard to an Azure SQL database. If you navigate to the Azure SQL server you created in Exercise 5.2, notice on the navigation pane there is a link to Manage Backups. Clicking that opens a blade that shows the backup policies and data retentions configurations. The Manage Backups blade may resemble Figure 5.48.

FIGURE 5.48   Azure SQL database backup and retention policy

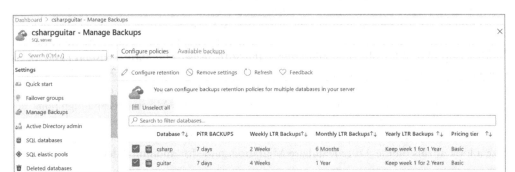

Azure SQL single and pooled databases as well as managed instances are backed up weekly automatically. The backups, which include full backups, differential backups, and transaction log backups, are stored in Azure Blob in a container using the redundancy option RA-GRS. As you can concur from Figure 5.48, PITR backups have a seven-day retention period; this is by default. The other retentions' settings for Weekly, Monthly, and Yearly were configured manually.

StorSimple

This product was purchased by Microsoft and is a cloud storage technology referred to as a *cloud-integrated storage (CiS)* device. This device helped manage on-premise applications to create and store backups of on-premise data to an off-premise (cloud) site. The speed at which the transfers occurred, the encryption capabilities, and its compression algorithms made the product an attractive alternative to the current existing products of that time period. To learn more about StorSimple, read through the online documentation at https://azure.microsoft.com/en-us/services/storsimple.

Azure Data Explorer (ADX)

Azure Data Explorer (ADX) is not to be confused with Azure Storage Explorer. Both have been introduced already, but a little more insight into ADX is still required. ADX is a highly scalable data service for storing logs and telemetry data for later exploration. There is no better way to learn about this than by creating one. Complete Exercise 5.7 to learn more about this Azure product.

EXERCISE 5.7

Creating an Azure Data Explorer Cluster and Database

1. Log in to the Azure Portal at portal.azure.com and then click the menu link in the top-left corner of the browser. When the menu opens, click + Create A Resource. Then click Analytics. Now click Azure Data Explorer and select the subscription and resource group into which you want to bind ADX, enter a cluster name, and select the region.

(The region you select should match the region of the resource group for consistency.) Select the Compute specifications. (I chose Dev(No SLA). . .it's the cheapest.) Click the Review + Create button then click the Create button.

2. Once the provision has completed, use the Overview blade and navigate to the cluster. Click the Create Database button, enter a database name (like `csharpguitar`), and leave the other settings at the defaults. Click the Create button.

3. In a browser, enter the following URL: **dataexplorer.azure.com**. Click the Add Cluster button. Enter the URL of the Azure Data Explorer Cluster that you just created and click the Add button. The URL will resemble the following HTTPS address, substituting the name you provided as the cluster name in step 1 (csharpguitar, in the example URL). Now check the region entry (southcentralralus in the example). Change the region name to the region in which you created the cluster, if necessary. You will find the value on the Overview tab for the Azure Data Explorer Cluster.

   `csharpguitar.southcentralus.kusto.windows.net`

4. Enter the following KUSTO query command. `show databases`, and click the Run button. The output should resemble that shown in Figure 5.49.

FIGURE 5.49 Azure Data Explorer clusters in the ADX Web user interface

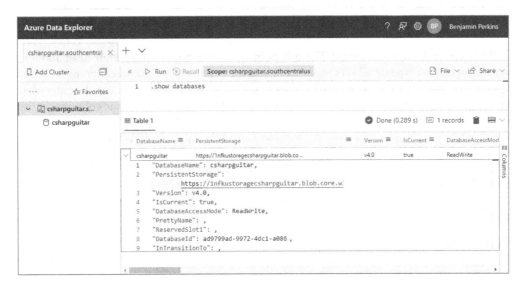

5. The following KUSTO queries can be downloaded from here:

   `github.com/benperk/ASA/tree/master/Chapter05/Ch05Ex07`

   Create a table in the database by executing the next KUSTO command. Make sure your database is selected (in focus) in the ADX Web UI before clicking the Run button.

   `.create`
   `table`

```
CsharpGuitarEventHub
    (TimeStamp: datetime, Name: string, Metric: int, Source:string)
```

6. Create an ingestion mapping using the next KUSTO command.

```
.create
table
CsharpGuitarEventHub ingestion json mapping
    'CsharpGuitarEventHubMapping'
    '[{"column":"TimeStamp","path":"$.timeStamp","datatype":"datetime"},
    {"column":"Name","path":"$.name","datatype":"string"},{"column":"Metric",
    "path":"$.metric","datatype":"int"},    {"column":"Source","path":"$.source",
    "datatype":"string"}]'
```

7. There is no data in the table yet; it will be added in the next chapter. However, you have experienced an example of a KUSTO query that will take 10 records from the table and sort them by TimeStamp.

```
CsharpGuitarEventHub
| sort by TimeStamp
| take 10
```

The exercise is straightforward. The two points you may be scratching your head about are the ingestion mapping KUSTO command and the next steps. When an endpoint is configured to send data to ADX, the data comes in the form of a JSON document. The ingestion mapping KUSTO command maps the elements in the JSON document to the columns on the table. Therefore, when an Event Hub sends information to ADX, the JSON file is parsed, and the elements are placed into a row on the table. Currently ADX supports three connection types, Event Hub, IOT Hub, and Blob storage, which are configurable via the Azure Portal. Microsoft also provides an ADX SDK so that you can send data to the cluster from any endpoint. As to what's next, in the next chapter, you will use the Event Hub created in Exercise 5.8, configure ADX to ingest data sent from the Event Hub, and then query ADX to view the results.

Import/Export

This Azure feature lets you send physical copies of your data or application directly to an Azure data center. This is useful for customers who have huge or gigantic amounts of data that cannot be sent over a network. The time required to send large amounts of data can take hours or even days, and the transfer might fail before it completes. Usually you have to start transfer over again from the beginning. Additionally, some customers may have security concerns with the transmission of data over a network, regardless of it being over a VPN or Express Route. Simply, if you have a large amount of data that you do not or cannot upload to the cloud over a network for any reason, the Import/Export option is a good choice.

Azure SQL

Keep in mind that backups are taken automatically when working with Azure SQL single and elastic pool databases. The same goes with SQL managed instances where they have built-in backups. The backups are stored on Azure Blobs using RA-GRS. You are covered if there is an outage in the region. This is not the case when you have chosen a SQL virtual machine. In that context, the scenario is the same as you would have when running the DBMS on-premise. For SQL VMs you take responsibility for the backups, storing, and managing. Note, however, that SQL Server Standard and Enterprise editions running on Azure VMs come with a service named SQL Server IaaS Agent Extension, which you can use to schedule backups. Additionally, using the Azure Backup product, it can be configured manually.

Cosmos DB

Like Azure SQL, the platform automatically takes backups of the data stored in your Azure Cosmos DB every four hours. The backups are stored on an Azure Blob container using the GRS redundancy option. There is currently no means for you to restore an Azure Cosmos database; if this is required, you must open a support request, and it will be handled for you. Database backups are stored for a maximum of 30 days. As you know, the most beneficial aspect of Azure Cosmos DB is its global replication capability. Knowing that there can be many, many copies of your database all over the world, it is unlikely you would ever need to restore. Excluding a scenario where you accidentally delete the database or container, then you would need a restore. The product also captures snapshots, which is helpful for rolling back updates that have corrupted a large amount of data. The query that performed the update is not rolled back; rather, a previous version of the database can be restored at a point prior to the data corruption.

Securing Azure Data

Security has never been anything but the number-one concern. That mentality hasn't changed and won't ever. Chapter 1 covered security first, because security is the highest priority, and therefore there is no problem with touching on that topic once again. You know about RBAC already; it is how you control access to provisioned Azure resources in the portal and AAD is what provides authentication into the Azure portal. It can also be embedded into application code to control access into the internet/web capabilities hosted on Azure. Connection security, authentication, authorization, and encryption are a restrained yet sophisticated set of principles for securing you data. From a connection security perspective, aspects such as connections strings and who can RDP to the server hosting the data have focus.

Sure, securing the data with complicated credentials provides some comfort, and where and how those credentials are stored are of great importance. Something called Azure Key Vault helps here. Historically, you would store a connection string in a `web.config` file, and if you were clever, you would encrypt it with `aspnet_regiis.exe` features. However, this was commonly only worthy when admin access to the machine hosting the website was also protected. If someone has admin access to a server, they can do everything on that server, including decrypting connection strings. The point is now an identity that isn't used to log in to the server can be used to access a key or secret in an Azure Key Vault that stores credentials and reduces password leaking. While the discussion is focused on this, let's define what is covered in this section and then proceed to the guts of password leaking. In this section, you will start by taking another look into data encryption and the Azure Key Vault; then you'll learn some more about other security options and capabilities you can implement on Azure. The following bullet points provide a bit more on what's to come:

- Data Encryption and Key Vault
- Azure Storage Security
- Shared Access Signature (SAS)
- Other Data and Storage Security Options

The topics in the list have been touched on already in previous chapters and sections; when applicable, references will make it easier to recall where they were introduced.

Data Encryption and Key Vault

After completing both Exercise 2.9 and Exercise 5.3, you have successfully created an Azure Key Vault that contained a key that you used to encrypt a column of data in an Azure SQL database. This kind of encryption is referred to as the encryption of data at rest. Data at rest is the security term that pertains to the encryption of data while it is not being used. This can be data stored in a database, but it can also be emails and files stored on a hard drive. To get a clear understanding, compare data at rest to its antonym—data in transit. Data in transit is not sitting idle on a hard disk or in a database. Rather, it is moving between a client and a server. The most obvious means for encrypting data in transit is by using the HTTPS protocol. In Chapter 2 these were discussed in a bit more detail. In Azure Confidential Computing, a third mode of data encryption was described. Security for data in use protects data that is stored in memory in case some malware got installed on the machine. Encryption has to do with cryptography and from a C# perspective is accessible in the `System.Security` `.Cryptography` class. That's way out of scope for this book, but take a look at that class and that term if this area interests you.

An important piece of data that needs all three of those encryption modes is a connection string. This is an important string of data because it contains the endpoint and credentials for connecting to a database or other resources like Azure Blobs or Event Hub, for example. Complete Exercise 5.8 exercise to create an Event Hub and update the Azure Key Vault Secret you created in Exercise 2.9, step 9.

EXERCISE 5.8

Creating an Event Hub and Updating the Azure Key Vault Secret value

1. Log in to the Azure Portal at `portal.azure.com` and click the menu link in the top-left corner of the browser. Click + Create A Resource and then search for Event Hubs. Press the Enter key, click the Create button and provide a name. Select Basic from the Pricing

tier drop-down list (it is the cheapest) and then select the subscription and resource group into which you want to place the Event Hub. Select the location. (The location you choose should match the location of the resource group.) Click the Create button.

2. Once provisioning completes, navigate to the Overview blade of the Event Hub. Select Shared Access Policies from the navigation menu; then select RootManageSharedAccessKey from the Share Access Policies blade. Copy the connection string-primary key.

3. Navigate to the Azure Key Vault you created in Exercise 2.9 and click the Secrets link in the navigation menu. Click the secret you created. Click the + New Version button, enter the Connection string-primary key into the Value text box, and click the Create button. The settings should resemble Figure 5.50.

FIGURE 5.50   Updating an Azure Key Vault secret in the Azure Portal

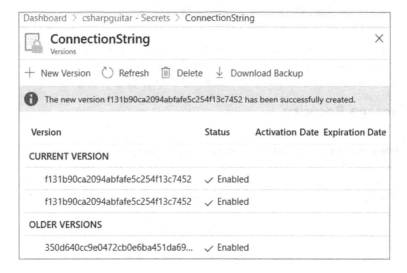

Take a look at the ASP.NET Core code located on GitHub here:

github.com/benperk/ASA/tree/master/Chapter05/DataEncryption

Specifically, pay attention to the index.cshtml.cs page. The code in this file provides an example of how to encrypt an Event Hub connection string, store it as an Azure Key Vault Secret, retrieve the encrypted connection string, decrypt it, and then use it to connect to an Event Hub. You can use this technique to encrypt, store, decrypt, and use for any Azure endpoint, including an Azure Blob. You would simply replace the Event Hub connection string with the Azure Blob one. As an alternative, you might consider a SAS key instead of the admin credentials in certain scenarios; see the next section. The code utilizes the following classes:

- `Microsoft.Azure.Services.AppAuthentication`
- `Microsoft.Azure.KeyVault`
- `System.Security.Cryptography`
- `Microsoft.Azure.EventHubs`

One note about this code is that it runs from within Visual Studio, which is a client. Getting authenticated using a managed identity and service principle against an AAD tenant is a challenge when you are working locally, but not so difficult when the code is hosted and running on the Azure platform itself. Therefore, you need to use something called *connected services*. You can read more about them here:

`docs.microsoft.com/en-us/azure/key-vault/` `vs-key-vault-add-connected-service`

Once you get over the authentication hurdle, using this code accomplishes the first two encryption modes, data at rest and data in transit. The remaining, data in use would require that you are running on Trusted Execution Environment (TEE); see Figure 2.51.

Azure Storage Security

When you upload data into a storage account, it is automatically encrypted and then decrypted when downloaded. This is achieved using a concept referred to as *Azure Storage Service Encryption (SSE)*, and it is completely transparent to users. You comply with any data-at-rest encryption requirements immediately/automatically. To achieve data in transit, you need to use the Windows Azure Storage client libraries and set the encryption policy. Basically, you set the key that is used to perform the encryption on the client before sending it to the storage account. As you might have guessed, the key is recommended to be stored in an Azure Key Vault. There are different clients for each of the storage account options, blob, files, queue, and table. Take note that encryption and decryption carry some performance overhead, but it is a necessary step required to keep things safe and secured. Another way to better enforce data in transit is to enable the Secure Transfer Required option, as shown in Figure 5.51.

When this is enabled, all communication using the Azure Storage REST APIs must come across HTTPS. Any request using HTTP only will be rejected. Also, it will enforce that all connections to an Azure File share using SMB will require encryption. Protecting who and how someone or some client can connect to your storage account is typically constrained to the authorization methods listed next.

- Azure Active Directory (AAD)
- Anonymous access
- Shared Keys
- Shared Access Signature (SAS)

FIGURE 5.51   Enabling secure transfer required option in the portal for an Azure
storage account

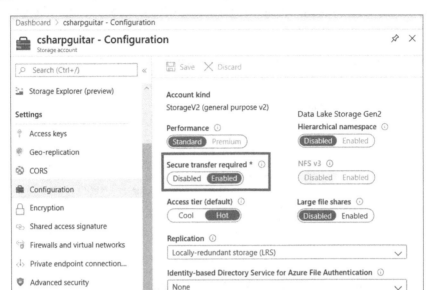

You should have some familiarity with all of those methods. With AAD you grant access
to the storage account using access control (IAM) and then authenticate a user's AAD credentials against the tenant using code in the client or cmdlets. If the user provides valid credentials, then they will gain access to the storage account. Anonymous access, as it pertains
to an Azure Blob, was illustrated in Figure 5.44. For development and test scenarios, this is
an acceptable setting, not so for production. You would instead change the access level to
prohibit anonymous and instead allow access only with an access key (shared key). Both of
those are similar in that they provide access to all options within a storage account and have
all CRUD-like permissions. To restrict access to specific storage account options and CRUD
permissions, use a shared access signature (SAS).

Shared Access Signature (SAS)

Any section that discusses Azure Storage security wouldn't be complete without having some
information about SAS. You just read that the access key provides full access to all options
in the Azure storage account. This isn't something you would necessarily want to provide
to clients who only require access to a specific blob container. Imagine a scenario where
you no longer know who has the token, and you have lost control over who has access, i.e.,
SAS leakage. You do have the option to regenerate the Access keys, but that's the same as
changing the password on a database. Doing so has great impact and would stop all clients
from being able to access. There are two access keys, key1 and key2, so if you are ever in
a situation where you must provide access keys and you have lost control you can provide

key2 to those who you know need access, give them some time to make the change, and then regenerate key1, which will result in you regaining control. When you create a SAS token, on the other hand, you have much more control over what can access and for how long (see Figure 5.52).

FIGURE 5.52   Shared access signature properties in the Azure Portal

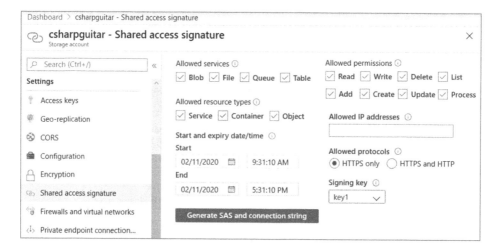

You can restrict access to a specific service option such as blob, files, queues, and tables. You can restrict a SAS token to a specific IP address or range of IP addresses by entering them into the Allowed IP Addresses text box. Additionally, you can restrict based on the CRUD operations like read, write, list, and delete. A powerful SAS attribute is the start and expiry date. This setting can also be useful in the case of SAS leakage because you would be confident that at some point the SAS token will expire. On the other hand, this causes some contention because if the client needs to continue using the SAS token after the planned expiry datetime, then it will need a new token. You need to set the expiration value based on the requirements of your solution. You also need to manage the process for regenerating tokens and providing the new token to clients. Just keep in mind that whoever or whatever has the token has the permissions to perform tasks provided by that token; watch out for that. Once you click the Generate SAS And Connection String button, you will see a connection string similar to the following. You can find a program on GitHub here:

```
https://github.com/benperk/AzureFunctionConsumer/releases
```

You can use that Azure Blob SAS connection string to add a blob to the container. The source code is also viewable on the GitHub repository if you are interested in seeing how the connection is made using the Microsoft.WindowsAzure.Storage SDK with C#. Figure 5.53 illustrates how that might look if you choose to attempt that.

```
BlobEndpoint=https://csharpguitar.blob.core.windows.net/?sv=2019-02-02&ss=
b&srt=sco&sp=rwdlac&se=2020-02-11T16:11:44Z&st=2020-02-11T08:11:44Z&spr=https&
sig=pl2qyK***************
```

FIGURE 5.53   Using a SAS blob connection string to upload a blob

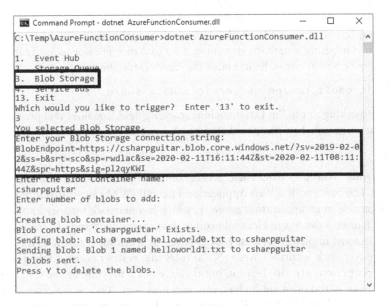

There is another technique for generating SAS access that is a bit more secure than using a SAS token. It is referred to as a *SAS signature* or user delegation. The primary difference is that the key used to sign the token is created using an Azure Active Directory (AAD) credential. Recall from Figure 5.52 that you need to select the signing key from a drop-down list. Key1 and key2 are the access keys that were generated by the Azure platform when the storage container was originally created. What you need to know from an Azure Solutions Architect exam perspective is that you can protect and secure an Azure Storage account using a SAS token, a SAS signature, and AAD. The level of security raises with each in the order they were just stated; a SAS token is the least secure due to SAS leakage, while using AAD with RBAC would be the most secure. Each have pros and cons that require knowledge of the application to which those security techniques need to be applied.

Other Data and Storage Security Options

There are a few additional data storage and data security options that need a mention here. Most of them you have already been introduced to. When reading them, consider it a refresher and a summary.

Azure Data Share

Azure Files as you learned is useful for sharing files like was commonly done in the past decades. Using the SMB protocol to share a directory and then having clients map a drive to that share is a standard practice. There can also be file share servers whose sole responsibility is to share files and documents. Azure Data Share does the same, but it is intended for sharing files in the context of big data. For example, if you get the data from a provider and the way they deliver it is in one large file, then email probably isn't a good way to deliver or receive it. If it is huge, then perhaps streaming it up to Azure Files or to an Azure Blob container isn't most optimal either. Read about the Azure Data Share here:

```
azure.microsoft.com/en-us/services/data-share/
```

If you are working in the Big Data/machine learning field, consider this product if it fits better in your scenario when compared to other Azure Storage options.

Firewalls

Firewalls provide protection from client access commonly based on IP address, protocol, and port number. The concept of a Web Application Firewall (WAF) was introduced in Chapter 2 and is configurable in an application gateway, which is a network security appliance. Additionally, in Chapter 3 the Azure Firewall product was introduced and also provides firewall capabilities. In most implementations, your compute is working within a VNet where you can configure Network Security Group (NSG) rules that restrict access to the resources within it. IP restrictions are also helpful, but they are not a firewall, as the restriction is only based on IP address and does not include protocol and port. Review the discussions about firewalls in Chapter 2 and Chapter 3 to learn more about this security feature.

Service Endpoints

Many Azure products expose a global endpoint, usually in the form of a URL. This means that access to it is fully discoverable by any device connected to the internet. It does not mean that anyone can access it. You can use firewalls and IP restrictions to prevent access to it. Another possibility to restrict access is by using service endpoints. You were introduced to service endpoints in Chapter 3 and enabled service endpoints in Exercise 3.2 and configured them for an Azure App Service later in Exercise 3.8. You learned that by setting up the endpoint, you restrict the access to the Azure App Service to only resources within the VNet. All other IP addresses are restricted. You also made a similar configuration in this chapter in Exercise 5.4 where you configured the service endpoint for an Azure SQL database, which resulted in the same restriction to allow access only from VMs in the given VNet. In all those scenarios, the global endpoint remains discoverable, but not usable; clients will receive an HTTP status of 403 if they attempt access or if using the SQLCMD client you'd receive an unable to connect exception; see Figure 3.34. There is a new feature in preview called *private endpoint connections*. Implementing this would hide the endpoint from discovery.

Summary

In this chapter, you learned about different kinds of database structures, specifically SQL versus NoSQL, and how their use cases differ. You learned about Azure SQL and Azure Cosmos DB, which are the most popular types of SQL and NoSQL Azure data store options. You learned about data partitioning, service endpoints, and global replication. Additionally, you learned about key/value pairs, Azure Cache for Redis, and numerous other Azure Data Store products. Azure Storage options include Azure Blobs, Azure Files, Azure Queues, and Azure Tables. Each has its own use case and data partitioning strategies. A must-know concept is Zone Replication, which includes LRS, ZRS, GRS, RA-GRS, GZRS, and RA-GZRS. The reason this is must-know is because those concepts, along with Azure Blobs, make up the backbone of many Azure products such as Azure SQL and Azure VMs.

Knowing how to migrate your on-premise database to Azure, which data store to choose and how to back up that data is a requirement of an Azure Solutions Architect. After reading this chapter, you should know how to pick the correct data store and which tools are available for making the migration a success. Finally, you had a review of many of the security concepts that were introduced in Chapter 2. The repeat had to do with scenarios specifically focused on data stores and data storage products. The many ways of protecting and encrypting your data hosted on Azure should now be solid in your mind.

Exam Essentials

Understand RDBMS (SQL) vs. NoSQL.   A database with tables, rows, columns, and relationships with other tables via a primary/foreign key relationship exposes traits similar to an RDBMS, relational database, or SQL database. Data commonly stored as a JSON document that has no or limited relationship with other data in the table is referred to as a NoSQL database.

Understand Azure SQL, SQL managed instance, SQL on VMs   Migrating to an on-premise SQL Server database to Azure confronts you with three options. Azure SQL should be considered when starting a new project or having a small database. A SQL managed instance has many benefits like automated backups, but if your database has a lot of customization, it may not migrate too easily. Running a SQL VM is the most like running on-premise.

Understand Azure Storage.   You may need to store more than just data in a database. Instead, you may need to store videos, messages, and VHDs, or create a network share with a global endpoint. Azure storage provides blobs, queues, tables, and file shares to meet those needs.

Understand Azure Storage Zone replication.   Redundancy is a necessity if you will need to run a mission-critical application. Having down time or corrupted data is not an option, and zone replication provides some features to prevent those events from happening. Each copy of the data does come with a cost, so use LRS for development and testing. Then decide how much more redundancy you need and if your application would benefit from reading from those copies.

Back up data.   If you lose data, then your company could go out of business. In most cases, your data is backed up automatically and replicated to another region. Therefore, if you need to recover from an outage, then you will have a backup. Even snapshots are taken by default, which means if your data gets corrupted by a rogue update, then you can fail back to a time before that update was performed.

Secure data.   Having your data exposed would be a catastrophe. You can sleep well knowing that Azure storage encrypts automatically all the data uploaded to it by default. Also, Azure SQL provides some capabilities for protecting your data at rest. Gaining access to the data using a global endpoint can be restricted with service endpoints, access tokens, and firewall rules. If you take the necessary precautions, your data will be safe on Azure.

Key Terms

Advanced Data Security (ADS)

Artificial Intelligence (AI)

Atomic, Consistent, Isolated, Durable (ACID)

AzCopy

Azure Analysis Services

Azure Data Explorer (ADX)

Azure Data Factory (ADF)

Azure Data Lake Store (ADLS)

Azure Database Migration Service (DMS)

Azure Storage REST APIs

Enterprise Data Warehouse (EDW)

Extract, Transform, Load (ETL)

First In First Out (FIFO)

Language Understanding Intelligent Service (LUIS)

Locally Redundant Storage (LRS)

Long-term Retention (LTR)

Microsoft Azure Storage Data Movement Library

Online Analytical Processing (OLAP)

Online Transaction Processing (OLTP)

Point-Time Restore (PITR)

Private endpoint connections

Azure Storage Service Encryption (SSE)

Binary Large Object (BLOB)

Cloud-integrated Storage (CiS)

Data Migration Assistant (DMA)

Database Administrator (DBA)

Database as a Service (DaaS)

Database Management System (RDBMS)

Database Throughput Unit (DTU)

Desktop as a Service (DaaS)

Document DB Data Migration Tool

Elastic Database Throughput Unit (eDTU)

Read-Access Geo-Redundant-Storage (RA-GRS)

Request Unit (RU)

SAS leakage

SAS signature

Search Engine Optimized (SEO)

Semantic Data Model (SDM)

Server Message Block (SMB)

SQL Server Integration Services (SSIS)

SQL Server Migration Assistant (SSMA)

User Defined Functions (UDF)

Virtual Network Appliances (VNA)

Review Questions

1. In which of the following can you store key/value pairs? (Select all that apply.)

   A. Azure SQL

   B. Azure Cosmos DB Table API

   C. Azure Table Storage

   D. Azure Storage Queue

2. Which Azure Data Store would you choose when performing a relational database lift-and-shift migration to Azure?

   A. Azure SQL

   B. SQL virtual machine

   C. Azure Blob Storage

   D. Azure Cosmos DB Gremlin API

3. Which Azure product offers data warehouse features?

   A. Azure Data Factory (ADF)

   B. Azure Data Bricks

   C. Azure Synapse Analytics

   D. Azure Storage Explorer

4. Which of the following provide automatic database backups? (Select all that apply.)

   A. Azure SQL single database

   B. Azure SQL elastic pool

   C. SQL managed instance

   D. SQL on a VM

5. Which of the following tools is best for identifying potential compatibility issues between Azure SQL and an on-premise SQL Server database?

   A. Import/Export

   B. Azure Backup/Restore

   C. SQL Server Migration Assistant (SSMA)

   D. Data Migration Assistant (DMA)

6. Which of the following Azure SQL products offer dynamic scaling? (Select all that apply.)

   A. Azure SQL

   B. SQL managed instances

   C. SQL virtual machines

7. If you wanted to store data in JSON format, which data store would you choose?

    A. Azure SQL

    B. Azure Cosmos DB

    C. Oracle

    D. Azure Blob Storage

8. Which of the following Azure Storage redundancy options provide redundancy in case of a data center zone outage? (Select all that apply.)

    A. LRS

    B. ZRS

    C. GRS

    D. RA-GZRS

9. Which of the following is not an Azure Storage product?

    A. Azure Blob

    B. Azure Queue

    C. Azure Kubernetes

    D. Azure Files

10. True or False: Providing an account key to protect an Azure Blob container is more restrictive than a SAS token.

    A. True

    B. False

Chapter

6

Hybrid, Compliance, and Messaging

EXAM AZ-303 OBJECTIVES COVERED IN THIS CHAPTER:

✓ **Implement and Monitor an Azure Infrastructure**

- Implement cloud infrastructure monitoring

✓ **Implement Management and Security Solutions**

- Implement and manage Azure governance solutions

EXAM AZ-304 OBJECTIVES COVERED IN THIS CHAPTER:

✓ **Design Infrastructure**

- Design an application architecture
- Design a network solution

✓ **Design Identity and Security**

- Design governance

✓ **Design Business Continuity**

- Design governance
- Design for high availability
- Design a solution for backup and recovery

✓ **Design Monitoring**

- Design a solution for logging and monitoring

A hybrid solution is something you as an Azure Solutions Architect Expert will surely be asked to describe and design at some point. A hybrid solution may last for only a short time, helping to "bridge the gap" while you migrate an entire workload to the Azure platform. Vladimir Lenin once said, "Trust is good, but control is better," which means that one should rely only on what has been verified. This leads greatly into discussions regarding compliance and governance techniques. Being compliant with government or regional regulations is a specialized and large area that encompasses many topics. You should have some introductory knowledge of underlying compliance themes as well as knowledge of Azure tools and documentation that provide compliance.

In Chapter 4, you learned about batch processing, which is a near real-time computing model. In the batch processing scenario, data is received and stored, and then at a scheduled frequency a batch job of some kind is triggered using the Command Run On (CRON) scheduler, which processes the data. That near real-time processing has evolved to something called *continuous computing*. This means that instead of storing data that typically would be processed using a batch job, the piece of data is processed immediately and continuously. This new computing approach is supported by Azure messaging services, such as Event Hub, Service Bus, and Azure Storage Queues. After reading this chapter, you will have a good understanding of these products.

Hybrid Solutions

Every chapter in this book so far has mentioned something about hybrid cloud solutions at least twice. Hybrid solutions were introduced in Chapter 1 as a use-case scenario for the API Management product. You learned that the API Management product can be configured to run within a VNet and use a VPN or Express Route to make the connection between on-premise resources and your workload hosted in Azure. An extra benefit of API Management is that you can expose a global endpoint and then configure the API manager to route to any backend endpoint. The backend endpoint can change without impacting consumers because the global API manager endpoint remains the same. This is beneficial when you are implementing a hybrid solution to "bridge the gap," meaning your hybrid solution may not be permanent. The workload or IT solution you are migrating to Azure may take weeks, months, or years. There may be data migrations that must be performed serially or constraints on planned business events such as a yearend sale that causes a delay in migrating some pieces of your solution. You can use something like API Management to support such a scenario. On the other hand, you may not ever be allowed to migrate all your security, compute, or data completely to the Azure platform for some compliance or legal reason. This would mean that you are forever in a state of running a hybrid solution, and that's fine. The point is you may never, completely, or partially be running in a hybrid state. The partial scenario may increase or decrease over time for many valid reasons. Azure provides some of the best, if not the best, set of features for running in a hybrid state, including the following:

- Hybrid security
- Hybrid networking
- Hybrid computing
- Hybrid data solutions

The remainder of this section provides some details about these hybrid solutions. There is also a good overview of all these hybrid cloud solution types located here:

azure.microsoft.com/en-us/solutions/hybrid-cloud-app

Hybrid Security

When you initially think about a hybrid security solution using Azure, the first things to come to your mind should be Azure AD Connect and Single Sign-On (SSO). If you want more details about AD Connect, check out the introduction of AD Connect in Chapter 1 and the section on this product in Chapter 2 (see Figure 2.11), with additional references and feature discussions throughout the chapter. In summary, AD Connect is used to synchronize an on-premise Active Directory with an Azure Active Directory (AAD) tenant. When AD Connect is used to synchronize users between two repositories, this provides an SSO scenario.

A *single sign-on (SSO)* allows a single entity to access multiple resources using the same set of credentials. An entity is typically a human. In Chapter 2 you read an analogy of the early IT days when you needed a different set of credentials for each application and how unproductive that was. As you have learned so far, though, an entity can also be a managed identity, or it can be a service principle. All three of those entity types will have not only credentials that are used for *authentication (AuthN)* but also permissions, for example CRUD on a data store or RBAC in the Azure Portal. Permissions are directly related to *authorization (AuthZ)*. Review password hash synchronization, pass-through authentication, and ADFS, which are SSO features and illustrated with Figure 2.15. Two other Azure products can help you manage and implement a hybrid security solution: Security Center and *Azure Sentinel*. Security Center will be covered later in this chapter.

Azure Sentinel utilizes AI to monitor behaviors of clients accessing your system. If you remember in Chapter 2, there was mention of such AI components that perform this behavioral monitoring and can notify and prevent access or notify and allow access. The notification is provided via the Security Center by default.

Hybrid Networking

This is where you will recognize that Azure excels in the hybrid cloud area when compared to other cloud service providers. Azure offers many products and features to achieve a hybrid network. All of the following hybrid Azure networking products and features were mentioned in Chapter 3. The following sections summarize each of the Azure networking products or features listed.

- Express Route and VPN Gateway (S2S)
- VNet integration
- Network Watcher
- API Management and Traffic Manager (ATM)
- Hybrid Connection Manager (HCM)

Express Route and VPN Gateway

When considering the implementation of a hybrid network, one serious consideration is the technology you will use to connect the two networks. The Azure products that provide this connectivity are Express Route and VPN Gateway. The primary difference between the two is that only Express Route (Figure 3.53) connections do not traverse the public internet. Therefore, Express Route network connections can offer faster connection speeds and a greater level of reliability. Just keep in mind that private connections come at a cost that is higher when compared to a VPN Gateway. You created a VPN gateway in Chapter 3; see Exercise 3.12. A VPN Gateway is primarily used when creating a site-to-site (S2S) connection between two data centers. It is possible to configure a point-to-site (P2S) connection using a VPN Gateway, and in most cases the configuration, management, and costs associated with a VPN Gateway are much less. Both are secure, and both are fully supported by Microsoft; the decision for one or the other is based on your application requirements and budget.

Other reasons for creating a hybrid network are for modernization and to increase bandwidth. If you are running in your own data centers that will include network devices and need to upgrade, you will certainly know the costs, risks, and impact the upgrade can have. Instead of making those changes, simply create your new compute resources on Azure and connect to them using Express Route or VPN Gateway. This way you gain access to the most sophisticated networking technology that exists, supported by some of the most experienced network engineers. Similarly, when bandwidth becomes an issue in your on-premise network, offload some of that traffic to your Azure network.

VNet Integration

Typically an Azure virtual network (VNet) is created when you begin your movement to the Azure platform—you cannot have an Azure VM without one. The VNet is the point of entry for accessing your IT solutions and for connecting any non-cloud-based (on-premise) resources. Not only can you connect to a VNet from outside of the Azure network, the following scenarios are also available:

- VNet-to-on-premise (just described)
- VNet-to-VNet
- VNet-to-Azure resources not in a VNet
- VNet-to-Internet

Within each VNet there can be multiple subnets that consist of a range of IP addresses. You created addresses by providing a CIDR value. When you configure a VNet-to-VNet connection, the resources in all subnets will have access to each other; it is important that there are no overlapping IP addresses, so choose your CIDR configuration with that in mind. You have learned about service endpoints and how they are used to grant and restrict access to Azure resource that do not exist within a VNet. The point here is the *restrict* part. It is possible to have public IP addresses for Azure VMs and other resources running within a VNet that expose the VM to the internet. Azure products such as an App Service, Azure SQL, or Azure Blob Storage have global endpoints by default. This makes the VNet-to-Internet connectivity relatively simple, but not as restrictive as you might like. To restrict those endpoints, use a VNet-to-Azure feature like service endpoints to make accessing those products more restrained. Azure VMs within a VNet do not have to expose a public IP address. Instead, you can configure only private IP addresses. Service endpoints support private IP addresses. Perform Exercise 3.2 to gain more experience in this area if you haven't already.

Network Watcher

You created and used Network Watcher in Exercise 3.1. There you reported latency values between an Azure region and any location around the world. This helps when you determine where you should place your Azure resource based on the responsiveness between the location where your customers are and the location of the Azure region where your resources are going to be. Network Watcher can also call out if you need to place additional resources into a new region for new customers who didn't exist during your initial deployment into an Azure region. If you originally deployed into South Central US because that was where most of your customers were, but you see some growth in Australia, then you can test to see how latent the connectivity would be between those two locations and determine whether you should place some Azure resources there.

Network Watcher is enabled by default and provides a visual representation of your resources in a VNet and how they are connected with each other. There are also diagnostics, one of which you used in Exercise 3.1. Capturing those metrics is useful for identifying contention points in your network topology. Some optimizations and reconfigurations may be needed. Network Watcher can also track the number of network resources you have created in your subscription per region and identify when you are approaching the limit. The metrics are stored and can be used as content for an in-portal dashboard that provides greater visual representation of your Azure resources and their behavior.

API Management and Traffic Manager

API Management provides many capabilities and features, but the one that specifically supports a hybrid network is its ability to act like a proxy. A proxy typically exposes an endpoint that is accessed by a client. The access is typically accomplished by an HTTPS request. The HTTPS request contains a domain name, some header information, and HTTP verbs like GET, POST, PUT, and the like. What the API Management product can do is route a request to the exposed endpoint for an Azure resource or to an on-premise resource, based on the contents in the request header. ATM is also used to route traffic to different endpoints, Azure or external. The difference is that ATM cannot analyze the data that is flowing through it. ATM uses location and health monitoring to route the request to the nearest and functional endpoint relative to the client's locale.

Hybrid Connection Manager

An S2S connection is used to connect two networks so that resources within each network can access each other. Using Express Route or a VPN Gateway are typically the products used for that. In Exercise 4.14, you created an HCM connection between an Azure App Service and a VNet. Testing the connection, you were able to access an Azure VM with no public IP address. That scenario is reflective of a P2S where the point was the Azure App Service and the site was the VNet. This product is quick and easy to configure and use and is based on the Azure Relay product.

The way HCM is effective in a hybrid solution is that you could place your compute in Azure (Azure App Service) and then host the data that the frontend uses in your on-premise private data center. Instead of making the HCM connection to a VNet, you can configure it to access the server in your data center. The fact that it uses HTTP/HTTPS means that it is highly probable the ports and protocols necessary to support the connection are already open on the company firewall.

Hybrid Computing

An interesting term, *cloud bursting*, was introduced in Chapter 4. Under normal circumstances, you can run your workload inside your private, on-premise data center. If you ever need to scale up your compute at a faster rate than possible in your data center, then you can manage this in Azure. A beneficial scenario of Azure App Service allows your website to be deployed but turned off, which would result in no charges. You could start it only if you needed it. You would need to create some kind of request routing scenario using API Management, ATM, or perhaps even Azure Front Door. This is a very cost-effective scenario for provisioning temporary compute.

You might also consider HCM in the context of a hybrid computing solution. In that scenario, you can utilize WebJobs to execute some batch processing against data stored on-premise. You can also have your frontends in Azure Connect and perform CRUD operations in data or files located in your private data center. A hybrid computing solution is one that utilizes cloud compute resources to perform all, part, or temporary required data processing. That, in combination with compute or data resources running in a private data center that provide your entire IT solution, constitutes a hybrid computing solution.

Hybrid Data Solutions

This is the same as a hybrid computing solution but in reverse. In the previous chapter you learned about the many data store and data storage options that are available to you. If you desire to store your data on Azure and then use compute resources in your private data center, then more power to you. You can accomplish this using, for example, an Azure SQL database, because it has a global endpoint. Using a SQL VM with a private IP address is also an option since the SQL VM will be in a VNet, and you could then use Express Route or a VPN Gateway to make the connection to the data store. Consider the option of loading large, huge, or gigantic datasets into a data store on Azure and then executing some processing or machine learning (ML) algorithms against it. The output can be a report that uses a subset of the dataset that can be quickly deleted or moved back on-premise.

If the dataset is a database, then you can use any of the data migration tools to move the data to Azure—permanently or temporarily. If the data is in the form of a large number of files or perhaps millions of JSON documents, you might consider using Azure Files, Azure Blob Storage, or Azure NetApp Files to store those files. You could then write some code to load them into a data store where your compute can access, analyze, and learn from them.

Azure Cloud Compliance Techniques

In general, compliance has to do with a set of rules and/or guidelines that you must adhere to in order to provide services to a specific customer. Customers or organizations working with governments, doing work in a variety of businesses, or engaging in activities in many locations around the world must conform to a set of standards. ISO 9001, Federal Information Processing Standard (FIPS), Payment Card Industry (PCI), and General Data Protection Regulation (GDPR) are examples of common compliance standards. There are many, many more.

In addition to offering compliance to the most popular and even singular standards, the Azure platform aspires to provide a cloud platform focused on these four principles:

- Compliance and governance
- Security
- Resiliency and reliability
- Privacy

Compliance and Governance

In addition to adhering to government, industry, and regional compliance requirements, Microsoft provides tools for achieving and governing your compliance obligations. Tools like *Microsoft Trust Center (MTC)*, *Service Trust Center*, and *Azure Blueprints* can all be utilized to achieve compliance. It goes without writing that you need to know which standards are required to run your IT solution to meet the conditions of a customer that consumes the IT solution. MTC is used by customers for guidance on how to attain certain certifications on Azure. It also provides transparency about Azure security and privacy on all Azure products and services. Here is a link to more information about MTC:

    aka.ms/trust-center

The Service Trust Center provides resources for you to run audit reports on Azure Security, trust documents, and compliance blueprints. The audit reports are useful for verifying the technical compliance of your Azure services. The Service Trust Center is accessible at the following internet address:

    servicetrust.microsoft.com/ComplianceManager

Finally, Azure Blueprints (accessible at haka.ms/getblueprints) provide additional guidelines and examples of ways to include key environment artifacts in your Azure deployments using ARM templates (ARM will be discussed in Chapter 8), resource groups, RBAC controls, and Azure policies (discussed later in this chapter). In summary, to achieve a specific government, regional, or industry certification, you must comply with the rules and regulations for the given certification. More is coming on how you can become compliant; however, there are also requirements for maintaining the certification after deployment, which falls into a category called *governance*.

You learned about RBAC in Chapter 2 and how it is useful for managing access to the resources in your Azure subscription. Unrestricted access to an Azure subscription would be more agile for teams requiring the provisioning of resources, but that would be risky and likely costly. Take a look at Figure 2.42 to refresh your memory about RBAC scope and where you can place RBAC restrictions. You can place RBAC restrictions on management groups, subscriptions, resource groups, and specific resources. Also take a look at Figure 2.43, which provides the kind of identities (such as user, group, managed identity, and service principle) you can use for granting access to those entities. Having a good RBAC strategy is one area that will help you govern your subscription and the resources within it. Governance is a continuous process; it never stops. Governance is focused on auditing, managing, and monitoring your Azure consumption; the design of the strategy for implementing those points has to do with your company's requirements and objectives. Additionally, if you have customers that require government, industry, or regional compliance, they will likely have ongoing governance requirements. There are some tools offered by Microsoft that are helpful for attaining and maintaining compliance and governance certification, shown here:

- Azure Status (see more in Chapter 9)
- Azure Monitor (learn more in Chapter 9)

- Azure Blueprints
- Azure Policy
- Tags

Both Azure Status and Azure Monitor are covered in detail in Chapter 9; however, they needed to be called out here because they are helpful in the context of compliance and governance. Azure Status provides you with a global view of the overall state of Azure globally and per region (status.azure.com/en-us/status). This is helpful for checking to see whether there is a known issue in the region where you have provisioned Azure resources. There may also be information on how to resolve any ongoing issue. Both Azure Health Monitor and Azure Monitor can be configured to notify you of events happening on Azure that would impact your resources. This notification capability is highly configurable and customizable to meet your needs. Azure Monitor focuses on a deeper level; it works with your applications directly. Therefore, if you want to know what is going on with Azure, check out Azure Status. If that checks out and you are still experiencing some problems, the next step is to use Azure Monitor as it might be an application issue and not an Azure platform one. You'll learn more about this in Chapter 9.

Azure Blueprints

Azure Blueprints are guidelines based on specific compliance standards that when followed lead to the adherence of the requirements of that standard (such as ISO 9001). A blueprint created specifically for an industry, government, or regional standard certification would call out different control mappings that identify the specific components required to achieve that standard. Examples of different control mapping topics are provided here:

- Separation of duties
- Remote access
- Least functionality
- Boundary protection
- Least privilege
- Malicious code protection
- Vulnerability scanning
- Account management
- Denial-of-service protection

Each of those control mappings would trigger some questions concerning how to implement such a control around the Azure products, features, and resources verifying compliance and achieving certification. This is exactly what MTC, Service Trust Center, and Azure Blueprint services provide. You will have a guideline for achieving a selected compliance standard. Reading through the previous list, however, you might recall some of the Azure products that you have learned about so far in this book as a means to achieve some of those control mappings. Take a few moments to reflect on them and which products you would implement to achieve compliance.

Azure Policy

Before you get into the text portion of learning about Azure Policy, complete Exercise 6.1 to view a list of Azure policies. This will help you get a picture of what's available and perhaps how it can be used.

EXERCISE 6.1

Viewing Azure Policies Using Azure PowerShell

1. Open Azure PowerShell IDE and log in using the following cmdlets:

```
Connect-AzAccount
$subscription = Get-AzSubscription -SubscriptionId "<SubscriptionId>"
Set-AzContext $subscription
```

2. Enter the following Azure PowerShell cmdlets that result in the output shown in Figure 6.1:

```
$azurePolicy = (Get-AzPolicyDefinition).Properties.metadata
$azurePolicy | Group-Object category | Select-Object Name, Count `
             | Sort-Object Count -Descending
```

FIGURE 6.1 Azure PowerShell output that renders a list of Azure policies

```
PS C:\> $azurePolicy = (Get-AzPolicyDefinition).Properties.metadata
PS C:\> $azurePolicy | Group-Object category | Select-Object Name, Count | Sort-Object Count -Descending

Name                   Count    Name                    Count
----                   -----    ----                    -----
Regulatory Compliance    728    backup                      2
Guest Configuration      123    Service Bus                 2
Security Center           70    App Configuration           2
Monitoring                47    Service Fabric              2
App Service               47    Batch                       2
SQL                       36    Container Registry          2
Network                   19    Internet of Things          1
Tags                      17    Lighthouse                  1
General                   13    Cache                       1
Compute                   12    Automation                  1
Key Vault                 11    Logic Apps                  1
Kubernetes service         9    Search                      1
Kubernetes                 9    Cosmos DB                   1
Storage                    8    Custom Provider             1
CSS                        5    Stream Analytics            1
Event Hub                  3    App Platform                1
Data Lake                  3    Managed Application         1
```

3. Execute the following Azure PowerShell cmdlet, which will list all the Azure policies that are targeted toward regulatory compliance. The output is illustrated in Figure 6.2.

```
(Get-AzPolicyDefinition).Properties `
    | where-object {$_.metadata.category -eq "Regulatory Compliance"} `
    | Format-Table displayName
```

FIGURE 6.2   Azure PowerShell output that renders a targeted list of Azure policies

```
PS C:\> (Get-AzPolicyDefinition).Properties | where-object {$_.metadata.category -eq "Regulatory Compliance"} | Format-Table displayName

displayName
-----------
Microsoft Managed Control 1599 - Developer Configuration Management | Software / Firmware Integrity Verification
Microsoft Managed Control 1375 - Incident Response Assistance | Automation Support For Availability Of Information / Support
Microsoft Managed Control 1605 - Developer Security Testing And Evaluation | Static Code Analysis
Microsoft Managed Control 1142 - Security Assessment And Authorization Policy And Procedures
Microsoft Managed Control 1099 - Security Training Records
Microsoft Managed Control 1285 - Telecommunications Services | Provider Contingency Plan
Microsoft Managed Control 1709 - Security Function Verification
Microsoft Managed Control 1052 - Session Lock
Microsoft Managed Control 1034 - Least Privilege
Microsoft Managed Control 1623 - Boundary Protection
Microsoft Managed Control 1515 - Personnel Termination
Microsoft Managed Control 1327 - Authenticator Management | Password-Based Authentication
Microsoft Managed Control 1229 - Information System Component Inventory | No Duplicate Accounting Of Components
Microsoft Managed Control 1123 - Audit Review, Analysis, And Reporting | Audit Level Adjustment
Microsoft Managed Control 1474 - Emergency Power | Long-Term Alternate Power Supply - Minimal Operational Capability
Microsoft Managed Control 1227 - Information System Component Inventory | Automated Unauthorized Component Detection
Microsoft Managed Control 1361 - Incident Handling
Microsoft Managed Control 1594 - Developer Configuration Management
Microsoft Managed Control 1572 - Acquisition Process
Microsoft Managed Control 1331 - Authenticator Management | Password-Based Authentication
Microsoft Managed Control 1132 - Protection Of Audit Information | Audit Backup On Separate Physical Systems / Components
Microsoft Managed Control 1223 - Information System Component Inventory
Microsoft Managed Control 1640 - Transmission Confidentiality And Integrity
Microsoft Managed Control 1420 - Maintenance Personnel
Microsoft Managed Control 1658 - Secure Name / Address Resolution Service (Recursive Or Caching Resolver)
```

In the next exercise, you will apply one of these Azure policies, but as you can see in Figure 6.1, there are a large number of Azure Policy definitions that you can apply at either the subscription or resource group level. The definitions represent a set of rules that include actions such as requiring that HTTPS be enabled on all app services or a limit on the number of subscription owners. The definitions are typically targeted toward fulfilling requirements for government, industry, or regional certification attainment. There are a lot of definitions and a lot of rules within them. It is up to you to know which certification you need and which template to use. Azure Blueprint should get you on the path fairly quickly. With Azure Policy you can get the actual restrictions applied fairly easily. If you need help, you can log a support case with Microsoft, and someone will help you through this. Additionally, if one of the built-in rules does not meet your requirements, guess what—you can create a custom Azure Policy and add your own group of rules to it.

In general, an Azure Policy enables the management, creation, and assignment of policy definitions. These policy definitions enforce the rules on your Azure resources. This enforcement helps you remain compliant with the service levels and standards of your company. Azure Policy also provides monitoring and scanning capabilities that identify any resource that is not in compliance with the policy. Take a look at Figure 6.3, which illustrates some of the reporting and management capabilities available to you.

The first thing I recognized as I started reviewing my Azure consumption footprint was how many resources I have provisioned. This just goes to show how quickly resources can be provisioned, and the overview of what you have can get lost. The Azure Policy Overview blade shows you the policy description. It also notes whether the resources to which it is applied are in compliance or not and the percentage of compliance for the given policy. Complete Exercise 6.2, where you will create and apply a custom policy definition.

FIGURE 6.3   Azure Policy overview in the Azure Portal

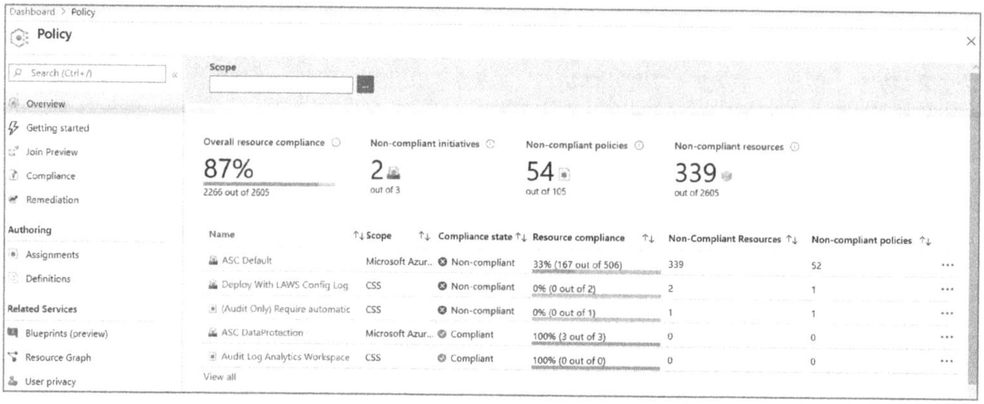

EXERCISE 6.2

Creating and Applying a Custom Policy Definition

1. Log in to the Azure Portal at portal.azure.com. In the search box at the top middle of the browser, enter **Policy**. Select Policy in the Authoring section on the navigation menu, click Definitions, and click + Policy Definition.

2. Click the ellipsis button to the right of Definition Location text box. Select the subscription from the Subscription drop-down text box into which you want to create the policy definition and click the Select button. Now provide a name for the policy definition (for example, Enforce HTTPS and TLS v 1.2), provide a description, and then select the Use Exiting radio button in the Category section. Select App Service and add the content of the csharpguitar.policy.json to the Policy Rule text block located here:

   github.com/benperk/ASA/tree/master/Chapter06/Ch06Ex02

   The final configuration should resemble Figure 6.4.

3. Click the Save button, and then in the Authoring section on the navigation menu, click the Assignments link. Click the Assign policy link and click the ellipsis button to the right of the Scope text box. Select the subscription and resource group where you want the policy applied and then click the Select button. Select the ellipsis button to the right of the Policy Definition text box and select the policy you created in step 2. Click the Select button, click the Review + Create button, and then click the Create button.

FIGURE 6.4   Creating a custom Azure Policy

4. Azure Policy will monitor and restrict the creation of Azure app services in the selected resource group based on the policy rules and show the compliance state on the Overview blade. Your result should be similar to that shown in Figure 6.3.

In step 3, where you selected the resource group you wanted to apply the policy to, you could have left that blank and applied it at the subscription level. The policy rule itself contained in the `csharpguitar.policy.json` file is a JSON document. It identifies the service to which you bound the rule (`Microsoft.Web`) as well as the field that it applies to within the service and its value. For example, `httpsOnly` and `minTlsVersion`, which you will find in the policy JSON file, were discussed in the previous exercise. The effect in this example is to deny the creation of an Azure Apps service unless `allOf` is true. It is not possible to create an Azure App Service unless it enables HTTPS Only and allows TLS 1.2 only. There is another effect named `audit`, which would allow the creation, but it would flag it on the Azure Policy Overview blade. You can create a rule that a *tag* is required when an Azure resource is provisioned as well, if desired.

Tags

There has been a lot of focus on the resource group as the means for logically grouping a set of provisioned Azure products together. The grouping could be based on location or the resources that provide an IT solution. Environments are an interesting scenario where *tags* can be utilized. It is common for IT organizations to have different environments such as development, *user acceptance testing (UAT)*, perhaps *integration and testing (I&T)*, and certainly a production environment. When you have only the concept of a resource group in your repertoire, you might consider placing all the Azure resources into a single resource group. That makes some sense because all the resources development through production make up the IT solution, but if you did that, you would surely end up with too many resources in the resource group. You would lose an overview quick, regardless if you give the resources distinct descriptive names. You could also consider creating a resource group to gather together the resources for each environment together, but that could become convoluted quickly too. The decision, like always, is dependent on your requirements.

An additional option you have is a tag. All Azure products support tagging. You will find a Tag option similar to that shown in Figure 6.5 in the navigation menu of each resource in the Azure Portal. There you can set a tag name and its value to use for querying.

FIGURE 6.5 Tag an Azure resource using the Azure Portal

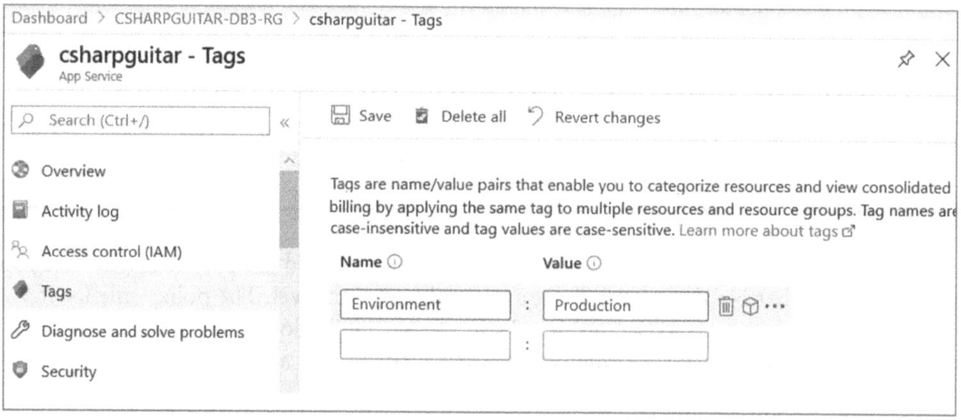

Once you set the tags, you can use the following Azure PowerShell cmdlets to query the resources using the tag name and tag value:

```
Get-AzResource -Tag @{ Environment="Production"} `
    | Format-Table Name, ResourceGroupName, ResourceType

Get-AzResource -Tag @{ Environment="Development"} `
    | Format-Table Name, ResourceGroupName, ResourceType
```

Figure 6.6 illustrates the output of these Azure PowerShell cmdlets. When reviewing Figure 6.6, note that a tag can span resource groups. This was done more to prove it is possible as opposed to making a recommendation to create such configurations. However, if your scenario requires it, know that it is possible to achieve it.

FIGURE 6.6   Querying on tag name and value using Azure PowerShell

```
PS C:\> Get-AzResource -Tag @{ Environment="Production"} | Format-Table Name, ResourceGroupName, ResourceType

Name                 ResourceGroupName    ResourceType
----                 -----------------    ------------
CSHARPGUITAR-VNET-A  CSHARPGUITAR-DB3-RG  Microsoft.Network/virtualNetworks
csharpguitar         CSHARPGUITAR-DB3-RG  Microsoft.web/sites
csharpguitar         CSHARPGUITAR-SN1-RG  Microsoft.DocumentDb/databaseAccounts


PS C:\> Get-AzResource -Tag @{ Environment="Development"} | Format-Table Name, ResourceGroupName, ResourceType

Name                  ResourceGroupName    ResourceType
----                  -----------------    ------------
csharpguitar-dar      CSHARPGUITAR-DB3-RG  Microsoft.keyVault/vaults
csharpguitar-table    CSHARPGUITAR-SN1-RG  Microsoft.DocumentDb/databaseAccounts
csharpguitar/csharp   CSHARPGUITAR-SN1-RG  Microsoft.Sql/servers/databases
```

There are numerous other queries you can run using a tag as the filter. For example, you can check how much the cost is for all the resources with a specific tag, as shown in Figure 6.7.

FIGURE 6.7   Filtering on tag name and value to see resource costs in the Azure Portal

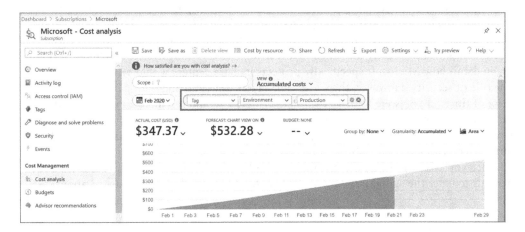

Listing all the resources with a specific tag, calculating costs, and grouping resources at a more granular level than a resource group are all nice features of tags. Use your creativity and find other reasons to use tags. For example, what are some your use cases for a tag with a name of Status and a value of Approved? You are limited only by your creativity and imagination.

Security

From a compliance perspective, the security elements in focus are physical protection, network security, infrastructure security, user access and identity, and data security. As you can see in Figure 6.8, the security element can be the responsibility of the customer, the responsibility of a cloud hosting provider, such as Azure/Microsoft, or a shared responsibility.

FIGURE 6.8   Security compliance roles and responsibilities by cloud service offering

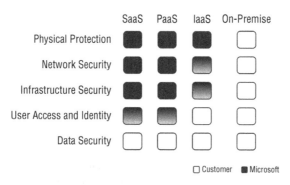

The location where the physical servers that run your workloads comprise a data center. Those data centers have doors, and those doors need to be protected. If you have some experience with security, you know that once someone gets physical access to a machine, it has historically been possible to log in to that machine. Planting a LAN turtle (a network implant) or simply causing some physical damage to machines and cables is enough to warrant significant security measures that restrict access to the physical machines. Explaining in detail how Microsoft specifically protects its data centers would violate the number-one rule of security. However, there are some layers to it, starting with parameter barriers. A lot of times, if you were to drive by a data center, it would resemble a military bunker, be surrounded by fences, or be located behind a small hill making it invisible. To enter, you would need to drive through a single point of entry, which is monitored, usually by a living human who checks credentials.

Once you pass that layer, there would be another check point that requires proper credentials to enter the actual building or data center. Once inside, as you learned about zones and fault and update domains in Chapter 4, the servers are segmented and separated from each other. There may be some areas in the data center that are more sensitive than others based on the impact of a bad actor gaining access. For example, power switches or emergency systems like a fire alarm need increased security. Thus, the final layer protects the console of the machine. This requires an additional and approved JIT credential for gaining access to the floor where the machine is running. In general, Microsoft is responsible for the physical protection of the workloads running in its data centers. Customer, running-on-premise workloads bear full responsibility for on-premise security.

Network security is the responsibly of Microsoft when it comes to SaaS and PaaS and a shared responsibility when it comes to IaaS. In all cases, you will not have physical access to any network switch, routers, or other network devices that run the Azure networking infrastructure. You do, however, get a virtual equivalent for each, like a virtual gateway or a virtual private network. The sharing of the networking security responsibility from an IaaS perspective has to do with the ability for a customer to create connectivity from an on-premise network to Azure-hosted workloads. Azure VMs, for example, exist within a VNet. If you wanted to make a secure connection to them from an on-premise network, then some of the protection to the VMs in the VNet lies with you. Remember, if your network is compromised, then there would be limited means for Microsoft to detect that. You create a trust relationship between the two networks, and trust means traffic between the two is allowed and expected to happen. Don't be alarmed because there are features that are monitoring for behaviors that exhibit patterns matching malicious activities. *Azure Sentinel* allows you to configure Security Center (discussed later), Azure Threat Protection, and the encrypting of communications between your endpoints. All are features you can use to safeguard your network.

An important aspect of security is the existence of antivirus and malware detection software. This is from the context of infrastructure security. All Azure VMs that are used to run the Azure infrastructure have native malware detection and antivirus software running. Do keep in mind that when you provision an Azure VM to run your workload, the provisioning doesn't include installing security software automatically. Also, some custom software products do not work well with antivirus and malware services because those applications have behavioral patterns that match algorithms that cause them to be quarantined. If you need an antivirus or malware service running on your Azure VM (IaaS), then you can install one. As per Figure 6.8, IaaS security is a shared responsibility, while PaaS, for example an Azure App Service, does have malware detection software that monitors the platform, but not the application. This is also the case with SaaS.

You are allowed to perform penetration testing on Azure without notifying Microsoft in advance. Keep in mind that you cannot try to hack other customers; your testing must be focused on your own resources. The only constraint is, if you find something, you need to notify Microsoft so the issue can be further analyzed and patched as required. Be certain that if you try to hack someone other than your own resources, there are large groups of teams and AI algorithms monitoring. Don't do it; you will lose. Keep in mind that even probing an endpoint to see whether it has a vulnerability is illegal, and attempting to exploit a discovered vulnerability will get you into deep, hot water. You will get caught.

In Chapter 2 there was a lot of coverage concerning user access and identity. Specifically, we covered security around RBAC and Azure Active Directory and some additional means for protecting your applications, such as multifactor authentication (MFA), JIT, and location-based access. In all identity scenarios you, as the customer, have a significant responsibility because you are the one that establishes the who, what, when, and where access to your workloads and application endpoints. This responsibility is shared for SaaS and PaaS because you do not have physical access to the machines that are running your workloads. Only Microsoft has this kind of access. However, you can grant anyone or any entity access to the code running on it. While IaaS and on-premise are totally owned by you, controlling remote and application access (the ability to run your custom code) is totally out of scope in IaaS and on-premise.

In the previous chapter, you learned about encrypting data on an Azure SQL database. You also learned about protecting data using SAS keys, Key Vault, firewalls, and service endpoints. All of those examples require you to perform the implementation and configuration. None of them is set up by default. They are optional features that allow additional protection from the unauthorized access to your data. Keys, tokens, locations, and credentials are all that is protecting your data and they need to be protected greatly, by you. The one exception occurs when you store content to an Azure Storage account (Azure Files and Azure Blob). Data there is encrypted by default. Microsoft cannot prevent you from exposing or sharing SAS keys, tokens, or other credentials; therefore, only best-case examples are provided as recommendations for implementation into your workloads. In all cases, the protection of your data is up to you. Don't confuse this with the physical, network, and infrastructure, etc., security, which is provided to you. The simple fact is that if your data is protected only by a simple user ID and password and that leaks, then your data is vulnerable, and there is nothing Microsoft can do about that.

Resiliency and Reliability

Performing backups, preparing for a disaster, and architecting your IT solution to maintain a high level of availability are all resiliency and reliability concepts that are applicable to the Azure platform. Additionally, making the code that runs in the cloud tolerant to transient issues also applies but is the responsibility of the company or individual who designs and writes the code. Taking backups of your database, your storage, and your Azure VM images have all been discussed in previous chapters and will be discussed in most detail later in Chapter 9. Backing and storing your data is a critical part of your *disaster recovery (DR)* strategy. As you learned in the previous chapter, Azure SQL and Azure Cosmos DBs are backed up automatically as part of the PaaS portfolio of default services. As well, you have learned that selecting LRS, ZRS, or GRS replication options results in copies of the storage contents existing in different zones or regions. Lastly, you learned that Azure VMs can be manually backed up, or you can create a schedule for regular backups. From a PaaS perspective, like Azure App Services or an Azure Function, you would want to focus mostly on keeping your source code in a safe and secured place versus focusing on the platform. Remember that with PaaS you are not responsible for the platform any longer. In Chapter 7 there will be some mention of source code repositories such as Azure DevOps and GitHub.

These are useful for storing, versioning, and protecting your code.

In Chapter 9, there will be more about *business continuity and disaster recovery (BCDR)*. Microsoft provides a tool named Azure Site Recovery, introduced in Chapter 1, as the recommend way to consume the *disaster recovery as a service (DRaaS)* solution offering. Following the guidelines and recommendations and using this tool provide the means for activating, executing, and recovering from an IT outage.

Azure Site Recovery (ASR) also provides the capabilities for testing your BCDR solution. This would be necessary if being compliant for a given certification requires the validation and execution of such a process. The point is, Azure Site Recovery is the recommended tool for implementing DRaaS if this kind of service is a requirement for your IT solution. Having a quality backup strategy, combined with the strategy for identifying and responding to scenarios that require the implementation of those backups, makes your solution resilient. *Resilient* means that your solution can withstand numerous kinds of failures and remain functional from the perspective of those who use the solution. When resiliency is achieved, the outcome of that is customers and employees begin to trust and rely on your solution. The result is reliability.

From an architectural perspective, products like Azure load balancers, Azure Traffic Manager (ATM), storage redundancy options (LRS, ZRS, GRS), availability sets, and availability zones are all built-in platform designs or are configurable Azure features to make your system resilient and reliable. Both Azure Load Balancer and ATM are useful for monitoring the health of an internet-based system to which the request is first sent. You would have numerous web servers sitting behind the ALB (aka LB) or ATM, sometimes in different regions. When a server is not responding, the two products are intelligent enough to stop routing traffic to it and send an alert to an administrator, if configured to do so. The storage redundancy story was covered in detail in the previous chapter, but even with the cheapest option, you will have three copies of the data stored in that account. An entire zone would need to become unavailable before you would be unable to connect or unable to recover. Remember that LRS is useful for development projects, and you should use at least ZRS for production workloads or for workloads that cannot easily recover from data loss. An availability set is the redundancy at the data center level. For example, if you have multiple instances of an Azure VM, they will be placed into different availability sets, each of which would have their own power supplies, networking infrastructure, and host update schedules. Availability zones encapsulate availability sets. There are multiple availability sets within an availability zone, and there are up to three availability zones per region. A region is North Europe (DB3) or South Central US (SN1). Finally, as you will learn in Chapter 7, there are also coding patterns, like the Retry or Circuit Breaker, which will make your applications more resilient.

Privacy

Privacy is built into Azure. Most people who use the internet know a little about privacy issues and how data is being captured while navigating the web. One of the leading regulations concerning online privacy is the General Data Protection Regulation (GDPR), which outlines stringent privacy standards and practices. As an Azure customer, you have control over your data, it is forever your data, you have complete control over it, and you must provide adequate privacy. Here are some key privacy points that highlight the commitment Microsoft has toward privacy:

- When you delete your Azure subscription, any leftover data is completely purged after a short timeframe.

- Your data remains located in the region where you deployed it.

- Your data is not transferred across international borders in accordance with the data protection laws of the country of origin.

- No one at Microsoft has default access to your data; most staff (actually almost all) will never come close to having access.

- If there is a security breach, Microsoft is committed to notifying you.

Here is a summarized list of privacy best practices that Microsoft is committed to applying toward the safeguarding of data:

- EU General Data Protection Regulation (GDPR)

- Personal Information Protection and Electronic Documents Act (PIPEDA)

- Personal Information Protection Act (PIPA)

- British Columbia Freedom of Information Protection of Privacy Act (BC FIPPA) (Canada)

- PDPA (Argentina)

- My Number Act (Japan)

- LOPD (Spain)

- Health Information Trust (HITRUST)

- Health Insurance Portability and Accountability Act (HIPAA)

- Family Educational Rights and Privacy Act (FERPA)

- EU-U.S. Privacy Shield

- EU Model Clauses

- ISO/IEC 27018

- California Consumer Privacy Act (CCPA)

Some tools that Microsoft provides for complying with privacy guidelines are *Azure Data Subject Request (DSR) Portal*, Azure Policy, and *Azure Information Protection (AIP)*. DSR is a guideline for providing the ability for individuals to access the data that has been captured and stored about them as per GDPR and CCPA regulations. Read more about DSR here:

docs.microsoft.com/en-us/microsoft-365/compliance/gdpr-dsr-azure

Azure Policy was discussed in a previous section, but in short, this provides the means for enforcing compliance with your corporate guidelines as they pertain to Azure resource provisioning. For example, in Exercise 6.1 you created an Azure policy that required HTTPS and TLS 1.2, which are necessary to comply with the PCI standard. AIP is a cloud-based solution that lets you apply a *label* to emails or documents in an effort to restrict and protect them against unauthorized access, even if unintentional. An administrator can create a label that defines a set of conditions and apply it to either email or documents. For example, only people in a specific organization (Luthiers) can read a document about the new model being created by Fender. Or perhaps an email is confidential and shouldn't be forwarded or printed because it contains the design document for C# version 12.

There is one more privacy concept to discuss before moving on. Many places on the Azure platform share resources with multiple customers. For example, when you provision an Azure VM, it was certainly at some point utilized by some other application previously. You should be certain and comfortable that any remnants of previous code running on the VM are removed and the system is wiped clean before it is put back into the pool of available compute power. A similar aspect is true for PaaS products such as Azure App Services and Azure Functions, especially Azure Functions because the compute lasts only as long as it is actually being invoked and executed. Networking components and network bandwidth may share some capacity and utilizations at some point. This might be an issue for some customers who need a greater level of isolation. True, a VNet is private and very secure, and an App Service Environment is also a secure and isolated environment, but some components can still be shared with other customers. This is simply the design in the cloud. The resources must be massively scaled and massively utilized to get the synergies required to make all the components profitably work together. The greatest isolation design runs your workloads in your on-premise data center, but if that were the objective, then there is no need for an Azure workload to begin with.

Azure Virtual Datacenter (VDC) is another product that can give you great isolation on the Azure platform. VDC runs on the Azure platform, like virtual machines, virtual networks, and virtual gateways. Like the other virtual products, the isolation applied by VDC remains static and private until deletion. Using what you know about VMs, VNets, and virtual gateways, recognize that although virtual product instances run on physical hardware, there is a virtual isolation wall between all of them. They are completely separate with absolutely no means of crossing that barrier.

Regulatory Boundaries

There have been multiple discussions about zones, twin zones, and the replication of data between them and also across other international borders. Many countries have regulations about how data owned by the citizens of that country can be stored. GDPR, PIPEDA, the German Federal Data Protection Act, and China's Cyber Security Law (CSL) all have stringent requirements about the storage and movement of data created and consumed within the country. In many cases, the capabilities to prevent erroneous data movement, data capturing, or storage must exist proactively on the platform. It cannot be left to enterprises or cloud hosts to comply. Microsoft and Azure are working hard on these tools and features. Most of the cases already have the capability to comply with the standards. Azure Blueprints, Azure Policy, and VDC are some of the tools available for enterprises to attain proper compliance. In addition to the high level of security available for those products on

Azure, the enforcement of policies at the subscription level and the Microsoft Trust Center containing steps for attaining compliance for a multitude of standards make Azure a top competitor in this area.

Security Center

This product was introduced in Chapter 2, which focused on the security aspects provided within it. Review that chapter and specifically Figure 2.49 to refresh your memory about it. As you will see, Security Center focuses on threat detection, advanced cloud defense, resource security hygiene, and the one that is in focus in this chapter, policy and compliance. Take a look at the Security Center in the Azure Portal by searching for it in the top middle search box. Then, click the Regulatory Compliance link on the navigation menu, and you will see something similar to Figure 6.9.

FIGURE 6.9 Security Center regulatory compliance overview report in the Azure Portal

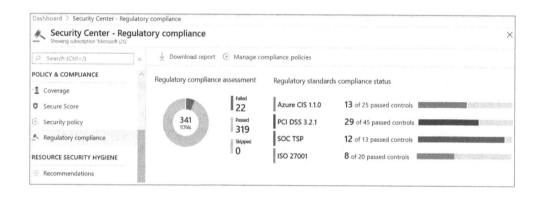

Notice that there is a list of regulatory compliance standards such as Azure CIS 1.1.0, PCI DSS 3.2.1, SOC TSP, and ISO 27001 that have been applied to the products in the subscription. Following those standards are bar graphs showing how far away the subscription is from complying with those standards. To the left of that is an overall status of regulatory compliance. Scroll down a bit on the Regulatory compliance blade, and you will notice tabs for each of the applied standards. Beneath each tab exists a report of the specific noncompliant attributes and some instruction on how to fix it. Check out Figure 6.10, which illustrates a summary of what you may see if you perform the same action on your subscription.

Notice that an action required for Azure CIS 1.1.0 compliance requires that all the Azure App Service products in the subscription must enforce the use of HTTPS. This encrypts all communication between clients and Azure App Service. By working through all the Azure products that failed the assessment and performing the identified action, you would be well on the way to achieving regulatory compliance for that standard. Lastly, if the standard is not in the list, take a look back at Figure 6.9 and notice the Manage Compliance Policies link. This is where you could add additional standards. Once added, an assessment would run automatically, allowing you to then work through the noncompliant resources.

FIGURE 6.10 Security Center regulatory compliance overview report in the Azure Portal

Before moving on to the next section, there are additional Security Center features that should be called out, such as Data & Storage, Compute & Apps, Networking, and Identity & Access. The latter two require no detailed explanation because the portal blade content provides a report similar to what you will see in Figure 6.12. Therefore, they aren't covered in more detail as there is no additional detail to cover. Take notice that the four available features are Identity (security), Networking, Compute, and Data, which are exactly what the previous four chapters covered. Those four components are specifically called out in Exercise 6.3. Keep these four components of Azure product and feature groupings in the back of your brain from now on and use them in the future as the model for the basis of your approach toward the creation of your Azure deployment strategy. The book is ordered in this way for that specific reason: they are ordered in the sequence of significance.

Data & Storage

A bit earlier you were introduced to Azure Information Protection (AIP), which uses a labeling mechanism to mark emails and documents with a classification. This classification is useful for making sure only those who are authorized can view, copy, share, or print the material. A similar feature, *SQL Information Protection*, also uses a labeling technique that is helpful for classifying columns in a database table. You might remember some discussion about this in the previous chapter in the discussion of Azure SQL and the Azure Data Security (ADS) features. Complete Exercise 6.3 to add a data classification (label) to the database you created in Exercise 5.2 and populated in Exercise 5.3.

EXERCISE 6.3

Configuring Data Discovery & Classification

1. Log in to the Azure Portal at `portal.azure.com`. Navigate to the SQL database you created in Exercise 5.2. Click the Advanced Data Security link in the navigation menu and click the Data Discovery & Classification graph on the blade. Select the Classification tab and click the + Add Classification link from the menu.

2. Leave the default Schema name (dbo) and select MODELS from the Table name drop-down list. Select MODEL from the Column Name drop-down list. Select Other from the Information Type drop-down list. Select Confidential from the Sensitivity Label drop-down list text box and click the Add Classification and Save buttons. The configuration should resemble that shown in Figure 6.11.

FIGURE 6.11   The configuration of a classification (label) on an Azure SQL database column

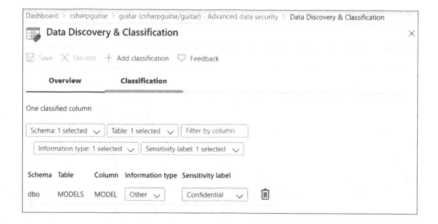

3. In the search box at the top middle of the Azure Portal, enter **Security Center**. Select Security Center from the search result and then select Data & Storage from the navigation menu (notice the other three, Compute & Apps, Data & Storage, and Identity & Access). The Data & Storage console should resemble something like Figure 6.12.

FIGURE 6.12   Data & Storage Security Center overview blade

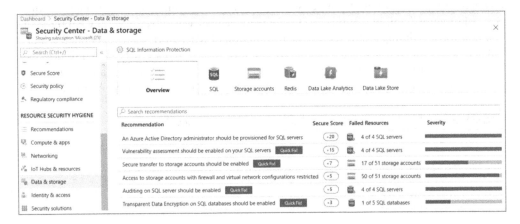

The content on the Data & Storage overview blade provides the same type of information as you see in Figure 6.10. You can click the recommendations to get instructions on how to resolve the compliancy issue. Additionally, in Figure 6.12, notice the SQL Information Protection link. In step 2 of Exercise 6.3, you selected the Sensitivity label with a value of Confidential. If you wanted to create or delete any of those labels, the SQL Information Protection feature is the place to do that. Now that you have classified that database column, when you enable auditing in Chapter 9, you will be able to check how often that column is queried and by whom.

Compute & Apps

When you navigate to the Compute & Apps blade in Security Center, you may see something similar to Figure 6.13 on the VM and Servers tab. You might be asking yourself if the image is correct because there are two VMs with the same name. The image is correct; those machines exist in different resource groups. This is a good example about the implementation of naming standards for your Azure resources. It is kind of easy to figure out the purpose of those two machines, but if there were hundreds, it's not so easy. Even if they were named differently, it might be challenging. Organization of your resources is an important design concern and useful in the compliance and policy context.

The report on the Compute & Apps blade is similar to the others where it lists the non-compliant configurations. What the missing or wrongly implemented configuration is and how to fix it are provided by clicking the VM name in the report list. While in this context of compute and apps, it is an appropriate time to discuss a few operational features available on Azure VMs that are helpful from a compliance, policy, and auditing perspective.

If you navigate to an Azure VM you created previously from within the Azure Portal, scroll down to the Operations section on the navigation menu, and you will see three features: Update Management, Inventory, and Change Tracking. Each of those features places their logs into a Log Analytics workspace, which was introduced in Chapter 1 and covered in more detail in Chapter 9. Update management was introduced in Chapter 4 and is useful for scheduling and tracking the installation of Microsoft Windows updates, aka KB patches. Many of those patches contain fixes for discovered security vulnerabilities, and having the record of the patch and when it was installed is a useful compliancy element. As just mentioned, the logs are written to Log Analytics and referenced from Azure Monitor.

FIGURE 6.13   Compute & Apps Security Center overview blade

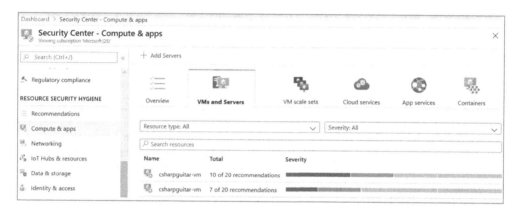

Inventory and Change tracking, see Figure 6.14, allow you to monitor activities on the VM that modify the configuration of the machine in some way. After enabling Inventory and Change tracking a baseline including state of the software, the Windows registry keys, the Windows services, and files on the computer are set. Then future assessments are able to call out whenever one or more of those elements have been modified.

FIGURE 6.14   Azure VM change tracking overview blade

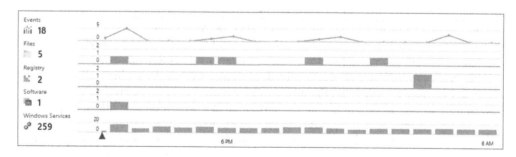

Microsoft Cloud App Security

This is a large topic worthy of its own book. What *Microsoft Cloud App Security (MCAS)* does is seamlessly merge all your Azure resources within your Azure Active Directory tenant with other consumed SaaS products. Take a look back at Figure 2.1 where it symbolizes how AAD can be used to authenticate and secure cross-SaaS. Expand on that figure to include not only authentication but also the following:

- Threat Detection
- Information Protection
- Cloud Discovery

Security is a big part of most compliancy standards; therefore, if you plan on attaining any industry standard, you will need to prove that your tools for monitoring and tracking compliance are competent. As you move your resources to the cloud, and by *cloud* I mean more than just Azure (see Figure 2.1), the ability to manage security holistically becomes even more complex. This is what MCAS is accomplishing by providing an overview and monitoring of those three previously listed concepts.

Threat Detection, which was covered in Chapter 2, is a set of algorithms that monitors the behaviors of clients utilizing your cloud resources. Think about an access from an unexpected location or a DDoS attack. When those events or other malicious behaviors are identified, they are logged, and, if configured, an administrator is alerted to the event in near real time.

Protecting the information, aka data, source code, and compute resources, requires some overview and capabilities too. Protection begins with an action such as setting the sensitivity classification of your data, as you did in Exercise 6.3 for a database column. AIP is also integrated with MCAS for email and file classifications. You then protect that data by being able to control access to it by granting and revoking permission to the data and information. MCAS provides those capabilities across all cloud apps configured within it.

Finding out which cloud applications exist within your portfolio is accomplished using the Cloud Discovery capability. Cloud Discovery uses your network traffic logs that flow through a proxy to determine the existence of cloud apps. It can also tell you who and how often those cloud apps are being utilized. If one of the cloud apps in the MCAS umbrella is found to expose some kind of vulnerability or perform a malicious activity, then access to that applications can be turned off.

Finally, policies, like those created using Azure Policy (see Exercise 6.1), can be applied across all cloud apps and cross-SaaS. MCAS is a tool that exists outside of Azure and requires a specific license for use. For more information about this product, read this online documentation:

docs.microsoft.com/en-us/cloud-app-security

Azure Messaging Services

Sending information between two or more systems isn't something that is new to computing; it's actually a fundamental concept. From a web application perspective, HTTP-based protocols such as SOAP, WCF, and REST are used for managing the communication between systems. Additionally, there are protocols such as *Microsoft Message Queuing (MSMQ)*, *Data Distribution Service (DDS)*, and *Advanced Message Queueing Protocol (AMQP)*, which are useful in scenarios that won't or don't function over HTTP. The implementation of those protocols into a solution requires some significant coding and testing efforts as the protocol provides the means of sending and queuing messages, but it is up to you to actually implement it. If you are scratching your head about the approach for implementing a messaging solution using any of those protocols, stop, because the products exiting in the Azure Messaging Services portfolio abstract that complexity away. All you need to do is design and configure the endpoints and then begin publishing and consuming the messages and responding to events. If you take a look in Chapter 1, you will see that Microsoft's portfolio of *messaging as a service (MaaS)* products, Event Hub, Service Bus, Azure Storage Queue, and Event Grid, were introduced. Take a look over that to get back into the messaging context. You also created an Event Hub in Chapter 5. In this section, you will learn the following:

- Event versus messaging
- How to choose the right messaging service
- Messaging patterns
- Event Hub, Service Bus, Azure Storage Queue, and Event Grid
- Logic App and Notification Hub

Before you get started on those topics, I wanted to reflect and expand on a comparison between what you learned about background jobs in Chapter 4 and what you will learn in this chapter. Remember, Azure Batch, HPC, and WebJobs are all products that allow you to process data based on a schedule or event trigger. In the scenario of background jobs, you typically have a large dataset that is either received all at once or built up over time. When the trigger happens, background processing usually processes large data sets. That processing usually consumes large amounts of I/O, CPU, or storage capacity. In contrast to batch and background processing, event and messaging data is processed in real time as soon as it arrives in the queue. If there are scenarios where you are running background jobs in short intervals, such as order processing or customer registration logic, then consider using one of these messaging products instead. You may find that some of the scheduled processing on large data sets can be optimized from a performance (speed of execution) and cost perspective, if instead the data could be processed in real time. From the perspective of many IT professionals, messaging is an evolution from scheduled background job execution to a continuous computing model.

Event vs. Messaging

You can determine which messaging products are event driven simply by name—Event Hub and Event Grid. The other two, Service Bus and Azure Storage Queue, are for managing messages. But what is the difference between an event and a message in this context? Take the Windows operating system as an example; Windows is event driven. In most cases, you boot up your computer, and if you do not do anything with it, then both of you simply sit there. You need to move the mouse, click the mouse, tap the screen, or tap some keys on the keyboard. Each of those actions triggers an event that is wired to a delegate that then triggers a function or method. Double-clicking the Edge icon tells the operating system to load the `MicrosoftEdge.exe` process into memory, which lets you surf the internet. Therefore, an event is a notification from a publisher that a change in state or condition has occurred. The question is who wants to know about that state or condition change? You'd guess it depends on what the event is reporting, which can be found by querying the metadata within the event object. If another system wants to be notified of such an event, that consumer can subscribe to the publisher and receive those event notifications. Take a quick look at Figure 4.4 for an illustration of the event publisher and event consumer flow. The glue between an event and a method is a delegate. In the Azure messaging service context, the glue between a publisher and a consumer is Event Hub or Event Grid. Once the consumer (function or method) is notified that it needs to run, it parses the content of the event metadata and executes code based on its findings—kind of in the same way when you call a method in C# where the method has a set of parameters sent based on the method definition. This is similar to the following, where you would expect the event calling the `GetGuitar()` method to pass along the number of strings, color, and body type:

```
GetGuitar(int numberOfStrings, string color, string bodyType)
```

Service Bus and Azure Storage Queue handle messages that you can visualize as an array of characters and strings. You likely send messages using What's App, Facebook, Snapchat, Apple, or Instagram messaging apps. In those scenarios, the size and complexity of the message may be less intense as messages sent, which require a service like Service Bus or an Azure Storage queue. By *intense*, I mean they may be large, there may be a million of them in a second, or they may be required to be stored and processed in order. However, the simplest description of message management services such as Service Bus and Azure Storage Queue is that they receive, queue, and track messages until they are consumed, processed, and deleted.

How to Choose the Right Messaging Service

In a few occasions so far, there have been examples of the decoupling of services from each other. Specifically, there was an example about running reports offline or the placing of product orders, where instead of running reports in real time or processing all the requirements for placing an order, the request is placed into a queue. The client or customer who placed the request gets an almost instantaneous response since the report isn't really run and the order isn't placed; it is instead queued for processing. Then, at a later moment, the report or order is processed offline, and a response is provided to the client or customer. This decoupling of services between the insertion and processing of data increased the probability of success and the response time. It increases the probability of success because, for one, the client isn't waiting for a response until the order is processed or the report is run. The longer you wait, the higher the probability the connection could get interrupted. Second, there is less source code required to enter the data into a queue than there is when compared to processing an order or when a report is executed and therefore less chance for race conditions, exceptions, and hangs. The reason for implementing this decoupling is clear, but which of the four messaging services work best in which scenarios? Figure 6.15 provides a simple decision tree that will help to get you on the right track. For more information on this topic, read the content on this web page:

docs.microsoft.com/en-us/azure/event-grid/compare-messaging-services

FIGURE 6.15 How to choose the right messaging service decision tree

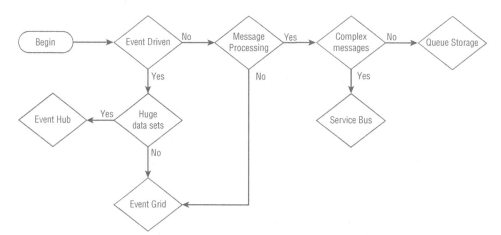

The primary decision to make is whether your solutions need to be triggered on an event or if you will be receiving or processing messages. There are many more complexities to making a fully educated decision about the correct message service; however, these are the most impactful decisions to make from the start. If you require event-driven capabilities and the amount of data needing processing is huge, like big data huge or perhaps you have a constant stream of data, then Event Hub is your choice. If not, go for Event Grid. If you require a messaging-driven capability with simple messages that are less than 64KB, then choose Azure Queue Storage. If the message is larger than 64KB and/or the messages require FIFO or you must guarantee processing, then a Service Bus is your best bet. As you attempt to digest that, keep in mind the sending of messages to the messaging service generally happens in the same way, by using the client SDK for the given type—Event Hub, Service Bus, Azure Storage Queue, and the like, each of which receives a character array of digits. The point is how the consumers get notified of the arrival of the message. Does the consumer receive an event that contains information about the message, or does the consumer receive the message? There is more detail coming in regarding each of these messaging services, so read on, and it will become clearer. Take a look at Table 6.1 for some side-by-side analysis of the messaging services, which are explained in more detail in their respective section later in this chapter.

TABLE 6.1   Comparing Azure Messaging Services

Event Hub	Event Grid	Service Bus	Azure Storage Queue
Event-driven	Event-driven	Message-based	Message-based
At least once	At least once	At least/most once	At least once
Pull	Push	Pull or push	Pull
Big data	Reactive	High-value messages	High-volume messages
Telemetry	Custom events	FIFO (w/ sessions)	Queue: 500TB

Before proceeding into the specifics of these Azure Messaging Services, read first about some messaging design patterns and guiding principles.

Messaging Patterns

In most components of technology, there are best-practice use patterns for achieving high availability, optimal scalability, resiliency, and performance. This applies to loosely coupled interconnected and asynchronous messaging systems, too. Some of the most popular patterns are listed here:

- Publisher/subscriber
- Asynchronous request/reply
- Queue-based load leveling
- Sequential convoy
- Competing consumers

In general, implementing a messaging service into your IT solution decouples systems that have numerous benefits. Decoupling, which improves reliability and scalability by being able to scale whichever component in the system needs the extra capacity instead of scaling the entire solution and the separations of concerns, reduces focus on infrastructure and instead places focus on the core business capabilities of the IT solution. For more information about these highlighted messaging patterns, read on. To learn about other patterns, visit this web page:

```
docs.microsoft.com/en-us/azure/architecture/patterns/category/
messaging
```

Publisher/Subscriber

Also commonly referred to as *pub/sub*, this pattern is similar to the one discussed earlier and visualized in Figure 4.4. However, to specialize it a bit more into the context of the Pub/Sub pattern, as illustrated in Figure 6.16.

FIGURE 6.16   Publisher/subscriber messaging pattern

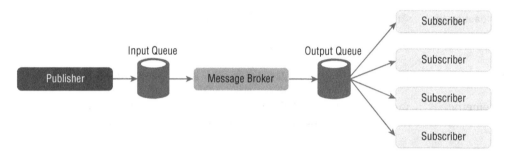

The benefit of this pattern is that the entity providing or creating the data must send it only to a single location. The "entity" is the publisher, and the location the data packet is sent to is inserted into an input data queue, which is an ultrafast ingestion data store. The message broker would then be responsible for managing the data packet and notifying the subscribers in the form of an event that there is a message for them. This pattern avoids having to send the information to multiple consumers or subscribers, which would take much longer than sending out a broadcast message from the publisher. As well, many notification systems are required to wait on a response from the receiver, which could fail or be slow due to load on the consumer. This pattern decouples systems, and by decoupling them, it makes them all the more reliable. The solution is more reliable because the ability for the publisher to send data to a consumer is no longer dependent on the consumer being available. The data is placed in a queue, and the consumer is notified and can come retrieve it whenever they want. This is a common pattern with IoT scenarios.

Asynchronous Request/Reply

When using the HTTP protocol, the client sending the request is expecting a response. The most common and most expected successful response from a sent request is a 200. However, if the request is asynchronous, then it is likely the response is sent before the code completes, so a 200 response code isn't the correct status. Instead, the response would be a 202, meaning that the request has been accepted but not necessarily completed. The status of the processing would need to be checked from time to time from the client, and once completed, the status check would respond with the results and a 200. In modern applications where web sockets are supported, the client and server can maintain a connection that allows the server to notify the client directly when the asynchronous request has completed successfully. This pattern is useful in legacy scenarios, scenarios that require HTTP, or where callbacks are not supported due to firewall restrictions on the client side.

Queue-Based Load Leveling

Queue-based load leveling is the pattern useful for systems that may experience bursts or carry heavy loads that may overload some backend system such as a data store like Azure SQL. This overload could cause orders from an online store to time out if the load is too high for the backend servers to respond in an appropriate time. See the left portion of Figure 6.17, which illustrates numerous clients, an Azure App Service, and an Azure Function all attempting to update data on an Azure SQL database. The dotted line represents a failure of an update because the data store is overloaded.

FIGURE 6.17   Queue-based load leveling messaging pattern

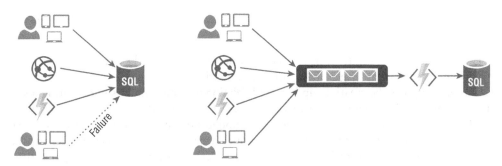

The illustration on the right side of Figure 6.17 represents the queue-based load leveling pattern. This pattern places a message queue, for example, Service Bus or Azure Storage Queue, between the clients and the database. Then there is an Azure Function, which monitors that queue and processes the messages, perhaps sequentially, in near real time or at a scheduled interval. In any case, the dotted line representing a failure due to the overloading of the backend data store is not present. This is because the orders are queued up instead of all attempting to be processed and stored at the same time. This is a one-way communication; the client will not automatically receive notification that the order has been processed. This is something you would need to build into your business logic.

Sequential Convoy

Many IT solutions require that transactions are processed in the order that they are received. At first glance, this may appear to be straightforward, because usually when you have a queue it is sequential, like when standing in a line; it's first come, first served. The complexity arises when there are multiple consumers processing the messages. What happens if consumer A for some reason can process faster than consumer B? Perhaps consumer A processes message 1, and consumer B processes message 2 but it hangs a little, and consumer A takes message 3 from the queue and completes it before message 2 is complete. Also consider a scenario where consumers can pull and process batches of messages at a time instead of one message at a time. What if multiple consumers can pull batches? It gets complicated, agreed? The solution is to implement a pattern similar to that shown in Figure 6.18, which is a visual representation of a sequential pattern.

FIGURE 6.18 Sequential convoy load leveling messaging pattern

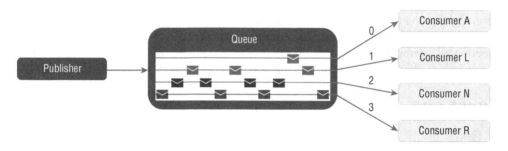

The trick, or the expectation, is that the messages being sent to the queue can be categorized into groups of messages. Take, for example, when you have an order management system that supports the creation, update, and deletion of orders and assumes that, in a scenario, all three of those happen in a close sequence. If you send all order creations to category 0, which are processed by Consumer A, all updates to category 1, which are processed by Consumer L, and all deletes to category 3, which are processed by Consumer R, and the orders are processing in the order in which they are received, there is then no way that the system could ever attempt to delete an order that hasn't yet been created.

Competing Consumers

This pattern can probably be visualized by reading its name. A consumer is a VM that has some code on it, whose purpose is to process messages entering a queue. It is certainly possible to have a single publisher that sends messages to a queue that are then processed by a single consumer. However, in larger solutions, there are multiple publishers and/or clients that are putting messages into the queue, and the number of messages may be too much for a single consumer to process. This would lead to a large backlog in the queue, and it is possible that the consumer never gets caught up. It may take hours or days to process all the events. If that happens, you can provision multiple consumers that pull messages from the queue and process them in parallel. Figure 6.19 illustrates that scenario and represents the competing consumers' messaging pattern.

FIGURE 6.19 Competing consumers' messaging pattern

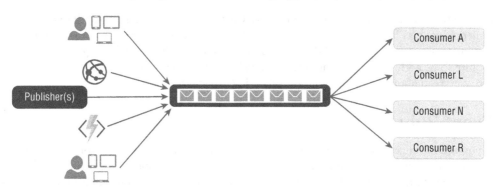

This pattern scales very well in that you can add consumers as the number of messages in the queue increases and also remove them when the backlog is small, which makes it a cost-effective solution. There are also some generic messaging concepts that you need exposure to when working with messaging services. Consider the following points as a guide for triggering some questions you may have for designers and developers as you begin building a decoupled asynchronous IT solution:

- **Message Ordering:** Does it matter if messages are processed in any order? For financial transactions, you would expect it does matter, but how important is it to your application?

- **Message Priority:** Are there any scenarios in which a message needs to jump to the top of the queue and be processed immediately? Consider the Priority Queue pattern.

- **Bidirectional Communication:** Does the system that is sending a message require a response? Pub/Sub is decoupled, but Request/Reply is not. How important is it to your solution to make sure the message is accepted and processed?

- **Poison Messages:** Data corruption can happen, and the message that arrives in the queue could be malformed. When a consumer retrieves and attempts to process it, there is a chance that processing will fail. Those messages should not be returned to the queue and instead moved to a poison queue so that other consumers are not impacted. However, how do you correct those messages, and how often?

- **Message Expiration:** How long is a message valid? What happens if there are numerous subscribers and consumers, but they have not all consumed the message, even after some hours, days, or weeks? Do you need to purge such messages from the queue for consumers after a certain timeframe?

- **Message Scheduling:** Do you need the ability to not process a message received until a specific time? For example, an earnings report may be queued for announcement, but it cannot be processed until after the closing bell.

Azure Cache for Redis

In Chapter 5, where you learned about Azure Cache for Redis, you may recall one of the bullet points was its ability to act as a queue. This is more of a "for your information." You can implement queuing and Pub/Sub messaging patterns with this technology. It would require some architectural configuration as well as custom code to implement. If this interests you, read about this capability at `redis.io/topics/pubsub`.

Event Hubs

If you need to ingest huge amounts of data in a short period of time from sources like IoT devices, anomaly detection algorithms, telemetry streamers, or big data generators, then consider using Event Hubs. This messaging service is capable of ingesting millions of events per second, which is huge. The most common pattern to be implemented using Event Hubs is the Pub/Sub messaging pattern. Take a look at Figure 6.20, and you will see the resemblance of the Pub/Sub pattern illustrated earlier in Figure 6.16.

FIGURE 6.20   Event Hub architecture components

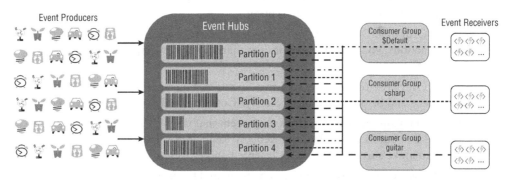

In Figure 6.20 you will find a visualization of the Event Hub architecture. There are numerous components that make up the architecture, for example the event producers (aka producers), which are depicted in the figure as IoT devices but can be anything that emits data. Your numerous partitions, multiple consumer groups, and event receivers (aka consumers) are also visualized. An event receiver can be any client that has subscribed in some way to get the Event Hub notification. Figure 6.20 shows Azure Functions as the event receivers, and the fact that there are numerous Azure Functions means that there can be multiple instances of an Azure Function, which can process events for a given consumer group and partition in parallel. Let's explain some of the terminology described in this paragraph a bit more, beginning with a namespace. In Exercise 5.8 you created an Event Hub namespace; the name you gave it is considered the namespace and is the unique portion of the Event Hub endpoint, for example, `<namespace>.servicebus.windows.net`. View an

Event Hub namespace as a container that contains one or more Event Hubs and where you configure security and monitoring features, which is similar to an Azure Storage account. In Exercise 6.4, you will create an Event Hub and two consumer groups.

EXERCISE 6.4

Creating an Event Hub and Two Consumer Groups

1. Log in to the Azure Portal at portal.azure.com. In the search box at the top middle of the browser, enter **Event Hubs**. Select Event Hubs and then select the Event Hub Namespace you created in Exercise 5.8. On the navigation menu, select Event Hubs and then click the + Event Hub link.

2. Enter an event hub name (for example, csharpguitar). Be sure the name you select is globally unique. Change the partition count to 3 and then click the Create button. Once it's provisioned, select it from the Event Hub list. Click the Consumer Groups link from the navigation menu. Notice that a default consumer group named $Default already exists. Click the + Consumer Group link, enter a consumer group name (for example, guitar), and then click the Create button. (Note that the Basic tier supports only a single consumer group.)

An Event Hub can have up to 32 partitions; a partition is the location the producers stream the data into for queuing and storage. Since the ingress of data into the Event Hub is expected to be huge, this is how the load is balanced and queued at such a high rate, meaning the incoming data is stored across the numerous provisioned partitions. If you have multiple partitions, recognize that there is no guarantee onto which partition the message is stored, nor is the order of receipt retained. It is possible to send the partition ID as part of the ingress that would force it to that specific partition; however, this is not recommended. Take a look now at Consumer Groups. Notice there are three shown in Figure 6.20, and the maximum is 20. Also notice the different patterns of lines connecting the consumers to the partitions. This means that each consumer connected to their given consumer group will have the ability to read the data stored in the partitions. You would not want to have consumers bound to different consumer groups processing events that will be stored in the same backend system. This would result in duplicates, because each consumer group gets access to all the partitions in the Event Hub. When an event or batch of events are consumed, they are not deleted from the partition. Instead, the consumer marks it as committed by using *offsets* or a process called *checkpointing*. An offset is like a pointer or a cursor that identifies where in the data stream your consumers are at in terms of differentiating what has and what has not been processed. Checkpointing is the responsibility of the consumer to notify the messaging service that the stream on that partition is no longer needed for the consumers bound to a given consumer group.

Complete the following exercise to configure ADX to ingest Event Hub information, add messages to the Event Hub you created in Exercise 6.4, and query ADX to view the logs.

EXERCISE 6.5

Configuring ADX to Receive

1. Log in to the Azure Portal at portal.azure.com. In the search box at the top middle of the browser, enter **Azure Data Explorer Clusters** and then select Azure Data Explorer Clusters. Select the Azure Data Explorer Cluster you created in Exercise 5.7. On the navigation menu, select Databases and then click the database you created in Exercise 5.7. Click the Data Ingestion link on the navigation menu and click the + Add Data Connection link.

2. Select Event Hub from the Select Connection Type drop-down list. Enter a name in the Data Connection Name text box (for example, csharpguitar-conn). Select the subscription in which the Event Hub exists and then select the Event Hub namespace you created in Exercise 5.8. Select the Event Hub you created in Exercise 6.4 and select $Default from the Consumer Group drop-down list. Select None from the Compression drop-down list.

3. Add the ADX table name that you created in Exercise 5.7 step 5 (for example, CsharpGuitarEventHub) and then select JSON from the Data Format drop-down list. Enter the Column mapping name that you created in Exercise 5.7 step 6 (for example, CsharpGuitarEventHubMapping). The final configuration should resemble that shown in Figure 6.21. Now click the Create button.

FIGURE 6.21   ADX to Event Hub Data connection configuration

4. Recall from Chapter 5 that there was an example using an Azure Function consumer; see Figure 5.53 as a refresher. You can download the tool here or view the source code and build one yourself:

   github.com/benperk/AzureFunctionConsumer/releases

5. Send messages to the Event Hub you created in Exercise 6.4. If you are not familiar with sending messages to an Event Hub, see Figure 6.22 as an example.

FIGURE 6.22   Adding messages to an Event Hub

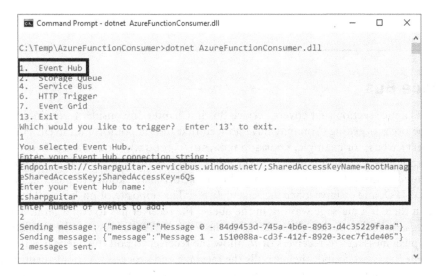

6. Navigate to your Azure Data Explorer Cluster located here:

   dataexplorer.azure.com/

   Execute these KUSTO queries and replace the table name with your table name. The output of the CsharpGuitarEventHub query (which is simply the table name and dumps out all data on that table) is illustrated in Figure 6.23.

   ```
   CsharpGuitarEventHub
   | count
   ```

   ```
   CsharpGuitarEventHub
   ```

FIGURE 6.23 KUSTO query output from Event Hub ADX configuration

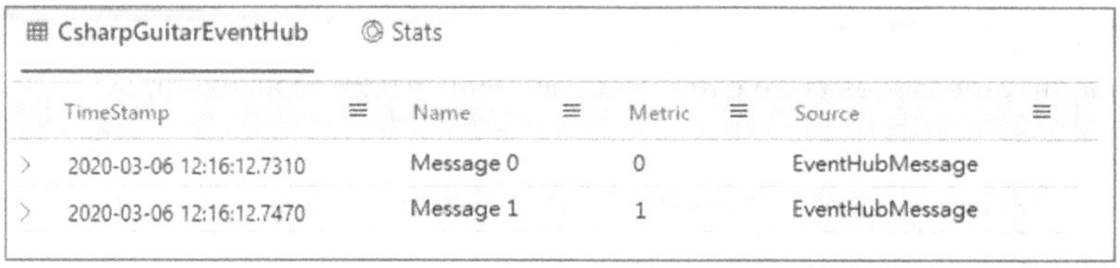

⊞ CsharpGuitarEventHub		⊙ Stats		
TimeStamp ≡	Name ≡	Metric ≡	Source ≡
> 2020-03-06 12:16:12.7310	Message 0	0	EventHubMessage
> 2020-03-06 12:16:12.7470	Message 1	1	EventHubMessage

Service Bus

There was a nice section that covers Service Bus in Chapter 1. Consider rereading that section before proceeding. You may have noticed that the endpoint for an Event Hub contains a service bus, for example, <namespace>.servicebus.windows.net. Event Hub is built on top of Service Bus; however, Service Bus provides three features that are not easily implemented in Event Hub. These are noted in Table 6.1 as the ability to push messages to receivers, FIFO, and at-most-once message delivery. The opposite of push is pull and means that when there is a message waiting in the queue, the receiver has to come get it. That pull or the message broker pushes the message to the receiver. Service Bus can be configured either to push messages to receivers or to allow the receiver to poll the queue length. If one or more messages are found, then it pulls the message and processes it. Implementing FIFO is achieved by implementing message sessions, which is the way the messaging service is able to order the messages. The internals of that are rather complex and not covered here, but you just need to know FIFO is possible with Service Bus, and the way you implement that is by enabling sessions on the Service Bus queue or topic. Finally, unlike the other three messaging services, Service Bus can guarantee that a message is delivered only once. This is handled by a feature called *duplication detection* and is achieved by having a message ID identified in the message data packet. The Service Bus logic keeps tabs on which message IDs have been received within a given timeframe. If a duplicate is found, the message will be accepted, but it will be ignored.

There are a few additional aspects of a Service Bus that need to be covered:

- Namespace
- Queues, topics, and subscriptions
- Sender and receiver
- Dead-letter queue, batching, and Peek-Lock

A namespace serves the same purpose in the Service Bus context as the namespace does for an Event Hub. A namespace is a container in which the queues and topics exist and allows an administrator to configure features such as encryption, geographical redundancies, change the pricing tier, and monitoring. As you can see in Figure 6.24, a Service Bus queue looks similar to Figure 6.16 (Publisher/Subscriber) where there is a sender (aka publisher) that sends messages to a queue, a message broker helps with the ingestion, and then receivers (aka consumers) that read the messages from the queue.

FIGURE 6.24 Service Bus queue architecture components

In Figure 6.24, the sender is illustrated by an Azure Web App and the receiver by an Azure Function. In practice, a sender can be any entity that has the ability to send a text-based message to the Service Bus endpoint. The same goes for a receiver. Any entity that has been granted access to the Service Bus can monitor the queue and, when a message is found, retrieve and process it. A scenario where you configure an Azure Function to monitor and process Service Bus queues is common. You can do the same with a Service Bus topic. Take a look at Figure 6.25, which illustrates a Service Bus topic; you might see some similarities between it and both Figure 6.16 (Publisher/Subscriber) and Figure 6.20, which illustrated the Event Hub architecture with multiple partitions.

FIGURE 6.25 Service Bus Topic architecture components

Notice that Figure 6.25 depicts a single sender; however, the messages are placed into four different queues. Those queues are referred to as *subscriptions*. When you configure a receiver to read from a Service Bus topic, it is required to provide the subscription name. Each subscription will receive a copy of the message that can then be processed by the subscribed receiver. This scenario may remind you of the Sequential Convoy pattern, as shown in Figure 6.18.

A few additional attributes available with a Service Bus are *dead-letter queue (DLQ)*, batching, and Peek-Lock. A DLQ is a queue where the Service Bus places messages that cannot be delivered. It would be prudent for a system designer to build in some logic that checks this queue from time to time to see whether there are any messages present in the DLQ. The DLQ ensures that no messages are lost. You will need to code the analysis of these DLQ messages into your application and find out for yourself why they failed.

Batching is an efficient concept. Instead of receiving one message, processing it, getting another, and processing it, the receiver can get a batch of messages, perhaps based on a timestamp range, and process them all in a single invocation. This saves some time when compared to making a network call for each message.

The last attribute is an interesting one named Peek-Lock (a nondestructive read). Peek-Lock is an approach that helps prevent the processing of a message in a Service Bus queue multiple times. To achieve this, you instruct a receiver to place a Peek-Lock on a message that includes a timed duration for how long the lock is valid. If the lock duration expires, then the message is again available for other receivers for processing. The timed duration is helpful for managing exceptions or timeouts during the processing of a message; this makes sure that if the receiver cannot successfully process the message that it gets back into the queue and isn't lost due to problems with the receiver or some resource the receiver relies on.

Azure Storage Queue

There was a lot discussed about Azure Storage Queue in the previous chapter. When you create an Azure Storage Queue, you create it in the context of an Azure Storage account, as you would for an Azure blob, an Azure file, or an Azure table. The architecture components for the flow of messages through an Azure Storage queue is similar to that shown in Figure 6.24, and you have already read some differences between Service Bus and an Azure Storage queue in Table 6.1. As you may recall from Table 6.1, the Service Bus and Azure Storage queues are message-based, but Service Bus has more capabilities like topics and FIFO. Some additional differences will make the decision on which one to use more straightforward. You will find them in Table 6.2.

TABLE 6.2   Comparing Azure Storage Queue and Service Bus

	Azure Storage Queue	Service Bus
Ordering	No	Yes
Atomic	No	Yes

	Azure Storage Queue	**Service Bus**
Push	No	Yes
Batch receive	Yes	Yes
Batch send	No	Yes
Duplicate detection	No	Yes
Max queue size	500TB	1GB to 80GB
Max message size	64KB	256KB to 1MB
HTTPS only	No	Yes
Automatic dead lettering	No	Yes
Delivery	At-least-once	At-least/most-once

There are many options to consider when choosing a message-driven messaging service. You should now be in good shape to make some good progress toward that. In the next section, you will learn about the other event-driven messaging services and then be able to decide between those two and ultimately all four of them.

Event Grid

When I attempt to describe what an Event Grid is, again I revert to the definition of a delegate. A delegate is a programming term, and it is the glue that binds an event to a method. The method triggered when an event is triggered is commonly referred to as an *event handler*. An event is the same thing as a notification in the real world. It's a single piece of information that many listeners might be interested in.

Before you get into the details, perform the next exercise, Exercise 6.6 where you will add an event to the Azure Blob Storage container created previously in Exercise 5.6. This event will trigger when you add a new blob to the container and then fire the Azure Function you created in Exercise 4.16.

EXERCISE 6.6

Configuring an Event Grid Service to Be Triggered When a Blob Is Added to a Container

1. Log in to the Azure Portal at portal.azure.com. In the search box at the top middle of the browser, enter **Function App**. Now, select Function App, and then select the Azure Function you created in Exercise 4.16. Click the + symbol next to the Functions

tree, as shown in Figure 6.26. Select Azure Event Grid Trigger on the blade and click the Install button. Enter a name for the function (for example, `csharpguitar-eg`) and click the Create button.

FIGURE 6.26   Creating an Event Grid–triggered Azure Function

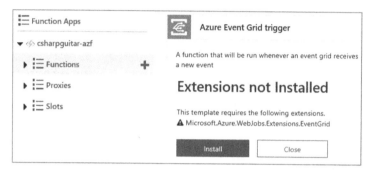

2. In the search box at the top middle of the browser you used to access the Azure Portal, enter **Storage accounts** and then select Storage accounts. Now, select the storage account you created in Exercise 5.6. On the navigation menu select Events, click the More Options link on the Storage accounts - Events blade, and then select Web Hook. Add a name for the Event Hub subscription and select only Blob Created from the Event Types drop-down list, as seen in Figure 6.27. Select Azure Function from the Endpoint Type drop-down list and click the Select An Endpoint link. Select the subscription, resource group, Function app, and the function, which you created in the previous step. Click the Confirm Selection button.

FIGURE 6.27   Configuring an Azure Blob Storage container to trigger an Event Hub event when created

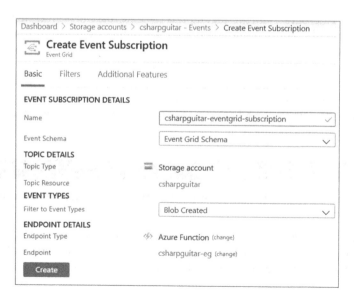

3. Navigate back to the Azure Function you created and expand the Log window, as shown in Figure 6.28. The Log window will be empty until you add the blob in the next step. Once the blob has been added, the details will be sent to the Event Grid and then to the Azure Function.

FIGURE 6.28   Azure Function log showing Event Grid and blob details

```
┌──────────────────────────────────────────────────────────────────────────────────┐
│  ∨  Logs   Console                     🔌 Reconnect  📋 Copy logs  ❚❚ Pause  🗑 Clear  ↗ Expand │
│  ──                                                                                │
│  2020-03-09T20:13:12.481 [Information] Executed 'Functions.csharpguitar-eg'        │
│  2020-03-09T20:13:43.247 [Information] Executing 'Functions.csharpguitar-eg'       │
│  09T20:13:43.2476700+00:00', Id=485c7752-3349-4e97-8f32-96f9367f3764)              │
│  2020-03-09T20:13:43.248 [Information] {                                           │
│    "api": "PutBlob",                                                               │
│    "contentType": "application/octet-stream",                                      │
│    "contentLength": 15,                                                            │
│    "blobType": "BlockBlob",                                                        │
│    "url": "https://csharpguitar.blob.core.windows.net/csharpguitar/helloworld0.txt",│
│    "storageDiagnostics": {                                                         │
│      "batchId": "2387d70a-1006-002f-004e-f69e7f000000"                             │
│    }                                                                               │
│  }                                                                                 │
│  2020-03-09T20:13:43.248 [Information] Executed 'Functions.csharpguitar-eg'        │
│  <                                                                                 │
└──────────────────────────────────────────────────────────────────────────────────┘
```

4. Add a blob to the blob container using the same command as shown in Figure 5.53. Check the contents of the blob container to confirm that it exists. You can achieve this by navigating to it from the Azure Portal. View the Event Subscriptions metrics on the Azure Storage Account Event blade, as depicted in Figure 6.29.

FIGURE 6.29   A view of an Azure Storage Event Grid Event metrics

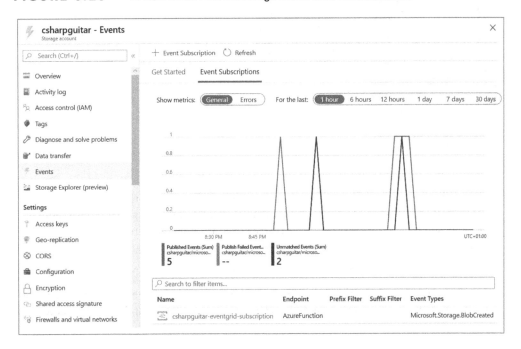

As you begin learning some Event Grid details, review Table 6.1 and then proceed to learning about these most common Event Grid terms:

- Event, publisher, source, and handler
- Domain, subscription, and topic

In the previous exercise, recognize that the event (aka notification) comes from the creation of a blob into the monitored source Azure Storage Blob container, as this is where the event happens. Notice again in Figure 6.27 that you selected Blob Created, which instructed the source to send the event notification to Event Grid. Event Grid then sends the event with the details, as shown in Figure 6.28 to the handler—an Azure Function. In the Exercise 6.5 scenario, you have the following:

- **Event:** Blob Created
- **Source:** Azure Storage
- **Handler:** Azure Function

As shown in Figure 6.30, many Azure products have built-in support for configuring and subscribing to Event Grid via the Events link on the navigation menu for the given Azure product.

FIGURE 6.30 A view of event grid sources and handlers

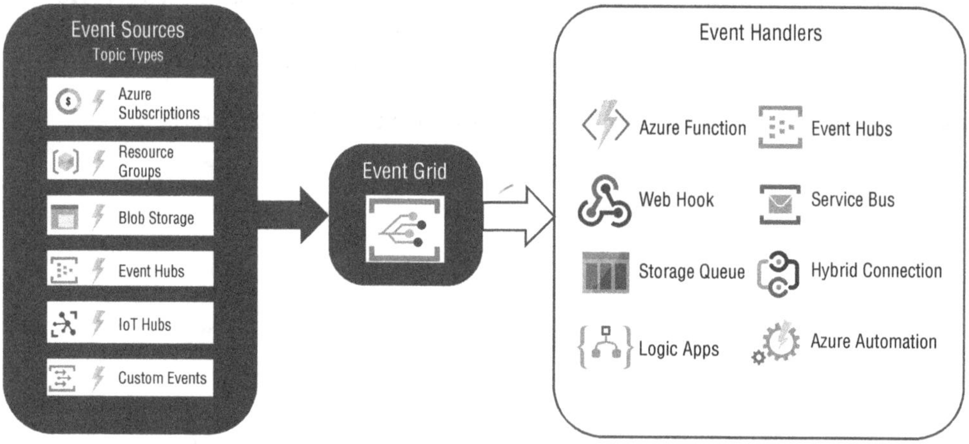

If the Azure product you want to send events to is an Event Grid that doesn't have the built-in ability to subscribe to Event Grid, then you need to manually create the Event Grid Topic. The same goes for the creation of custom events. When you create an Event Grid Topic, it exposes a global endpoint, which is similar to the following:

```
<topicName>.westeurope-1.eventgrid.azure.net/api/events
```

The Event Grid Topic exposes an API to which you can send JSON documents that contain information about the event, as well as some data that the Event Grid sends on to the event handler. Therefore, an Event Grid Topic is an HTTP/HTTPS endpoint. Another way of explaining it is that it's the location to which information about an event is sent. Then, as you did in Exercise 6.5, step 2 (Figure 6.27), you create an Event Grid subscription, which defines where the Event Grid will send the event details. That location is the event handler and can be a web hook when it's a custom event or one of the event handlers shown previously in Figure 6.30. Note that a topic is created by the publisher, who is an individual, organization, or company. Finally, you can visualize an Event Grid domain in the same way you would a resource group. An Event Grid domain is a shell container for managing a large number of Event Grid topics. The topics are usually all related to the same application and are similar to the way you would organize your Azure resources into a resource group. By the way, Event Grid topics support tags too, just in case resource groups or domains are not specific enough for your deployment needs.

Logic Apps

We cannot begin a discussion about Logic Apps without knowing what a workflow is. In simple terms, it is a repeatable pattern of activity or a sequence of small isolated operations that, when followed, result in the completion of a more complex process. Take, for example, the creation of an Azure Policy, which was discussed earlier in this chapter. Many large organizations would have a chain of creation, testing, and approval steps required to place an Azure Policy into production. It usually isn't the responsibility of a single person to create, test, approve, and deploy something with this level of impact. Know that changing an Azure Policy may result in a breach of some compliance standard law, which could have serious results that justify having a formal process for managing and approving changes. Therefore, you would want to have a defined flow of steps required to change and apply an Azure Policy. See Figure 6.31 as an example of a business process workflow.

FIGURE 6.31   Business process workflow diagram example

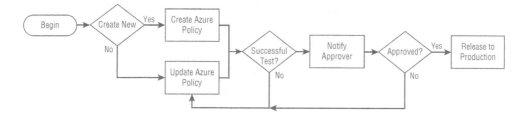

A product named Microsoft Flow runs on top of Azure Logic Apps. While Microsoft Flow is considered a SaaS offering, Azure Logic Apps falls into the category of serverless computing, like Azure Functions. Both products perform close to the same thing in that they provide graphical interfaces that expose connectors, triggering mechanisms, and controls to manage your workflows. Connectors can be Office 365 Outlook, SharePoint Online, Azure Blob Storage, and Dynamics 365 to name a few. Think for a moment about how you could use those connectors to implement the workflow process identified in Figure 6.31. You would use Outlook to send requests for approval and approval emails. You could use SharePoint online as a place to store details about the changes. Azure Blob Storage can store the actual Azure Policy JSON document. Perhaps even, after approval, you could insert an Azure Blob to trigger an Azure Function and then perform the deployment to production. Figure 6.32 shows an example of the Logic Apps Designer blade in the Azure Portal. It illustrates a two-step process to send an email when a new file is added, modified, or some content is changed on a SharePoint site.

FIGURE 6.32 Business process workflow diagram example

A trigger is some action or event that kicks off the workflow such as an HTTP request to an API from a client, scheduled or from another Logic App. In the workflow scenario example, this may be triggered via an email sent to a specific email alias that contains the requested change or creation to the Azure Policy. That email then triggers notifications to those who can work on, test, and ultimately approve the application of the policy into your Azure subscription. This interface reminds me of a programming technique called Snap! (snap.berkeley.edu) where you can drag and drop logical controls into a graphical interface, separated by actions such as for each, if-then-else, switch cases, and while loops. The same is possible with Logic Apps and would be necessary to implement in the workflow example used here. In short, you use the graphical user interface to drag and drop the connections and the actions required to successfully process your workflow, and the code is generated for you behind the scenes.

Also, you would use Azure Logic Apps when you want to automate workflows that have historically been performed manually, like gaining expense approvals, hiring new employees, vacation approvals, or the fulfillment of a purchase order. The days of having a large stack of papers waiting in an inbox or emails waiting in an inbox for approval are over. These types of activities can be automated using Azure Logic Apps. It is one of the driving forces behind the concept of digitalization of the enterprise and workforce.

Notification Hubs

This tool is used to send push notifications to mobile devices running your mobile app. Have you ever received a notification on your phone that someone sent you a What's App text, liked one of your posts on Facebook, or that the stock market climbed over 1,500 points? Well, either they used Notification Hub to perform that or they used a product similar to it. Notification Hub supports the sending of pop-up messages to clients running Android, iOS, and Windows.

Notification Hubs are tightly integrated with App Service Mobile Apps, which was introduced in Chapter 4. In that section, you learned that Mobile Apps is deprecating. However, it is important for legacy and potentially an exam question perspective to know at least a little about the integrated Azure products, Mobile Apps, and Notification Hub.

Summary

This chapter provided the finishing touches to understand a hybrid solution. The concept was touched in many chapters before this one, and in this chapter you got clarity about security, networking, compute, and data hybrid solutions. Hybrid solutions are the combination of resources existing in cloud and private data centers. Azure Blueprint, Azure Policy, and Security Center are all tools that can help you meet compliance standards such as GDPR, PIPA, and ISO/IEC 27018. These tools help by providing an outline of what Azure procedures are required to meet a certification standard specifically one like Azure Blueprint. Azure Policy provides the means for applying and enforcing those described procedures and Security Center monitors and alerts and provides feedback on noncompliant configurations in near real time.

In the second part of this chapter, you learned about Azure's MaaS offerings and some message patterns used to decouple large IT solutions. Decoupling makes a computer system more reliable, as the dependency between previously linked systems are detached from each other. Instead of placing an order directly into an OLTP database, the order can be placed into a queue and processed offline. You learned why you would use Service Bus, Azure Storage queues, Event Hub, or Event Grid. Messaging is not a new concept and is something that is getting more traction as legacy applications retire and are refreshed with new technology and design patterns. The digital transformation happening in many companies and one of Microsoft's major areas of operations can be mostly achieved by digitizing historically manual workflows with Azure Logic Apps.

Exam Essentials

Understand hybrid solutions.   Hybrid solutions are a combination of resources in the cloud and the ones that you run in an on-premise or other private data center. Hybrid solutions can be, but are not entirely limited to, security, networking, compute, and data.

Understand Azure Policy.   This a feature that allows an administrator to enforce restrictions on a management group, subscription, or resource group. The restrictions can be aligned with a compliance standard or just something your enterprise requires, for example, requiring TLS 1.2 on all endpoints that expose an HTTP interface.

Know how to use tags.   You can use these as another means of organizing your provisioned Azure resources. When a resource group doesn't quite meet your requirements, or even within the same resource group, use tags as an additional means for marking your resources, whether the resource is a development, test, or production environment.

Know how to use Security Center.   This is the place where you manage most of your security configurations and monitor your Azure resources. You receive reports of compliance issues, compliance scores, and instructions on how to configure the resources that are not compliant.

Know how to use Service Bus.   Service Bus is a messaging-based storage queue used for decoupling IT solutions from each other. A sender places a message into a queue that can be monitored for duplicates and stored and processed in the received order. There can be multiple receivers that process messages in the same queue in parallel, or by using a Service Bus topic, multiple receivers can receive and process the messages for their own purpose.

Know how to use Event Grid.   Use this product for the ingress of telemetric, streaming, or huge big data message processing. Your Event Hub can have a single partition, which a producer adds messages into, with a single consumer group and a single receiver to process them. You can have a maximum of 32 partitions and a consumer for each one, which makes the processing of such data extremely parallel, fast, and efficient for these high-level throughput operations.

Key Terms

Advanced Message Queueing Protocol (AMQP)	disaster recovery (DR)
allOf	disaster recovery as a service (DRaaS)
authentication (AuthN)	integration and testing (I&T)
authorization (AuthZ)	label

Azure Blueprints

Azure Data Subject Request (DSR) Portal

Azure Information Protection (AIP)

Azure Sentinel

Azure Site Recovery (ASR)

Azure Virtual Data Center (VDC)

Business Continuity and Disaster
Recovery (BCDR)

checkpointing

data distribution service (DDS)

dead-letter queue (DLQ)

messaging as a service (MaaS)

Microsoft Cloud App Security (MCAS)

Microsoft Message Queuing (MSMQ)

Microsoft Trust Center (MTC)

offsets

Service Trust Center

single sign-on (SSO)

SQL Information Protection

tag

user acceptance testing (UAT)

Review Questions

Many questions can have more than a single answer. Please select all choices that are true.

1. Which of the following can you not create a hybrid solution with using Azure products?

    A. Azure Active Directory

    B. Azure Virtual Network

    C. Azure Policy

    D. Azure Virtual Machine

2. Which networking products are helpful for creating a hybrid networking solution?

    A. API Management

    B. Network Watcher

    C. Hybrid Connection Manager

    D. Single-sign on

3. Which of the following are helpful for implementing and monitoring compliance standards?

    A. Azure Compliance Standards

    B. Azure Policy

    C. Security Center

    D. Azure Blueprint

4. Which of the following are helpful for grouping resources that help with management and overview?

    A. Resource groups

    B. Event Grid domains

    C. Subscriptions

    D. Tags

5. True or False? Reliability means that a system can recover quickly from a transient outage. Resiliency is the outcome of a reliable system.

    A. True

    B. False

6. True or False? GDPR and PIPA are data privacy compliance standards.

    A. True

    B. False

7. Which of the following features are configurable in Security Center?

    A. Policy and compliance analysis

    B. Resource security hygiene

    C. Multifactor authentication (MFA)

    D. Threat detection

8. True or False? Security Center automatically enforces compliance standards once an Azure product configuration is flagged as noncompliant to its associated compliance standard.

    A. True

    B. False

9. If you wanted to ingest streaming data or telemetry information into a data source and you wanted to queue that data using a messaging service, which one would you use?

    A. Event Grid

    B. Event Hub

    C. Service Bus

    D. Azure Storage Queue

10. If you need to process messages that arrive in a queue in the order they are received, which Azure messaging service would you choose?

    A. Azure Storage Queue

    B. Event Hub

    C. Event Grid

    D. Service Bus

Chapter

7

Developing for the Cloud

EXAM AZ-303 OBJECTIVES COVERED IN THIS CHAPTER:

✓ **Implement Management and Security Solutions**

 ▪ Manage security for applications

✓ **Implement Solutions for Apps**

 ▪ Implement an application infrastructure

EXAM AZ-304 OBJECTIVES COVERED IN THIS CHAPTER:

✓ **Design Identity and Security**

 ▪ Design authentication

 ▪ Design security for applications

✓ **Design Business Continuity**

 ▪ Design for high availability

✓ **Design Infrastructure**

 ▪ Design an application architecture

 ▪ Design a compute solution

✓ **Design Data Storage**

 ▪ Design a solution for databases

At the start of Chapter 5, I told you to take for granted that you have an application. That application could be a simple snippet of code or a complicated enterprise system that uses inheritance, interfaces, and third-party functional libraries. No matter how well you designed, implemented, and configured the security, networking, compute, and data stores, if your code is bad, the other components don't matter so much. Well, from a security perspective, that's not 100% true, because security always matters, but I think you get what I am trying to say here. In short, there are coding patterns that you can follow that will increase the probability of success in the cloud. This chapter shares some of those patterns and provides some coding examples. It also covers IDEs, source code repositories, and more about coding for security.

Don't expect many, if any, questions about coding on the exam. This chapter is present more for making you the best Azure Solutions Architect Expert than it is for helping you prepare for the exam. As Ian Stewart once said, "There are 10 kinds of people in the world: those who understand binary numerals and those who don't." In this chapter, you will learn some coding patterns and tools for creating and managing source code.

Architectural Styles, Principles, and Patterns

In this section, you will find information about the following topics:

- Architectural styles
- Design principles
- Cloud design patterns

Patterns have been called out in a few chapters in various phases of IT solution design and configuration.

- Architectural styles such as multitiered applications
- Enterprise data warehouse (EDW) designs such as snowflake and star schemas
- Design principles such as partitioning

There are design patterns that should be implemented into your code when running in the cloud. This chapter provides guidelines and suggestions for implementing all the best-practice styles, principles, and patterns into the solutions that you plan on moving or creating on the Azure platform.

Architectural Styles

The most common or traditional architecture style is called *multitiered* (aka *n*-tier), which is illustrated in Figure 7.1. In this design, you will see the existence of a client that connects to a web server, which is one of the tiers. The web server then can make connections to an application server and/or a database server.

FIGURE 7.1 A multitiered architecture

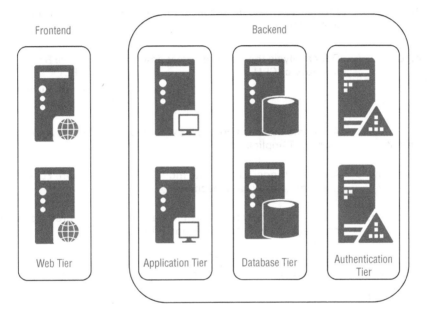

Table 7.1 lists some of the other common architectural styles.

TABLE 7.1 Azure Architecture Styles

Architectural Style	Description	Azure Product
Multitiered (*n*-tier)	A division of application roles by physical machines	Azure Virtual Machines
Big Data	Unstructured data collection and analysis	Azure Cosmos DB Azure Synapse Analytics Data Lake Analytics

TABLE 7.1   Azure Architecture Styles *(continued)*

Architectural Style	Description	Azure Product
Microservices	A division of business logic by service exposed via an API	Service Fabric Azure Kubernetes Service (AKS)
Web-queue-worker	Decoupling of IT solutions using a messaging queue	Service Bus Azure Storage Queue
Event-driven	Producers create data; consumers receive and process it	Event Hub Event Grid
Big Compute	Data analysis that requires great amounts of memory or CPU	Azure Batch (aka HPC) Azure Virtual Machines
Workflow management	Automate business processes with your current IT applications	Logic Apps
Serverless computing	An event-triggered compute model without the need to provision machines	Azure Functions
Web applications	Applications that are accessible via the internet that work with the HTTP and HTTPS protocol	Azure App Service

The following is a list of figures in the book that can provide more context about these styles:

There are many more architectural styles not mentioned here. The ones provided here are the most common. As the concept of a hybrid model is not an unfamiliar term for you, using bits and pieces of each style to build the one you require is by all means a valid approach. Keep in mind that these styles are best-practice recommendations. If you choose to take your own path, great, but recognize that it comes at a risk. Following best-practice recommendations is the path that leads you toward success.

Design Principles

When designing your solution on the Azure platform or in any data center, there are some guiding principles to align with during this design phase. They are provided in the following list and discussed afterward in more detail:

- Redundancy, resiliency, and reliance
- Self and automatic healing
- Scaling and decoupling
- Use SaaS, PaaS, and IaaS, in that order
- Design for change

The list is ordered based on the relevance and impact they have on running workloads successfully on the Azure platform.

Redundancy, Resiliency, and Reliance

These three concepts shouldn't be new to you now. Take a moment to go over them in your head and then see whether what you have learned so far matches the descriptions that follow:

Redundancy   Redundancy has to do with having multiple copies of your system configurations, source code, and data in many places. This is important in the case of mid- to long-term outages and, in some cases, helpful in recovery in the case of permanent data loss. To implement redundancies in Azure, concepts such as Availability Zones, fault and update domains, failover database instances and ZRS and GRS storage options should all be considered.

Resiliency   Resiliency has to do with the next section that discusses recovering from transient issues automatically. How well does your application respond and recover from failures? One pattern discussed later, the Retry pattern, will wait for a few seconds if an error is received when attempting to execute code and then try it again. That is a much more resilient experience than simply throwing an exception stating, "Something unexpected happened; please try again later."

Reliance   The experiences users, customers, employees, or clients have with the application determine how much they can rely on the system. If they lose faith in it, meaning they don't know if the system will be working or not when they need it, you have failed in making the system resilient because it is not reliable. Reliance is the outcome of a system that is resilient and redundant.

Self and Automatic Healing

The components used in the cloud are commoditized. Their lifespan may not be what you would expect from a trademarked brand of computer components. When a commoditized memory module, for example, fails, it is simply replaced instead of trying to find out why it failed and fixing it. Simply replacing it is much faster than performing root-cause analysis and fixing it, and the latter really isn't possible at cloud speed anyway. When there is a failure of a hardware component, there will be a disruption. How large of a disruption is dependent on how heavily your application depends on the component that failed. Regardless, you need to place code into your applications to manage these kinds of short disruptions. Making sure that your transactions are ACID compliant (atomic, consistent, isolated, and durable) will help your application respond better in these situations.

If your software fails for some reason, make sure to catch the exception. This results in a handled exception and provides an interface for responding and retrying the execution. If you do not catch exceptions and one happens (an unhandled exception), it has the likelihood of crashing the process. When a process such as W3WP.exe crashes, it is possible that it will not be respawned automatically. It may require a reboot or manual restart to get all the bits realigned. There are platform features on Azure that monitor the health of the operating system and sometimes the application itself. When the OS or application appears to be unhealthy, the platform monitor may trigger a reimage of the VM on which your application is (or was) running. Simply, your application must be able to handle sudden stoppages in the execution of your transactions. It will happen, and if you don't manage it, your application will not be reliant!

Scaling and Decoupling

One of the primary features in the cloud and on Azure is the ability to provision and scale on demand. You can use large amounts of compute when required and then deallocate the computer when the demand diminishes. Your application needs to be able to work in that scenario, for example, if your web application requires state to be maintained throughout an operation. When a customer is placing an order online, then the process is usually fulfilled across numerous pages and numerous steps. Do any of these steps store some of the information on the server? If yes, then you need to make sure requests are sent back to the same server each time if you have multiple servers running. This can be achieved by a context called *client affinity* or *sticky sessions*. Those simply make sure that once a session is started on a specific server, all additional requests route to the same server for that session. There are scenarios in which your scaling is automated and will scale in or out the number of instances your workload is consuming. However, there is some built-in intelligence that waits some time before reimaging and returning the VM to the pool. Long-running tasks, like a WebJob, a batch job, or a background job, might get shut down in midprocess. You need to code for that by perhaps having some startup logic in the background job to check that everything is OK before proceeding with normal operations. The logic is application-specific. Making sure everything is OK could be as simple as having a processing status column on a row in a database and checking that status at startup. If the status shows "in process" for a long period, the code likely failed, and the data needs reprocessing.

The next topic discussed in this section covers decoupling and has a lot to do with the messaging services discussed in Chapter 6. It also has to do with removing long-running or resource-intensive jobs like a WebJob, batch job, or another background job to an offline service. For example, the multitiered (*n*-tiered) architecture style is a tightly coupled process. In that scenario, the client would wait for the request to the web server to flow through the application server and to the database server and then back before proceeding further. One of the problems with that architecture is that a successful response is dependent on the availability of all three of those tiers. If you could somehow decouple that flow by implementing the web-queue-worker model, then a request from a client wouldn't be dependent on the availability and resiliency of many systems. Your application would appear more reliant.

Use SaaS, PaaS, and IaaS, in That Order

You would likely agree that the fewer tasks you are directly responsible for, the higher probability of being successful in the areas where your responsibilities increase. In other words, if you can focus your efforts more directly on what you feel is the most important and be successful at those few things, then overall you will be more successful. If you can offload the management of your network infrastructure, the configuration, and the maintenance of your computer hardware, as well as the administration of the operating system, then by all means do that. If all you need is the product, then take that one too. The point is, if you can run your workload on PaaS, choose that one over IaaS. There is less to worry about. In reality, if you are like me, you can always find things to worry about. Even if you have only two tasks, not having to worry about network, hardware, and operating system administration is great. Then you can worry about just the important aspects of your work.

Design for Change

Things change, and sometimes they change fast. Can you recall any mention of the cloud five or ten years ago? Think about where we were then and what we have now. Designing for change is focused on, but not limited to, factors such as decoupling, asynchronous models, and microservice/serverless concepts. In short, the more you can isolate a specific piece of logic from the whole, the easier it is to change. Recall the discussion about NoSQL databases like Azure Cosmos DB and how quickly you can get a container to store data into it. Contrast that with a relational database where the tables and columns have an applied meaning, and the changes would likely have greater impact. When compared to a nonrelational data source, making a change to a relational model is possible, but it would take much longer and require much more application knowledge.

Cloud Design Patterns

From a coding perspective, there are many patterns that are worthy of a book on their own. Therefore, only five patterns will be discussed in detail. These five have the most impact when running your workloads on Azure:

- Retry
- Gatekeeper
- Throttling
- Sharding
- Circuit Breaker

Some additional coding patterns worthy of honorable mention are Health Endpoint Monitoring, Bulkhead, Valet Key, and *Command and Query Responsibility Segregation (CQRS)*. If any of those trigger any interest, search for information online. There is a plethora of information available.

Retry

The Retry pattern is probably the most important one to implement. You can implement the pattern in all code running on all kinds of platforms, but it is of additional importance when the code is running in the cloud. This is because of the higher probability of transient faults. Historically, there have been patterns that recommend catching exceptions using a code snippet like the following:

```
try
{ ...}
catch (Exception ex)
{...}
```

The interesting fact about this pattern is that in many cases there is no coded logic added inside the `catch` expression to perform any kind of recovery activity. I cannot explain this behavior; however, I review a lot of code, and this is the scenario I see often. The more sophisticated applications do at least log the `ex.Message` that is included in the `Exception` and maybe provide it back to the client that triggered the transaction, but nothing more. When running in the cloud, transient faults may happen more often when compared to running on-premise, trademarked hardware. Here, you should now implement some code within the `catch` expression to retry the transactions that triggered the exception. You need to define a retry policy that describes the scenario in which a retry should happen and the actions to take on retry.

The `Exception` defined in the previous code snippet is considered a catchall exception; however, there are numerous kinds of exceptions. This is not the place to cover all the possible exceptions. One that can be called out is an `HttpRequestException`. This kind of exception is one that could be successful if you were to try it again after waiting a few seconds. Some pseudocode that defines how a retry would look is shown here:

```
catch (HttpRequestException ex)
{
    writeLog($"This exception happened {ex.Message}")
    if currentRetryCount < allowedRetryCount && IsTransient(ex)
        await Task.Delay(5000)
        theMethodWhichFailed()
}
```

The retry policy applied in the previous code snippet requires that:

- The exception be logged
- The retry happen only a specific number of times

- The retry validate the exception to confirm it may be transient
- The retry wait for five seconds and then recall the method again

The example provided here was one that would occur when using the `System.Net` `.Http.HttpClient` class. When you use Azure product-specific SDKs for communicating with, for example, AAD, Azure Storage, or Cosmos DB, the SDKs typically have built-in retry capabilities. For a list of products that have built-in retry capabilities, take a look at

https://docs.microsoft.com/en-us/azure/architecture/best-practices/ retry-service-specific

Gatekeeper

It makes a lot of sense to name things that perform the action it actually performs. The Gatekeeper pattern does exactly as the name implies, like an orchestrator orchestrates and like a programmer inherits attributes from a parent class. A gatekeeper monitors an entry point to some service and makes sure that only those who should have access to it actually do. The location of the gatekeeper is in front of the resource that it protects so that unauthorized entities attempting to access it can be denied access before they are inside or close to being inside. (If it had been up to me, I would have named this Bouncer, which seems a bit cooler, but I guess Gatekeeper is acceptable.)

There are many Azure resources that have a global endpoint that in the given scenario is already too close to the protected resource for comfort. The measurement of "too close" depends greatly on the sensitivity and criticality of the data and application. However, let's assume doing authentication on a service that runs in full trust mode is, for you, too much of a risk. You may know that when you have a process (like `W3WP.exe`) running on an operating system, it runs within the context of an identity. Some identities have full access, while other custom identities may have restricted access only to the specific resources required to do a job. In reality, the latter is hard to do, but the most common scenario is somewhere in between with a tendency to provide too much privilege. Therefore, if for some reason the entry point at your front door is compromised, then full access to the house is a relative certainty. It's interesting that I used "front door" there because there is an Azure product named *Azure Front Door* that can be used to protect endpoints from an architectural perspective. You may be thinking, well, what about service endpoints, NSGs, and IP restrictions? You can achieve the Gatekeeper pattern by using Azure Firewall, a service endpoint, and some other Azure products. As illustrated in Figure 7.2, any Azure product or feature that can act as a firewall is an option for implementing this pattern.

FIGURE 7.2   Gatekeeper design pattern

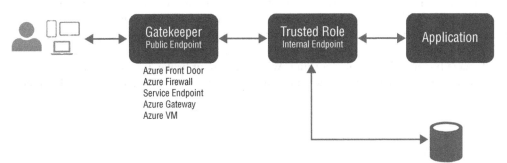

IP restrictions and NSGs (default Azure VM configurations) are typically configured on the resource themselves, which negates the purpose of the pattern. The purpose is to keep the tier that exposes a public endpoint separate from the tier that runs the sensitive or mission-critical processing.

Throttling

There is an HTTPS status code that exists just for this scenario; it's a status code of 429 and means Too Many Requests. This is usually handled by some custom code or third-party application that is monitoring the number of requests to a website for a specific period of time. What throttling does is limit the number of requests or amount of compute resources for a given time period. In Internet Information Services (IIS), it is possible to restrict the amount of consumed CPU for a given time frame. When the threshold is breached, any requests going to that specific process are not processed and instead return an error. This kind of setting can also be useful in a distributed denial-of-service (DDoS) scenario (intentional or not) where a large number of requests are coming from a specific IP address. The feature is called Dynamic IP Restrictions (DIPR), and it counts the number of concurrent connections or the number of total connection in a given time frame from the same IP address. When that restriction is breached, DIPR no longer allows access from that IP address for a configurable amount of time. Throttling is an important pattern that needs some attention, not only preventing it when it happens to your system but also preventing your system from inadvertently doing it to another system.

Sharding

Sharding was covered in many data storage scenarios in Chapter 5. The concept of sharding is the division of large sets of data into smaller, logically structured subsets. Review Figure 5.14 and Figure 5.15, which demonstrate examples of horizontal and vertical sharding. Horizontal sharding may break the data into rows depending on the alphabetical order of the row key. If you know there is an actual division of load across data starting and ending with A–K, L–P, and Q–Z, then it would make sense to configure three horizontal shards to improve performance and stability. On the other hand, if you see no pattern of such data access but instead notice there are three or four columns on each row that are retrieved much more frequently than the others, you can consider a vertical shard and separate the data structure into data columns that are accessed frequently versus a shard with columns that are not accessed as often.

Circuit Breaker

I was trimming my hedges once with an electric trimmer, and somehow the cord got between the blades and the leaves and—boom—it got cut, and the electricity shut off. To get the electricity flowing again, I had to switch the circuit back on. Had the circuit breaker not reacted, there would have been electricity flowing out the end of the electric cord causing damage but effectively doing nothing. When the circuit broke, it automatically caused the stoppage of electricity flow, which happened in less than a second. The Circuit Breaker pattern from a cloud design pattern operates in the same context. When one of the remote resources or services is not available, then the flow of all communications to them stop. You might be thinking that this is the same as the Retry pattern, and you are right—almost. The difference here is that you are certain that the resource or service your application is remotely connecting to is unavailable, and you have no idea when it will be back online. In this scenario, it doesn't make as much sense to retry. In the trimmer scenario, I knew something happened, and I knew trying to use the trimmer wouldn't work, so it was worthless to try. The outage took some time to resolve as I traversed down into the basement and found the switch needing administration. It took about 10 minutes; imagine how many exceptions your application would throw if your IT processes 100 or more transactions per second. Also, imagine how those using the application would feel getting the exceptions over and over again. They would think your system is unreliable. You could make the application more resilient by implementing the Circuit Breaker pattern.

A method for implementing a circuit breaker is to monitor the state of the dependent resources or services. For example, perhaps you look at the Closed, Open, and Half-Open states. If the state is Closed, the dependent resources are functional, just like if an electric circuit is closed, it is all flowing as expected, and there are no breaks in the connectivity. If there is a break, then the state changes to Open and requests that the dependent resource stop. In that scenario, you should have code that displays a temporary out-of-service page or routes and stores the transaction details to a temporary location for offline processing when the service comes back online. Half-Open is the state in which the exception has stopped occurring and the resource is likely back online, but it's in the early stages, so you throttle the number of requests you are passing through. After a given threshold based on a configured time frame is breached, the state is set back to Closed and you are back in business.

Antipatterns

When you are coding and designing your application, keep in mind the antipatterns, listed here:

- Superfluous Fetching
- Not Caching
- Synchronous I/O
- Monolithic Persistence
- Improperly Instantiating Objects

The first one, Superfluous Fetching, has to do with a concept called *projection*. This means you need to have only the columns that perform your task in the SELECT clause. You will need a very tight WHERE clause, as well. You do not want to retrieve any more data from a data store than is absolutely necessary. The same goes for caching. Don't store more data in a cache than the application needs to run because data loaded into the cache consumes memory. RAM has a cost in the cloud, sometimes a variable one. By all means, cache when you can. Give caching some close analysis and load only the data that is often retrieved from a data source into cache. This not only reduces load on your data store but also decreases the latency of your application since it doesn't have to perform unnecessary queries on the database to retrieve the same data over and over again.

When you are using a library in your programming and there exists asynchronous methods, by all means use them. When you use synchronous methods for performing I/O tasks such as accessing content on a hard disk or performing a task where the thread needs to pause for a response from some service on another server as the thread waits, that thread remains blocked until a response is returned from the I/O task. You must understand that the number of threads a process can generate is finite, and you should take actions where you can to reduce the number of them. Some latency happens when the process needs to create a new thread. When you use asynchronous methods that employ the `async/await` keywords, which make I/O calls, then the thread is not stuck waiting on the response. It is instead reallocated to the thread pool for other tasks to use. Once the I/O function is complete, the thread is pulled from the pool and is used to complete the action. Use asynchronous coding patterns when possible.

Monolithic Persistence has to do with having all your data stored on the same data store regardless of whether the data is related. When possible, you should separate online transactional processing (OLTP) data stores from data stores that contain logging, telemetry, or historical data used for reporting purposes. The reason for this is that OLTP data stores need to be responsive. They could be impacted if a large annual sales report is run against the same data store that orders are placed into. Separating them would likely have a positive impact on performance.

When you make a connection to a database or to a REST API, part of that process is to instantiate a connection object. Running your application on-premise, where you likely have almost unrestricted outbound connections, the most common pattern creates the connection within a `using` statement, like the following:

```
using (var httpClient = new HttpClient())
{
   ...
}
```

This pattern follows a guideline for scoping the use of the `httpClient` object. As soon as the code execution leaves the closing bracket, the `httpClient` is marked for garbage collection. The negative aspect of this is that for every invocation of this code block, an object needs to be instantiated and a new connection made. That implementation is improper and will not scale in the cloud, from a performance perspective, but mostly from a connection perspective. Remember from Chapter 3 there was a discussion about SNAT ports. Recognize that there are rather stringent limitations on the number that you can have concurrently open. The previous pattern where the `httpClient` was instantiated has a high probability of using many SNAT ports under high load. The alternative and recommended best practice creates a static instance in your class and instantiates it in the constructor.

```
public class CsharpGuitarHttpClientController : ApiController
{
    private static readonly HttpClient httpClient;
```

```
static CsharpGuitarHttpClientController()
{
    httpClient = new HttpClient();
}
public async Task<Product> GetTheCoolestGuitarEver(string id)
{
    ...
}
}
```

When you do this, the same connection object is used for all outbound connections to the same server. The pattern is the same when you are making connections to an Azure SQL database, an Azure Cosmos DB, or any system that requires the instantiation of a connection object.

An Introduction to Coding for the Cloud

Throughout the book there have been references to Chapter 7 as the place where you will see how to actually implement some of the concepts. In this section, you will see those examples or get some tips on how to proceed with them. The following examples will be provided:

- Triggering a background job
- Connecting to regional/global database instances
- Working with the Azure Queue Storage SDK
- Using Forms Authentication, certificates, Windows Authentication, MFA, Open Standards, managed identities, and service principle authentication
- Reading encrypted data from a database

Triggering a Background Job

A background job is a snippet of code that typically require high CPU, high memory, or long-running activities. Really, code snippets do anything that takes too long to trigger the background job and then wait for a response in real time. There are two primary ways in which a background job can be triggered: by an event or by a schedule. In the context of a WebJob, for example, an event trigger calls its exposed REST API. As you may recall, WebJobs are background job processors that run in the Azure App Service (PaaS) context. Assume you have an Azure App Service named csharpguitar that has the following endpoint:

```
csharpguitar.azurewebsites.net
```

A WebJob can be triggered using a similar endpoint. That endpoint would be similar to the following:

```
https://csharpguitar.scm.azurewebsites.net/api/triggeredwebjobs/
<webjobName>/run
```

These can be called from a browser manually or from another application that uses the `HttpClient` class. The other option is the use a scheduler like a CRON job that will trigger the execution of a batch job or a WebJob at certain intervals.

Connecting to Regional/Global Database Instances

In Chapter 5 you learned about the global replication capabilities of the Azure Cosmos DB. The question was, how can you make code intelligent enough to connect to the read-only instances closest to the location of the client? A class in the Azure Cosmos DB SDK named `ConnectionPolicy` exposes a property called `PreferredLocations`. Preferred locations are used when creating the client that is used to make the connection to the database. Code within the SDK itself chooses the most optimal location. That is very cool. The snippet of code that achieves this is provided here:

```
ConnectionPolicy connectionPolicy = new ConnectionPolicy();
connectionPolicy.PreferredLocations.Add(LocationNames.SouthCentralUS);
connectionPolicy.PreferredLocations.Add(LocationNames.NorthEurope);
DocumentClient docClient =
    new DocumentClient(accountEndPoint, accountKey, connectionPolicy);
```

Working with the Azure Queue Storage SDK

Some principles that are important to know about Azure Queue Storage are related to these three methods: `PeekMessage()`, `GetMessage()`, and `DeleteMessage()`. These methods, as well as the client code required to utilize them, are downloadable as a NuGet package from here:

www.nuget.org/packages/Microsoft.Azure.Storage.Queue

Installation instructions for Visual Studio are also available at that URL.

The `PeekMessage()` method is called with the following code snippet. Please note that there is code required before and after this snippet to make it work. For example, you must instantiate the storage account, instantiate the storage client, and identify the storage queue. This example/pseudocode is useful only for the explanation of the following implementation concept.

```
CloudQueueMessage peekedMessage = queue.PeekMessage();
```

Here is a snippet of code that calls the `GetMessage()` method and its asynchronous alternative `GetMessageAsync()`:

```
CloudQueueMessage message = queue.GetMessage();
CloudQueueMessage retrievedMessage = await queue.GetMessageAsync();
```

The difference between the `PeekMessage()` and `GetMessage()` methods is that the `GetMessage()` method, when called, blocks the thread and waits until a message arrives in the queue before returning. The thread will be hung in a waiting state, which may not be a huge issue since there wouldn't be any messages to process if the method call had to wait. Nonetheless, it is always good practice to release and not block threads in most, if not all, scenarios.

The benefit that `PeekMessage()` provides is that, when called, it tells you if there is a message in the queue waiting to be processed without blocking the thread or waiting on a message to arrive. Therefore, it is not necessary to call `GetMessage()` unless `PeekMessage()` returns with a status stating there is a message available for processing. `PeekMessage()` does not set any locks on the message and does not modify it in any way.

You may also consider calling the `GetMessageAsync()` method that would release the thread, but it would wait via `await` until there is a message in the queue ready for processing. Which process to use is up to the application requirements. One thing to note about using asynchronous methods is that all methods that include the `await` keyword must be asynchronous themselves (all the way up). It is not recommended to ever call `Result()` or `Wait()` in the async classes. This can cause serious blocking and hangs.

After one of the get message methods is called from your application, you need to call `DeleteMessage()` so that the queue knows the message has been processed. Notice that there is also an asynchronous version of this method and that it doesn't return a value; it will, however, return a catchable exception if the deletion fails.

```
queue.DeleteMessage(retrievedMessage);
await queue.DeleteMessageAsync(retrievedMessage);
```

If there is an exception in your code and the message is not processed, then at some point the message would become unlocked and available for processing once again. The only way in which the queue knows that the message has been successfully processed is by you calling the `DeleteMessage()` method from your code after the processing is complete. You should seriously consider placing your code within a `try{} ... catch{}` block and in the `catch` expression perform some code to attempt a reprocess, place the message into a poison queue, log it for sure, and decide what you want to do with it later. It is possible that the message is malformed and would fail over and over again, so simply reprocessing the message isn't the most optimal unless you have good logic in your `catch` expressions and handle them appropriately.

Forms, Certificate, Windows, MFA, Open Standard, Managed Identities, and Service Principle Authentication

There are numerous methods for implementing authentication into your application. Some have been covered in detail; others have not. We will briefly cover several types, starting with Forms Authentication.

Forms Authentication

Forms Authentication is implemented into an ASP.NET application starting with the installation of the IIS module. Then, its configuration is installed into the web.config file using syntax similar to the following snippet:

```
<configuration>
    <system.web>
        <authentication mode="Forms" />
    </system.web>
</configuration>
```

Figure 7.3 shows that the IIS module for Forms Authentication is installed but not yet enabled.

FIGURE 7.3 IIS authentication providers

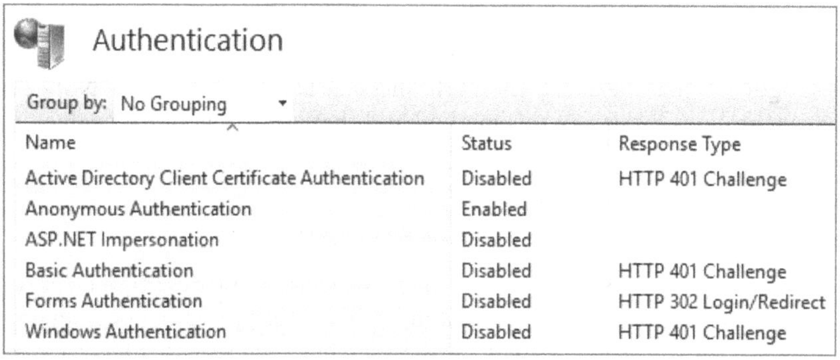

Enabling the IIS module and the web.config file results in the authentication provider being enabled. The scope of this configuration is for the website running within and underneath the directory structure in direct relation to the location of the physical web .config file.

The reason for the note about where the configuration is applied in relation to the location of the web.config file is that this authentication provider can be enabled on the web server, but it's not used unless you enabled it specifically on a website. In addition to configuring web.config, you must also have an *Authentication (AuthN)*, in which your custom user identity database stores the credentials. Any group associations that define whether the user has access to specific resources within the application once authenticated, would utilize *Authorization (AuthZ)* to confirm the access. The code required to perform the AuthN and AuthZ procedure must be written by a developer working in the application itself. This is not an "out-of-the-box" authentication solution. It is, however, a solid, sophisticated, and valid approach for implementing security into an internet application.

Certificate Authentication

A certificate is a file that contains an encrypted key or token that is created and administered by a *certificate authority (CA)*. Recall from Chapter 5, which covered cryptography, that you encrypted a column on an Azure SQL database in Exercise 5.3. Certificate authentication falls into the same category and is related to cryptography. Something to call out here specifically has to do with public and private keys. Here are the fundamental concepts:

- A private key is used to encrypt data.
- The private key decrypts data encrypted by the public key.

Based on those definitions of public and private keys, it may be obvious that the private key is the one that needs the greatest protection. Making it possible to encrypt data using a key wouldn't cause any harm; however, the ability to decrypt that data and use it is something that needs greater control. Let's not go much deeper into this as it was mentioned before; this area of technology is career worthy and book worthy, but not essential for the exam. Some knowledge here is helpful. Certificate authentication has dependencies on public and private keys because those keys must be validated against the certificate to consider the certificate authentication successful. Look at Figure 7.3. You will see an authentication provider is installed as well. Figure 7.4 illustrates the process of this authentication (recall also from Figure 2.28 that a certificate was called out as a means for validating an identity using MFA).

FIGURE 7.4   Client certificate authentication flow

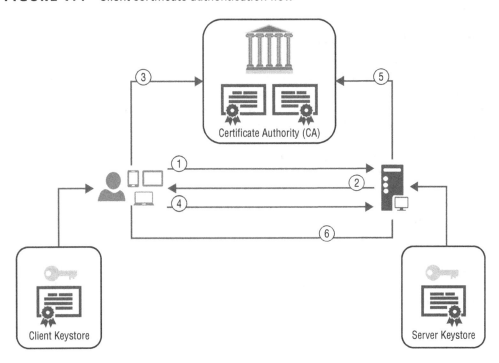

An interesting point regarding the previous figure is that it isn't always just the server side that is concerned about the identity of the client/user making the connection. You should also be aware and confident that you are connecting to the server that you really intend to. It is easy to scrape a web page from a bank that includes the user ID and password textbox. You enter them on my page, and I store them when you click the submit button and then redirect you to the real bank site so you can reenter them and access. Having this client-server certificate validation is helpful for both parties, not just the server side. The process of client certification is as follows:

1. The client requests a protected resource.
2. The server returns a server certificate.
3. The client validates the certificate with the CA.
4. The client sends a client certificate.
5. The server validates the certificate with the CA.
6. The server grants or denies access based on the validation.

Notice that the client makes a request to the resource before sending the certificate. This makes sense because you wouldn't want to send a certificate with each request unless it is required to do so. This would increase the data transmission with each request. However, there is a feature called `uploadReadAheadSize` that defines how much of the data body content can be sent along with the certificate from the client in step 4. This improves performance as the data transmission can be optimized by utilizing all the available transmission buffer.

Windows Authentication

Both NTLM and Kerberos were introduced in Chapter 2 when discussing Azure Active Directory Domain Services. Both of those security protocols, NTLM and Kerberos, are included when you enable Windows Authentication for an intranet website. The key point here is that Windows Authentication is used with intranets and not the internet because intranets typically require an Active Directory (AD) and some additional infrastructure to implement. As you can see in Figure 7.3, there is an authentication provider named Windows Authentication aka *Integrated Windows Authentication (IWA)*. If you want to enable IWA, you need to disable Anonymous Authentication to protect your website. Recall from the previous section where you learned that the initial request from the client to the server is an anonymous one. This is because the client doesn't yet know which security protocol the server requires for access to the requested resource. Therefore, if anonymous authentication is enabled, IIS uses that one as the default; once authentication is granted, it doesn't proceed to check for other enabled authentication providers.

Integrated Windows Authentication does support NTLM but mostly uses Kerberos, which is the default as it is more secure. You can see this in the advanced settings for IWA in the IIS Management console, as shown in Figure 7.5.

FIGURE 7.5   Kerberos and NTLM settings in IIS for IWA

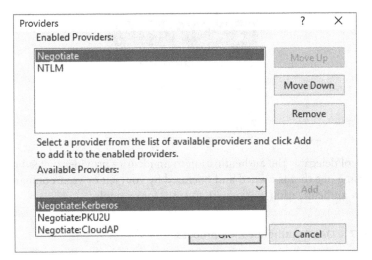

IWA provides a single sign-on (SSO) solution. When an employee successfully logs into their Windows workstation, they receive a Kerberos token. This token is cached and can again be used when accessing a website without having to log in again. In most cases, the browser that is used to access the intranet site has the code necessary to check whether the website is an intranet and then look and use the Kerberos token automatically. If you are coding a custom client application that is not web-based or doesn't use a browser, then you would need to code this logic into your app manually.

Multifactor Authentication

There isn't much more to add about multifactor authentication (MFA) that hasn't already been covered in Chapter 2 (see Figure 2.28). In summary, MFA is an added level of security that takes place after someone successfully provides a user ID and password, which is something they know. The second layer is based on something they have, such as a certificate, a fingerprint, or a code sent to a mobile device in your possession. These days, you need to strongly consider MFA as a default because the user ID and password security solution has many vulnerabilities and should no longer be solely depended on.

Open Standards

Protocols like OAuth and OpenID are used mostly for delegated authentication of internet-based applications. If you have a Google, Apple, Microsoft, or Facebook account and have clicked a button similar to those shown in Figure 7.6, then you have been authenticated using an open standard authentication protocol.

FIGURE 7.6   Open standard authentication protocols

This protocol delegates the authentication to an identity provider instead of your application using one that is owned and operated by yourself or your company. Figure 7.7 illustrates how authentication works with OAuth, for example.

FIGURE 7.7   OAuth authentication process

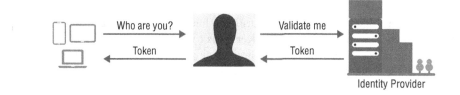

Identity Provider

In this example, you try to access some application that is protected by an identity provider, as shown in Figure 7.6. You select the one that you will use, which triggers a routing of the request to the selected identity provider. If the credentials are not cached locally already, then you are prompted to enter those necessary for the selected provider. If the credentials are cached on your machine already, then they get used. If the credentials are valid, then the identity provider returns a token that must then be validated by the application code to which you want access. In some respects, this is like Forms Authentication without the need to store user credentials in your own data store. You will, however, need to have logic to enforce authorization access, using groups, claims, and permissions.

Managed Identities

Managed Identities (MI) are in many ways a service principle. The difference is that they can be used only with Azure resources. Chapter 2 includes a section about managed identities, so take a look at that. In a majority of cases, credentials usually identify a human individual. Some scenarios let you give an application an identity and grant the application access to the application instead of granting access to individuals. A scenario in which MI is used is to access Azure Key Vault where a connection string or token is stored to access some other resource such as a database or an Event Hub partition. Using Managed Identity can prevent credential leaking since the developer and/or administrator of the application never sees the credentials of the resource that are stored in the Azure Key Vault.

Service Principal Authentication

A service principal is an identity that is used to access a resource but isn't linked to any living being. It is simply an account with a user ID and password that applications can use to make sure whatever is accessing it is allowed to. In the service principal scenario, someone has created the account and will need to manage it. For example, someone must be made responsible for resetting the password and performing other tasks. Doing that may cause some disruption if you are unaware of all the applications using it. You need to notify them all and give them the new password and the date and time, and it will change so they can update the connected systems. In summary, using a service principle requires some management, which is why the abstracted layer around the service principal is called a *managed identity*. All the creation and administration tasks of the service principal identity are managed for you. The approach to use depends on your needs.

Reading Encrypted Data from a Database

Encrypting your data at rest is something you should really consider. If your data source's integrity is compromised or stolen, the impact can be greatly reduced by simply encrypting the sensitive data. I confess to not being the best hacker in the world, but compromising a data source from the outside is extremely difficult. The reality is that many malicious activities happen by exploiting the trust or greed of an individual who has access to the resources you want. Most of the time the user ID and password are enough to get copies of the database onto a thumb drive and out it goes. But if the data is encrypted, like you did in Exercise 5.3, and no single person has access to the data source credentials and the encryption key, then the probability of a breach is greatly reduced.

In Exercise 2.9 you created an Azure Key Vault and generated a key, likely named DAR if you completed the exercises. If you take a look at your Azure Key Vault key now in the Azure Portal, it should resemble that shown in Figure 7.8.

FIGURE 7.8   An Azure Key Vault key

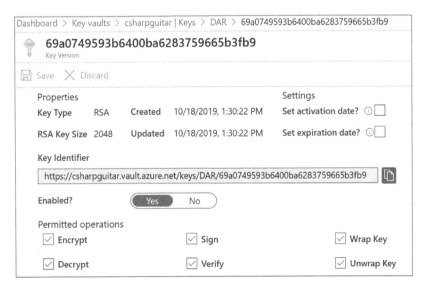

You will not be able to call the Key Identifier shown in Figure 7.8 because you do not have permission. Permission can be granted to a managed identity, which would make sure no individual or developer had direct access to the key. Instead, only the application would. If you are the administrator, for example, and you were the one who created the key, then you could access it using Azure CLI with the following command:

```
az keyvault key show --id https://<name>.vault.azure.net/keys/DAR/69 ... 0bb9
```

Executing that would result in the encryption key being returned and stored to a variable named n. The key is accessible via C# code using syntax like the following. The GitHub link at the end of the next paragraph allows you to view the entire class.

```
var publicKey = Convert.ToBase64String(key.Key.N);
```

You used that key in Exercise 5.3 to encrypt the MODEL column on the MODELS table contained in an Azure SQL database. Take a look at Figure 5.30 if you forgot what that data looked like. In Exercise 5.8, you added an unencrypted Event Hub connection string to an Azure Key Vault secret, but later you learned how you could encrypt and store the connection string using some C# code. Take a look at it again if desired.

github.com/benperk/ASA/tree/master/Chapter05/DataEncryption

To use the code in that example to store and retrieve the encrypted data, you would need to perform the following:

1. Create the connection to the database using either ADO.NET or Entity Framework.
2. On INSERT, get the Azure Key Vault key using the managed identity credentials. Call the EncryptText() method, which encrypts the data. Write the data to the database.
3. On SELECT, get the Azure Key Vault key using the Managed Identity credentials. Call the DecryptText() method that decrypts the data. Display the data to the authenticated client.

If you completed Exercise 5.3, then you would only need to decrypt the data on selection because the data was encrypted when it was inserted by the configurations you made in that exercise. Another good use for this scenario is when you implemented Forms Authentication and need to store passwords in a database. For sure you would want to encrypt this column. However, you wouldn't want to send the plain-text password from the client to the server; even if TLS is enabled, it would still feel unsecure by doing that. Instead, you can make sure the passwords are encrypted using the Azure Key Vault key before it leaves the client and store it encrypted. Then, instead of comparing the plain-text password, encrypt the password on the client, and compare the encrypted value with the encrypted value on the database.

IDEs and Source Code Repositories

With all the programming languages and technologies that can be deployed on the Azure platform, you might have some questions about the most commonly used *integrated development environments (IDEs)* and source code repositories. The most common IDE by far is Visual Studio followed by Visual Studio Code, which is rapidly growing in popularity. Visual Studio is typically used for larger enterprises because it comes with a lot of debugging and testing capabilities. C# is the most common programming language, but C++ and Visual Basic are also popular. Visual Studio Code is used for many open source and cross-platform languages such as JavaScript, Python, and .NET Core. It is free but does lack some of the more sophisticated features found in full Visual Studio versions such as the Professional and Enterprise versions. Figure 7.9 shows the IDE for Visual Studio Community 2019. IntelliJ and NetBeans are two of the common IDEs used for developing Java-based applications.

FIGURE 7.9   The Visual Studio Community IDE

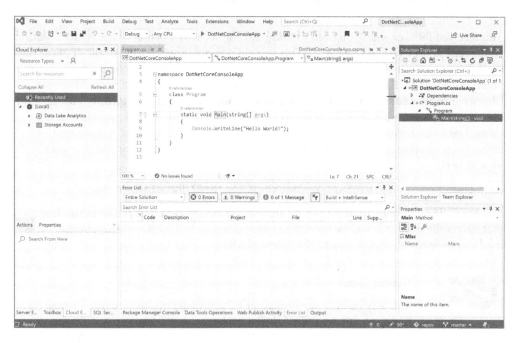

Backing up your data has been covered in much detail, and the reasons to do so are very clear. Now think about backing up the source code that analyzes, creates, or manipulates that data. If you lose the code, then all you have is a big data set but nothing to do with it or learn from it. Therefore, having a backup of your code is important. Additionally, having a change log so you can see who made changes and incorporating the ability to roll back to a previous version in case of bugs or regressions are helpful features. Some years ago, a Microsoft product named Visual Source Safe (VSS) provided these kinds of capabilities. These days the Microsoft tool for such a purpose is the Repository feature within the Azure DevOps portfolio, which used to be called *Team Foundation Services (TFS)*, aka VSTS. There will be more on this in Chapter 8. There are many other source code repositories; a popular one is GitHub, which Microsoft recently purchased. Others like Bitbucket or a local Git repository are tightly integrated with Azure and can be used to implement deployment concepts like *continuous integration/continuous deployment (CI/CD)* deployment flows.

Implementing Security

You received 99% of what you need to know for the security portion of the Azure Solutions Architect Expert exam in Chapter 2. This section is more targeted toward the application itself. The content in this chapter is good to know if your goal is to become a great Azure Solutions Architect Expert. In this section, you will implement and configure Managed Identity into an Azure App Service to give your Azure App Service an identity and use that identity in creating and configuring an Azure Key Vault key secret and provide access to other Azure resources. The code that will use that identity to get a database connection string from an Azure Key Vault secret and an encryption key to encrypt and decrypt can be viewed here:

```
github.com/benperk/ASA/tree/master/Chapter07/DataEncryption
```

That code will not be discussed in detail because coding isn't part of the exam. But note that this is the code that will be used in the next chapter. In Chapter 8, this application is used as you learn how to deploy to the Azure platform.

 Source Code

You may need to perform several steps to get the code to run, such as installing the dependent NuGet packages. Additionally, you will need to update the code to point to your Azure Key Vault. If you have any questions, start an issue on GitHub.

In addition to Managed Identity and Azure Key Vault access policies, you will configure EasyAuth. EasyAuth (introduced in Chapter 2) is a quick and easy way to implement Authentication (AuthN) using Azure Active Directory within the context of Azure App Service or Azure Function.

Let's get started. In Exercise 7.1 you will enable Managed Identity in the Azure App Service you created in Exercise 3.8 and then grant the identity access to an Azure Key Vault secret. (You created an Azure Key Vault in Exercise 2.9.)

EXERCISE 7.1

Enabling Managed Identity and Allowing Access to the Azure Key Vault Secret

1. Log in to the Azure Portal at portal.azure.com.

2. Navigate to the Azure App Service you created in Exercise 3.8; then click the Identity link in the navigation menu. Set the Status to On, and click the Save button. Your configuration should resemble Figure 7.10.

FIGURE 7.10   Enabling Managed Identity on an Azure App Service

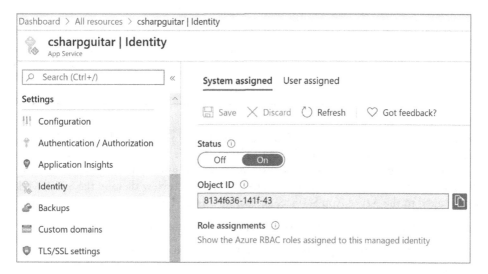

3. Navigate to the Azure Key Vault you created in Exercise 2.9 and click the Access Policies link in the navigation menu. Click the + Add Access Policy link, select the Get check box in the Secret Permissions list, select the Get and Decrypt check boxes in the Key Permissions list, and then select the name of the Azure App Service where you enabled Managed Identity in the Principle Member list. Click the Add button and click the Save button. Your configuration should resemble Figure 7.11.

FIGURE 7.11   Adding an access policy to an Azure Key Vault

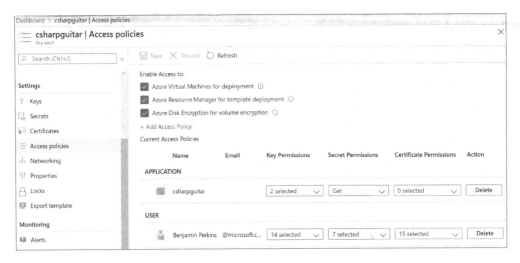

That wasn't so hard, was it? Just a few clicks in the portal, and you have enabled Managed Identity for an Azure App Service. The procedure for many other Azure products is of the same complexity. Behind the scenes, the configuration creates two environment variables, MSI_ENDPOINT and MSI_SECRET. You can review them in the SCM/KUDU console linked to the Azure App Service, accessible using a URL similar to the following:

```
https://<appName>.scm.azurewebsites.net/Env.cshtml
```

The values are used by the platform to get an authentication token on behalf of the principle.

If you were to deploy the updated GitHub code with the required packages, after completing the previous exercise, then when you access the ASP.NET Core application, the following will take place:

1. A token for the application principle is retrieved.

2. An Azure Key Vault client is created and authenticated.

3. A database connection string is retrieved from an Azure Key Vault secret.

4. An Azure Key Vault key is retrieved and used to encrypt a guitar brand.

5. A connection is made to a database, and the encrypted value is inserted into the database, as shown in Figure 7.12.

6. The inserted row is then retrieved, decrypted, and displayed on the web page.

FIGURE 7.12   An encrypted data element on a database table

csharpguitar.guitar - dbo.GUITARS ⊕ ×	
GUITAR_ID	BRAND
1	Fender
2	Gibson
3	IIIVjFGSCkXd8cNKI1x1DTyTt8DN/Ch55i2/bJHgI0SuNDVp4fxJ9eCyCevFKdiET2zBbbJ2WgWVxAPRumw8qS4Ji...
▶* *NULL*	NULL

At the moment, the web page is open and accessible to anyone who comes across the page or discovers the endpoint. To prevent this, implement EasyAuth to make sure only authenticated users associated with an Azure Active Directory tenant can view the page. See Exercise 7.2.

EXERCISE 7.2

Enabling Easy Auth

1. Log in to the Azure Portal at `portal.azure.com`.

2. Navigate to the Azure App Service where you configured Managed Identity and Azure Key Vault in Exercise 7.1. Click the Authentication/Authorization link in the navigation menu, set App Service Authentication to On, and select Azure Active Directory from the Authentication Providers section.

3. Select Express from the Management mode selection area, set Grant Common Data Services Permissions to On, click the OK button, and finally click the Save button. The configuration should resemble Figure 7.13.

FIGURE 7.13   Configuring EasyAuth in Azure App Service

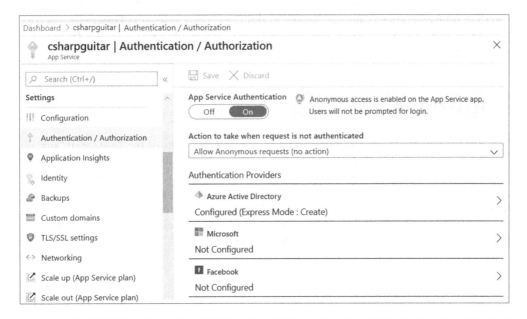

That's easy and is why it's named EasyAuth. When you now access the Azure App Service, based on the Allow Anonymous Requests setting in the configuration, the client will have access to the main page. You need to make code changes to protect the content of your application, such as implementing Authorization (AuthZ). If you take a look at the source code provided earlier, specifically the index.cshtml file, you will notice an if.. else.. statement that checks to see that an authentication token exists and is not null. If the token doesn't exist, then you see the links to log in with AAD. Clicking that captures the credentials, authenticates, and then dumps out some of the details about the token. You need to check whether the client is authenticated and has a valid token in each one of your web pages that needs restricted access. Additionally, and most importantly, you also need to build your own authorization logic into the application. EasyAuth doesn't provide that feature. When all is configured correctly, your client is authenticated, and the screen shown in Figure 7.14 is rendered in the browser.

FIGURE 7.14   EasyAuth Azure Active Directory successful login

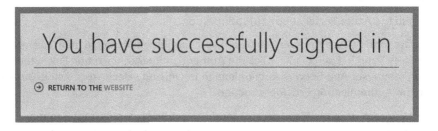

Security is an important aspect when it comes to IT and creating applications. There are many components in an IT solution, each of which should be reviewed from a security perspective. In addition to the hardware and infrastructure components, the code and the entry point into the code require professional skill, expertise, and experience in the security area. In all cases, consult a security expert when you have doubts about the integrity of your IT footprint.

Summary

You will not find many questions on the exam about the contents of this chapter. In any case, knowing architectural styles and coding patterns that are optimal for the cloud will only make you a better architect. You gained some knowledge of the IDEs used for developing and testing applications and the importance of protecting and tracking your application source code. There were some examples about different types of authentication, such as Forms, IWA, and OAuth. In addition, you learned about encryption, enabling EasyAuth, and configuring Managed Identity on an Azure App Service.

Exam Essentials

Know what *lift* and *shift* means.   This term has to do with moving an application that is running in an on-premise data center and moving it to the cloud without making any changes. Having read this chapter, you will recognize there are some cloud-only issues you may face and some optimal patterns and styles to follow that will improve the chances of being successful in the cloud. They include Retry and creating a reusable static connection object.

Understand authentication protocols.   There are numerous methods for protecting your application by checking for credentials: Forms Authentication, certificate authentication, Windows Authentication (Kerberos), and OAuth. These are protocols that protect the application entry point, which then allow the client to execute the code. You need to implement some logic to authenticate and authorize access to the application and to the features running within it.

Understand encryption.   This area has to do with the concept of cryptography. The examples provided in this book focused on the encryption of data on a given column in an Azure SQL database table. This is an example of encrypting your data at rest. The data is encrypted when inserted, the data is selected from the database encrypted, and then the client can use an encryption key to decrypt and view the value. This kind of operation can add latency, so implement it only on very sensitive data.

Key Terms

authentication (AuthN)

authorization (AuthZ)

Azure Front Door

certificate authority (CA)

Command and Query Responsibility Segregation (CQRS)

continuous integration/continuous deployment (CI/CD)

integrated development environments (IDE)

Integrated Windows Authentication (IWA)

Team Foundation Services (TFS)

Review Questions

1. Which of the following cloud concepts would you expect to occur more in the cloud than on-premise? (Select all that apply.)

   A. Auto healing

   B. Datacenter outage

   C. Transient outages

   D. Data loss

2. If your application running on an Azure App Service or Azure Function is receiving a `SocketException` or experiencing SNAT port exhaustion, which coding pattern would you implement?

   A. Gatekeeper

   B. Sharding

   C. Create private static connection objects

   D. Use asynchronous methods

3. What coding pattern would you use to recover from transient issue?

   A. Retry

   B. Gatekeeper

   C. Circuit breaker

   D. Throttling

4. Which of the following are user authentication mechanisms you can use to protect your internet-based application? (Select all that apply.)

   A. Forms authentication

   B. Certificate authentication

   C. Windows authentication

   D. Service principle

5. Which of the following is not a valid IDE for building applications that run on Azure?

   A. Visual Studio Community

   B. IntelliJ

   C. Visual Studio Code

   D. Visio Studio

6. Which of the following is true concerning Managed Identity (MI)? (Select all that apply.)

   A. Can be used to access Azure Key Vault

   B. Cannot be used with an ASP.NET Core application

    C. Represents the identity of an Azure product

    D. Managed Identity is enabled by default on all supported Azure products

7. Which of the following authority providers does EasyAuth support? (Select all that apply.)

    A. Facebook

    B. Google

    C. Microsoft

    D. GitHub

8. Which product would you choose to implement a Big Data solution? (Select all that apply.)

    A. Data Lake Analytics

    B. Azure Cosmos DB

    C. Event Grid

    D. Azure Kubernetes Service (AKS)

9. Which product would you choose to implement a decoupled IT solution? (Select all that apply.)

    A. Service Bus

    B. Azure Cosmos DB

    C. Azure Batch

    D. Azure Storage Queue

10. Which product would you choose to implement a big compute solution? (Select all that apply.)

    A. Service Fabric

    B. Azure Virtual Machines

    C. Azure Batch (aka HPC)

    D. Azure Functions

Chapter

8

Migrate and Deploy

EXAM AZ-303 OBJECTIVES COVERED IN THIS CHAPTER:

✓ **Implement and Monitor an Azure Infrastructure**

- Automate deployment and configuration of resources

✓ **Implement Management and Security Solutions**

- Manage workloads in Azure

✓ **Implement Solutions for Apps**

- Implement an application infrastructure

EXAM AZ-304 OBJECTIVES COVERED IN THIS CHAPTER:

✓ **Design Infrastructure**

- Design migrations

If you have progressed through all the chapters so far, you will realize that everything is now ready for you to move your workloads onto the Azure platform. You earned all the prerequisites required to get to this point, for example, security, networking, compute, data and storage, compliance strategies, messaging services, and cloud coding patterns. The moment of truth has arrived, and it's now time to migrate your workload to Azure. In this chapter, you can gain the skills necessary to do the following:

- Migrate Azure Virtual Machines and your data store.
- Deploy source code to PaaS products.
- Deploy using an ARM template.
- Deploy using Visual Studio.
- Deploy using Azure DevOps.

The most common migrations move your Azure Virtual Machines and your data store. ARM templates are useful for automating deployments. They tie well into an Azure feature called Azure Automation. Azure DevOps support projects that require or desire CI/CD deployment models. Lastly, deploying code from Visual Studio to a PaaS product like Azure App Service is tightly integrated with the IDE. It is quick and easy to get a website running and accessible to anyone from anyplace in the world with internet access. Let's get right to it, starting with learning a bit about migration concepts and some tools useful for migrating compute and data resources.

Migrating to Azure

Moving an existing IT solution to a new platform is a big deal. Even if you are moving only a part of the solution, it takes more than knowing which tools are recommended for each resource type; it takes a plan. What I mean by "resource type" is your compute (dependent on CPU), memory, and operating systems requirements. Additionally, you need to know your targeted data store, such as SQL Server, Oracle, or MySQL, for example. What you're trying to migrate to Azure—for example, an application that uses only storage, only compute, only a data store versus a complete IT solution that requires all of those and perhaps others—will drive the migration planning. Like many other technical contexts, there is a pattern that if used as a model increases your probability for success. That pattern and recommended tools that should be used to migrate your specific resource type are also discussed in this chapter. The Azure Solutions Architect Expert exam is more focused on the tools than the plan, but both are important to know.

As shown in Figure 8.1, a migration of your resources to the Azure platform can be broken down into four phases: assessment, migration, optimization, and security and management. The assessment phase is where you clearly define your objectives and priorities. It is similar to a design phase where you document what you want and then plan the steps required to achieve them. This is where you would want to engage a project manager who would break down the objectives into steps and apply a timeline. The timeline would include the items identified as priorities to make sure they are by all means completed when required.

FIGURE 8.1   Azure migration phases

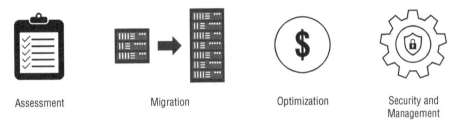

| Assessment | Migration | Optimization | Security and Management |

From a technical perspective, you need to assess which changes, if any, are required for the migration to be successful. For example, does your workload require a specific version of an operating system, require registry changes, or require some kind of third-party framework? This is the phase to discover such things and then identify which compute resource or group of resources are available and/or required to successfully migrate the workload to Azure. There are some tools that can analyze your current solution and generate a report containing some issues you may have with your migration. Consider employing the following:

- Azure Migrate for a compute server assessment
- Azure Data Migration Assistant (DMA) to examine your data stores
- Azure App Service migration assessment for your web applications
- Azure Data Migration Service (DMS)

Additionally, the output of the tool may contain some tips on possible issues that require further investigation. The tools are all covered in more detail later in this chapter. All were introduced in earlier chapters.

In addition to performing assessments, the tools can be used for the actual migration in the next phase. The migration phase is where you execute the plan you created in the assessment phase. How you execute the deployment has much to do with whether you have decided to lift and shift or perform a variety of refactoring, rearchitecting, or rebuilding one or more components of your workload solution. Look back at Figure 4.2, which illustrated a decision tree for choosing the best-fitting compute offering. To remind you, lift and shift means that you do not plan on making any changes to your workload and want to run it just like it works on-premise but on the Azure platform. When doing a lift and shift, the range of possible changes you can make are limited to only a few cloud optimizations, such as increasing the amount of available compute power like CPU and RAM. Life and shift can go directly to PaaS in many cases, and there are real benefits to doing so, such as autoscaling no longer being required for load balancing and delegating the responsibility for the management of operating systems and software libraries. The other end of the spectrum is completely rearchitecting and rebuilding your current IT solution to be cloud optimized. That would include options such as containerization with Azure Kubernetes (AKS) and Azure Container Instances (ACI) or the implementation of new technologies such as Azure Functions and Azure Cosmos DB. Some tools helpful for actually performing the migration follow:

- Azure Site Recovery
- Azure Migrate
- Azure Data Migration Service (DMS)
- Import/Export

Those are, by all means, not the only available migration tools; there are many other tools you would need for a large number of scenarios and technologies. Using the *File Transfer Protocol (FTP)* is an example of a basic but useful tool for moving files of many different types and purposes between servers. There may also be some activities for which there exists no deployment tool. Their deployment must be performed manually via a *Remote Desktop Protocol (RDP)* connection to an Azure virtual machine. The execution phase, during which you actually perform the migration, is the time where your skills, the skills of your team, and your planning all come together. Consider including the definition of an escalation path as part of the assessment and planning phase to identify how long someone should attempt to resolve an issue before escalation. Also, here you define the path and process the person having the technical issue should follow when they hit a roadblock. By all means consider reaching out to Microsoft Support if you come to a standstill. Microsoft is dedicated to making customers successful on the Azure platform, and you will receive a high level of support from them. Also recognize that there are other cloud companies that specialize in helping customers migrate to Azure. If your workload and the Azure footprint is large, consider consulting with a third party specialized in migrating from on-premise to Azure. Doing this increases the speed and decreases possible unexpected impacts on your business and customers. Have a look at this page, which can help you find a Microsoft partner for consulting in this area:

azure.microsoft.com/en-us/migration/migration-partners

Congratulations, once your workload is transferred to the Azure platform and all is running as expected, take a moment to pat yourself and team on the back for successfully bringing your IT into the 21st century. OK, that's long enough, there is much more work to do.

Now it is time to optimize your workloads to make sure your consumption and costs are falling in line with expectations. Two ways to achieve optimization are *Azure Hybrid*

Benefit and *Azure Reserved Virtual Machine Instances.* Both offers are discussed in the "Migrating Azure Virtual Machines" section. The other way to optimize is by using Azure Cost Management and Cloudy, both of which were introduced in Chapter 1. Remember, forecasting, monitoring, and controlling costs is of utmost significance. If your company runs out of money, then you go out of business. You can view a useful report on your spending based on subscription in the Azure Portal, similar to Figure 8.2.

FIGURE 8.2   Azure Cost Management

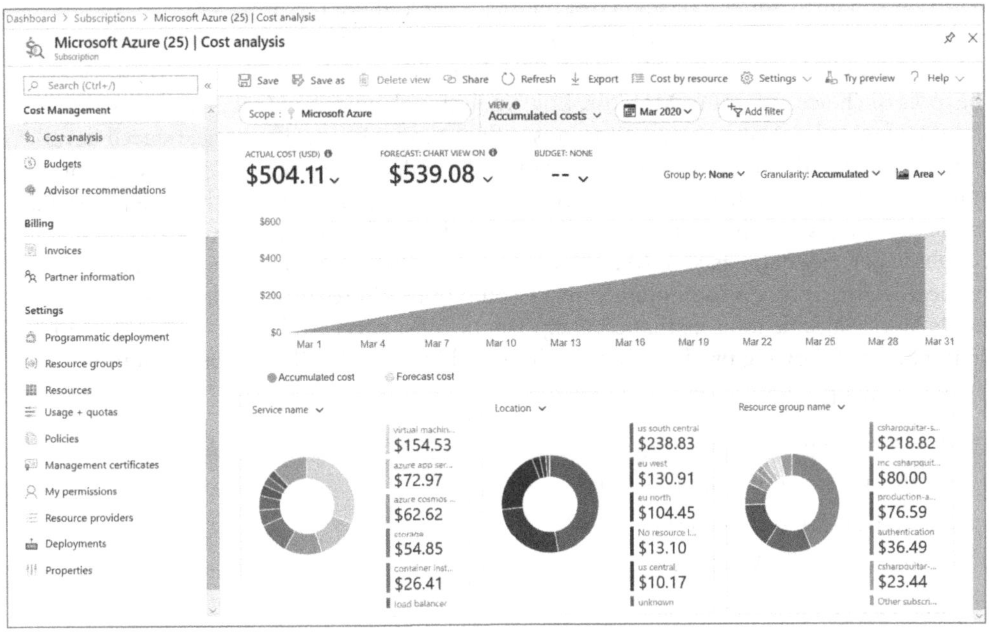

Navigate to the Subscription blade and select the Azure subscription that you want to assess. Click the Cost Analysis link in the navigation menu. Notice that it provides both a current and forecasted view of the charges. A nice feature is located toward the bottom of the Cost Analysis blade. Here you will find the breakdown of charges based on the service name such as Azure VM, App Service, Azure Cosmos DB, and the like; the location such as South Central US (SN1), North Europe (DB3), and others; and the resource group name. All three of these cost breakdown reports will provide you great insights into where your Azure spend is being consumed. Then you can match that with the expectations you defined at the beginning of the migration process in the assessment phase.

The final phase of the migration is making sure the workloads remain secure and functional. From a security perspective, you should test often. Ensure that your RBAC restrictions still restrict CRUD activities within your subscription. Regularly check that your Azure Policies are still in compliance with your corporate and industry requirements. Check that your MFA and JIT access providers are working and that any new applications are compliant with the storage of credentials on Azure Key Vault. Verify that the utilization of Managed Identities (MI) is happening. Lastly, consider the implementation of malware detection and other security-related IT solutions into your workloads. Keep in mind that although Azure has great security policies and procedures in place, they are primarily focused toward the protection of the platform and not so much toward applications running on it. Security Center is for customers to customize and define in greater detail what should and what shouldn't be considered a malicious behavioral pattern. Microsoft cannot know if the behaviors on your application are expected or not and if Microsoft takes an action that shuts down your workloads wrongly, which would be a problem. Therefore, application security is primarily the responsibility of the customer and not the provider.

The management of your IT solution on Azure has to do with the monitoring and recovery capabilities of your applications. Those details are covered in the next chapter. The tools of choice are Azure Monitor, Log Analytics, Application Insights, and Azure Backup. Having worked in support for most of my career, I have often experienced developers who believed that the project is over once the code is delivered and in production. In reality, once the code is live and being used, the project begins. Keeping the code running, troubleshooting issues, performance tuning, upgrades, and making sure we can recover without losing any data lasts, in some cases, decades. Now that you know the phases of a typical, generic process to migrate your IT solution to Azure, read further to get more details on the specific toolsets that can help you be more successful in the execution and planning. The following products will be discussed in more detail in the next sections:

- Azure Site Recovery
- Azure Migrate
- Migrating Azure Virtual Machines
- Azure Data Migration Service (DMS)
- Migrating Azure App Services
- Import/Export

Before moving on, I'd like to call out a comment by Arthur C. Clarke. He said, "Any sufficiently advanced technology is indistinguishable from magic." As you become more experienced, you may find yourself scratching your head, wondering how something worked, and wondering why it didn't work last time even though you followed the same steps again. I wouldn't call it magic, because when you execute a process, it simply runs the code it was programmed to do. It does still amaze me how all the bits and bytes align to complete my desired outcome. Maybe there is an aspect to magic to it, but maybe it has more to do with us being IT wizards and magicians after all.

Azure Site Recovery

Azure Site Recovery (ASR) was introduced in Chapter 1. Read through the chapter if you haven't already done so; there is much information there. Also, take a look at Figure 1.8, which illustrates this kind of configuration. There is also a comparison between Azure Site

Recovery and Azure Backup in Chapter 4. What I am getting at is that this shouldn't be the first place you are reading or learning about this. If it is, you need to read those other discussions first. You will notice that mostly Azure Site Recovery is used for BDCR scenarios, but you can also move production workloads to Azure with it. In reality, you may be forced to move a workload to it, if the on-premise version requires a failover when your BDCR is configured in a way to do so.

A process for migrating an on-premise VMware, a Hyper-V virtual machine, or a physical machine to Azure can be achieved by using the Azure Site Recovery tool. You achieve the migration by configuring a disaster recovery scenario between the on-premise machine and one on the Azure platform. Once configured and tested, you could purposely trigger a failover that would move the workload to the Azure platform. That is a valid migration approach and may be less impactful than using Azure Migrate. Consider the point that if you failover and it doesn't work, then you have the option of flicking a switch and the traffic is set back to the original on-premise architecture. Depending on how you managed the migration using Azure Migrate, being able to fail back onto your on-premise compute may not be an option.

The configuration of a BDCR is relatively complicated, but it relies heavily on the kind of compute environment you are migrating from. There is more on that in the next section. However, consider that planning a migration is different when your source migration location is a Hyper-V VM, a VMware VM, or a physical server. Azure Site Recovery also supports the migration from *Azure Stack* workloads, which is a product for enterprises to run Azure in their own private data centers. There will be a bit more to come about Azure Site Recovery in the next chapter. What you need to know now is that this product can be used for migration purposes if Azure Migrate doesn't meet all your requirements. Before moving on to Azure Migrate, there is one more tool that needs mentioning. The *ASR Deployment Planner* can help migrate VMware virtual machines to Azure. This tool will help analyze the existing VM from a disk number, disk size, IOPS, BIOS, and OS version to help determine whether the VM is compliant with Azure VMs. In conclusion, use Azure Site Recovery for migrations only if Azure Migrate features do not meet your needs.

Azure Migrate

Migration of existing resources to Azure has been a theme in many chapters up to now. Both Azure Site Recovery and Azure Migrate were introduced in Chapter 1 and discussed further in Chapter 4. Azure Migrate is accessible via the Azure Portal. The overview blade resembles something similar to Figure 8.3.

Notice that there are features and tools for discovering, assessing, and migrating on-premise data center applications to Azure. The discovery aspect would result in the identification of all servers in your data center so that you get some kind of idea of how many servers and how much compute resource you currently consume. It used to be the case that you had to know which operating systems and hardware configurations were supported by manually comparing what you have with what Azure offers and then map them together. This is how it was mentioned in Chapter 4, specifically Tables 4.1, 4.2, 4.4, 4.5,

FIGURE 8.3 Azure Migrate Overview blade

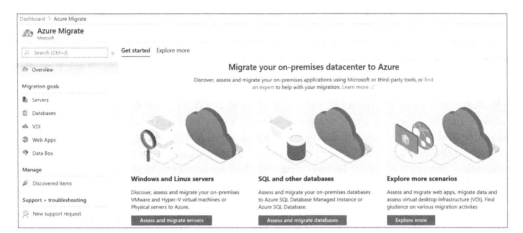

and 4.6. These tables provide a list of Azure VM sizes, supported operating system versions, and the recommended VM size for the selected operating system. Because all of that data is accessible via REST APIs, it makes a lot of sense that someone has coded a tool to automate such decisions. An interesting point about the manual mapping of OS to Azure VM, which Azure Migrate can now do for you, is that you learn some of the reasons for the decisions made on your behalf. Also, you can recognize the complexities behind the logic that would help very much in scenarios where Azure Monitor doesn't provide a migration path for you. In that case, you would have the knowledge now to proceed with a manual process for making the decision and progressing the migration forward.

The actual migration of your VMware, Hyper-V, or physical machines running either Windows Server or Linux will be executed for you. Be aware that the configuration of migration is quite significant. An interesting point you may find when setting this up is the reliance Azure Migrate has on Azure Site Recovery. Behind the scenes, when preparing the on-premise machines for migration, a Recovery Services vault is created to store the VHD that is used for building the Azure VM. Additionally, a tool named Azure Site Recovery Provider must be installed on all Hyper-V instances to complete a migration successfully. A Recovery Services vault can be seen in the Azure Portal and looks something similar to that shown in Figure 8.4. You would expect to see information about your deployments on this blade as you progress through the discovery (aka assessment) phase and the migration phase.

This useful tool is moving in the right direction with regard to simplifying the migration of enterprise data centers to the Azure platform. If you need to migrate only a few VMs or physical machines, the overhead incurred by using a Recovery Services vault may be too much for you.

For the exam, you need to know about Azure Monitor and its features. What you have learned about it here and in the previous chapter will greatly increase the probability of successfully answering any question you may encounter on the exam. Read on to get some hands-on experience with the migration of an on-premise VM to the Azure platform.

FIGURE 8.4   Recovery Services vault

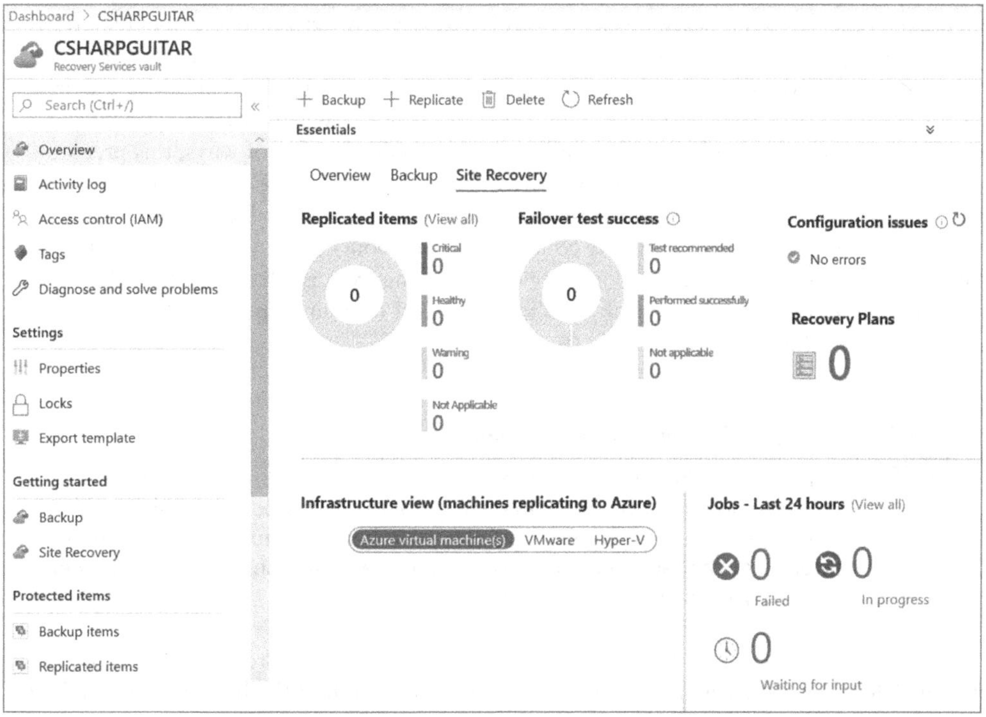

Migrating Azure Virtual Machines

In Exercise 3.3 you created your first Azure VM. You did this in Chapter 3 because it became a little complicated to discuss virtual networks, subnets, and NSGs without having something to apply those concepts to. You can have a virtual network without Azure VM in it, but you cannot have Azure VM without a virtual network. Therefore, before you attempt to migrate an on-premise workload to an Azure virtual machine, you will need a virtual network and a subnet like the one you created in Exercise 3.2. It is certainly possible to run a vast variety of both Windows Server and Linux versions on Azure VM. The source location of those on-premise machines can be running on VMware, Hyper-V, Azure Stack, and even AWS. Yes, there is a documented procedure that walks you through moving your IaaS workloads from AWS to Azure. Why not? The point here is that each of those sources requires some different steps to prepare and migrate. Most of them were discussed and provided in the previous chapters and discussions. For a hands-on example of migrating and deploying a single Hyper-V virtual machine instance to an Azure virtual machine, continue to the next section.

Hyper-V/VMware

Both Hyper-V and VMware are server virtualization management software. These products allow you to allocate a specific number of CPUs, an amount of Memory, an amount of hard disk storage, and then install an operating system. This is how you would usually create a virtual machine running on your workstation or on a server in a private data center. What you are going to do in this section is learn that regardless of your VM deployment source, VMware or Hyper-V, the file that must be deployed has to be a VHD. If you are deploying from a physical server where there is no virtualization, you need to use Azure Migrate or, if it is easier, virtualize the server before migrating. This is useful when Azure Migrate is too much overhead versus simply doing the migration manually. In a lot of ways, this preparation and building process is similar to what you did in Exercise 4.6. There you had a snapshot of an Azure virtual machine you created on Azure and used it to build other identical instances of that VM image. Again, the concept you are about to learn has close relation to that previously discussed concept. Complete the following exercise, Exercise 8.1, where you will convert a VMware image (.vmdk) to VHD, deploy it to Azure, and use it to build an Azure virtual machine.

Regional Dependencies in Exercise 8.1

Make sure the Azure Blob container into which you upload the VHD exists in the same region you want the Azure VM to be located. Also, the Azure VM must be in the same region as its targeted Azure virtual network. Simply place all the resources created in Exercise 8.1 into the same region; otherwise, you will not be successful.

There are no steps provided for the extraction of the VM image from VMware; the example VKMD was provisioned from the internet. You can find the links for that and all other referenced downloads here:

github.com/benperk/ASA/tree/master/Chapter08/Ch08Ex01

EXERCISE 8.1

Migrating a VMware Image to an Azure Virtual Machine

1. Export the server from the VMware management console in the form of a vmdk file or acquire one from the internet. Being a wannabe hacker, I downloaded Metasploitable from Rapid7. (The link to it is available from the previously provided URL; you do not need to make any exports from VMware.) After the download completes, extract the vmdk image into another directory.

2. Download and install Microsoft Virtual Machine Converter 3.0 into the default directory. The download link is provided in the same place as the previous link. Open PowerShell and enter the following command:

```
Import-Module "C:\Program Files\Microsoft Virtual Machine Converter\
MvmcCmdlet.psd1"
```

3. Execute the following PowerShell command to convert the vmdk to vhd. This may take some minutes to complete. The output should resemble that shown in Figure 8.5.

```
ConvertTo-MvmcVirtualHardDisk `
        -SourceLiteralPath "C:\Temp\Metasploitable.vmdk" `
        -DestinationLiteralPath "C:\Temp\Metasploitable.vhd" `
        -VhdType FixedHardDisk -VhdFormat Vhd
```

FIGURE 8.5   VMDK to VHD conversion

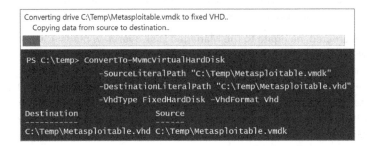

4. Execute the following PowerShell Azure CLI to upload the VHD to an Azure Blob Storage container. The output will resemble something similar to that shown in Figure 8.6. Be sure to update the parameter values to match your own. This can take some minutes depending on the speed of your connection.

```
Add-AzVhd -ResourceGroupName "<ResoureGroupName>" -Destination `
    "https://<name>.blob.core.windows.net/<container>/Metasploitable.vhd" `
    -LocalFilePath "C:\Temp\Metasploitable.vhd"
```

FIGURE 8.6   Uploading a VHD to an Azure Blob container using Azure CLI

```
Uploading.
  6.8% complete; Remaining Time: 00:16:43; Throughput: 18.6Mbps, 00:16:43 remaining.

PS C:\Temp> Add-AzVhd -ResourceGroupName "CSHARPGUITAR-SN1-RG"
            -Destination "https://csharpguitar.blob.core.windows.net/csharp/Metasploitable.vhd"
            -LocalFilePath "C:\Temp\Metasploitable.vhd"
MD5 hash is being calculated for the file  C:\Temp\Metasploitable.vhd.
MD5 hash calculation is completed.
Elapsed time for the operation: 00:00:36
Creating new page blob of size 8589935104...
Detecting the empty data blocks in the local file.
Detecting the empty data blocks completed.
Elapsed time for upload: 00:10:27

LocalFilePath             DestinationUri
-------------             --------------
C:\Temp\Metasploitable.vhd https://csharpguitar.blob.core.windows.net/csharp/Metas...
```

5. Once the upload is complete, log in to the Azure Portal at portal.azure.com. Click the menu button at the top-left area of the browser; then click + Create a Resource. Search for and click Managed Disks. Click the Create button and enter the subscription and resource group. Provide a disk name (I used METASPLOITABLE-DISK). Now, select the region and the Storage blob from the Source type drop-down list. Browse to the location where you uploaded the VHD in the previous step and select the VHD from the container. Click the Select button, and then select Linux for OS Type. Click the Review + Create button, and click the Create button.

6. Once that's created, navigate to the Managed Disk overview blade. Click + Create VM, and select the desired subscription and resource group. Enter a virtual machine name (mine was METASPLOITABLE-VHD1). Confirm that the image created in the previous step is selected from the Image drop-down list box, click the Select Size link, and choose the Azure VM size (for example, D2s_v3). Click the Next : Disks button, click Next : Networking, and select the virtual network (for example, CSHARPGUITAR-VNET-A). Select the subnet (for example, csharp), click the Review + Create button, then click the Create button.

7. You can then SSH to the virtual machine and test it. The credentials are the ones you used to access it when running on-premise. A note of caution, this VHD is exploitable. Consider not having a public IP or any means for someone other than yourself to access.

That is pretty straightforward, no? The previously described process works well if you only want to test how an individual virtualized server works when running on an Azure virtual machine within an Azure virtual network. Exercise 8.1 is not the path for large enterprises that intend on moving large numbers of VMs or have large requirements for Azure compute. If that is the case, i.e., that you expect to have a large Azure compute footprint, then as stated already, use Azure Migrate or Azure Site Recovery if for some reason Azure Migrate doesn't work for you to move your workloads to the Azure platform.

If you are coming from the VMware world, there is another tool set that will interest you called *Azure VMware Solutions*. This tool set lets you continue to use the same or similar VMware management console so that you or your team do not need to be reskilled. The features available when running VMware in your private data center remain available to you, for example, vSAN, vSphere, and vCenter. From a Hyper-V perspective, both generation 1 (VHD) and generation 2 (VHDX) VMs are supported. However, the VHDX needs to be converted to VHD format and cannot be greater than 1,023GB in size. You can first export the VM from the Hyper-V management console using the Export wizard, as illustrated in Figure 8.7.

FIGURE 8.7   Exporting a virtualized server in Hyper-V

Once exported, if required, you can convert the VHDX to VHD by using the following PowerShell command:

```
Convert-VHD -Path "C:\Temp\Metasploitable.vhdx" `
          -DestinationPath "C:\Temp\Metasploitable.vhd" -VHDType Fixed
```

Windows Server/Linux Workloads

A simple way to find the most common or most recommended versions of operating systems that are available by Microsoft for Azure VMs is to look at the default list of images when creating one. Table 8.1 is the current list as of this writing that you would find in that drop-down list.

Note that just below the Image drop-down list there is a link to browse all public and private images. There exists a huge number of choices, so the list provided in Table 8.1 is a summary and by no means a complete list. The list will contain third-party images as well, so the list isn't static, and therefore this book is not a place to attempt the creation of a complete list. Just remember two things here. First, Linux is open source, which means anyone can create and customize a version of it. Second, those customizations may or may not work when you deploy them to an Azure virtual machine. This is why you'd want to use one of the versions already on the platform and/or use a version of Linux that is endorsed aka blessed. You will find a list of them here:

docs.microsoft.com/en-us/azure/virtual-machines/linux/endorsed-distros.

TABLE 8.1   Recommended Azure VM Operating Systems

Type	Version
Linux	Ubuntu Server 10.04 LTS
Linux	Red Hat Enterprise Linux 7.7
Linux	SUSE Enterprise Linux 15 SP1
Linux	CentOS-Based 7.7
Linux	Debian 10 "Buster" with backports kernel
Linux	Oracle Linux 7.7
Linux	Ubuntu Server 16.04 LTS
Windows	Server 2019 Datacenter
Windows	Server 2016 Datacenter
Windows	Server 2012 R2 Datacenter
Windows	10 Pro, Version 1809

From a Windows Server perspective, you should expect that all currently supported versions of that operating system will work on the Azure platform. In some rare and expensive cases, Microsoft will provide companies the option of using Windows NT, Windows 2000, or Windows Server 2003 on Azure. If you need that, then consider contacting Microsoft Support for advice. It is certainly not recommended to remain running on those ancient operating systems, but it does still happen. The list of Windows operating systems in Table 8.1 does represent all currently supported versions for this type. Finally, take another look at Table 4.2 and Table 4.6. They call out recommended Azure VM sizes based on the selected operating system. I would expect something like this to be built into Azure Migrate and perhaps to get some recommendations in the portal. However, in the assessment and design phases of the project, you must recognize this and plan for it because there are additional costs when a larger VM is required to run a specific OS. That cost can influence the decision-making process.

Azure Hybrid Benefit

Don't underestimate the complexities of software licensing. There are so many options, bundles, agreements, and teams surrounding and attempting to apply licensing terms and conditions. But be sure to recognize that in some way, shape, or form you will pay for using Microsoft software. The question that often arises is what to do with or how to transfer the licenses you have for running your on-premise data center to Azure. Software license charges on Azure are typically built into the overall consumption charge of the compute platform. If you already have a license, then you could expect some kind of discount by using that license you already have. Makes sense, right? The *Azure Hybrid Benefit* program exists for just this reason. If you already have Windows Server and/or SQL Server licenses, then you could expect compute cost savings of between 40% and 55% when migrating the workloads to Azure. You may be able to increase that savings to 80% when you combine this benefit program with *Azure Reserved VM Instances (RI)*, discussed next.

Azure Reserved VM Instances

The default pricing model you typically find in the cloud is based on your consumption. When you need a lot of compute or other Azure resource, it is there for you. When you don't need it anymore, the hardware and infrastructure is still there, but you are not billed for it if you do not use it. That's good for you and one of the great benefits of the cloud concepts. From the cloud service provider perspective, having infrastructure and compute resources idle is not cost effective. A solution for this is to kind of share the cost of idle hardware. The means for this sharing is realized with RIs. The resources that currently support this model can be seen in the Reservations blade in the Azure Portal. Your Reservations blade should be similar to that shown in Figure 8.8.

FIGURE 8.8   Azure Reserved Instances

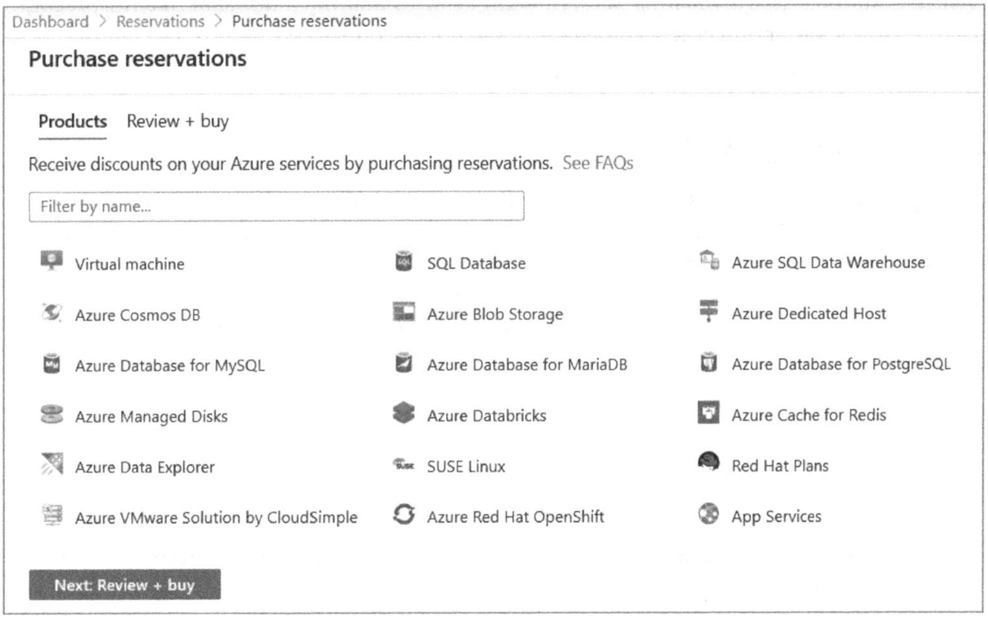

Instead of incurring pay-as-you-go charges based on unplanned consumption, you commit to a specific spend amount over a 7-day, 30-day, 60-day, or longer time frame. It would need to be less than if you were charged solely based on usage but a bit more than if you had less than expected usage during the same time frame. The overall cost average would be less for the customer but more cost effective for the cloud provider. The infrastructure isn't simply sitting idle doing nothing and generating no revenue. Take a look at the costs incurred when using RIs, compare that to the cost of dynamic pay-as-you-go consumption charges, and, if you save, then by all means take advantage of it.

Containers

If you want to lift and shift one quick way is using a container. In case you forgot about this model, take a look at the container as a service (CaaS) visualized in Figure 4.1. Also, review the decision tree illustrated in Figure 4.2 to again refresh yourself on the rationale for choosing containers as a deployment or migration option. If you get into a bind or have exhausted all effort to migrate your workloads to Azure because of currently unsupported customization in your application, don't ignore or forget this option. Seriously consider contacting Microsoft Support; seriously, now is the time to work with Microsoft Support. They want your business and want you to be successful on Azure.

In summary, a container lets you isolate your application completely away from a VM and an operating system. Either or both of those layers may be the reason your deployments or migration plans are not progressing as expected. Removing them may be the quickest solution. Take a warning here, though. Prior to making a decision like this, recognize the significant architectural changes and the impact on skillset required to migrate and support such architectures.

Database Migration

The migration of your data stores and data storage needs to follow the structural process used to migrate your compute. Refer to Figure 8.1 where the phases of assessment, migration, optimization, and security and management are called out. As with assessing and migrating, specific tools exist for the assessment and migration of your database. You can, by all means, use Azure Migrate to help discover and inventory the machines that you want to migrate.

A significant decision point that dictates your approach has much to do with the data source.

> Is the data source Microsoft SQL Server, or is it another of the many other data sources, like Oracle, MySQL, Cosmos DB, and Mongo?

> Do you plan on migrating those non-Microsoft SQL Server databases to one of the SQL Server offerings on Azure?

> Are you moving what you have to Azure, or are you moving to Azure and changing DBMS?

If you are moving from an on-premise Microsoft SQL Server installation to a SQL Server product on Azure, then a good place to start is with the *Database Management Assistant (DMA)*.

Database Management Assistant

DMA is a tool that will help you identify compatibility issues between the currently running version of SQL Server and the one you are targeting for the migration. Table 8.2 provides an overview of supported source database versions and supported target database versions.

TABLE 8.2   SQL Server–Supported Sources and Targets

Location	Version
Source	SQL Server 2005
Source	SQL Server 2008
Source	SQL Server 2008 R2
Source	SQL Server 2012
Source	SQL Server 2014
Source	SQL Server 2016
Source	SQL Server 2017 on Windows
Source	SQL Server 2019
Target	SQL Server 2012
Target	SQL Server 2014
Target	SQL Server 2016
Target	SQL Server 2017 Windows / Linux
Target	SQL Server 2019
Target	Azure SQL single database
Target	SQL Server manages instance
Target	SQL Server on an Azure virtual machine

You might agree that if your source database is SQL Server 2005 and the target is SQL Server 2019, there may have been some features that were deprecated along the way. DMA specifically calls out deprecated features, changes in behaviors, and breaking changes. Most of those would require redesign or rework to have a successful migration. DMA provides some tips on how to work around them, as well, and specifically shows additional recommendations in regard to security, performance, and storage. Notice in Table 8.2 that the oldest targetable version of SQL Server on Azure is SQL Server 2012; therefore, if you are running an older version than 2012, using DMA prior to migration is highly recommended. If you wanted to migrate to one of the targeted SQL Server versions from a DBMS other than SQL Server, then you would want to use a tool called *SQL Server Migration Assistant (SSMA)*.

SQL Server Migration Assistant

If you decided to move from a non-Microsoft SQL Server product to Azure and at the same time migrate the DMBS to SQL Server, then SSMA is the tool for helping you achieve that. The supported source data stores as of this writing are provided in the following list:

- Microsoft Access
- SAP ASE
- Oracle
- MySQL
- DB2

The SSMA tool can automate a comparison of many steps in a migration from discovery and assessment of the existing implementation and the targeted location. Because of the vast variety and customization of source DBMSs, there may be some issues that are not resolvable by a simple patch or code modification. There may be some issues found that may require a fundamental rethink about the design and purpose of an application's implementation. The point is, don't underestimate a migration like this. Make sure you have the right skilled specialist working on this kind of migration. Now that you are covered from SQL Server to SQL Server and non-SQL Server to SQL Server, take a look at DMS aka ADMS.

Azure Data Migration Service

The DMS tool was introduced in Chapter 1, with some additional discussion (and rightly so) in Chapter 5. Chapter 5 is where you learned about data and storage, and a chapter on that couldn't exist without a little bit about DMS. Some nice details about this service are accessible at datamigration.microsoft.com. DMS is optimal for scenarios where there are a large number of database to be migrated. The differences between DMA, SSMA, and DMS are as follows:

- DMA is used for small datasets, compatibility reports, and SQL Server to Azure SQL Server migrations.
- SSMA accommodates small to medium datasets, compatibility reports, and non–SQL Server to Azure SQL migrations.

- DMS is intended for large datasets and many sources to many target migration scenarios.

Before you get too deep into DMS, complete Exercise 8.2 and create an Azure Data Migration Service.

EXERCISE 8.2

Creating an Azure Data Migration Service

1. Log in to the Azure Portal at portal.azure.com.

2. Select the menu button on the top-left corner of the web page and click the + Create A Resource Link. Now, select Databases, and then select Azure Database Migration Service. (It is/was at the bottom of the list.)

3. Select the subscription and resource group into which you want to place DMS and select the location. Consider the location you choose as the location where you would migrate your database(s) to, as well. Enter a migration service name and click the Next : Networking button.

4. Select an existing virtual network/subnet or create a new one. The virtual network must exist in the same region as DMS. Click the Review + Create button, click the Create button, and once created navigate to the DMS Overview blade that would resemble Figure 8.9.

FIGURE 8.9   The Azure Database Migration Service Overview blade as shown in the Azure Portal

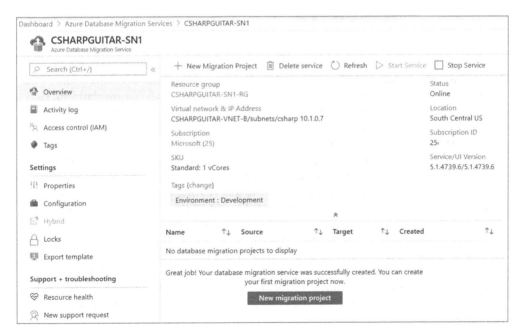

5. Click the + New Migration Project link at the top of the Overview blade and take a look at the listed database products in the Source Server Type drop-down list. Also, take a look at the listed database products in the Target Server Type drop-down list. Change the source server type to match the source version of your database. Select the target server types and notice that the options change. See Table 8.3 for those mappings. Select Choose Type Of Activity to view the list contents. The New Migration Project blade now resembles the screen shown in Figure 8.10.

FIGURE 8.10 DMS New Migration Project blade

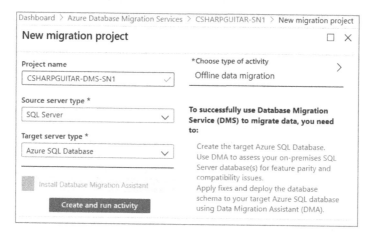

You may have noticed during the creation of DMS that there are two DMS modes, Azure and Hybrid (Preview). When you select Azure from the drop-down list it means that the worker on which the target database will exist on resides on the Azure platform. In contrast, you can create a DMS for usage with hybrid models where the target database is hosted on-premise. When a feature is tagged with "(Preview)," it means that feature is in a beta or testing phase. You would not want to use any product or feature in this mode for live production scenarios. However, the purpose of making those features available for consumption is for testing and discovering new features.

The Azure Database Migration Service (DMS aka ADMS) is useful for moving a large number of DBMS source versions to a supported target on the Azure platform. Table 8.3 lists the supported sources and their recommended target instance on Azure.

As you navigate through the Source Server Type options in the drop-down, you may also see tips for performing the selected migration between the source and target. For example, in Figure 8.10, you see the source is SQL Server and the target is Azure SQL Database. Some tips and links are shown under the bolded text "To successfully use Database Migration Service (DMS) to migrate data, you need to." Those are very helpful to read and learn from.

TABLE 8.3 Source/Target Database for DMS

Source	Target
SQL Server	Azure SQL Virtual Machine
	Azure SQL Managed Instance
	Azure SQL Database
MongoDB	Azure Cosmos DB (MongoDB API)
MySQL	Azure Database for MySQL
	SQL Server 2008–2017
	Azure SQL Database
AWS RDS for MySQL	Azure Database for MySQL
PostgreSQL	Azure Database for PostgreSQL
AWS RDS for PostgreSQL	Azure Database for PostgreSQL
Oracle	Azure Database for PostgreSQL
AWS RDS for SQL Server	Azure SQL Database

The contents of the Choose Type Of Activity drop-down list change based on the selected source/target mapping. You may recall the definition of a schema in Chapter 5, illustrated in Figure 5.5. A schema is the database structure that contains the tables and the relationships between them; no data is migrated if you select a schema activity. Other activities include the following:

- Schema-only migration
- Offline data migration
- Online data migration
- Create project only

Deciding whether you can perform the migration while the database is still allowing CRUD operations is one that depends on your requirements. If you are performing a migration while the database is online, then you need to plan for handling disruptions and updating any tables that temporarily store data during the different data migration phases. Also note that DMS has different pricing tiers, and online migration is available only with Premium tier. You will see the SKU is Standard in Figure 8.9. Notice also that there is an associated amount of compute allocated to the SKU. Recognize that DMS requires compute power to perform the migration. If you sense that the migration is slow, it is likely caused from the amount of compute you chose during the provisioning of DMS.

Cosmos DB Data Migration Tool

If you choose Azure Cosmos DB as the location where you intend on storing JSON documents, content from an Azure Storage table, CSV files, or many other similar types of unstructured data, then consider using this tool. You can find more information about this here:

    docs.microsoft.com/en-us/azure/cosmos-db/import-data

After installing the tool, you identify the source, which could be a directory full of JSON documents, and you select the target and execute the migration. Unstructured data, although it can be large, is in many cases a simple cut-and-paste exercise in contrast to an RDBMS, where replications can fail due to primary/foreign key violations.

Azure Databox

This product includes some interesting hardware components. For more details, take a look here:

    azure.microsoft.com/en-us/services/databox

Azure Databox devices are useful for moving large datasets to Azure. Azure Databox works in the context of Edge computing, where you typically have IoT devices capturing and streaming data that need real-time or near real-time ingestion, analysis, and alerting capabilities. The product comes in offline and online models where the offline model imitates the Import/Export product introduced in Chapter 5 and discussed in numerous other locations. With this tool, Microsoft sends you a hardware device to securely store your data. Once you have securely sent your data and the device to a Microsoft data center, the data is uploaded onto the Azure platform. In that scenario a massive amount of data needs to be migrated, and sending it over a network of any kind would be too great a task.

The online data transfer option includes a virtual device called a Data Box Gateway. This device helps to capture and transmit large datasets across the network. It is useful for archiving hundreds of terabytes of data, real-time ingestion of streaming data from the edge, and perhaps bulk data transfers of a large database migration, if the migration needs to happen online.

Database Experimentation Assistant

There is a testing concept known as A/B testing where you send some of your users to the new version of your application and some to the current version. The *Database Experimentation Assistant (DEA)* provides this kind of testing scenario between different versions of SQL Server. DEA will execute and capture a defined scenario on your source SQL Server instance and then replay them on the target instances. When both are completed, the tool will analyze the differences and provide a report. The report will help identify any compatibility issues or errors that are happening between the two SQL Server versions.

Database Access Migration Toolkit

This tool is one that will analyze the source code and target the specific areas that can be impacted by database changes. This tool is in (preview) and currently supports only SQL Server and Oracle DBMSs. Java, C#, JSON, and SQL files are the supported coding languages and file types. You would use this tool in collaboration with DMA.

Migrating Azure App Services

There is much focus on the migration of workloads to Azure Virtual Machines and data migration tools and methods on the Azure Solutions Architect Expert exam. Make sure you spend a lot of time in that area. One area not covered so much was Azure App Service (PaaS). As you know, Azure VMs and SQL Server on VMs are IaaS offerings. Sure, Azure SQL and SQL Server on Managed Instances is a bit more PaaS, but be certain that Azure App Service is a PaaS and dedicated to running websites. Azure App Service was introduced in Chapter 1, and you created your first one in Chapter 3. Lots of information was provided in Chapter 4, as well. Consider taking another look at Figure 4.2 (a decision tree) to see under which scenarios you would choose to provision an Azure App Service instance. The biggest difference between running a website on an Azure virtual machine versus an Azure App Service lies in the fundamental differences between IaaS and PaaS. In IaaS you have more flexibility, but more responsibility, while in PaaS you have less flexibility and less responsibility. That is the reason you need to utilize an App Service Migration Assistant for ASP.NET applications. You may have some configurations or dependencies that are not supported or allowed on Azure App Services. Recognize now that you can run Azure App Services with Containers; this will get you past most sandboxed restrictions. It may not be an option, however, due to the requirement of reskilling your IT support, deployment, and development staff. Containers are just an option and not necessarily the recommendation. Note that if you choose to proceed with what you have, then use the App Service Migration Assistant tool located at aka.ms/AppMigrate. The online tool will resemble that shown in Figure 8.11.

The figure calls out a few interesting points. First, the analysis happens when you enter the current URL of the web application you want to migrate to an Azure App Service. The App Service Migration Assistant tool will check the website and return the framework (like ASP.NET), how/where the website with the current URL you entered is being hosted, and the web server (IIS, for example). If there are any unsupported aspects found, then the report would call them out. Once the assessment is complete, you can download a migration assistant to help progress the movement. Also worthy of calling out is the link to Azure Migrate toward the bottom of the page. The more often you see specific tools, the more weight their usage and implementation should be.

FIGURE 8.11   DMS New Migration Project blade

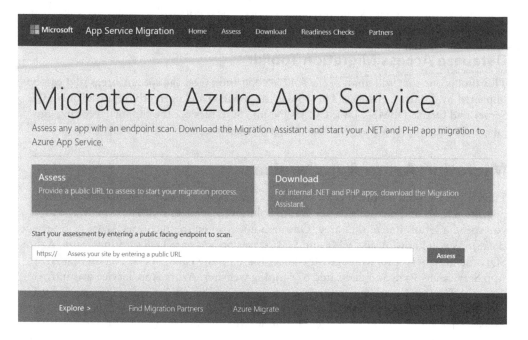

Import/Export

There is a detailed paragraph about this feature in Chapter 5. It was discussed there because when the size of database is huge and the real-time transmission of it across a network is not possible, then this product is an option. There isn't much more frustrating than sending a 50GB file between two servers and the connection brakes after 49.78GB and after 19 hours waiting for the copy to complete. When that happens you usually have to restart the copy procedure and hope it works this time. But you likely wouldn't even consider transferring such a large file like that anyway. It is just an example, but one that I am sure you relate to even with smaller file sizes. Read the description in Chapter 5; it's the same product. It is added here as well just in case you skipped Chapter 5 and came straight here.

In summary, the Import/Export tool lets you create a physical copy of the data and send it to an Azure data center. Someone human at that data center will take the physical device and load it onto the platform in a secure location where you can access and perform the required actions on it. This product seems similar to Azure Databox, which was discussed earlier. These two products may merge at some point, so keep an eye out in this area if migrations of this kind are in your role, scope, or of particular interest.

Moving Resources in Azure

Here is another topic that was covered in a previous chapter. Migration and moving resources around does require significant planning and skill. This topic is also one that is covered in some detail in the Azure Solution Architect Expert exam, so in Chapter 4, which covered compute, I called out the migration specifically in regard to Azure VMs. There is an entire section called "Change Resource Groups, Subscriptions, Regions, or Zones." Figure 4.31 shows that an Azure virtual machine can be moved with relative ease between resource groups because that is a logical grouping. This does not involve the physical movement of the Azure VM. Instead, you will see the resource group named CSHARPGUITAR-DB3-RG, which is in North Europe aka DB3 but physically located in South Central US aka SN1. Making that migration between resource groups is as simple as updating a value in the database.

The questions now are how to actually move the Azure VM, a database, or an Azure App Service to another subscription, region, or zone. Let's first make sure we remember what a subscription is. It is a means for organizing groups of resources, similar to a resource group, but the billing occurs at the subscription level. If you were to need to move a physical resource to another subscription, you should first contact Microsoft Support. If you're not working with Microsoft Support, you can consider using one of the tools we'll cover in the following pages. One serious decision point has to do with if both the source and target subscriptions are owned by a single administrator. If this is the case, then the transfer should be relatively easy. Execute these Azure CLI commands, and if the tenant matches, you have access to both.

```
az account show --subscription <source-subscription> --query tenantId
az account show --subscription <destination-subscription> --query tenantId
```

Additionally, in the portal you can navigate to the resource you would want to move to another subscription or resource group and click the Move link on the Overview blade. See Figure 8.12 that illustrates the selection option. What you see there is for an Azure SQL server, but the same exists for Azure VMs and Azure App Service. You should expect that capability exists for all Azure products.

FIGURE 8.12 Moving Azure resources between subscriptions and resource groups

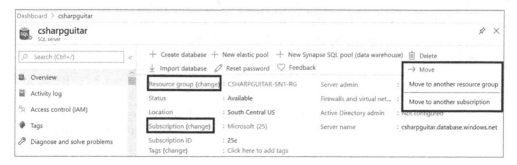

Also notice in Figure 8.12 that there are links next to the resource group (change) and subscription (change), which will take you to the same location as if you had clicked the links in the Move menu. Those are the easy ones, because you are really only updating some data in a database. A real physical move of Azure products such as Azure virtual machines, databases, or Azure App Service apps requires more work. The work required would be similar to a migration from on-premise, excluding the step where you assess the application-specific configurations. The configurations on your on-premises installation might not be supported on the Azure location you are migrating to. That should not cause problems for your move because you are already on Azure. Let's discuss the following in more detail:

- Moving Azure App Services
- Moving Azure Virtual Machines

Each scenario will be a little different because of the platform design for each product when it comes to moving the physical resource between regions or zones. For example, currently Azure App Service apps do not support zones, so you wouldn't be able to do a migration like that. There is work to change this, but it is not clear if you would be ever able to pick the zone specifically or if it would be managed by the PaaS-focused platform code.

Moving Azure App Services

Remember that Azure App Service apps run on an *App Service Plan (ASP)*, which is synonymous with a VM. You can have multiple app services on an ASP, which means you have multiple websites running on a VM. An alternative for moving an app service is a concept called *cloning*. Using this feature won't move the website, but instead it will make an identical copy of it so you can then move and install the copy into another location that you specify. Once the site is moved and tested, you can remap the custom domain name to the new location and turn off the old one. If you navigate to the app service you want to relocate, you will find a link named Clone App in the navigation menu. The logic in the portal then walks you through the cloning process.

Some Azure PowerShell cmdlets result in the same outcome. Here are some example cmdlets:

```
$srcapp = Get-AzWebApp -ResourceGroupName SrcResGrp -Name source-webapp
$destasp = New-AzAppServicePlan -Location "North Central US" `
        -ResourceGroupName DestinationAzureResourceGroup `
        -Name DestinationAppServicePlan -Tier Standard
New-AzWebApp -ResourceGroupName DestResGrp -Name dest-webapp `
        -Location "South Central US" -AppServicePlan $destasp `
        -SourceWebApp $srcapp
```

Basically, the cmdlet retrieves the configuration details of the web app (aka app service) and stores it in the variable named $srcapp. $srcapp then is used as the source for the creation of the new app service. This assumes you have an existing ASP retrieved and stored in the `$destasp` variable, as shown in the code snippet. An ASP is created instead of retrieved. If an `AzAppServicePlan` already exists, you can use the `Get-AzAppServicePlan` cmdlet instead of the `New-AzAppServicePlan` Azure Power-Shell cmdlet. You cannot physically move an ASP because it is a VM on physical computer hardware. You can only move the websites that exist on the ASP. You could certainly get fancy and loop through all the web apps that exist on the ASP and then migrate them one by one within a PowerShell `foreach` statement so they all get moved in one cmdlet invocation.

Moving Azure Virtual Machines

A tool that you have already been exposed to in this chapter is used to perform this kind of movement. Can you think of what it would be? Remember, you are not doing a migration; rather, you are moving an Azure virtual machine that has already been migrated to the platform. Some reasons you would want to move the application or database running on an Azure virtual machine can be one or more of the following:

- The user base of application has moved further away from the original region and closer to another one.

- There are features that do not exist in the region where your VM is running, but they are available in another region.

- Your company has merged, and the data stored on a VM in that region is no longer allowed per compliance and governance restrictions.

- The role of a VM has changed, and it needs to move to another VNET to simplify management and release processes, as shown in Figure 8.13.

FIGURE 8.13   Relocating an Azure virtual machine to another VNET in the same Azure region

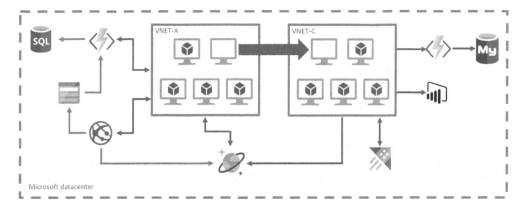

The tool you should seriously consider using to move an Azure virtual machine to another region or virtual network is Azure Site Recovery (ASR). The best way to learn about this migration is by doing it. Complete Exercise 8.3 where you will move a VM to another virtual network in the same region. In Exercise 8.4 you will replicate an Azure virtual machine to another region.

EXERCISE 8.3

Moving an Azure Virtual Machine to Another Virtual Network in the Same Region

1. Log in to the Azure Portal at portal.azure.com.

2. Click the menu button on the top-left corner of the web page, click the + Create A Resource link, click IT & Management Tools, select Backup and Site Recovery, and enter the subscription and resource group into which you want the Recovery Service vault placed. Provide a vault name, enter the region, and click the Review + Create button. Now, click the Create button.

3. Once the provision has completed, navigate to the resource's Overview blade and click the + Backup menu item. Select Azure and Virtual Machine from the drop-down lists, as illustrated in Figure 8.14; then click the Backup button.

FIGURE 8.14   Configuring the Azure Site Recovery service vault

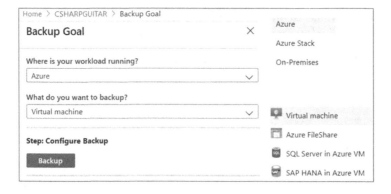

4. On the Select Virtual Machines blade, click the OK button to accept the default backup policy. Select the Azure VM(s) that you want to back up, as illustrated in Figure 8.15; then click the OK and Enable Backup buttons.

FIGURE 8.15   Setting up a backup policy in Azure Site Recovery

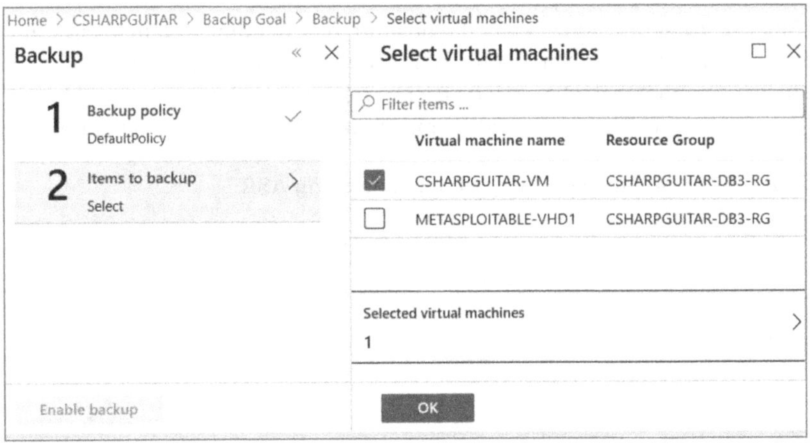

5.   Once the backup is complete (this can take some time), click the Backup Items link on the navigation menu. Next, click the Azure Virtual Machine link under the Backup Management Type column heading and select the Azure VM you backed up in step 4. The current blade should resemble Figure 8.16.

FIGURE 8.16   Restoring an Azure virtual machine using ASR

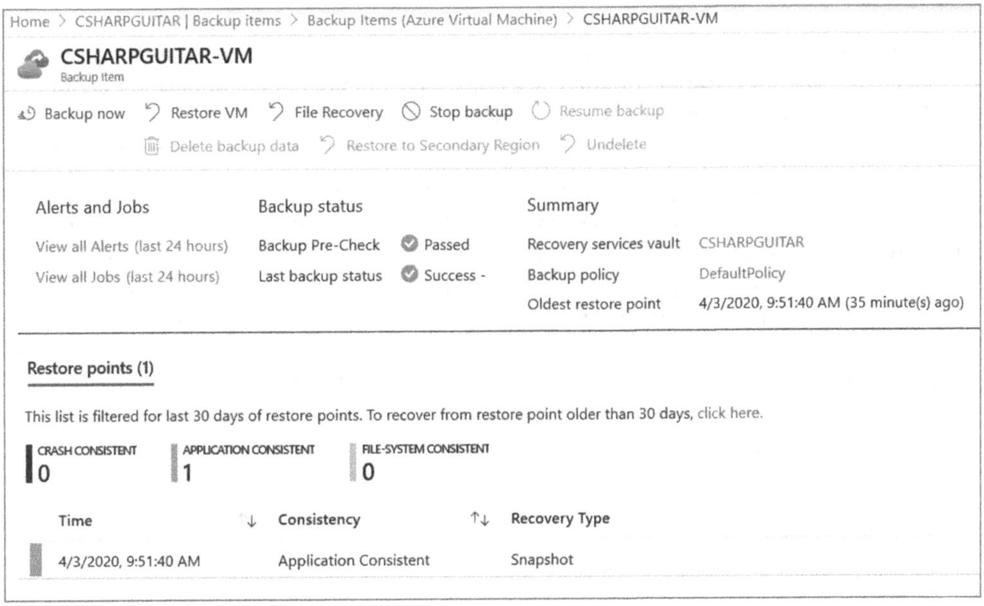

6. Click the Restore VM menu item, select the desired restore point, and then click the OK button. Enter a virtual machine name, select a resource group, select a virtual network, select a subnet, select a storage account, then click the OK button. Now, click the Restore button. The configuration may resemble that shown in Figure 8.17.

FIGURE 8.17   Restoring an Azure virtual machine using ASR

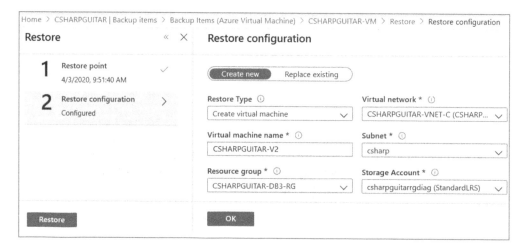

7. Once the restore is complete, navigate to the new Azure VM, confirm the change in VNET, and test the new Azure VM. Once testing is complete, decommission the old Azure VM by shutting it down and deleting it.

You might recognize this product from the earlier discussion in the Azure Site Recovery (ASR) section, as the Site Recovery Overview blade for ASR was shown in Figure 8.4. Take a look at the Backup Overview blade now (I assume you are reading on waiting for Exercise 8.3 step 5 to complete), and you will see some actions have taken place. After the next exercise, review them, and you will see the activities you performed tracked within them. It is also prudent to review Figure 8.14. You should see the options you have when configuring this backup. The following is an output of the values presented to you as options for the source of the backup and the types of backups this feature supports:

-   Where is your workload running?

    -   Azure

    -   Azure Stack

    -   On-Premise

- What do you want to back up?
  - Virtual Machine
  - Azure FileShare
  - SQL Server in Azure VM
  - SAP HANA in Azure VM

You had the option in step 6 to create a new or replace existing virtual machines. If you select to replace the existing ones, then it is the disk that is moved and no VM instance is provisioned. Also, if there are no values in the virtual network, subnet, or staging location, then it is likely that those specific resources don't exist in the region you are working in. All resources being configured here are required and need to be in the same region to successfully perform this operation. If they do not exist, you can create them manually, one by one, until you see them as options in the drop-down lists. Finally, the exercise moved an Azure virtual machine (which existed in the virtual network/subnet named CSHARPGUITAR-VNET-A/csharp) into CSHARPGUITAR-VNET-C/guitar. Both of those virtual networks existed within the same North Europe (DB3) region.

Windows Azure Guest Agent

The Azure VM must be running, and the Windows Azure Guest Agent service must be installed and running on the VM in order to be backed up successfully. Both scenarios are the default when you create the VM from a marketplace image. However, if you lift and shift or use your own custom image, you will need to manually install them. See this page:

docs.microsoft.com/en-us/azure/backup/
backup-azure-arm-vms-prepare#install-the-vm-agent

In Exercise 8.4, you will move an Azure virtual machine to a different Azure region. Pay special attention to this exercise as it is the scenario you will see again in the next chapter in the context of recovery and BCDR scenarios. Before you begin, note the following. In the previous exercise, the location of the *Azure Recovery Service Vault* happened in the resource group CSHARPGUITAR-DB3-RG, which was bound to the North Europe region. You will not be able to perform a recovery/replication into the same region as the location of the resource group. From a BCDR perspective, this makes sense as the outage would happen in a region (data center) in a scenario where the BCDR feature is warranted. Replicating to the same region wouldn't bring relief because those machines would be collocated in the same data center and also may be experiencing a disruption. Take a look back at Figure 1.8, which illustrates this. Also take a look at Figure 8.18. Figure 1.8 shows the use of Azure Site Recovery to replicate between on-premise and an Azure region and also replicate between two Azure regions. There is no illustration of replication within the same region. You would use the backup and restore process you learned in Exercise 8.3 for that. Figure 8.18 illustrates an Azure virtual machine in North Europe (DB3) in Availability Zone 2 migrating to South Central US (SN1) to Availability Zone 1.

FIGURE 8.18 Relocating an Azure virtual machine to another Azure region

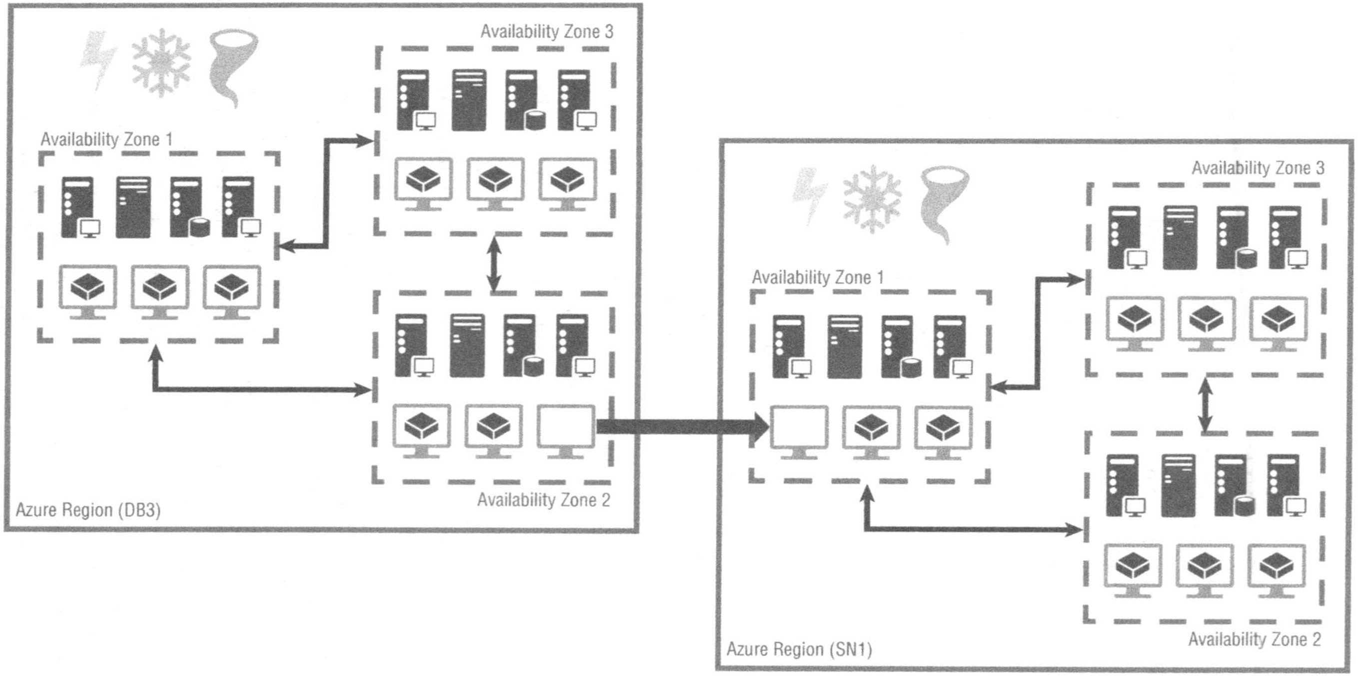

More information about availability zone concepts and movement, unsupported scenarios, and what activities should be left to the platform is discussed later. For now, do Exercise 8.4 where you will move an Azure virtual machine to another region.

EXERCISE 8.4

Moving an Azure Virtual Machine to Another Region

1. Log in to the Azure Portal at portal.azure.com.

2. Select the menu button at the top-left corner of the web page and then click the + Create A Resource link. Select IT & Management Tools and then select Backup and Site Recovery. Enter the subscription and resource group where you want the Recovery Service vault placed. (Note: the resource group must exist in a location other than the one you want to replicate the VM to (for example, West Europe - AM2). Provide a vault name, enter the region (for example, (Europe) West Europe - AM2), and click the Review + Create and the Create buttons. (It will become clear why you chose AM2 here in a moment.)

3. Once that's completed, navigate to the Overview blade and press the + Replicate menu item. Select Azure from the Source drop-down list and (Europe) North Europe from the Source location drop-down list. Select the resource group of the VM you want to replicate, and consider using the same resource group as you backed up in Exercise 8.3 step 5, as illustrated in Figure 8.15. See Figure 8.19, which represents a sample configuration. Now click the OK button.

FIGURE 8.19 ASR replication configuration

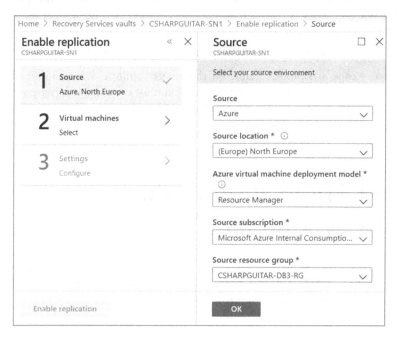

4. Select the Azure VM that you would like to replicate and then click the OK button. Select (Europe) West Europe from the Target location drop-down list and then expand the list in the drop-down and view your options. Click the Create Target Resource button and then click the Enable Replication button.

You might be wondering why you were all of a sudden instructed to create an Azure resource group in West Europe (AM2). It may have become obvious when, in step 4, you saw the list of available target locations. The fact is, this replication is intended to be used for BCDR scenarios, and if you wanted to create a failover instance of your application, you would logically put it in a location closest to your users. It wouldn't be logical to use the infrastructure in South Central US (SN1) as a failover for your infrastructure in North Europe (DB3). You might be able to create a configuration like that, but it wouldn't be performant for your clients that were used to the performance without having to make the connection across the Atlantic Ocean during a failover. Also, as you saw, the target location in the drop-down list is in the same geography.

In Chapter 3, you learned about data centers, zones, regions, and geographies. Within geographies there are regions that are referred to as sister, twin, or most commonly named paired regions. This list you were presented with was considered the paired regions for the selected source location, as illustrated in Figure 8.19. From an Availability Zone perspective, moving Azure VMs or other products that support them is better left to the logic that runs on the platform. When you create an Azure virtual machine and choose Availability Zone as the availability option, you then pick which zone to place the VM into, for example, Zone 1, Zone 2 or Zone 3. You can also set the zone at the time of creation by using an Azure CLI command similar to the following:

```
az vm create -n MyVm -g MyResourceGroup --image Centos --zone 1
```

There is neither a --zone attribute available for the az vm update command set nor the option to update it via the Azure Portal. Therefore, you must conclude it is not possible and it makes sense not to expose such capabilities and leave it to the platform. If you choose Availability Sets from the availability option, then you are going into the VMSS direction where the zones are managed by the platform and cannot be changed.

Deploying Application Code and Azure Resources

At some point after the initial deployment, code needs to change and be updated due to changes in requirements, new requirements, to fix bugs, or to patch security vulnerabilities. You will learn about the following topics in this section:

- Deploying with Visual Studio
- Deploying with ARM templates
- Working with DevOps and Azure DevOps

But before starting on those topics, it is a good idea to provide a bit of history about development and deployment topics because there is a lot of it, going back to the 1970s. Having a successful development process depends on many factors, and there are many books written that go into great detail. This content isn't meant to replace or compete with those. There are, however, some common activities that can be applied to all development team processes. A few of them have already been exposed to you and are also applicable to general project management terminology, as well. The common or core activities are as follows:

- Requirements gathering
- Design
- Construction
- Testing
- Debugging
- Deployment
- Maintenance

Since you know about hybrid models, you can conceptually apply bullet points onto these activities listed previously that can be modified and enhanced based on the changing software techniques, methodologies, frameworks, and practices. Small changes to that preceding set of bullet points results in the creation of a new hybrid technique, methodology, or coding model. For example, structured programming, *object-oriented programming (OOP)*, SCRUM, *rapid application development (RAD)*, agile, and now DevOps models using the *continuous integration/continuous delivery (CI/CD)* practice are all hybrid concepts built on learning and optimizations from previous activities. Each of those techniques still exists, and when you find yourself working within them, recognize that you are following code patterns, techniques, and methods from that given era. In many ways, you can learn the age of an IT application based on the model in which it operates. Here is a potentially debatable and summarized timeline.

- **1970s/80s:** Waterfall
- **1990s:** OOP, RAD, and Scrum
- **2000s:** Agile
- **2010s:** DevOps

Now that you have a little bit of history, recognize there is a lot of it and that this is an area where teams and large groups of highly skilled people work together to achieve great things. If this interests you, get into that field and go for it. You will focus a bit more on DevOps later in this section, for now let's begin with a simple deployment approach using Visual Studio.

Deploying with Visual Studio

If you are an individual developer working on a project alone, then this is by far the easiest way to get a relatively complex application deployed to Azure App Service. You can create an app service on Azure App Service directly in the Azure Portal. Using Visual Studio can be a bit challenging, so those who master it will also master the creation of complex code. Exercise 8.5 will guide you through the deployment of the code that you were introduced to in the previous chapter.

EXERCISE 8.5

Deploying an Azure App Service Using Visual Studio

1. Open Visual Studio and click Create A New Project. Select ASP.NET Core Web Application and enter a project name. Select .NET Core, select ASP.NET Core 3.1, select Web Application, and you should see something similar to Figure 8.20.

FIGURE 8.20   Creating an ASP.NET Core application in Visual Studio

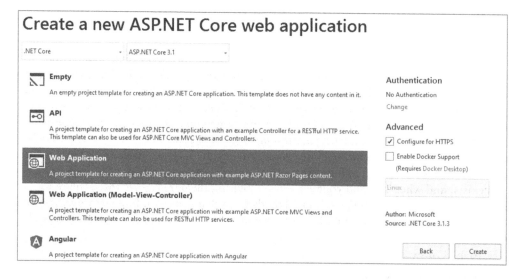

2. Replace the following files with the code found here:

    github.com/benperk/ASA/tree/master/Chapter08/Ch08Ex04

    (You must update the code to use your Azure Key Vault, namespace, and the Azure SQL details.)

    Program.cs

    Startup.cs

Pages/Index.cshtml

Pages/Index.cshtml.cs

3. Install the following NuGet packages. Select Tools from the menu: NuGet Package Manager, Package Manager Console, and enter the following commands, one after the other:

```
install-package Microsoft.Azure.KeyVault
install-package Microsoft.Azure.Services.AppAuthentication
install-package System.IdentityModel.Tokens.Jwt
install-package Microsoft.Extensions.Configuration.AzureKeyVault
install-package System.Data.SqlClient
```

4. Press Ctrl+Shift+B to compile the Visual Studio solution. Now, right-click your Visual Studio project and select Publish from the pop-up menu. Select App Service, select Existing, and then click the Create Profile button. (See Figure 8.21.)

FIGURE 8.21 Publishing an ASP.NET Core application in Visual Studio to an app service

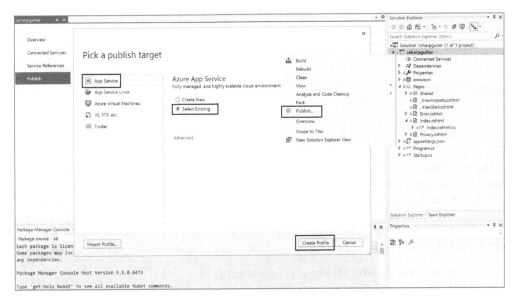

5. Select the subscription, resource group, and web app where you want to deploy the code, and then click the OK button. Now, click the Publish button.

6. You will need to additionally perform Exercise 7.1 (configuring a managed identity) and Exercise 7.2 (configuring EasyAuth) to render the application as expected. Look forward a bit at Figure 8.31, which illustrates the managed identity, key vault access policy, and EasyAuth configuration requirements.

That's it. Take a look at Figure 8.21 again; in addition to deploying to an app service, there are also options for deploying an app service to Linux, for deploying an Azure virtual machine to IIS, and for deploying to a folder. Had you selected an Azure virtual machine, you would have been prompted to select the targeted VM to deploy the code onto, something similar to Figure 8.22.

FIGURE 8.22   Publishing an ASP.NET Core application in Visual Studio to an Azure virtual machine

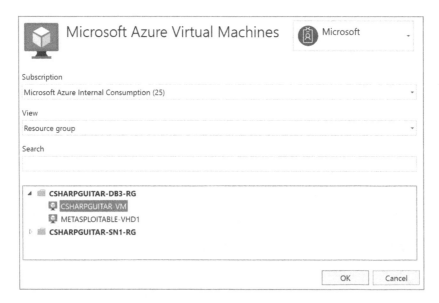

There are two prerequisites to deploying to a virtual machine from Visual Studio. The requirements are the same if you were to deploy to any machine, whether on the Azure platform or not. First be sure the Azure virtual machine has an endpoint that you can deploy to. Ideally this would be a public domain or IP address. Second, the Azure VM must be configured to support ASP.NET web deployments. This means you need to have the Web Deploy module installed and configured on the Azure VM. You can find more details about that here:

www.iis.net/downloads/microsoft/web-deploy

This capability is already configured and ready to receive your deployment by default on Azure App Service. Isn't that PaaS offering nice?

Deploying with ARM Templates

You have learned a few methods for making deployments that use the same images, snapshots, backups, and disks. *Azure Resource Manager (ARM)* templates are another means for achieving this. ARM templates are JSON documents that describe your Azure resource in script form. Take a look at the file named `ARM-template-VM.json` located here:

> github.com/benperk/ASA/tree/master/Chapter08

You can extract it by clicking the Download A Template For Automation link on the Review + Create blade, similar to Figure 8.23.

FIGURE 8.23   Downloading a template for automation

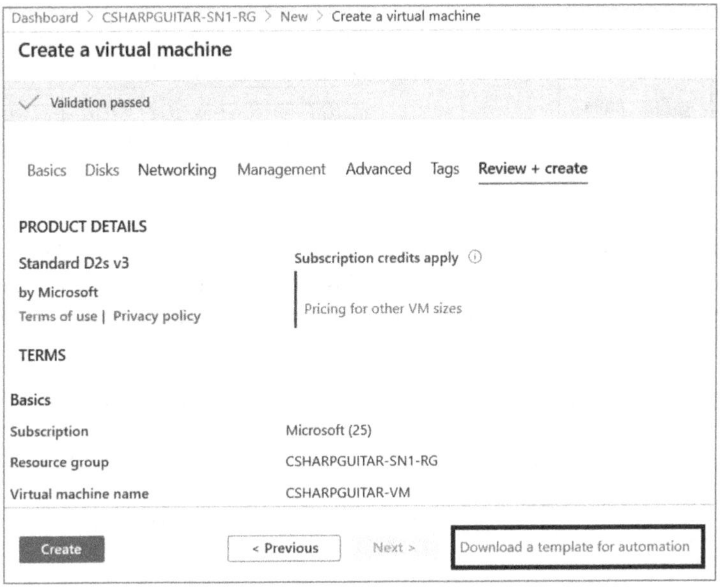

That link to download the ARM template is present for a majority of Azure products, but it represents a default provision state template for the given resource. If you need or want to get the ARM template after the resources have been created, there is a link in the navigation menu named Export Template. A benefit of using the Export template is that if you make some configurations such as, for example, requiring HTTPS or allowing only TLS 1.2, then those configurations will be included in the ARM template. This is important because if you require HTTPS and TLS 1.2 due to the Azure Policy you created in Exercise 6.2, attempting to create those resources without those properties set fails. Take a look at file `ARM-template-APP-SERVICE.json` located on GitHub in the same location as the one provided earlier for a VM. Navigate through it, and you will see both `"httpsOnly": true` and `"minTlsVersion": "1.2"` set correctly in the template. There are numerous ways in which you can organize your ARM templates for deployment. The examples provided so far, with the example templates on GitHub, represent a VM template, an App Service template, and an Azure SQL template (see `ARM-template-AZURE-SQL.json`). That scenario represents the deployment of multi-tiered Azure products into the same resource group. Each resource is manually provisioned following a predetermined order.

You can see a visual representation of that on the left side of Figure 8.24. If you are running the same multi-tiered environment and wanted the products in different resource groups, see the right side of Figure 8.24. Again, each resource is deployed individually.

FIGURE 8.24   Deploying an ARM template to a single or multiple resource groups

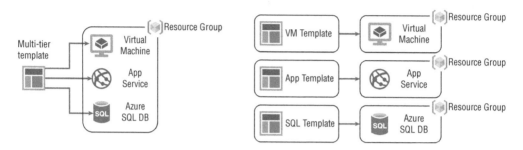

Another deployment approach has to do with all the resources being deployed at the same time into the same resource group. As illustrated in Figure 8.25, you would achieve this by creating a parent ARM template with internally embedded children (nested) templates.

FIGURE 8.25   Deploying an ARM template with nested templates

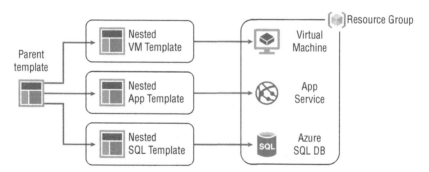

It is possible to export an ARM template from the Resource Group blade. On the Resource Group blade you will find an Export template navigation menu item. Once you get all your resources configured to be deployed again at a later time the way you want them, you can export the resource configurations contained with the resource group. In the following three sections, you will learn the components required to support, deploy, and execute the provisioning of Azure resources using an ARM template. They are the Azure Resource Manager (ARM) template and the Azure Resource Manager. Their relationship is represented in Figure 8.26.

FIGURE 8.26   Implementing a template for automation

management.azure.com

You might recognize that relationship a little bit because it was introduced in Chapter 2 in the context of RBAC. This relationship will be summarized again in the Azure Resource Manager section later. In preparation for that, take a look back at Figure 2.45, which illustrates this relationship in a similar but different manner. Read on to get more details about each of those components.

Azure Resource Manager (ARM) Templates

ARM templates are not a coding language, but they can be complicated. The following is a standard summarized ARM template that will create a single resource in isolation:

```
"https://schema.management.azure.com/schemas/deploymentTemplate.json"
{
  "resources": [
    {
      "type": "Microsoft.Web/sites",
      "apiVersion": "2018-11-01",
      "name": "csharpguitar",
      "location": "North Europe",
      "tags": { "Environment": "Production" },
      "kind": "app",
      "properties": { "httpsOnly": true }
    },
    {
      "type": "Microsoft.Web/sites/config",
      "apiVersion": "2018-11-01",
      "dependsOn": [
        "[resourceId('Microsoft.Web/sites', 'csharpguitar')]"
      ],
      "properties": {
        "autoHealEnabled": false,
        "http20Enabled": true,
        "minTlsVersion": "1.2"
      }}]
}
```

The content of an ARM template is in the form of a JSON document. At the top, you will find a reference to a schema. Like a database schema, which textually describes the structure of a database, the JSON document schema defines the structure of the file and its supported attributes. There are a few attributes in the previous ARM template example that need some additional information, specifically, type, apiVersion, and dependsOn.

The type attribute is the resource that will be provisioned and configured by the template. These are considered resource providers, which are discussed later in the chapter in more detail. The value bound to the type attribute may look familiar to you already as it isn't a new concept or structural pattern at this point. Read the "Resource Providers" section now if you want to dig deeper into this.

apiVersion identifies the version of the REST API used by the Azure Resource Manager to provision the product. (See Figure 8.26.) There is an exercise later in the chapter where you will use an ARM template to provision resources. When the ARM template is sent to the Azure Resource Manager, it is translated into an HTTPS request that is assembled using the JSON document contents. The type and apiVersion attributes would resemble something similar to the following:

```
PUT
https://management.azure.com/subscriptions/{subscriptionId}/resourceGroups/
{resourceGroupName}/providers/Microsoft.Web/sites/csharpguitar?api-version=2018-11-01
REQUEST BODY
{
  "location": "North Europe",
  "tags": { "Environment": "Production" },
  "kind": "app",
  "properties": { "httpsOnly": true }
}
```

For each type and respective configuration content for that type, an additional HTTPS request is sent to the resource provider for provisioning and configuration.

Now let's return to the first sentence of this section where I stated this could become complicated. Consider if you have exported the template for all the products in a resource group. Think about how many HTTPS calls from the Azure Resource Manager to the resource provider per resource would be required to provision and deploy all those products, features, and configurations. With large ARM deployments, there are two topics that you should know about. The first one is the dependsOn attribute. As shown in the previous ARM template example, setting these App Service properties (autoHealEnabled, http20Enabled, minTlsVersion) is dependent on the existence of the app service. This makes sense because you cannot modify something that doesn't yet exist. The same goes for binding a network interface to an Azure virtual machine or for adding an NSG to a subnet. Those configurations have dependencies on each other, and they will not succeed unless the required resources are available. It can be a challenge when some resources are successful, but the overall deployment fails partially through its execution. This is indeed a challenging area that continues to improve over time. I exported the CSHAPRGUITAR_ SN1_RG ARM template for all products and configurations in the resource group, and it was almost 4,000 lines long with 155 dependsOn attributes. That's big and complex.

With an ARM deployment that is so large, you need to keep in mind that there are limits to the number of requests to the Azure Resource Manager per hour. They are a relatively high number, but your deployment could get throttled if you are doing some big deployments or other activities that utilize the Azure Resource Manager. The limits are in the area of 1,200 writes and 12,000 reads per hour. You should seriously consider making smaller deployments, using multiple templates coordinated by some custom code to execute them in a specific order and over an extended time frame, when possible. There is a lot to learn in regard to ARM templates; have a look at aka.ms/arm-template, to learn the internals and more on techniques, structure, and troubleshooting guides.

Content Deployment

Before moving to the next section, note that the discussion about ARM templates up to now has been focused on the provisioning of Azure products. There has been no discussion about deploying application code along with the compute provisioning from the ARM template. As you learned in Exercise 8.5, you can deploy your content using Visual Studio to an Azure App Service and an Azure virtual machine. In both cases, the deployment uses Web Deploy (msdeploy) behind the scenes to make that happen. An msdeploy extension inside an ARM template can perform content deployments. The JSON document snippet shown here includes content in the ARM template:

```
"resources": [
  {
    "apiVersion": "2016-08-01",
    "name": "MSDeploy",
    "type": "Extensions",
    "dependsOn": [
    "[concat('Microsoft.Web/Sites/', 'csharpguitar')]"],
    "properties": {
      "addOnPackages" : [
      {
        "packageUri":
           "https://<n>.blob.core.windows.net/csharp/webdeploy_package.zip",
 "AppOffline": true}}]}}]
```

This feature uses the addOnPackages schema element to identify where the code is located. The code location is provided by the packageUri property, which points to a zip file stored on an Azure Blob Storage container. Notice also the dependsOn attributes that ensure that the app service exists before attempting to deploy code to it. You will configure and deploy this later in Exercise 8.6.

Resource Providers

There exists a corresponding resource provider for every Azure product, feature, and service. There are more than 100 of them for certain. Table 8.4 summarizes the resource providers and their matching services that are referenced in this book. As there are more products and features added or modified on Azure often, the list may change. If you ever need to find additional resource providers, take a look here:

```
docs.microsoft.com/en-us/azure/azure-resource-manager/management/
azure-services-resource-providers
```

You can also search for documentation on the internet, specifically at `docs.microsoft`
`.com`. Also, consider using this Azure CLI command:

```
Get-AzResourceProvider
```

That command lists all the current Azure resource providers and is kept up-to-date. The result also provides the region(s) where the resource is available and whether your account is registered to use the resource provider. If you are not registered and/or do not have access to the resource provider, then you will not be able to create or configure that Azure resource. To see which resource providers you have access to in the Azure Portal, navigate to your subscription and click the Resource Providers navigation menu link. See Figure 8.27 for an example of how that might look.

FIGURE 8.27 Available resource providers via the Azure Portal

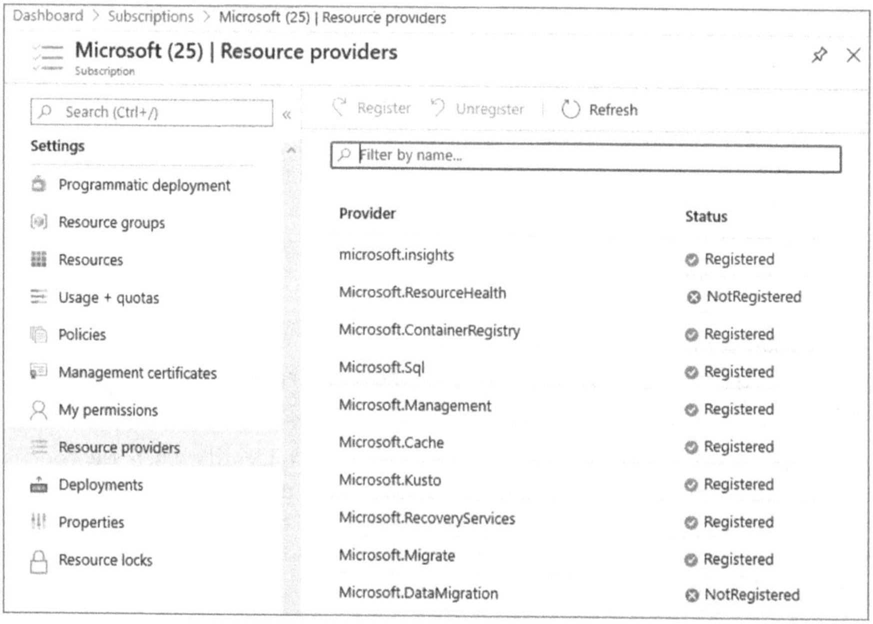

TABLE 8.4   Common Resource Providers and Services

Resource Provider	Service
Microsoft.AAD	Azure Active Directory Domain Services
Microsoft.AlertsManagement	Azure Monitor
Microsoft.AnalysisServices	Azure Analysis Services
Microsoft.ApiManagement	API Management
Microsoft.Authorization	Azure Resource Manager
Microsoft.Automation	Automation
Microsoft.AzureActiveDirectory	Azure Active Directory B2C
Microsoft.Batch	Batch
Microsoft.Billing	Cost Management and Billing
Microsoft.Blueprint	Azure Blueprints
Microsoft.Cache	Azure Cache for Redis
Microsoft.Cdn	Content Delivery Network
Microsoft.Compute	Virtual Machines
Microsoft.Compute	Virtual Machine Scale Sets
Microsoft.Consumption	Cost Management
Microsoft.ContainerInstance	Container Instances
Microsoft.ContainerRegistry	Container Registry
Microsoft.ContainerService	Azure Kubernetes Service (AKS)
Microsoft.CostManagement	Cost Management
Microsoft.DataBox	Azure Databox
Microsoft.Databricks	Azure Databricks
Microsoft.DataFactory	Data Factory

TABLE 8.4 Common Resource Providers and Services *(continued)*

Resource Provider	Service
Microsoft.DataLakeAnalytics	Data Lake Analytics
Microsoft.DataMigration	Azure Database Migration Service
Microsoft.DBforMariaDB	Azure Database for MariaDB
Microsoft.DBforMySQL	Azure Database for MySQL
Microsoft.DBforPostgreSQL	Azure Database for PostgreSQL
Microsoft.DesktopVirtualization	Windows Virtual Desktop
Microsoft.DevOps	Azure DevOps
Microsoft.DevSpaces	Azure Dev Spaces
Microsoft.DocumentDB	Azure Cosmos DB
Microsoft.EventGrid	Event Grid
Microsoft.EventHub	Event Hubs
Microsoft.HDInsight	HDInsight
Microsoft.HybridCompute	Azure Arc
Microsoft.ImportExport	Azure Import/Export
microsoft.insights	Azure Monitor
Microsoft.KeyVault	Key Vault
Microsoft.Kubernetes	Azure Kubernetes Service (AKS)
Microsoft.Kusto	Azure Data Explorer
Microsoft.Logic	Logic Apps
Microsoft.Maintenance	Azure Maintenance
Microsoft.ManagedIdentity	Managed identities for Azure resources
Microsoft.Management	Management Groups

Resource Provider	Service
Microsoft.Migrate	Azure Migrate
Microsoft.NetApp	Azure NetApp Files
Microsoft.Network	Application Gateway
Microsoft.Network	Azure Bastion
Microsoft.Network	Azure DDoS Protection
Microsoft.Network	Azure DNS
Microsoft.Network	Azure ExpressRoute
Microsoft.Network	Azure Firewall
Microsoft.Network	Azure Front Door Service
Microsoft.Network	Azure Private Link
Microsoft.Network	Load Balancer
Microsoft.Network	Network Watcher
Microsoft.Network	Traffic Manager
Microsoft.Network	Virtual Network
Microsoft.Network	VPN Gateway
Microsoft.NotificationHubs	Notification Hubs
Microsoft.OperationalInsights	Azure Monitor
Microsoft.OperationsManagement	Azure Monitor
Microsoft.PolicyInsights	Azure Policy
Microsoft.Portal	Azure Portal
Microsoft.PowerBI	Power BI
Microsoft.RecoveryServices	Azure Site Recover
Microsoft.Relay	Azure Relay

TABLE 8.4   Common Resource Providers and Services *(continued)*

Resource Provider	Service
Microsoft.ResourceGraph	Azure Resource Graph
Microsoft.ResourceHealth	Azure Service Health
Microsoft.Resources	Azure Resource Manager
Microsoft.Scheduler	Scheduler
Microsoft.Security	Security Center
Microsoft.SecurityInsights	Azure Sentinel
Microsoft.ServiceBus	Service Bus
Microsoft.ServiceFabric	Service Fabric
Microsoft.Sql	Azure SQL Database
Microsoft.Sql	Azure Synapse Analytics
Microsoft.SqlVirtualMachine	SQL Server on Azure Virtual Machines
Microsoft.Storage	Storage
Microsoft.StorageCache	Azure HPC Cache
Microsoft.StorageSync	Storage
Microsoft.StorSimple	StorSimple
Microsoft.Synapse	Azure Synapse Analytics
Microsoft.VirtualMachineImages	Azure Image Builder
microsoft.visualstudio	Azure DevOps
Microsoft.Web	App Service
Microsoft.Web	Azure Functions
Microsoft.WorkloadMonitor	Azure Monitor

This is a list of all the Azure products, services, and features that have been either covered in detail or summarized in this book. If you wanted to interface with an Azure product using an ARM template or directly through the REST API from some HTTP client application, then the resource providers listed in Table 8.4 provide a starting point.

The Azure Resource Manager and resource providers were introduced in Chapter 2 in the context of granting permissions to users using role-based access control (RBAC) capabilities. Each resource provider exposes a set of permissions that you can then grant users access to such as read, write and delete. Take a look at Figure 2.28 and compare them to the resource providers listed in Table 8.4. You will recognize a few of them. In many locations and in many exercises throughout this book, you have been exposed to resource providers as they are the basis for accessing, configuring, and provisioning Azure resources. Specifically, in Exercise 3.2, you enabled the `Microsoft.Web` resource provider and granted it access to a subnet; see Figure 3-8. Notice in Figure 8.28 that the endpoints available for a service endpoint configuration are based on resource providers.

This means only the services within that resource provider are supported with service endpoints. There are many such examples of the use of resource provider consumption for configuring dependencies and links between Azure resources.

FIGURE 8.28   Available resource providers for configuration with a service endpoint

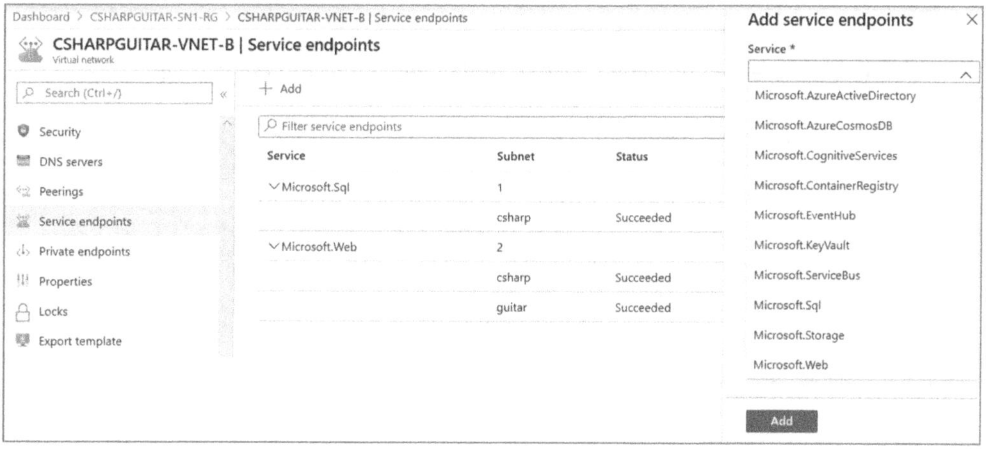

Azure Resource Manager

The final piece of the puzzle is the Azure Resource Manager, which is the platform service and compute power behind management.azure.com. Any and all supported clients, represented in Figure 2.45 and Figure 8.26, send instructions for the provisioning and management of Azure products and features. The Azure Portal, Azure CLI, Azure PowerShell, and any custom coded program can interface with the Azure Resource Manager to perform the requested actions. Requests to the Resource Manager are authenticated, authorized, and executed by the Azure Resource Manager. Complete Exercise 8.6 and deploy an Azure App Service using an ARM template.

EXERCISE 8.6

Deploying an App Service Using an ARM Template

1. The first part of the exercise requires you to create a zip deployment. To do this, you need to have completed Exercise 8.5. Take a look again at Figure 8.21. Instead of selecting App Service, select Folder. In Visual Studio right-click the project, select Publish from the pop-up menu, select Folder, click the Create Profile button (see Figure 8.29), click the Publish button, and finally, navigate to the folder where the application was published.

2. Select all the contents within the bin\Release\netcoreapp3.1\publish directory (Ctrl+A), right-click the selected files, select Send to, and select Compressed (zipped) folder. Rename the zip file (I used csharpguitar.zip). Log in to the Azure Portal at portal.azure.com, navigate to an Azure Blob storage container you created previously, and then upload the compressed zip file. After a successful upload, you should see something similar to Figure 8.30.

FIGURE 8.29   Publishing a Visual Studio web application to a folder

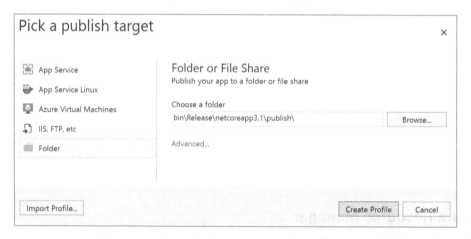

3. Download the ARM-template-APP-SERVICE.json file located here:

github.com/benperk/ASA/tree/master/Chapter08/Ch08Ex05

Modify the appName and the serverFarm directory path with your subscription, resource group, and App Service Plan, and of course modify the msdeployPackageUrl that points to your zipped application created and uploaded in the previous steps. Open PowerShell, connect to Azure, and execute this Azure CLI command. Be sure to change the `--resource-group` and `--template-file` values so they reflect your resource group name and location of the JSON file.

```
az deployment group create --resource-group "<resGroup>" `
    --template-file "C:\Temp\ARM-template-APP-SERVICE.json"
```

FIGURE 8.30 Uploading a compressed .net core application to an Azure Blob storage container

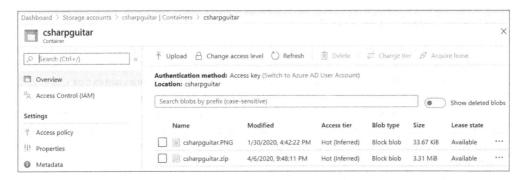

4. As with Exercise 8.5, you must perform the processes in Exercise 7.1 (configuring a managed identity) and Exercise 7.2 (configuring EasyAuth) to get the application to render as expected. Figure 8.31 illustrates the managed identity, key vault access policy, and EasyAuth configuration requirements.

FIGURE 8.31 Configuring Managed Identity, EasyAuth and Key Vault

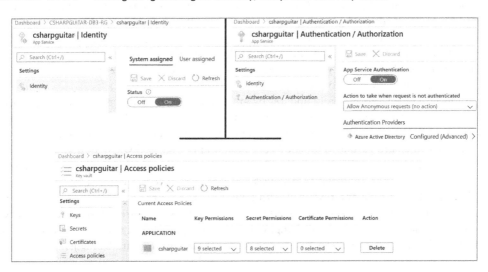

Although it would be possible to configure managed identity and EasyAuth within the ARM template, that's more complicated. Those kinds of actions would be better provided in a book written about ARM template deployments. This example illustrated how to deploy an app service to an existing App Service Plan (ASP) and deploy content to the ASP that is hosted in an Azure Blob storage container. That is a sophisticated and technically challenging exercise. If you were successful, then you are well on your way. If you experience an issue, you can log an issue on the GitHub site where you downloaded the JSON file from. Now that you can deploy to Azure using Visual Studio, Azure CLI, and ARM templates, it is time to focus a bit more on DevOps.

Working with DevOps

The acronym DevOps comes from the words *software development* (Dev) and *information technology operations* (Ops). It is a software development methodology that is intended to shorten delivery timelines. In practice, you would see it in the same context as CI/CD, which stands for continuous integration/continuous delivery and which can reduce the time between completion of a code change and the time to a production/live environment for execution by clients, consumers, and/or customers. It focuses greatly between the construction and deployment phases of a common *software development life cycle (SDLC)*. I have mentioned a few times about Python being a language that is greatly related to the machine learning (known as AI or ML) and Big Data industries. As well, Azure Cosmos DB is useful at capturing large sets of unstructured data really fast versus a relational database structure. DevOps works and falls seamlessly into ML, AI, and Big Data projects. All of those technical components work well with the "store the data now, real fast, and figure out what to do with it later" concept. With DevOps, the goals are to increase the frequency of releases, decrease the time to fix bugs, and automate testing.

Recall from Figure 4.61 where you were first introduced to a few Azure DevOps services. Specifically, you saw how Azure Repos (a source code repository) and Azure Pipelines worked with GitHub, AKS, and container images. Azure DevOps is a tool that is useful for achieving the desired goals expected from a DevOps methodology. As you can see in Figure 8.32, Azure DevOps is the product that stores your application code. It builds it and then provides a means for performing the deployment. Figure 8.32 illustrates a made-up, hypothetical solution. It's kind of amazing how you can put all these Azure products together to build any kind of IT solution imaginable.

The example hypothetically updates by an Azure DevOps deployment that targets an Azure app service. The app service accepts data from users over the internet and inserts, updates, or deletes data in an Azure SQL database and, under some circumstances, inserts data into an Azure Cosmos DB. An Azure Function is triggered when an item is inserted into an Azure Cosmos DB container. The function inserts the item into an Azure Data Warehouse that gets analyzed by Analysis Services. The report generated by Analysis Services can then be seen and reviewed with Power BI. The point of the illustration is to show the central point role that Azure DevOps plays in that architecture solution. Azure DevOps compiles and then deploys code changes onto Azure App Service, which is the entry point of the solution. Figure 8.33 shows the services provided with Azure DevOps.

FIGURE 8.32   The role of Azure DevOps in an Azure workload

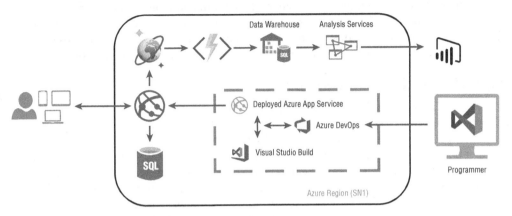

FIGURE 8.33   Azure DevOps services

Table 8.5 lists the details of each Azure DevOps. Keep in mind that this tool is targeted for development teams inside a company or enterprise. If you are an individual, the effort required to implement such a process wouldn't gain much more than the experience of setting it up. You might consider a GitHub repository if you are working on projects yourself as a one-person organization.

TABLE 8.5   Azure DevOps Service Descriptions

Service	Description
Boards	Provides an interface for work item assignment and tracking
Repos	The location to store and manage your application source code
Pipelines	An interface for building, testing, and deploying your application
Test Plans	A location to create and store application testing modules and plans
Artifacts	A single location to store application-dependent packages

When you are working on a team of developers, the work assignment process can be ambiguous. Using Azure Boards can help clarify who is responsible for what and when the delivery is expected. The unit of assignment is referred to as a work item. Azure Artifacts is a place to store the dependent versions of packages, for example from *Node Package Manager (npm)*, NuGet, and Python public sources. It is not uncommon for a dependent version of a library or runtime to be removed from public consumption. Azure Artifacts is a place where you can store them for future internal consumption. The other Azure DevOps services listed in Table 8.5 are self-explanatory or have already been covered at some point earlier.

Deploying with Azure DevOps

Now that you know what Azure DevOps is, it's time for an exercise to use it for deploying an application. Before you begin you will need an Azure DevOps account. Please follow the instructions at aka.ms/devops and click the Try For Free button to create one. I do recognize that not everyone reading this book is a programmer and the following exercise may be stretching your skills a bit. This exercise does require some prerequisites that won't be covered in detail but will be called out when they happen. The most important takeaways from this is to know what Azure DevOps is, what it can do, and why and when to use it. The actual execution of the work could be left to a specialist in this area. If you feel challenged, then perform Exercise 8.7. If you get stuck, log an issue on GitHub where you can get the code example.

EXERCISE 8.7

Deploying an Application from Azure DevOps

1. Use the application you created in Exercise 8.5 or create a new one using the same instructions. Open the project/solution in Visual Studio, select View Team Explorer from the menu, and click the Manage Connection button on the Team Explorer menu. (It looks like a plug adapter. See Figure 8.37 as an example.) Connect to the Azure DevOps instance you created at aka.ms/devops (as mentioned in the paragraph just before this exercise). Click the Synchronize button and publish the code to Azure DevOps. Once that's complete, the Azure DevOps Repo will look like Figure 8.34.

FIGURE 8.34   Azure DevOps Repos

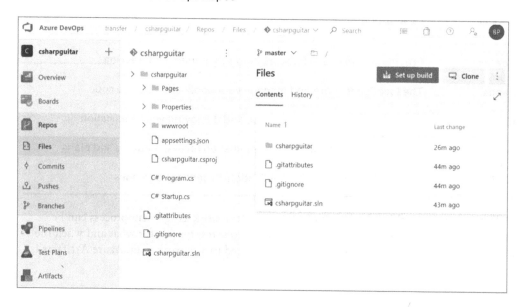

2. In the Azure DevOps portal, select Pipelines from the navigation menu. Click the Create Pipeline button, select Azure Repos Git from the list (note the mention of YAML, I told you it would come up again later), and select the repository (it will be the one you create in step 3, for example, csharpguitar). Now, select ASP.NET Core as the template for your pipeline. (See Figure 8.35.)

FIGURE 8.35   Azure DevOps Pipeline template

3. View the YAML syntax click the Save & Run button; you would see something similar to that shown in Figure 8.36.

FIGURE 8.36   Azure DevOps Pipeline save and run status

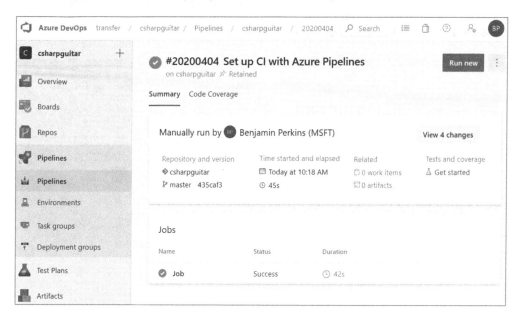

4. Click the Pipelines link in the navigation menu and select the pipeline that you just created. Click the Edit button, and update the azure-pipeline.yml file with the one located here:

    github.com/benperk/ASA/tree/master/Chapter08/Ch08Ex06

Click the Save button and then click the Run button. If you experience any issues, please log an issue on the GitHub site where you downloaded this YAML file.

5. As with Exercise 8.5 and Exercise 8.6, you must additionally perform Exercises 7.1 (configuring a managed identity) and 7.2 (configuring EasyAuth) to get the application to render as expected. Refer to Figure 8.31, which illustrates the managed identity, key vault access policy, and EasyAuth configuration requirements.

6. To prove CI/CD is working, by default make a change to line 33 of the `index.cshtml` so that it modifies the following text color to red.

```
<h5 style="color: red">A JWT Token Does Not Exist</h5>
```

7. Take a look at Figure 8.37 that illustrates the following instructions. Save the `index .cshtml` file. Notice the check mark next to the file name. Click the Team Explorer tab, click the Changes option, add a comment (for example, Made H5 red), and then click the Commit All button. Click the Home button located toward the top of the Team Explorer tab; then click the Sync button. Now, click the Push link under the Outgoing Commits heading and monitor the Pipeline Runs tab. Once the Run completes, refresh the App Service page in the browser to confirm the update was published automatically.

FIGURE 8.37 Azure DevOps Pipeline CI/CD process flow

Azure DevOps and the integration of the product and the DevOps methodology is something you should get engaged in and learn much more about. The information here barely scratches the surface. Keep in mind that there are numerous other source code repositories. Two that come quickly to mind are GitHub and Jenkins. You could easily swap either of them with Azure DevOps and achieve the same kind of CI/CD and DevOps process. It simply comes down to which tool you want to use. There may be a few subtle differences or benefits that exist only in the tool you choose; however, the author of this book doesn't know them. You would need to become a specialist in using those tools to find them, which is not necessary to pass the Azure Solutions Architect Expert exam.

Lastly, YAML expertise will soon become a nice skill to have in your pocket. YAML was introduced to you in Chapter 4 within the discussion of development and deployments of AKS. When using YAML, it seems like another bridge is being built between Microsoft and the open source community. AKS being open source and dependent on YAML files and the fact that YAML is used to configure the deployment of a .NET Core application from Azure DevOps are signs of Microsoft moving toward open source. It is an interesting area to spend some time and learn on your quest to becoming a great Azure Solutions Architect Expert. It is not so important, however, in regard to passing the exam.

Other Deployment Options

There are a few other deployment-related topics that need to be touched on. The first one has to do with deploying straight into production. In the examples provided in this chapter, that is what happened, but in the real world that is risky. It is risky because the deployment could fail halfway through or there may be a bug introduced that wasn't caught in testing. You should seriously consider using failovers when doing database upgrades, so if you need to roll back, you fail back over to the original instance. For Azure VM, perhaps make the instance of the application installed on your preproduction environment the production one by changing the IP address bound to the VM or DNS entry. Lastly, when deploying to an Azure app service, there is a feature called *deployment slots* where you can deploy your application. Once testing passes, you swap the slot so the testing slot becomes production and the production slot becomes testing. The point is, it is bad practice to deploy changes directly into production; it simply has too much impact and can result in some serious downtime.

There is a feature in the Azure Portal useful for deployment that is found by searching for "Deploy a custom template." As shown in Figure 8.38, the feature allows you to create an ARM template online. You could also take the template used in Exercise 8.6, cut and paste it into the portal, click Save, and publish it. It is a nice feature.

FIGURE 8.38   Azure Portal custom deployments

Finally, there is a project template in Visual Studio called Azure Resource Group that provides a graphical interface for creating ARM templates. See Figure 8.39.

FIGURE 8.39 Creating ARM templates in Visual Studio

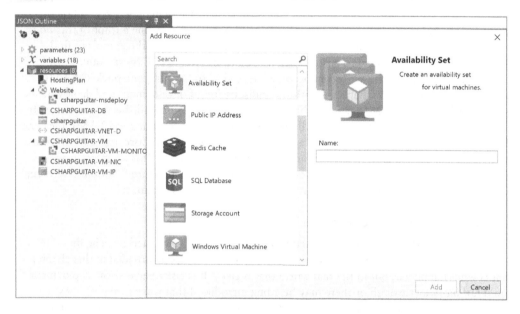

The JSON document is outlined for you, and by right-clicking parameter, variables, or resources, you get the option to create, update, or delete them. It is much easier than doing it in Notepad. You might also consider pasting an ARM template example you downloaded from some website into the IDE and see how the JSON Outline graphically interprets it.

Learning Azure Automation

As you learn and ramp up your knowledge of Azure and cloud computing in general, your footprint would be initially small. No one should be put into a position to sink or swim, and leaders should always aspire to create an environment geared toward success. As your company grows or as you take up more challenging projects having to do with the cloud and Azure, the number of resources under management can and will grow. That is one of the gotchas in the cloud, it is so easy to provision a resource and then end up with a large number in a short amount of time. Look back at Figure 6.3, which gives you a look into my personal subscription that somehow ended up with more than 2,600 resources—and that's just me. Luckily, there are no production or mission-critical applications running in them; otherwise, I would be lost. My point with all this is that in the beginning when you have a low number of provisioned Azure resources, managing them manually is possible. That footprint can quickly grow to a point to where manually managing your cloud products is no longer feasible. Also, if you wait until the "ah-ha" moment, the effort to go back and rework an automated approach for managing all your Azure products could be too great. You need to have this perspective, and the perspective that a single mind or a group of great minds is still not enough to manage massive compute scale. You must use compute itself to manage your provisioned resources. You and your team manage the products and features that manage your compute and workloads.

Microsoft understands that and has a set of tools and services that help you manage cloud-scale compute footprints. It begins with a service portfolio called *Azure Automation*. Azure Automation is concentrated on the elimination of manual Azure-related management tasks. A list of Azure Automation capabilities is provided in the following list:

- Process automation
- Configuration management
- Update management

Before going into the details of those capabilities, an exercise awaits you. In Exercise 8.8 you will view numerous Azure Automation modules to get an understanding of what is available. Then you will create a simple "Hello CSHARPGUITAR" Process Automation Runbook.

EXERCISE 8.8

Creating a Process Automation Account and Runbook

1. Log in to the Azure Portal at portal.azure.com. Click the menu button on the top-left corner of the web page, click + Create A Resource, select IT & Management Tools, select Automation, enter a name, select the subscription and resource group into which you want the Automation Account to exist, and select the region. (You should strongly consider placing the Automation account into the resource group that contains the products you want to automate. Also, choose the same location as the resource and resource group for the Automation account.) Select a Location from the drop-down list box and click the Create button.

2. Once the provisioning is complete, navigate to the Overview blade of the Azure Automation account; see Figure 8.40.

3. In the navigation menu, click the Runbooks Gallery link. Take a look at some of the examples, some which are of particular interest are listed here:

    - Stop-Start-AzureVM, Stop-Start-VMSS
    - Backup Azure SQL Database to Blob Storage
    - Delete Azure blobs older than X number of days
    - Stop-Start-Scale Websites (App services)

EXERCISE 8.8 *(continued)*

- Check SSL expiration and notify per email.

- Disable expired Active Directory accounts.

- Azure RBAC Report

- Vertically scale Azure SQL Database.

- Onboard Azure VMs for update management and change tracking

- Remove empty Resource Groups.

FIGURE 8.40 The Azure Automation account Overview portal blade

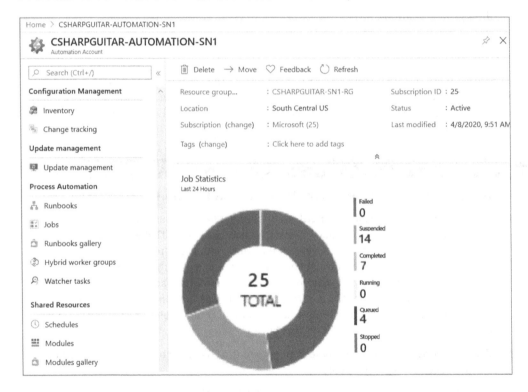

4. Select Runbooks from the navigation menu, click + Create A Runbook, and enter a runbook name. Select PowerShell from the Runbook Type drop-down list, enter a description, click the Create button, and enter the following code snippet into the editor, as illustrated in Figure 8.41. It is downloadable from here:

```
github.com/benperk/ASA/tree/master/Chapter08/Ch08Ex07
param
```

```
(
    [Parameter(Mandatory=$false)]
    [String] $Name = "CSHARPGUITAR"
)
"Hello $Name!"
```

FIGURE 8.41   Creating an Automation runbook in the Azure Portal

5.   Click the Save button, click the Test Pane button, enter a name, and click the Start button. See Figure 8.42.

FIGURE 8.42   Testing an Automation runbook in the Azure Portal

6.   Close the Test blade by clicking the X in the upper-right corner of the blade, click the Publish button, and click the Yes button. You can then schedule, run, export, and edit the runbook as required from the, for example, Hello-CSHARPGUITAR Runbook overview blade.

Read on to discuss a bit more about this exercise and some other Azure Automation capabilities.

Process Automation

In Exercise 8.8 you created a simple process automation runbook. However, when you observed the gallery of example templates, you certainly learned and became aware of the power, capabilities, and opportunities this Azure product can offer. The purpose of process automation is to automate tasks that take significant time, tasks that are at high risk of error, tasks that have high impact or activities, and tasks that happen frequently. Those benefits make your workloads more resilient and reliant if automated because once the actions are perfected and coded, then the odds of error or forgetting to perform the tasks are greatly reduced. Take, for example, the runbook template you saw in Exercise 8.8, which checks the expiry date of an SSL certificate. I cannot count the number of times I have received escalations causing massive high-scale downtime where the reason is an expired certificate. That kind of issue shuts down a system completely and is 100% avoidable by this process automation runbook task.

In the previous exercise, you created a runbook using the PowerShell syntax. When you selected PowerShell from the Runbook Type drop-down list, you may have noticed some other supported types such as Python and a graphical, workflow diagram-like option. Supporting more options for the creation of runbooks increases the probability of organizations having the skill set required to create such automation. Additionally, once the runbook is created, you can create a web hook to trigger the execution of the runbook. If you recall the discussion of Event Grid in Chapter 6, you will remember how it can be triggered from or can trigger web hooks based on events. Consider the automation of the deployment of an Azure virtual machine using an ARM template or from Azure DevOps, which includes the triggering of this web hook. This feature allows you to be notified when provisions happen and also have the ability to run a runbook report against the product and confirm it complies to your corporate mandates, compliance, and governance constraints or guidelines.

There are many examples and scenarios that can be implemented using runbooks and process automation. One area I like to go back to often is security. Take a look, for example, at the runbook that had to do with RBAC listed in the previous exercise. If you have granted others administrative privileges, which is a big deal, and you are a control freak like me, then you would want to check to make sure they retain control themselves. Once you lose control of security, your subscription or IT solution has no integrity; therefore, you must maintain control. Running reports and seeing how they look numerous times per month or weeks will help security specialists and subscription administrators sleep at night. If you find accounts that are not used, the existence of a large number of new accounts, or accounts that have expired passwords, part of the runbook script can suspend and then ultimately remove those accounts.

Configuration Management

Take a look at the navigation menu options under the Configuration Management heading in Figure 8.40. Inventory and change tracking may look familiar to you since Chapter 6 discussed the monitoring of changes and tracking inventory of your Azure VMs and other supported Azure products. Figure 6.14 illustrates how a change tracking report looks in the Azure Portal. You will find the same inventory and change tracking navigation menu items on the Azure VM blade; however, this option in the Automation Account blade can have greater scope than a single Azure VM or product. Having that visibility would be helpful in checking what changes were made, when and where they were made, and other helpful pieces of information for performance of availability troubleshooting.

Another menu item found on the Azure Automation blade is the State Configuration (DSC) link. *Desired State Configuration (DSC)* is, in its original form, a Windows-based PowerShell platform for managing the configuration of your on-premise IT and development infrastructure with declarative code. This means you can create your own PowerShell-like cmdlets, something like `CreateVM`, and it would then create a VM using a predefined configuration that contains application-specific settings.

Take that same context and apply it to the Azure platform, and this is what you get when you configure state configuration (DSC) in Azure Automation. Click the link in the navigation menu and look through the options. (See Figure 8.43.)

FIGURE 8.43 Azure Automation desired state configuration

Home > CSHARPGUITAR-AUTOMATION-SN1 | State configuration (DSC) > Compose configuration

Compose configuration
/resourceGroups/CSHARPGUITAR-SN1-RG/providers/Microsoft.Automation/automationAccounts/CSHARPGUITAR-AUTOMATION-SN1

Basics   **Source code**   Parameters

The following PowerShell script will define the state of your VM's configuration as code:

```
 1    Configuration CSHARPGUITAR_DSC {
 2
 3    param(
 4        [String[]] $ComputerRename_DependsOn,
 5        [String] $ComputerRename_description,
 6        [PSCredential] $ComputerRename_PsDscRunAsCredential,
 7        [Parameter(Mandatory=$true)]
 8        [ValidateNotNullOrEmpty()]
 9        [String] $ComputerRename_computerName
10    )
11        # resource import
12        Import-DscResource -ModuleName StateConfigCompositeResources
13
14        Node local {
15            ComputerRename ComputerRename {
16
17
```

Next

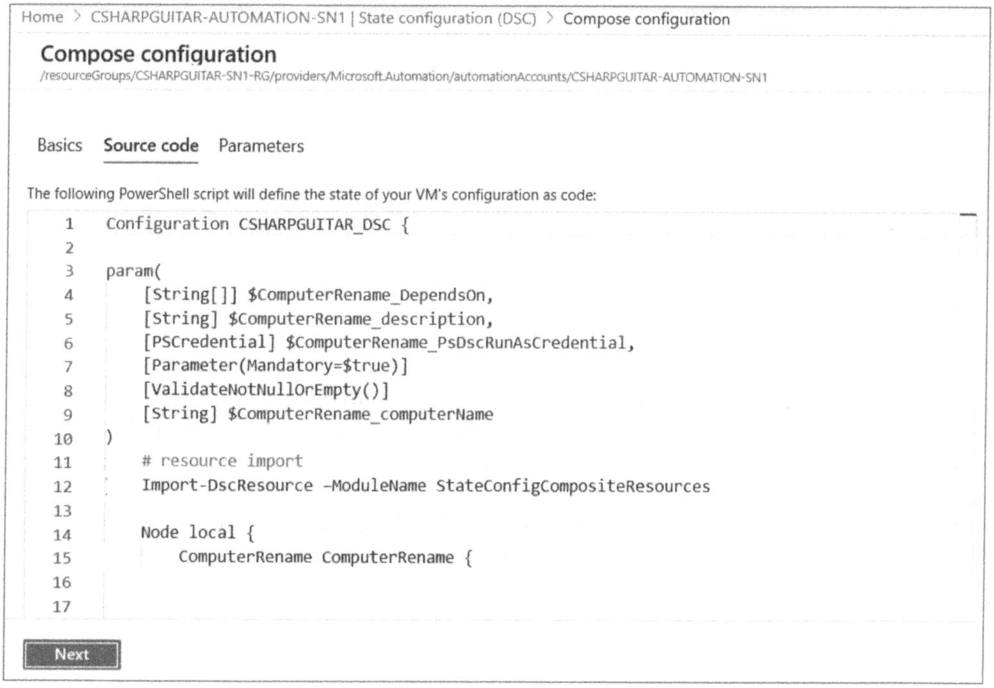

There are some example templates, a place for coding the configuration, setting parameters, and testing the script. There is likely a need for this kind of capability; otherwise, it wouldn't exist. However, consider this a scenario for large enterprises, which has very high Azure consumption and footprints.

Update Management

This Azure Automation feature, update management, was introduced in Chapter 4 in the context of an Azure virtual machine. As mentioned earlier in regard to change management, update management can be configured to have a much larger scope than a single Azure VM. As shown in Figure 8.44, the report can analyze multiple kinds of Azure resources, including *Azure Arc* resources. Log Analytics is the place where the information is stored into and drawn from for reporting. You'll learn more about Logs Analytics in Chapter 9.

FIGURE 8.44   Azure Automation update management

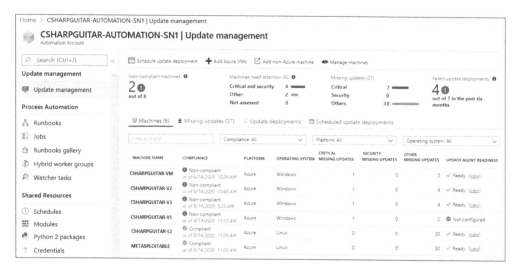

As shown in Figure 8.44, there is a clear report that identifies which Azure VMs are compliant and which are not. You can also see which machines are missing patches, have errors, and require an update. This would lead to an action on your part to schedule the installation of the patch or troubleshoot the errored patch, resolve the issue, and then get the solution installed. This is a powerful and useful tool that will help customers with large Azure footprints and workloads function optimally on the platform.

Azure Arc

You know what Azure is, you know what on-premise means, you know what private data centers are, and you know that a hybrid cloud is a combination of all of those. Increase the scope to other cloud hosting providers and SaaS in the mix and you have Azure Arc.

Other Automation Resources

Azure Automation isn't the only tool that Microsoft has for helping you mechanize manual compute activities. Two other tools are *System Center Orchestrator* and *Service Management Automation*. Table 8.6 describes each in a bit more detail.

TABLE 8.6   Microsoft Automation Tools

Automation Tool	Description
Azure Automation	Intended to run automated runbooks in the public cloud, specifically Azure
Service Management Automation	An automation engine targeted at running configuration and provisioning activities in a private cloud, for example, when using Windows Azure Pack or Stack
System Center Orchestrator	An automation engine aimed at running on-premise configuration and provisioning activities. Scripting is not required as it offers a graphical interface for creating runbooks.

The final topic in regard to Azure Automation that needs to be covered is the set of features under the Shared Resources header in the navigation menu. See Figure 8.44, which shows a few of them on the Azure Automation Azure Portal blade. The following is a completed list of them and a brief description:

Schedules   Set up a schedule and then link runbooks to be executed based on the time, date, and frequency.

Modules   Similar to a DSC script in that it is simple to execute but does a great deal of work behind the scenes

Modules Gallery   A list of modules for use as templates, similar to the bullet list provided in Exercise 8.8

Python 2 Packages   Like the modules, but written in Python

Credentials   A place to store sensitive information required to execute runbooks

Connections   Your automation task may need connection details such as IP addresses, endpoints, and access tokens; this is the place to store them.

Certificates   If the automation tasks require certificate authentication, store the certificates in this secure location.

Variables   When a runbook needs to access some value available in another executing runbook, this is how you can pass those values between them.

There is no simple way to keep all your machines in optimal shape. Teams of people and organizations exist just to support the infrastructure on which applications run. Don't underestimate the complexities, importance, and effort required in this area. Your IT solutions need ongoing maintenance to remain reliant.

Summary

In this chapter, you learned that Azure Migrate is the starting point to begin your movement of resources from on-premise to Azure. Consider the Azure Migrate service as well when moving resources within Azure to different regions, subscriptions, or resource groups, but don't forget about the useful Azure Site Recovery (ASR) tool. The resources that are most commonly moved are compute resources such as Azure VMs and Azure App Services, but SQL Server on VMs need special attention for changing their location. Making a backup or an image snapshot of the VMs and their contents and then recovering them on the new instance is a valid migration and movement approach.

You learned numerous methods for migrating code to Azure compute products. As well, you learned how to continuously make updates to the application code after its initial deployment. Visual Studio, ARM templates, and Azure DevOps are a few sources for making those deployments. Azure DevOps specifically has numerous other features that support the assignment of development work, their testing, and then deployment onto the Azure compute product of choice. You now know that you shouldn't deploy directly into production, but instead to a deployment slot or a pre-production instance.

Exam Essentials

Start with Azure Migrate.   Start here when you begin your journey into the cloud. This service is helpful for assessing and migrating your workloads from on-premise to the Azure platform. Azure virtual machines, databases, web applications, and data storage are the workloads that will gain the most benefit from Azure Migrate.

Understand Azure Site Recovery (ASR).   The name defines its purpose. Its primary role is to provide the backbone of your BCDR strategy. It is useful for performing backups and replication of workloads from on-premise to Azure and between Azure regions.

Understand Azure Data Migration Service (DMS).   When you need to migrate your data store, aka the database, begin with this service. This tool can assess existing on-premise database configurations and compare them with a targeted Azure data store product. It then provides you with a report of possible conflicts for further analysis and correction. In many cases, tips are provided to resolve the conflict.

Understand Azure Resource Manager (ARM).   Performing changes to your Azure product and resource within the Azure Portal requires resources. When you change a configuration of an Azure SQL database, app service, or VM, the platform must authenticate, validate, and update those products' configurations. ARM is the resource that performs that duty.

Understand Azure Resource Provider.   `Microsoft.Web`, `Microsoft.Sql`, and `Microsoft.Compute` are examples of what an Azure resource provider looks like. These provide the structure for RBAC, service principle, user access valida-tion, resource provisioning, and resource configuration. It represents the structure behind the ARM.

Understand Azure DevOps.   DevOps is a methodology that aligns well with some of the newer technologies gaining momentum in the IT industry such as open source, unstructured data storage, AI, and the very rapid release of new code-based features. Azure DevOps is a product that provides customers and companies with the frame-work to implement such an IT development methodology.

Key Terms

App Service Plan (ASP)

ASR Deployment Planner

Azure Arc

Azure Automation

Azure Hybrid Benefit

Azure Recovery Service Vault

Azure Reserved Virtual Machine Instances

Azure Reserved VM Instances (RI)

Azure Resource Manager (ARM)

Azure Stack

Azure VMware Solutions

Continuous Integration / Continuous Delivery (CI/CD)

Database Experimentation Assistant (DEA)

Database Management Assistant (DMA)

Deployment Slots

Desired State Configuration (DSC)

File Transfer Protocol (FTP)

Node Package Manager (npm)

Object-Oriented Programming (OOP)

Rapid Application Development (RAD)

Remote Desktop Protocol (RDP)

Service Management Automation

Software Development Life Cycle (SDLC)

SQL Server Migration Assistant (SSMA)

System Center Orchestrator

Review Questions

1. Which of the following tools are helpful for migrating on-premise workloads to the Azure platform?

    A. Azure Blueprint

    B. Azure Monitor

    C. Azure Migrate

    D. Azure Deployment Assistant (ADA)

2. Before migrating an on-premise virtual machine, it must be migrated to and then exported from Hyper-V, which is Microsoft's virtualization platform.

    A. True

    B. False

3. When migrating a data store, aka database, from on-premise to the Azure platform, the source and destination DBMS version must be identical, once migrated, and only then can you upgrade the DBMS version.

    A. True

    B. False

4. Which of the following tools are helpful for migrating on-premise data stores to the Azure platform?

    A. Database Management Assistant (DMA)

    B. Azure Migrate

    C. Azure Data Migration Service (DMS)

    D. Azure Deployment Assistant (ADA)

5. Moving an Azure product into a different subscription or resource group can be achieved by which of the following tools? (Choose two.)

    A. Azure Portal

    B. Azure Deployment Assistant (ADA)

    C. Azure CLI

    D. Azure Site Recovery (ASR)

6. Which of the following can you move Azure products and resources between after they have been provisioned?

    A. Azure regions

    B. Azure zones

    C. Azure subscriptions

    D. Azure resource groups

7. You need an Azure subscription to deploy an app service from Visual Studio.

   A. True

   B. False

8. Azure DevOps is primarily intended to support which of the following deployment and development methodologies?

   A. Continuous integration/continuous delivery (CI/CD)

   B. Waterfall

   C. Object-oriented programming (OOP)

   D. Agile

9. Which of the following are true about ARM templates?

   A. Implemented using YAML-based syntax

   B. Implemented using JSON-based syntax

   C. Can only provision and configure Azure products and/or features

   D. Useful for provisioning and configuring Azure product, features, and deploying application code

10. Which of the following is a realized benefit of Azure Automation?

   A. Templates that describe the most optimal configuration of Azure products

   B. Increase the manageability of larger cloud workload footprints.

   C. Monitor the installation status of operating system patches across an entire subscription

   D. Proactive monitoring of malicious activities happening on provisioned resourcesj

Chapter

9

Monitor and Recover

EXAM AZ-303 OBJECTIVES COVERED IN THIS CHAPTER:

✓ **Implement and Monitor an Azure Infrastructure**

■ Implement cloud infrastructure monitoring

EXAM AZ-304 OBJECTIVES COVERED IN THIS CHAPTER:

✓ **Design Monitoring**

■ Design for cost optimization

■ Design a solution for logging and monitoring

✓ **Design Business Continuity**

■ Design a solution for backup and recovery

■ Design for high availability

This chapter covers some tools and scenarios that are helpful for monitoring the Azure platform. Take special note of the "for monitoring the Azure platform" phrasing because this is what the monitoring capabilities you will find on Azure are intended for. There may be a few places in this chapter where a tool is pointed out that may be useful for monitoring your application, but not so much. This is important to point out because you need to know what logs and metrics your applications need to produce and store to gauge its health. Azure Monitor will provide logs and metrics for the products and features your application runs on and not much more. Also, in this chapter, you will learn about disaster recovery and failover tools. But again, the focus is on the tools; you will need to determine what the application needs to continue working if one piece of your solution becomes unavailable. The most important Azure services that you need to know about in regard to monitoring and recovery are Azure Monitor, Azure Backup, and Azure Site Recovery (ASR). Each of these was introduced in Chapter 1 and in numerous other chapters throughout this book.

The monitoring and recovery portions of the lifecycle of an IT solution are typically owned by a support organization. The thing about support is that, by nature, IT support engineers are reactive. That means support team members usually wait until something is broken before taking an action, and typically there are enough broken things to keep them more than busy. It is a common behavior for support organizations to take on programs that focus on preventative support activities, where they aspire to lessen the reactive nature of the organization, i.e., try to become proactive. But unfortunately, the limitations of the human support resources often result in falling short of those aspirations. Monitoring is an absolute necessity if you aspire to take proactive actions on your production IT resources. A monitoring strategy must be created that requires direct financial investment because there are limited metrics available by default. You commonly have CPU and memory logs that might help you solve a number of issues, but those alone are not good enough.

In my many decades of work in the IT industry, mostly in a support role, I have never executed a full-blown disaster recovery plan. The team has spent many hours on preparing and testing BCDR plans, but never have I completely moved a production application to another environment. I think it historically had to do with the cost of having an identical copy of a production environment sitting idle just in case it's needed. In most cases, when we triggered the disaster recovery plan, the issue mostly got resolved before we passed the point of no return. When I think back on those scenarios, I do not remember ever having a sense of confidence in the environment that we had built to act as the DR production environment. Perhaps this is the reason a complete move to the DR environment never actually happened. Remember that it is the support team that not only troubleshoots production issues but are also commonly responsible for executing the BCDR plan. If there was no confidence in the DR production environment actually working, then the support team would focus on fixing the issues instead of failing over. This lack of confidence would unfortunately result in longer downtimes and a more stressed support organization.

Those were challenging times that may never happen again since the cost of those failover environments are no longer significant. That means you can have an exact replica of your production environment ready to roll in a short time frame. Not only will you gain confidence by having the existence of an identical production environment for DR, but also Azure provides the tools required to perform the failover quickly and easily. You simply need to now build that BCDR culture into your support organization. Mitch Radcliff said, "A computer lets you make more mistakes faster than any other invention." So, make sure you always have a backup plan for any action you take on a computer. Have metrics that you can use to measure the impact of those changes, and have a plan to fail back or roll over to another instance of your environment when things go wrong. Azure Monitor, Azure Backup, and ASR can help you achieve exactly that.

Monitoring Azure Resources

To begin with, you need to think about why you want to monitor the workloads you have running on Azure. Clearly define your objective in written form and then break that down into distinct measurable items and organize them in the order of importance. Then think about how you can measure those items, what metrics and tools exist that supply some kind of comparative value, and what value is an acceptable threshold. In reality, why you want to monitor is an easy question to answer. You must know how the platform and how your applications running on the platform are behaving. Your objective is to meet the *service level agreements (SLAs)* you have guaranteed to your customers, partners, and/ or the business organization within your company. SLAs were introduced in Chapter 2 in case you want to refresh that now. In addition to meeting an SLA, you also should desire an IT solution that is both reliant and resilient. To achieve those objectives, focus your monitoring strategy on the following monitoring aspects:

- Availability/SLA monitoring
- Collecting, storing, and reporting
- Auditing
- Health monitoring
- Performance monitoring
- Security monitoring
- Usage monitoring

The definition of application availability is simply the amount of time the application is accessible for use. Calculating the availability of an application is achieved by using the following algorithm:

```
percent_availability = ((total_time - total_downtime) / total_time) * 100
```

Common values for `percent_availability` are, for example, 99.9%, 99.95%, 99.99%, and 99.999%. The last one is referred to as *five nines* and is the holy grail of availability because it is difficult and expensive to achieve. An IT application rarely exists on a single server, and it is rarely dependent only on itself. In Chapter 6, you learned about decoupling systems in an effort to make them more available. Without decoupling your systems, the calculation of availability for one tier of your IT solutions becomes a bit more complicated, especially when you want to need to pinpoint the root cause of `total_downtime`. Pinpointing the root cause of downtime is important for making improvements and not for finger-pointing or blaming. The point is, the `total_downtime` value may not be caused by the application being accessed itself; rather, it's caused by one of its dependencies. There are certainly tools and metrics that can help you track the availability metric. Unfortunately, though, like many other topics summarized in this book, how to find why the availability issue is happening and how to fix it is another career-worthy profession and is also worth a book of its own.

The Azure portfolio offers the following services for collecting, storing, and reporting details about your workloads:

- Azure Monitor
- Log Analytics
- Application Insights
- Azure Data Explorer (ADX)

In Figure 9.1, you see how the previous Azure services all fit together. You can see that Azure Monitor is in place to monitor the products running on the Azure platform and feed that data into Log Analytics for reporting. As well, monitoring data can be fed directly into Azure Data Explorer (ADX) or into some custom logging source. Application Insights is a tool that is useful for capturing logs that are more application-specific, i.e., not platform-specific. This monitoring data can be fed into numerous repositories and analyzed from the portal where the information is graphically presented. Or you can query the data using KUSTO-like SQL queries aka KQL.

Logging can be configured to track and monitor Azure VMs, containers, security, Azure Active Directory, and subscriptions. Just about all Azure products and features have the capability to create logs and expose an interface to retrieve and analyze them. Reviewing the log/monitor data is possible through numerous endpoints, starting within the Azure Portal. Additionally, there are dashboards and views in Application Insights, Log Analytics, and ADX that allow you to customize the data to analyze and customize the presentation of it. Each of those dashboards is presented to you later in this chapter. Keep in mind also that Power BI is a valid tool for the graphical representation of large complicated datasets. Azure Monitor is the main component you need to know and focus on when building your monitoring strategy, but you will learn a lot more as you proceed through this chapter.

FIGURE 9.1 Azure Monitoring overview

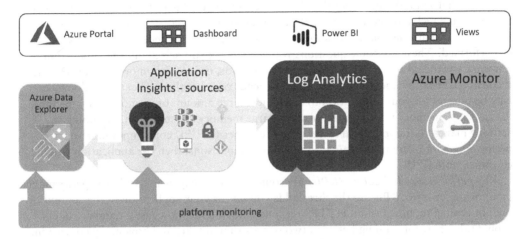

You learned in Chapter 6 what you need to know when it comes to auditing. Being compliant with industry regulations and government privacy laws cannot be achieved without knowing what exists in your Azure footprint, what each resource does, and whether they are secure. There are some helpful tools in Security Center for auditing as well. In addition to Security Center, Azure Policy and Azure Blueprint are helpful in making sure your solutions remain compliant. Finally, remember that in Chapter 5 and Chapter 6 you worked with the MODEL column on the MODELS Azure SQL database table. In those exercises, you encrypted and labeled the MODEL column as confidential. You will later learn how to enable auditing on a database column and track who and how often that piece of data is being accessed. This is important if the data is extremely sensitive and perhaps there isn't a need to see it often. Therefore, when that data is accessed, it will show up on an audit report.

The next monitoring aspect has to do with health monitoring. What exactly is health monitoring? Think about it in the actual sense of a human, in that a human can perform a task even when unhealthy. However, if the individual were healthier, the effort required to perform the task would be less, leaving more energy to perform additional activities and making them more productive. The same is applicable with IT resources, in that if you have a bad piece of code that consumes an unnecessary amount of CPU or memory, then the compute can perform fewer computations over the same time frame when compared to the same process running a more optimal version of the code. Remember that in the cloud model where you pay for consumption, that is an important point. Bad, inefficient code can result in higher average costs since they consume more cloud resources. Health monitoring is generally constructed using colors. Green is when all is good, yellow is for partially good, and red is for not good. The thing is that you, the application owner, must know what is considered green, yellow, and red, because what is green for you may not be for someone else. Consider metrics such as CPU utilization, memory consumption, and how fast your application responds to requests. Logging the health data in a tool to interpret the data and report it for action is totally application-dependent and outside the scope of Azure. However, the tools in Figure 9.1 are helpful to capture, store, and report the findings from that kind of data, from the platform perspective. One of the metrics mentioned is the speed in which a request to the application responds to a request made to it. How fast should it be, what is normal, and what is a threshold where you believe an action should be performed? These are some questions you need to ask yourself about the application. Is it normal for the response to come back in ten seconds, or is 500ms more the norm? What is considered healthy and what is not again depends on what the application is doing. It may be normal for your application to consume a large amount of memory. Caching large datasets into memory will typically result in large memory consumption, but doing so actually makes your application faster. The same goes for CPU consumption; if you are performing a lot of complex regular expression comparisons, then the application would consume more CPU.

Key performance indicators (KPIs) are something you may hear within the performance monitoring scenario. KPIs are the thresholds you set for your application in the context of, but not limited to, how fast an HTTPS response should take, how fast a database query should take, how long a ping between two servers should take, and how many concurrent connections is normal. When any of those KPIs are breached, then alerts need to be sent and analysis done to find out what happened and implement a solution to keep it from happening again if it caused downtime. If it didn't cause downtime or any disruption, then you should consider changing the KPIs so that it reflects "normal production activity." The kind of information attained from this scenario is also helpful for managing growth by making some tweaks to the autoscaling rules you have implemented into your compute or data workloads.

There is no shortage of security-related monitoring you will find in Azure; you already know there is an entire product offering named Security Center. Take a look at Chapter 2 to get more information about Security Center; specifically look at Figure 2.49. From a security monitoring perspective, some of the areas of interest are from a user access perspective. Azure Active Directory (AAD) provides some features under the Monitoring header on the AAD blade. There are also reports to run and manage an RBAC, User, Group, sign-on, and audit logs, which describe what actions were taken under those login activities. Keep in mind that these security reports are targeted toward what is going on in the Azure Portal; if you need more information about what is happening in your application, there is more on that in the later section named "Monitoring Security." However, a lot of the security-related application responsibilities sit with you, the user of Azure products and services.

The last monitoring scenario discussed here has to do with usage. A useful usage monitoring report is available for you already; take a look back at Figure 8.2. It is the Cost Analysis report for a given Azure subscription. This report is broken down by resource group, region, and event to specific Azure products. This is helpful for you not only to see where you are having the most cost, but also where you have the most activity. Remember, cloud computing charges you based on consumption. The products and features with the most usage will typically result in the highest cost. But that can also be helpful to identify your most popular product or service. Why that is important comes down to making sure there is enough available resources allocated to it, especially if it is a revenue generator. There are throttling rules you can place on resources and subscriptions, and when the limit is breached, Azure can be instructed to stop allocating additional resources. You would not want to do that when it comes to your most popular product, right? A usage report is helpful in identifying those resources; then you can determine what limitations need to be applied to each. Instead of constraining a popular revenue-generating application, manage spend versus consumption versus revenue and tune it for growth.

The remainder of this section is broken into two subsections. The first one has to do with Azure Service Health followed by the most important Azure Monitor service. You'll learn about Azure Service Health and then get ready to get your hands dirty with Azure Monitor.

Azure Service Health

Your migration or creation of IT solutions onto the Azure platform begins with trust. You are handing over a lot of responsibility to Microsoft, which can have a great impact on the success of your solution and company. In many cases, once you migrate to Azure, the success of your entire business is in the hands of Microsoft; perhaps all the revenue that your company makes is driven through the applications now running on Azure. If that's the case and there is a problem on the Azure platform, then you also have a problem. You can trust Microsoft Azure, and you can rely on the platform; it is truly the best suite of cloud products and features available. It is a stable platform, but it would be good practice to know and keep track of its general status. You want to know if there are any platform issues or changes that have impacted you, and you want to find out why those changes or transient issues had impact. Knowing and learning how Azure works will lead to an understanding that Azure is not only some architecture; there is also a massive amount of code and technologies working behind the scenes that keep all the components working together. The more you can learn about that, the more you can design and tweak your application to run on the platform. Azure Service Health is a tool that you can use to monitor what is happening on the platform. Take a look at Figure 9.2, which illustrates how Azure Service Health aka Service Health appears in the Azure Portal.

The output from this Azure feature is a report of service events, planned maintenance, health advisories, and security advisories. There exists also a feature for filtering and the history of platform health–related events by subscription, region, and service, where the service is something like Azure Virtual Machines, Azure SQL, or Event Hubs. To achieve this, select the option from the drop-down lists shown in Figure 9.2. This filtering is helpful when performing root-cause analysis of a disruption that was logged by one of your workloads running on the Azure platform. You could check the history, listed at the bottom of Figure 9.2, to see whether any of your services had an event that happened around the same time as your application incident. There is also a feature named Health Alerts, which you can see on the navigation menu in Figure 9.2. Access this feature either from the navigation menu or by clicking + Add Service Health Alert on the main overview blade, also shown in Figure 9.2. This feature will proactively send you information about any incident based on event type, i.e., service issues, planned maintenance, health advisories, and security advisories, that might have an impact on your Azure workloads. You can project the notifications by selecting specific subscriptions, regions, and services for those events and even send those events to specific people or groups for notification and possible reaction.

FIGURE 9.2   Azure Service Health Azure Portal blade

The concept of resource health has been a common theme throughout the book. In Chapters 4 and 6, application health was called out. In Chapter 6, there was a mention of Azure Health Monitor aka Azure Monitor and Azure Status, which should have provided clarity. As a reminder, Azure Status is located at status.azure.com and is useful for getting an overall view of what is going on with Azure.

In summary, Azure Service Health is focused on monitoring the Azure platform. If provides you with capabilities for being alerted when a platform event may have impacted your provisioned Azure products. It will also, in many cases, provide a *root-cause analysis (RCA)* of what happened, why, and what is being done to prevent it in the future. Those messages are helpful for status meetings with management or business leaders. Also, in many cases there will be some tips on how you could better configure your workload to better react and respond to these kinds of events. Let's now get into Azure Monitor, which is helpful for logging and analyzing the Azure platform and some aspects of your IT solutions running on Azure.

Azure Monitor

This is the Azure service to start with when you want to design your Azure monitoring strategy. As you learned in the previous section, Azure Monitor is focused more on the platform than on the application. The word *application* has been used a lot in this book and can be a bit ambiguous. Some might interpret an application to mean the custom source code that you or your development team wrote that is running on a server. Others might abstract the meaning up or out a few layers. Are dependent code libraries or hardware drivers considered the application or part of the application? It would be generally accepted to consider an application as one component of your IT solution in totality. What you are going to learn in the following exercise is how to monitor the later definition of what an application is. An application is not the platform, and it's not the code; rather, it's a shared space between the two. With that understanding, recognize that the information placed into Log Analytics is mostly platform diagnostics. The diagnostics are metrics such as the number of connections, CPU, Azure resource CRUD operations, auto-scale events, etc. Those metrics are not embedded into your custom code; they are generated from the operating system or platform.

It has been a common theme in the book that Microsoft is responsible for monitoring the platform and not the code running your application. You must include the log creation logic within your source code to track, log, and manage code exceptions. What you will learn in this section is that Azure Monitor and Log Analytics are a step closer to your code, but there is nothing in your application code to log unless you specifically placed it there. You will learn later, though, that Application Insights (AI) provides you with some metrics that are closer to the code than Azure Monitor or Log Analytics via a *software development kit (SDK)* to place unique code-specific logging logic directly into your code. That data is then written into Log Analytics, which will support the querying of raw data or data that is graphically viewed in the Azure Portal. Complete Exercise 9.1 where you will configure an Azure Monitor and enable diagnostic monitoring.

EXERCISE 9.1

Creating and Reviewing Azure Monitor Details

1. Log in to the Azure Portal at portal.azure.com.

2. Enter **Monitor** in the search box at the top center of the portal, select the Monitor service, and click the Activity Log link in the navigation menu. You will see, as illustrated in Figure 9.3, a list of activities that have taken place on your Azure workloads for the selected subscription and time frame.

FIGURE 9.3   Azure Monitor Activity Log report—portal

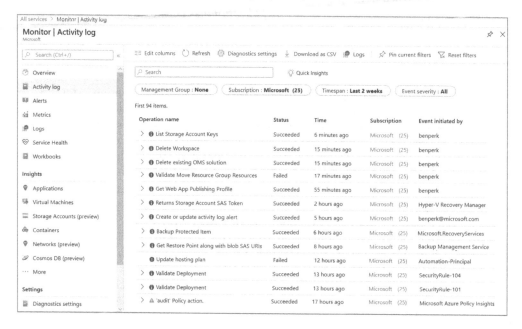

3. Execute the following Azure CLI cmdlet via the PowerShell console to check it for a given resource group over the last day. Figure 9.4 shows the summarized output.

```
az monitor activity-log list --resource-group "CSHARPGUITAR-SN1-RG" `
   --offset 1d --query `
      '[].{Operation: operationName.value, Status: status.value}'
```

FIGURE 9.4   Azure Monitor Activity Log report—Azure CLI

```
PS C:\> az monitor activity-log list --resource-group "CSHARPGUITAR-SN1-RG" --offset 1d --query
'[].{Operation: operationName.value, Status: status.value, SubStatus: subStatus.localizedValue}'
[
  {
    "Operation": "Microsoft.Storage/storageAccounts/listKeys/action",
    "Status": "Succeeded",
    "SubStatus": "OK (HTTP Status Code: 200)"
  },
  {
    "Operation": "microsoft.insights/activityLogAlerts/write",
    "Status": "Succeeded",
    "SubStatus": ""
  },
  {
    "Operation": "Microsoft.Resources/deployments/validate/action",
    "Status": "Succeeded",
    "SubStatus": "OK"
  },
  {
    "Operation": "Microsoft.Authorization/policies/deployIfNotExists/action",
    "Status": "Succeeded",
    "SubStatus": ""
  },
```

4. Click the Virtual Machines link on the navigation menu under the Insights heading. Click Monitored ➤ Not Monitored ➤ Workspace Configuration. Navigate back to Not Monitored, and you would see something similar to that shown in Figure 9.5.

FIGURE 9.5   Azure Monitor - Virtual Machine insights

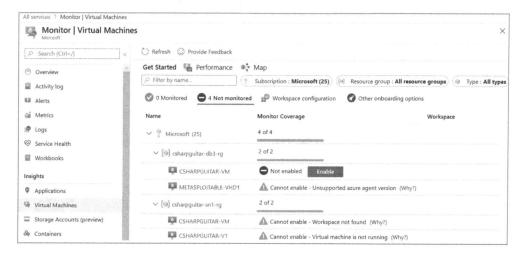

5. To enable Azure Monitor on one of the Azure VMs in the list shown in Figure 9.5, click the Enable button next to the Azure VM for which you want to enable Azure Monitor, click the Enable button again on the pop-up blade, select the subscription, select the Log Analytics workspace or create a new one, click the Enable button a final time, and navigate to the Monitored tab. See Figure 9.6.

FIGURE 9.6   Azure Monitor Virtual Machine monitored

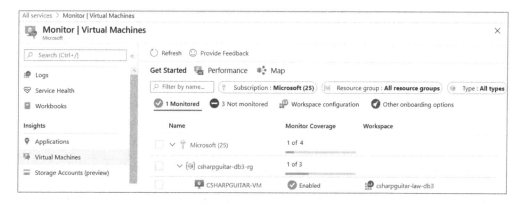

6. Click the Performance link toward the top of the Monitor | Virtual Machines blade and review the details such as CPU Util, Memory, Bytes sent/Received, and Disk Space. Click Map to see a graphical representation of the Azure VM including the process list, ports, IP address, OS version, events, etc. See Figure 9.7.

FIGURE 9.7 Azure Monitor Virtual Machine map

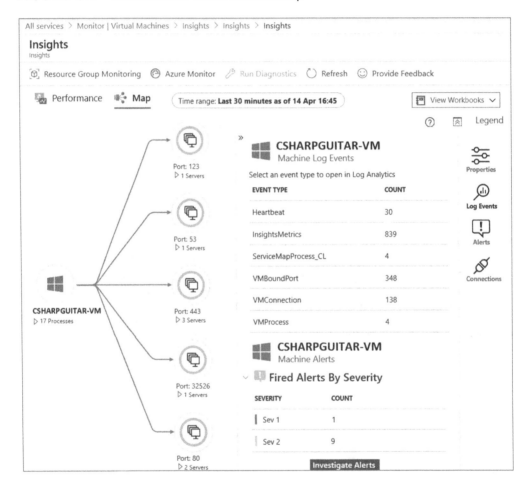

7. In the navigation menu, select Diagnostics Settings, select a resource that you want to enable diagnostics, click the + Add Diagnostic setting, enter a Diagnostics Settings name, select the log details you want to log, check the Send To Log Analytics, select the subscription, and select the Log Analytics workspace where you want store the log. See Figure 9.8.

FIGURE 9.8   Azure Monitor Diagnostics settings

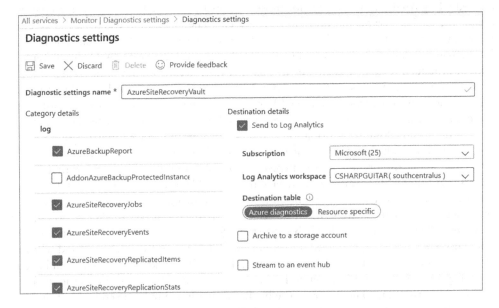

8.   Click the Save button, and navigate back to the Diagnostics blade. You will see something similar to that shown in Figure 9.9.

FIGURE 9.9   Azure Monitor Diagnostics settings overview

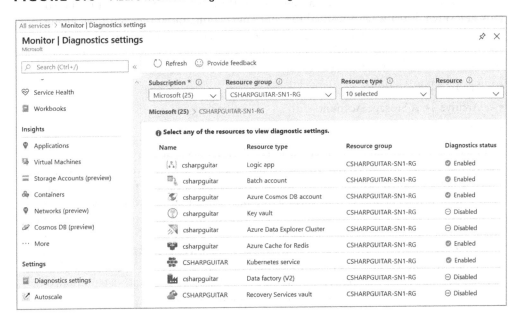

That's good work—you configured some insights for an Azure virtual machine, you created a Log Analytics workspace for those insights to be stored into, and you configured diagnostic settings for one or more Azure resources. The first action you took in Exercise 9.1 was to look at the *activity logs* of Azure resources across the subscription. The Activity Logs navigation menu item is available on each Azure product Overview blade. If you have a lot of products, reviewing them one by one isn't feasible, so you have this Azure Monitor interface for seeing what is going on across the subscriptions. You also learned that you can retrieve the activity logs using Azure CLI and target a specific resource group. In all cases, there is a large amount of data. Therefore, it would be prudent to optimize your queries toward the specific kind of information you seek. Perhaps only look for errors or updates to Key Vault private keys; the tool is flexible but is up to you to decide what your application requires. An interesting point to call out in Figure 9.5 is that the METASPLOITABLE-VHD1 Azure Virtual Machine isn't able to be monitored. Monitoring requires a service to be installed on machines for monitoring, something like what was discussed shortly after Exercise 8.3 (i.e., Windows Azure Guest Agent). The reason for the message in Figure 9.5 is most likely because the OS that was deployed to the Azure VM is not considered a blessed, endorsed, or supported Linux image. Keep that in mind when you troubleshoot this kind of configuration running Linux OS, make sure the OS is endorsed.

In Figures 9.5, 9.6, and 9.7, you will see toward the top of the image items shown as Performance and Map. The Performance blade, as mentioned in the exercise, will show you the basic, default server metrics such as CPU utilization, memory consumption, and throughout. These metrics are useful and can be used as the early warning signs that there may be some trouble brewing. The other item is Map, which is illustrated nicely in Figure 9.7. This is a nice representation of the Azure VM properties, events, alerts, and connections. When you see visualizations such as this, the important aspect is that you look at it often, learn what is normal for your application, and if the picture suddenly looks different, take an action to find out why. There is another point to call out that you experienced in Exercise 9.1, specifically in step 7 where you configured the Destination detail for the Diagnostics settings, as shown in Figure 9.8. There were three options.

- Send To Log Analytics
- Archive To A Storage Account
- Stream To An Event Hub

In the exercise, you chose to place the selected logs to be sent to a Log Analytics workspace. You will learn more about that in the next section; however, you could have also chosen to place them into an Azure Blob storage container in JSON format. You could then write a custom application to query and report using that JSON document. The other option is to stream the logs into an Event Hub. You learned about Event Hubs in Chapter 6 and that it's a messaging service. The data wouldn't/shouldn't exist long in that location, so if you choose this one, there needs to be a consumer that will process the messages being sent to the Event Hub. This is an option where you might need to be analyzing and alerting application health in almost real time. Finally, note that there are some default limits for Azure Monitor; see Table 9.1 as a sample of the limits.

TABLE 9.1   Azure Monitor Limits

Resource	Default Limit
Alerts	2000 per subscription
Email alert notifications	100 per hour
SMS	1 every 5 minutes
KUSTO Queries	200 per 30 seconds
Storage limit	500MB–unlimited
Data retention	7–730 days

If you ever find that some logs are missing, then that may be due to one of the default limits. These limits are in place to protect you because the consumption of this resource has a cost; it is not free. If you need more than the defaulted limit, you can create a support case with Microsoft, and the limits can be increased or some feedback given on how to optimize your logging strategy. Keep in mind also that some limits are based on the pricing tier you selected when creating the Log Analytics workspace. Storage limits and data retentions are based on the pricing tier, so take a look at them when you need to determine your need. The pricing tier can be changed after creation, so perhaps begin small and grow as your needs require.

Log Analytics

Like many other Azure products, this isn't the first time you are exposed to Log Analytics. As you approach the end of the book, a big majority of the cloud concepts, Azure products, and features have already been covered. In the previous exercise, specifically in step 5 you created a Log Analytics workspace. Its creation was simple, in that it required only a location, a name, and a pricing tier. As you can see in Figure 9.1, it is the place where the logs and metrics are stored for reporting and alerting capabilities. The Log Analytics workspace has a lot of features, so take a look at them in the Azure Portal. Navigate to the workspace you created previously. There shouldn't be many options in the navigation menu that are unknown. Click the Logs navigation menu item. You will see something similar to that shown in Figure 9.10.

In the previous exercise, you enabled Diagnostic settings for one or more Azure products. It takes some minutes for the data to begin flowing into the workspace, but once it starts flowing, you can query the information by using the following query. The query and the output are also visualized in Figure 9.10. Clicking the Run button executes the query.

```
AzureDiagnostics
| project Category
```

```
| summarize Count = count() by Category
| order by Count desc nulls last
```

FIGURE 9.10 Querying diagnostics in the Log Analytics workspace

The data for update management, change tracking, inventory, and other compliance and tracking data are also logged in a Log Analytics workspace. All the data is bound together in some way; this area is still evolving but is useful for getting some information about how your applications and application dependencies are behaving. Those kinds of metrics are helpful in taking proactive measures to manage growth and consumption as well; they are helpful in troubleshooting a current issue or finding a root cause of a historical issue. There are also limitations when it come to the Log Analytics workspace, as provided in Table 9.2.

TABLE 9.2 Log Analytics Limits

Resource	Default Limits
Workspace limit	10–unlimited
Returned rows in portal	10000
Max columns in a table	500
Max column name length	500
Data export	No supported
Data Ingestion	6GB/min

There is a free tier for a Log Analytics workspace, which is the one that has a limit on the number of workspaces per subscription. Also notice that it is currently not possible to export the data you store into the workspace. This is the current situation; it might change in the future. Lastly, the more diagnostic logging you configure, the more data that is generated. Note that there is a limit on the amount of data that can be placed into the workspace per minute.

Application Insights

Application Insights has a rather large set of capabilities. To begin with, you already know the difference between Log Analytics and Application Insights, right? Take a moment to remind yourself in what scenario you would look into Log Analytics data versus Application Insights. Figure 9.11 shows some additional differentiation, specifically, table names into which metric data is stored.

FIGURE 9.11   Application Insights versus Log Analytics workspace logs

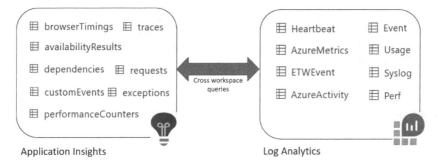

Earlier there was an attempt to compare these two components that have been merged into the Azure Monitor service. I tried to explain how Log Analytics stores more platform-specific information, while Application Insights stores application and code data. Specifically calling out that the Event table shown for Log Analytics is more platform-related, you would expect to find within it what you see in the Event Viewer on a Windows server. Exceptions or request tables accessible through Application Insights are, simply by name, more associated to the code and an application than to a platform. It is hopeful now that the relation (or lack of relation) between the two is clearer. Also, as illustrated in Figure 9.11, it is possible to perform queries across the two data repositories, both of which are ADX clusters. This will become more obvious later.

Take a look back at Figure 9.9, and you will see the Applications link in the navigation menu. Navigate back to the Azure Monitor blade and click that link. On that link you will be provided with the ability to add a new Application Insights service. It is a simple process and requires only a subscription, a resource group, and a name. Once created, navigate to it and click the View Application Insights data link and notice two specific items. The first one is on the Overview blade; there is an attribute called the Instrumentation Key that looks a lot like a GUID. This is the piece of information that uniquely identifies your AI logs. The Instrumentation Key is a necessary, required piece of information for configuring AI logging from within application code. In an ASP.NET Core application, you wire the two together in a configuration file; it resembles something similar to the following:

```
{    "ApplicationInsights": {
        "InstrumentationKey": "appInsightsInstrumentationKey"
    },
    "Logging": {
        "LogLevel": {
            "Default": "Warning"
        }}}
```

Then you install and configure the `Microsoft.ApplicationInsights.AspNetCore` NuGet package to create logs into the AI service as desired. This is what is truly meant by "application code monitoring" because the logging capability is really inside of the custom code running on the Azure platform. Next, take a look at the navigation menu items available for AI, and you will find one named Logs. Click Logs, and you will have the same query interface as you see in Figure 9.10; however, the tables you will see are those specific to AI, as shown in Figure 9.11. On the Overview blade for AI, you will see an Application Dashboard link. Click it, and you will see some impressive default information. See Figure 9.12.

FIGURE 9.12 Application Insights—Application Dashboard

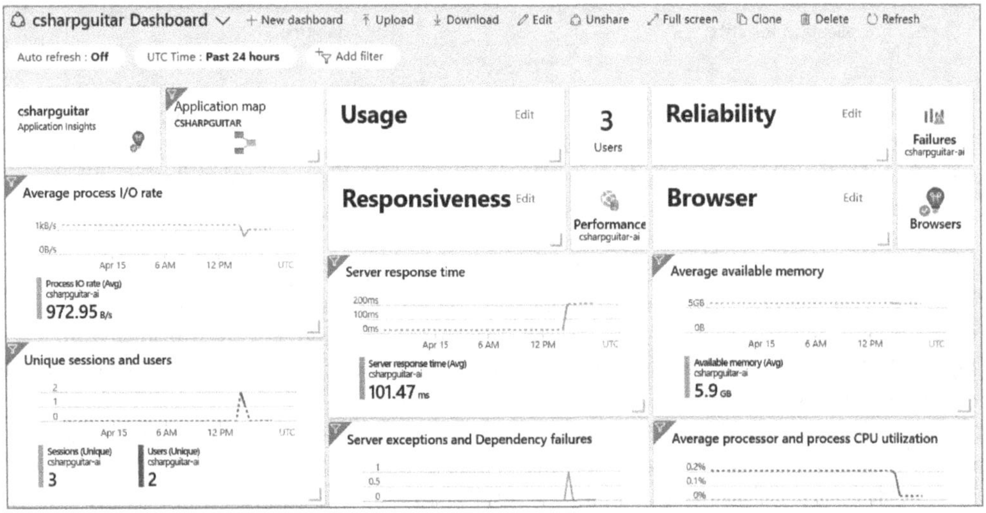

Before continuing to the next section, be aware that for all Azure products there will exist a Monitoring section in the navigation menu in the Azure Portal. The contents in that section are standard and contain something similar to Figure 9.13. Note that in most cases all of them use the same backend technology for storing the data. Those tools allow you to configure, view, and in many cases manipulate the data. It also supports direct access so you can create your own tools and reports based on your exact requirements.

FIGURE 9.13   Monitoring section in Azure Portal

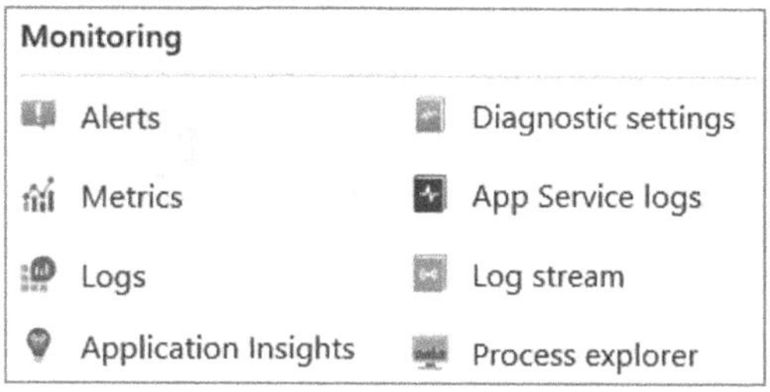

At the moment, only Azure App Services and Azure Functions have built-in, default support for Application Insights. When creating either of those in the portal, you will notice a step is to enable that feature. Application Insights can be enabled later for those Azure products and can be enabled for any application by creating an AI service and using the Instrumentation Key within your code.

Azure Data Explorer

If you wanted to build your own custom monitoring and reporting system, this is a good place to begin that journey. You might have already realized that both Log Analytics and Application Insights, which are components within Azure Monitor, store the data onto the same type of data source. This storage location is commonly referred to as a *KUSTO cluster* or *ADX cluster*. Take a look at Figure 9.14.

You see that the cluster that Azure Monitor uses is a shared cluster, which means all Azure products that you have configured to use Azure Monitor will store their logs into that cluster. This is the location of the log storage which you created in Exercise 9.1, specifically, in step 5 where you enabled the monitoring for an Azure VM and selected a Log Analytics workspace. Behind the scenes, it configured and linked to an ADX cluster. Application Insights does similar work behind the scenes when you create it. In the Application Insights scenario, the ADX cluster is bound only to the clients that have the Instrumentation Key and is therefore considered private. Lastly, recall from Exercise 5.7 where you created a stand-alone ADX cluster and database; then later in Exercise 6.5 you configured Event Hub to send information to the cluster. IoT Hubs and Azure Blob containers, in addition to Event Hub, have built-in support for ADX integration. There exists also an Azure Data Explorer SDK; its NuGet package is named `Microsoft.Azure.Kusto .Ingest.NETStandard` and can be used from any client to send logs to the cluster. You have already had some exposure to the *Kusto Query Language (KQL)* in previous chapters and also in this one. If you would like to learn more about this query language, take a look here:

docs.microsoft.com/en-us/azure/data-explorer/kusto/query

FIGURE 9.14   Shared, virtual, and private ADX clusters

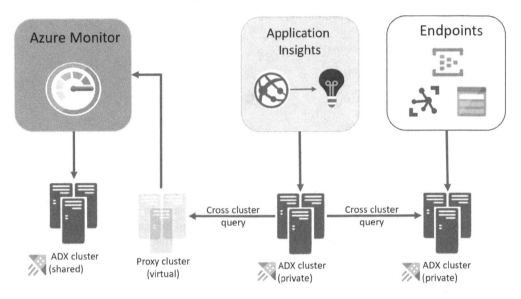

KQL has a lot of capabilities and feels similar to SQL. I haven't used KQL enough to find any significant differences it has with SQL or limitations. Both have worked well in the scenarios that they are designed for, and I have no complaints. Becoming an expert with KQL is an area where you will need to branch off from the book and investigate more in that area if it interests you. This seems like a good time for an exercise. In Exercise 9.2, you will add the Log Analytics workspace you created in Exercise 9.1 to Azure Monitor in ADX at dataexplorer.azure.com. You did a similar activity in Exercise 5.7 when you created a stand-alone ADX cluster. Additionally, you will add Application Insights to the ADX cluster. By adding these to ADX, you will be able to visibly see them all in one place, which will be helpful when you create cross-cluster queries. You can visualize cross-cluster queries in Figure 9.14, as well as a proxy cluster. A proxy cluster is something you must create to query the shared instance of the ADX cluster.

Adding ADX Clusters to Azure Data Explorer

1. Open this URL in a browser: dataexplorer.azure.com.

2. Click the Add Cluster button, and enter your Log Analytics and Application Insights endpoints. They will resemble something similar to the following. Replace <sub-id>, <resource-group>, and <*-name> with your values.

   ade.loganalytics.io/subscriptions/<sub-id>/resourcegroups/
   <resource-group>/providers/microsoft.operationalinsights/
   workspaces/<workspace-name>

   ade.applicationinsights.io/subscriptions/<sub-id>/
   resourcegroups/<resource-group>/providers/microsoft.insights/
   components/<ai-app-name>

3. Select the database for your Log Analytics workspace endpoint, and enter the query you see in Figure 9.15. The output will be similar to Figure 9.15.

FIGURE 9.15 Shared, virtual, and private ADX clusters

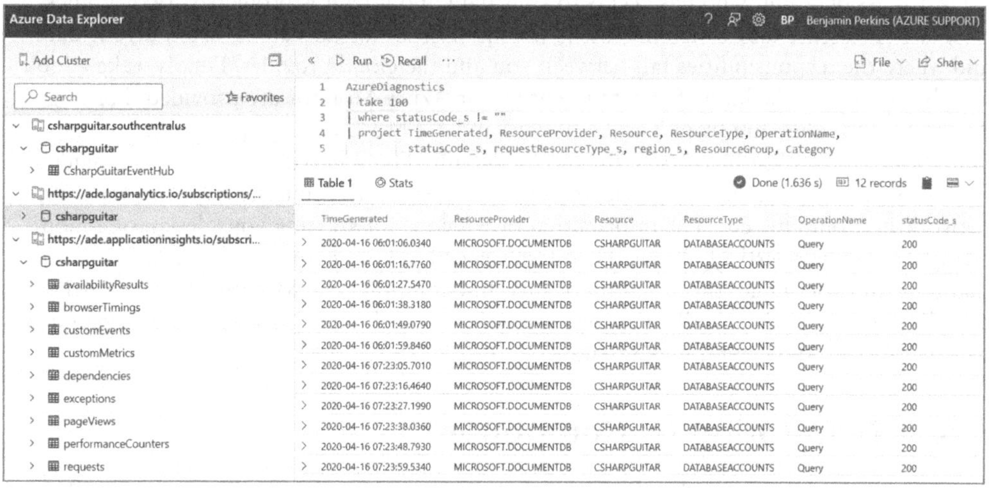

4. The power of this configuration is that it allows you to join the logs that exist in more than a single cluster. The following KQL query is an example of how to achieve that:

   ```
   let LA1 = 'https://ade.loganalytics.io/subscriptions/...';
   union <AI1-ADX table>, cluster(LA1).database(<workspace-name>).<table name>
   ```

That query is a template only and is intended to provide you with an example. You can probably recognize the possibilities and complexities with this. It is an interesting area. Before moving on to the next section, it is important to discuss the data retention and security topics regarding logged metric data. In Chapter 6, where you learned about governance and compliance, one of the topics had to do with the location, protection, and storage of data. When you create the Log Analytics workspace or an Application Insights monitor, part of the creation is the selection of its location, and you have control over that. Any Azure product or resource from any location will be able to write into the data store regardless of location. That means your data can remain in a specific geographical location regardless of where the data producers are located. Remember also that when you configured Azure Monitor for an Azure VM, part of the configuration was the selection of a Log Analytics workspace that is also bound, i.e., created in a chosen region. The point is that you have control of the location into which your metric and tracing data is stored. You might also consider an Azure Policy to prohibit the creation of a Log Analytics workspace into any region, which results in noncompliance to any of your privacy regulations.

The data that exists in the ADX data clusters is encrypted at rest by default. As well, all data communications between the SDKs and the portal happen over HTTPS, which means the data is encrypted in transit as well. Take a look back in Chapter 2 if you need a reminder of what the encryption of data at rest and data in transit mean. Also discussed in Chapter 6, specifically in the "Azure Cloud Compliance Techniques" section, there is some discussion about who has access to your data and how it is protected. Take a quick look back at Figure 6.8, which illustrates the different kinds of security around your data and where the responsibilities fall between you and the cloud provider. Finally, take a look at Table 9.1 where the limits for data retention for Azure Monitor are provided. For Log Analytics, the values are from 7 and 730 days and are based on your pricing tier or configuration. Application Insights is 90 days by default. The following sections are intended to show some of the monitoring features available per Azure component such as security, networking, compute, etc. The information provided is for starting your design of a monitoring strategy per vertical. As you have experienced in your career, monitoring is an area that typically doesn't get the attention or investment it deserves. Monitoring is a rather complicated area and typically has great impact on troubleshooting and forecasting and is worthy of focus and capital investment.

Azure Monitoring by Component

This book is organized in a way that your migration or initial consumption is performed on the Azure cloud platform. The order in which you design the deployment of your workloads onto Azure will have a higher probability of success if your plan flows in the same sequence, i.e., security, network, compute, data, etc. Knowing what is going on with your IT solutions after deployment to Azure is complete is a must-have component. You probably cannot imagine running an IT organization without some kind of reporting and metrics that explain how things are going. The following will provide some insights into monitoring features per Azure components. You should consider including these monitoring concepts into the initial design of your approach for each component and then build your customization on top of them. Waiting until the end of your project to consider monitoring, after the workloads are running on Azure, may result in not receiving the investment required to complete this important part of your IT support model. You might find yourself in a troubleshooting scenario and not have any information to help you resolve the issue.

Monitoring Security

There are three fundamental areas to monitor regarding security on Azure. They are Azure Active Directory, RBAC, and your Azure products. There is one additional, your application security; however, that is dependent on your application requirements and behaviors, so that's not covered much here. Like many other Azure products, you will find the Diagnostic settings and Logs menu item on the navigation blade; it exists for Azure Active Directory as well. Once Diagnostic settings are configured, the logs are placed into a Log Analytics workspace and become available for KQL querying. There are two tables added to the data store when you enable Azure Active Directory (AAD) diagnostics, `AuditLogs` and `SigninLogs`. The audit logs provide information about an identity that can then be linked to activities performed in the portal, for example. If you wanted to see who made a change to an RBAC group, you could analyze this table to find that out. The sign-in logs will provide just that, namely, who attempted to sign in and what was the status. Table 9.3 summarizes the current `AuditLogs` and `SigninLogs` table schema.

TABLE 9.3 AAD Diagnostic Log Table Schema

AuditLogs	SigninLogs
AADOperationType	AADTenantId
AADTenantId	AppDisplayName
ActivityDateTime	AppId
ActivityDisplayName	Category
AdditionalDetails	ClientAppUsed
Category	ConditionalAccessPolicies
CorrelationId	ConditionalAccessStatus
DurationMs	CorrelationId
Id	CreatedDateTime
Identity	DeviceDetail

TABLE 9.3 AAD Diagnostic Log Table Schema *(continued)*

AuditLogs	SigninLogs
InitiatedBy	DurationMs
Level	Id
Location	Identity
LoggedByService	IPAddress
OperationName	IsRisky
OperationVersion	Level
Resource	Location
ResourceGroup	LocationDetails
ResourceId	OperationName
ResourceProvider	OperationVersion
Result	OriginalRequestId
ResultDescription	Resource
ResultReason	ResourceProvider
ResultSignature	ResourceGroup
ResultType	RiskDetail
SourceSystem	RiskLevelDuringSignIn
TargetResources	RiskState
TimeGenerated	UserId
Type	UserPrincipleName

Those table columns should give you an idea of what is stored and how the data within them could be used. The information stored in the AuditLogs .ResourceProvider column, for example, would show the Azure resource an action was taken on. The `SigninLogs.RiskLevelDuringSignIn` column would determine how risky the login was. In Chapter 2, you learned that the values for this risk can be High, Medium, or Low and are calculated by sophisticated Azure platform security algorithms for you. Consider the following KUSTO query and recall from Figure 9.10 the + New Alert Rule feature; you see it also in Figure 9.16. That feature will allow you to configure an alert when the specified query retrieves a specific number of results in a given timeframe.

```
SigninLogs
| where RiskLevelDuringSignIn == "High"
```

FIGURE 9.16   Log Analytics altering

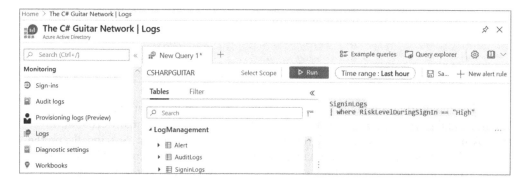

There are many options for creating queries and setting alerts based on their findings. It is only a matter of your requirements, your creativity, and the cost. Keep in mind that these alerts will cost, because some compute power is required to execute and analyze the result on your behalf. From a role-based access control (RBAC) perspective, the best way to monitor that is by selecting the Activity Log navigation menu item. For example, click the Activity Log navigation on a resource group, a specific Azure service, or at the Azure subscriptions level to get the report of what happened at each of those levels. Add a filter to the log and look for the following operations:

- Creating A Role Assignment
- Deleting A Role Assignment
- Creating Or Updating A Custom Role Definition
- Deleting A Custom Role Definition

Figure 9.17 shows the output of such a query using the activity log feature for an Azure subscription. You can click the results and filter down into the details of the log. You will also notice the Logs link, which will open the Log Analytics workspace console where you can pull the same information using KQL queries.

FIGURE 9.17 RBAC activity log in the Azure Portal

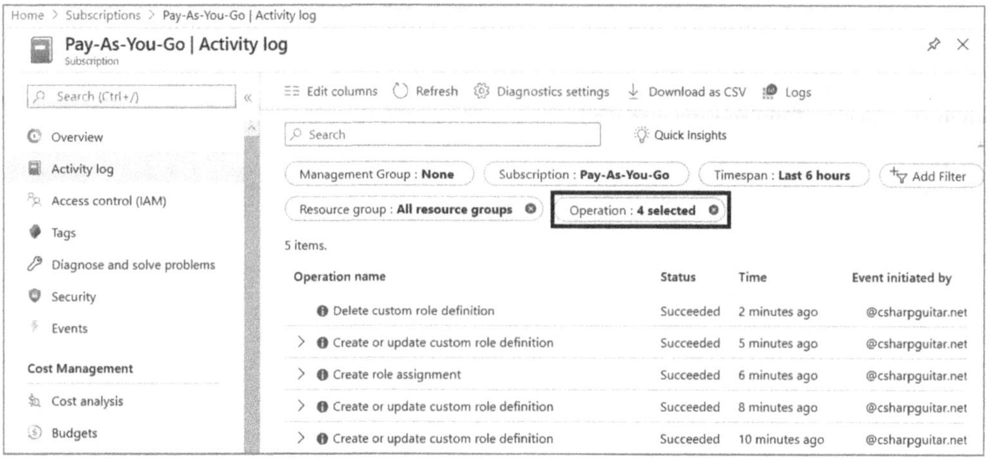

The last monitoring component for security has a focus on your Azure products, resources, and platform. You know about Security Center, which has many capabilities for looking after your workloads and resource in your Azure footprint. Specifically, on the Security Center blade, you will see a navigation menu item named Security Alerts under the Threat Protection header. Click this to see occurrences where the platform has identified suspicious behaviors, for example, the identification of accesses from an unknown location or IP address range. There is also a platform feature named Azure Sentinel that was introduced in Chapter 2 and more in Chapter 6. Azure Sentinel is a *security information and event management (SIEM)* security system that utilizes artificial intelligence to monitor the platform for activities matching known malicious behaviors.

Monitoring Network

With both IaaS and PaaS, the networking aspects of your IT department have been outsourced once you are running on Azure. Therefore, you need not worry too much about that, that is, until you start getting some latency issues and have reviewed everything else and haven't found the reason. If that is the case, a go-to tool is Network Watcher. With Network Watcher you can diagnose VM routing problems and log VM network traffic. You performed an exercise in Chapter 3, Exercise 3.1, where you utilized Network Watcher. In that exercise, you worked with it via Azure PowerShell, but there is also a rich set of capabilities available in the Azure Portal. Take a look at Figure 3.48 where you see how Network Watcher rendered a topology of your network. On the Network Monitor blade, you will find a link in the navigation menu called Connection Monitor. This feature will provide you with the means for monitoring connectivity and latency metrics between two Azure VMs, as well as track any changes to the network topology. You will find numerous additional troubleshooting tools in the Network Monitor navigation menu.

There is also a nice feature that hasn't been discussed up until now. It's called Metrics, which you will find on the Azure Monitor blade; see Figure 9.18. In my pursuit to find more options for monitoring networking and the connectivity between machines, I found this web page: docs.microsoft.com/en-us/azure/azure-monitor/platform/ metrics-supported. It describes all the supported metrics based on resource provider; see Table 8.4 as well as a refresher on the products covered in this book. The resource provider of interest is Microsoft.Network/*.

FIGURE 9.18   Azure Monitor metrics

As you see in Figure 9.18, Microsoft.Network/networkInterfaces and Microsoft .Network/networkWatchers are added to the metric. Table 9.4 shows the metrics available for each.

TABLE 9.4   Networking Azure Monitor metrics

Network Interfaces	Network Watcher
Bytes Received	% Probes Failed
Bytes Sent	Avg. Round-trip Time (ms)
Packets Received	Checks Failed Percent
Packets Sent	Round-Trip Time (ms)

There exists a lot of information to capture, store, and analyze your Azure products. You will need to spend some time on this to find the reports and products that provide the information required to answer the questions you are being asked or are asking yourself. Interpreting the data into an actionable set of tasks comes with experiences not only with the technology but with the product that you are analyzing. All applications have their own unique behaviors that can only be learned over time while working with them.

There is one more networking appliance that needs to be covered in this section, and it is the WAF/Application Gateway. In many scenarios, this is the entry point into your internet-accessible Azure workloads. The endpoint is globally accessible and therefore likely needs some additional monitoring. Be certain that if you have configured Security Center and/or Azure Sentinel that you get malicious behavior notifications and preventative tips/actions by default. If for some reason those features are too costly, you can monitor some Application Gateway behaviors using the Azure Monitor metrics. As you saw in Figure 9.18 and earlier, there is a link, + New Alert Rule, on the Metrics blade. Once you identify a baseline that describes the normal behavior for your appliance, if there is something that exists outside of this normalcy, then you can be alerted or send alerts to the team, which should take the action.

Monitoring Compute

The Monitoring component is where I think you will spend most of your time configuring, optimizing, and analyzing metrics. This is where your application is running and is the location where your customers, users, clients, or employees will report as the source of the problem. Not only is it important to have the metrics configured, alerts created, and your IT support team notified, it is crucial to have actions in place to respond to those alerts and take actions when they occur. When designing a monitoring solution for Azure compute, it would be a good approach to categorize compute into the following cloud service models. These models were introduced in Chapter 4; see also Figure 4.1 as a refresher.

- **IaaS:** Azure Virtual Machines
- **CaaS:** AKS and ACI
- **PaaS:** Azure App Services
- **FaaS:** Azure Functions

Azure Virtual Machines, as you may have noticed, is the odd one out when it comes to the available features for monitoring. When I say odd, I really mean best. As you learned in Exercise 9.1 versus what you have seen when configuring other Azure resources in Azure Monitor, Azure Virtual Machines works a little different. This is mostly because of legacy technology; Azure Virtual Machines was the first product offering Azure had, and many customers are dependent on how it currently runs, so making a change to how they operate and log metrics isn't to be taken lightly. However, over time the Azure team has learned some lessons and identified opportunities for optimization and simplifications and then made enhancements based on those findings. Some of those enchantments cannot be added to Azure VM metrics due to compatibilities, which is the reason for the differences.

The monitoring features I refer to are the following and have already been covered in great detail throughout this book:

- Update management (Figure 8.44)
- Change tracking (Figure 6.14)
- Configuration management
- Inventory
- Security Center: Compute & Apps (Figure 6.13)

For the other Azure compute products, the monitoring capabilities exist as shown in Figure 9.13 and listed here:

- Insights aka Application Insights
- Metrics
- Logs
- Diagnostic settings
- Alerts

In addition, do not forget about Azure Automation runbooks, which can be used to monitor not only Azure compute but most anything imaginable. Take a look at Figure 9.19, which illustrates the search results for Process Automation Runbooks, filtered where an associated tag equals Monitor. You can reuse them or modify them a bit to meet exactly what you want to monitor.

FIGURE 9.19   Azure Automation Monitor runbook templates

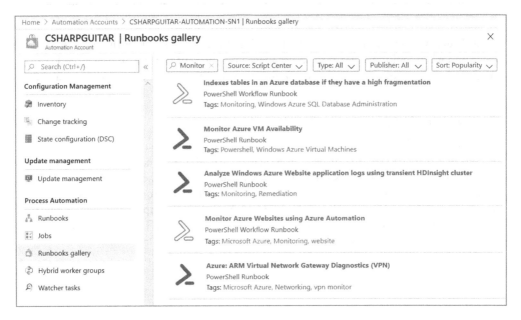

When configuring the Metrics feature for Azure App Services and Azure Functions, you will find them to be similar, especially when the Azure Functions trigger is from HTTP. Find some examples of metrics for the `Microsoft.Web/sites` resource provider in Table 9.5.

TABLE 9.5 Azure App Service and Azure Functions Metrics

Azure App Service	Azure Function
Http5xx	Http5xx
MemoryWorkingSet	MemoryWorkingSet
Gen0-2Collections	Gen0-2Collections
HealthCheckStatus	Health check status
Requests	FunctionExecutionUnit
ResponseTime	FunctionExecutionCount
Handles	RequestsInApplicationQueue
Threads	FileSystemUsage
CurrentAssemblies	CurrentAssemblies

For Azure App Service metrics, you will find that they have much of the same details you would find when looking at IIS web server logs. There is a lot of information stored that can give you a good overview of what is going on with that product and, in some cases, the application.

Monitoring Data

Monitoring your data store has a lot to do with the cloud model on which it is hosted and the kind of DBMS. If you're running a SQL Server virtual machine, then you would want to make a hybrid monitoring solution using what you learned in the previous compute section combined with stand-alone SQL Server metrics. If the data store is an Azure SQL or Azure Cosmos DB, then you can use the common monitoring components such as Metrics, Diagnostic settings, and Logs (i.e., Log Analytics). Take a look at Table 9.6, which summarizes the metrics available for Azure SQL and Azure Cosmos DB data stores.

TABLE 9.6   Azure SQL and Azure Cosmos DB Metrics

Azure SQL	Azure Cosmos DB
allocated_data_storage	DataUsage
blocked_by_firewall	DocumentCount
connection_failed	DocumentQuota
connection_successful	IndexUsage
cpu_percent	RegionFailover
deadlock	ReplicationLatency
dtu_consumption_percent	ServiceAvailability
dtu_used	TotalRequests
storage_used	UpdateAccountKeys

The Azure Cosmos DB has a nice graphical representation of the metrics in the portal, as shown in Figure 9.20.

FIGURE 9.20   Azure Cosmos DB metrics

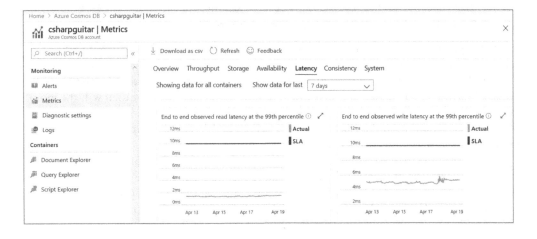

Notice the tabs across the top of the Metrics blade: Overview, Throughput, Storage, Availability, Latency, Consistency, and System. Those metrics and their visualization should give you a good overview of what is going on with your Azure Cosmos DB. From an Azure SQL perspective, you will find similar metrics and diagnostics. What I want to follow up on here is the exercise that you performed in Chapter 6, which had to do with setting sensitivity levels on specific columns on a database table. Take a look back at Exercise 6.3 and view Figure 6.11, which may help you remember. You might take a moment and execute this Azure PowerShell cmdlet to confirm you have settings like this on an Azure SQL table and to see what the settings are. The output would resemble something similar to that shown in Figure 9.21.

FIGURE 9.21   Azure SQL sensitivity level

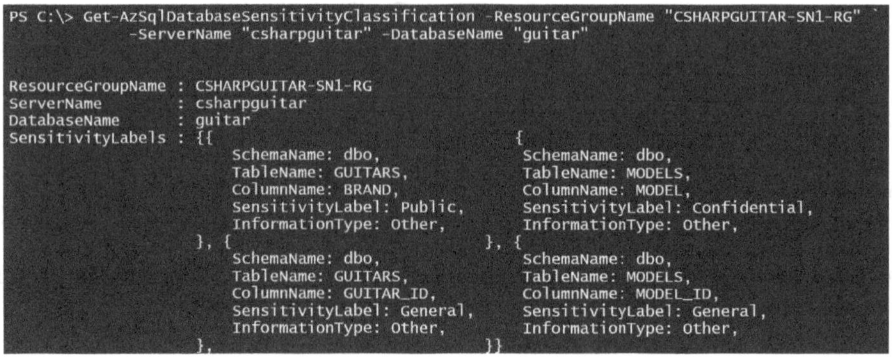

```
PS C:\> Get-AzSqlDatabaseSensitivityClassification -ResourceGroupName "CSHARPGUITAR-SN1-RG" `
        -ServerName "csharpguitar" -DatabaseName "guitar"


ResourceGroupName : CSHARPGUITAR-SN1-RG
ServerName        : csharpguitar
DatabaseName      : guitar
SensitivityLabels : {{
                        SchemaName: dbo,                  {
                        TableName: GUITARS,                  SchemaName: dbo,
                        ColumnName: BRAND,                   TableName: MODELS,
                        SensitivityLabel: Public,            ColumnName: MODEL,
                        InformationType: Other,              SensitivityLabel: Confidential,
                    }, {                                     InformationType: Other,
                        SchemaName: dbo,              }, {
                        TableName: GUITARS,                  SchemaName: dbo,
                        ColumnName: GUITAR_ID,               TableName: MODELS,
                        SensitivityLabel: General,           ColumnName: MODEL_ID,
                        InformationType: Other,              SensitivityLabel: General,
                    },                                       InformationType: Other,
                                                      }}
```

```
Get-AzSqlDatabaseSensitivityClassification -ResourceGroupName "<rgName>" `
    -ServerName "<sName>" -DatabaseName "<dName>"
```

That is great, but what about monitoring who is accessing it and how often it gets accessed. This can be monitored by using the Auditing feature for the Azure SQL database. You will find this feature in the portal on the Azure SQL database blade under the Security header. It is disabled by default, and you will first need to enable it; only then will the monitoring of the access be logged. Once enabled, notice a menu item named View Audit Log at the top of the Auditing blade. Click it and then click the View dashboard link, and you will be presented with an overview, as illustrated in Figure 9.22.

When you compare the settings in Figure 9.21 and in Figure 9.22, you will get an understanding of how they fit together. To create that report and generate the audit logs, I ran a SELECT query numerous times against the MODEL table on the guitar database. To get more access details, click the Azure SQL – Access to Sensitive Data metric, as shown in Figure 9.22. You will find information about who performed the query and from which client; see Figure 9.23. There are certainly ways to find out which columns and tables the queries were accessing using KQL on Log Analytics too. Which database, table, and query that are running are important pieces of information, but they are apparently not part of the default reporting feature. Instead, only the numbers of times access to tables and columns with this type of status are provided, i.e., not the table and column names specifically. However, you can get them manually using Log Analytics and KQL and then export the result as CSV and create your own reports in Power BI or Excel.

FIGURE 9.22   Azure SQL sensitivity-level overview

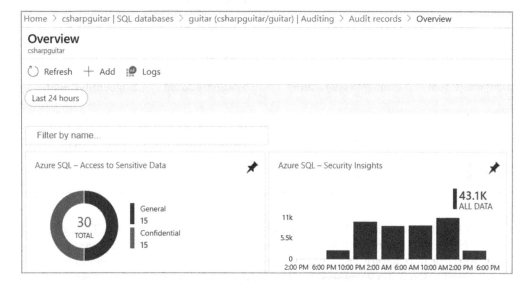

FIGURE 9.23   Azure SQL sensitivity level who, how often, and from where

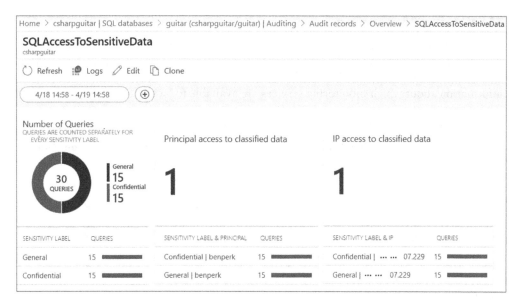

There are also many metrics for data storage products such as Azure Blob containers, Azure Queues, Azure Files, and Azure Tables; see Table 9.7 for a summarized list of existing, helpful metrics for monitoring Azure storage.

TABLE 9.7   Blob, Queue, and Table Storage Metrics

Azure Blob	Azure Queue	Azure Files	Azure Table
BlobCapacity	QueueCapacity	FileCapacity	TableCapacity
BlobCount	QueueCount	FileCount	TableCount
ContainerCount	QueueMessageCount	FileShareCount	TableEntityCount
Transactions	Transactions	Transactions	Transactions
Ingress/Egress	Ingress/Egress	Ingress/Egress	Ingress/Egress
Availability	Availability	Availability	Availability

Don't forget about Storage Explorer, which was introduced in Chapter 5. Take a look back at Figure 5.10 and read about that product more there. Those tools give you some good overview and monitoring capabilities. Additionally, activity logs are helpful for data storage products and show you specifically which actions have recently been taken on the configuration of the specific Azure storage product. You will find the Activity Logs navigation menu item on all Azure product blades in the Azure Portal.

Monitoring Messaging

As you learned in Chapter 6, there are four Azure messaging services: Event Hub, Service Bus, Azure Storage Queue, and Event Grid. The common monitoring features are found for each of the messaging services on their respective Azure Portal blade. See Table 9.8 for information about which monitoring services are available for which messaging service.

TABLE 9.8   Azure Messaging Monitoring Support

Monitor	Event Hub	Service Bus	Storage Queue	Event Grid
Alerts	✓	✓	✓	✓
Metrics	✓	✓	✓	✓
Diagnostic settings	✓	✓	×	✓
Logs	✓	✓	×	✓
Insights	×	×	✓	×

An important aspect to consider with those Azure products is at which level you want to monitor. Event Hubs and Service Buses have a namespace into which you place hubs for Event Hubs and queues or topics for a Service Bus. An Azure Storage Queue exists within a storage account, and an Event Grid can contain one or more topics existing within an Event Grid domain. You would probably like to have some monitoring metrics on the applicable namespace, account, or domain and the part of the product that is receiving and managing the events or messages. This is something you need to take specific actions to differentiate and configure. You should again look at the available metrics here to determine which specific logs you need:

`docs.microsoft.com/en-us/azure/azure-monitor/platform/`
`metrics-supported`

As you see in Figure 9.24, there are some metrics available on the Overview blade for each of the messaging services by default.

FIGURE 9.24   Azure Messaging metrics examples

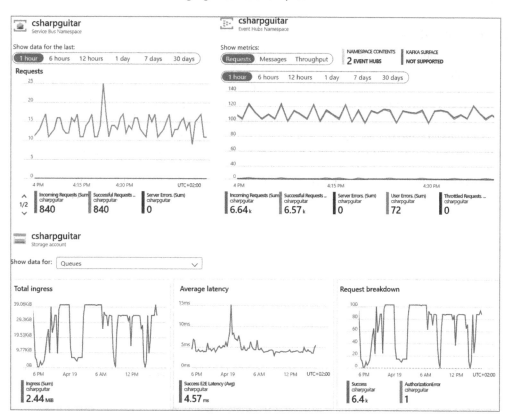

Monitoring Compliance

Once you have implemented your compliance and governance rules, the whole idea behind it is monitoring those rules and making sure people and IT systems adhere to the rules. In Chapter 6, you were introduced to Azure Policy and saw in Figure 6.3 that the entire Policy Overview blade is dedicated to showing you the status of the policies that you have created and applied. You also learned that when you are not in compliance that the Azure Policy feature will provide you some tips that define some steps to help you become compliant. There also exists some details and metrics, in regard to policy and compliance within Security Center. Take a look back at Figure 2.49 and Figure 6.9, which show metrics concerning regulatory compliance.

Additional Monitoring Topics

You can monitor numerous additional areas. In this section, you'll find a short summary of monitoring deployments and how tags and labels contribute to a better monitoring experience.

Deployment Logs

If you ever wanted to get an overview of the deployments that are happening within your subscription, there are two places to look. This is not concerning the monitoring of application code deployments that was discussed in Chapter 7, rather, deployments of and to Azure products, features, and services. One interesting point is checking the deployments that happen within a resource group. As you can see in Figure 9.25, there is a header named Deployments that exists on the resource group's Overview blade. Beneath the header there is a link that shows the number of failed and successful deployments.

FIGURE 9.25   A view of deployment status from the Azure Portal

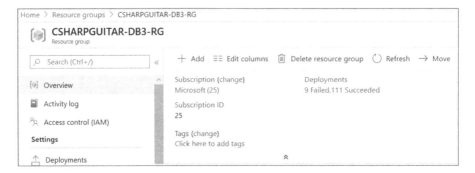

If you click the link, you will get the details of each deployment. There is also a navigation menu item named Deployments, also shown in Figure 9.25, which will direct you to

the same list of failed or successful deployment details. The activity log will show you all operations that have taken place in the select context for the selected timeframe. Context means, for example, that a resource group and timeframe is perhaps the previous six hours. The same list of operations can also be run in the subscription context where you would get a wider view on what has taken place.

Tags and Labels

Both tags and labels were introduced in Chapter 6 and are helpful from a monitoring perspective. They are helpful simply because tags and labels provide an extra queryable attribute to the metrics or logs that your Azure product, features, or your software applications generate. From a tag perspective, the example used in Chapter 6 had to do with identifying Azure resources by environment where the product could be production, testing, or development. Someone who has hands-on and real-time engagement with a specific application would likely know which servers and which Azure products are the production ones and which are not. It is common to place the environment of a server into its name; for example, naming an Azure VM as CSHARPGUITAR-PRO or CSHARPGUITAR-DEV would help identify them. However, what happens if you failover or the role of the server changes? Then this approach isn't so appealing. Having these tags are helpful for newcomers or people who are not actively engaged in the project to get some understanding of the environments quickly and safely. The labeling concept has to do with setting sensitivity levels of data or the management of documents that can or should be shared only with certain groups of people. You have been shown how to audit these kinds of elements that can help you remain in control and, of course, govern your Azure workloads and IT solutions and remain compliant with regulations.

That is all for monitoring. The most important takeaway is that you know what Azure Monitor, Log Analytics, and Application Insights are and with which use cases you would use them. It's now time to move onto the final section of this book.

Recover Azure Resources

If you reflect back a bit in your IT career up to now or perhaps to a time in your studies, you may remember losing a file. Perhaps it was a picture, a document, or a research paper that you didn't save for a while and your PC locked up. Either way, I think we have all had those moments. These are moments where you think, why didn't I back that up or why didn't I save more often? After some time, in most cases, you forget about it and recover from it, but did you really take any action to prevent it from happening again? Probably not. It is likely you rewrote what you lost, and, over time, you simply moved on. The unfortunate reality is that this behavior is often carried over into the professional IT industry; however, the impact is much greater, and the ability to simply move on is in some cases not possible. What does a company move on from if it has lost its data and source code? Starting over is not an option when there are high costs and multiple people or organizations involved in doing so.

To avoid losing business IT data or applications, you need to have backups, redundancies, and disaster recovery plans. Running a company without having those three DR aspects embedded into the culture of the IT organization is a great risk. Azure provides products and features that help customers to design, test, implement, and maintain BCDR solutions. Azure Backup and Azure Site Recovery (ASR) were introduced in Chapter 1, so take a look over them again; both are covered again later as well. This section isn't the first time you would have read about BCDR; there are discussions in Chapter 3, Chapter 5, Chapter 6, and numerous other places in the book. Don't overlook this important aspect of IT and read further to learn more about the product and features Microsoft Azure provides for helping customers prevent catastrophic events that can destroy your business.

What Is BCDR?

When there is a disruption in your IT systems that impact your business operations, you need to have a plan of what to do, by implementing a business continuity and disaster recovery (BCDR) plan. The first step is to identify what constitutes as a disruption. Is it a disruption caused by a transient issue, is it an outage that might take several minutes or hours to resolve, or does it look like there will be some long-term downtime? The first step is to have good monitoring, so you know what is really going on and then define the metrics that determine when to activate your BCDR plan. Once the metrics are clarified and the thresholds breached, you then execute the plan that can include changing routing on Azure Front Door, using Azure Traffic Manager (ATM), or making a DNS change to route a web address to a new IP address. It is also possible to failover to a replica of your production environment into a different region. There are many scenarios, and each plan needs to be described in detail based on the application requirement and maintained with ongoing updates to reflect any changes in the application architecture and behavior. Finally, once you have executed the failover and all is well, you need to determine whether you will now run your business in this state or whether you will work on getting the previous production back up and functional and then reroute your customers or employees back to it. There is so much work, stress, and complexities in those previous words having to do with the actual execution of a BCDR plan. Anyone who has ever been in that situation knows this; without a plan it is worse and very chaotic, but read through the remaining sections, and you will get some tips on how to make a situation like this more tolerable. Let's start with a closer look into business continuity specifically.

Business Continuity

Scenarios where you need these kinds of procedures are usually intense and complicated. They are complicated because in most cases no one has actually ever executed a BCDR process and the risks are high. The best way to uncomplicate any scenario is to break it down into smaller pieces and then learn and execute them one after the other. The concept of business continuity has to do not only with IT continuity, but as the name implies, it describes how the business will operate if there is a disruption and isn't necessarily a technical aspect. Consider that your company works with partners that place orders for your product and the internet portal for them to do this is down. Is it possible to increase human resources in a call center to manually take these orders on paper and then enter them into the system later when it is back up? Another aspect would be to find out how long this business continuity process can exist before you need to activate your disaster recovery plan. How much impact the outage has on your business and how long it can remain in this state define the time when you begin to perform configurations on your production environment to route customers and employees to another instance of your application. Ideally, you have this environment and the plan to use it; otherwise, it's too late to build one when you are in crisis mode. Not having a plan is risky and would reflect badly on the IT organization if one is required and found not to exist.

Disaster Recovery

This portion of the BCDR plan is focused on the IT aspects and is much more low level. It starts when the thresholds that define an IT disruption are breached and means it's time to execute the plan. There is no going back from this point; making a decision like this is a huge risk because you most likely don't know if what you're about to do will be successful. Your IT organization has likely spent years if not decades getting the solution to work as it does now on its current environment, and you are now going to attempt to replicate that environment over the next few hours. These references are coming from a historical perspective driven by on-premise or private data center scenarios. In those days the IT solutions were run on expensive trademarked hardware, and having a duplicate of production sitting idle was a conversation that couldn't get started; it was simply too expensive. However, in the cloud, where you can configure a disaster recovery (DR) environment and not use it, at a reasonable cost, changes the landscape a lot. Remember in the cloud you are charged only when the product or feature is consumed. Having a DR environment in the cloud has opened the DR conversation channel and resolves the main stopping point for having a BCDR plan, i.e., the cost. But you still need to plan; the plan needs to include thresholds, and the plan needs to be tested and maintained as required. The following section will provide you with some means for creating, testing, and executing the BCDR plan if ever you are required to do so.

Azure Recovery Services

The remainder of this chapter will cover some Azure products and features that are helpful with creating, testing, and executing a BCDR plan. The design part is too application-specific, so that part will need to be done on a case-by-case basis. Some topics you might need to design, just for an example, are having a clear overview of what Azure resources you have that make up your IT solution. This is one area that has been pushed in many places throughout the book in regard to resource groups and tags, both of which are a useful feature for grouping together Azure resources that make up your IT solution. Once you know what you have, you need to determine whether you will create an exact replica of the environment or only parts of it. Remember one example in the previous chapter called out that you can export an ARM template that contains all of your Azure resources for a given resource group. That would only contain the provisioning piece of the Azure footprint, but it could be a start. If you decide to re-provision the same workloads in another region, then using the ARM template might be an option. It wouldn't be recommended to attempt to deploy using the template while you are actually executing the BCDR plan. That approach would need to be completed beforehand because after provisioning you would then need to make configurations to the new platform. That's too much work to do in crisis mode.

If you only need to failover specific pieces of an application, then you need to identify them and make a plan to do so. Azure Traffic Manager (ATM) can do this for you automatically if you configure it to do so. For example, if one of your web servers becomes unhealthy, ATM will stop sending traffic to it, and if you have other web servers in other regions configured as failover, then you would experience only a transient outage. The same goes for your data stores such as Azure SQL, Azure Cosmos DB, or a SQL Server virtual machine. Each of those would have a different BCDR plan. The plan wouldn't only cover how to get the database back up and accessible but also how to make sure all the clients that connect to it are updated or notified of the new connection requirements. The next sections begin with a discussion concerning how you can capture an overview of what you have running on Azure. Ideally, you have those pieces organized in a way that make this easy. Then you will learn about backups that, if you make them, will get you into a position to recover from an incident that triggered the BCDR plan. Finally, you will perform some tasks that simulate a failover that would be one of the actions taken in a real-world BCDR recovery plan creation. The last section in this chapter will give some details about specific recovery options per Azure product, similar to what was provided for monitoring previously in this chapter.

Azure Resource Graph

This Azure feature is helpful for determining what you currently have provisioned and running on the Azure platform. There is a tool named Azure Resource Graph Explorer where you can execute KUSTO queries (KQL) to gather information about your resources. As shown in Figure 9.26, a query can be executed to find all the resources that have a tag named Environment that is equal to Production.

You can also query for the same output as seen in Figure 9.26 using Azure CLI and the following command:

```
az graph query -q "Resources | where tags.Environment=~'Production' `
| project name, type, location"
```

Once you get all the Azure resources you need in order to have a complete replica of your production environment, then you need to decide which ones you will include in the BCDR plan. Once that's decided, go through them all and make sure you know the schedules and the locations for all their backups. Take a look at the Azure Backup feature that can help you manage backups of your provisioned Azure resources.

FIGURE 9.26   Azure Resource Graph Explorer KQL query

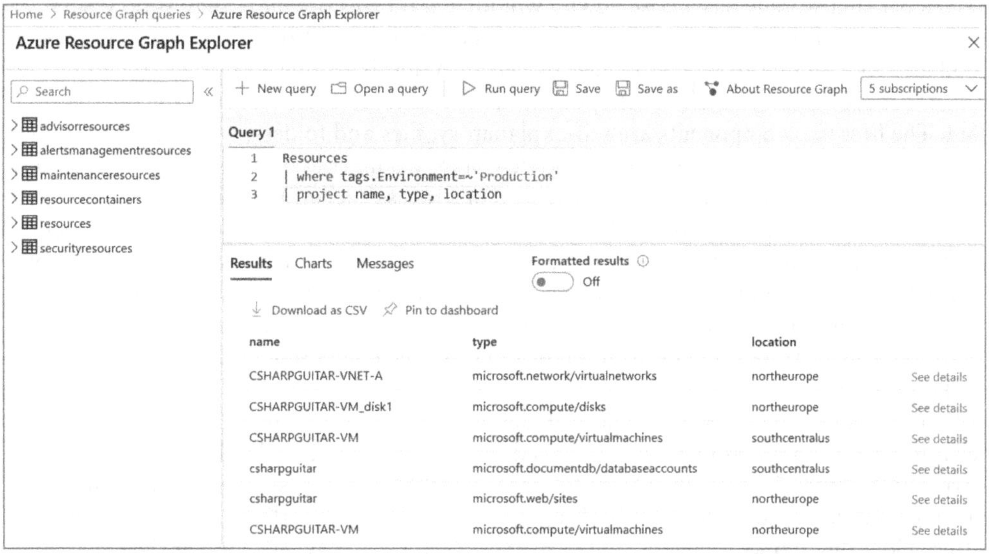

Azure Backup

Before you can recover from data loss, a server crash, or an all-out disaster, you must have something to recover from. You typically use a backup to recover from an incident where you have lost data or a server. Azure Backup is the tool you should choose for capturing backups for Azure VMs, Azure Files, and SQL Server virtual machine. Some details about creating backups have been covered in previous chapters, such as Chapter 4 for Azure VMs and Chapter 5 for data stores. Take a look at those chapters as a refresher in case you are jumping straight to this section and want more information. For this section, the following topics are discussed from an Azure platform perspective:

- Description of a backup
- How backups work on Azure
- Storing and managing backups
- Backing up other products
- Linux versus Windows backups

Like many other activities that are required to run a successful IT organization, making backups is a complicated endeavor. There is nothing simple about taking, managing, and restoring a system from a backup. You first begin by determining which specific servers you need to back up, as discussed previously. After that, you need to determine whether everything on that server is required to be backed up.

Description of a Backup

Remember that storage has a cost, so you wouldn't want to store more than is necessary. Storage is not one of the more expensive products available on Azure; however, it is never a good idea to spend more than you must. When an Azure Backup is performed on an Azure VM, the most common updated components are the files, folders, system state, and app data. The first two components are self-explanatory, files and folders, which is what you see in Windows Explorer, for example. The system state would contain the registry, which may contain custom settings, environment settings, or process execution paths. You would agree that many applications have dependencies on other assemblies that are located in a specific location. Those configurations are considered the state of the system and are backed up by default when you configure Azure Backup. App data is commonly used for local temporary storage and to store application-specific information. For example, if the application needs to parse a file, that file needs to be stored someplace temporary while the process works with it.

From a data store perspective, like SQL Server, the Azure VM on which it is running needs to be backed up, as just discussed, as does the database. The database itself, as you learned in Chapter 5, is simply a large file that the DBMS manages access to. Therefore, backing up a database is all about backing up a file and any specialized database configuration. How that works is covered in the next section; right now let's look at the different types of backup, which are provided in Table 9.9.

TABLE 9.9   Azure Backup Types

Backup Type	Azure Product	Description
Full	VM/SQL	A complete backup of the entire source
Incremental	VM	A backup of changes since last backup
Differential	SQL	A backup of changes since last backup
Transactional	SQL	A log which enabled PITR restoration

The difference between an incremental and differential backup is that a differential backup requires a full backup to perform a restore, because unchanged data is not included. When a differential backup is performed, only the data that has been modified is backed up. A differential backup decreases the storage requirements, network consumption, and time required to perform the backup, when compared to the other Azure Backup types. It is supported to perform a full data backup every day; however, you need to determine whether it is required in your scenario. Keep in mind, again, that storage has an associated cost, and if you have a 5GB database that you back up each day, the cost, like the amount of required storage space, could get big, fast. Watch out for that and make sure you optimize what and how often you back up. As you may recall point-in-time restore (PITR) from Chapter 5; see Figure 5.48, which is where you were exposed to this concept. PITR allows you to recover a database to its state up to a specific second. In contrast, an incremental or differential backup supports either daily or weekly schedules, meaning you could lose a day's worth of data without transactional backups. Can you live with that? Is it worth the cost? Those are questions you need to decide based on the criticality of the data and the impact its loss would have on your company.

How Backups Work on Azure?

Azure Backup relies on a number of different Azure products and services to perform a backup. The simplest way to back up an Azure VM or a SQL Server virtual machine is to utilize the Azure Backup extension, which is installed into the Azure VM agent running on the VM. After configuring Azure Backup for your VM, as you will do in Exercise 9.3, when you navigate to the Extensions blade in the Azure Portal for the VM, you will see the Microsoft Monitoring Agent installed; this is previously referred to as the agent.

In the previous chapter, you learned that *Microsoft Azure Recovery Services (MARS)* can be useful for deploying workloads to the Azure platform. The same is true for performing backups; take a look back at Figure 1.8 also, which illustrates the use of MARS for backing up both on-premise and Azure VMs and storing them on Azure. *Microsoft Azure Backup Server (MARS)* and *System Center Data Protection Manager (DPM)* are useful tools for backing up on-premise VMs to Azure. Both MARS and DPM require installation and configuration of server software and either the provisioning of an Azure VM or an on-premise machine to run the server software. If you currently have a DPM license, then you or your company would already have the skillset required to perform those kinds of backups. In the case where you already have DPM, you would need to change the location where you store the backup to be on the Azure platform. If you do not have a DPM license, then you can use MARS for achieving the same backup capabilities as DPM. The benefit of DPM is that it is part of the System Center suite of tools. To learn more about System Center, read this page: www.microsoft.com/en-us/system-center.

Another option for performing backups and restores is to use an Azure Automation script. Azure Automation was discussed in the previous chapter. Scripting your backup activities would increase the scope of VMs you could maintain all at once and reduce the complexity and the chance of making any mistakes. In Exercise 9.3, you will configure a backup for an Azure VM; the configuration is performed on a single VM. If you have many Azure VMs and/or a SQL Server virtual machine that needs to be backed up, doing this one at a time wouldn't be feasible. Instead, you could script the backup process using a PowerShell script executed with Azure Automation. Complete Exercise 9.3 to learn how to configure an Azure Backup for an Azure virtual machine.

EXERCISE 9.3

Configuring Azure Backup for an Azure VM

1. Log in to the Azure Portal at portal.azure.com.

2. Navigate to one of the Azure virtual machines that you have created in a previous exercise or create a new one. Make sure the VM is running, click the Backup link from the navigation menu, click the Create New radio button, enter a name, enter the resource group into which you want the Recovery Service vault to be placed into, and click the Create (or Edit) A New Policy link under the Choose Backup Policy drop-down list.

3. Enter a policy name; configure the Backup schedule by choosing a frequency, time, and time zone; click the OK button; and click the Enable Backup button.

In the exercise, one of the steps required to configure Azure Backup was the creation of a backup policy. It contained three components: the backup schedule, snapshot recovery, and retention ranges. The backup schedule defines the frequency (daily or weekly), time, and time zone for which a backup is taken. As you may recall from Chapter 4, a *snapshot* is a copy of a disk that is bound to the VM and can be used to build replicas or, in this case, recover from a server crash. A snapshot doesn't carry with it the configurations and environment settings as they are when a backup is performed using Azure Backup. The amount of time a backup must be retained may be driven by a compliance or governance requirement. If your scenario has no reliance on either of those, then you need to determine how far back it would make sense to recover to. The timeframes would be different based on usage and how often the configuration or data changes over a given timeframe. How often you back up and for how long you retain the backup are unique to your application's scenario. However, in my experience and without being bound by any compliance, legal, or governance constraint, I wouldn't consider recovering to a database state more than one to two weeks ago. There are many constraints and conditions you need to consider; take the time to figure out what works best in your scenario.

After a few backups have run from the Azure Backup configuration, you performed in Exercise 9.3, clicking the Backup link in the navigation menu will render something similar to that shown in Figure 9.27. You will see three states of restore points: Crash Consistent, Application Consistent, and File-System Consistent.

When taking a backup of a data store or a VM, the best state in which it can be in is off. From a data store perspective, off means that the database is not accessible, and from a VM perspective, it means no client is connecting to it, and there are no jobs or services running on it. If the service that you are backing up is in use when a backup is run, then attempting to back up a file that is being accessed can hang, which can result in only partial data being backed up or only some of the expected content/configuration being backed up. All of those scenarios would result in some issues if you attempted to restore using one of the partially successful backups. Unless you take preemptive actions to make sure that your services being backed up are "off" when the scheduled backup is run, then you need to expect and plan for some troubleshooting when you attempt to restore it. This is the reason and purpose of those three consistency status codes. The reason is that you know how good the backup is, which helps you determine the probability of success if they are used to recover from an outage or crash.

FIGURE 9.27   Azure VM configured Azure Backup

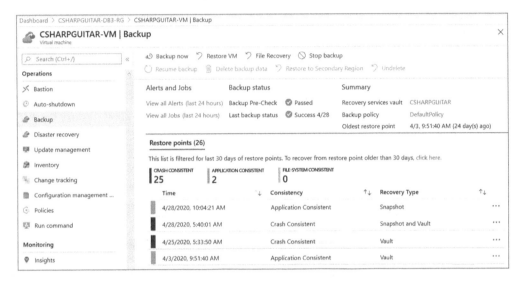

Crash consistent wouldn't be considered a good backup. It means that the backup ran when the VM is in a stopped or deallocated state. The VM needs to be running but "off" in order to get a good backup, where "off" means that there are no activities happening, no programs running, and no user is accessing anything on the VM.

You may be able to recover and boot from one of these backups, but if that is all you see on the Backup blade, consider running a backup manually to make sure you have at least one. Application Consistent is the status you want to see. This one means that the backup was successful, and all aspects of the backup were successful. Using a backup in this state for a restore would offer the highest probability of success. As you might expect then, File-System Consistent is between the two and means some or part of the backup failed. The reason for the failure can be caused by the VM not being "off" when the backup is executed. Not being "off" can cause issues like the ones mentioned earlier, one of which is a file, which is currently being accessed and is therefore locked and cannot be accessed by the backup process.

Storing and Managing Backups

When you configured Azure Backup for an Azure VM in Exercise 9.3, part of the configuration was the provisioning of an Azure Recovery Services Vault. A recovery vault was also called out in Chapter 8 and shown using Figure 8.4, which shows the Site Recovery dashboard, which is also discussed later. The dashboard of interest now is the one focused on the Backup tab and is illustrated with Figure 9.28.

FIGURE 9.28   Azure Backup, Azure Recovery Services Vault

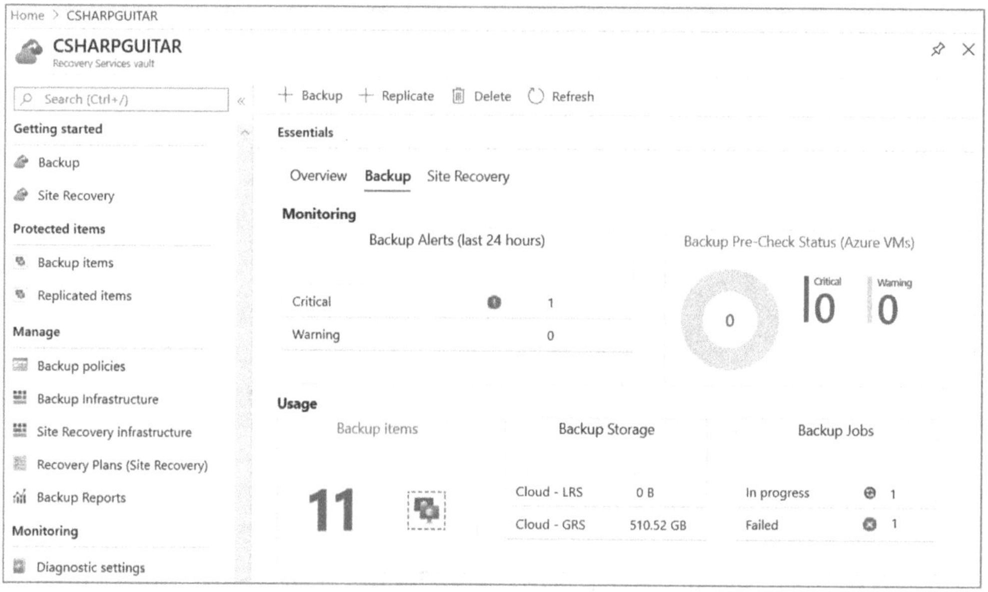

The Backup dashboard provides you with an overview of the current state of any Azure Backup that is in progress or in a failed state. It identifies how many backups have been performed and stored in the Recovery Services vault. If you were to click the Backup Items link in the Usage text block, near the number 11, you would be presented with a list of how many of each backup types have been performed. See Figure 9.29.

If you then click a specific backup management type, for example, Azure Virtual Machines, a detailed list of specific VMs that were backed up is provided. For example, you will see the VM name, the resource group in which is exists, and its status. One last detail from the Backup dashboard from Figure 9.28 is the Backup Storage text box. This shows how much storage your backups are consuming. Both LRS and GRS storage types should seem familiar. You learned in Chapter 5 about the different Azure Storage redundancy types. Based on that information shown on the Backup dashboard, you can conclude that your backups are stored as Azure Blobs in an Azure Blob Storage container and by default uses the GRS redundancy type. As a quick review, GRS means that your backup is backed up three times in your primary region and then again in a secondary region.

FIGURE 9.29   Azure Backup Items in Azure Recovery Services Vault

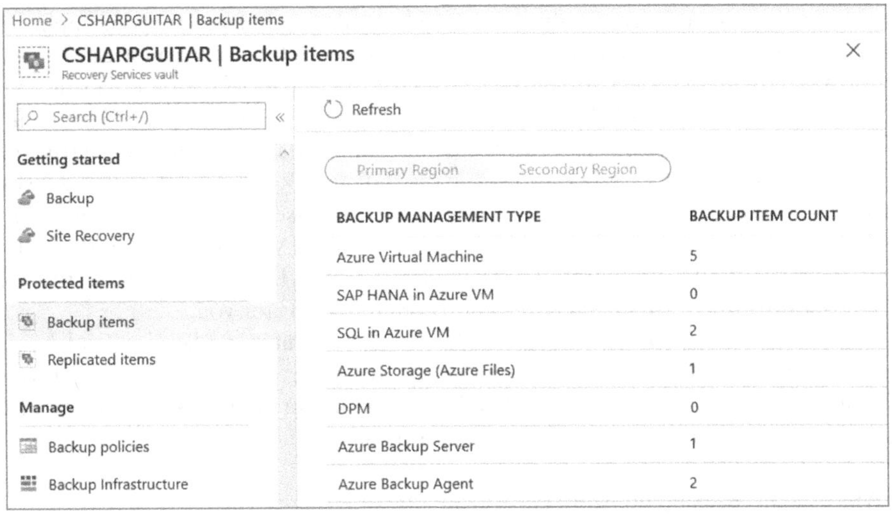

Now you know how Azure Backup works, it uses an agent running on the VM for VMs on Azure. You then configure a backup policy that defines the frequency and retention of the backup. Use MARS/DPM for backing up VMs to Azure that are running in an on-premise data center. When you configure either of those agents for backing up VMs, the backups are stored into an Azure Blob storage account. The Recovery Services vault is the location from which you can then monitor and manage your backups. From a management perspective, there are two points that are important to cover: security and management of the backups. From a security perspective, all data is encrypted in transit and at rest, which means there is no way for anyone, if they happen to get a copy of your backup, to use it. Backup data is sent over an HTTPS link, and when the backup is stored using the Recovery Service vault, it is stored encrypted. From a management perspective, if you no longer want to perform a backup, you can disable the backup by clicking Stop Backup, which exists on the Azure VM Backup blade, as shown earlier in Figure 9.27. When you click the Stop Backup button, you are asked if you want to retain or delete the backup data. If you choose to retain the data for some time and then want to delete it later, you can return to the Backup blade for the Azure VM and click the Delete Backup Data menu option, also shown in Figure 9.27. It is grayed out there because the backup is still enabled; however, when the backup is stopped, it will be enabled. Remember that your old backups are deleted automatically based on the retention settings you provided when creating the backup policy.

Backing Up Other Products

In the previous sections, you learned about backing up Azure VMs and SQL Server virtual machines, but what about other Azure products and features? The approach toward answering this question is greatly linked to the kind of cloud hosting service that you work with. Azure VMs are IaaS, and because you have taken responsibility for the platform, you are responsible for managing it, which includes backing it up. The same is not true when you run on a PaaS cloud hosting service such as Azure App Services, Azure Functions, Azure SQL, or Azure Cosmos DB. Your only concerns when running in PaaS are your application and your data, and therefore you only need to back up that. When you deploy an Azure App Service or Azure Function, their configurations are stored as part of the product offering and are backed up automatically by the platform. For example, if your application requires .NET Core binaries, if it allows HTTP or the name and value in an application setting connection string, basically any configurations you see in Figure 9.30 under the Setting header are stored and protected by the platform. This must be the case; since that configuration information is what's used to scale out additional instances of your application, they all need the same source code and configurations. The point is, unlike IaaS, PaaS provides the backing up of your operating system and application configurations for you.

There exists both backup and snapshot capabilities for Azure App Services and Azure Functions, as shown in Figure 9.30. Those will help you improve the speed at which your application could be recovered if required. When you configure the backup, you can also configure it to include any database that the application is connected to.

FIGURE 9.30 Backing up Azure PaaS products

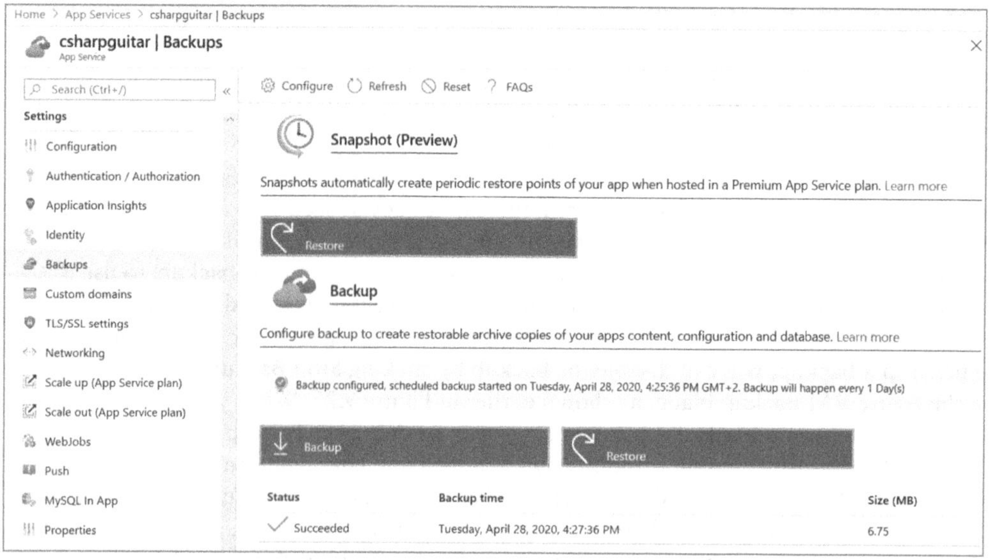

Like Azure Backup and the Recovery Services vault, an Azure App Service or Azure Functions backup is placed onto an Azure Blob Storage container. You select which one when you configure the backup by clicking the Configure menu link, also shown in Figure 9.30. Remember to be careful to store your content and code in a source code repository such as Azure DevOps or GitHub, for example. Because, as you know, there is a difference between the source code and the code that runs on a server. The difference is the one on the server is compiled and you cannot make bug fixes or code enhancements to it. I am just calling that out to make sure it is recognized; sometimes when people hear the word *backup*, they think it means everything is backed up, but there are many components that need to be backed up, as you have learned.

The way I see this PaaS backup process implemented is because it simplifies the backup of any associated database. This is good, but as you learned in Chapter 5, both Azure SQL and Azure Cosmos DB are backed up automatically for you. Therefore, the benefit of the backup feature for Azure App Services and Azure Functions comes mostly from the simplification of management by having a single point of entry into it. That means you can manage your PaaS and your backups (application and data) from the same set of Azure Portal blades. However, as your Azure consumption and footprint grow, so would the complexities of managing your backups. This would lead to a desire to have a greater overview of all your backups in a single location. That location is found within an Azure Recovery Services vault; this approach is for companies or individuals with smaller Azure footprints.

Linux vs. Windows Backup

When you are planning your backup strategy, you will need to know some details about what is supported and what is not. There are a number of differences between what is supported in regard to the operating system of the VM that you want to back up. Table 9.10 provides some details about what is and what is not supported when backing up Linux versus Windows operating systems. Performing Azure Backups on Linux requires that it is an endorsed or blessed version. This topic was discussed previously in Chapter 4, specifically on Table 4.5; also consider referring to docs.microsoft.com/en-us/azure/virtual-machines/linux/endorsed-distros, which lists the currently endorsed Linux distributions on Azure.

TABLE 9.10   Linux vs. Windows Azure Backups

Feature	Linux	Windows
32-bit operating system	×	✓
64-bit operating system	✓	✓
On-premise MARS	×	✓
On-premise MABS	✓	✓
On-premise DPM	✓	✓
Azure MARS	×	✓
Azure MABS	×	✓

TABLE 9.10   Linux vs. Windows Azure Backups *(continued)*

Feature	Linux	Windows
Azure DPM	✕	✓
File-system consistent is default	✓	✕
Application consistent is default	✕	✓

Microsoft Azure Recovery Services (MARS) is supported only on Windows machines, and therefore you can by default exclude that tool when you are discussing machines running Linux. If you need to back up one of the endorsed versions of Linux that is running in an on-premise data center to Azure, then you would choose either Microsoft Azure Backup Server (MABS) or Data Protection Manager (DPM). However, neither MABS nor DPM can be used to back up an Azure VM running Linux, rather, only on-premise. Using Azure Backup will work; take note that for Linux the default restore point status is File-System Consistent. Microsoft does provide customers running Linux with an option to configure Azure Backup so that application-consistent restore points are captured. For more information about that, read docs.microsoft.com/en-us/azure/backup/backup-azure-linux-app-consistent.

The ability to capture application-consistent restore points boils down to the Microsoft feature used to take such a backup. That feature is a Windows Server service named *Volume Shadow Copy Service (VSS)*, which is supported only on Windows. From a Linux perspective, you will need to have Python installed and utilize a feature named fsFreeze. You can find more information about those two services provided here:

- **VSS:** docs.microsoft.com/en-us/windows-server/storage/file-server/volume-shadow-copy-service

- **fsFreeze:** github.com/Azure/azure-linux-extensions/tree/master/VMBackup

In addition to different backup support between Linux and Windows operating systems, like other Azure products, there are limitations that exist for Azure Backups in general. Table 9.11 provides some details about them pertaining to both Linux and Windows. Remember that in most cases, default limits are in place to protect you from unknowingly triggering a task that attempts to consume infinite resources that result in astronomical charge. If you need more, open a support case with Microsoft, and they will surely increase the limit for you.

The default limitations are generous with supporting the backup of 500,000 machines per subscription. That would be a lot of machines and a rare scenario for any company to run up against that, but never say never. If you quickly did the math for the Azure App Service entry and calculated that if backups are limited to once per hour, then the maximum could only be 24, so why is 50 supported? First, the ability to do backups on an Azure

App Service depends on the pricing tier. Only Azure App Services running in Standard or greater can perform backups, and in Standard, 12 backups per day is the maximum and one backup every two hours. The math there works; the difference is that you are also allowed to take manual backups. Therefore, if you take scheduled backups every hour and then 26 manual backups in 24 hours, you would still be OK.

TABLE 9.11   Azure Backup Limits

Product/Feature	Limit per Subscription
Recovery Services vault	500
Machines per vault	1000
Azure Backup of Azure VM	Once per day
Backup using DPM/MABS to Azure	Twice per day
Backup using MARS	Three times per day
Azure App Service (premium tier)	50 per day, once per hour

Azure Site Recovery

Let's assume now that you have all the Azure products identified that make up your production environment, and you have them backed up just in case you ever have to restore them. Let's hope you never need to do this. ASR is a tool that can help you move the resources from one region or one location to another region or location. The location is specifically called out here because ASR not only supports moving VMs hosted in Azure; it also supports customers who are running their workload on-premise, i.e., in private data centers. In the scenario where customers are running on-premise, when an outage happens, they could use ASR to move their workloads to Azure until the on-premise incident is resolved.

Take a look in Chapter 1 where ASR was first introduced. Figure 1.8 illustrates how ASR can be used to back up and restore VMs already within Azure or from on-premise to Azure. In Chapter 4, you learned about the differences between Azure Backup and ASR. Additionally, you learned that ASR is a helpful tool when it comes to migrating an on-premise VM to the Azure platform. And again, ASR was discussed in Chapter 8 where you learned it can be used not only for migrating Windows and Linux VM running on either Hyper-V or VMware, but also stand-alone, nonvirtualized servers. The final piece of ASR that remains is the actual execution of a failover. In Exercise 8.3 you used the Backup and Restore capabilities provided to you within the Recovery Services vault. Then in Exercise 8.4 you used the replication feature, which is ASR, to move an Azure VM from one region to another. Exercise 8.4 was straightforward and required only four steps; it was not a complicated activity. In Exercise 9.4, you will use the Site Recovery feature within the Recovery Services vault to recover an Azure VM running in West Europe (AM2) to North Europe (DB3). You will see the navigation menu item named Site Recovery in both Figure 9.28 and Figure 9.29 provided earlier.

EXERCISE 9.4

Recovering an Azure VM Using Azure Site Recovery

1. Log in to the Azure Portal at `portal.azure.com`.

2. Navigate to your Recovery Services vault that you created in Exercise 9.3 and click the Site Recovery navigation menu item. Figure 9.31 shows how the page will look. Click Step 1: Replicate Application.

FIGURE 9.31   Azure Site Recovery, Replicate Application

3. Select Azure from the Source drop-down list, select (Europe) West Europe from the Source Location drop-down list, select Resource Manager from the Azure Virtual Machine Deployment Model drop-down list, select the Source subscription, select the source resource group where the Azure VM you want to recover exists, and click the OK button.

4. Check the check box next to the VM or group of VMs you want to recover. Click the OK button, select (Europe) North Europe from the Target location drop-down list, click the Create Target Resources button, and click the Enable replication button. The blade looks the same as from Exercise 8.4's Figure 8.19.

5. While the Site Recovery configuration is being deployed, take a look back at Figure 9.31. Notice Step 2, which is about managing recover plans. Once the

deployment has completed, click the navigation menu item named Recover Plans (Site Recovery), clicking either Step 2: Manage Recover Plans or the navigation menu link. The same blade is rendered either way. Click the + Recovery Plan menu item, enter a name, select West Europe from the Source drop-down list, select North Europe from the Target drop-down list, and select Resource Manager from the Allow Items With Deployment Model drop-down list. Click the Select Items link, and check the check box for the VMs that you want to add to the recovery plan. Figure 9.32 illustrates the configuration.

FIGURE 9.32 Azure Site Recovery, creating a recovery plan

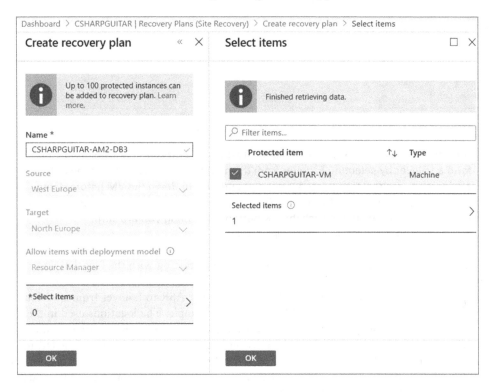

6. Click the OK button twice. Once the recovery plan is created, it will show up in the list of recovery plans. Click the ellipsis dots for the just created recovery plan, and select Test Failover from the pop-up menu. See Figure 9.33. Select the VNET into which you want to test the failover from the Azure Virtual Network drop-down list from the rendered Test Failover blade and click the OK button.

FIGURE 9.33   Azure Site Recovery test failover

7. Once the test is a success, select Cleanup Test Failover from the pop-up menu, perform a failover by selecting Failover from the menu pop-up menu, leave the default settings (i.e., source, target, recovery point and to shut down the VM before doing the failover), and click the OK button. Once the failover is completed, select Commit from the pop-up menu and click the OK button confirming you are sure.

There are a few things to call out from that exercise starting with the fact that you can only failover to regions in the same geography. This was mentioned once before but is worthy of stating again. It would not be possible to use ASR to failover from a VM in North Europe (DB3) to South Central US (SN1), for example. The locations used in the exercise are for example only, and you would want to choose the ones required in your scenario. Also, if you were setting up Site Recovery so you can use Azure VMs as DR for your on-premise workloads, you would choose the Azure region closest to your private data center. This will speed up the failover and also avoid any compliance and governance data issues if they are relevant in your scenario. The next point is the description and purpose of the recovery plan you created in Exercise 9.4.

The recovery plan is a template that is used to define the source, target, and items that need to be failed over when the failover process is executed. Exercise 9.4 was a simple example that contained only a single Azure VM. In real-world scenarios the number of Azure VMs and the relationships between them are much more complicated. This is why there is a Customize pop-up menu item that lets you tailor the recovery plan to your specific needs. One reason for this customization being important is if there are any requirements on the order in which you failover, shut down, or start up your workloads in a BCDR scenario. For example, if you have a batch job that will start feeding a database with data as soon as you start it up, you need to make sure the database is ready to receive the data; otherwise, you may create another mess that requires cleanup. Perhaps the batch job itself has a dependency on a system for attributes required for correctly processing the data. If those data parameters are not available, you may get corrupted data on your database, which is another problem you'd need to resolve. This customization capability is present for just these kinds of reasons. The reason is that defining in which order VMs need to be shut down, moved, and then restarted has great impact on the successful execution of a BCDR plan.

In practice, it wouldn't be a good idea to actually perform the failover until it is actually required; if you do, the VMs identified in the recovery plan would be moved into that other region. You should consider only performing the test that would confirm that if the time ever comes where you need to really failover to another region, that it will work. If you do need to perform an actual failover, then as you learned in Exercise 9.4 you select Failover from the pop-up menu. You are not completely finished with the failover once the process triggered by selecting Failover from the pop-up menu completes. Two additional pop-up menu items you may have noticed are Commit and Re-protect. If you recall, if you selected Failover, part of the information required was the selection of the recovery point for the given VM. The contents of the Recovery Point drop-down list are the following:

- Latest (Lowest RPO)
- Latest Processed (Low RTO)
- Latest App-Consistent

What *app-consistent* means should be clear because it was already discussed. An app-consistent status means all aspects of the backup were successful. This is the status you want to have because it has the greatest probability of being successful when deployed. The *recovery point objective (RPO)* and *recovery time object (RTO)* are measurements that identify the amount of data you are willing to lose based on the backup schedule and how much time is required to get your backup running again. An RPO consideration is one that can be linked to the decision between daily or weekly backups. If you were to choose a weekly backup schedule and your VM crashes six days from the last backup, you lose six days' worth of data. An RTO consideration has to do with available network bandwidth, the size of your backup that would require transfer, and the speed of the disks bound to the VM. RTO is focused on getting your VMs and other services up and running as fast as possible. Latest Processed (Low RTO) is the default. Therefore, you should conclude the most common objective from those executing a BCDR plan is to get the DR environment deployed, set up, and running as fast as possible. Make the selection wisely; you can use the test failover capability to see which works out best for your given scenario. Be conscious of the fact that after a real failover, once you commit, you cannot change this recovery point. But until the commitment is enacted, by selecting the Commit menu option, you will have these other recovery points, which you can use in case there are problems with any of the other recovery points.

If you are using Azure as the platform for your DR compute requirements from an on-premise data center, then re-protect is relevant to you. In many scenarios, a DR failover is only a temporary solution until the actual production environment is back up and running again. When you are ready to fail back from your DR on Azure into your on-premise data center, you must first select Re-protect. Once the Re-protect process is completed, you would see a pop-up menu item called Unplanned Failover, and clicking that would initiate the process for moving the workloads from Azure back into your on-premise data center. To perform a fail back, all the VMs in your recovery plan must have at least one recovery point on Azure. Therefore, you need to make sure you run at least one backup while you are running the DR machines on Azure. This is likely a good step to add to your overall BCDR plan, specifically, to create a backup before triggering a failback.

Two final points before moving onto the next section have to do with Azure Automation and the monitoring of your site recovery activities. You created a simple Azure Automation script in the previous chapter, and as shown in Figure 9.19, you can write scripts to automate many activities you perform on Azure. The scripts can perform monitoring activities, and what is relevant here is that the failover process can be scripted too. Although Exercise 9.4 was not a complicated one, it would be simplified by scripting it. Imagine instead of the numerous steps to perform a real-world, complicated failover, you could instead execute a single PowerShell cmdlet. In scenarios where you have a large number of resources, dependencies, and complexities, you should consider scripting the failover process. From a monitoring perspective, take a look back at Figure 8.4. That figure illustrates the Site Recovery dashboard within the Recovery Services vault. That dashboard provides an overview of how many failovers you have performed and their status. This overview can be helpful, especially if you are using Azure Automation to perform the failovers automatically when specific events occur that warrant such an action.

Site Recovery Deployment Planner

As introduced in Chapter 1, Site Recovery Deployment Planner (SRDP) is a command-line tool useful for analyzing on-premise virtual machines you want to potentially failover to Azure. This tool works with both Hyper-V and VMware virtualization scenarios. The output of the analysis will identify any compatibility issues, such as number of disks, IOPS, disk sizes, boot type (EFI/BIOS), and OS version. If there are any issues, you will be notified and would be able to take an action to make the on-premise VMs compatible. The amount of bandwidth required to perform the operation is also provided as output from the tool. This information will help you decide if you need to create an ExpressRoute connection or VPN or if you can simply replicate over the internet. Information about your storage requirements and the number of VMs required to execute the recovery plan will be a helpful tool in the calculation of the cost if you are ever required to trigger the failover.

Azure Recovery by Product Type

Most of the information required to back up, recover, or build in redundancies for our Azure products and features have already been covered. The contents in this section are provided for an additional review and may contain some supplementary tips, procedures, or diagrams that are helpful for building a reliant IT solution on Azure.

Recovering Azure Networking

The networking backbone on which Azure Functions is fully supported by Microsoft for all cloud hosting models. You wouldn't need to take any proactive activities from a networking infrastructure perspective. Because of that, from a BCDR perspective, you should focus on two other aspects. The first one has to do with your IaaS-based Azure products that are supported specifically by ASR. From a networking perspective, notice in Figure 9.34 that when you test a failover, you select the Azure virtual network into which you want to place the recovered items. If one doesn't exist in the target region, you are prompted to create one.

FIGURE 9.34   Azure Site Recovery Test failover VNET creation

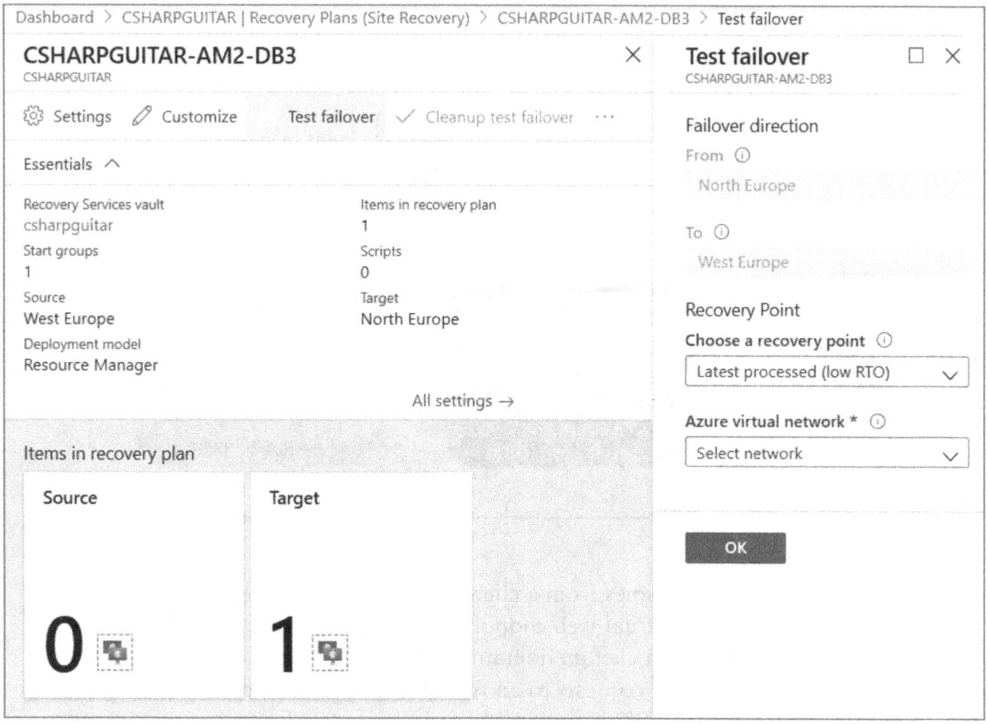

Once the test is successful and you need to actually trigger a failover, the virtual network in the target region is the place where your VMs will be placed into. That virtual network is ready to support the compute resources running within it. The other aspect concerns the utilization of the plethora of network virtual appliances (NVAs) available to you from Azure. Mostly in Chapter 3 where networking was covered, you learned about the API Management, Azure Front Door, Azure Traffic Manager (ATM), and Web Application Firewall (WAF) capabilities running in collaboration with Azure Application Gateway. All of those Azure networking products are mostly in place to help failover scenarios instead of requiring a failover scenario themselves. A WAF would need to be manually configured to reroute traffic from one endpoint to another; this isn't the case for ATM. An ATM can be configured to monitor the health of an endpoint, and when the configured threshold is breached, perhaps based on response time, an ATM can redirect all traffic to another endpoint running the same application, as illustrated in Figure 9.35.

FIGURE 9.35   How Azure Traffic Manager works

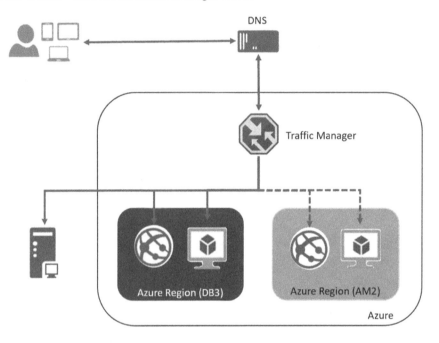

Notice that when a request comes from a client, the request is routed to the Azure Traffic Manager instead of an actual web endpoint running an application. The DNS has a CNAME, which would route a custom domain to the ATM endpoint, which is configured, as per Figure 9.35 to route requests to an Azure App Service and/or an Azure VM running in the North Europe (DB3) region. ATM can also be configured to route traffic to an endpoint not hosted in Azure. If the health monitor finds that the endpoints in DB3 are not responding as expected, West Europe (AM2) automatically begins accepting traffic from clients.

Recovering Azure VMs

The approach for recovering an Azure virtual machine is dependent on whether you are using Azure as a DR environment for your on-premise workloads or if the VMs are already hosted on Azure. If you are using Azure as your DR environment, then it should already be clear which tools you use for setting up and executing any failover. The tools are provided here for clarity.

- Azure Backup
- Site Recovery Deployment Planner (SRDP)
- Azure Site Recovery (ASR)
- Recovery Services Vault

When your workloads are already running on Azure, you have an additional option for setting up and maintaining a resilient application. Snapshots are a useful concept, discussed in Chapter 4, that let you not only backup the disks bound to the VM but also use them to build identical replicas. Those additional replicas are helpful for adding redundancies to your Azure workload. A snapshot is, in a majority of scenarios, a copy of the drive which bound to your VM that is running the operating system. That means the snapshot, once bound to a VM, is bootable, which is a similar attribute as an image. You would find the concept of an image with Azure Container Instances (ACI), Azure Kubernetes Services (AKS), and Virtual Machine Scale Sets (VMSS). This is called out specifically because if you navigate to any of those Azure products, i.e., ACI, AKS, or VMSS, in the Azure Portal, you will not find any navigation menu items focused on backup and recovery. The reason for that is that the disk image is what should be protected and stored versus an actual backup of one or more of the machines. Remember in Chapter 4's Exercise 4.1 that you created a Docker image. Like the source code, you would want to safely store the scripts and dependent components for that image. If you ever needed to redeploy the image, it could be done by following the instructions provided in Exercise 4.4.

Two more items to call out in this section, the Disaster Recovery navigation menu item on the Azure VM blade and partially restoring files from a backup. The Disaster Recovery navigation menu item is visible in a previous image, Figure 9.27. Clicking that navigation menu item opens the Replicated Items blade, which is identical to the one you would see if you navigated to it from the Recovery Services Vault blade, as shown in Figure 9.36.

You would notice that you also have the capability from that blade to execute a test failover or perform an actual BCDR failover plan if required. On a side note, if you find features duplicated in multiple locations, you can be certain they all call the same Resource Manager REST API on the backend. Therefore, use the approach and procedures for their use that are easiest and most logical for your specific scenario. Let's move on to the next topic of restoring only a portion of a VM. There may be a scenario where you only need a file or folder from a backup and not the entire thing. In that case, by using the blade shown in Figure 9.27, click the ellipsis dots, and you will see Restore VM and File Recovery contained within the pop-up menu. Click File Recovery, and you are prompted to download and run an executable named `IaaSVMILRExeForWindows.exe`, which will connect to a snapshot of the disk. Figure 9.37 shows the output of the executable.

FIGURE 9.36   Azure virtual machine disaster recovery

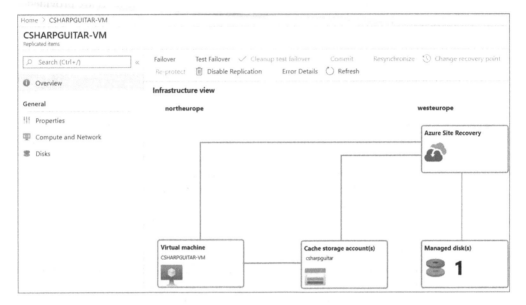

FIGURE 9.37   Azure virtual machine file recovery

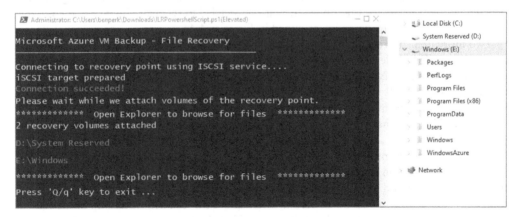

The executable mounts the disks from the recovery point as local drives. Notice in Figure 9.37 that there is a `D:\` drive and an `E:\` drive, which allows you to navigate through the content and copy the files or directories that you want to retrieve. On the same blade that provided you with the ability to mount the drive, there also exists an Unmount Disks button. Click that button when you have completed your recovery, and the drive will remain mounted for 12 hours and unmount automatically, in case you forget.

Recovering Azure App Services

This one is pretty well covered; you need to remember that when running on a PaaS cloud hosting model, the provider owns the operating system. The primary focus for you is to make sure your application code is secure and that you have a document that contains the configurations you made to the application after deploying it to PaaS, i.e., an Azure App Service. Although the configuration is stored safely and securely, it makes sense to have a document that describes any custom configuration in your possession. Azure App Services do provide the feature to perform and recover from backups; see Figure 9.30 as a reminder about what that looks like. Also, take a look back over Figure 9.35, which discusses ATM as a recovery option for responding to incidents that may require the execution of a BCDR plan.

Recovering Azure Data Services

Azure data services consist within two primary groups, data stores that are databases and data storage that concern files or documents. The data stores that have been focused on in this book and likely on the exam are Azure SQL and Azure Cosmos DB. The data storage products are those that exist within an Azure Storage account, specifically, Azure Blobs, Azure Tables, and Azure Files. Azure queues also reside within an Azure Storage account; however, Azure Queues are there for legacy reasons more than anything else. Let's make sure you know as much as possible about the backup, recovery, and redundancy capabilities available for each of these Azure products. Note that much of this content has already been covered in Chapter 5; the content here is just to close out any possible loose ends.

- Azure SQL, SQL managed instances, and SQL virtual machines
- Azure Cosmos DB
- Azure Storage

From a data recovery perspective, an important concept is data retention. This is the amount of time that you plan on keeping the copy of the backup. You have learned concepts such as LTR and PITR that dictate the frequency of a backup and for how long the backup will be stored; the maximum is 10 years. By default, Azure SQL databases are backed up every 12 hours, and transaction logs are taken every 5 to 10 minutes. Recall from Figure 5.48 where you will see a custom configuration of the database backup schedule. If you ever want to restore one of those backups, you would find a Restore menu item on the Azure SQL or SQL managed instance's Overview blade in the Azure Portal, as illustrated with Figure 9.38. After clicking Restore, you are provided the options to select the most recent PITR backup or LTR backup.

FIGURE 9.38   Azure SQL or Azure managed instance restore

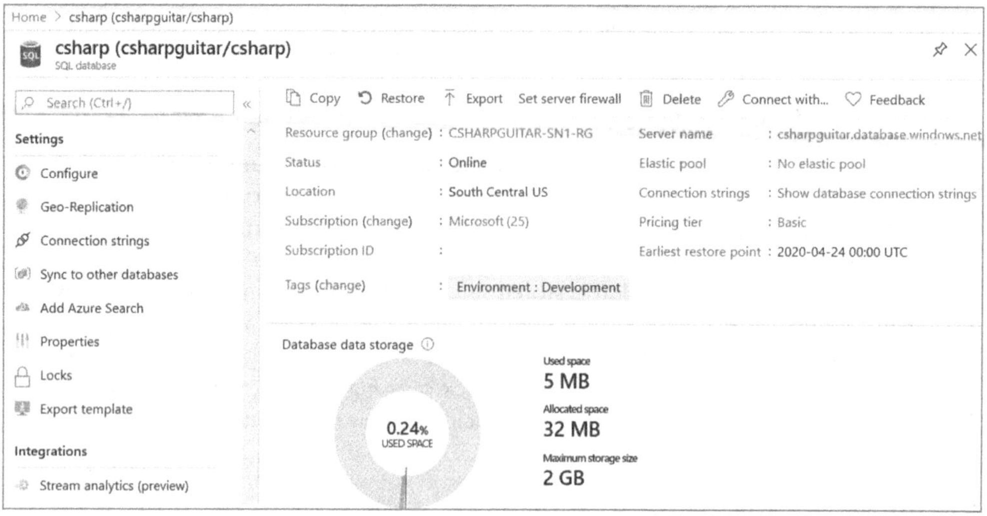

When you select LTR, you are provided with a drop-down list that allows you to select the specific backup you would like, based on date. From a SQL virtual machine perspective, you know this already, but a backup of the database is performed along with the backup of the Azure VM on which it runs. Azure Backup and Azure Site Recovery Services (ASR) are the tools that do this on VMs and have just recently been covered. From an Azure Cosmos DB perspective, take a look at Figure 5.41, which shows the Replicate Data Globally blade for an Azure Cosmos DB. Once you enable replication, the Manual Failover menu item would become enabled. If you were to identify any issue on your primary Azure Cosmos DB instance, you can use the Manual Failover menu to make another instance the primary one. Or, consider enabling Automatic Failover, which will monitor the DB in that region, and, if it is determined to be unhealthy, the platform will perform the failover to another region for you. When configuring Automatic Failover, you will identify which region is preferred as the failover instance. Azure Cosmos DB databases are backed up automatically by the platform every four hours. If you ever get into a situation where you must restore your database from a backup, you will need to contact Microsoft Support. There is currently no online functionality to support this scenario.

When your Azure Storage account is running in the GRS or RA-GRS service tier, you can configure georeplication, as shown in Figure 9.39. As you can see, the primary Azure Storage account is in West Europe (AM2) with the secondary in North Europe (DB3).

If your primary Azure Storage account, which includes blobs, tables, and files, begins to experience problems or there is an outage, click the Prepare For Failover button to begin the failover procedure. The procedure would simply make the storage in North Europe the primary and redirect all the storage endpoints to the instance in that new region. Remember that your Azure Storage endpoints resemble the following:

- **Blob:** `https://*.blob.core.windows.net`
- **Files:** `https://*.file.core.windows.net`

- Queue: `https://*.queue.core.windows.net`
- Tables: `https://*.table.core.windows.net`
- Static Website: `https://*.z6.web.core.windows.net`

FIGURE 9.39   Azure Storage account georeplication

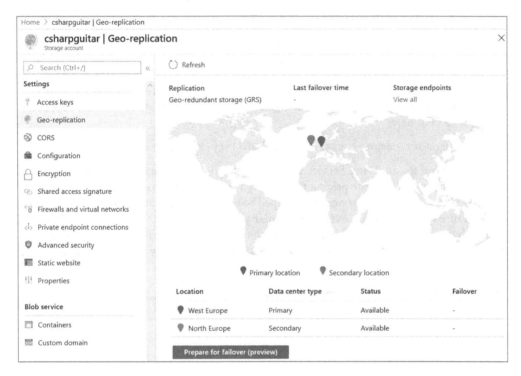

You can also perform the failover of a storage account using the following Azure CLI command:

```
az storage account show --name <accountName> --expand geoReplicationStats
az storage account failover --name <accountName>
```

Replace *<accountName>* with your Azure Storage account name. The first command will display the primary and secondary information as you saw previously in Figure 9.39. The second command will perform the actual failover process.

Recovering Azure Messaging Services

There was not a lot about backup and recovery in Chapter 6 where the Azure Messaging services were covered in detail. From a conceptual perspective, in many ways the need for taking a backup doesn't make a lot of sense. It doesn't make a lot of sense because the data that is present in the queues wouldn't remain there for long. The purpose of messaging services is to store a piece of information and to notify a consumer that information is present for processing. Once the message is processed, it is removed from the messaging service queue. Therefore, your primary consideration from a recovery perspective in the context of messaging should focus on redundancies. Meaning, if you have an outage in a region, make sure you can quickly divert producers and consumers to an available endpoint in a different region.

From an Azure Storage Queue perspective, the redundancy approach was just provided in the previous section. Azure Queue Storage is contained within an Azure Storage account, so if you need to perform a failover, you have that feature after enabling georeplication, which requires GRS or RA-GRS. With regard to both an Azure Service Bus and an Event Hub, you can choose to make them zone redundant during their initial provisioning only. Zone redundancy, as you recall, means that the product is deployed into all data centers within a region; the typical number of data centers per region is three. All regions do not support availability zones; you can find an up-to-date list of which Azure regions support Availability Zones here:

docs.microsoft.com/en-us/azure/availability-zones/az-overview

Georeplication for an Azure Service Bus is available only when using the premium pricing tier. For an Event Hub, the pricing tier required for georeplication is standard. The reason these two messaging services are lumped together is because the process and georeplication Azure Portal blade are extremely similar to each other. Both Azure Service Bus and Event Hub have a georeplication blade similar to that shown in Figure 9.40. You will certainly see the resemblance between Figure 9.39 and Figure 9.40 as well, which makes sense, as the goal for this feature is the same, i.e., redundancy.

FIGURE 9.40   Azure Service Bus georeplication

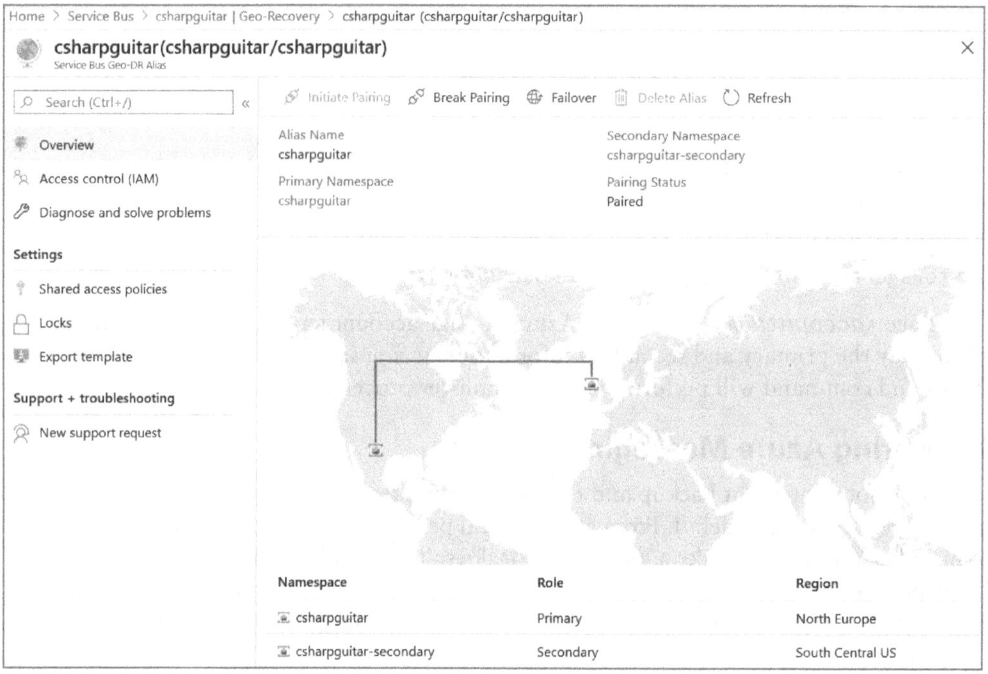

The last messaging service is Event Grid, which has built-in redundancy. A failover happens automatically when the Event Grid endpoint becomes unavailable in a region. For an Event Grid, remember that it doesn't actually store any messages; instead, it sends an event notification to its subscribers. That notification can inform a consumer that there is a message in an Event Hub ready for processing, for example. In the Event Grid scenario, you can therefore build redundancies into the producers that are monitored by Event Grid by provisioning an identical endpoint in two or more different regions. The producers can then attempt to notify the Event Grid endpoint in the primary region. If that fails, the code would attempt to use the secondary region. Ensuring both endpoints are configured the same, no notifications would be lost.

Summary

In this chapter, you learned about Azure Monitor, which consists of two Azure tools, Application Insights and Log Analytics. Application Insights is targeted toward the application and can be embedded into the application code. Log Analytics is platform-focused but is useful for monitoring the state of almost all Azure products and features. The monitor data can be visualized using the Azure Monitor blade in the Azure Portal, or you can use KUSTO queries (KQL) to query the data via Azure Data Explorer (ADX). The other portion of the chapter covered backup and recovery tools and concepts. Azure Backup is the tool used for backing up Azure virtual machines and SQL virtual machines. You also learned that Azure Backup is useful for on-premise virtualized or physical servers running Linux or Windows on VMware or Hyper-V. Lastly, you learned about Azure Site Recovery and how it can be used to take a backup and use it to recover the VM into another region as part of a BCDR plan.

Going forward, if you want to keep up with all the changes and plans for future Azure products and features, read the page azure.microsoft.com/en-us/updates regularly. I learned a lot while writing this book. I actually passed the AZ-300 and AZ-301 exams without any kind of preparation. This is a benefit I got by working with the technology every day for some years. I am confident that if you have read all the pages and worked all the exercises that you too will be able to clear this exam. If you made it all the way through this book, you deserve recognition and the Azure Solutions Architect Expert is exactly the recognition you deserve. I wish you success, and I am hopeful that this book will not only help you clear the exam, but also make you a great Azure Solutions Architect Expert.

In each chapter, I provided a quote from a famous person that I found somewhat relevant to the content of the chapter or section. I asked my son to provide the final quote for me. His quote was simple, clear, and direct: Noa Perkins said, "The End."

Exam Essentials

Understand Azure Monitor.   This is a tool that collects, analyzes, and provides insights into the performance and availability aspect of your cloud and on-premise workloads. Azure Monitor can proactively identify issues with your provisioned Azure products and resources, as well as those they depend on.

Understand Log Analytics.   This product is merged into Azure Monitor and is the location where your telemetric data is stored. Using KUSTO Queries (KQL) and Azure Data Explorer (ADX), you can extract data in the exact format you require. The data stored in this repository is focused on the platform and IaaS cloud offerings. Some key metrics are CPU utilization, memory, and IOPS.

Understand Application Insights.   This is another logging, analyzing, and reporting Azure product that is useful for capturing performance and availability metrics. This product, as its name implies, is focused a bit more on the application and PaaS cloud offerings. This feature also has an SDK so that you can embed it directly into your application code, which will provide greater insights into the behaviors of your solution.

Understand business continuity and disaster recovery (BCDR).   A BCDR plan is focused on what actions you will take if there is an outage that renders your workloads inaccessible. Business continuity is focused on keeping the business moving forward in scenarios when the computer systems are not available such as taking orders by phone and writing them down on paper until the systems come back online. The disaster recovery portion is focused on the computer systems running your database, compute, and/or messaging services. Having your backups taken and your recovery plan created in advance will help you perform failovers to other Azure regions or from on-premise to Azure, when there is a requirement to do so.

Understand Azure Backup.   Like the name suggests, this feature is what performs the backup of your provisioned workloads. What the name does not imply is that it performs recoveries as well. This is the go-to tool for scheduling, performing, and managing your backup and recovery needs in Azure and on-premise.

Understand Azure Site Recovery (ASR).   This product is not only helpful in migration scenarios but is the backbone for the execution of the DR part of your BCDR plan. With the help of a Recovery Services vault, you can create and replicate backups of your Azure and on-premise workloads. Additionally, you can use this product to test failover scenarios, execute a real failover, and, once the incident is resolved, use it to fail back to your actual production environment.

Review Questions

1. Azure Service Health monitors all Azure products' performance and availability in all regions globally.

    A. True

    B. False

2. Activity logs that are accessible via the portal or Azure PowerShell provide what kind of information? (Choose all that apply.)

    A. Deployment to an Azure App Service

    B. A login attempt on an Azure VM

    C. Removal of Azure resources via the portal

    D. An access to a Key Vault Key

3. Which of the following is true about Log Analytics? (Choose all that apply.)

    A. Supports custom querying using KUSTO queries (KQL)

    B. Supports custom querying using GUSTO queries (GQL)

    C. Provides insights into application code exceptions and memory consumption

    D. Is queryable from Azure Data Explorer (ADX)

4. Which metric would you not expect to see when analyzing Application Insights logs?

    A. Exceptions

    B. ETWEvent

    C. Requests

    D. Syslog

5. To use Azure Automation runbooks in the context of monitoring, only PowerShell scripting can be used.

    A. True

    B. False

6. Which of the following backup/restore scenarios are not supported by Azure Backup?

    A. Azure to Azure

    B. Azure to on-premise

    C. On-premise to Azure

    D. On-premise to on-premise

7. Which of the following does Azure Backup support when backing up VMs or physical machines running Linux by default? (Choose all that apply.)

   A. 32-bit operating system

   B. Application-consistent backups

   C. 64-bit operating system

   D. File-system-consistent backups

8. Which of the following backup status is most desired?

   A. Application consistent

   B. Crash consistent

   C. File system consistent

9. Azure Site Recovery (ASR) is useful in the following scenarios? (Choose all that apply.)

   A. Monitoring

   B. Migration from on-premise to Azure

   C. Migration between Azure regions

   D. Testing and executing BCDR plans

10. Which of the following products support georeplication? (Choose all that apply.)

    A. Azure Cosmos DB

    B. Azure Service Bus

    C. Azure Storage Account

    D. Event Hub

Appendix

Answers to Review Questions

Chapter 1: Gaining the Azure Solutions Architect Certification

1. A, D. Azure Active Directory and single sign-on (SSO) can protect Azure App Service from unauthorized internet access. RBAC manages access to Azure resources in Azure Portal, and Managed Identity is a feature for applications to securely communicate with each other.

2. A, C. Azure VM and Azure Functions are compute resources. ExpressRoute and API Management are not compute resources.

3. A, B, C. A custom domain can be bound to Azure App Service, Azure Storage Account, and Azure VM. You cannot bind a custom domain to an Azure SQL endpoint.

4. A, B and C. Azure Storage does consist of blob, queues, file and table service types.

5. B. A zone-redundant solution is the cheapest given the requirements. LRS is the cheapest, but there is no redundancy.

6. C. Only managed identity provides that capability.

7. A. Only Azure Availability Sets provide business continuity capabilities.

8. D. TLS 1.3 is the most current; however, it is not widely implemented yet.

9. A. All are supported except P2P.

10. C. `*.onmicrosoft.com` is correct. The others are not valid domain extensions for AAD, unless owned by the customer and configured.

11. C. Azure Functions might be considered; however, it has a limit of 1.5GB and therefore will not work. Therefore, WebJobs is best suited for the scenario.

12. B. Although option C seems relevant, the best answer is something you know and something you have. There are questions like this on the exam, where numerous options seem possible. You need to pick the best of the possible options.

13. A. The product that provides the most coverage is Azure Monitor. Application Insights does monitor and provide metrics, but it is specific to Azure App Service for now.

14. A, B, C, D. All are valid features for Azure VM.

15. B. CORS is a security feature that makes sure during the rendering of a web page on the client that no unexpected scripts from other sites are executed.

16. B, C. API Management use cases are to help manage integration as it exposes a single global endpoint that acts as a proxy allowing the redirection to other endpoints. It also provides access management capabilities.

17. A. It is not possible to automatically scale up.

18. C. Azure VM allows registration of an assembly into the Global Assembly Cache (GAC). Azure Functions and Azure App Service run within a sandbox that doesn't support access to the GAC.

19. A, C, D. A RESTful API supports cross-platform software, typically converses using JSON, and is supported by Cosmos DB. There is no relation or dependency between WCF and REST.

20. B, D. An Azure Web App for Containers instance is compatible with Azure files, and can consume GPU resources. There are no statistics to prove the speed at which the startup happens, and GPU resources are not available with Azure containers.

Chapter 2: Security and Identity

1. A, B, D. AAD does not provide retinal scanning capabilities. This capability would need to be developed and implemented into an application manually.

2. D. I love these both, neither, and none questions and so do the people who write the Azure Solutions Architect Expert exam. You must admit that they really test your knowledge and create doubt. There are numerous scenarios where data at rest is encrypted; however, in the list of possible answers, only D is correct.

3. C. There is no charge for RBAC, but you need to know what costs money and what does not in many scenarios. Knowing which tier of the product has which features and which are free is a common theme on the exam.

4. C. This is a good example of a question you might see. I would think you can eliminate option A pretty easily. But option B seems possible even though you have never read or seen any information about it. So, I am torn between C and D, because I am confident option C is something AAD Connect does. If you have some good experience and have read documentation about AAD Connect and you feel you have never read anything about option B, then go with C.

5. A. Although conditional access can be configured to enforce numerous vulnerable scenarios, location of login attempt is the only one here that is correct.

6. D. `Microsoft.Authorization/roleDefinition/read` and `Microsoft.Authorization/roleDefinition/write` can do it if combined, but only `Microsoft.Authorization/roleDefinition/*` is the correct answer.

7. A. ARM ensures clients like the Azure Portal, Azure PowerShell, Azure CLI, and any client consuming the REST APIs are authenticated. Managing resources on Azure depends on ARM.

8. B. It does not encrypt *all* data in memory; it encrypts only the data that is defined within an enclave.

9. C. You can use a SAS key for user authentication on Azure Blob Storage Container. There is no Azure Message Storage Container product, and the other options do not support a SAS token as a valid authentication token.

10. D. Secrets, keys, and certificates (i.e., PFX) can be stored and protected in Azure Key Vault.

Chapter 3: Networking

1. A. The smaller the routing prefix, the more IP addresses that will be allocated. A routing prefix of 8 is equal to 2^{24}, which equals 16,777,216. You can calculate the power by subtracting it from 32, where $2^{32} - 2^8 = 2^{24}$.

2. D. The Application Gateway and Azure Front Door services offer SSL termination.

3. A. Azure Firewall works at layer 3, not 7. Azure Front Door does work on layer 7, but it is too large for a small company; in other words, the cost is too much, and most of the other features wouldn't be needed. Therefore, the WAF provided by Application Gateway is the best choice.

4. B. There can be only one gateway subnet per VNet. The name of the gateway subnet is GatewaySubnet, so neither A nor C is correct.

5. A. By default, there are inbound and outbound NSG rules that allow all traffic where the source and destination are VirtualNetwork.

6. A. Option B can seem legitimate, but the word *global* is missing from the proposed solution. Therefore, the correct answer is that VNet peering connects two or more VNets that exist in the same region.

7. C. OSI layer 3 provides access to a TCP session, and only Azure Firewall operates on the layer. The other options do not operate at that OSI layer.

8. C. It is possible to connect a frontend like App Service to a backend like SQL Azure; however, it is not a textbook-defined networking configuration.

9. C. A DNS server to provide host name to IP resolution is optional and is not required.

10. A. Azure CDN does not have the feature to route requests to specific servers in a backend pool.

Chapter 4: Compute

1. A, C

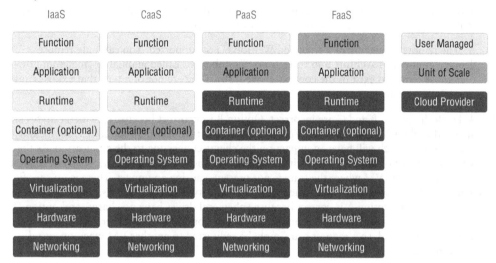

Figure shows the different layers of the IT stack that the cloud provider has versus that of the customer. You will see that IaaS and CaaS allow customers to choose the version of runtime that the hosted application targets. For example, .NET Core 3 or Python 3.8.

2. C. Azure VMs would end up costing more because there is a flat fee applied when one is provisioned; you are charged regardless whether it is used or not. Also, more maintenance is required as you own the operating systems, which would require you to keep it up-to-date. Azure Functions' primary purpose is not intended to host Web APIs rather to run small snippets of code when triggered. Azure Batch would not expose an API and is intended for HPC models; therefore, Azure App Service is the only remaining choice. It is intended to be used for Web APIs and Web Application hosting.

3. A, B. An Azure Container Registry is not a compute product; it is a repository like Docker Hub used to store images, and Azure Functions does not support container. The other two options support containers.

4. D. During the provision of both VMs and container instances, you select the VM series on which the workload will run. Both VMs and containers can autoscale based on load. Therefore, both options A and B are not correct. Option C is also not correct because you can change the VM series at any time without redeploying and rebuilding the VM.

5. A, C. The `Stop-AzVM` PowerShell cmdlet does deallocate the VM as does the execution of `Remove-AzResourceGroup` because it deletes all the contents contained within the resource group when executed. The Azure CLI command `az vm stop` does not deallocate the VM, so `az vm deallocate` is the correct command. Logging off of a VM using the Remote Desktop Connection (RDP) does not shut down nor deallocate the VM.

6. C. There is no such limit on the number of Availability Zone into which you can place your VMSS. However, the maximum is three; there exists only a possibility of three. Since option C is the opposite of option B, option B is not correct. The described architecture is best suited for availability sets. Finally, scaling out new instances of an application does manage state and can have a negative impact. If clients with a session on instance X are suddenly directed to instance Y, then their state would not exist on that server.

7. A. The remote debugging of a triggered WebJob is not supported. You can only remote debug a continuous WebJob, and there is no WebJob types called manual or singleton; however, those terms do exist in the context of WebJobs. They are not of a type that exposes any capability to enable or necessitate debugging.

8. A, D. Both options B and C are incorrect. Option B is incorrect because ephemeral drives are attached to the VM, and when the VM gets reimaged, it will flush all the state from memory and it's gone, which will have an impact on the clients connecting to the application. As the VM is taken out of the pool for a reimage, the state is not shared to another VM; the request is routed to a new VM where the state is not present, causing an impact. There is no specific limit issue based on that amount when it comes to the two storage options; therefore, option C is not correct. Option A is correct because ephemeral drives have no charge, and option D is true because it is the opposite of option B. They are opposite in that there is no state on the VM being reimaged, so a request can simply be redirected to another VM when one is taken out of the pool.

9. A, B, C, D. All of the options are true. All of the declared components are required.

10. A. All of the options are required to implement a Windows Virtual Desktop solution.

11. B, C. Because option C is true, option A cannot be true. An ephemeral drive (option D) is one that is physically connected to an Azure VM and offers better performance because of its direct connection with managed disks.

12. A, B. Option C would be better suited for an Azure App Service, and option D would be better suited for Azure Batch. Both options A and B are valid use cases for an Azure VM.

13. B, C, D. Azure App Services does not support the installation of EXE or MSI programs that install binaries. When running on PaaS, you cannot make any changes at the OS level.

14. A, B, D. If you wanted to run PHP or Node on a Windows machine, you wouldn't choose an App Service Web App for Containers because they would work on the plain Azure App Services. The other options are valid reasons for choosing Web Apps for Containers.

15. B. An Azure Function is limited to one CPU and 1.5GB of memory. If your compute requirement per invocation requires more than this, you shouldn't use this product. Since Functions is serverless, if it is not used, then the VM gets deallocated, which means the first request may take a bit because the VM needs to be provisioned and started up. Azure Functions is for running small snippets of programming logic and not for hosting content.

16. B. The opposite is true.

17. A, B. ACI supports both Windows and Linux and does not currently provide any orchestration capability that is comparable to AKS.

18. A, B, D. YAML is the syntax used to configure AKS, not JSON. Both AKS and Service Fabric are designed for running microservices and do offer similar capabilities.

19. D. ACR has a capability that supports the georeplication of images to other regions. It is available in the Premium pricing tier only.

20. A, B, D. A primary use case for Windows Virtual Desktop is to optimize the use of compute resources. When companies are required to purchase expensive in-house workstations, some of the compute resources may sit idle, which is not optimal. If you implement Windows Virtual Desktop, then the in-house workstations can be to a smaller specification, and you use the compute resources on Azure and pay for only what you use.

Chapter 5: Data and Storage

1. A, B, C. The Azure Cosmos DB Table API is the best solution; however, you can store key/value pairs in an Azure SQL database. Azure Table Storage is what the Azure Cosmos DB Table API is based on and can be used without the Azure Cosmos DB wrapper.

2. B. SQL VMs offer the most probable level of success when performing a lift-and-shift migration of a relational database. Azure SQL may be too constrained as it runs in the PaaS context, Azure Blob Storage is for storing blobs, and the Azure Cosmos DB Gremlin API is for Graph Databases.

3. C. Azure Data Factory and Azure Data Bricks are products that help with the analysis of the data hosted on Azure Synapse Analytics. Azure Storage Explorer is used for reviewing the contents in an Azure storage account.

4. A, B, C. The only one that doesn't provide automatic backups is SQL on a VM. This is because a VM is IaaS and the automatic database backup is a PaaS-like offering.

5. D. The first two options may help with the migration, but there is no feature within them that will check for compatibility issues. SSMA is used when the source database is not SQL Server but the target database is. DMA is the correct answer.

6. A, B. Dynamic scaling is a common PaaS feature and supported by both Azure SQL and SQL managed instances. SQL VM is IaaS, and the scaling would need to be performed manually or manually configured to scale using a script or program.

7. B. Remember that you always need to choose the "best" or "recommended" answer when there are multiple options that could be correct. You could store a JSON document in any of those data stores, but for JSON documents, an Azure Cosmos DB is the recommended data store.

8. B, C, D. Only locally redundant storage (LRS) does not provide replication to a remote location that can be used in case of a data center, i.e., zone outage.

9. C. Azure Blob, Azure Table, Azure Queue, and Azure Files are all contained within an Azure Storage account and are therefore considered Azure Storage products. Azure Kubernetes Service (AKS) is a compute product.

10. B. SAS tokens can be configured to restrict access to a specific Azure Blob container, as well. CRUD operations can be restricted using a SAS token. An account key gives full access to all storage options in the storage account.

Chapter 6: Hybrid, Compliance, and Messaging

1. A, B, D. Azure Policy is not useful in the creation of a hybrid cloud solution. Azure Policy is utilized in the compliance and policy context.

2. A, B, C. Single sign-on might help with the simplification of implementing authentication of workloads on-premise and in the cloud, but it is not a networking product.

3. B, C, D. There is no product or feature in Azure named Azure Compliance Standards.

4. All of the above. The tricky one is Event Grid domains, but it does group together Event Topics and Event Subscriptions. Event domains help grouping and manageability for Event Grid consumptions. Namespaces and storage accounts group together Azure resources and features as well.

5. B. It is the other way around. The outcome of having a resilient application makes it reliable.

6. A. Both are focused on defining data privacy standards. For more information about GDPR and PIPA, view the following pages: en.wikipedia.org/wiki/General_Data_Protection_Regulation en.wikipedia.org/wiki/PROTECT_IP_Act

7. A, B, D. MFA is not available to configure through Security Center; the others are.

8. B. There is a feature in Security Center that will analyze the vulnerabilities and configurations that may be in noncompliance with a list of selected compliance standards. They are highlighted, and recommended solutions are provided; however, the implementation of those suggestions is manual.

9. B. Event Hub is specifically designed for that scenario.

10. D. Service Bus is specifically designed for that scenario.

Chapter 7: Developing for the Cloud

1. A, C. Datacenter outages are rare in both cases, but due to Availability Zones you would expect them to impact less in the cloud, assuming you have built that into your cloud solutions. You would not expect much to any data loss if you are running in the proper pricing tiers that perform automatic backups. Many products perform backups by default, so data loss is rare.

2. C. The number of outbound connections is limited when running on PaaS. Connections can be reused if the connection object is created at the class level instead of created for each request.

3. A. The retry pattern is the optimal pattern for working with issues that should recover within a short period of time. A transient issue is one that happens but then self-corrects; these kinds of issues are hard to troubleshoot.

4. A, B, C. Although Windows authentication is historically used for intranet applications, it is possible to make Integrated Windows Authentication (IWA) work over the internet. However, you wouldn't use a service principle to authenticate users for your application.

5. D. Visio Studio is not an IDE for developing code, running, or testing applications.

6. A, C. You can use authentication code from within an ASP.NET Core application to access information stored in an Azure Key Vault. Managed Identity is not enabled by default on supported Azure products. It must be enabled and configured for each product.

7. A, B, C, D. All of those listed are provided via EasyAuth.

8. A, B. Event Grid is used to manage messages sent by message publishers and then send them to endpoints that have subscribed to receive them. AKS is a compute product for running microservice-designed programs. Therefore, only Data Lake Analytics and Azure Cosmos DB are correct.

9. A, D. Both Service Bus and Azure Storage Queue receive messages for processing offline. That kind of offline processing is a common practice of decoupling IT systems. The other two options, Azure Cosmos DB and Azure Batch, are not considered products that will help with the decoupling of IT applications.

10. B, C. Service Fabric is designed for microservices, and Azure Functions is a serverless capability; therefore, those options are not correct. Azure Virtual Machines and Azure Batch are both capable of running large compute workloads.

Chapter 8: Migrate and Deploy

1. C. Azure Blueprint is helpful in the governance area of migration and not in the migration of workloads. Neither is Azure Monitor, which is focused on health and availability of your workloads once on the platform. There is no tool named Azure Deployment Assistance (ADA), which leaves only Azure Migrate as the correct answer.

2. B. The exported image must be in VHD format that can be achieved using VMware.

3. B. Not only can you upgrade the version of DBMS, for example, SQL Server 2005 to SQL Server 2019, you can also migrate from Oracle to Azure SQL during the migration.

4. A, B, C. All of them are helpful, except the Azure Deployment Assistant, which isn't a service at all.

5. **A, C.** Moving an Azure product into a different subscription can be achieved via the Azure Portal and Azure CLI. Any tool that can access the ARM can update this data. No physical move of resource is required to change the subscription or resource group. Although ASR would result in the resource likely being in a new resource group or subscription, you wouldn't choose that tool for making the migration. There is no tool named Azure Deployment Assistance (ADA).

6. **A, C, D.** You cannot move resources into a specific Azure zone after it has provisioned; this is a role performed by the platform. At creation time you can choose how many zones you want your product placed into but cannot change it later.

7. **A.** You must have an Azure subscription to provision and access any Azure resource.

8. **A.** Both waterfall and agile approaches are organizational models and not methodologies. OOP is a coding pattern and not a deployment technique. Azure DevOps is intended to provide the ability to execute the CI/CD methodology. Azure DevOps can support the Agile model as well, but it is not its primary targeted model.

9. **B, D.** ARM templates are JSON documents and the most common means for transferring data to a REST API. ARM templates can deploy application code using the `msdeploy` extension when embedded into the document.

10. **B, C.** Azure Automation does not provide recommendations about how to configure Azure products. That is dependent on your requirements and not something Microsoft would attempt to drive. There are some recommendations, but not in the context of Azure Automation. There are also no security-related capabilities built into Azure Automation; that is better performed in the Security Center context.

Chapter 9: Monitor and Recover

1. **A.** Azure Service Health is a web page that monitors the performance and availability status of all Azure products globally.

2. **A, C, D.** Activity logs are logged when clients use the REST APIs exposed by the Resource Manager. Logging into a provisioned Azure VM would use RDP or SSH, neither of which is related to Resource Manager.

3. **A, D.** KQL is the query language for running customer queries against Log Analytics; there is no GQL language. Log Analytics focuses on platform metrics and will not log an application exception generated from custom code.

4. **B, D.** ETW stands for Event Tracing for Windows and wouldn't be something you would expect to see in application logs. The same goes for a Syslog aka system logs. Both options B and D are system/platform-focused and not application-focused. Both ETWEvents and SysLogs are Log Analytics metrics.

5. **B.** This is not a requirement. PowerShell scripts, graphical runbooks, PowerShell workflows, and Python scripts are all supported.

6. D. Azure Backup supports backup and restore scenarios within Azure, from on-premise onto the Azure platform and the recovery from Azure to on-premise.

7. C, D. 32-bit Linux versions are not supported, and due to the absence of VSS for Linux, application-consistent backups are not supported by default when running Linux.

8. A. Application-consistent is the most desired. Special configuration is required to get to this status for Linux.

9. B, C, D. ASR is not useful for monitoring backups, recoveries, and failovers. You would find that information on the Recovery Services vault dashboards for Backups and Site Recovery.

10. A, B, C, D. All of them support the replication of data between different regions. The purpose of georeplication is to provide a secondary endpoint for your Azure product, which becomes accessible when the region containing your primary endpoint becomes unavailable.

Index

A

E

Y

Z

Comprehensive Online Learning Environment

Register to gain one year of FREE access to the online interactive learning environment and test bank to help you study for your Azure Architect Technologies and Design certification exam—included with your purchase of this book!

The online test bank includes the following:

- **Assessment Test** to help you focus your study to specific objectives
- **Chapter Tests** to reinforce what you've learned
- **Practice Exams** to test your knowledge of the material
- **Digital Flashcards** to reinforce your learning and provide last-minute test prep before the exam
- **Searchable Glossary** to define the key terms you'll need to know for the exam

Register and Access the Online Test Bank

To register your book and get access to the online test bank, follow these steps:

1. Go to bit.ly/SybexTest.
2. Select your book from the list.
3. Complete the required registration information, including answering the security verification to prove book ownership. You will be emailed a pin code.
4. Follow the directions in the email or go to www.wiley.com/go/sybextestprep.
5. Enter the pin code you received and click the "Activate PIN" button.
6. On the Create an Account or Login page, enter your username and password, and click Login. A "Thank you for activating your PIN!" message will appear. If you don't have an account already, create a new account.
7. Click the "Go to My Account" button to add your new book to the My Products page.